Problem
Solving
with

C++

The
Object
of Programming

Third
Edition

WALTER SAVITCH
University of California at San Diego

Addison
Wesley

Boston San Francisco New York
London Toronto Sydney Tokyo Singapore Madrid
Mexico City Munich Paris Cape Town Hong Kong Montreal

Senior Acquisitions Editor: Susan Hartman Sullivan
Assistant Editor: Lisa Kalner
Executive Marketing Manager: Michael Hirsch
Project Management: Diane Freed
Composition: Michael and Sigrid Wile
Copyeditor: Roberta Lewis
Proofreader: Holly McLean Aldis
Text and Cover Design: Regina Hagen
Media Producer: Jennifer Pelland
Prepress and Manufacturing: Caroline Fell
Cover art © PhotoDisc

Access the latest information about Addison-Wesley Computer Science titles from our World Wide Web site: http://www.awl.com/cs

Much of the material in Chapter 16 was adapted from *Java, An Introduction to Computer Science and Programming* by Walter Savitch, copyright 1999 by Prentice-Hall.

Library of Congress Cataloging-in-Publication Data

Savitch, Walter J., 1943–
    Problem solving with C++ : the object of programming / Walter Savitch.—3rd ed.
      p. cm.
    Includes bibliographical references and index.
    ISBN 0-201-70390-4 (pbk.)
    1. C++ (Computer program language)   I. Title.

QA76.73.C153 S34 2001
005.13'3—dc21
                                                00-045111

This book was typeset in QuarkXpress 4.1 on a Power Macintosh G4-500. The fonts used were Times, Futura, Lucida, Kaufmann, Arbitrary, and Remedy. It was printed on New Era Matte.

2 3 4 5 6 7 8 9 10-CRW-04030201

Preface

This book is meant to be used in a first course in programming and computer science using the C++ language. It assumes no previous programming experience and no mathematics beyond high school algebra. It could also be used as a text for a course designed to teach C++ to students who have already had some other programming course.

If you have used an earlier edition of this book, you should read the following section that explains the changes to this third edition, and then you can skip the rest of this preface. If you are new to this book, the rest of this preface will give you an overview of the book.

Changes to the Third Edition

This third edition presents the same programming philosophy and uses the same outline of topics as the second edition. If you are an instructor already using the second edition, you can continue to teach your course almost without change. You will need to update some details in some code, but, in most cases, the general thrust of the examples remains the same as in the previous edition. (Updating to the new C++ standard requires some changes.) This third edition does offer an opportunity for adding topics to a course. This third edition has been updated to match the latest ANSI/ISO C++ standard, including expanded coverage of the new string and bool types, coverage of and use of namespaces, and use of the new header files for standard libraries. For this edition, the chapters on templates and inheritance have been completely rewritten to make them more accessible and complete. This edition also includes a new final chapter on exception handling.

Choose Your Own Ordering of Topics

Most introductory textbooks that use C++ have a very detailed agenda that instructors must follow to use the book in their courses. If you are an instructor, this book adapts to the way you teach, rather than making you adapt to the book. This book explains C++ and basic programming techniques in a way suitable for beginning students, but it does not tightly prescribe the order in which your course must cover topics. You can easily change the order in which chapters and sections are covered without loss of continuity in reading the book. The details about rearranging material are explained later in the preface in the flexibility section.

Although this book uses libraries and teaches students the importance of libraries, it requires no nonstandard libraries. This book only uses libraries that are provided with essentially all C++ implementations.

ANSI/ISO C++ Standard

This edition has been updated for use with compilers that meet the new ANSI/ISO C++ Standard. Among other things, this means that we use the new library file names and that we teach and use namespaces. The previous edition already used the new types string and bool, and that use is expanded in this edition.

Unfortunately, many compilers still do not conform or do not fully conform to the new standard. So, although we wrote to the new standard, we did include some provisions to accommodate older compilers. There is an appendix with a table matching old and new library header file names. If your compiler does not use the new library names, you can substitute the old library names. Other brief accommodations for older compilers are also integrated into the book. You can use the accommodations when they are needed, but stay as close to the new standard as your compiler allows.

Early Classes

There are at least two ways that a book can introduce classes early: A book can teach students how to *design* their own classes early in the book or it can merely teach them how to *use* classes early without defining them. This book teaches students to define their own classes early and does not merely teach them how to use classes early. To effectively design classes, a student needs basic tools such as some simple control structures and function definitions. Thus, this book starts out covering these basics in Chapters 2, 3, and 4. It then moves immediately to classes. In Chapter 5, file I/O streams are used to teach students how to use classes. In Chapter 6, students learn how to write their own classes.

This book uses a measured approach to teaching classes. It teaches students to write some very simple classes, and then it adds constructors, then overloading simple operators, then overloading the I/O operators << and >>, and so forth. This measured approach keeps the student from being overwhelmed with a long list of complicated constructions and concepts. However, one goal of this book is to get students to write realistic class definitions as soon as possible, and not to have them spend time writing classes that are artificially simple. By the end of Chapter 8, students are writing essentially the same kinds of classes that they will be writing when they finish the course.

Inheritance is covered briefly in Chapter 5 so that students become aware of the concept. However, this book does not teach students how to write their own derived classes until later in the book. This is because the examples that strongly motivate inheritance and derived classes often do not arise naturally at the beginning of a first course using C++. Chapter 15 does teach students how to define and use derived classes, including the use of virtual functions. Some instructors may choose to leave that material for a second course. Other instructors will want to integrate this inheritance coverage into their course.

Even though we postpone a complete discussion of inheritance, the classes that are used early in the book are very sophisticated, and some would argue that they are too complicated to be covered so early in a first programming course. After all, in addition to the basic notions of member variables and member functions, beginning students reading this book will learn all of the following topics very early: public and private members, function overloading, operator overloading, friend functions, returning a reference so that they can overload the I/O operators << and >>, constructors for automatic initialization, constructors for type conversion, and a number of smaller issues. Some would argue that this is too much to give students so early. We have class tested this material, however, and found that the examples become unrealistic or poorly behaved if we omit any of these topics. Moreover, in class testing we found that students respond to early classes in basically the same way that they respond to early functions. Certainly the material presents some problems. However, students are as capable of learning the material early in the course as they will be later in the course. Moreover, covering classes early leaves students with a better working knowledge of classes. Students have a strong loyalty to the first technique they learn for solving a problem. So, if you want them to really use a technique, then you need to teach it early. Moreover, classes are not the hardest topic the students encounter. For example, classes are more intuitive and better behaved than ordinary (C-style) arrays, which they learn later in the course.

Having made the case for early classes, we are still aware that not everybody wants to introduce classes as early as we do, so we have written the book to allow instructors to move coverage of classes to later in the course. This is discussed in the flexibility section in this preface.

Accessible to Students

It is not enough for a book to present the right topics in the right order. It is not even enough for it to be clear and correct when read by an instructor or other experienced programmer. The material needs to be presented in a way that is accessible to beginning students. In this series of introductory textbooks, I have endeavored to write in a way that students find clear and friendly. Reports from the many students who have used the earlier editions of this book confirm that this style makes the material clear and often even enjoyable to students.

Advanced Topics

Many "advanced topics" are becoming part of a standard CS1 course. Even if they are not part of a course, it is good to have them available in the text as enrichment material. This book offers a number of advanced topics that can be integrated into a course or left as enrichment topics. It gives thorough coverage of C++ templates, inheritance, including virtual functions, and exception handling. The two chapters on templates and exception handling have been completely rewritten for this edition. The chapter on exception handling is new to this edition.

Summary Boxes

Each major point is summarized in a boxed section. These boxed sections are spread throughout each chapter.

Self-Test Exercises

Each chapter contains numerous Self-Test Exercises at strategic points in the chapter. Complete answers for all the Self-Test Exercises are given at the end of each chapter.

Class Tested

Over 100,000 students have used the first two editions of this book. Many of these students and many of their instructors have given me feedback about what worked and what did not work for them. The vast majority of the comments were extremely positive and indicated that they liked the book pretty much as it was, but suggestions for some changes were made. All suggestions for changes were carefully considered. That valuable feedback was used to revise this edition so that it fits students' and instructors' needs even better than the previous editions.

Flexibility in Topic Ordering

This book was written to allow instructors wide latitude in reordering the material. To illustrate this flexibility, we suggest a number of alternative ways to order the topics. There is no loss of continuity when the book is read in any of these ways. To ensure this continuity when you rearrange material, you may need to move sections rather than entire chapters. However, only large sections in convenient locations are moved. To help customize a particular order to any class's needs, the dependency chart, which follows this preface, describes many more possible ways in which the chapters and sections can be ordered without loss of continuity.

Reordering 1: Late Classes

This version essentially covers all of a traditional ANSI C course before going on to cover classes. The only thing that is much like C++ before the introduction of classes is the use of streams for I/O. Because stream I/O does require some use of namespaces, coverage of namespaces is integrated into the first few chapters. (If you are using an older compiler, you can ignore the references to namespaces.)

Basics: Chapters 1, 2, 3, 4, 5, and 7 (omitting Chapter 6 on defining classes). This material covers all of control structures, function definitions, and basic file I/O.

Arrays: Chapter 9, omitting the last section (Section 9.4), which uses classes. Chapter 10, omitting the last section (Section 10.2), which covers the STL string class.

Pointers and Dynamic Arrays: Chapter 11, omitting the last section (Section 11.3), which covers material on classes.

Recursion: Chapter 12, omitting the programming example on classes that ends the chapter. (Alternatively, recursion may be moved to later in the course.)

Structures and Classes: Chapters 6, 8, and the last sections of Chapters 9, 10, and 11.

Pointers and Linked Lists: Chapter 14

Plus any subset of the following chapters:

Templates: Chapter 13

Inheritance: Chapter 15

Exception Handling: Chapter 16

Reordering 2: Classes Slightly Earlier

This version covers all control structures and the basic material on arrays before doing classes, but classes are covered somewhat earlier than the previous reordering.

Basics: Chapters 1, 2, 3, 4, 5, and 7 (omitting Chapter 6 on defining classes). This material covers all of control structures, function definitions, and basic file I/O.

One-Dimensional Arrays: Chapter 9, omitting the last section (Section 9.4), which uses classes.

Structures and Classes: Chapters 6, 8, and the last sections of Chapter 9.

Multidimensional Arrays and Strings: Chapter 10

Pointers and Dynamic Arrays: Chapter 11

Recursion: Chapter 12

Pointers and Linked Lists: Chapter 14

Plus any subset of the following chapters:
> Templates: Chapter 13
> Inheritance: Chapter 15
> Exception Handling: Chapter 16

Reordering 3: Early Classes, but with All Control Structures Covered before Classes:

This is almost the regular ordering of the book. You only need to move Chapter 7 so that you cover Chapter 7 before Chapter 6.

Variations:

The first two sections of Chapter 12 (which cover basic recursion) can be covered anytime after Chapter 4. The first two sections on pointers (in Chapter 11) can be covered before Chapter 10, which covers multidimensional arrays and strings. Most of the first section of Chapter 13, which covers function templates, can be covered anytime after Chapter 4. The first two sections of Chapter 15 (15.1 and 15.2), which cover the basics of defining and using derived classes, can be covered anytime after Chapter 10. Other possible variations are shown in the dependency chart at the end of this preface.

Support Material

The following support material is available from the publisher:

Programs from the Text: All the programs in the text are available by following the links at the following Web site:
> http://www.awl.com/cssupport

Alternatively, you can find the programs by going to the author's Web site, given below, and following the links there.
> http://www-cse.ucsd.edu/users/savitch/

Instructor's Resource Guide: A chapter-by-chapter instructor's guide includes numerous teaching hints, quiz questions with solutions, and solutions to many programming exercises.

The instructor's guide is for qualified instructors only. It is available through your Addison-Wesley sales representative or by sending an e-mail message to aw.cse@awl.com.

E-mail Contact

I would very much like to hear your comments so that I can continue to improve this book to make it better fit your needs. Please send your comments to the following e-mail address:

    wsavitch@ucsd.edu

I want to know how you like the book and I want suggestions for changes, but unfortunately I am not able to provide students with an e-mail consulting or tutoring service. The volume of e-mail has gotten too large for this. In particular, I cannot provide solutions to exercises in this book or to other exercises provided by your instructor. I simply do not have enough time to answer the numerous requests that I get for such detailed assistance. I also do not want to interfere with any instructor's plans for how students should go about solving programming problems. As at least a partial consolation to those who desire such help, this book does include complete answers to all of the Self-Test Exercises. Also, the instructor's guide does provide instructors with some answers to Programming Projects, but that material is only available to college and university instructors who adopt the book, and it cannot be given out to students. Finally, many questions can be answered by visiting the following Web site, which has answers to some frequently asked questions:

    http://www-cse.ucsd.edu/users/savitch/

Click on the link for this book.

Acknowledgments

Numerous individuals and groups have provided me with suggestions, discussions, and other help in preparing this textbook. Much of the first edition of this book was written while I was visiting the Computer Science Department at the University of Colorado in Boulder. The remainder of the writing on the first edition and the work on the second and third editions was done in the Computer Science and Engineering Department at the University of California, San Diego (UCSD). I am grateful to these institutions for providing a conducive environment for teaching this material and writing this book.

David Teague deserves special acknowledgment. I very much appreciate his hard work, good insights, and careful researching for many sections of the book. He assisted in updating the material to match the new ANSI/ISO C++ Standard.

The list of other individuals who have contributed critiques for earlier editions and drafts of this book is too long to thank each contributor in the unique way that she or he deserves. So I must simply list them (in alphabetical order) and extend my deepest thanks to them all. Comments and reviews for the first two editions have helped tremendously with this edition as well. For reviews and critiques provided for writing the first two editions I thank: Claire Bono, Andrew Burt, Karla Chaveau, Joel Cohen, Doug Cosman, Joe Faletti, Paulo Franca, Len Garrett, Jerrold Grossman, Dennis Heckman, Bob Holloway, Bruce Johnston, Thomas Judson, Michael Keenan, Barney MacCabe, Steve Mahaney, Michael Main, John Marsaglia, Nat Martin, Jesse Morehouse, Lt. Donald Needham, Dung Nguyen, Ken Rockwood, John Russo, and Jerry Weltman. For comments and reviews for this edition I thank: Scot Drysdale, Dartmouth College, Alex Feldman, Boise State University, Eitan M. Gurari, Ohio State University, Matt Johnson, University of Missouri-Rolla, Paul J. Kaiser, Lewis University, Walter A. Manrique, SUNY New Paltz, Anne Marchant, George Mason University, Bob Matthews, University of Puget Sound, Joseph D. Oldham, George-town College, Amber Settle, DePaul University, Naomi Shapiro, Georgian Court College, John J. Westman, UCLA, and Linda F. Wilson, Dartmouth College.

I extend a special thanks to the many instructors who used early editions of this book. Their comments provided some of the most helpful reviewing that the book received. In particular, I'd like to offer a special thanks to Paul Kube, Susan Seitz, and David Teague for their valuable feedback after class testing material from earlier editions of this book.

I again thank David Teague. This time for his excellent work in preparing the instructor's guide.

I thank Prentice-Hall for allowing me to adapt some material from my book *Java, An Introduction to Computer Science and Programming* so that I could use the adapted material in Chapter 16 of this book.

I thank all the individuals at Addison-Wesley who supported my work on this edition. I thank Lisa Kalner for coordinating reviews, coordinating communication with production, and coordinating just about everything else. She was the critical communication node that made this edition possible. I thank Diane Freed for an excellent job of handling production under very tight time constraints. I thank Frank Ruggirello for his encouragement and support. I thank my editor Susan Hartman Sullivan who provided the reviewers, as well as the encouragement that allowed this third edition to be produced in a timely fashion.

Finally, I thank Christina for putting up with my working late on the book and even offering encouragement and critiques on the content.

W.S.
http://www-cse.ucsd.edu/users/savitch/

Dependency Chart

The dependency chart on the next page shows possible orderings of chapters and subsections. A line joining two boxes means that the upper box must be covered before the lower box. Any ordering that is consistent with this partial ordering can be read without loss of continuity. If a section number or numbers are given in a box, then the box refers only to those sections and not to the entire chapter.

Dependency Chart

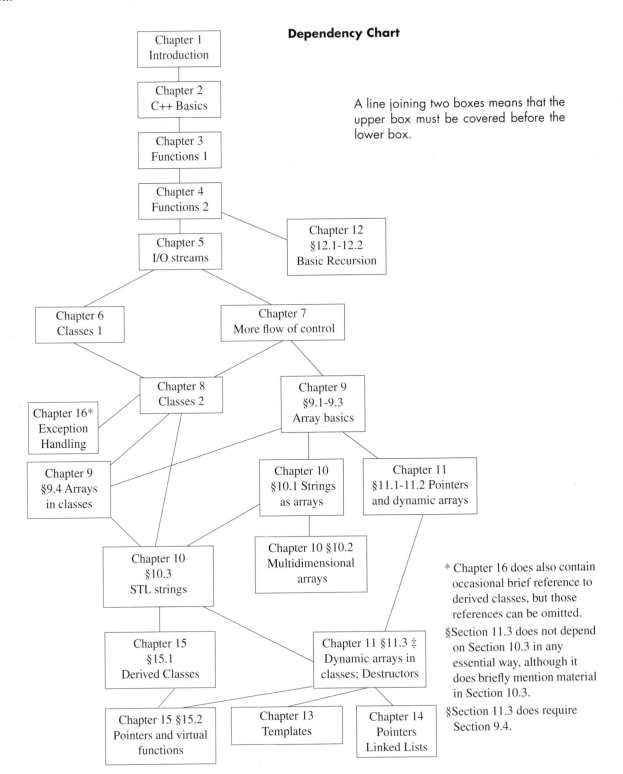

A line joining two boxes means that the upper box must be covered before the lower box.

Chapter 1
Introduction

Chapter 2
C++ Basics

Chapter 3
Functions 1

Chapter 4
Functions 2

Chapter 12
§12.1-12.2
Basic Recursion

Chapter 5
I/O streams

Chapter 6
Classes 1

Chapter 7
More flow of control

Chapter 8
Classes 2

Chapter 9
§9.1-9.3
Array basics

Chapter 16*
Exception
Handling

Chapter 9
§9.4 Arrays
in classes

Chapter 10
§10.1 Strings
as arrays

Chapter 11
§11.1-11.2 Pointers
and dynamic arrays

Chapter 10
§10.3
STL strings

Chapter 10 §10.2
Multidimensional
arrays

Chapter 15
§15.1
Derived Classes

Chapter 11 §11.3 ‡
Dynamic arrays in
classes; Destructors

Chapter 15 §15.2
Pointers and virtual
functions

Chapter 13
Templates

Chapter 14
Pointers
Linked Lists

* Chapter 16 does also contain occasional brief reference to derived classes, but those references can be omitted.

§Section 11.3 does not depend on Section 10.3 in any essential way, although it does briefly mention material in Section 10.3.

§Section 11.3 does require Section 9.4.

Dependency Chart

The dependency chart on the next page shows possible orderings of chapters and subsections. A line joining two boxes means that the upper box must be covered before the lower box. Any ordering that is consistent with this partial ordering can be read without loss of continuity. If a section number or numbers are given in a box, then the box refers only to those sections and not to the entire chapter.

Dependency Chart

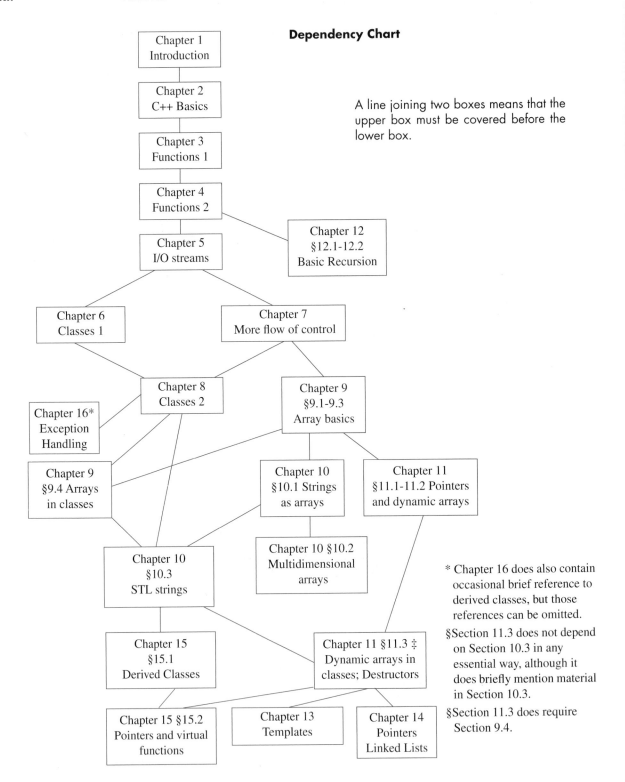

A line joining two boxes means that the upper box must be covered before the lower box.

* Chapter 16 does also contain occasional brief reference to derived classes, but those references can be omitted.

§Section 11.3 does not depend on Section 10.3 in any essential way, although it does briefly mention material in Section 10.3.

§Section 11.3 does require Section 9.4.

Contents

CHAPTER 7

MORE FLOW OF CONTROL   365

CHAPTER 1

Introduction to Computers and C++ Programming

1 Introduction to Computers and C + + Programming

The whole of the development and operation of analysis are now capable of being executed by machinery ... As soon as an Analytical Engine exists, it will necessarily guide the future course of science.

CHARLES BABBAGE (1792–1871)

Introduction

In this chapter we describe the basic components of a computer, as well as the basic technique for designing and writing a program. We then show you a sample C++ program and describe how it works.

1.1 Computer Systems

software

hardware

A set of instructions for a computer to follow is called a **program.** The collection of programs used by a computer is referred to as the **software** for that computer. The actual physical machines that make up a computer installation are referred to as **hardware.** As we will see, the hardware for a computer is conceptually very simple. However, computers now come with a large array of software to aid in the task of programming. This software includes editors, translators, and managers of various sorts. The resulting environment is a complicated and powerful system. In this book we are concerned almost exclusively with software, but a brief overview of how the hardware is organized will be useful.

Hardware

PCs, mainframes, and workstations

There are three main classes of computers: *PCs*, *workstations*, and *mainframes*. A **PC (personal computer)** is a relatively small computer designed to be used by one person at a time. Most home computers are PCs, but PCs are also widely used in business, industry, and science. A **workstation** is essentially a larger and more powerful PC. You can think of it as an "industrial-strength" PC. A **mainframe** is an even larger computer that typically requires some support staff and generally is shared by more than one user. The distinctions between PCs, workstations, and mainframes are

Display 1.1 Main Components of a Computer

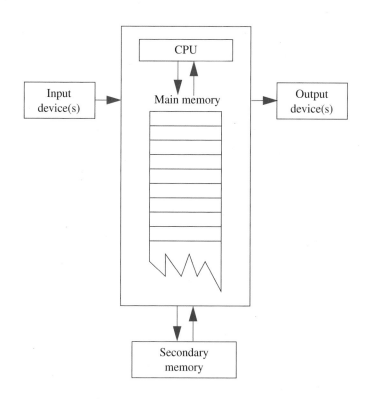

not precise, but the terms are commonly used and do convey some very general information about a computer.

A **network** consists of a number of computers connected, so they may share resources, such as printers, and may share information. A network might contain a number of workstations and one or more mainframes, as well as shared devices such as printers. For our purposes in learning programming it will not matter whether you are working on a PC, a mainframe, or a workstation. The basic configuration of the computer, as we will view it, is the same for all three types of computers.

network

The hardware for most computer systems is organized as shown in Display 1.1. The computer can be thought of as having five main components: the *input device(s)*, the *output device(s)*, the *central processing unit (CPU)*, the *main memory*, and the *secondary memory*. The CPU, main memory, and sometimes even secondary memory are normally housed in a single cabinet. The CPU and main memory form the heart of a computer, and can be thought of as an integrated unit. Other components connect to the main memory and operate under the direction of the CPU. The arrows in Display 1.1 indicate the direction of information flow.

input devices

An **input device** is any device that allows a person to communicate information to the computer. Your primary input devices are likely to be a keyboard and a mouse. Among other things, a mouse is used to point to and choose one of a list of alternatives displayed on the screen. The device is called a *mouse* because the cord connecting it to the terminal makes it look somewhat like a mouse with a long tail.

output devices

An **output device** is anything that allows the computer to communicate information to you. The most common output device is a display screen, referred to as a *video display screen* or a *monitor.* Quite often, there is more than one output device. For example, in addition to the display screen, your computer probably has a printer for producing output on paper. The keyboard and display screen are frequently thought of as a single unit called a *video display terminal*, which is usually abbreviated with the initials *VDT* or the single word *terminal.*

In order to store input and to have the equivalent of scratch paper for performing calculations, computers are provided with *memory*. The program that the computer executes is also stored in this memory. A computer has two forms of memory called *main memory* and *secondary memory*. The program that is being executed is kept in main memory, and main memory is, as the name implies, the most important mem-

main memory

ory. **Main memory** consists of a long list of numbered locations called *memory locations*; the number of memory locations varies from one computer to another, ranging from a few thousand to many millions, and sometimes even into the billions. Each memory location contains a string of zeros and ones. The contents of these locations can change. Hence, you can think of each memory location as a tiny blackboard on which the computer may write and erase. In most computers, all memory locations contain the same number of zero/one digits. A digit that can assume only

bit

the values zero or one is called a **binary digit** or a **bit.** The memory locations in most computers contain eight bits (or some multiple of eight bits). An eight-bit por-

byte

tion of memory is called a **byte,** so we may refer to these numbered memory locations as *bytes*. To rephrase the situation, you can think of the computer's main memory as a long list of numbered memory locations called *bytes*. The number that

address

identifies a byte is called its **address.** A data item, such as a number or a letter, can be stored in one of these bytes and the address of the byte is then used to find the data item when it is needed.

If the computer needs to deal with a data item (such as a large number) that is too large to fit in a single byte, it will use several adjacent bytes to hold the data item. In this case the entire chunk of memory that holds the data item is still called a

memory location

memory location. The address of the first of the bytes that make up this memory location is used as the address for this larger memory location. Thus, as a practical matter, you can think of the computer's main memory as a long list of memory loca-

Display 1.2 Memory Locations and Bytes

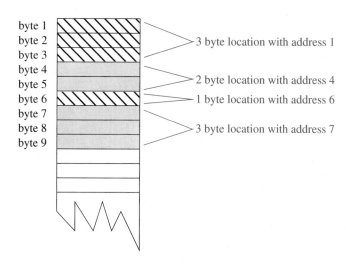

tions of *varying sizes*. The size of each of these locations is expressed in bytes and the address of the first byte is used as the address (name) of that memory location. Display 1.2 shows a picture of a hypothetical computer's main memory. The sizes of the memory locations are not fixed, but can change when a new program is run on the computer.

Bytes and Addresses

Main memory is divided into numbered locations called **bytes.** The number associated with a byte is called its **address.** A group of consecutive bytes is used as the location for a data item, such as a number or letter. The address of the first byte in the group is used as the address of this larger memory location.

The fact that the information in a computer's memory is represented as zeros and ones need not be of great concern to you when programming in C++ (or in most any other programming language). There is, however, one point about this use of zeros and ones that will concern us as soon as we start to write programs. The computer needs to interpret these strings of zeros and ones as numbers, letters, instructions, or other types of information. The computer performs these interpretations automatically according to certain coding schemes. A different code is used for each different type of item that is stored in the computer's memory: one code for letters,

---

Why Eight?

A **byte** is a memory location that can hold eight bits. What is so special about eight? Why not ten bits? There are two reasons why eight is special. First, eight is a power of 2. (8 is 2^3.) Since computers use bits, which only have two possible values, powers of two are more convenient than powers of 10. Second, it turns out that it requires eight bits (one byte) to code a single character (such as a letter or other keyboard symbol).

---

another for whole numbers, another for fractions, another for instructions, and so on. For example, in one commonly used set of codes, 01000001 is the code for the letter A and also for the number 65. In order to know what the string 01000001 in a particular location stands for, the computer must keep track of which code is currently being used for that location. Fortunately, the programmer seldom needs to be concerned with such codes and can safely reason as though the locations actually contained letters, numbers, or whatever is desired.

The memory we have been discussing up until now is the main memory. Without its main memory, a computer can do nothing. However, main memory is only used while the computer is actually following the instructions in a program. The computer also has another form of memory called *secondary memory* or *secondary storage*. (The words *memory* and *storage* are exact synonyms in this context.)

secondary memory

Secondary memory is the memory that is used for keeping a permanent record of information after (and before) the computer is used. Some alternative terms that are commonly used to refer to secondary memory are *auxiliary memory*, *auxiliary storage*, *external memory*, and *external storage*.

files

Information in secondary storage is kept in units called **files,** which can be as large or as small as you like. A program, for example, is stored in a file in secondary storage and copied into main memory when the program is run. You can store a program, a letter, an inventory list, or any other unit of information in a file.

Several different kinds of secondary memory may be attached to a single computer. The most common forms of secondary memory are *hard disks*, *diskettes*, and *tapes*. (Diskettes are also sometimes referred to as *floppy disks*.) Computer tapes and computer tape drives are similar to the tapes and tape drives used to record and play music. Information is stored on hard disks and diskettes in basically the same way as it is stored on tapes, but the information is in concentric rings on a disk rather than on a long tape. **Hard disks** are fixed in place and are normally not removed from the disk drive. **Diskettes** can be easily removed from the disk drive and carried to another computer. Diskettes have the advantages of being inexpensive and portable, but hard disks hold more data and operate faster.

disks and diskettes

Other, newer forms of secondary memory are rapidly coming into wide use. For example, a **CD-ROM** is essentially the same thing as a CD (compact disk) used to play music on a home stereo system. The initials *CD-ROM* stand for *compact disk with read only memory.* The memory on a CD-ROM cannot be changed, but it can be very large. CD-ROM is used for things that do not change (or only change very rarely), such as dictionaries. Other forms of secondary memory are also available, but this list covers most forms that you are likely to encounter.

CD-ROM

Main memory is often referred to as **RAM** or **random access memory.** It is called *random access* because the computer can immediately access the data in any memory location. Secondary memory often requires **sequential access,** which means that the computer must look through all (or at least very many) memory locations until it finds the item it needs. (Do not confuse the term *RAM* and the term *ROM*, as in *CD-ROM*. They are two different terms.)

RAM

The **central processing unit,** or **CPU,** is the "brain" of the computer. The CPU follows the instructions in a program and performs the calculations specified by the program. The CPU is, however, a very simple brain. All it can do is follow a set of simple instructions provided by the programmer. Typical CPU instructions say things like "Interpret the zeros and ones as numbers, and then add the number in memory location 37 to the number in memory location 59, and put the answer in location 43," or "Read a letter of input, convert it to its code as a string of zeros and ones, and place it in memory location 1298." The CPU can add, subtract, multiply, and divide and can move things from one memory location to another. It can interpret strings of zeros and ones as letters and send the letters to an output device. The CPU also has some primitive ability to rearrange the order of instructions. CPU instructions vary somewhat from one computer to another. The CPU of a modern computer can have as many as several hundred available instructions. However, these instructions are typically all about as simple as those we have just described.

CPU

Software

You do not normally talk directly to the computer, but communicate with it through an *operating system*. The **operating system** allocates the computer's resources to the different tasks that the computer must accomplish. The operating system is actually a program, but it is perhaps better to think of it as your chief servant. It is in charge of all your other servant programs, and it delivers your requests to them. If you want to run a program, you tell the operating system the name of the file that contains it, and the operating system runs the program. If you want to edit a file, you tell the operating system the name of the file and it starts up the editor to work on that file. To most users the operating system is the computer. Most users never see the computer without its operating system. The names of some common operating systems are *UNIX, DOS, Linux, Windows, Macintosh*, and *VMS*.

operating system

Display 1.3 Simple View of Running a Program

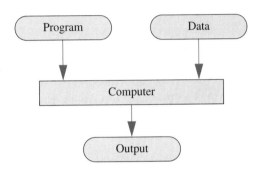

program

A **program** is a set of instructions for a computer to follow. As shown in Display 1.3, the input to a computer can be thought of as consisting of two parts, a program and some data. The computer follows the instructions in the program, and in that way, performs some process. The **data** is what we conceptualize as the input to the program. For example, if the program adds two numbers, then the two numbers are the data. In other words, the data is the input to the program, and both the program and the data are input to the computer (usually via the operating system). Whenever we give a computer both a program to follow and some data for the program, we are said to be **running** the program on the data, and the computer is said to **execute** the program on the data. The word *data* also has a much more general meaning than the one we have just given it. In its most general sense it means any information available to the computer. The word is commonly used in both the narrow sense and the more general sense.

data

running a program

executing a program

High-Level Languages

There are many languages for writing programs. In this text we will discuss the C++ programming language and use it to write our programs. C++ is a high-level language, as are most of the other programming languages you are likely to have heard of, such as C, Java, Pascal, FORTRAN, BASIC, COBOL, Lisp, Scheme, and Ada. **High-level languages** resemble human languages in many ways. They are designed to be easy for human beings to write programs in and to be easy for human beings to read. A high-level language, such as C++, contains instructions that are much more complicated than the simple instructions a computer's CPU is capable of following.

high-level language

The kind of language a computer can understand is called a **low-level language.** The exact details of low-level languages differ from one kind of computer to another. A typical low-level instruction might be the following:

low-level
language

```
ADD X Y Z
```

This instruction might mean "Add the number in the memory location called X to the number in the memory location called Y, and place the result in the memory location called Z." The above sample instruction is written in what is called **assembly language.** Although assembly language is almost the same as the language understood by the computer, it must undergo one simple translation before the computer can understand it. In order to get a computer to follow an assembly language instruction, the words need to be translated into strings of zeros and ones. For example, the word ADD might translate to 0110, the X might translate to 1001, the Y to 1010, and the Z to 1011. The version of the above instruction that the computer ultimately follows would then be:

assembly
language

```
0110 1001 1010 1011
```

Assembly language instructions and their translation into zeros and ones differ from machine to machine.

Programs written in the form of zeros and ones are said to be written in **machine language,** because that is the version of the program that the computer (the machine) actually reads and follows. Assembly language and machine language are almost the same thing, and the distinction between them will not be important to us. The important distinction is that between machine language and high-level languages like C++: any high-level language program must be translated into machine language before the computer can understand and follow the program.

machine
language

Compilers

A program that translates a high-level language like C++ to a machine language is called a **compiler.** A compiler is thus a somewhat peculiar sort of program, in that its input or data is some other program, and its output is yet another program. To avoid confusion, the input program is usually called the **source program** or **source code,** and the translated version produced by the compiler is called the **object program** or **object code.** The word **code** is frequently used to mean a program or a part of a program, and this usage is particularly common when referring to object programs. Now, suppose you want to run a C++ program that you have written. In order to get the computer to follow your C++ instructions, proceed as follows. First, run the compiler using your C++ program as data. Notice that in this case your C++ program is not being treated as a set of instructions. To the compiler, your C++ program

source program
object program
code

**Display 1.4 Compiling and Running a C++ Program
(Basic Outline)**

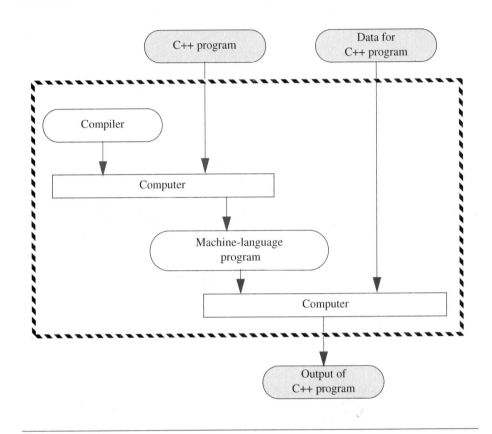

is just a long string of characters. The output will be another long string of characters, which is the machine-language equivalent of your C++ program. Next, run this machine-language program on what we normally think of as the data for the C++ program. The output will be what we normally conceptualize as the output of the C++ program. The basic process is easier to visualize if you have two computers available, as diagrammed in Display 1.4. In reality, the entire process is accomplished by using one computer two times.

linking

The complete process of translating and running a C++ program is a bit more complicated than what we showed in Display 1.4. Any C++ program you write will use some operations (such as input and output routines) that have already been programmed for you. These items that are already programmed for you (like input and output routines) are already compiled and have their object code waiting to be com-

---

Compiler

A **compiler** is a program that translates a high-level language program, such as a C++ program, into a machine-language program that the computer can directly understand and execute.

---

bined with your program's object code to produce a complete machine-language program that can be run on the computer. Another program, called a **linker,** combines the object code for these program pieces with the object code that the compiler produced from your C++ program. The interaction of the compiler and the linker are diagrammed in Display 1.5. In very routine cases, many systems will do this linking for you automatically. Thus, you may not need to worry about linking in very simple cases.

Linking

The object code for your C++ program must be combined with the object code for routines (such as input and output routines) that your program uses. This process of combining object code is called **linking** and is done by a program called a **linker.** For simple programs linking may be done for you automatically.

SELF-TEST EXERCISES

1 What are the five main components of a computer?

2 What would be the data for a program to add two numbers?

3 What would be the data for a program that assigns letter grades to students in a class?

4 What is the difference between a machine-language program and a high-level language program?

5 What is the role of a compiler?

6 What is a source program? What is an object program?

7 What is an operating system?

8 What purpose does the operating system serve?

9 Name the operating system that runs on the computer you use to prepare programs for this course.

Display 1.5 Preparing a C++ Program for Running

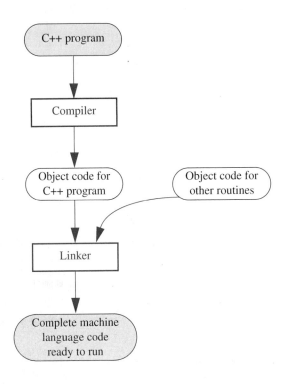

10 What is linking?

11 Find out whether linking is done automatically by the compiler you use for this course.

History Note

Charles Babbage

The first truly programmable computer was designed by Charles Babbage, an English mathematician and physical scientist. Babbage began the project sometime before 1822 and worked on it for the rest of his life. Although he never completed the construction of his machine, the design was a conceptual milestone in the history of computing. Much of what we know about Charles Babbage and his computer design comes from the writings of his colleague Ada Augusta, daughter of the poet Byron and the Countess of Lovelace. Ada Augusta is frequently given the title of the first computer programmer. Her comments, quoted in the opening of the next section, still apply to the process of solving problems on a computer. Computers are not

Ada Augusta

magic and do not, at least as yet, have the ability to formulate sophisticated solutions to all the problems we encounter. Computers simply do what the programmer orders them to do. The solutions to problems are carried out by the computer, but the solutions are formulated by the programmer. Our discussion of computer programming begins with a discussion of how a programmer formulates these solutions.

1.2 Programming and Problem-Solving

The Analytical Engine has no pretensions whatever to originate anything. It can do whatever we know how to order it to perform. It can follow analysis; but it has no power of anticipating any analytical relations or truths. Its province is to assist us in making available what we are already acquainted with.

ADA AUGUSTA, COUNTESS OF LOVELACE

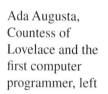

Ada Augusta, Countess of Lovelace and the first computer programmer, left

Charles Babbage, right

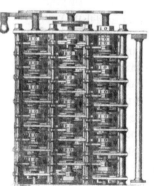

A Model of Babbage's computer

In this section we describe some general principles that you can use to design and write programs. These principles are not particular to C++. They apply no matter what programming language you are using.

Algorithms

When learning your first programming language it is easy to get the impression that the hard part of solving a problem on a computer is translating your ideas into the specific language that will be fed into the computer. This definitely is not the case. The most difficult part of solving a problem on a computer is discovering the method of solution. After you come up with a method of solution, it is routine to translate your method into the required language, be it C++ or some other programming language. It is therefore helpful to temporarily ignore the programming language and to concentrate instead on formulating the steps of the solution and writing them down in plain English, as if the instructions were to be given to a human being rather than a computer. A sequence of instructions expressed in this way is frequently referred to as an *algorithm*.

algorithm
     A sequence of precise instructions which leads to a solution is called an **algorithm.** Some approximately equivalent words are *recipe*, *method*, *directions*, *procedure*, and *routine*. The instructions may be expressed in a programming language or a human language. Our algorithms will be expressed in English and in the programming language C++. A computer program is simply an algorithm expressed in a language that a computer can understand. Thus, the term *algorithm* is more general than the term *program*. However, when we say that a sequence of instructions is an algorithm we usually mean that the instructions are expressed in English, since if they were expressed in a programming language we would use the more specific term *program*. An example may help to clarify the concept.

sample algorithm
     Display 1.6 contains an algorithm expressed in rather stylized English. The algorithm determines the number of times a specified name occurs on a list of names. If the list contains the winners of each of last season's football games and the name is that of your favorite team, then the algorithm determines how many games your team won. The algorithm is short and simple but is otherwise very typical of the algorithms with which we will be dealing.

     The instructions numbered 1 through 5 in our sample algorithm are meant to be carried out in the order they are listed. Unless otherwise specified, we will always assume that the instructions of an algorithm are carried out in the order in which they are given (written down). Most interesting algorithms do, however, specify some change of order, usually a repeating of some instruction again and again such as in instruction 4 of our sample algorithm.

origin of the word algorithm
     The word *algorithm* has a long history. It derives from the name of a ninth-century Persian mathematician and astronomer Al-Khowarizmi. He wrote a famous

Display 1.6 An Algorithm

**Algorithm that determines how many times
a name occurs in a list of names:**

1. Get the list of names.
2. Get the name being checked.
3. Set a counter to zero.
4. Do the following for each name on the list:
   Compare the name on the list to the name being checked,
   and if the names are the same, then add one to the counter.
5. Announce that the answer is the number indicated by the counter.

textbook on the manipulation of numbers and equations. The book was entitled *Kitab al-jabr w'almuqabala*, which can be translated as *Rules for reuniting and reducing*. The similar sounding word *algebra* was derived from the arabic word *al-jabr*, which appears in the title of the book and which is often translated as *reuniting* or *restoring*. The meanings of the words *algebra* and *algorithm* used to be much more intimately related than they are today. Indeed, until modern times, the word *algorithm* usually referred only to algebraic rules for solving numerical equations. Today the word *algorithm* can be applied to a wide variety of kinds of instructions for manipulating symbolic as well as numeric data. The properties that qualify a set of instructions as an algorithm now are determined by the nature of the instructions rather than by the things manipulated by the instructions. To qualify as an algorithm a set of instructions must completely and unambiguously specify the steps to be taken and the order in which they are taken. The person or machine carrying out the algorithm does exactly what the algorithm says, neither more nor less.

Algorithm

An **algorithm** is a sequence of precise instructions that leads to a solution.

Program Design

Designing a program is often a difficult task. There is no complete set of rules, no algorithm to tell you how to write programs. Program design is a creative process. Still, there is the outline of a plan to follow. The outline is given in diagrammatic form in Display 1.7. As indicated there, the entire program-design process can be divided into two phases, the *problem-solving phase* and the *implementation phase*. The result of the **problem-solving phase** is an algorithm, expressed in English, for solving the problem. To produce a program in a programming language such as C++, the algorithm is translated into the programming language. Producing the final program from the algorithm is called the **implementation phase.**

problem-solving phase

implementation phase

The first step is to be certain that the task—that you want your program to do—is completely and precisely specified. Do not take this step lightly. If you do not know exactly what you want as the output of your program, you may be surprised at what your program produces. Be certain that you know what the input to the program will be and exactly what information is supposed to be in the output, as well as what form that information should be in. For example, if the program is a bank accounting program, you must know not only the interest rate, but also whether interest is to be compounded annually, monthly, daily, or whatever. If the program is supposed to write poetry, you need to determine whether the poems can be in free verse or must be in iambic pentameter or some other meter.

Many novice programmers do not understand the need to design an algorithm before writing a program in a programming language, such as C++, and so they try to short-circuit the process by omitting the problem-solving phase entirely, or by reducing it to just the problem definition part. This seems reasonable. Why not "go for the mark" and save time? The answer is that *it does not save time!* Experience has shown that the two-phase process will produce a correctly working program faster. The two-phase process simplifies the algorithm design phase by isolating it from the detailed rules of a programming language such as C++. The result is that the algorithm design process becomes much less intricate and much less prone to error. For even a modest size program it can represent the difference between a half day of careful work and several frustrating days of looking for mistakes in a poorly understood program.

The implementation phase is not a trivial step. There are details to be concerned about, and occasionally some of these details can be subtle, but it is much simpler than you might at first think. Once you become familiar with C++ or any other programming language, the translation of an algorithm from English into the programming language becomes a routine task.

As indicated in Display 1.7, testing takes place in both phases. Before the program is written, the algorithm is tested and if the algorithm is found to be deficient, then the algorithm is redesigned. That desktop testing is performed by mentally going through the algorithm and executing the steps yourself. On large algorithms this will require a pencil and paper. The C++ program is tested by compiling it and running it on some sample input data. The compiler will give error messages for certain kinds of errors. To find other types of errors, you must somehow check to see if the output is correct.

Display 1.7 Program Design Process

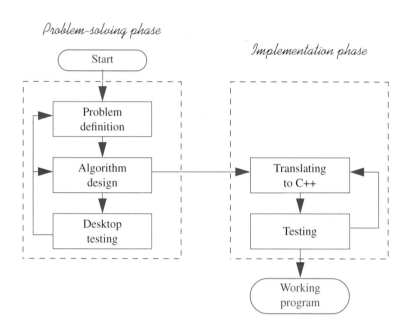

The process diagrammed in Display 1.7 is an idealized picture of the program design process. It is the basic picture you should have in mind, but reality is sometimes more complicated. In reality mistakes and deficiencies are discovered at unexpected times, and you may have to back up and redo an earlier step. For example, testing the algorithm may reveal that the definition of the problem was incomplete. In such a case you must back up and reformulate the definition. Occasionally, deficiencies in the definition or algorithm may not be observed until a program is tested. In that case you must back up and modify the definition or algorithm and all that follows them in the design process.

The Software Life Cycle

Designers of large software systems, such as compilers and operating systems, divided the software development process into six phases known as the **software life cycle.** The six phases of this life cycle are:

1. Analysis and specification of the task (problem definition);
2. Design of the software (algorithm design);

3. Implementation (coding);

4. Testing;

5. Maintenance and evolution of the system; and

6. Obsolescence

We did not mention the last two phases in our discussion of program design because they take place after the program is finished and put into service. However, they should always be kept in mind. You will not be able to add improvements or corrections to your program unless you design it to be easy to read and easy to change. Designing programs so that they can be easily modified will be an important topic that we will discuss in detail when we have developed a bit more background and a few more programming techniques. The meaning of obsolescence is obvious, but it is not always easy to accept. When a program is not working as it should and cannot be fixed with a reasonable amount of effort, it should be discarded and replaced with a completely new program.

SELF-TEST EXERCISES

12 An algorithm is approximately the same thing as a recipe, but some kinds of steps that would be allowed in a recipe are not allowed in an algorithm. Which steps in the following recipe would be allowed?

Place 2 teaspoons of sugar in mixing bowl.

Add 1 egg to mixing bowl.

Add 1 cup of milk to mixing bowl.

Add 1 ounce of rum, if you are not driving.

Add vanilla extract to taste.

Beat until smooth.

Pour into a pretty glass.

Sprinkle with nutmeg.

13 What is the first step you should take when creating a program?

14 The program design process can be divided into two main phases. What are they?

15 Explain why the problem-solving phase should not be slighted.

1.3 Introduction to C++

Language is the only instrument of science ...

SAMUEL JOHNSON

In this section we introduce you to the C++ programming language, which is the programming language used in this book.

Origins of the C++ Language

The first thing that people notice about the C++ language is its unusual name. Is there a C programming language, you might ask? Is there a C– or a C–– language? Are there programming languages named A and B? The answers to most of these questions is no. But the general thrust of the questions is on the mark. There is a B programming language; it was not derived from a language called A, but from a language called BCPL. The C language was derived from the B language, and C++ was derived from the C language. Why are there two pluses in the name C++? As you will see in the next chapter, ++ is an operation in the C and C++ languages so using ++ produces a nice pun. The languages BCPL and B will not concern us. They are earlier versions of the C programming language. We will start our description of the C++ programming language with a description of the C language.

The C programming language was developed by Dennis Ritchie of AT&T Bell Laboratories in the 1970s. It was first used for writing and maintaining the UNIX operating system. (Up until that time UNIX systems programs were written either in assembly language or in B, a language developed by Ken Thompson who is the originator of UNIX.) C is a general-purpose language that can be used for writing any sort of program, but its success and popularity are closely tied to the UNIX operating system. If you wanted to maintain your UNIX system, you needed to use C. C and UNIX fit together so well that soon, not just systems programs, but almost all commercial programs that ran under UNIX were written in the C language. C became so popular that versions of the language were written for other popular operating systems; so its use is not limited to computers that use UNIX. However, despite its popularity, C was not without its shortcomings.

The C language is peculiar because it is a high-level language with many of the features of a low-level language. C is somewhere in between the two extremes of a very high-level language and a low-level language, and therein lies both its strengths and its weaknesses. Like (low-level) assembly language, C language programs can directly manipulate the computer's memory. On the other hand, C has the features of a high-level language, which makes it easier to read and write than assembly language. This makes C an excellent choice for writing systems programs, but for other programs (and in some sense even for systems programs) C is not as easy to understand as other languages; also it does not have as many automatic checks as some other high-level languages.

To overcome these and other shortcomings of C, Bjarne Stroustrup of AT&T Bell Laboratories developed C++ in the early 1980s. Stroustrup designed C++ to be a better C. Most of C is a subset of C++, and so most C programs are also C++ programs. (The reverse is not true; many C++ programs are definitely not C programs.) Unlike C, C++ has facilities to do *object-oriented programming,* which is a recently developed and very powerful programming technique.

A Sample C++ Program

Display 1.8 contains a simple C++ program and the screen display that might be generated when a *user* runs and interacts with this program. The person who runs a program is called the **user.** The text typed in by the user is shown in boldface to distinguish it from the text written by the program. On the actual screen both texts would look alike. The person who writes the program is called the **programmer.** Do not confuse the roles of the user and the programmer. The user and the programmer may or may not be the same person. For example, if you write and then run a program, you are both the programmer and the user. With professionally produced programs the programmer (or programmers) and the user are usually different persons.

In the next chapter we will explain in detail all the C++ features you need to write programs like the one in Display 1.8, but to give you a feel for how a C++ program works, we will now give a brief description of how this particular program works. If some of the details are a bit unclear, do not worry. In this section, we just want to give you a feel for what a C++ program is.

The beginning and end of our sample program contain some details that need not concern us yet. The program begins with the following lines:

user

programmer

beginning of program

```
#include <iostream>
using namespace std;

int main( )
{
```

For now we will consider these lines to be a rather complicated way of saying "The program starts here."

The program ends with the following two lines:

return 0;

```
    return 0;
}
```

For a simple program, these two lines simply mean "The program ends here."

Display 1.8 A Sample C++ Program

```cpp
#include <iostream>
using namespace std;

int main( )
{
    int number_of_pods, peas_per_pod, total_peas;

    cout << "Press return after entering a number.\n";
    cout << "Enter the number of pods:\n";
    cin >> number_of_pods;
    cout << "Enter the number of peas in a pod:\n";
    cin >> peas_per_pod;

    total_peas = number_of_pods * peas_per_pod;

    cout << "If you have ";
    cout << number_of_pods;
    cout << " pea pods\n";
    cout << "and ";
    cout << peas_per_pod;
    cout << " peas in each pod, then\n";
    cout << "you have ";
    cout << total_peas;
    cout << " peas in all the pods.\n";

    return 0;
}
```

Sample Dialogue

```
Press return after entering a number.
Enter the number of pods:
10
Enter the number of peas in a pod:
9
If you have 10 pea pods
and 9 peas in each pod, then
you have 90 peas in all the pods.
```

The lines in between these beginning and ending lines are the heart of the program. We will briefly describe these lines, starting with the following line:

```
int number_of_pods, peas_per_pod, total_peas;
```

variable declarations

variables

This line is called a **variable declaration.** This variable declaration tells the computer that `number_of_pods`, `peas_per_pod`, and `total_peas` will be used as names for three *variables*. Variables will be explained more precisely in the next chapter, but it is easy to understand how they are used in this program. In this program, the **variables** are used to name numbers. The word that starts this line, `int`, is an abbreviation for the word *integer* and it tells the computer that the numbers named by these variables will be integers. An **integer** is a whole number, like 1, 2, –1, –7, 0, 205, –103, and so forth.

statements

The remaining lines are all instructions that tell the computer to do something. These instructions are called **statements** or **executable statements.** In this program each statement fits on exactly one line. That need not be true, but for very simple programs, statements are usually listed one per line.

`cin` *and* `cout`

Most of the statements begin with either the word `cin` or `cout`. These statements are input statements and output statements. The word `cin`, which is pronounced "see-in," is used for input. The statements that begin with `cin` tell the computer what to do when information is entered from the keyboard. The word `cout`, which is pronounced "see-out," is used for output, that is, for sending information from the program to the terminal screen. The letter `c` is there because the language is C++. The arrows, written `<<` or `>>`, tell you the direction that data is moving. The arrows, `<<` and `>>`, are called 'insert' and 'extract,' or 'put to' and 'get from,' respectively. For example, consider the line:

```
cout << "Press return after entering a number.\n";
```

\n

This line may be read, 'put "Press...number.\n" to `cout`'. If you think of the word `cout` as a name for the screen (the output device), then the arrows tell the computer to send the string in quotes to the screen. As shown in the sample dialogue, this causes the text contained in the quotes to be written to the screen, The \n at the end of the quoted string tells the computer to start a new line after writing out the text. Similarly, the next line of the program also begins with `cout`, and that program line causes the following line of text to be written to the screen:

```
Enter the number of pods:
```

The next program line starts with the word `cin` so it is an input statement. Let's look at that line:

```
cin >> number_of_pods;
```

This line may be read, 'get number of pods from `cin`'.

If you think of the word `cin` as standing for the keyboard (the input device), then the arrows say that input should be sent from the keyboard to the variable `number_of_pods`. Look again at the sample dialogue. The next line shown has a `10` written in bold. We use bold to indicate something typed in at the keyboard. If you type in the number `10`, then the `10` appears on the screen. If you then press the return key (which is also sometimes called the *enter key*), that makes the `10` available to the program. The statement which begins with `cin` tells the computer to send that input value of `10` to the variable `number_of_pods`. From that point on, `number_of_pods` has the value `10`; when we see `number_of_pods` later in the program, we can think of it as standing for the number `10`.

Consider the next two program lines:

```
cout << "Enter the number of peas in a pod:\n";
cin >> peas_per_pod;
```

These lines are similar to the previous two lines. The first sends a message to the screen asking for a number. When you type in a number at the keyboard and press the return key, that number becomes the value of the variable `peas_per_pod`. In the sample dialogue, we assume that you type in the number 9. After you type in 9 and press the return key, the value of the variable `peas_per_pod` becomes 9.

The next nonblank program line, shown below, does all the computation that is done in this simple program:

```
total_peas = number_of_pods * peas_per_pod;
```

The asterisk symbol, *, is used for multiplication in C++. So this statement says to multiply `number_of_pods` and `peas_per_pod`. In this case, `10` is multiplied by 9 to give a result of `90`. The equal sign says that the variable `total_peas` should be made equal to this result of `90`. This is a special use of the equal sign; its meaning here is different than in other mathematical contexts. It gives the variable on the left-hand side a (possibly new) value; in this case it makes `90` the value of `total_peas`.

The rest of the program is basically more of the same sort of output. Consider the next three nonblank lines:

```
cout << "If you have ";
cout << number_of_pods;
cout << " pea pods\n";
```

These are just three more output statements that work basically the same as the previous statements that begin with `cout`. The only thing that is new is the second of these three statements, which says to output the variable `number_of_pods`. When a variable is output, it is the value of the variable that is output. So this statement causes a `10` to be output. (Remember that in this sample run of the program, the variable `number_of_pods` was set to 10 by the user who ran the program.) Thus, the output produced by these three lines is:

```
If you have 10 pea pods
```

Notice that the output is all on one line. A new line is not begun until the special instruction \n is sent as output.

The rest of the program contains nothing new and if you understand what we have discussed so far, you should be able to understand the rest of the program.

● PITFALL   **Using the Wrong Slash in** $\backslash\text{n}$

backslash

When you use a \n in a `cout`-statement be sure that you use the **backslash,** which is written \. If you make a mistake and use /n rather than \n, the compiler will not give you an error message. Your program will run, but the output will look peculiar.

~ PROGRAMMING TIP
Input and Output Syntax

If you think of `cin` as a name for the keyboard or **in**put device and think of `cout` as a name for the screen or the **out**put device, then it is easy to remember the direction of the arrows >> and <<. They point in the direction that data moves. For example, consider the statement

```
cin >> number_of_pods;
```

In the above statement, data moves from the keyboard to the variable `number_of_pods`, and so the arrow points from `cin` to the variable.

On the other hand, consider the output statement

```
cout << number_of_pods;
```

In this statement the data moves from the variable `number_of_pods` to the screen so the arrow points from the variable `number_of_pods` to `cout`.

● PITFALL   **Putting a Space before the**
`include` **File Name**

Be certain that you do not have any extra space between the < and the `iostream` file name or between the end of the file name and the closing >. The compiler `include` directive is not very smart: it will search for a file name that starts or ends with a space! The file name will not be found, producing an error that is quite difficult to find. You should make this error deliberately in a small program, then compile it. Save the message your compiler produces and the error for your catalog of errors and error messages. (You will be asked to create this catalog in an exercise.)

Layout of a Simple C++ Program

The general form of a simple C++ program is shown in Display 1.9. As far as the compiler is concerned, the line breaks and spacing need not be as shown there and in our examples. The compiler will accept any reasonable pattern of line breaks and indentation. In fact, the compiler will even accept most unreasonable patterns of line breaks and indentation. However, a program should always be laid out so that it is easy to read. Placing the opening brace, {, on a line by itself and also placing the closing brace, }, on a line by itself will make these punctuations easy to find. Indenting each statement and placing each statement on a separate line makes it easy to see what the program instructions are. Later on, some of our statements will be too long to fit on one line and then we will use a slight variant of this pattern for indenting and line breaks. You should follow the pattern set by the examples in this book, or follow the pattern specified by your instructor if you are in a class.

line breaks and spaces

In Display 1.8, the variable declarations are on the line that begins with the word `int`. As we will see in the next chapter, you need not place all your variable declarations at the beginning of your program, but that is a good default location for them. Unless you have a compelling reason to place them somewhere else, place them at the start of your program as shown in Display 1.9 and in the sample program in Display 1.8. The **statements** are the instructions that are followed by the computer.

statement

Display 1.9 Layout of a Simple C++ Program

```
#include <iostream>
using namespace std;

int main( )
{
    Variable_Declarations

    Statement_1
    Statement_2
       . . .
    Statement_Last

    return 0;
}
```

executable statement

In Display 1.8, the statements are the lines that begin with `cout` or `cin`, and the one line that begins with `total_peas` followed by an equal sign. Statements are often called **executable statements.** We will use the terms *statement* and *executable statement* interchangeably. Notice that each of the statements we have seen ends with a semicolon. The semicolon in statements is used in more or less the same way that the period is used in English sentences; it marks the end of a statement.

`#include`

For now you can view the first few lines as a funny way to say "this is the beginning of the program." But we can explain them in a bit more detail. The first line

```
#include <iostream>
```

include directive

is called an `include` **directive.** It tells the compiler where to find information about certain items that are used in your program. In this case `iostream` is the name of a library that contains the definitions of the routines that handle input from the keyboard and output to the screen; `iostream` is a file that contains some basic information about this library. The linker program that we discussed earlier in this chapter combines the object code for the library `iostream` and the object code for the program you write. For the library `iostream` this will probably happen automatically on your system. You will eventually use other libraries as well, and when you use them, they will have to be named in directives at the start of your program. For other libraries, you may need to do more than just place an `include` directive in your program, but in order to use any library in your program, you will always need to at least place an `include` directive for that library in your program. Directives always begin with the symbol #. Some compilers require that directives have no spaces around the #; so it is always safest to place the # at the very start of the line and not include any space between the # and the word `include`.

The following line further explains the `include` directive that we just explained.

```
using namespace std;
```

The above line says that the names defined in `iostream` are to be interpreted in the "standard way" (`std` is an abbreviation of "standard"). We will have more to say about this line a bit later in this book.

`int main( )`

The third and fourth nonblank lines, shown below, simply say that the main part of the program starts here:

```
int main( )
{
```

The correct term is *main function*, rather than *main part*, but the reason for that subtlety will not concern us until Chapter 3. The braces { and } mark the beginning and end of the main part of the program. They need not be on a line by themselves, but that is the way to make them easy to find and we will always place each of them on a line by itself.

The next-to-last line

return 0;

```
return 0;
```

says to "end the program when you get to here." This line need not be the last thing in the program, but in a very simple program it makes no sense to place it anywhere else. Some compilers will allow you to omit this line and will figure out that the program ends when there are no more statements to execute. However, other compilers will insist that you include this line, so it is best to get in the habit of including it, even if your compiler is happy without it. This line is called a **return-statement** and is considered to be an (executable) statement because it tells the computer to do something; specifically, it tells the computer to end the program. The number 0 has no intuitive significance to us yet, but must be there; its meaning will become clear as you learn more about C++. Note that, even though the return-statement says to end the program, you still must add a closing brace } at the end of the main part of your program.

return-statement

Compiling and Running a C++ Program

In the previous section you learned what would happen if you ran the C++ program shown in Display 1.8. But where is that program and how do you make it run? We now discuss such issues.

You write a C++ program using a text editor in the same way that you write any other document such as a term paper, a love letter, a shopping list, or whatever. The program is kept in a file just like any other document you prepare using a text editor. There are different text editors and the details of how to use the text editor will vary from one text editor to another; so we cannot say too much more about your text editor. You will need to consult the documents for your editor.

The way that you compile and run a C++ program also depends on the particular system you are using, so we will discuss these points in only a very general way. You will need to learn how to give the commands to compile, link, and run a C++ program on your system. These commands can be found in the manuals for your system and by asking people who are already using C++ on your system. When you give the command to compile your program this will produce a machine-language translation of your C++ program. This translated version of your program is called the *object code* for your program. The object code for your program must be linked (i.e., combined) with the object code for routines (such as input and output routines) that are already written for you. It is likely that for your first few simple programs this linking will be done automatically, so you do not need to worry about linking. But on some systems, you may be required to make a separate call to the linker. Again, you will need to consult your manuals or a local expert. Finally, you give the command to run your program; how you give that command also depends on the system you are using, so check with the manuals or a local expert.

↝ *PROGRAMMING* TIP
Getting Your Program to Run

Different compilers and different environments might require a slight variation in some details of how you set up a file with your C++ program. Obtain a copy of the program in Display 1.10. It is available for downloading over the Internet. (See the preface for details.) Alternatively, *very carefully* type in the program yourself. Compile the program. If you get an error message, check your typing, fix any typing mistakes, and recompile the file. Once the program compiles with no error messages, try running the program.

If you get the program to compile and run normally, you are all set. You do not need to do anything different from the examples shown in the book. If this program will not compile or will not run normally, then read on. In what follows we offer some hints for dealing with your C++ setup. Once you get this simple program to run normally, you will know what small changes to make to your C++ program files in order to get them to run on your system.

If your program seems to run, but you do not see the output line

```
Testing 1, 2, 3
```

then, in all likelihood, the program probably did give that output, but it disappeared before you could see it. Try adding the following to the end of your program, just

Display 1.10 Testing Your C++ Setup

```cpp
#include <iostream>
using namespace std;

int main()
{
    cout << "Testing 1, 2, 3\n";
    return 0;
}
```

If you cannot compile and run this program, then see the programming tip entitled "Getting Your Program to Run." It suggests some things you might do to get your C++ programs to run on your particular computer setup.

Sample Dialogue

```
Hello out there!
```

before the line with `return 0;` these lines should stop your program to allow you to read the output.

```
char letter;
cout << "Enter a letter to end the program:\n";
cin >> letter;
```

The part in braces should then read as follows:

```
cout << "Testing 1, 2, 3\n";
char letter;
cout << "Enter a letter to end the program:\n";
cin >> letter;
return 0;
```

For now you need not understand these added lines, but they will be clear to you by the end of Chapter 2.

If the program will not compile or will not run at all, then try changing

```
#include <iostream>
```

by adding a `.h` to the end of `iostream`, so it reads as follows:

```
#include <iostream.h>
```

If your program still does not compile and run normally, try deleting.

```
using namespace std;
```

If your program still does not compile and run, then check the documentation for your version of C++ to see if any more "directives" are needed for "console" input/output.

If all this fails, consult your instructor if you are in a course. If you are not in a course or you are not using the course computer, check the documentation for your C++ compiler or check with a friend who has a similar computer setup. The necessary change is undoubtedly very small and, once you find out what it is, very easy.

SELF-TEST EXERCISES

16 If the following statement were used in a C++ program it would cause something to be written on the screen. What would it cause to be written on the screen?

```
cout << "C++ is easy to understand.";
```

17 What is the meaning of the symbols \n as used in the following statement (which appears in Display 1.8)?

```
cout << "Enter the number of peas in a pod:\n";
```

18 What is the meaning of the following statement (which appears in Display 1.8)?

```
cin >> peas_per_pod;
```

19 What is the meaning of the following statement (which appears in Display 1.8)?

```
total_peas = number_of_pods * peas_per_pod;
```

20 What is the meaning of this directive?

```
#include <iostream>
```

21 What, if anything, is wrong with the following #include directives?

    a. `#include <iostream >`
    b. `#include < iostream>`
    c. `#include <iostream>`

1.4 Testing and Debugging

"And if you take one from three hundred and sixty-five, what remains?"
"Three hundred and sixty-four, of course."
Humpty Dumpty looked doubtful. "I'd rather see that done on paper," he said.

    LEWIS CARROLL, *Through the Looking-Glass*

bug

A mistake in a program is usually called a **bug,** and the process of eliminating bugs is called **debugging.** There are several stories about the origin of this terminology. The most colorful is that the terms originated in the early days of computing, when computer hardware was extremely sensitive. Rear Admiral Grace Murray Hopper (1906–1992) was "the third programmer on the world's first large-scale digital computer." (Denise W. Gurer, "Pioneering women in computer science" CACM 38(1):45–54, January 1995.) While Hopper was working on the Harvard Mark I computer under the command of Harvard Professor Howard H. Aiken, an unfortunate moth caused a relay to fail. Hopper and the other programmers taped the deceased moth in the logbook with the note "First actual case of bug being found." The logbook is currently on display at the Naval Museum in Dahlgren, Virginia. This was the first documented computer bug. Professor Aiken would come into the facility during a slack time and inquire if any numbers were being computed. The programmers would reply that they were debugging the computer. For more information about Admiral Hopper and other persons in computing, see Robert Slater, *Portraits in Silicon,* MIT Press, 1987. Today, a bug is a mistake in a program. In this section we will describe the three main kinds of programming mistakes and give some hints on how to correct them.

Kinds of Program Errors

The compiler will catch certain kinds of mistakes and will write out an error message when it finds a mistake. It will detect what are called **syntax errors** since they are, by and large, violation of the syntax (i.e., the grammar rules) of the programming language, such as omitting a semicolon.

syntax error

If the compiler discovers that your program contains a syntax error, it will tell you where the error is likely to be and what kind of error it is likely to be. If the compiler says your program contains a syntax error, you can be confident that it does. However, the compiler may be incorrect about either the location or the nature of the error. It does a better job of determining the location of an error, to within a line or two, than it does of determining the source of the error. This is because the compiler is guessing at what you meant to write down and can easily guess wrong. After all, the compiler cannot read your mind. Error messages subsequent to the first one have a higher likelihood of being incorrect with respect to either the location or the nature of the error. Again, this is because the compiler must guess your meaning. If the compiler's first guess was incorrect, this will affect its analysis of future mistakes, since the analysis will be based on a false assumption.

If your program contains something that is a direct violation of the syntax rules for your programming language, the compiler will give you an **error message.** However, sometimes the compiler will give you only a **warning message,** which indicates that you have done something that is not, technically speaking, a violation of the programming language syntax rules, but that is unusual enough to indicate a likely mistake. When you get a warning message, the compiler is saying, "Are you sure you mean this?" At this stage of your development, you should treat every warning as if it were an error until your instructor approves ignoring the warning.

error messages versus warning messages

There are certain kinds of errors that the computer system can detect only when a program is run. Appropriately enough, these are called **run-time errors.** Most computer systems will detect certain run-time errors and output an appropriate error message. Many run-time errors have to do with numeric calculations. For example, if the computer attempts to divide a number by zero, that is normally a run-time error.

run-time error

logic error

If the compiler approved of your program and the program ran once with no run-time error messages, this does not guarantee that your program is correct. Remember, the compiler will only tell you if you wrote a syntactically (i.e., grammatically) correct C++ program. It will not tell you whether the program does what you want it to do. Mistakes in the underlying algorithm or in translating the algorithm into the C++ language are called **logic errors.** For example, if you were to mistakenly use the addition sign + instead of the multiplication sign * in the program in Display 1.8, that would be a logic error. The program would compile and run normally, but would give the wrong answer. If the compiler approves of your program and there are no run-time errors, but the program does not perform properly, then undoubtedly your program contains a logic error. Logic errors are the hardest kind to diagnose, because the computer gives you no error messages to help find the error. It cannot reasonably be expected to give any error messages. For all the computer knows, you may have meant what you wrote.

◆ PITFALL   Assuming Your Program Is Correct

In order to test a new program for logic errors, you should run the program on several representative data sets and check its performance on those inputs. If the program passes those tests, you can have more confidence in it, but this is still not an absolute guarantee that the program is correct. It still may not do what you want it to do when it is run on some other data. The only way to justify confidence in a program is to program carefully and so avoid most errors.

SELF-TEST EXERCISES

22   What are the three main kinds of program errors?

23   What kinds of errors are discovered by the compiler?

24   If you omit a punctuation symbol (such as a semicolon) from a program, then this produces an error. What kind of error?

25   If you omit the final brace } from a program, then this produces an error. What kind of error?

26   Suppose your program has a situation about which the compiler reports a warning. What should you do about it? Give the text's answer, and your local answer if it is different from the text's. Identify your answers as the text's or as based on your local rules.

27 Suppose you write a program that is supposed to compute the interest on a bank account at a bank that computes interest on a daily basis, and suppose you incorrectly write your program so that it computes interest on an annual basis. What kind of program error is this?

CHAPTER SUMMARY

- The collection of programs used by a computer is referred to as the **software** for that computer. The actual physical machines that make up a computer installation are referred to as **hardware.**

- The five main components of a computer are: the input device(s), the output device(s), the central processing unit (CPU), the main memory, and the secondary memory.

- A computer has two kinds of memory: main memory and secondary memory. Main memory is only used while the program is running. Secondary memory is used to hold data that will stay in the computer before and/or after the program is run.

- A computer's main memory is divided into a series of numbered locations called **bytes.** The number associated with one of these bytes is called the **address** of the byte. Often several of these bytes are grouped together to form a larger memory location. In that case, the address of the first byte is used as the address of this larger memory location.

- A **byte** consists of eight binary digits, each either zero or one. A digit that can only be zero or one is called a **bit.**

- A **compiler** is a program that translates a program written in a high-level language like C++ into a program written in the machine language which the computer can directly understand and execute.

- A sequence of precise instructions that leads to a solution is called an **algorithm.** Algorithms can be written in English or in a programming language, like C++. However, the word *algorithm* is usually used to mean a sequence of instructions written in English (or some other human language, such as Spanish or Arabic).

- Before writing a C++ program, you should design the algorithm (method of solution) that the program will use.

- Programming errors can be classified into three groups: syntax errors, runtime errors, and logic errors. The computer will usually tell you about errors in the first two categories. You must discover logic errors yourself.

- The individual instructions in a C++ program are called **statements.**

- A variable in a C++ program can be used to name a number. (Variables are explained more fully in the next chapter.)

- A statement in a C++ program that begins with cout << is an output statement, which tells the computer to output to the screen whatever follows the <<.

- A statement in a C++ program that begins with cin >> is an input statement.

Answers to Self-Test Exercises

1   The five main components of a computer are the input device(s), the output device(s), the central processing unit (CPU), the main memory, and the secondary memory.

2   The two numbers to be added.

3   The grades for each student on each test and each assignment.

4   A machine-language program is written in a form the computer can execute directly. A high-level language program is written in a form that is easy for a human being to write and read. A high-level language program must be translated into a machine-language program before the computer can execute it.

5   A compiler translates a high-level language program into a machine-language program.

6   The high-level language program that is input to a compiler is called the source program. The translated machine-language program that is output by the compiler is called the object program.

7   An operating system is a program, or several cooperating programs, but is best thought of as the user's chief servant.

8   An operating system's purpose is to allocate the computer's resources to different tasks the computer must accomplish.

9   Among the possibilities are the Macintosh operating system, Windows 95, MS DOS, VMS, Solaris, SunOS, Unix (or perhaps one of the Unix-like operating systems such as Linux). There are many others.

10   The object code for your C++ program must be combined with the object code for routines (such as input and output routines) that your program uses. This process of combining object code is called *linking.* For simple programs this linking may be done for you automatically.

11 The answer varies, depending on the compiler you use. Most Unix and Unix-like compilers link automatically, as do the compilers in most integrated development environments for Windows and Macintosh operating systems.

12 The following instructions are too vague for use in an algorithm:

Add vanilla extract to taste.
Beat until smooth.
Pour into a pretty glass.
Sprinkle with nutmeg.

The notions of "to taste," "smooth," and "pretty" are not precise. The instruction "Sprinkle" is too vague, since it does not specify how much nutmeg to sprinkle. The other instructions are reasonable to use in an algorithm.

13 The first step you should take when creating a program is to be certain that the task to be accomplished by the program is completely and precisely specified.

14 The problem-solving phase and the implementation phase.

15 Experience has shown that the two-phase process produces a correctly working program faster. In part this is because there are two stages for finding and correcting errors in the design of the solution of a program. The process is divided into a design phase and a coding phase. You can spend a half day of careful work instead of several frustrating days of looking for mistakes in a poorly understood program that solves a poorly understood problem.

16   `C++ is easy to understand.`

17 The symbols \n tell the computer to start a new line in the output so that the next item output will be on the next line.

18 This statement tells the computer to read the next number that is typed in at the keyboard and to send that number to the variable named `peas_per_pod`.

19 This statement says to multiply the two numbers in the variables `number_of_pods` and `peas_per_pod`, and to place the result in the variable named `total_peas`.

20 The `#include <iostream>` directive tells the compiler to fetch the file `iostream`. This file contains declarations of `cin`, `cout`, the insertion (`<<`) and extraction (`>>`) operators for input and output. This enables correct linking of the object code from the iostream library with the I/O statements in the program.

21 a. The extra space after the `iostream` file name causes a *file-not-found* error message.

 b. The extra space before the `iostream` file name causes a *file-not-found* error message.

 c. This one is correct.

22 The three main kinds of program errors are syntax errors, run-time errors, and logic errors.

23 The compiler detects syntax errors. There are other errors that are not technically syntax errors that we are lumping with syntax errors. You will learn about these later.

24 A syntax error.

25 A syntax error.

26 The text states that you should take warnings as if they had been reported as errors. You should ask your instructor for the local rules on how to handle warnings.

27 A logic error.

Programming Projects

1 Using your text editor, enter (i.e., type in) the C++ program shown in Display 1.8. Be certain to type the first line exactly as shown in Display 1.8. In particular, be sure that the first line begins at the left-hand end of the line with no space before or after the # symbol. Compile and run the program. If the compiler gives you an error message, correct the program and recompile the program. Do this until the compiler gives no error messages. Then run your program.

2 Modify the C++ program you entered in the Programming Project 1. Change the program so that it first writes the word `Hello` to the screen and then goes on to do the same things that the program in Display 1.8 does. You will only have to add one line to the program to make this happen. Recompile the changed program and run the changed program. Then, change the program even more. Add one more line that will make the program write the word `Good-bye` to the screen at the end of the program. Be certain to add the symbols \n to the last output statement so that it reads as follows:

```
cout << "Good-bye\n";
```

(Some systems require that final \n and your system may be one of the systems that requires a final \n.) Recompile and run the changed program.

3 Modify the C++ program that you entered in Programming Project 1 or 2. Change the multiplication sign * in your C++ program to an addition sign +. Recompile and run the changed program. Notice that the program compiles and runs perfectly fine, but the output is incorrect. That is because this modification is a logic error.

4 Write a C++ program that reads in two integers and then outputs both their sum and their product. One way to proceed is to start with the program in Display 1.8 and to then modify that program to produce the program for this project. Be certain to type the first line of your program exactly the same as the first line in Display 1.8. In particular, be sure that the first line begins at the left-hand end of the line with no space before or after the # symbol. Also, be certain to add the symbols \n to the last output statement in your program. For example, the last output statement might be the following:

```
cout << "This is the end of the program.\n";
```

(Some systems require that final \n and your system may be one of the systems that requires a final \n.)

5 The purpose of this exercise is to produce a catalog of typical syntax errors and error messages that will be encountered by a beginner, and to continue acquainting the student with the programming environment. This exercise should leave the student with a knowledge of what error to look for when given any of a number of common error messages.

Your instructor may have a program for you to use for this exercise. If not, you should use a program from one of the Programming Projects above.

You are to deliberately introduce errors to the program, compile, record the error and the error message, fix the error, compile again (to be sure you have the program corrected), then introduce another error. Keep the catalog of errors and add program errors and messages to it as you continue through this course.

The sequence of suggested errors to introduce is:

a. put an extra space between the < and the iostream file name.

b. Omit one of the < or > symbols in the include directive.

c. Omit the int from int main().

d. Omit or misspell the word `main`.

e. Omit one of the (), then omit both the ().

f. Continue in this fashion, deliberately misspelling identifiers (`cout`, `cin`, and so on). Omit one or both of the << in the cout >> statement; leave off the ending curly brace }.

CHAPTER

2

C++ Basics

2. C·· Basics

Introduction

In Chapter 1 we gave a brief description of one sample C++ program. (If you have not read the description of that program, you may find it helpful to do so before reading this chapter.) In this chapter we explain some additional sample C++ programs and present enough details of the C++ language to allow you to write simple C++ programs.

2.1 Variables and Assignments

Once a person has understood the way variables are used in programming, he has understood the quintessence of programming.

E. W. DIJKSTRA, NOTES ON STRUCTURED PROGRAMMING

Programs manipulate data such as numbers and letters. C++ and most other common programming languages use programming constructs known as *variables* to name and store data. Variables are at the very heart of a programming language like C++, so that is where we start our description of C++. We will use the program in Display 2.1 for our discussion and will explain all the items in that program. While the general idea of that program should be clear, some of the details are new and will require some explanation.

Variables

A C++ variable can hold a number or data of other types. For the moment, we will confine our attention to variables that hold only numbers. These variables are like small blackboards on which the numbers can be written. Just as the numbers written on a blackboard can be changed, so too can the number held by a C++ variable be changed. Unlike a blackboard that might possibly contain no number at all, a C++

variable is guaranteed to have some value in it, if only a garbage number left there by the last program that used the variable. The number or other type of data held in a variable is called its **value;** that is, the value of a variable is the item written on the figurative blackboard. In the program in Display 2.1, `number_of_bars`, `one_weight`, and `total_weight` are variables. For example, when this program is run with the input shown in the sample dialogue, `number_of_bars` has its value set equal to the number 11 with the statement

value of a variable

```
cin >> number_of_bars;
```

Later, the value of the variable `number_of_bars` is changed to 12 when a second copy of the same statement is executed. We will discuss exactly how this happens a little later in this chapter.

Of course, variables are not blackboards. In programming languages, variables are implemented as memory locations. The compiler assigns a memory location (of the kind discussed in Chapter 1) to each variable name in the program. The value of the variable, in a coded form consisting of zeros and ones, is kept in the memory location assigned to that variable. For example, the three variables in the program shown in Display 2.1 might be assigned the memory locations with addresses 1001, 1003, and 1007. The exact numbers will depend on your computer, your compiler, and a number of other factors. We do not know, or even care, what addresses the compiler will choose for the variables in our program. We can think as though the memory locations were actually labeled with the variable names.

variables are memory locations

Cannot Get Programs to Run?

If you cannot get your C++ programs to compile and run, read the Pitfall section of Chapter 1 entitled "Getting Your Program to Run." This section has tips for dealing with variations in C++ compilers and C++ environments.

Names: Identifiers

The first thing you might notice about the names of the variables in our sample programs is that they are longer than the names normally used for variables in mathematics classes. To make your program easy to understand, you should always use meaningful names for variables. The name of a variable (or other item you might define in a program) is called an **identifier.** An identifier must start with either a letter or the underscore symbol, and all the rest of the characters must be letters, digits, or the underscore symbol. For example, the following are all valid identifiers:

```
x x1 x_1 _abc ABC123z7 sum RATE count data2 Big_Bonus
```

Display 2.1 A C++ Program *(part 1 of 2)*

```cpp
#include <iostream>
using namespace std;
int main( )
{
    int number_of_bars;
    double one_weight, total_weight;

    cout << "Enter the number of candy bars in a package\n";
    cout << "and the weight in ounces of one candy bar.\n";
    cout << "Then press return.\n";
    cin >> number_of_bars;
    cin >> one_weight;

    total_weight = one_weight * number_of_bars;

    cout << number_of_bars << " candy bars\n";
    cout << one_weight << " ounces each\n";
    cout << "Total weight is " << total_weight << " ounces.\n";

    cout << "Try another brand.\n";
    cout << "Enter the number of candy bars in a package\n";
    cout << "and the weight in ounces of one candy bar.\n";
    cout << "Then press return.\n";
    cin >> number_of_bars;
    cin >> one_weight;

    total_weight = one_weight * number_of_bars;

    cout << number_of_bars << " candy bars\n";
    cout << one_weight << " ounces each\n";
    cout << "Total weight is " << total_weight << " ounces.\n";

    cout << "Perhaps an apple would be healthier.\n";

    return 0;
}
```

Display 2.1 A C++ Program *(part 2 of 2)*

Sample Dialogue

```
Enter the number of candy bars in a package
and the weight in ounces of one candy bar.
Then press return
11 2.1
11 candy bars
2.1 ounces each
Total weight is 23.1 ounces.
Try another brand.
Enter the number of candy bars in a package
and the weight in ounces of one candy bar.
Then press return
12 1.8
12 candy bars
1.8 ounces each
Total weight is 21.6 ounces.
Perhaps an apple would be healthier.
```

All of the previously mentioned names are legal and would be accepted by the compiler, but the first five are poor choices for identifiers, since they are not descriptive of the identifier's use. None of the following are legal identifiers and all would be rejected by the compiler:

```
12  3X  %change  data-1  myfirst.c  PROG.CPP
```

The first three are not allowed because they do not start with a letter or an underscore. The remaining three are not identifiers because they contain symbols other than letters, digits, and the underscore symbol.

C++ is a case-sensitive language; that is, it distinguishes between uppercase and lowercase letters in the spelling of identifiers. Hence the following are three distinct identifiers and could be used to name three distinct variables:

uppercase and lowercase

```
rate  RATE  Rate
```

However, it is not a good idea to use two such variants in the same program, since that might be confusing. Although it is not required by C++, variables are often spelled with all lowercase letters. The predefined identifiers, such as `main`, `cin`, `cout`, and so forth, must be spelled in all lowercase letters. We will see uses for identifiers spelled with uppercase letters later in this chapter.

A C++ identifier can be of any length, although some compilers will ignore all characters after some specified number of initial characters. You can safely assume that your compiler uses at least the first six letters of every identifier.

Identifiers

Identifiers are used as names for variables and other items in a C++ program. An identifier must start with either a letter or the underscore symbol, and the remaining characters must all be letters, digits, or the underscore symbol.

---

keywords

There is a special class of identifiers, called **keywords** or **reserved words,** that have a predefined meaning in C++ and that you cannot use as names for variables or anything else. In this book keywords are written in a different type font like so: *int*, *double*. (And now you know why those words were written in a funny way.) A complete list of keywords is given in Appendix 1.

You may wonder why the other words that we defined as part of the C++ language are not on the list of keywords. What about words like `cin` and `cout`? The answer is that you are allowed to redefine these words, although it would be confusing to do so. These predefined words are not keywords; however, they are defined in libraries required by the C++ language standard. The library in which `cin` and `cout` are defined has been added to C++ as part of the officially defined core language. We will discuss libraries later in this book. For now, you need not worry about libraries. Needless to say, using a predefined identifier for anything other than its standard meaning can be confusing and dangerous, and thus should be avoided. The safest and easiest practice is to treat all predefined identifiers as if they were keywords.

Variable Declarations

Every variable in a C++ program must be *declared*. When you **declare** a variable you are telling the compiler—and, ultimately, the computer—what kind of data you will be storing in the variable. For example, the following two declarations from the program in Display 2.1 declare the three variables used in that program:

```
int number_of_bars;
double one_weight, total_weight;
```

When there is more than one variable in a declaration, the variables are separated by commas. Also, note that each declaration ends with a semicolon.

The word *int* in the first of these two declarations is an abbreviation of the word *intege*r. (But, in a C++ program you must use the abbreviated form *int*. Do not write out the entire word *integer.*) This line declares the identifier `number_of_bars` to be a variable of *type* `int`. This means that the value of `number_of_bars` must be a whole number, such as 1, 2, –1, 0, 37, or –288.

type

The word *double* in the second of these two lines declares the two identifiers `one_weight` and `total_weight` to be variables of type *double*. A variable of type *double* can hold numbers with a fractional part, such as 1.75 or –0.55. The kind of data that is held in a variable is called its **type** and the name for the type, such as *int* or *double*, is called a **type name.**

Variable Declarations

All variables must be declared before they are used. The syntax for variable declarations is as follows:

Syntax:

> *Type_Name Variable_Name_1, Variable_Name_2, • • •;*

Example:

> *int* count, number_of_dragons, number_of_trolls;
> *double* distance;

Every variable in a C++ program must be declared before the variable can be used. There are two natural places to declare a variable: either just before it is used or at the start of the `main` part of your program right after the lines

where to place variable declarations

> *int* main( )
> {

Do whatever makes your program clearer.

Variable declarations provide information the compiler needs in order to implement the variables. Recall that the compiler implements variables as memory locations and that the value of a variable is stored in the memory location assigned to that variable. The value is coded as a string of zeros and ones. Different types of variables require different sizes of memory locations and different methods for coding their values as a string of zeros and ones. The computer uses one code to encode integers as a string of zeros and ones. It uses a different code to encode numbers that have a fractional part. It uses yet another code to encode letters as strings of zeros and ones. The variable declaration tells the compiler—and, ultimately, the computer—what size memory location to use for the variable and which code to use when representing the variable's value as a string of zeros and ones.

Assignment Statements

The most direct way to change the value of a variable is to use an *assignment statement*. An **assignment statement** is an order to the computer saying "set the value of this variable to what I have written down." The following line from the program in Display 2.1 is an example of an assignment statement:

```
total_weight = one_weight * number_of_bars;
```

This assignment statement tells the computer to set the value of `total_weight` equal to the number in the variable `one_weight` multiplied by the number in `number_of_bars`. (As we noted in Chapter 1, * is the sign used for multiplication in C++.)

An assignment statement always consists of a variable on the left-hand side of the equal sign and an expression on the right-hand side. An assignment statement ends with a semicolon. The expression on the right-hand side of the equal sign may be a variable, a number, or a more complicated expression made up of variables, numbers, and arithmetic operators such as * and +. An assignment statement instructs the computer to evaluate (i.e., to compute the value of) the expression on the right-hand side of the equal sign and to set the value of the variable on the left-hand side equal to the value of that expression. A few more examples may help to clarify the way these assignment statements work.

You may use any arithmetic operator in place of the multiplication sign. The following, for example, is also a valid assignment statement:

```
total_weight = one_weight + number_of_bars;
```

This statement is just like the assignment statements in our sample program except that it performs addition rather than multiplication. This statement changes the value of `total_weight` to the sum of the values of `one_weight` and `number_of_bars`. Of course, if you made this change in the program in Display 2.1, the program would give incorrect output, but it would still run.

In an assignment statement, the expression on the right-hand side of the equal sign can simply be another variable. The statement

```
total_weight = one_weight;
```

changes the value of the variable `total_weight` so that it is the same as that of the variable `one_weight`. If you were to use this in the program in Display 2.1, it would give out incorrectly low values for the total weight of a package (assuming there is more than one candy bar in a package), but it might make sense in some other program.

As another example, the following assignment statement changes the value of `number_of_bars` to 37:

```
number_of_bars = 37;
```

A number, like the 37 in this example, is called a **constant,** because, unlike a variable, its value cannot change.

constant

Since variables can change value over time and since the assignment operator is one vehicle for changing their values, there is an element of time involved in the meaning of an assignment statement.   First, the expression on the right-hand side of the equal sign is evaluated.   After that, the value of the variable on the left side of the equal sign is changed to the value that was obtained from that expression. This means that a variable can meaningfully occur on both sides of an assignment operator. For example, consider the assignment statement

same variable on both sides of =

```
number_of_bars = number_of_bars + 3;
```

This assignment statement may look strange at first. If you read it as an English sentence it seems to say "the `number_of_bars` is equal to the `number_of_bars` plus three." It may seem to say that but what it really says is, "Make the *new* value of `number_of_bars` equal to the *old* value of `number_of_bars` plus three." The equal sign in C++ is not used the same way that it is used in English or in simple mathematics.

Assignment Statements

In an assignment statement, first the expression on the right-hand side of the equal sign is evaluated and then the variable on the left-hand side of the equal sign is set equal to this value.

Syntax:

> *Variable* = *Expression*;

Examples:

```
distance = rate * time;
count = count + 2;
```

● PITFALL   Uninitialized Variables

A variable has no meaningful value until a program gives it one. For example, if the variable minimum_number has not been given a value either as the left-hand side of an assignment statement or by some other means (such as being given an input value with a cin-statement), then the following is an error:

```
desired_number = minimum_number + 10;
```

This is because minimum_number has no meaningful value and so the entire expression on the right-hand side of the equal sign has no meaningful value. A variable like minimum_number that has not been given a value is said to be **uninitialized.** This situation is, in fact, worse than it would be if minimum_number had no value at all. An uninitialized variable, like minimum_number, will simply have some "garbage value." The value of an uninitialized variable is determined by whatever pattern of zeros and ones was left in its memory location by the last program that used that portion of memory. Thus if the program is run twice, an uninitialized variable may receive a different value each time the program is run. Whenever a program gives different output on *exactly* the same input data and without *any* changes in the program itself, you should suspect an uninitialized variable.

One way to avoid an uninitialized variable is to initialize variables at the same time they are declared. This can be done by adding an equal sign and a value, as follows:

```
int minimum_number = 3;
```

This both declares minimum_number to be a variable of type int and sets the value of the variable minimum_number equal to 3. You can use a more complicated expression involving operations such as addition or multiplication when you initialize a variable inside the declaration in this way. However, a simple constant is what is most often used. You can initialize some, all, or none of the variables in a declaration that lists more than one variable. For example, the following declares three variables and initializes two of them:

```
double rate = 0.07, time, balance = 0.00;
```

C++ allows an alternative notation for initializing variables when they are declared. This alternative notation is illustrated by the following, which is equivalent to the preceding declaration:

```
double rate(0.07), time, balance(0.00);
```

Whether you initialize a variable when it is declared or at some later point in the program depends on the circumstances. Do whatever makes your program the easiest to understand.

Initializing Variables in Declarations

You can initialize a variable (i.e., give it a value) at the time that you declare the variable.

Syntax:

> *Type_Name Variable_Name_1 = Expression_for_Value_1,*
> *Variable_Name_2 = Expresssion_for_Value_2,* **. . .;**

Examples:

> *int* count = 0, limit = 10, fudge_factor = 2;
> *double* distance = 999.99;

Alternative syntax for initializing in Declarations:

> *Type_Name Variable_Name_1 (Expression_for_Value_1),*
> *Variable_Name_2 (Expression_for_Value_2),* **. . .;**

Examples:

> `int count(0), limit(10), fudge_factor(4);`
> `double distance(5.723), zymurgy_constant(1.234);`

↪ PROGRAMMING TIP
Use Meaningful Names

Variable names and other names in a program should at least hint at the meaning or use of the thing they are naming. It is much easier to understand a program if the variables have meaningful names. Contrast

```
x = y * z;
```

with the more suggestive:

```
distance = speed * time;
```

The two statements accomplish the same thing, but the second is easier to understand.

SELF-TEST EXERCISES

1 Give the declaration for two variables called `feet` and `inches`. Both variables are of type *int* and both are to be initialized to zero in the declaration. Use both initialization alternatives.

2   Give the declaration for two variables called count and distance. count is of type *int* and is initialized to zero. distance is of type *double* and is initialized to 1.5.

3   Give a C++ statement that will change the value of the variable sum to the sum of the values in the variables n1 and n2. The variables are all of type *int*.

4   Write a program that contains statements that output the value of five or six variables that have been defined, but not initialized. Compile and run the program. What is the output? Explain.

5   Give good variable names for each of the following:

a. A variable to hold the speed of an automobile.
b. A variable to hold the pay rate for an hourly employee.
c. A variable to hold the highest score in an exam.

2.2   Input and Output

Garbage in means garbage out.

PROGRAMMER'S SAYING

There are several different ways that a C++ program can perform input and output. We will describe what are called *streams*. An **input stream** is simply the stream of input that is being fed into the computer for the program to use. The word *stream* suggests that the program processes the input in the same way no matter where the input comes from. The intuition for the word *stream* is that the program sees only the stream of input and not the source of the stream, like a mountain stream whose water flows past you but whose source is unknown to you. In this section we will assume that the input comes from the keyboard. In Chapter 5 we will discuss how a program can read its input from a file; as you will see there, you can use the same kinds of input statements to read input from a file as those that you use for reading input from the keyboard. Similarly, an **output stream** is the stream of output generated by the program. In this section we will assume the output is going to a terminal screen; in Chapter 5 we will discuss output that goes to a file.

input stream

output stream

Output Using cout

The values of variables as well as strings of text may be output to the screen using cout. There may be any combination of variables and strings to be output. For example, consider the following line from the program in Display 2.1:

```
cout << number_of_bars << " candy bars\n";
```

This statement tells the computer to output two items: the value of the variable `number_of_bars` and the quoted string `" candy bars\n"`. Notice that you do not need a separate copy of the word `cout` for each item output. You can simply list all the items to be output preceding each item to be output with the arrow symbols `<<`. The above single `cout`-statement is equivalent to the following two `cout`-statements:

```
cout << number_of_bars;
cout << " candy bars\n";
```

You can include arithmetic expressions in a `cout`-statement as shown by the following example, where `price` and `tax` are variables:

expression in a
`cout`-*statement*

```
cout << "The total cost is $" << (price + tax);
```

The parentheses around arithmetic expressions, like `price + tax`, are required by some compiler, so it is best to include them.

The symbol `<` is the same as the "less than" symbol. The two `<` symbols should be typed without any space between them. The arrow notation `<<` is often called the **insertion operator.** The entire `cout`-statement ends with a semicolon.

insertion operator

Whenever you have two `cout`-statements in a row, you can combine them into a single long `cout`-statement. For example, consider the following lines from Display 2.1:

```
    cout << number_of_bars << " candy bars\n";
    cout << one_weight << " ounces each\n";
```

These two statements can be rewritten as the single statement shown below, and the program will perform exactly the same:

```
  cout << number_of_bars << " candy bars\n" << one_weight << " ounces each\n";
```

If you want to keep your program lines from running off the screen, you will have to place such a long `cout`-statement on two or more lines. A better way to write the above long `cout`-statement is:

```
cout << number_of_bars << " candy bars\n"
        << one_weight << " ounces each\n";
```

You should not break a quoted string across two lines, but otherwise you can start a new line anywhere you can insert a space. Any reasonable pattern of spaces and line breaks will be acceptable to the computer, but the above example and the sample programs are good models to follow. A good policy is to use one `cout` for each group of output that is intuitively considered a unit. Notice that there is just one semicolon for each `cout`, even if the `cout`-statement spans several lines.

Pay particular attention to the quoted strings that are output in the program in Display 2.1. Notice that the strings must be included in double quotes. The double quote symbol used is a single key on your keyboard; do not type two single quotes. Also, notice that the same double quote symbol is used at each end of the string; there are not separate left and right quote symbols.

spaces in output

Also, notice the spaces inside the quotes. The computer does not insert any extra space before or after the items output by a cout-statement. That is why the quoted strings in the samples often start and/or end with a blank. The blanks keep the various strings and numbers from running together. If all you need is a space and there is no quoted string where you want to insert the space, then use a string that contains only a space, as in the following:

```
cout << first_number << " " << second_number;
```

new lines in output

As we noted in Chapter 1, \n tells the computer to start a new line of output. Unless you tell the computer to go to the next line, it will put all the output on the same line. Depending on how your screen is set up, this can produce anything from arbitrary line breaks to output that runs off the screen. Notice that the \n goes inside of the quotes. In C++ going to the next line is considered to be a special character (special symbol) and the way you spell this special character inside a quoted string is \n, with no space between the two symbols in \n. Although it is typed as two symbols, C++ considers \n to be single character that is called the **new-line character.**

new-line character

Include Directives and Namespaces

We have started all of our programs with the following two lines:

```
#include <iostream>
using namespace std;
```

These two lines make the library iostream available. This is the library that includes, among other things, the definitions of cin and cout. So, if your program uses either cin or cout you should have these two lines at the start of the file that contains your program.

include directive

The following line is known as an **include directive**. It "includes" the library iostream in your program so that you have cin and cout available:

```
#include <iostream>
```

The operators cin and cout are defined in a file named iostream and the above include directive is equivalent to copying that named file into your program. The second line is a bit more complicated to explain.

namespace

C++ divides names into **namespaces**. A namespace is a collection of names, such as the names cin and cout. A statement that specifies a namespace in the way illustrated by the following is called a *using* **directive**.

```
using namespace std;
```

This particular *using* directive says that your program is using the std ("standard") namespace. This means that the names you use will have the meaning defined for them in the std namespace. In this case, the important thing is that when names such as cin and cout were defined in iostream, their definitions said they were in the std namespace. So to use names like cin and cout, you need to tell the compiler you are *using namespace* std;.

That is all you need to know (for now) about namespaces, but a brief clarifying remark will remove some of the mystery that might surround the use of *namespace*. The reason that C++ has namespaces at all is because there are so many things to name. As a result, sometimes two or more items receive the same name; that is, a single name can get two different definitions. To eliminate these ambiguities, C++ divides items into collections so that no two items in the same collection (the same namespace) have the same name.

Note that a namespace is not simply a collection of names. It is a body of C++ code that specifies the meaning of some names, such as some definitions and/or declarations. The function of namespaces is to divide all the C++ name specifications into collections (called namespaces) such that each name in a namespace has only one specification (one "definition") in that namespace. A namespace divides up the names, but it takes a lot of C++ code along with the names.

What if you want to use two items in two different namespaces, such that both items have the same name? It can be done and is not too complicated, but that is a topic for later in the book. For now, we do not need to do this.

Some versions of C++ use the following, older form of the include directive (without any *using namespace*):

alternative form

```
#include <iostream.h>
```

If your programs do not compile or do not run with

```
#include <iostream>
using namespace std;
```

then try using the following line instead of the previous two lines:

```
#include <iostream.h>
```

Escape Sequences

The \ preceeding a character tells the compiler that the sequence following the \ does not have the same meaning as the character appearing by itself. Such a sequence is called an **escape sequence.** The sequence is typed in as two characters with no space between the symbols. Several escape sequences are defined in C++.

If you want to put a backslash, \, or a " into a string constant, you must escape the ability of the " to terminate a string constant by using \", or the ability of the \ to escape, by using \\. The \\ tells the compiler you mean a real backslash, \, not an escape sequence, or \" means a real quote, not a string constant end.

A stray \, say \z, in a string constant will on one compiler simply give back a z; on another it will produce an error. The ANSI Standard provides that the unspecified escape sequences have undefined behavior. This means a compiler can do anything its author finds convenient. The consequence is that code that uses undefined escape sequences is not portable. You should not use any escape sequences other than those provided. We list a few here.

new-line	\n
horizontal tab	\t
alert	\a
backslash	\\
double quote	\"

For completeness, we mention that if the character following the backslash is not one of the characters: n, t, v, b, r, a, \, ?, :, ", \000 (octal digits) or \xhhh (hex digits) the behavior is undefined.

If you wish to insert a blank line in the output, you can output the new-line character \n by itself:

```
cout << "\n";
```

Another way to output a blank line is to use endl, which means essentially the same thing as "\n". So you can also output a blank line as follows:

```
cout << endl;
```

Although "\n" and endl mean the same thing, they are used slightly differently; \n must always be inside of quotes and endl should not be placed in quotes.

deciding between
\n and endl

A good rule for deciding whether to use \n or endl is the following: If you can include the \n at the end of a longer string, then use \n as in the following

```
cout << "Fuel efficiency is "
     << mpg << " miles per gallon\n";
```

On the other hand, if the \n would appear by itself as the short string "\n", then use endl instead:

```
cout << "You entered " << number << endl;
```

Starting New Lines in Output

To start a new output line, you can include \n in a quoted string, as in the following example:

```
cout << "You have definitely won\n"
     << "one of the following prizes:\n";
```

Recall that \n is typed as two symbols with no space in-between the two symbols.
    Alternatively, you can start a new line by outputting end1. An equivalent way
to write the above cout-statement is as follows:

    cout << "You have definitely won" << end1
         << "one of the following prizes:" << end1;

➤ *PROGRAMMING* *TIP*
End Each Program with a \n *or* end1

It is a good idea to output a new-line instruction at the end of every program. If the
last item to be output is a string, then include a \n at the end of the string; if not, output an end1 as the last action in your program. This serves two purposes. Some compilers will not output the last line of your program unless you include a new-line
instruction at the end. On other systems, your program may work fine without this
final new-line instruction, but the next program that is run will have its first line of
output mixed with the last line of the previous program. Even if neither of these
problems occurs on your system, putting a new-line instruction at the end will make
your programs more portable.

Formatting for Numbers with a Decimal Point

When the computer outputs a value of type *double*, the format may not be what you
would like. For example, the following simple cout-statement can produce any of a
wide range of outputs:

format for
double values

    cout << "The price is $" << price << end1;

If price has the value 78.5, the output might be

    The price is $78.500000

or it might be

    The price is $78.5

or it might be output in the following notation (which we will explain in section 2.3):

    The price is $7.850000e01

But, it is extremely unlikely that the output will be the following, even though this is the format that makes the most sense:

```
The price is $78.50
```

To ensure that the output is in the form you want, your program should contain some sort of instructions that tell the computer how to output the numbers.

magic formula

There is a "magic formula" that you can insert in your program to cause numbers that contain a decimal point, such as numbers of type *double*, to be output in everyday notation with the exact number of digits after the decimal point that you specify. If you want two digits after the decimal point, use the following magic formula:

```
cout.setf(ios::fixed);
cout.setf(ios::showpoint);
cout.precision(2);
```

outputting money amounts

If you insert the preceding three statements in your program, then any `cout`-statement that follows these three statements will output values of type *double* in ordinary notation, with exactly two digits after the decimal point. For example, suppose the following `cout`-statement appears somewhere after this magic formula and suppose the value of `price` is `78.5`:

```
cout << "The price is $" << price << endl;
```

The output will then be as follows:

```
The price is $78.50
```

You may use any other nonnegative whole number in place of 2 to specify a different number of digits after the decimal point. You can even use a variable of type *int* in place of the 2.

We will explain this magic formula in detail in Chapter 5. For now you should think of this magic formula as one long instruction that tells the computer how you want it to output numbers that contain a decimal point.

If you wish to change the number of digits after the decimal point so that different values in your program are output with different numbers of digits, you can repeat the magic formula with some other number in place of 2. However, when you repeat the magic formula, you only need to repeat the last line of the formula. If the magic formula has already occurred once in your program, then the following line will change the number of digits after the decimal point to 5 for all subsequent values of type *double* that are output:

```
cout.precision(5);
```

Outputting Values of Type *double*

If you insert the following "magic formula" in your program, then all numbers of type *double* (or any other type that allows for digits after the decimal point) will be output in ordinary everyday notation with 2 digits after the decimal point:

```
cout.setf(ios::fixed);
cout.setf(ios::showpoint);
cout.precision(2);
```

You can use any other nonnegative whole number in place of the 2 to specify a different number of digits after the decimal point. You can even use a variable of type *int* in place of the 2.

Input Using cin

You use cin for input more or less the same way you use cout for output. The syntax is similar, except that cin is used in place of cout and the arrows point in the opposite direction. For example, in the program in Display 2.1, the variables number_of_bars and one_weight were filled by the following cin-statements (shown along with the cout-statements that tell the user what to do):

```
cout << "Enter the number of candy bars in a package\n";
cout << "and the weight in ounces of one candy bar.\n";
cout << "Then press return.\n";
cin >> number_of_bars;
cin >> one_weight;
```

You can list more than one variable in a single cin-statement. So, the above lines could be rewritten to the following:

```
cout << "Enter the number of candy bars in a package\n";
cout << "and the weight in ounces of one candy bar.\n";
cout << "Then press return.\n";
cin >> number_of_bars >> one_weight;
```

If you prefer, the above cin-statement can be written on two lines as follows:

```
cin >> number_of_bars
    >> one_weight;
```

Notice that, as with the cout-statement, there is just one semicolon for each occurrence of cin.

When a program reaches a cin-statement, it waits for input to be entered from the keyboard. It sets the first variable equal to the first value typed at the keyboard,

how cin works

the second variable equal to the second value typed, and so forth. However, the program does not read the input until the user presses the return key. This allows the user to backspace and correct mistakes when entering a line of input.

separate numbers with spaces

Numbers in the input must be separated by one or more spaces or by a line break. If, for instance, you want to enter the two numbers **12** and **5** and instead you enter the numbers without any space between them, then the computer will think you have entered the single number **125.** When you use cin-statements, the computer will skip over any number of blanks or line breaks until it finds the next input value. Thus, it does not matter whether input numbers are separated by one space or several spaces or even a line break.

---

cin-Statements

A cin-statement sets variables equal to values typed in at the keyboard.

Syntax:

```
cin >> Variable_1 >> Variable_2 >> . . . ;
```

Examples:

```
cin >> number >> size;
cin >> time_to_go
    >> points_needed;
```

Designing Input and Output

I/O

Input and output, or as it is often called **I/O,** is the part of the program that the user sees, so the user will not be happy with a program unless the program has well-designed I/O.

prompt lines

When the computer executes a cin-statement, it expects some data to be typed in at the keyboard. If none is typed in, the computer simply waits for it. The program must tell the user when to type in a number (or other data item). The computer will not automatically ask the user to enter data. That is why the sample programs contain output statements like the following:

```
cout << "Enter the number of candy bars in a package\n";
cout << "and the weight in ounces of one candy bar.\n";
cout << "Then press return.\n";
```

These output statements prompt the user to enter the input. Your programs should always prompt for input.

echoing input

When entering input from a terminal, the input appears on the screen as it is typed in. Nonetheless, the program should always write out the input values some time before it ends. This is called **echoing the input,** and it serves as a check to see that the input was read in correctly. Just because the input looks good on the screen when it is typed in, that does not mean that it was read correctly by the computer. There could be an unnoticed typing mistake or other problem. Echoing input serves as a test of the integrity of the input data.

➦ *PROGRAMMING* *TIP*
Line Breaks in I/O

It is possible to keep output and input on the same line, and sometimes it can produce a nicer interface for the user. If you simply omit a \n or endl at the end of the last prompt line, then the user's input will appear on the same line as the prompt. For example, suppose you use the following prompt and input statements:

```
cout << "Enter the cost per person: $";
cin >> cost_per_person;
```

When the cout-statement is executed, the following will appear on the screen:

```
Enter the cost per person: $
```

When the user types in the input, it will appear on the same line, like this:

```
Enter the cost per person: $1.25
```

SELF-TEST EXERCISES

6 Give an output statement that will produce the following message on the screen:

```
The answer to the question of
Life, the Universe, and Everything is 42.
```

7 Give an input statement that will fill the variable the_number (of type *int*) with a number typed in at the keyboard. Precede the input statement with a prompt statement asking the user to enter a whole number.

8 What statements should you include in your program to ensure that, when a number of type *double* is output, it will be output in ordinary notation with 3 digits after the decimal point?

9 Write a complete C++ program that writes the phrase `Hello world` to the screen. The program does nothing else.

10 Give an output statement that produces the new-line character and a tab character.

11 Write a short program that declares and initializes *double* variables one, two, three, four, and five to the values 1.000, 1.414, 1.732, 2.000, and 2.236, respectively. Then write output statements to generate the following legend and table. Use the tab escape sequence \t to line up the columns. If you are unfamiliar with the tab character, you should experiment with it while doing this exercise. A tab works like a mechanical stop on a typewriter. A tab causes output to begin in a next column, usually a multiple of 8 spaces away. Many editors and most word processors will have adjustable tab stops. Our output does not.

The output should be:

```
N       Square Root
1       1.000
2       1.414
3       1.732
4       2.000
5       2.236
```

2.3 Data Types and Expressions

They'll never be happy together. He's not her type.

OVERHEARD AT A COCKTAIL PARTY

The Types *int* and *double*

Conceptually the numbers 2 and 2.0 are the same number. But C++ considers them to be of different types. The whole number 2 is of type *int*; the number 2.0 is of type *double*, because it contains a fraction part (even though the fraction is 0). Once again, the mathematics of computer programming is a bit different from what you may have learned in mathematics classes. Something about the practicalities of computers makes a computer's numbers differ from the abstract definitions of these numbers. The whole numbers in C++ behave as you would expect them to. The type *int* holds no surprises. But values of type *double* are more troublesome. Because it can store only a limited number of significant digits, the computer stores numbers of type *double* as approximate values. Numbers of type *int* are stored as exact values. The precision with which *double* values are stored varies from one computer to another, but you can expect them to be stored with 14 or more digits of accuracy. For most applications this is likely to be sufficient, though subtle problems can occur even in simple cases. Thus, if you know that the values in some variable will always be whole numbers in the range allowed by your computer, it is best to declare the variable to be of type *int*.

Number constants of type *double* are written differently from those of type *int*. Constants of type *int* must not contain a decimal point. Constants of type *double* may be written in either of two forms. The simple form for *double* constants is like the everyday way of writing decimal fractions. When written in this form a *double* constant must contain a decimal point. There is, however, one thing that constants of type *double* and constants of type *int* have in common: No number in C++ may contain a comma.

The more complicated notation for constants of type *double* is frequently called **scientific notation** or **floating point notation** and is particularly handy for writing very large numbers and very small fractions. For instance,

e notation

3.67×10^{17}, which is the same as 367000000000000000.0,

is best expressed in C++ by the constant 3.67e17. The number

5.89×10^{-6}, which is the same as 0.00000589,

is best expressed in C++ by the constants and 5.89e–6. The e stands for *exponent* and means "multiply by 10 to the power that follows."

This e notation is used because keyboards normally have no way to write exponents as superscripts. Think of the number after the e as telling you the direction and number of digits to move the decimal point. For example, to change 3.49e4 to a numeral without an e, you move the decimal point 4 places to the right to obtain 34900.0 which is another way of writing the same number. If the number after the e is negative, you move the decimal point the indicated number of spaces to the left, inserting extra zeros if need be. So, 3.49e–2 is the same as 0.0349.

The number before the e may contain a decimal point, although it is not required. However, the exponent after the e definitely must *not* contain a decimal point.

Since computers have size limitations on their memory, numbers are typically stored in a limited number of bytes (i.e., a limited amount of storage). Hence, there is a limit to how large the magnitude of a number can be, and this limit is different for different number types. The largest allowable number of type *double* is always much larger than the largest allowable number of type *int*. Just about any implementation of C++ will allow values of type *int* as large as 32767 and values of type *double* up to about 10^{308}.

What is doubled?

Why is the type for numbers with a fraction part called *double*? Is there a type called "single" that is half as big? No, but something like that is true. Many programming languages traditionally used two types for numbers with a fractional part. One type used less storage and was very imprecise (that is, it did not allow very many significant digits). The second type used *double* the amount of storage and so was much more precise; it also allowed numbers that were larger (although programmers tend to care more about precision than about size). The kind of numbers that used twice as much storage were called *double precision* numbers; those that used less storage were called *single precision*. Following this tradition, the type that (more or less) corresponds to this double precision type was named *double* in C++. The type that corresponds to single precision in C++ was called *float*. C++ also has a third type for numbers with a fractional part, which is called *long double*. These types are described in the subsection entitled "Other Number Types." However, we will have no occasion to use the types *float* and *long double* in this book.

Other Number Types

C++ has other numeric types besides *int* and *double*. Some are described in Display 2.2. The various number types allow for different size numbers, and for more or less precision (that is, more or fewer digits after the decimal point). In Display 2.2, the values given for memory used, size range, and precision are only one sample set of values, intended to give you a general feel for how the types differ. The values vary from one system to another, and may be different on your system.

Although some of these other numeric types are spelled as two words, you declare variables of these other types just as you declare variables of types *int* and *double*. For example, the following declares one variable of type *long double*:

long double big_number;

long double

The type names *long* and *long int* are two names for the same type. Thus, the following two declarations are equivalent:

long

```
long big_total;
    and the equivalent
long int big_total;
```

Of course, in any one program, you should use only one of the above two declarations for the variable big_total, but it does not matter which one you use. Also, remember that the type name *long* by itself means the same thing as *long int*, not the same thing as *long double*.

Display 2.2 Some Number Types

Type Name	Memory Used	Size Range	Precision
short (also called *short int*)	2 bytes	–32,767 to 32,767	(not applicable)
int	4 bytes	–2,147,483,647 to 2,147,483,647	(not applicable)
long (also called *long int*)	4 bytes	–2,147,483,647 to 2,147,483,647	(not applicable)
float	4 bytes	approximately 10^{-38} to 10^{38}	7 digits
double	8 bytes	approximately 10^{-308} to 10^{308}	15 digits
long double	10 bytes	approximately 10^{-4932} to 10^{4932}	19 digits

These are only sample values to give you a general idea of how the types differ. The values for any of these entries may be different on your system. *Precision* refers to the number of meaningful digits, including digits in front of the decimal point. The ranges for the types *float*, *double*, and *long double* are the ranges for positive numbers. Negative numbers have a similar range, but with a negative sign in front of each number.

Note: Machines that primarily use a 16-bit word length (Intel processors running MS-DOS and Windows 3.1, for example) use a 2-byte *int* that has the same range of values as the short int mentioned here. Machines with a 32-bit word length (most Unix, recent Windows with Intel processors, Mac, Sun) use 4-byte integers. The advent of 64-bit processors and compilers that use this feature will result in a change to this table!

The types for whole numbers, such an *int* and similar types, are called **integer types.** The type for numbers with a decimal point—such as the type *double* and similar types—are called **floating-point types.** They are called *floating-point* because when the computer stores a number written in the usual way, like 392.123, it first converts the number to something like e notation, in this case something like 3.92123e2. When the computer performs this conversion, the decimal point *floats* (that is, moves) to a new position.

integer types

floating-point types

You should be aware of the fact that there are other numeric types in C++. However, in this book, we will use only the types *int*, *double*, and occasionally *long*. For most simple applications, you should not need any types except *int* and *double*. However, if you are writing a program that uses very large whole numbers, then you might need to use the type *long*.

The Type *char*

We do not want to give you the impression that computers and C++ are used only for numeric calculations, so we will introduce one nonnumeric type now, though eventually we will see other more complicated nonnumeric types. Values of the type *char*, which is short for *character*, are single symbols such as a letter, digit, or punctuation mark. Values of this type are frequently called *characters* in books and in conversation, but in a C++ program this type must always be spelled in the abbreviated fashion *char*. For example, the variables symbol and letter of type *char* are declared as follows:

        char symbol, letter;

A variable of type *char* can hold any single character on the keyboard.   So, for example, the variable symbol could hold an 'A' or a '+' or an 'a'. Note that uppercase and lowercase versions of a letter are considered different characters.

strings and characters

There is a type for strings of more than one character, but we will not introduce that type for a while, although you have seen, and even used, values that are strings. The strings in double quotes that are output using cout are string values. For example, the following, which occurs in the program in Display 2.1, is a string:

        "Enter the number of candy bars in a package\n"

quotes

Be sure to notice that string constants are placed inside of double quotes, while constants of type *char* are placed inside of single quotes. The two kinds of quotes mean different things. In particular, 'A' and "A" mean different things. 'A' is a value of type *char* and can be stored in a variable of type *char*. "A" is string of characters. The fact that the string happens to contain only one character does *not* make "A" a value of type *char*. Also notice that, for both strings and characters, the left and right quotes are the same.

The use of the type *char* is illustrated in the program shown in Display 2.3. Notice that the user types a space between the first and second initials. Yet the program skips over the blank and reads the letter **B** as the second input character. When you use cin to read input into a variable of type *char*, the computer skips over all blanks and line breaks until it gets to the first nonblank character and reads that nonblank character into the variable. It makes no difference whether there are blanks in the input or not. The program in Display 2.3 will give the same output whether the user types in a blank between initials as shown in the sample dialogue or the user types in the two initials without a blank, like so:

    JB

The Type bool

The final type we discuss here is the type *bool*. This type was recently added to the C++ language by the ISO/ANSI (International Standards Organization/American National Standards Organization) committee. Expressions of type *bool* are called Boolean after George Boole, who formulated the rules of mathematical logic.

Boolean expressions evaluate to one of the two values *true* or *false*. Boolean expressions are used in branching and looping statements that we study in the next section. We will say more about Boolean expressions and the type *bool* in that section.

Type Compatibilities

As a general rule, you cannot store a value of one type in a variable of another type. For example, most compilers will object to the following:

```
int int_variable;
int_variable = 2.99;
```

The problem is a type mismatch. The constant 2.99 is of type *double* and the variable int_variable is of type *int*. Unfortunately, not all compilers will react the same way to the above assignment statement. Some will issue an error message, some will give only a warning message, and some compilers will not object at all. But even if the compiler does allow you to use the above assignment, it will probably give int_variable the *int* value 2, not the value 3. Since you cannot count on your compiler accepting the above assignment, you should not assign a *double* value to a variable of type *int*.

The same problem arises if you use a variable of type *double* instead of the constant 2.99. Most compilers will also object to the following:

```
int int_variable;
double double_variable;
double_variable = 2.00;
int_variable = double_variable;
```

The fact that the value 2.00 "comes out even" makes no difference. The value 2.00 is of type *double*, not of type *int*. As you will see shortly, you can replace 2.00

Display 2.3 The type *char*

```
#include <iostream>
using namespace std;
int main( )
{
    char symbol1, symbol2, symbol3;

    cout << "Enter two initials, without any periods:\n";
    cin >> symbol1 >> symbol2;

    cout << "The two initials are:\n";
    cout << symbol1 << symbol2 << endl;

    cout << "Once more with a space:\n";
    symbol3 = ' ';
    cout << symbol1 << symbol3 << symbol2 << endl;

    cout << "That's all.";

    return 0;
}
```

Sample Dialogue

```
Enter two initials, without any periods:
J B
The two initials are:
JB
Once more with a space:
J B
That's all.
```

with 2 in the above assignment to the variable double_variable, but even that is not enough to make the above acceptable. The variables int_variable and double_variable are of different types, and that is the cause of the problem.

Even if the compiler will allow you to mix types in an assignment statement, in most cases you should not. Doing so makes your program less portable, and it can be confusing. For example, if your compiler lets you assign 2.99 to a variable of type *int*, the variable will receive the value 2.00, rather than 2.99, which can be confusing since the program seems to say the value will be 2.99.

There are some special cases where it is permitted to assign a value of one type to a variable of another type. It is acceptable to assign a value of type *int* to a variable of type *double*. For example, the following is both legal and acceptable style:

```
double double_variable;
double_variable = 2;
```

The above will set the value of the variable named double_variable equal to 2.0.

Although it is usually a bad idea to do so, you can store an *int* value such as 65 in a variable of type *char* and you can store a letter such as 'Z' in a variable of type *int*. For many purposes, the C language considers the characters to be small integers, and perhaps unfortunately, C++ inherited this from C. The reason for allowing this is that variables of type *char* consume less memory than variables of type *int* and so doing arithmetic with variables of type *char* can save some memory. However, it is clearer to use the type *int* when you are dealing with integers and to use the type *char* when you are dealing with characters.

The general rule is that you cannot place a value of one type in a variable of another type—though it may seem that there are more exceptions to the rule than there are cases that follow the rule. Even if the compiler does not enforce this rule very strictly, it is a good rule to follow. Placing data of one type in a variable of another type can cause problems, since the value must be changed to a value of the appropriate type and that value may not be what you would expect.

Values of type *bool* can be assigned to variables of an integer type (*short*, *int*, *long*) and integers can be assigned to variables of type *bool*. However, it is poor style to do this and you should not use these features. For completeness and to help you read other people's code, we do give the details: When assigned to a variable of type *bool*, any nonzero integer will be stored as the value *true*. Zero will be stored as the value *false*. When assigning a *bool* value to an integer variable, *true* will be stored as 1 and *false* will be stored as 0.

Arithmetic Operators and Expressions

In a C++ program, you can combine variables and/or numbers using the arithmetic operators + for addition, – for subtraction, * for multiplication, and / for division. For example, the following assignment statement, which appears in the program in Display 2.1, uses the * operator to multiply the numbers in two variables. (The result is then placed in the variable on the left-hand side of the equal sign.)

```
total_weight = one_weight * number_of_bars;
```

All of the arithmetic operators can be used with numbers of type *int*, numbers of type *double*, and even with one number of each type. However, the type of the value produced and the exact value of the result depends on the types of the numbers being combined. If both operands (i.e., both numbers) are of type *int*, then the result of combining them with an arithmetic operator is of type *int*. If one, or both, of the operands is of type *double*, then the result is of type *double*. For example, if the variables base_amount and increase are of type *int*, then the number produced by the following expression is of type *int*:

```
base_amount + increase
```

However, if one or both of the two variables is of type *double*, then the result is of type *double*. This is also true if you replace the operator + with any of the operators –, *, or /.

division
        The type of the result can be more significant than you might suspect. For example, 7.0/2 has one operand of type *double*, namely 7.0. Hence, the result is the type *double* number 3.5. However, 7/2 has two operands of type *int* and so it yields the type *int* result 3. Even if the result "comes out even," there is a difference. For example, 6.0/2 has one operand of type *double*, namely 6.0. Hence, the result is the type *double* number 3.0, which is only an approximate quantity. However, 6/2 has two operands of type *int*; so it yields the result 3 which is of type *int* and so is an exact quantity. The division operator is the operator that is affected most severely by the type of its arguments.

integer division
        When used with one or both operands of type *double*, the division operator, /, behaves as you might expect. However, when used with two operands of type *int*, the division operator, /, yields the integer part resulting from division. In other words, integer division discards the part after the decimal point. So, 10/3 is 3 (not 3.3333...), 5/2 is 2 (not 2.5), and 11/3 is 3 (not 3.6666...). Notice that the number *is not rounded;* the part after the decimal point is discarded no matter how large it is.

the % operator
        The operator % can be used with operands of type *int* to recover the information lost when you use / to do division with numbers of type *int*. When used with values of type *int*, the two operators / and % yield the two numbers produced when you perform the long division algorithm you learned in grade school. For example, 17 divided by 5 yields 3 with a remainder of 2. The / operation yields the number of times one number "goes into" another. The % operation gives the remainder. For example, the statements

```
cout << "17 divided by 5 is " << (17/5) << endl;
cout << "with a remainder of " << (17%5) << endl;
```

yield the following output:

```
17 divided by 5 is 3
with a remainder of 2
```

Display 2.4 illustrates how / and % work with values of type *int*.

Display 2.4 Integer Division

When used with negative values of type *int*, the result of the operators / and % *negative integers* can be different for different implementations of C++. Thus, you should use / and % *in division* with *int* values only when you know that both values are nonnegative.

Any reasonable spacing will do in arithmetic expressions. You can insert spaces *spacing* before and after operations and parentheses, or you can omit them. Do whatever produces a result that is easy to read.

You can specify the order of operations by inserting parentheses, as illustrated in *parentheses* the following two expressions:

```
(x + y) * z
x + (y * z)
```

To evaluate the first expression, the computer first adds x and y and then multiplies the result by z. To evaluate the second expression, it multiplies y and z and then adds the result to x. Although you may be used to using mathematical formulas that contain square brackets and various other forms of parentheses, that is not allowed in C++. C++ allows only one kind of parentheses in arithmetic expressions. The other varieties are reserved for other purposes.

If you omit parentheses, the computer will follow rules called **precedence rules** *precedence rules* that determine the order in which the operators, such as + and *, are performed. These precedence rules are similar to rules used in algebra and other mathematics classes. For example,

```
x + y * z
```

is evaluated by first doing the multiplication and then the addition. Except in some standard cases, such as a string of additions or a simple multiplication embedded inside an addition, it is usually best to include the parentheses, even if the intended order of operations is the one dictated by the precedence rules. The parentheses make the expression easier to read and less prone to programmer error. A complete set of C++ precedence rules are given in Appendix 2.

Display 2.5 Arithmetic Expressions

Mathematical Formula	C++ Expression
$b^2 - 4ac$	b*b - 4*a*c
$x(y+z)$	x*(y + z)
$\dfrac{1}{x^2+x+3}$	1/(x*x + x + 3)
$\dfrac{a+b}{c-d}$	(a + b)/(c - d)

Display 2.5 shows some examples of common kinds of arithmetic expressions and how they are expressed in C++.

◆ PITFALL   **Whole Numbers in Division**

When you use the division operator / on two whole numbers, the result is a whole number. This can be a problem if you expect a fraction. Moreover, the problem can easily go unnoticed, resulting in a program that looks fine but is producing incorrect output without your even being aware of the problem. For example, suppose you are a landscape architect who charges $5,000 per mile to landscape a highway, and suppose you know the length of the highway you are working on in feet. The price you charge can easily be calculated by the following C++ statement:

```
total_price = 5000 * (feet/5280.0);
```

This works because there are 5,280 feet in a mile. If the stretch of highway you are landscaping is 15,000 feet long, this formula will tell you that the total price is

```
5000 * (15000/5280.0)
```

Your C++ program obtains the final value as follows: 15000/5280.0 is computed as 2.84. Then the program multiplies 5000 by 2.84 to produce the value 14200.00.

With the aid of your C++ program, you know that you should charge $14,200 for the project.

Now suppose the variable `feet` is of type *int*, and you forget to put in the decimal point and the zero, so that the assignment statement in your program reads:

```
total_price = 5000 * (feet/5280);
```

It still looks fine, but will cause serious problems. If you use this second form of the assignment statement, you are dividing two values of type *int*, so the result of the division `feet/5280` is `15000/5280` which is the *int* value 2 (instead of the value 2.84 which you think you are getting). So the value assigned to `total_cost` is `5000*2`, or `10000.00`. If you forget the decimal point, you will charge $10,000. However, as we have already seen, the correct value is $14,200. A missing decimal point has cost you $4,200. Note that this will be true whether the type of `total_price` is *int* or *double*; the damage is done before the value is assigned to `total_price`.

SELF-TEST EXERCISES

12 Convert each of the following mathematical formulas to C++ expression:

$$3x \qquad\qquad 3x + y \qquad\qquad \frac{x + y}{7} \qquad\qquad \frac{3x + y}{z + 2}$$

13 What is the output of the following program lines, when embedded in a correct program that declares all variables to be of type *char*?

```
a = 'b';
b = 'c';
c = a;
cout << a << b << c << 'c';
```

14 What is the output of the following program lines (when embedded in a correct program that declares number to be of type *int*)?

```
number = (1/3) * 3;
cout << "(1/3) * 3 is equal to " << number;
```

15 Write a complete C++ program that reads two whole numbers into two variables of type *int*, and then outputs both the whole number part and the remainder when the first number is divided by the second. This can be done using the operators / and %.

16   Given the following fragment that purports to convert from degrees Celsius to degrees Fahrenheit, answer the following questions:

```
double c = 20;
double f;
f = (9/5) * c + 32.0;
```

    a. What value is assigned to f?

    b. Explain what is actually happening, and what the programmer likely wanted.

    c. Rewrite the code as the programmer intended.

More Assignment Statements

There is a shorthand notation that combines the assignment operator (=) and an arithmetic operator so that a given variable can have its value changed by adding, subtracting, multiplying by, or dividing by a specified value. The general form is

    Variable Operator = Expression

which is equivalent to

    Variable = Variable Operator (Expression)

The *Expression* can be another variable, a constant, or a more complicated arithmetic expression. Below are examples:

Example:	Equivalent to:
`count += 2;`	`count = count + 2;`
`total -= discount;`	`total = total - discount;`
`bonus *= 2;`	`bonus = bonus * 2;`
`time /= rush_factor;`	`time = time/rush_factor;`
`change %= 100;`	`change = change % 100;`
`amount *= cnt1 + cnt2;`	`amount = amount * (cnt1 + cnt2);`

2.4 Simple Flow of Control

> *"If you think we're wax-works," he said, "you ought to pay, you know. Wax-works weren't made to be looked at for nothing. Nohow!"*
> *"Contrariwise," added the one marked "DEE," "if you think we're alive, you ought to speak."*
>
> LEWIS CARROLL, THROUGH THE LOOKING-GLASS

The programs you have seen thus far each consist of a simple list of statements to be executed in the order given. However, to write more sophisticated programs you will also need some way to vary the order in which statements are executed. The order in which statements are executed is often referred to as **flow of control.** In this section we will present two simple ways to add some flow of control to your programs. We will discuss a branching mechanism that lets your program choose between two alternative actions, choosing one or the other depending on the values of variables. We will also present a looping mechanism that lets your program repeat an action a number of times.

flow of control

A Simple Branching Mechanism

Sometimes it is necessary to have a program choose one of two alternatives, depending on the input. For example, suppose you want to design a program to compute a week's salary for an hourly employee. Assume the firm pays an overtime rate of one-and-one-half times the regular rate for all hours after the first forty hours worked. As long as the employee works forty or more hours, the pay is then equal to

```
rate*40 + 1.5*rate*(hours - 40)
```

However, if there is a possibility that the employee will work less than forty hours, this formula will unfairly pay a negative amount of overtime. (To see this just substitute 10 for hours, 1 for rate, and do the arithmetic. The poor employee will get a negative pay check.) The correct pay formula for an employee who works less than forty hours is simply:

```
rate*hours
```

If both more than forty hours and less than forty hours of work are possible, then the program will need to choose between the two formulas. In order to compute the employee's pay, the program action should be

Decide whether or not (hours > 40) is true.

If it is, do the following assignment statement:

```
gross_pay = rate*40 + 1.5*rate*(hours - 40);
```

If it is not, do the following:

```
gross_pay = rate*hours;
```

There is a C++ statement that does exactly this kind of branching action. The *if-else*-**statement** chooses between two alternative actions. For example, the wage calculation we have been discussing can be accomplished with the following C++ statement:

```
if (hours > 40)
    gross_pay = rate*40 + 1.5*rate*(hours - 40);
else
    gross_pay = rate*hours;
```

A complete program that uses this statement is given in Display 2.6.

Two forms of an *if-else*-statement are described in Display 2.7. The first is the simple form of an *if-else*-statement; the second form will be discussed in the subsection entitled "Compound Statements." In the first form shown, the two statements may be any executable statements. The *Boolean_Expression* is a test that can be checked to see if it is true or false, i.e., to see if it is satisfied or not. For example, the *Boolean_Expression* in the above *if-else*-statement is

```
hours > 40
```

When the program reaches the *if-else*-statement, exactly one of the two embedded statements is executed. If the *Boolean_Expression* is true (that is, if it is satisfied), then the *Yes_Statement* is executed; if the *Boolean_Expression* is false (that is, if it is not satisfied), then the *No_Statement* is executed. Notice that the *Boolean_Expression must be enclosed in parentheses.* (This is required by the syntax rules for if-else-statements in C++.) Also notice that an *if-else*-statement has two smaller statements embedded in it.

Boolean expression

A **Boolean expression** is any expression that is either true or false. An *if-else*-statement always contains a *Boolean_Expression*. The simplest form for a *Boolean_Expression* consists of two expressions, such as numbers or variables, that are compared with one of the comparison operators shown in Display 2.8. Notice that some of the operators are spelled with two symbols, for example, ==, !=, <=, >=. Be sure to notice that you use a double equal == for the equal sign, and you use the two symbols != for not equal. Such two-symbol operators should not have any space between the two symbols. The part of the compiler that separates the characters into C++ names and symbols will see the !=, for example, and tell the rest of the compiler that the programmer meant to test for INEQUALITY. When an *if-else*-statement

Display 2.6 An *if-else*-Statement

```
#include <iostream>
using namespace std;
int main( )
{
    int hours;
    double gross_pay, rate;

    cout << "Enter the hourly rate of pay: $";
    cin >> rate;
    cout << "Enter the number of hours worked,\n"
         << "rounded to a whole number of hours: ";
    cin >> hours;

    if (hours > 40)
        gross_pay = rate*40 + 1.5*rate*(hours - 40);
    else
        gross_pay = rate*hours;

    cout.setf(ios::fixed);
    cout.setf(ios::showpoint);
    cout.precision(2);
    cout << "Hours = " << hours << endl;
    cout << "Hourly pay rate = $" << rate << endl;
    cout << "Gross pay = $" << gross_pay << endl;

    return 0;
}
```

Sample Dialogue 1

```
Enter the hourly rate of pay: $20.00
Enter the number of hours worked,
rounded to a whole number of hours: 30
Hours = 30
Hourly pay rate = $20.00
Gross pay = $600.00
```

Sample Dialogue 2

```
Enter the hourly rate of pay: $10.00
Enter the number of hours worked,
rounded to a whole number of hours: 41
Hours = 41
Hourly pay rate = $10.00
Gross pay = $415.00
```

Display 2.7 Syntax for an *if-else*-**Statement**

A Single Statement for Each Alternative:

if (*Boolean_Expression*)
>   *Yes_Statement*

else
>   *No_Statement*

A Sequence of Statements for Each Alternative:

if (*Boolean_Expression*)
{
>   *Yes_Statement_1*
>   *Yes_Statement_2*
>   . . .
>   *Yes_Statement_Last*

}
else
{
>   *No_Statement_1*
>   *No_Statement_2*
>   . . .
>   *No_Statement_Last*

}

---

is executed, the two expressions being compared are evaluated and compared using the operator. If the comparison turns out to be true, then the first statement is performed. If the comparison fails, then the second statement is executed.

&& means "and"   You can combine two comparisons using the "and" operator, which is spelled **&&** in C++. For example, the following Boolean expression is true (i.e., is satisfied) provided x is greater than 2 *and* x is less than 7:

>   (2 < x) && (x < 7)

When two comparisons are connected using a **&&**, the entire expression is true, provided both of the comparisons are true (i.e., provided both are satisfied); otherwise, the entire expression is false.

|| means "or"   You can also combine two comparisons using the "or" operator, which is spelled **||** in C++. For example, the following is true provided y is less than 0 *or* y is greater than 12:

>   (y < 0) || (y > 12)

Display 2.8 Comparison Operators

Math Symbol	English	C++ Notation	C++ Sample	Math Equivalent
=	equal to	==	x + 7 == 2*y	$x + 7 = 2y$
≠	not equal to	!=	ans != 'n'	$ans \neq \text{'n'}$
<	less than	<	count < m + 3	$count < m + 3$
≤	less than or equal to	<=	time <= limit	$time \leq limit$
>	greater than	>	time > limit	$time > limit$
≥	greater than or equal to	>=	age >= 21	$age \geq 21$

When two comparisons are connected using a ||, the entire expression is true provided that one or both of the comparisons are true (i.e., satisfied); otherwise, the entire expression is false.

Remember that when you use a Boolean expression in an *if-else*-statement, the Boolean expression must be enclosed in parentheses. Therefore, an *if-else*-statement that uses the **&&** operator and two comparisons is parenthesized as follows:

parentheses

```
if ( (temperature >= 95) && (humidity >= 90) )
    . . .
```

The inner parentheses around the comparisons are not required, but they do make the meaning clearer and we will normally include them.

You can negate any Boolean expression using the **!** operator. If you want to negate a Boolean expression, place the expression in parentheses and place the **!** operator in front of it. For example, !(x < y) means "x is *not* less than y." Since the Boolean expression in an *if-else*-statement must be enclosed in parentheses, you should place a second pair of parentheses around the negated expression when the negated expression is used in an *if-else*-statement. For example, an *if-else*-statement might begin as follows:

```
if (!(x < y))
    . . .
```

The "and" operator &&

You can form a more elaborate Boolean expression by combining two simple tests using the "and" operator &&.

Syntax (for a Boolean Expression Using &&):

(*Comparison_1*) && (*Comparison_2*)

Example (within an *if-else*-**statement):**

```
if ( (score > 0) && (score < 10) )
    cout << "score is between 0 and 10\n";
else
    cout << "score is not between 0 and 10.\n";
```

If the value of score is greater than 0 and the value of score is also less than 10, then the first cout-statement will be executed; otherwise, the second cout-statement will be executed.

The "or" operator ||

You can form a more elaborate Boolean expression by combining two simple tests using the "or" operator ||.

Syntax (for a Boolean Expression Using ||):

(*Comparison_1*) || (*Comparison_2*)

Example (within an *if-else*-**statement):**

```
if ( (x == 1) || (x == y) )
    cout << "x is 1 or x equals y.\n";
else
    cout << "x is neither 1 nor equal to y.\n";
```

If the value of x is equal to 1 or the value of x is equal to the value of y (or both), then the first cout-statement will be executed; otherwise, the second cout-statement will be executed.

The ! operator can usually be avoided. For example, our hypothetical *if-else*-statement can instead begin with the following, which is equivalent and easier to read:

```
if (x >= y)

    . . .
```

We will not have much call to use the ! operator until later in this book and so we postpone any detailed discussion of the ! operator until then.

Sometimes you want one of the two alternatives in an *if-else*-statement to do nothing at all. In C++ this can be accomplished by omitting the *else* part. These sorts of statements are referred to as *if*-**statements** to distinguish them from *if-else*-statements. For example, the first of the following two statements is an *if*-statement:

omitting else

```
if (sales >= minimum)
    salary = salary + bonus;
cout << "salary = $" << salary;
```

If the value of `sales` is greater than or equal to the value of `minimum`, the assignment statement is executed and then the following `cout`-statement is executed. On the other hand, if the value of `sales` is less than `minimum`, then the embedded assignment statement is not executed, so the *if*-statement causes no change (that is, no bonus is added to the base salary), and the program proceeds directly to the `cout`-statement.

◆ PITFALL   Strings of Inequalities

Do not use a string of inequalities such as the following in your program:

```
if (x < z < y)              Do not do this!
    cout << "z is between x and y.";
```

If you do use the above, your program will probably compile and run, but it will undoubtedly give incorrect output. We will explain why this happens after we learn more details about the C++ language. The same problem will occur with a string of comparisons using any of the comparison operators; the problem is not limited to < comparisons. The correct way to express a string of inequalities is to use the "and" operator && as follows

```
if ( (x < z) && (z < y) )          correct form
    cout << "z is between x and y.";
```

◆ PITFALL   Using = in place of ==

Unfortunately, you can write many things in C++ that you would think are incorrectly formed C++ statements but turn out to have some obscure meaning. This means that if you mistakenly write something that you would expect to produce an error message, you may find out that the program compiles and runs with no error messages, but gives incorrect output. Since you may not realize you wrote something incorrectly, this can cause serious problems. By the time you realize something is wrong, the mistake may be very hard to find. One common mistake is to use the symbol = when you mean ==. For example, consider an *if-else*-statement that begins as follows:

```
if (x = 12)
      Do_Something
else
      Do_Something_Else
```

Suppose you wanted to test to see if the value of x is equal to 12 so that you really meant to use == rather than =. You might think the compiler will catch your mistake. The expression

```
x = 12
```

is not something that is satisfied or not. It is an assignment statement, so surely the compiler will give an error message. Unfortunately, that is not the case. In C++ the expression x = 12 is an expression that returns (or has) a value, just like x + 12 or 2 + 3. An assignment expression's value is the value transferred to the variable on the left. For example, the value of x = 12 is 12. We saw in our discussion of Boolean value compatibility that *int* values may be converted to *true*. If you use x = 12 as the Boolean expression in an *if* statement, the yes clause is always executed.

This error is very hard to find, because it *looks right!* The compiler can find the error without any special instructions if you put the 12 on the left side of the comparison, as in:

```
if(12==x)
    Yes_clause;
else
    No_clause;
```

Remember that dropping one of the = in an == is a common error that is not caught by many compilers, is very hard to see, and is almost certainly not what you wanted. In C++, many executable statements can also be used as almost any kind of expression, including as a Boolean expression for an *if-else*-statement. If you put an assignment statement where a Boolean expression is expected, the assignment statement will be interpreted as a Boolean expression. Of course, the result of the "test" will undoubtedly not be what you intended as the Boolean

Display 2.9 Compound Statements Used with *if-else*

```
if (my_score > your_score)
{
    cout << "I win!\n";
    wager = wager + 100;
}
else
{
    cout << "I wish these were golf scores.\n";
    wager = 0;
}
```

expression. The above *if-else*-statement looks fine at a quick glance and it will compile and run. But, in all likelihood, it will produce puzzling results when it is run.

Compound Statements

You will often want the branches of an *if-else*-statement to execute more than one statement each. To accomplish this, enclose the statements for each branch between a pair of braces, { and }, as indicated in the second syntax template in Display 2.7. This is illustrated in Display 2.9. A list of statements enclosed in a pair of braces is called a **compound statement.** A compound statement is treated as a single statement by C++ and may be used anywhere that a single statement may be used. (Thus, the second syntax template in Display 2.7 is really just a special case of the first one.) Display 2.9 contains two compound statements, embedded in an *if-else*-statement. The compound statements are in color.

Syntax rules for *if-else* demand that the Yes Statement and No Statements be exactly one statement. If more are desired, these must be enclosed in curly braces to make them one statement. If two statements not enclosed by curly braces are placed between the *if* and the *else*, then the compiler will give an error message.

if-else with
multiple statements

compound statement

SELF-TEST EXERCISES

17 Write an *if-else*-statement that outputs the word High if the value of the variable score is greater than 100 and Low if the value of score is at most 100. The variable score is of type *int*.

18 Suppose savings and expenses are variables of type *double* that have been given values. Write an *if-else*-statement that outputs the word Solvent, decreases the value of savings by the value of expenses, and sets the value of expenses to zero, provided that savings is at least as large as expenses. If, however, savings is less than expenses, the *if-else*-statement simply outputs the word Bankrupt, and does not change the value of any variables.

19 Write an *if-else*-statement that outputs the word Passed provided the value of the variable exam is greater than or equal to 60 and also the value of the variable programs_done is greater than or equal to 10. Otherwise, the *if-else*-statement outputs the word Failed. The variables exam and programs_done are both of type *int*.

20 Write an *if-else*-statement that outputs the word Warning provided that either the value of the variable temperature is greater than or equal to 100, or the value of the variable pressure is greater than or equal to 200, or both. Otherwise, the *if-else*-statement outputs the word OK. The variables temperature and pressure are both of type *int*.

21 Consider a quadratic expression, say

$$x^2 - x - 2$$

Describing where this quadratic is positive (i.e., greater than 0), involves describing a set of numbers that are either less than the smaller root (which is -1) or greater than the larger root (which is $+2$). Write a C++ Boolean expression that is true when this formula has positive values.

22 Consider the quadratic expression

$$x^2 - 4x + 3$$

Describing where this quadratic is negative involves describing a set of numbers that are simultaneously greater than the smaller root ($+1$) and less than the larger root ($+3$). Write a C++ Boolean expression that is true when the value of this quadratic is negative.

23 What is the output of the following `cout` statements embedded in these *if-else* statements? You are to assume that these are embedded in a complete correct program. Explain your answer.

a. `if(0)`
```
    cout << "0 is true";
else
    cout << "0 is false";
cout << endl;
```

b. `if(1)`
```
    cout << "1 is true";
else
    cout << "1 is false";
cout << endl;
```

c. `if(-1)`
```
    cout << "-1 is true";
else
    cout << "-1 is false";
cout << endl;
```

Note: This is an exercise only. This is *not* intended to illustrate programming style you should follow.

Simple Loop Mechanisms

Most programs include some action that is repeated a number of times. For example, the program in Display 2.6 computes the gross pay for one worker. If the company employs one hundred workers, then a more complete payroll program would repeat this calculation one hundred times. A portion of a program that repeats a statement or group of statements is called a **loop.** The C++ language has a number of ways to create loops. One of these constructions is called a *while*-**statement** or *while*-**loop.** We will first illustrate its use with a short toy example and then do a more realistic example.

while-statement

The program in Display 2.10 contains a simple *while*-statement shown in color. The portion between the braces { and }, is called the **body** of the *while*-loop; it is the action that is repeated. The statements inside the braces are executed in order, then they are executed again, then again, and so forth until the *while*-loop ends. In the first sample dialogue, the body is executed three times before the loop ends, so the program outputs `Hello` three times. Each repetition of the loop body is called an **iteration** of the loop, and so the first sample dialogue shows three iterations of the loop.

loop body

iteration

Display 2.10 A *while***-Loop**

```cpp
#include <iostream>
using namespace std;
int main( )
{
    int count_down;

    cout << "How many greetings do you want? ";
    cin >> count_down;

    while (count_down > 0)
    {
        cout << "Hello ";
        count_down = count_down - 1;
    }

    cout << endl;
    cout << "That's all!\n";

    return 0;
}
```

Sample Dialogue 1

```
How many greetings do you want? 3
Hello Hello Hello
That's all!
```

Sample Dialogue 2

```
How many greetings do you want? 1
Hello
That's all!
```

Sample Dialogue 3

```
How many greetings do you want? 0

That's all!
```

The loop body is executed zero times.

The meaning of a *while*-statement is suggested by the English word *while*. The loop is repeated *while the Boolean expression in the parentheses is satisfied*. In Display 2.10 this means that the loop body is repeated as long as the value of the variable count_down is greater than 0. Let's consider the first sample dialogue and see how the *while*-loop performs. The user types in **3** so the cin-statement sets the value of count_down to 3. Thus, in this case, when the program reaches the *while*-statement it is certainly true that count_down is greater than 0 and so the statements in the loop body are executed. Every time the loop body is repeated the following two statements are executed:

```
cout << "Hello ";
count_down = count_down - 1;
```

Therefore, every time the loop body is repeated, "Hello " is output and the value of the variable count_down is decreased by one. After the computer repeats the loop body three times, the value of count_down is decreased to 0 and the Boolean expression in parentheses is no longer satisfied. So, this *while*-statement ends after repeating the loop body three times.

The syntax for a *while*-statement is given in Display 2.11. The Boolean_Expressions allowed are exactly the same as the Boolean expressions allowed in an *if-else*-statement. Just as in *if-else*-statements, the Boolean expression in a *while*-statement must be enclosed in parentheses. In Display 2.11 we have given the syntax templates for two cases: the case when there is more than one statement in the loop body and the case when there is just a single statement in the loop body. Note that when there is only a single statement in the loop body, you need not include the braces { and }.

Let's go over the actions performed by a *while*-statement in greater detail. When the *while*-statement is executed, the first thing that happens is that the Boolean expression following the word *while* is checked. It is either true or false. For example, the comparison

```
count_down > 0
```

is true if the value of count_down is positive. If it is false, then no action is taken and the program proceeds to the next statement after the *while*-statement. If the comparison is true, then the entire body of the loop is executed. At least one of the expressions being compared typically contains something that might be changed by the loop body, such as the value of count_down in the *while*-statement in Display 2.10. After the body of the loop is executed, the comparison is again checked. This process is repeated again and again as long as the comparison continues to be true. After each iteration of the loop body the comparison is again checked and if it is

Display 2.11 Syntax of the *while*-**Statement**

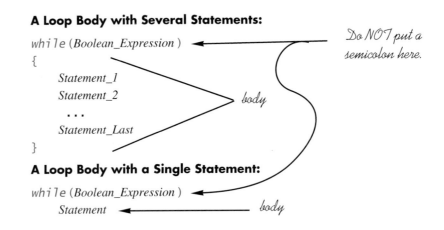

A Loop Body with Several Statements:

while (*Boolean_Expression*)
{
    Statement_1
    Statement_2
    . . .
    Statement_Last
}
                                  body

Do NOT put a semicolon here.

A Loop Body with a Single Statement:

while (*Boolean_Expression*)
    Statement   *body*

---

true, then the entire loop body is executed again. When the comparison is no longer true, the *while*-statement ends.

executing the loop body zero times

    The first thing that happens when a *while*-statement is executed is that the Boolean expression is checked. If the Boolean expression is not true when the *while*-statement begins, then the loop body is never executed. That is exactly what happens in Sample Dialogue 3 of Display 2.10. In many programming situations you want the possibility of executing the loop body zero times. For example, if your *while*-loop is reading a list consisting of all the failing scores on an exam and nobody failed the exam, then you want the loop body to be executed zero times.

do-while-statement

    As we just noted, a *while*-loop might execute its loop body zero times, which is often what you want. If on the other hand you know that *under all circumstances* your loop body should be executed at least one time, then you can use a *do-while*-statement. A *do-while*-statement is similar to a *while*-statement except that the loop body is always executed at least once. The syntax for a *do-while*-statement is given in Display 2.12. A program with a sample *do-while*-loop is given in Display 2.13. In that *do-while*-loop, as in any *do-while*-loop, the first thing that happens is that the statements in the loop body are executed. After that first iteration of the loop body, the *do-while*-statement behaves the same as a *while*-loop. The Boolean expression is checked. If the Boolean expression is true, the loop body is executed again; the Boolean expression is checked again, and so forth.

Display 2.12 Syntax of the *do-while*-Statement

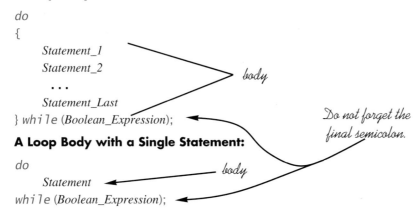

A Loop Body with Several Statements:

do
{
    Statement_1
    Statement_2
    . . .
    Statement_Last
} while (*Boolean_Expression*);

body

Do not forget the final semicolon.

A Loop Body with a Single Statement:

do
    Statement
while (*Boolean_Expression*);

body

Increment and Decrement Operators

We discussed binary operators in the section entitled "Arithmetic Operators and Expressions." Binary operators have two operands. Unary operators have only one operand. You already know of two unary operators, + and -, as used in the expressions +7 and –7. The C++ language has two other very common unary operators, ++ and --. The ++ operator is called the **increment operator** and the -- operator is called the **decrement operator.** They are usually used with variables of type *int*. If n is a variable of type *int*, then n++ increases the value of n by one and n-- decreases the value of n by one. So n++ and n-- (when followed by a semicolon) are executable statements. For example, the statements

++ and --

```
int n = 1, m = 7;
n++;
cout << "The value of n is changed to " << n << endl;
m--;
cout << "The value of m is changed to " << m << endl;
```

yield the following output:

```
The value of n is changed to 2
The value of m is changed to 6
```

Display 2.13 A *do-while-***Loop**

```
#include <iostream>
using namespace std;
int main( )
{
    char ans;

    do
    {
        cout << "Hello\n";
        cout << "Do you want another greeting?\n"
             << "Press y for yes, n for no,\n"
             << "and then press return: ";
        cin >> ans;
    } while (ans == 'y' || ans == 'Y');

    cout << "Good-Bye\n";

    return 0;
}
```

Sample Dialogue

```
Hello
Do you want another greeting?
Press y for yes, n for no,
and then press return: y
Hello
Do you want another greeting?
Press y for yes, n for no,
and then press return: Y
Hello
Do you want another greeting?
Press y for yes, n for no,
and then press return: n
Good-Bye
```

And now you know where the "++" came from in the name "C++."

Increment and decrement statements are often used in loops. For example, we used the following statement in the *while*-loop in Display 2.10:

```
count_down = count_down - 1;
```

However, most experienced C++ programmers would use the decrement operator rather than the assignment statement, so that the entire *while*-loop would read as follows:

```
while (count_down > 0)
{
    cout << "Hello ";
    count_down--;
}
```

In fact, most experienced C++ programmers would simplify this *while*-loop even more than this, but we will leave that discussion until later.

◀)) PROGRAMMING EXAMPLE
Charge Card Balance

Suppose you have a bank charge card with a balance owed of $50 and suppose the bank charges you 2% per month interest. How many months can you let pass without making any payments before your balance owed will exceed $100? One way to solve this problem is to simply read each monthly statement and count the number of months that go by until your balance reaches $100 or more. Better still, you can calculate the monthly balances with a program rather than waiting for the statements to arrive. In this way you will obtain an answer without having to wait so long (and without endangering your credit rating).

After one month the balance would be $50 plus 2% of $50, which is $51. After two months the balance would be $51 plus 2% of $51, which is $52.02. After three months the balance would be $52.02 plus 2% of $52.02, and so on. In general, each month increases the balance by 2%. The program could keep track of the balance by storing it in a variable called `balance`. The change in the value of `balance` for one month can be calculated as follows:

```
balance = balance + 0.02*balance;
```

If we repeat this action until the value of `balance` reaches (or exceeds) `100.00` and we count the number of repetitions, then we will know the number of months it will take for the balance to reach `100.00`. To do this we need another variable to count the number of times the balance is changed. Let us call this new variable `count`. The final body of our *while*-loop will thus contain the following statements:

```
balance = balance + 0.02*balance;
count++;
```

In order to make this loop perform correctly, we must give appropriate values to the variables `balance` and `count` before the loop is executed. In this case, we can initialize the variables when they are declared. The complete program is shown in Display 2.14.

⬢ *PITFALL*   **Infinite Loops**

infinite loop

A *while*-loop or *do-while*-loop does not terminate as long as the Boolean expression after the word *while* is true. This Boolean expression normally contains a variable that will be changed by the loop body, and usually the value of this variable eventually is changed in a way that makes the Boolean expression false and therefore terminates the loop. However, if you make a mistake and write your program so that the Boolean expression is always true, then the loop will run forever. A loop that runs forever is called an **infinite loop.**

First let's describe a loop that does terminate. The following C++ code will write out the positive even numbers less than 12. That is, it will output the numbers 2, 4, 6, 8 and 10, one per line, and then the loop will end.

```
x = 2;
while (x != 12)
{
    cout << x << endl;
    x = x + 2;
}
```

The value of x is increased by 2 on each loop iteration until it reaches 12. At that point, the Boolean expression after the word *while* is no longer true, so the loop ends.

Now suppose you want to write out the odd numbers less than 12, rather than the even numbers. You might mistakenly think that all you need do is change the initializing statement to

```
x = 1;
```

But this mistake will create an infinite loop. Because the value of x goes from 11 to 13, the value of x is never equal to 12; so the loop will never terminate.

Display 2.14 Charge Card Program

```cpp
#include <iostream>
using namespace std;
int main( )
{
    double balance = 50.00;
    int count = 0;

    cout << "This program tells you how long it takes\n"
         << "to accumulate a debt of $100, starting with\n"
         << "an initial balance of $50 owed.\n"
         << "The interest rate is 2% per month.\n";

    while (balance < 100.00)
    {
        balance = balance + 0.02 * balance;
        count++;
    }

    cout << "After " << count << " months,\n";
    cout.setf(ios::fixed);
    cout.setf(ios::showpoint);
    cout.precision(2);
    cout << "your balance due will be $" << balance << endl;

    return 0;
}
```

Sample Dialogue

```
This program tells you how long it takes
to accumulate a debt of $100, starting with
an initial balance of $50 owed.
The interest rate is 2% per month.
After 36 months,
your balance due will be $101.99
```

This sort of problem is common when loops are terminated by checking a numeric quantity using == or !=. When dealing with numbers, it is always safer to test for passing a value. For example, the following will work fine as the first line of our *while*-loop:

```
while (x < 12)
```

With this change, x can be initialized to any number and the loop will still terminate.

A program that is in an infinite loop will run forever unless some external force stops it. Since you can now write programs that contain an infinite loop, it is a good idea to learn how to force a program to terminate. The method for forcing a program to stop varies from system to system. The keystrokes control-C will terminate a program on many systems. (To type a control-C hold down the control key while pressing the C key.)

SELF-TEST EXERCISES

24 What is the output produced by the following (when embedded in a correct program with x declared to be of type *int*)?

```
x = 10;
while (x > 0)
{
    cout << x << endl;
    x = x - 3;
}
```

25 What output would be produced in the previous exercise if the > sign were replaced with <?

26 What is the output produced by the following (when embedded in a correct program with x declared to be of type *int*)?

```
x = 10;
do
{
    cout << x << endl;
    x = x - 3;
} while (x > 0);
```

27 What is the output produced by the following (when embedded in a correct program with x declared to be of type *int*)?

```
x = -42;
do
{
    cout << x << endl;
    x = x - 3;
} while (x > 0);
```

28 What is the most important difference between a *while*-statement and a *do-while*-statement?

29 What is the output produced by the following (when embedded in a correct program with x declared to be of type *int*)?

```
x = 10;
while (x > 0)
{
    cout << x << endl;
    x = x + 3;
}
```

2.5 Program Style

> *In matters of grave importance,*
>   *style, not sincerity, is the vital thing.*
>
> OSCAR WILDE, THE IMPORTANCE OF BEING EARNEST

All the variable names in our sample programs were chosen to suggest their use. Our sample programs were laid out in a particular format. For example, the declarations and statements were all indented the same amount. These and other matters of style are of more than aesthetic interest. A program that is written with careful attention to style is easier to read, easier to correct, and easier to change.

Indenting

A program should be laid out so that elements that are naturally considered a group are made to look like a group. One way to do this is to skip a line between parts that are logically considered separate. Indenting can also help to make the structure of the program clearer. A statement within a statement should be indented. In particular, *if-else*-statements, *while*-loops, and *do-while*-loops should be indented either as in our sample programs or in some similar manner.

The braces { } determine a large part of the structure of a program. Placing each brace on a line by itself, as we have been doing, makes it easy to find the matching pairs. Notice that we have indented some pairs of braces. When one pair of braces is embedded in another pair, the embedded braces are indented more than the outer braces. Look back at the program in Display 2.14. The braces for the body of the *while*-loop are indented more than the braces for the main part of the program.

There are at least two schools of thought on where you should place braces. The first, which we use in this book, is to reserve a separate line for each brace. This form is easiest to read. The second school of thought holds that the opening brace for a pair need not be on a line by itself. If used with care this second method can be effective, and it does save space. The important point is to use a style that shows the structure of the program. The exact layout is not precisely dictated, but you should be consistent within any one program.

Comments

In order to make a program understandable, you should include some explanatory notes at key places in the program. Such notes are called **comments.** C++ and most other programming languages have provisions for including such comments within the text of a program. In C++ the symbols // are used to indicate the start of a comment. All of the text between the // and the end of the line is a comment. The compiler simply ignores anything that follows // on a line. If you want a comment that covers more than one line, place a // on each line of the comment. The symbols // are two slashes (without a space between them).

In this book, comments will always be written in italic so they stand out from the program text. Some text editors indicate comments by showing them in a different color from the rest of the program text.

There is another way to insert comments in a C++ program. Anything between the symbol pair /* and the symbol pair */ is considered a comment and is ignored by the compiler. Unlike the // comments, which require an additional // on each line, the /* to */ comments can span several lines like so:

```
/*This is a comment that spans
three lines. Note that there is no comment
symbol of any kind on the second line.*/
```

Comments of the /* */ type may be inserted anywhere in a program that a space or line break is allowed. However, they should not be inserted anywhere except where they are easy to read and do not distract from the layout of the program. Usually comments are only placed at the ends of lines or on separate lines by themselves.

There are differing opinions on which kind of comment is best to use. Either variety (the // kind or the /* */ kind) can be effective if used with care. We will use the // kind in this book.

It is difficult to say just how many comments a program should contain. The only correct answer is "just enough," which of course conveys little to the novice programmer. It will take some experience to get a feel for when it is best to include a comment. Whenever something is important and not obvious, it merits a comment. However, too many comments are as bad as too few. A program that has a comment on each line will be so buried in comments that the structure of the program is hidden in a sea of obvious observations. Comments like the following contribute nothing to understanding and should not appear in a program:

when to comment

```
distance = speed * time; //Computes the distance traveled
```

Notice the comment given at the start of the program in Display 2.15. All programs should begin with a comment similar to the one shown there. It gives all the essential information about the program: what file the program is in, who wrote the program, how to contact the person who wrote the program, what the program does, the date that the program was last modified, and any other particulars that are appropriate, such as the assignment number, if the program is a class assignment. Exactly what you include in this comment will depend on your particular situation. For example, if you do not have an electronic mail (Email) address, then you might use your phone number. We will not include such long comments in the programs in the rest of this book, but you should always begin your programs with such a comment.

Naming Constants

There are two problems with numbers in a computer program. The first is that they carry no mnemonic value. For example, when the number 10 is encountered in a program, it gives no hint of its significance. If the program is a banking program, it might be the number of branch offices or the number of teller windows at the main office. In order to understand the program, you need to know the significance of each constant. The second problem is that when a program needs to have some numbers changed, the changing tends to introduce errors. Suppose that 10 occurs twelve times in a banking program, that four of the times it represents the number of branch offices, and that eight of the times it represents the number of teller windows at the main office. When the bank opens a new branch and the program needs to be updated, there is a good chance that some of the 10's that should be changed to 11 will not be, or some that should not be changed will be. The way to avoid these problems is to name each number and use the name instead of the number within your program. For example, a banking program might have two constants with the names BRANCH_COUNT and WINDOW_COUNT. Both these numbers might have a value of 10,

Display 2.15 Comments and Named Constants

```
//File Name: health.cxx (Your system may require some suffix other than cxx.)
//Author: Your Name Goes Here.
//Email Address: you@yourmachine.bla.bla
//Assignment Number: 2
//Description: Program to determine if the user is ill.
//Last Changed: September 23, 2001

#include <iostream>
using namespace std;
int main( )
{
    const double NORMAL = 98.6;//degrees Fahrenheit
    double temperature;

    cout << "Enter your temperature: ";
    cin >> temperature;

    if (temperature > NORMAL)
    {
        cout << "You have a fever.\n";
        cout << "Drink lots of liquids and get to bed.\n";
    }
    else
    {
        cout << "You don't have a fever.\n";
        cout << "Go study.\n";
    }

    return 0;
}
```

Your programs should always begin with a comment similar to this one.

Sample Dialogue

```
Enter your temperature: 98.6
You don't have a fever.
Go study.
```

but when the bank opens a new branch, all you need do in order to update the program is to change the definition of BRANCH_COUNT.

How do you name a number in a C++ program? One way to name a number is to initialize a variable to that number value, as in the following example:

```
int BRANCH_COUNT = 10;
int WINDOW_COUNT = 10;
```

There is, however, one problem with this method of naming number constants: You might inadvertently change the value of one of these variables. C++ provides a way of marking an initialized variable so that it cannot be changed. If your program tries to change one of these variables it produces an error condition. To mark a variable declaration so that the value of the variable cannot be changed, precede the declaration with the word *const* (which is an abbreviation of *constant*). For example:

const

```
const int BRANCH_COUNT = 10;
const int WINDOW_COUNT = 10;
```

If the variables are of the same type, it is possible to combine the above lines into one declaration, as follows:

```
const int BRANCH_COUNT = 10, WINDOW_COUNT = 10;
```

However, most programmers find that placing each name definition on a separate line is clearer. The word *const* is often called a **modifier,** because it modifies (restricts) the variables being declared.

A variable declared using the *const* modifier is often called a **declared constant.** Writing declared constants in all uppercase letters is not required by the C++ language, but it is standard practice among C++ programmers.

declared constants

Once a number has been named in this way, the name can then be used anywhere the number is allowed, and it will have exactly the same meaning as the number it names. To change a named constant, you need only change the initializing value in the *const* variable declaration. The meaning of all occurrences of BRANCH_COUNT, for instance, can be changed from 10 to 11 simply by changing the initializing value of 10 in the declaration of BRANCH_COUNT.

Although unnamed numeric constants are allowed in a program, you should seldom use them. It often makes sense to use unnamed number constants for well-known, easily recognizable, and unchangeable quantities, such as 100 for the number of centimeters in a meter. However, all other numeric constants should be given names in the fashion we just described. This will make your programs easier to read and easier to change.

Display 2.15 contains a simple program that illustrates the use of the declaration modifier *const*.

Naming Constants with the *const* Modifier

When you initialize a variable inside a declaration, you can mark the variable so that the program is not allowed to change its value. To do this place the word *const* in front of the declaration, as described below:

Syntax:

const Type_Name Variable_Name = Constant;

Examples:

const int MAX_TRIES = 3;
const double PI = 3.14159;

SELF-TEST EXERCISES

30 The following *if-else*-statement will compile and run without any problems. However, it is not laid out in a way that is consistent with the other *if-else*-statements we have used in our programs. Rewrite it so that the layout (indenting and line breaks) matches the style we used in this chapter.

```
if (x < 0) {x = 7; cout << "x is now positive.";} else
{x = -7; cout << "x is now negative.";}
```

31 What output would be produced by the following two lines (when embedded in a complete and correct program)?

```
//cout << "Hello from";
cout << "Self-Test Exercise 31";
```

CHAPTER SUMMARY

- Use meaningful names for variables.

- Be sure to check that variables are declared to be of the correct data type.

- Be sure that variables are initialized before the program attempts to use their value. This can be done when the variable is declared or with an assignment statement before the variable is first used.

- Use enough parentheses in arithmetic expressions to make the order of operations clear.

- Always include a prompt line in a program whenever the user is expected to enter data from the keyboard, and always echo the user's input.

- An *if-else*-statement allows your program to choose one of two alternative actions. An *if*-statement allows your program to decide whether or not to perform some one particular action.

- A *do-while*-loop always executes its loop body at least once. In some situations a *while*-loop might not execute the body of the loop at all.

- Almost all number constants in a program should be given meaningful names that can be used in place of the numbers. This can be done by using the modifier *const* in a variable declaration.

- Use an indenting, spacing, and line break pattern similar to the sample programs.

- Insert comments to explain major subsections or any unclear part of a program.

Answers to Self-Test Exercises

1 `int feet = 0, inches = 0;`
  `int feet(0), inches(0);`

2 `int count = 0;`
  `double distance = 1.5;`

3 `sum = n1 + n2;`

4 The actual output from a program such as this is dependent on the system and the history of the use of the system.

```
#include <iostream>
using namespace std;
int main()
{
  int first, second, third, fourth, fifth;
  cout << first << " " << second << " " third
      << " " fourth << " " << fifth << endl;
  return 0;
}
```

5 There is no unique right answer for this one. Below are possible answers:

a. speed
b. pay_rate
c. highest or max_score

6

```cpp
cout << "The answer to the question of\n"
     << "Life, the Universe, and Everything is 42.\n";
```

7

```cpp
cout << "Enter a whole number and press return: ";
cin >> the_number;
```

8

```cpp
cout.setf(ios::fixed);
cout.setf(ios::showpoint);
cout.precision(3);
```

9

```cpp
#include <iostream>
using namespace std;
int main( )
{
    cout << "Hello world\n";
    return 0;
}
```

10

```cpp
cout << endl << "\t";
```

11

```cpp
#include <iostream>
using namespace std;
int main( )
{
  double one(1.0), two(1.414), three(1.732), four(2.0),
  five(2.236);
  cout << "\tN\tSquare Root\n";
  cout << "\t1\t" << one << endl
       << "\t2\t" << two << endl
       << "\t3\t" << three << endl
       << "\t4\t" << four << endl
       << "\t5\t" << five << endl;
  return 0;
}
```

12 3*x
    3*x + y
    (x + y)/7   Note that x + y/7 is not correct.
    (3*x + y)/(z + 2)

13   bcbc

14   (1/3) * 3 is equal to 0

Since 1 and 3 are of type *int*, the / operator performs integer division, which discards the remainder, so the value of 1/3 is 0, not 0.3333.... This makes the value of the entire expression 0 * 3, which of course is 0.

15

```
#include <iostream>
using namespace std;

int main( )
{
    int number1, number2;

    cout << "Enter two whole numbers: ";
    cin >> number1 >> number2;
    cout << number1 << " divided by " << number2
         << " equals " << (number1/number2) << endl
         << "with a remainder of " << (number1%number2)
         << endl;
    return 0;
}
```

16 a. 52.0

    b. 9/5 has *int* value 1, since numerator and denominator are both *int*, integer division is done; the fractional part is discarded.

    c. f = (9.0/5) * c + 32.0;
       or this
       f = 1.8 * c + 32.0;

17

```
if (score > 100)
    cout << "High";
else
    cout << "Low";
```

You may want to add \n to the end of the above quoted strings depending on the other details of the program.

18

```
if (savings >= expenses)
{
    savings = savings - expenses;
    expenses = 0;
    cout << "Solvent";
}
else
{
    cout << "Bankrupt";
}
```

You may want to add \n to the end of the above quoted strings depending on the other details of the program.

19

```
if ( (exam >= 60) && (programs_done >= 10) )
    cout << "Passed";
else
    cout << "Failed";
```

You may want to add \n to the end of the above quoted strings depending on the other details of the program.

20

```
if ( (temperature >= 100) || (pressure >= 200) )
    cout << "Warning";
else
    cout << "OK";
```

You may want to add \n to the end of the above quoted strings depending on the other details of the program.

21 (x < -1 || (x > 2)

22 (1 < x) && (x < 3)

23 a. 0 is `false`. In the section on type compatibility, it is noted that the `int` value 0 converts to `false`.

b. 1 is `true`. In the section on type compatibility, it is noted that a nonzero `int` value converts to `true`.

c. -1 is `true`. In the section on type compatibility, it is noted that a nonzero `int` value converts to `true`.

24
```
10
7
4
1
```

25 There would be no output, since the Boolean expression (x < 0) is not satisfied and so the *while*-statement ends without executing the loop body.

26 The output is exactly the same as it was for Self-Test Exercise 24.

27 The body of the loop is executed before the Boolean expression is checked, the Boolean expression is false, and so the output is

```
-42
```

28 With a *do-while*-statement the loop body is always executed at least once. With a *while*-statement there can be conditions under which the loop body is not executed at all.

29 This is an infinite loop. The output would begin with the following and go on forever:

```
10
13
16
19
```

30

```
if (x < 0)
{
    x = 7;
    cout << "x is now positive.";
}
else
{
    x = -7;
    cout << "x is now negative.";
}
```

31 The first line is a comment and is not executed. So the entire output is just the following line:

Self-Test Exercise 31

Programming Projects

1   A metric ton is 35,273.92 ounces. Write a program that will read the weight of a package of breakfast cereal in ounces and output the weight in metric tons as well as the number of boxes needed to yield one metric ton of cereal. Your program should allow the user to repeat this calculation as often as the user wishes.

2   A government research lab has concluded that an artificial sweetener commonly used in diet soda pop will cause death in laboratory mice. A friend of yours is desperate to lose weight but cannot give up soda pop. Your friend wants to know how much diet soda pop it is possible to drink without dying as a result. Write a program to supply the answer. The input to the program is the amount of artificial sweetener needed to kill a mouse, the weight of the mouse, and the weight of the dieter. To ensure the safety of your friend, be sure the program requests the weight at which the dieter will stop dieting, rather than the dieter's current weight. Assume that diet soda contains 1/10th of one percent artificial sweetener. Use a variable declaration with the modifier *const* to give a name to this fraction. You may want to express the percent as the *double* value 0.001. Your program should allow the calculation to be repeated as often as the user wishes.

3   Workers at a particular company have won a 7.6% pay increase retroactive for six months. Write a program that takes an employee's previous annual

salary as input, and outputs the amount of retroactive pay due the employee, the new annual salary, and the new monthly salary. Use a variable declaration with the modifier *const* to express the pay increase. Your program should allow the calculation to be repeated as often as the user wishes.

4 Negotiating a consumer loan is not always straightforward. One form of loan is the discount installment loan, which works as follows. Suppose a loan has a face value of $1,000, the interest rate is 15%, and the duration is 18 months. The interest is computed by multiplying the face value of $1,000 by 0.15, to yield $150. That figure is then multiplied by the loan period of 1.5 years to yield $225 as the total interest owed. That amount is immediately deducted from the face value, leaving the consumer with only $775. Repayment is made in equal monthly installments based on the face value. So the monthly loan payment will be $1,000 divided by 18 which is $55.56. This method of calculation may not be too bad if the consumer needs $775 dollars, but the calculation is a bit more complicated if the consumer needs $1,000. Write a program that will take three inputs: the amount the consumer needs to receive, the interest rate, and the duration of the loan in months. The program should then calculate the face value required in order for the consumer to receive the amount needed. It should also calculate the monthly payment. Your program should allow the calculations to be repeated as often as the user wishes.

5 Write a program that determines whether a meeting room is in violation of fire law regulations regarding the maximum room capacity. The program will read in the maximum room capacity and the number of people to attend the meeting. If the number of people is less than or equal to the maximum room capacity, the program announces that it is legal to hold the meeting and tells how many additional people may legally attend. If the number of people exceeds the maximum room capacity, the program announces that the meeting cannot be held as planned due to fire regulations and tells how many people must be excluded in order to meet the fire regulations. For a harder version write your program so that it allows the calculation to be repeated as often as the user wishes. If this is a class exercise, ask your instructor if you should do this harder version or not.

6 An employee is paid at a rate of $16.78 per hour for regular hours worked in a week. Any hours over that are paid at the overtime rate of one and one half times that. From the worker's gross pay 6% is withheld for social security tax, 14% is withheld for federal income tax, 5% is withheld for state income tax, and $10 per week is withheld for union dues. If the worker has three or more dependents, then an additional $35 is withheld to cover the extra cost of

health insurance beyond what the employer pays. Write a program that will read in the number of hours worked in a week and the number of dependents as input, and will then output the worker's gross pay, each withholding amount, and the net take-home pay for the week. For a harder version write your program so that it allows the calculation to be repeated as often as the user wishes. If this is a class exercise, ask your instructor if you should do this harder version or not.

7   It is difficult to make a budget that spans several years, because prices are not stable. If your company needs 200 pencils per year, you cannot simply use this year's price as the cost of pencils two years from now. Due to inflation the cost is likely to be higher than it is today. Write a program to gauge the expected cost of an item in a specified number of years. The program asks for the cost of the item, the number of years from now that the item will be purchased, and the rate of inflation. The program then outputs the estimated cost of the item after the specified period. Have the user enter the inflation rate as a percentage, like 5.6 (percent). Your program should then convert the percent to a fraction, like 0.056 and should use a loop to estimate the price adjusted for inflation. (Hint: This is similar to computing interest on a charge card account, which was discussed in this chapter.)

8   You have just purchased a stereo system that cost $1000 on the following credit plan: No down payment, an interest rate of 18% per year (and hence 1.5% per month), and monthly payments of $50. The monthly payment of $50 is used to pay the interest and whatever is left is used to pay part of the remaining debt. Hence, the first month you pay 1.5% of $1000 in interest. That is $15 in interest. So, the remaining $35 is deducted from your debt, which leaves you with a debt of $965.00. The next month you pay interest of 1.5% of $965.00, which is $14.48. Hence, you can deduct $35.52 (which is $50 − $14.48) from the amount you owe. Write a program that will tell you how many months it will take you to pay off the loan, as well as the total amount of interest paid over the life of the loan. Use a loop to calculate the amount of interest and the size of the debt after each month. (Your final program need not output the monthly amount of interest paid and remaining debt, but you may want to write a preliminary version of the program that does output these values.) Use a variable to count the number of loop iterations and hence the number of months until the debt is zero. You may want to use other variables as well. The last payment may be less than $50 if the debt is small, but do not forget the interest. If you owe $50, then your monthly payment of $50 will not pay off your debt, although it will come close. One month's interest on $50 is only 75 cents.

CHAPTER

3

Procedural Abstraction and Functions That Return a Value

3 Procedural Abstraction and Functions That Return a Value

There was a most ingenious Architect who had contrived a new method for building Houses, by beginning at the Roof, and working downward to the Foundation.

JONATHAN SWIFT, GULLIVER'S TRAVELS

Introduction

A program can be thought of as consisting of subparts such as obtaining the input data, calculating the output data, and displaying the output data. C++, like most programming languages, has facilities to name and code each of these subparts separately. In C++ these subparts are called **functions.** In this chapter we present the basic syntax for one of the two main kinds of C++ functions—namely those designed to compute a single value. We also discuss how these functions can aid in program design. We begin with a discussion of a fundamental design principle.

3.1 Top-Down Design

Remember that the way to write a program is to first design the method that the program will use and to write out this method in English, as if the instructions were to be followed by a human clerk. As we noted in Chapter 1, this set of instructions is called an *algorithm.* A good plan of attack for designing the algorithm is to break down the task to be accomplished into a few subtasks, decompose each of these subtasks into smaller subtasks, and so forth. Eventually the subtasks become so small that they are trivial to implement in C++. This method is called **top-down design.** (The method is also sometimes called **stepwise refinement,** or, more graphically, **divide and conquer.**)

   Using the top-down method, you design a program by breaking the program's task into subtasks and solving these subtasks by subalgorithms. Preserving this top-down structure in your C++ program would make the program easier to understand, easier to change if need be and, as will become apparent, easier to write, test, and debug. C++, like most programming languages, has facilities to include separate subparts inside of a program. In other programming languages these subparts are called *subprograms* or *procedures.* In C++ these subparts are called *functions.*

One of the advantages of using functions to divide a programming task into sub-tasks is that different people can work on the different subtasks. When producing a very large program, such as a compiler or office-management system, this sort of teamwork is needed if the program is to be produced in a reasonable amount of time. We will begin our discussion of functions by showing you how to use functions that were written by somebody else.

functions for teamwork

3.2 Predefined Functions

C++ comes with libraries of predefined functions that you can use in your programs. Before we show you how to define functions, we will first show you how to use these functions that are already defined for you.

Using Predefined Functions

We will use the `sqrt` function to illustrate how you use predefined functions. The `sqrt` function calculates the square root of a number. (The square root of a number is that number which when multiplied by itself will produce the number you started out with. For example, the square root of 9 is 3 because 3^2 is equal to 9.) The function `sqrt` starts with a number, such as 9.0, and computes its square root, in this case 3.0. The value the function starts out with is called its **argument.** The value it computes is called the **value returned.** Some functions may have more than one argument, but no function has more than one value returned. If you think of the function as being similar to a small program, then the arguments are analogous to the input and the value returned is analogous to the output.

argument
value returned

The syntax for using functions in your program is simple. To set a variable named `the_root` equal to the square root of 9.0, you can use the following assignment statement:

```
the_root = sqrt(9.0);
```

The expression `sqrt(9.0)` is called a **function call** (or if you want to be fancy you can also call it a **function invocation**). An argument in a function call can be a constant, such as 9.0, or a variable, or a more complicated expression. A function call is an expression that can be used like any other expression. You can use a function call wherever it is legal to use an expression of the type specified for the value returned by the function. For example, the value returned by `sqrt` is of type *double*. Thus, the following is legal (although perhaps stingy):

function call

```
bonus = sqrt(sales)/10;
```

`sales` and `bonus` are variables that would normally be of type *double*. The function call `sqrt(sales)` is a single item, just as if it were enclosed in parentheses. Thus, the above assignment statement is equivalent to:

```
bonus = (sqrt(sales))/10;
```

You can also use a function call directly in a `cout`-statement, as in the following:

```
cout << "The side of a square with area " << area
     << " is " << sqrt(area);
```

Display 3.1 contains a complete program that uses the predefined function `sqrt`. The program computes the size of the largest square dog house that can be built for the amount of money the user is willing to spend. The program asks the user for an amount of money, and then determines how many square feet of floor space can be purchased for that amount of money. That calculation yields an area in square feet for the floor area of the dog house. The function `sqrt` yields the length of one side of the dog house floor.

Function Call

A function call is an expression consisting of the function name followed by arguments enclosed in parentheses. If there is more than one argument, the arguments are separated by commas. A function call is an expression that can be used like any other expression of the type specified for the value returned by the function.

Syntax:

Function_Name(*Argument_List*)
   where the *Argument_List* is a comma-separated list of arguments:
Argument_1, *Argument_2*, . . . , *Argument_Last*

Examples:

```
side = sqrt(area);
cout << "2.5 to the power 3.0 is "
     << pow(2.5, 3.0);
```

Notice that there is another new element in the program in Display 3.1:

```
#include <cmath>
```

Display 3.1 A Function Call

```
//Computes the size of a dog house that can be purchased
//given the user's budget.
#include <iostream>
#include <cmath>
using namespace std;

int main( )
{
    const double COST_PER_SQ_FT = 10.50;
    double budget, area, length_side;

    cout << "Enter the amount budgeted for your dog house $";
    cin >> budget;

    area = budget/COST_PER_SQ_FT;
    length_side = sqrt(area);

    cout.setf(ios::fixed);
    cout.setf(ios::showpoint);
    cout.precision(2);
    cout << "For a price of $" << budget << endl
         << "I can build you a luxurious square dog house\n"
         << "that is " << length_side
         << " feet on each side.\n";

    return 0;
}
```

Sample Dialogue

```
Enter the amount budgeted for your dog house $25.00
For a price of $25.00
I can build you a luxurious square dog house
that is 1.54 feet on each side.
```

That line looks very much like the line

    #include <iostream>

and, in fact, these two lines are the same sort of thing. As we noted in Chapter 2, such lines are called `include` **directives.** The name inside the angular brackets < > is the name of a file known as a **header file.** A header file for a library provides the compiler with certain basic information about the library, and an `include` directive delivers this information to the compiler. This enables the linker to find object code for the functions in the library so that it can correctly link the library to your program. For example, the library iostream contains the definitions of `cin` and `cout`, and the header file for the iostream library is called `iostream`. The math library contains the definition of the function `sqrt` and a number of other mathematical functions, and the header file for this library is `cmath`. If your program uses a predefined function from some library, then it must contain a directive that names the header file for that library, such as the following:

    #include <cmath>

Be sure to follow the syntax illustrated in our examples. Do not forget the symbols < and >; they are the same symbols as the less-than and greater-than symbols. There should be no space between the < and the filename, nor between the filename and the >. Also, some compilers require that directives have no spaces around the #, so it is always safest to place the # at the very start of the line and to not put any space between the # and the word `include`. These `#include` directives are normally placed at the beginning of the file containing your program.

As we noted before, the directive

    #include <iostream>

requires that you also use the following *using* directive:

    using namespace std;

This is because the definitions of names like `cin` and `cout`, which are given in `iostream`, define those names to be part of the `std` namespace. This is true of most standard libraries. If you have an `include` directive for a standard library such as

    #include <cmath>

then you probably need the *using* directive:

    using namespace std;

There is no need to use multiple copes of this *using* directive when you have multiple include directives.

Usually, all you need to do to use a library is to place an `include` directive and a *using* directive for that library in the file with your program. If things work with just the include directive and *using* directive, you need not worry about doing anything else. However, for some libraries on some systems you may need to give additional instructions to the compiler or to explicitly run a linker program to link in the library. Early C and C++ compilers did not automatically search all libraries for linking. The details vary from one system to another, so you will have to check your manual or a local expert to see exactly what is necessary.

Some people will tell you that include directives are not processed by the compiler but are processed by a **preprocessor.** They're right, but the difference is more of a word game than anything that need concern you. On almost all compilers the preprocessor is called automatically when you compile your program.

preprocessor

A few predefined functions are described in Display 3.2. More predefined functions are described in Appendix 4. Notice that the absolute value functions abs and

Display 3.2 Some Predefined Functions

Name	Description	Type of Arguments	Type of Value Returned	Example	Value	Library Header
sqrt	square root	*double*	*double*	sqrt(4.0)	2.0	cmath
pow	powers	*double*	*double*	pow(2.0,3.0)	8.0	cmath
abs	absolute value for *int*	*int*	*int*	abs(−7) abs(7)	7 7	cstdlib
labs	absolute value for *long*	*long*	*long*	labs(−70000) labs(70000)	70000 70000	cstdlib
fabs	absolute value for *double*	*double*	*double*	fabs(−7.5) fabs(7.5)	7.5 7.5	cmath
ceil	ceiling (round up)	*double*	*double*	ceil(3.2) ceil(3.9)	4.0 4.0	cmath
floor	floor (round down)	*double*	*double*	floor(3.2) floor(3.9)	3.0 3.0	cmath

abs *and* labs

labs are in the library with header file cstdlib, so any program that uses either of these functions must contain the following directive:

```
#include <cstdlib>
```

All the other functions listed are in the library with header file cmath, just like sqrt.

fabs

Also notice that there are three absolute value functions. If you want to produce the absolute value of a number of type *int*, you use abs; if you want to produce the absolute value of a number of type *long*, you use labs; and if you want to produce the absolute value of a number of type *double*, you use fabs. To complicate things even more, abs and labs are in the library with header file cstdlib, while fabs is in the library with header file cmath. fabs is an abbreviation for *floating-point absolute value*. Recall that numbers with a fraction after the decimal point, such as numbers of type *double*, are often called *floating-point numbers*.

pow

Another example of a predefined function is pow, which is in the library with header file cmath. The function pow can be used to do exponentiation in C++. For example, if you want to set a variable result equal to x^y, you can use the following:

```
result = pow(x, y);
```

Hence, the following three lines of program code will output the number 9.0 to the screen, because $(3.0)^{2.0}$ is 9.0:

```
double result, x = 3.0, y = 2.0;
result = pow(x, y);
cout << result;
```

arguments have a type

Notice that the above call to pow returns 9.0, not 9. The function pow always returns a value of type *double*, not of type *int*. Also notice that the function pow requires two arguments. A function can have any number of arguments. Moreover, every argument position has a specified type and the argument used in a function call should be of that type. In many cases, if you use an argument of the wrong type, then some automatic type conversion will be done for you by C++. However, the results may not be what you intended. When you call a function, you should use arguments of the type specified for that function. One exception to this caution is the automatic conversion of arguments from type *int* to type *double*. In many situations, including calls to the function pow, you can safely use an argument of type *int* when an argument of type *double* is specified.

restrictions on pow

Many implementations of pow have a restriction on what arguments can be used. In these implementations, if the first argument to pow is negative, then the second argument must be a whole number. Since you probably have enough other things to worry about when learning to program, it might be easiest and safest to use pow only when the first argument is nonnegative.

◆ PITFALL   Problems with Library Names

The C++ language is currently in transition. A new standard has come out with, among other things, new names for libraries. If you are using a compiler that has not yet been revised to meet the new standard, then you will need to use different library names.

If the following does not work

```
#include <iostream>
```

use

```
#include <iostream.h>
```

Similarly, if

```
#include <cmath>
```

does not work, then try

```
#include <math.h>
```

And if

```
#include <cstdlib>
```

does not work, then try

```
#include <stdlib.h>
```

In all probability, either all the new library names will work or else you will need to use all old library names. It is unlikely that only some of the library names have been made up to date on your system. If you use the older library names (the ones that end in .h), you do *not* need the *using* directive:

```
using namespace std;
```

Type Changing Functions

Recall that 9/2 is integer division, and evaluates to 4, not 4.5. If you want division to produce an answer of type *double* (i.e., including the fractional part after the decimal point), then at least one of the two numbers in the division must be of

Division may require the

type *double*. For example, 9/2.0 evaluates to 4.5. If one of the two numbers is given as a constant, you can simply add a decimal point and a zero to one (or both) numbers, and the division will then produce a value that includes the digits after the decimal point.

But what if both of the operands in a division are variables, as in the following?

```
int total_candy, number_of_people;
double candy_per_person;
  <The program somehow sets the value of total_candy to 9
     and the value of number_of_people to 2.
   It does not matter how the program does this.>
candy_per_person = total_candy/number_of_people;
```

Unless you convert the value in one of the variables total_candy or number_of_people to a value of type *double*, then the result of the division will be 4, not 4.5 as it should be. The fact that the variable candy_per_person is of type *double* does not help. The value of 4 obtained by division will be converted to a value of type *double* before it is stored in the variable candy_per_person, but that will be too late. The 4 will be converted to 4.0 and the final value of candy_per_person will be 4.0, not 4.5. If one of the quantities in the division were a constant, you could add a decimal point and a zero to convert the constant to type *double*, but in this case both quantities are variables. Fortunately, there is a way to convert from type *int* to type *double* that you can use with either a constant or a variable.

double used
as a function

In C++ you can tell the computer to convert a value of type *int* to a value of type *double*. The way that you write "Convert the value 9 to a value of type *double*" is

```
double(9)
```

The type name *double* can be used as if it were a predefined function that converts a value of some other type, such as 9, to a value of type *double*, in this case 9.0. When it is used in this way, the type name *double* is a kind of predefined function. However, it is not normally referred to as a function. Using the type name *double* in

type casting

this way is called **type casting.** You can use other type names besides *double* for type casting, but we will postpone that topic until later.

For example, in the following we use a type cast to change the type of 9 from *int* to *double* and so the value of answer is set to 4.5:

```
double answer;
answer = double(9)/2;
```

Type casting applied to a constant, such as 9, can make your code easier to read, since it makes your intended meaning clearer. But, type casting applied to constants of type *int* does not give you any additional power. You can use 9.0 instead of *double*(9) when you want to convert 9 to a value of type *double*. However, if the division involves only variables, then type casting may be your only sensible alternative. Using type casting, we can rewrite our earlier example so that the variable candy_per_person receives the correct value of 4.5, instead of 4.0; the only change is the word *double* and two parentheses in the last line:

```
int total_candy, number_of_people;
double candy_per_person;
   <The program somehow sets the value of total_candy to 9
      and the value of number_of_people to 2.
      It does not matter how the program does this.>
candy_per_person = double(total_candy)/number_of_people;
```

Notice the placement of parentheses in the type casting used in the above code.   *Warning!*
You want to do the type casting before the division so that the division operator is working on a value of type *double*. If you wait until after the division is completed, then the digits after the decimal point are already lost. If you mistakenly use the following for the last line of the above code, then the value of candy_per_person will be 4.0, not 4.5.

```
candy_per_person = double(total_candy/number_of_people); //WRONG!
```

A Function to Convert from *int* to *double*

The type name *double* can be used as a predefined function and it will convert a value of some other type to a value of type *double*. For example, *double*(2) returns 2.0. This is called **type casting**. (Type casting can be done with type names other than *double*, but until later in this book, we will only do type casting with the type *double*.)

Syntax:

```
double(Expression_of_Type_int)
```

Example:

```
int total_pot, number_of_winners;
double your_winnings;
   . . .
your_winnings = double(total_pot)/number_of_winners;
```

◆ PITFALL   **Integer Division Drops the Fractional Part**

In integer division, such as computing 11/2, it is easy to forget that 11/2 gives 5, not 5.5. The result is the next lower integer, regardless of the subsequent use of this result. For example,

> *double* d;
> d = 11/2;

Here, the division is done using integer divide; the result of the division is 5, which is converted to *double*, then assigned to d. The fractional part is not generated. Observe that casting to *double* after the division is complete has no effect on the result.

SELF-TEST EXERCISES

1 Determine the value of each of the following arithmetic expressions:

sqrt(16.0)	sqrt(16)	pow(2.0, 3.0)
pow(2, 3)	pow(2.0, 3)	pow(1.1, 2)
abs(3)	abs(-3)	abs(0)
fabs(-3.0)	fabs(-3.5)	fabs(3.5)
ceil(5.1)	ceil(5.8)	floor(5.1)
floor(5.8)	pow(3.0, 2)/2.0	pow(3.0, 2)/2
7/abs(-2)	(7 + sqrt(4.0))/3.0	sqrt(pow(3, 2))

2 Convert each of the following mathematical expressions to a C++ arithmetic expression:

$$\sqrt{x+y} \qquad x^{y+7} \qquad \sqrt{area+fudge}$$

$$\frac{\sqrt{time+tide}}{nobody} \qquad \frac{-b+\sqrt{b^2-4ac}}{2a} \qquad |x-y|$$

3 Write a complete C++ program to compute and output the square root of PI; PI is approximately 3.14159. The *const double* PI is predefined in `cmath`. You are encouraged to use this predefined constant.

4 Write and compile short programs to test the following issues:

   a. Determine if your compiler will allow the `#include <iostream>` anywhere on the line, or if the # needs to be flush with the left margin.

   b. Determine whether your compiler will allow space between the # and the `include`.

3.3   Programmer-Defined Functions

A custom tailored suit always fits better than one off the rack.

MY UNCLE, THE TAILOR

In the previous section we told you how to use predefined functions. In this section we tell you how to define your own functions.

Function Definitions

You can define your own functions, either in the same file as the `main` part of your program or in a separate file so that the functions can be used by several different programs. The definition is the same in either case, but for now, we will assume that the function definition will be in the same file as the `main` part of your program.

Display 3.3 contains a sample function definition in a complete program that demonstrates a call to the function. The function is called `total_cost`. The function takes two arguments—the price for one item and number of items for a purchase. The function returns the total cost, including sales tax, for that many items at the specified price. The function is called in the same way a predefined function is called. The description of the function, which the programmer must write, is a bit more complicated.

The description of the function is given in two parts that are called the *function prototype* and the *function definition*. The **function prototype**[1] describes how the function is called. C++ requires that either the complete function definition or the function prototype appears in the code before the function is called. The prototype

function prototype

---

[1]Many C++ textbooks call a function prototype a *function declaration.* We follow the usage that derives from the C forebearer of C++ and call this bit of C++ syntax a *prototype.*

Display 3.3 A Function Definition *(part 1 of 2)*

```
#include <iostream>
using namespace std;

double total_cost(int number_par, double price_par);        function prototype
//Computes the total cost, including 5% sales tax,
//on number_par items at a cost of price_par each.

int main( )
{
    double price, bill;
    int number;

    cout << "Enter the number of items purchased: ";
    cin >> number;
    cout << "Enter the price per item $";
    cin >> price;
                                              function call
    bill = total_cost(number, price);

    cout.setf(ios::fixed);
    cout.setf(ios::showpoint);
    cout.precision(2);
    cout << number << " items at "
         << "$" << price << " each.\n"
         << "Final bill, including tax, is $" << bill
         << endl;
                                                          function
    return 0;                                             heading
}
double total_cost(int number_par, double price_par)
{
    const double TAX_RATE = 0.05; //5% sales tax
    double subtotal;                                    function        function
                                                        body           definition
    subtotal = price_par * number_par;
    return (subtotal + subtotal*TAX_RATE);
}
```

Display 3.3 A Function Definition (part 2 of 2)

Sample Dialogue

```
Enter the number of items purchased: 2
Enter the price per item: $10.10
2 items at  $10.10 each.
Final bill, including tax, is $21.21
```

for the function `total_cost` is in color at the top of Display 3.3 and is reproduced below:

```
double total_cost(int number_par, double price_par);
```

The function prototype tells you everything you need to know in order to write a call to the function. It tells you the name of the function; in this case `total_cost`. It tells you how many arguments the function needs and what type the arguments should be; in this case, the function `total_cost` takes two arguments, the first one of type *int* and the second one of type *double*. The identifiers `number_par` and `price_par` are called *formal parameters*. A **formal parameter** is used as a kind of blank, or placeholder, to stand in for the argument. When you write a function prototype you do not know what the arguments will be, so you use the formal parameters in place of the arguments. The names of the formal parameters can be any valid identifiers, but for a while we will end our formal parameter names with _par so that it will be easier for us to distinguish them from other items in a program. Notice that a function prototype ends with a semicolon.

formal parameter

The first word in a function prototype specifies the type of the value returned by the function. Thus, for the function `total_cost`, the type of the value returned is *double*.

type for value returned

As you can see, the function call in Display 3.3 satisfies all the requirements given by its function prototype. Let's take a look. The function call is in the following line:

```
bill = total_cost(number, price);
```

The function call is the expression on the right-hand side of the equal sign. The function name is `total_cost`, there are two arguments, the first argument is of type *int*, the second argument is of type *double*, and since the variable `bill` is of type *double*, it looks like the function returns a value of type *double* (which it does do). All that detail is determined by the function prototype.

Function Prototype

A **function prototype** tells you all you need to know to write a call to the function. A prototype is required to appear in your code prior to a call to a function whose definition has not yet appeared. Function prototypes are normally placed before the main part of your program.

Syntax:

Type_Returned   Function_Name(Parameter_List) ;   ← *Do not forget this semicolon.*
Prototype_Comment

where the *Parameter_List* is a comma-separated list of parameters:
        Type_1 Formal_Parameter_1 , *Type_2 Formal_Parameter_2* , . . .
                                . . . , *Type_Last Formal_Parameter_Last*

Example:

```
double total_weight(int number, double weight_of_one);
//Returns the total weight of number items that
//each weigh weight_of_one.
```

---

prototype comment

The compiler does not care whether there's a comment along with the function prototype, but you should always include a comment that explains what value is returned by the function.

function definition

In Display 3.3 the function definition is in color at the bottom of the display. A **function definition** describes how the function computes the value it returns. If you think of a function as a small program within your program, then the function definition is like the code for this small program. In fact, the syntax for the definition of a function is very much like the syntax for the main part of a program. A function definition consists of a *function header* followed by a *function body*. The **function header** is written the same way as the function prototype, except that the header does *not* have a semicolon at the end. This makes the header a bit repetitious, but that's OK.

function header

Although the function prototype tells you all you need to know to write a function call, it does not tell you what value will be returned. The value returned is determined by the statements in the *function body*. The **function body** follows the function header and completes the function definition. The function body consists of declarations and executable statements enclosed within a pair of braces. Thus, the function body is just like the body of the main part of a program. When the function is called, the argument values are plugged in for the formal parameters and then the statements in the body are executed. The value returned by the function is

function body

determined when the function executes a *return-statement*. (The details of this "plugging in" will be discussed in a later section.)

A **return-statement** consists of the keyword *return* followed by an expression. The function definition in Display 3.3 contains the following *return*-statement:

return-statement

```
return (subtotal + subtotal*TAX_RATE);
```

When this *return*-statement is executed, the value of the following expression is returned as the value of the function call:

```
(subtotal + subtotal*TAX_RATE)
```

The parentheses are not needed. The program will run exactly the same if the *return*-statement is written as follows:

```
return subtotal + subtotal*TAX_RATE;
```

However, on larger expressions, the parentheses make the *return*-statement easier to read. For consistency, some programmers advocate using these parentheses even on simple expressions. In the function definition in Display 3.3 there are no statements after the *return*-statement, but if there were, they would not be executed. When a *return*-statement is executed the function call ends.

A Function Is Like a Small Program

To understand functions, keep the following three points in mind:

- A function definition is like a small program and calling the function is the same thing as running this "small program."

- A function uses formal parameters, rather than cin, for input. The arguments to the function are the input and they are plugged in for the formal parameters.

- A function (of the kind discussed in this chapter) does not send any output to the screen, but it does send a kind of "output" back to the program. The function returns a value, which is like the "output" for the function. The function uses a *return*-statement instead of a cout-statement for this "output."

Let's see exactly what happens when the following function call is executed in the program shown in Display 3.3:

anatomy of a function call

```
bill = total_cost(number, price);
```

First, the values of the arguments `number` and `price` are plugged in for the formal parameters; that is, the values of the arguments `number` and `price` are substituted in `number_par` and `price_par`. In the Sample Dialogue `number` receives the value 2 and `price` receives the value `10.10`. So 2 and `10.10` are substituted for `number_par` and `price_par`, respectively. This substitution process is known as the **call-by-value mechanism,** and the formal parameters are often referred to as **call-by-value formal parameters,** or simply as **call-by-value parameters.** There are three things that you should note about this substitution process:

call-by-value

1 It is the values of the arguments that are plugged in for the formal parameters. If the arguments are variables, the values of the variables, not the variables themselves, are plugged in.

2 The first argument is plugged in for the first formal parameter in the parameter list, the second argument is plugged in for the second formal parameter in the list, and so forth.

3 When an argument is plugged in for a formal parameter (for instance when 2 is plugged in for `number_par`), the argument is plugged in for *all* instances of the formal parameter that occur in the function body (for instances 2 is plugged in for `number_par` each time it appears in the function body).

The entire process involved in the function call shown in Display 3.3 is described in detail in Display 3.4.

Alternate Form for Function Prototypes

You are not required to list formal parameter names in a function prototype. The following two prototypes are equivalent:

> `double total_cost(int number_par, double price_par);`

and the equivalent

> `double total_cost(int, double);`

We will always use the first form so that we can refer to the formal parameters in the comment that accompanies the function prototype. However, you will often see the second form in manuals that describe functions.[2]

This alternate form applies only to function prototypes. *Function headers must always list the formal parameter names.*

---

[2]All C++ needs to be able to enable your program to link to the library or your function is the function name and sequence of types of the formal parameters. The formal parameter names are important only to the function definition. However, programs should communicate to programmers as well as to compilers. It is frequently very helpful in understanding a function to use the name that the programmer attaches to the function's data.

Display 3.4 Details of a Function Call *(part 1 of 2)*

Anatomy of the Function Call in Display 3.3

0 Before the function is called, the values of the variables number and price are set to 2 and 10.10, by cin statements (as you can see in the Sample Dialogue in Display 3.3).

1 The following statement, which includes a function call, begins executing:

```
bill = total_cost(number, price);
```

2 The value of number (which is 2) is plugged in for number_par and the value of price (which is 10.10) is plugged in for price_par:

```
double total_cost(int number_par, double price_par)
{
    const double TAX_RATE = 0.05; //5% sales tax
    double subtotal;

    subtotal = price_par * number_par;
    return (subtotal + subtotal*TAX_RATE);
}
```

plug in value of number

plug in value of price

producing the following:

```
double total_cost(int 2, double 10.10)
{
    const double TAX_RATE = 0.05; //5% sales tax
    double subtotal;

    subtotal = 10.10 * 2;
    return (subtotal + subtotal*TAX_RATE);
}
```

Display 3.4 Details of a Function Call *(part 2 of 2)*

Anatomy of the Function Call in Display 3.3 *(concluded)*

3 The body of the function is executed, i.e., the following is executed:

```
{
    const double TAX_RATE = 0.05; //5% sales tax
    double subtotal;

    subtotal = 10.10 * 2;
    return (subtotal + subtotal*TAX_RATE);
}
```

4 When the *return*-statement is executed, the value of the expression after *return* is the value returned by the function. In this case when

```
    return (subtotal + subtotal*TAX_RATE);
```

is executed, the value of (subtotal + subtotal*TAX_RATE), which is 21.21, is returned by the function call

```
    total_cost(number, price)
```

and so the value of bill (on the left-hand side of the equal sign) is set equal to 21.21 when the following statement finally ends:

```
    bill = total_cost(number, price);
```

◆ PITFALL   Arguments in the Wrong Order

When a function is called, the computer substitutes the first argument for the first formal parameter, the second argument for the second formal parameter, and so forth. It does not check for reasonableness. If you confuse the order of the arguments in a function call, the program will not do what you want it to do. In order to see what can go wrong, consider the program in Display 3.5. The programmer who wrote that program carelessly reversed the order of the arguments in the call to the function grade. The function call should have been

```
    letter_grade = grade(score, need_to_pass);
```

Display 3.5 Incorrectly Ordered Arguments *(part 1 of 2)*

```
//Determines user's grade. Grades are Pass or Fail.
#include <iostream>
using namespace std;

char grade(int received_par, int min_score_par);
//Returns 'P' for passing, if received_par is
//min_score_par or higher. Otherwise returns 'F' for failing.

int main( )
{
    int score, need_to_pass;
    char letter_grade;

    cout << "Enter your score"
         << " and the minimum needed to pass:\n";
    cin >> score >> need_to_pass;

    letter_grade = grade(need_to_pass, score);

    cout << "You received a score of " << score << endl
         << "Minimum to pass is " << need_to_pass << endl;

    if (letter_grade == 'P')
        cout << "You Passed. Congratulations!\n";
    else
        cout << "Sorry. You failed.\n";

    cout << letter_grade
         << " will be entered in your record.\n";

    return 0;
}

char grade(int received_par, int min_score_par)
{
    if (received_par >= min_score_par)
        return 'P';
    else
        return 'F';
}
```

Display 3.5 Incorrectly Ordered Arguments *(part 2 of 2)*

Sample Dialogue

```
Enter your score and the minimum needed to pass:
98 60
You received a score of 98
Minimum to pass is 60
Sorry. You failed.
F will be entered in your record.
```

This is the only mistake in the program. Yet, some poor student has been mistakenly failed in a course because of this careless mistake. The function grade is so simple that you might expect this mistake to be discovered by the programmer when the program is tested. However, if grade were a more complicated function, the mistake might easily go unnoticed.

If the type of an argument does not match the formal parameter, then the compiler may give you a warning message. Unfortunately, not all compilers will give such warning messages. Moreover, in a situation like the one in Display 3.5, no compiler will complain about the ordering of the arguments, because the function argument types will match the formal parameter types no matter what order the arguments are in.

Function Definition-Syntax Summary

Function prototypes are normally placed before the main part of your program and function definitions are normally placed after the main part of your program (or, as we will see later in this book, in a separate file). Display 3.6 gives a summary of the syntax for a function prototype and definition. There is actually a bit more freedom than that display indicates. The declarations and executable statements in the function definition can be intermixed, as long as each variable is declared before it is used. The rules about intermixing declarations and executable statements in a function definition are the same as they are for the main part of a program. However, unless you have reason to do otherwise, it is best to place the declarations first, as indicated in Display 3.6.

return-statement

Since a function does not return a value until it executes a *return*-statement, a function must contain one or more *return*-statements in the body of the function. A function definition may contain more than one *return*-statement. For example, the body of the code might contain an *if-else*-statement, and each branch of the *if-*

Display 3.6 Syntax for a Function that Returns a Value

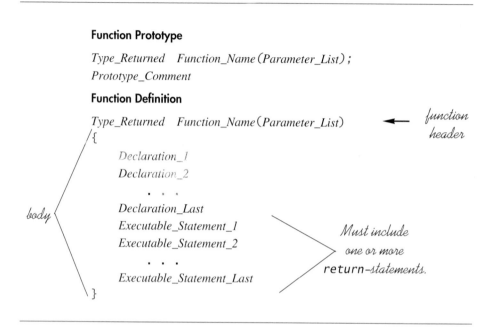

Function Prototype

Type_Returned   Function_Name (Parameter_List) ;
Prototype_Comment

Function Definition

Type_Returned   Function_Name (Parameter_List)   ⟵ *function header*

{

   Declaration_1
   Declaration_2
         . . .
   Declaration_Last
   Executable_Statement_1   *Must include*
   Executable_Statement_2   *one or more*
         . . .   *return-statements.*
   Executable_Statement_Last

}

body

else-statement might contain a different *return*-statement, as illustrated in Display 3.5.

Any reasonable pattern of spaces and line breaks in a function definition will be accepted by the compiler. However, you should use the same rules for indenting and laying out a function definition as you use for the `main` part of a program. In particular, notice the placement of braces {} in our function definitions and in Display 3.6. The opening and closing braces that mark the ends of the function body are each placed on a line by themselves. This sets off the function body.

spacing and line breaks

More About Placement of Function Definitions

We have discussed where function definitions and function prototypes are normally placed. Under normal circumstances these are the best locations for the prototypes and function definitions. However, the compiler will accept programs with the function definitions and prototypes in certain other locations. A more precise statement of the rules is as follows: Each function call must be preceded by either a function prototype for that function or the definition of the function. For example, if you place all of your function definitions before the `main` part of the program, then you need not include any function prototypes. Knowing this more general rule will help you to understand C++ programs you see in some other books, but you should follow the example of the programs in this book. The style we are using sets the stage for learning how to build your own libraries of functions, and is the style that most C++ programmers use.

SELF-TEST EXERCISES

5   What is the output produced by the following program?

```
#include <iostream>
using namespace std;
char mystery(int first_par, int second_par);
int main( )
{
    cout << mystery(10, 9) << "ow\n";
    return 0;
}
char mystery(int first_par, int second_par)
{
    if (first_par >= second_par)
        return 'W';
    else
        return 'H';
}
```

6   Write a function prototype and a function definition for a function that takes three arguments, all of type *int*, and that returns the sum of its three arguments.

7   Write a function prototype and a function definition for a function that takes one argument of type *double*. The function returns the character value 'P' if its argument is positive and returns 'N' if its argument is zero or negative.

8   Carefully describe the call-by-value parameter mechanism.

9   List the similarities and differences between use of a predefined (i.e., library) function and a user-defined function.

3.4 Procedural Abstraction

The cause is hidden, but the result is well known.

Ovid, METAMORPHOSES IV

The Black Box Analogy

A person who uses a program should not need to know the details of how the program is coded. Imagine how miserable your life would be if you had to know and remember the code for the compiler you use. A program has a job to do, such as compile your program or check the spelling of words in your paper. You need to know *what* the program's job is so that you can use the program, but you do not (or at least should not) need to know *how* the program does its job. A function is like a small program and should be used in a similar way. A programmer who uses a function in a program needs to know *what* the function does (such as calculate a square root or convert a temperature from degrees Fahrenheit to degrees Celsius), but should not need to know *how* the function accomplishes its task. This is often referred to as treating the function like a *black box*.

Calling something a **black box** is a figure of speech intended to convey the image of a physical device that you know how to use but whose method of operation is a mystery, because it is enclosed in a black box and you cannot see inside the box (and cannot pry it open!). If a function is well designed, the programmer can use the function as if it were a black box. All the programmer needs to know is that if he or she puts appropriate arguments into the black box, then an appropriate returned value will come out of the black box. Designing a function so that it can be used as a black box is sometimes called **information hiding** to emphasize the fact that the programmer acts as if the body of the function were hidden from view.

black box

information hiding

Display 3.7 contains the prototype and two different definitions for a function named `new_balance`. As the prototype comment explains, the function `new_balance` calculates the new balance in a bank account when simple interest is added. For instance, if an account starts with $100, and 4.5% interest is posted to the account, then the new balance is $104.50. Hence, the following code will change the value of `vacation_fund` from `100.00` to `104.50`:

```
vacation_fund = 100.00;
vacation_fund = new_balance(vacation_fund, 4.5);
```

It does not matter which of the implementations of `new_balance` shown in Display 3.7 that a programmer uses. The two definitions produce functions that return exactly the same values. We may as well place a black box over the body of the function definition so that the programmer does not know which implementation is being used. In order to use the function `new_balance`, all the programmer needs to read is the function prototype and the accompanying comment.

Writing and using functions as if they were black boxes is also called **procedural abstraction.** When programming in C++ it might make more sense to call it *functional abstraction.* However, *procedure* is a more general term than *function.* Computer scientists use the term *procedure* for all "function like" sets of instructions

procedural abstraction

Display 3.7 Definitions that Are Black-Box Equivalent

Prototype

```
double new_balance(double balance_par, double rate_par);
//Returns the balance in a bank account after
//posting simple interest. The formal parameter balance_par is
//the old balance. The formal parameter rate_par is the interest rate.
//For example, if rate_par is 5.0, then the interest rate is 5%
//and so new_balance(100, 5.0) returns 105.00.
```

Definition 1

```
double new_balance(double balance_par, double rate_par)
{
    double interest_fraction, interest;

    interest_fraction = rate_par/100;
    interest = interest_fraction*balance_par;
    return (balance_par + interest);
}
```

Definition 2

```
double new_balance(double balance_par, double rate_par)
{
    double interest_fraction, updated_balance;

    interest_fraction = rate_par/100;
    updated_balance = balance_par*(1 + interest_fraction);
    return updated_balance;
}
```

and so they use the term *procedural abstraction*. The term *abstraction* is intended to convey the idea that, when you use a function as a black box, you are abstracting away the details of the code contained in the function body. You can call this technique *the black box principle* or *the principle of procedural abstraction* or *information hiding*. The three terms mean the same thing. Whatever you call this principle, the important point is that you should use it when designing and writing your function definitions.

Procedural Abstraction

When applied to a function definition, the principle of **procedural abstraction** means that your function should be written so that it can be used like a **black box.** This means that the programmer who uses the function should not need to look at the body of the function definition to see how the function works. The function prototype and the accompanying comment should be all the programmer needs to know in order to use the function. To ensure that your function definitions have this important property, you should strictly adhere to the following rules:

How to Write a Black-Box Function Definition (that Returns a Value)

- The prototype comment should tell the programmer any and all conditions that are required of the arguments to the function and should describe the value that is returned by the function when called with these arguments.

- All variables used in the function body should be declared in the function body. (The formal parameters do not need to be declared, because they are listed in the function prototype.)

➤ PROGRAMMING TIP
Choosing Formal Parameter Names

The principle of procedural abstraction says that functions should be self-contained modules that are designed separately from the rest of the program. On large programming projects a different programmer may be assigned to write each function. The programmer should choose the most meaningful names he or she can find for formal parameters. The arguments that will be substituted for the formal parameters may well be variables in the main part of the program. These variables should also be given meaningful names, often chosen by someone other than the programmer who writes the function definition. This makes it likely that some or all arguments will have the same names as some of the formal parameters. This is perfectly acceptable. No matter what names are chosen for the variables that will be used as arguments, these names will not produce any confusion with the names used for formal parameters. After all, the functions will use only the values of the arguments. When you use a variable as a function argument, the function takes only the value of the variable and disregards the variable name.

Now that you know you have complete freedom in choosing formal parameter names, we will stop placing a "_par" at the end of each formal parameter name. For example, in Display 3.8 we have rewritten the definition for the function total_cost from Display 3.3 so that the formal parameters are named number and

Display 3.8 Simpler Formal Parameter Names

Prototype

```
double total_cost(int number, double price);
//Computes the total cost, including 5% sales tax, on
//number items at a cost of price each.
```

Function Definition

```
double total_cost(int number, double price)
{
    const double TAX_RATE = 0.05; //5% sales tax
    double subtotal;

    subtotal = price * number;
    return (subtotal + subtotal*TAX_RATE);
}
```

price rather than number_par and price_par. If you replace the prototype and definition of the function total_cost that appear in Display 3.3 with the versions in Display 3.8, then the program will perform in exactly the same way even though there will be formal parameters named number and price and there will be variables in the main part of the program that are also named number and price.

Case Study   Buying Pizza

The large "economy" size of an item is not always a better buy than the smaller size. This is particularly true when buying pizzas. Pizza sizes are given as the diameter of the pizza in inches. However, the quantity of pizza is determined by the area of the pizza and the area is not proportional to the diameter. Most people cannot easily estimate the difference in area between a ten-inch pizza and a twelve-inch pizza, and so cannot easily determine which size is the best buy—that is, which size has the lowest price per square inch. In this case study we will design a program that compares two sizes of pizza to determine which is the better buy.

PROBLEM DEFINITION

The precise specification of the program input and output are as follows:

INPUT:
The input will consist of the diameter in inches and the price for each of two sizes of pizza.

OUTPUT:
The output will give the cost per square inch for each of the two sizes of pizza and will tell which is the better buy, that is, which has the lowest cost per square inch. (If they are the same cost per square inch, we will consider the smaller one to be the better buy.)

ANALYSIS OF THE PROBLEM
We will use top-down design to divide the task to be solved by our program into the following subtasks:

Subtask 1: Get the input data for both the small and large pizzas.
Subtask 2: Compute the price per square inch for the small pizza.
Subtask 3: Compute the price per square inch for the large pizza.
Subtask 4: Determine which is the better buy.
Subtask 5: Output the results.

Notice subtasks 2 and 3. They have two important properties: *subtasks 2 and 3*

(i) They are exactly the same task. The only difference is that they use different data to do the computation. The only things that change between subtask 2 and subtask 3 are the size of the pizza and its price.
(ii) The result of subtask 2 and the result of subtask 3 are each a single value, the price per square inch of the pizza.

Whenever a subtask takes some values, such as some numbers, and returns a   *when to define*
single value, it is natural to implement the subtask as a function. Whenever two or   *a function*
more such subtasks perform the same computation, they can be implemented as the same function called with different arguments each time it is used. We therefore decide to use a function called unitprice to compute the price per square inch of a pizza. The prototype and explanatory comment for this function will be as follows:

```
double unitprice(int diameter, double price);
//Returns the price per square inch of a pizza. The formal
//parameter named diameter is the diameter of the pizza in
// inches.
//The formal parameter named price is the price of the pizza.
```

ALGORITHM DESIGN
Subtask 1 is straightforward. The program will simply ask for the input values and   *subtask 1*
store them in four variables, which we will call diameter_small, diameter_large, price_small, and price_large.

Subtask 4 is routine. To determine which pizza is the best buy, we just compare   *subtasks 4 and 5*
the cost per square inch of the two pizzas using the less-than operator. Subtask 5 is a routine output of the results.

subtasks 2 and 3

Subtasks 2 and 3 are implemented as calls to the function `unitprice`. Next, we design the algorithm for this function. The hard part of the algorithm is determining the area of the pizza. Once we know the area, we can easily determine the price per square inch using division, as follows:

```
price/area
```

where `area` is a variable that holds the area of the pizza. The above expression will be the value returned by the function `unitprice`. But, we still need to formulate a method for computing the area of the pizza.

A pizza is basically a circle (made up of bread, cheese, sauce, and so forth). The area of a circle (and hence of a pizza) is πr^2, where r is the radius of the circle, and π is the number called "pi," which is approximately equal to 3.14159. The radius is one half of the diameter.

The algorithm for the function `unitprice` can be outlined as follows:

Algorithm Outline for the Function `unitprice`

1. Compute the radius of the pizza.
2. Compute the area of the pizza using the formula πr^2.
3. Return the value of the expression (`price/area`).

pseudocode

We will give this outline a bit more detail before translating it into C++ code. We will express this more detailed version of our algorithm in *pseudocode*. **Pseudocode** is a mixture of C++ and ordinary English. Pseudocode allows us to make our algorithm precise without worrying about the details of C++ syntax. We can then easily translate our pseudocode into C++ code. In our pseudocode, `radius` and `area` will be variables for holding the values indicated by their names.

Pseudocode for the Function `unitprice`

```
radius = one half of diameter;
area = π * radius * radius;
return (price/area);
```

That completes our algorithm for `unitprice`. We are now ready to convert our solutions to subtasks 1 through 5 into a complete C++ program.

CODING

Coding subtask 1 is routine, so we next consider subtasks 2 and 3. Our program can implement subtasks 2 and 3 by the following two calls to the function `unitprice`:

```
unitprice_small = unitprice(diameter_small, price_small);
unitprice_large = unitprice(diameter_large, price_large);
```

where `unitprice_small` and `unitprice_large` are two variables of type *double*. One of the benefits of a function definition is that you can have multiple calls to the function in your program. This saves you the trouble of repeating the same (or almost the same) code. But we still must write the code for the function `unitprice`.

When we translate our pseudocode into C++ code, we obtain the following for the body of the function `unitprice`:

```
{//First draft of the function body for unitprice
    const double PI = 3.14159;
    double radius, area;

    radius = diameter/2;
    area = PI * radius * radius;
    return (price/area);
}
```

Notice that we made `PI` a named constant using the modifier *const*. Also, notice the following line from the above code:

```
radius = diameter/2;
```

This is just a simple division by two, and you might think that nothing could be more routine. Yet, as written, this line contains a serious mistake. We want the division to produce the radius of the pizza including any fraction. For example, if we are considering buying the "bad luck special," which is a 13-inch pizza, then the radius is 6.5 inches. But the variable `diameter` is of type *int*. The constant 2 is also of type *int*. Thus, as we saw in Chapter 2, this line would perform integer division and would compute the radius 13/2 to be 6 instead of the correct value of 6.5, and we would have disregarded a half inch of pizza radius. In all likelihood this would go unnoticed, but the result could be that millions of subscribers to the Pizza Consumers Union could be wasting their money by buying the wrong size pizza. This is not likely to produce a major worldwide recession, but the program would be failing to accomplish its goal of helping consumers find the best buy. In a more important program, the result of such a simple mistake could be disastrous.

How do we fix this mistake? We want the division by two to be regular division that includes any fractional part in the answer. That form of division requires that at least one of the arguments to the division operator / must be of type *double*. We can use type casting to convert the constant 2 to a value of type *double*. Recall that dou-*ble*(2), which is called a *type casting*, converts the *int* value 2 to a value of type *double*. Thus, if we replace 2 by *double*(2), that will change the second argument

double(2)

in the division from type *int* to type *double* and the division will then produce the result we want. The rewritten assignment statement is:

```
radius = diameter/double(2);
```

The complete corrected code for the function definition of unitprice, along with the rest of the program, is shown in Display 3.9.

The type cast *double*(2) returns the value 2.0 so we could have used the constant 2.0 in place of *double*(2). Either way, the function unitprice will return the same value. However, by using *double*(2) we make it conspicuously obvious that we want to do the version of division that includes the fractional part in its answer. If we instead used 2.0, then when revising or copying the code, we can easily make the mistake of changing 2.0 to 2, and that would produce a subtle problem.

We need to make one more remark about the coding of our program. As you can see in Display 3.9, when we coded tasks 4 and 5, we combined these two tasks into a single section of code consisting of a sequence of cout-statements followed by an *if-else*-statement. When two tasks are very simple and are closely related, it sometimes makes sense to combine them into a single task.

PROGRAM TESTING

Just because a program compiles and produces answers that look right does not mean the program is correct. In order to increase your confidence in your program you should test it on some input values for which you know the correct answer by some other means, such as working out the answer with paper and pencil or by using a hand-held calculator. For example, it does not make sense to buy a two-inch pizza, but it can still be used as an easy test case for this program. It is an easy test case because it is easy to compute the answer by hand. Let's calculate the cost per square inch of a two-inch pizza that sells for $3.14. Since the diameter is two inches, the radius is one inch. The area of a pizza with radius one is $3.14159*1^2$ which is 3.14159. If we divide this into the price of $3.14, we find that the price per square inch is 3.14/3.14159 which is approximately $1.00. Of course, this is an absurd size for a pizza and an absurd price for such a small pizza, but it is easy to determine the value that the function unitprice should return for these arguments.

Having checked your program on this one case, you can have more confidence in your program, but you still cannot be certain your program is correct. An incorrect program can sometimes give the correct answer, even though it will give incorrect answers on some other inputs. You may have tested an incorrect program on one of the cases for which the program happens to give the correct output. For example, suppose we had not caught the mistake we discovered when coding the function unitprice. Suppose we mistakenly used 2 instead of *double*(2) in the following line:

```
radius = diameter/double(2);
```

Display 3.9 Buying Pizza *(part 1 of 2)*

```
//Determines which of two pizza sizes is the best buy.
#include <iostream>
using namespace std;

double unitprice(int diameter, double price);
//Returns the price per square inch of a pizza. The formal
//parameter named diameter is the diameter of the pizza in inches.
//The formal parameter named price is the price of the pizza.

int main( )
{
    int diameter_small, diameter_large;
    double price_small, unitprice_small,
           price_large, unitprice_large;

    cout << "Welcome to the Pizza Consumers Union.\n";
    cout << "Enter diameter of a small pizza (in inches): ";
    cin >> diameter_small;
    cout << "Enter the price of a small pizza: $";
    cin >> price_small;
    cout << "Enter diameter of a large pizza (in inches): ";
    cin >> diameter_large;
    cout << "Enter the price of a large pizza: $";
    cin >> price_large;

    unitprice_small = unitprice(diameter_small, price_small);
    unitprice_large = unitprice(diameter_large, price_large);

    cout.setf(ios::fixed);
    cout.setf(ios::showpoint);
    cout.precision(2);
    cout << "Small pizza:\n"
         << "Diameter = " << diameter_small << " inches\n"
         << "Price = $" << price_small
         << " Per square inch = $" << unitprice_small << endl
         << "Large pizza:\n"
         << "Diameter = " << diameter_large << " inches\n"
         << "Price = $" << price_large
         << " Per square inch = $" << unitprice_large << endl;
```

Display 3.9 Buying Pizza *(part 2 of 2)*

```
    if (unitprice_large < unitprice_small)
        cout << "The large one is the better buy.\n";
    else
        cout << "The small one is the better buy.\n";
    cout << "Buon Appetito!\n";

    return 0;
}

double unitprice(int diameter, double price)
{
    const double PI = 3.14159;
    double radius, area;

    radius = diameter/double(2);
    area = PI * radius * radius;
    return (price/area);
}
```

Sample Dialogue

```
Welcome to the Pizza Consumers Union.
Enter diameter of a small pizza (in inches): 10
Enter the price of a small pizza: $7.50
Enter diameter of a large pizza (in inches): 13
Enter the price of a large pizza: $14.75
Small pizza:
Diameter = 10 inches
Price = $7.50 Per square inch = $0.10
Large pizza:
Diameter = 13 inches
Price = $14.75 Per square inch = $0.11
The small one is the better buy.
Buon Appetito!
```

So that line reads as follows:

```
radius = diameter/2;
```

As long as the pizza diameter is an even number, like 2, 8, 10, or 12, the program gives the same answer whether we divide by 2 or by *double*(2). It is unlikely that it would occur to you to be sure to check both even and odd size pizzas. However, if you test your program on several different pizza sizes, then there is a better chance that your test cases will contain samples of the relevant kinds of data.

⤳ PROGRAMMING TIP
Use Pseudocode

Algorithms are typically expressed in *pseudocode*. **Pseudocode** is a mixture of C++ (or whatever programming language you are using) and ordinary English (or whatever human language you are using). Pseudocode allows you to state your algorithm precisely without having to worrying about all the details of C++ syntax. When the C++ code for a step in your algorithm is obvious, there is little point in stating it in English. When a step is difficult to express in C++, the algorithm will be clearer if the step is expressed in English. You can see an example of pseudocode in the previous case study, where we expressed our algorithm for the function `unitprice` in pseudocode.

pseudocode

SELF-TEST EXERCISES

10 What is the purpose of the comment that accompanies a function prototype?

11 What is the principle of procedural abstraction as applied to function definitions?

12 What does it mean when we say the programmer who uses a function should be able to treat the function like a black box? (This question is very closely related to the previous question.)

13 Carefully describe the process of program testing.

14 Consider two possible definitions for the function `unitprice`. One is the definition given in Display 3.9. The other definition is the same except that the type cast *double*(2) is replaced with the constant 2.0, in other words, the line

```
radius = diameter/double(2);
```

is replaced with the line

```
radius = diameter/2.0;
```

Are these two possible function definitions black-box equivalent?

3.5 Local Variables

He was a local boy,
  not known outside his home town.

COMMON SAYING

In the last section we advocated using functions as if they were black boxes. In order to define a function so that it can be used as a black box, you often need to give the function variables of its own that do not interfere with the rest of your program. These variables that "belong to" a function are called *local variables*. In this section we describe local variables and tell you how to use them.

The Small Program Analogy

Look back at the program in Display 3.1. It includes a call to the predefined function sqrt. We did not need to know anything about the details of the function definition for sqrt in order to use this function. In particular, we did not need to know what variables were declared in the definition of sqrt. A function which you define is no different. Variable declarations in function definitions that you write are as separate as those in the function definitions for the predefined functions. Variable declarations within a function definition are the same as if they were variable declarations in another program. If you declare a variable in a function definition and then declare another variable of the same name in the main part of your program (or in the body of some other function definition), then these two variables are two different variables, even though they have the same name. Let's look at a program that does have a variable in a function definition with the same name as another variable in the program.

The program in Display 3.10 has two variables named average_pea; one is declared and used in the function definition for the function est_total, and the other is declared and used in the main part of the program. The variable average_pea in the function definition for est_total and the variable average_pea in the main part of the program are two different variables. It is the same as if the function est_total were a predefined function. The two variables named average_pea will not interfere with each other anymore than two variables in two completely different programs would. When the variable average_pea is

Display 3.10 Local Variables *(part 1 of 2)*

```
//Computes the average yield on an experimental pea growing patch.
#include <iostream>
using namespace std;

double est_total(int min_peas, int max_peas, int pod_count);
//Returns an estimate of the total number of peas harvested.
//The formal parameter pod_count is the number of pods.
//The formal parameters min_peas and max_peas are the minimum
//and maximum number of peas in a pod.

int main( )
{
    int max_count, min_count, pod_count;
    double average_pea, yield;

    cout << "Enter minimum and maximum number of peas in a pod: ";
    cin >> min_count >> max_count;
    cout << "Enter the number of pods: ";
    cin >> pod_count;
    cout << "Enter the weight of an average pea (in ounces): ";
    cin >> average_pea;

    yield =
          est_total(min_count, max_count, pod_count) * average_pea;

    cout.setf(ios::fixed);
    cout.setf(ios::showpoint);
    cout.precision(3);
    cout << "Min number of peas per pod = " << min_count << endl
         << "Max number of peas per pod = " << max_count << endl
         << "Pod count = " << pod_count << endl
         << "Average pea weight = "
         << average_pea << " ounces" << endl
         << "Estimated average yield = " << yield << " ounces"
         << endl;

    return 0;
}
```

This variable named average_pea *is local to the* main *part of the program.*

Display 3.10 Local Variables *(part 2 of 2)*

```
double est_total(int min_peas, int max_peas, int pod_count)
{
    double average_pea;

    average_pea = (max_peas + min_peas)/2.0;
    return (pod_count * average_pea);
}
```

This variable named average_pea *is local to the function* est_total.

Sample Dialogue

```
Enter minimum and maximum number of peas in a pod: 4 6
Enter the number of pods: 10
Enter the weight of an average pea (in ounces): 0.5
Min number of peas per pod = 4
Max number of peas per pod = 6
Pod count = 10
Average pea weight = 0.500 ounces
Estimated average yield = 25.000 ounces
```

given a value in the function call to est_total, this does not change the value of the variable in the main part of the program that is also named average_pea. (The details of the program in Display 3.10, other than this coincidence of names, are explained in the Programming Example section that follows this section.)

local to a function

Variables that are declared within the body of a function definition are said to be **local to that function** or to have that function as their **scope.** Variables that are defined within the main body of the program are said to be **local to the main part of the program** or to have the main part of the program as their **scope.** There are other

scope

kinds of variables that are not local to any function or to the main part of the program, but we will have no use for such variable. Every variable we will use is either local to a function definition or local to the main part of the program. When we say

local variable

that a variable is a **local variable** without any mention of a function and without any mention of the main part of the program, we mean that the variable is local to some function definition.

Local Variables

Variables that are declared within the body of a function definition are said to be **local to that function** or to have that function as their **scope.** Variables that are defined within the main part of the program are said to be **local to the** main **part of the program** or to have the main part of the program as their **scope.** When we say that a variable is a **local variable** without any mention of a function and without any mention of the main part of the program, we mean that the variable is local to some function definition. If a variable is local to a function, then you can have another variable with the same name that is declared in the main part of the program or in another function definition and these will be two different variables, even though they have the same name.

◼)) *PROGRAMMING EXAMPLE*
Experimental Pea Patch

The program in Display 3.10 gives an estimate for the total yield on a small garden plot used to raise an experimental variety of peas. The function `est_total` returns an estimate of the total number of peas harvested. The function `est_total` takes three arguments. One argument is the number of pea pods that were harvested. The other two arguments are used to estimate the average number of peas in a pod. Different pea pods contain differing numbers of peas so the other two arguments to the function are the smallest and the largest number of peas that were found in any one pod. The function `est_total` averages these two numbers and uses this average as an estimate for the average number of peas in a pod.

Global Constants and Global Variables

As we noted in Chapter 2, you can and should name constant values using the *const* modifier. For example, in Display 3.9 we used the following declaration[3] to give the name PI to the constant 3.14159:

```
const double PI = 3.14159;
```

In Display 3.3, we used the *const* modifier to give a name to the rate of sales tax with the following declaration:

```
const double TAX_RATE = 0.05; //5% sales tax
```

---

[3]The declaration
    const double PI = 3.14159;
appears in cmath, so you need not use this declaration in a file in your program if you already have the following directive in your file:
    #include <cmath>

As with our variable declarations, we placed these declarations for naming constants inside the body of the functions that used them. This worked out fine because each named constant was used by only one function. However, it can easily happen that more than one function uses a named constant. In that case you can place the declaration for naming a constant at the beginning of your program, outside of the body of all the functions and outside the body of the main part of your program. The named constant is then said to be a **global named constant** and the named constant can be used in any function definition that follows the constant declaration.

Display 3.11 shows a program with an example of a global named constant. The program asks for a radius and then computes both the area of a circle and the volume of a sphere with that radius. The programmer who wrote that program looked up the formulas for computing those quantities and found the following:

$$area = \pi \times (radius)^2$$
$$volume = (4/3) \times \pi \times (radius)^3$$

Both formulas include the constant π, which is approximately equal to 3.14159. The symbol π is the Greek letter called "pi." In previous programs we have used the following declaration to produce a named constant called PI to use when we convert such formulas to C++ code:

const double PI = 3.14159;

In the program in Display 3.11 we use the same declaration but place it near the beginning of the file, so that it defines a global named constant that can be used in all the function bodies.

The compiler allows you wide latitude in where you place the declarations for your global named constants, but to aid readability you should place all your include directives together, all your global named constant declarations together in another group, and all your function prototypes together. We will follow standard practice and place all our global named constant declarations after our include directives and before our function prototypes.

Placing all named constant declarations at the start of your program can aid readability even if the named constant is used by only one function. If the named constant might need to be changed in a future version of your program, it will be easier to find if it is at the beginning of your program. For example, placing the constant declaration for the sales tax rate at the beginning of an accounting program will make it easy to revise the program should the tax rate increase.

global variables

It is possible to declare ordinary variables, without the *const* modifier, as **global variables,** which are accessible to all function definitions in the file. This is done the same way that it is done for global named constants, except that the modifier *const* is not used in the variable declaration. However, there is seldom any need to use such global variables. Moreover, global variables can make a program harder to understand

Display 3.11 A Global Named Constant *(part 1 of 2)*

```
//Computes the area of a circle and the volume of a sphere.
//Uses the same radius for both calculations.
#include <iostream>
#include <cmath>
using namespace std;

const double PI = 3.14159;

double area(double radius);
//Returns the area of a circle with the specified radius.

double volume(double radius);
//Returns the volume of a sphere with the specified radius.

int main( )
{
    double radius_of_both, area_of_circle, volume_of_sphere;

    cout << "Enter a radius to use for both a circle\n"
         << "and a sphere (in inches): ";
    cin >> radius_of_both;

    area_of_circle = area(radius_of_both);
    volume_of_sphere = volume(radius_of_both);

    cout << "Radius = " << radius_of_both << " inches\n"
         << "Area of circle = " << area_of_circle
         << " square inches\n"
         << "Volume of sphere = " << volume_of_sphere
         << " cubic inches\n";

    return 0;
}
```

Display 3.11 A Global Named Constant *(part 2 of 2)*

```
double area(double radius)
{
    return (PI * pow(radius, 2));
}
double volume(double radius)
{
    return ((4.0/3.0) * PI * pow(radius, 3));
}
```

Sample Dialogue

```
Enter a radius to use for both a circle
and a sphere (in inches): 2
Radius = 2 inches
Area of circle = 12.5664 square inches
Volume of sphere = 33.5103 cubic inches
```

and maintain, so we will not use any global variables. Once you have had more experience designing programs, you may choose to occasionally use global variables.

Call-by-Value Formal Parameters Are Local Variables

Formal parameters are more than just blanks that are filled in with the argument values for the function. Formal parameters are actually variables that are local to the function definition, so they can be used just like a local variable that is declared in the function definition. Earlier in this chapter we described the call-by-value mechanism which handles the arguments in a function call. We can now define this mechanism for "plugging in arguments" in more detail. When a function is called, the formal parameters for the function (which are local variables) are initialized to the values of the arguments. This is the precise meaning of the phrase "plugged in for the formal parameters" which we have been using. Typically, a formal parameter is used only as a kind of blank, or placeholder, that is filled in by the value of its corresponding argument; occasionally, however, a formal parameter is used as a variable whose value is changed. In this section we will give one example of a formal parameter used as a local variable.

The program in Display 3.12 is the billing program for the law offices of Dewey, Cheatham, and Howe. Notice that, unlike other law firms, the firm of Dewey,

Display 3.12 Formal Parameter Used as a Local Variable (part 1 of 2)

```
//Law office billing program.
#include <iostream>
using namespace std;

const double RATE = 150.00; //Dollars per quarter hour.

double fee(int hours_worked, int minutes_worked);
//Returns the charges for hours_worked hours and
//minutes_worked minutes of legal services.

int main( )
{
    int hours, minutes;
    double bill;

    cout << "Welcome to the offices of\n"
         << "Dewey, Cheatham, and Howe.\n"
         << "The law office with a heart.\n"
         << "Enter the hours and minutes"
         << " of your consultation:\n";
    cin >> hours >> minutes;

    bill = fee(hours, minutes);

    cout.setf(ios::fixed);
    cout.setf(ios::showpoint);
    cout.precision(2);
    cout << "For " << hours << " hours and " << minutes
         << " minutes, your bill is $" << bill << endl;

    return 0;
}

double fee(int hours_worked, int minutes_worked)
{
    int quarter_hours;

    minutes_worked = hours_worked*60 + minutes_worked;
    quarter_hours = minutes_worked/15;
    return (quarter_hours*RATE);
}
```

The value of minutes is not changed by the call to fee.

minutes_worked is a local variable initialized to the value of minutes.

Display 3.12 Formal Parameter Used as a Local Variable *(part 2 of 2)*

Sample Dialogue

```
Welcome to the offices of
Dewey, Cheatham, and Howe.
The law office with a heart.
Enter the hours and minutes of your consultation:
2 45
For 2 hours and 45 minutes, your bill is $1650.00
```

Cheatham, and Howe does not charge for any time less than a quarter of an hour. That is why it's called "the law office with a heart." If they work for one hour and fourteen minutes, they only charge for four quarter hours, not five quarter hours as other firms do; so you would pay only $600 for the consultation.

Notice the formal parameter `minutes_worked` in the definition of the function `fee`. It is used as a variable and has its value changed by the following line, which occurs within the function definition:

```
minutes_worked = hours_worked*60 + minutes_worked;
```

Do not add a declaration for a

Formal parameters are local variables just like the variables you declare within the body of a function. However, you should not add a variable declaration for the formal parameters. Listing the formal parameter `minutes_worked` in the function prototype also serves as the variable declaration. The following is the *wrong way* to start the function definition for `fee` as it declares `minutes_worked` twice:

```
double fee(int hours_worked, int minutes_worked)
{
    int quarter_hours;
    int minutes_worked;         ←——————  Do NOT do this!
        . . .
```

Namespaces Revisited

Thus far, we have started all of our programs with the following two lines:

```
#include <iostream>
using namespace std;
```

However, the start of the file is not the best location for the line.

```
using namespace std;
```

We will eventually be using more namespaces than just `std`. In fact, we may be using different namespaces in different function definitions. If you place the directive

```
using namespace std;
```

inside the brace { that starts the body of a function definition, then the *using* directive applies to only that function definition. This will allow you to use two different namespaces in two different function definitions, even if the two function definitions are in the same file and even if the two namespaces have some name(s) with different meanings in the two different namespaces.

Placing a *using* directive inside a function definition is analogous to placing a variable declaration inside a function definition. If you place a variable definition inside a function definition, the variable is local to the function; that is, the meaning of the variable declaration is confined to the function definition. If you place a *using* directive inside a function definition, the *using* directive is local to the function definition; in other words, the meaning of the *using* directive is confined to the function definition.

It will be some time before we use any namespace other than `std` in a *using* directives, but it will be good practice to start placing these *using* directives where they should go.

In Display 3.13 we have rewritten the program in Display 3.11 with the *using* directives where they should be placed. The program in Display 3.13 will behave exactly the same as the one in Display 3.11. In this particular case, the difference is only one of style, but when you start to use more namespaces, the difference will affect how your programs perform.

(If you are using an older version of C++ that does not use namespaces, just ignore the references to namespaces.)

Display 3.13 Using Namespaces *(part 1 of 2)*

```cpp
//Computes the area of a circle and the volume of a sphere.
//Uses the same radius for both calculations.
#include <iostream>
#include <cmath>//Some compilers may use math.h instead of cmath.

const double PI = 3.14159;

double area(double radius);
//Returns the area of a circle with the specified radius.

double volume(double radius);
//Returns the volume of a sphere with the specified radius.

int main( )
{
    using namespace std;

    double radius_of_both, area_of_circle, volume_of_sphere;

    cout << "Enter a radius to use for both a circle\n"
         << "and a sphere (in inches): ";
    cin >> radius_of_both;

    area_of_circle = area(radius_of_both);
    volume_of_sphere = volume(radius_of_both);

    cout << "Radius = " << radius_of_both << " inches\n"
         << "Area of circle = " << area_of_circle
         << " square inches\n"
         << "Volume of sphere = " << volume_of_sphere
         << " cubic inches\n";

    return 0;
}
```

Display 3.13 Using Namespaces *(part 2 of 2)*

```
double area(double radius)
{
    using namespace std;

    return (PI * pow(radius, 2));
}
double volume(double radius)
{
    using namespace std;

    return ((4.0/3.0) * PI * pow(radius, 3));
}
```

The sample dialogue for this program would be the same as the one for the program in Display 3.11.

SELF-TEST EXERCISES

15 If you use a variable in a function definition where should you declare the variable? In the function definition? In the `main` part of the program? Anyplace that is convenient?

16 Suppose a function named `Function1` has a variable named `Sam` declared within the definition of `Function1` and a function named `Function2` also has a variable named `Sam` declared within the definition of `Function2`. Will the program compile (assuming everything else is correct)? If the program will compile, will it run (assuming that everything else is correct)? If it runs, will it generate an error message when run (assuming everything else is correct)? If it runs and does not produce an error message when run, will it give the correct output (assuming everything else is correct)?

17 The following function is supposed to take as arguments a length expressed in feet and inches and return the total number of inches in that many feet and inches. For example, `total_inches(1, 2)` is supposed to return 14, because

1 foot and 2 inches is the same as 14 inches. Will the following function perform correctly? If not, why not?

```
double total_inches(int feet, int inches)
{
    inches = 12*feet + inches;
    return inches;
}
```

■)) *PROGRAMMING* EXAMPLE
The Factorial Function

Display 3.14 contains the prototype and definition for a commonly used mathematical function known as the *factorial* function. In mathematics texts, the factorial function is usually written *n*!, and is defined to be the product of all the integers from 1 to *n*. In traditional mathematical notation, you can define *n*! as follows:

$$n! = 1 \times 2 \times 3 \times \ldots \times n$$

In the function definition we perform the multiplication with a *while*-loop. Note that the multiplication is performed in the reverse order to what you might expect. The program multiplies by n, then n–1, then n–2, and so forth.

*formal parameter used
as a local variable*

The function definition for `factorial` uses two local variables: `product`, which is declared at the start of the function body, and the formal parameter n. Since a formal parameter is a local variable, we can change its value. In this case we change the value of the formal parameter n with the decrement operator n--. (The decrement operator was discussed in Chapter 2.)

Each time the body of the loop is executed, the value of the variable `product` is multiplied by the value of n, and then the value of n is decreased by one using n--. If the function `factorial` is called with 3 as its argument, then the first time the loop body is executed the value of `product` is 3, the next time the loop body is executed the value of `product` is 3*2, the next time the value of `product` is 3*2*1, and then the *while*-loop ends. Thus, the following will set the variable x equal to 6 which is 3*2*1:

```
x = factorial(3);
```

Notice that the local variable `product` is initialized to the value 1 when the variable is declared. (This way of initializing a variable when it is declared was introduced in Chapter 2.) It is easy to see that 1 is the correct initial value for the variable `product`. To see that this is the correct initial value for `product` note that, after executing the body of the *while*-loop the first time, we want the value of `product` to be equal to the (original) value of the formal parameter n; if `product` is initialized to 1, then this will be what happens.

Display 3.14 Factorial Function

Function Prototype

```
int factorial(int n);
//Returns factorial of n.
//The argument n should be nonnegative.
```

Function Definition

```
int factorial(int n)
{
    int product = 1;
    while (n > 0)
    {
        product = n * product;
        n--;                        formal parameter n
    }                               used as a local variable

    return product;
}
```

3.6 Overloading Function Names

> "...—and that shows that there are three hundred and sixty-four days when you
>   might get un-birthday presents—"
> "Certainly," said Alice.
> "And only one for birthday presents, you know. There's glory for you!"
> "I don't know what you mean by 'glory,' " Alice said.
> Humpty Dumpty smiled contemptuously, "Of course you don't—till I tell you. I
>   mean 'there's a nice knock-down argument for you!' "
> "But 'glory' doesn't mean 'a nice knock-down argument,' " Alice objected.
> "When I use a word," Humpty Dumpty said, in rather a scornful tone, "it means just
>   what I choose it to mean—neither more nor less."
> "The question is," said Alice, "whether you can make words mean so many different
>   things."
> "The question is," said Humpty Dumpty, "which is to be master—that's all."
>
> LEWIS CARROLL, THROUGH THE LOOKING-GLASS

C++ allows you to give two or more different definitions to the same function name, which means you can reuse names that have strong intuitive appeal across a variety of situations. For example, you could have three functions called max: one that computes the largest of two numbers, another that computes the largest of three numbers, and yet another that computes the largest of four numbers. When you give two (or more) function definitions for the same function name, that is called **overloading** the function name. Overloading does require some extra care in defining your functions, and should not be used unless it will add greatly to your program's readability. But when it is appropriate, overloading can be very effective.

Introduction to Overloading

Suppose you are writing a program that requires you to compute the average of two numbers. You might use the following function definition:

```
double ave(double n1, double n2)
{
    return ((n1 + n2)/2.0);
}
```

Now suppose your program also requires a function to compute the average of three numbers. You might define a new function called ave3 as follows:

```
double ave3(double n1, double n2, double n3)
{
    return ((n1 + n2 + n3)/3.0);
}
```

This will work, and in many programming languages you have no choice but to do something like this. Fortunately, C++ allows for a more elegant solution. In C++ you can simply use the same function name ave for both functions. In C++ you can use the following function definition in place of the function definition ave3:

```
double ave(double n1, double n2, double n3)
{
    return ((n1 + n2 + n3)/3.0);
}
```

so that the function name ave then has two definitions. This is an example of overloading. In this case we have overloaded the function name ave. In Display 3.15 we have embedded these two function definitions for ave into a complete sample program. Be sure to notice that each function definition has its own prototype.

Display 3.15 Overloading a Function Name

```
//Illustrates overloading the function name ave.
#include <iostream>

double ave(double n1, double n2);
//Returns the average of the two numbers n1 and n2.

double ave(double n1, double n2, double n3);
//Returns the average of the three numbers n1, n2, and n3.

int main()
{
    using namespace std;
    cout << "The average of 2.0, 2.5, and 3.0 is "
         << ave(2.0, 2.5, 3.0) << endl;

    cout << "The average of 4.5 and 5.5 is "
         << ave(4.5, 5.5) << endl;

    return 0;
}
double ave(double n1, double n2)
{
    return ((n1 + n2)/2.0);
}

double ave(double n1, double n2, double n3)
{
    return ((n1 + n2 + n3)/3.0);
}
```

two arguments

three arguments

Output

```
The average of 2.0, 2.5, and 3.0 is 2.50000
The average of 4.5 and 5.5 is 5.00000
```

Overloading is a great idea. It makes a program easier to read. It saves you from going crazy trying to think up a new name for a function just because you already used the most natural name in some other function definition. But how does the compiler know which function definition to use when it encounters a call to a function name that has two or more definitions? The compiler cannot read a programmer's mind. In order to tell which function definition to use, the compiler checks the number of arguments and the types of the arguments in the function call. In the program in Display 3.15, one of the functions called ave has two arguments and the other has three arguments. To tell which definition to use, the compiler simply counts the number of arguments in the function call. If there are two arguments, it uses the first definition. If there are three arguments it uses the second definition.

determining which definition applies

Whenever you give two or more definitions to the same function name, the various function definitions must have different specifications for their arguments; that is, any two function definitions that have the same function name must use different numbers of formal parameters or use formal parameters of different types (or both). Notice that when you overload a function name, the prototypes for the two different definitions must differ in their formal parameters. *You cannot overload a function name by giving two definitions that differ only in the type of the value returned.*

Overloading a Function Name

If you have two or more function definitions for the same function name, that is called **overloading.** When you overload a function name, the function definitions must have different numbers of formal parameters or some formal parameters of different types. When there is a function call, the compiler uses the function definition whose number of formal parameters and types of formal parameters match the arguments in the function call.

Overloading is not really new to you. You saw a kind of overloading in Chapter 2 with the division operator /. If both operands are of type *int*, as in 13/2, then the value returned is the result of integer division, in this case 6. On the other hand, if one or both operands are of type *double*, then the value returned is the result of regular division; for example, 13/2.0 returned the value 6.5. There are two definitions for the division operator /, and the two definitions are distinguished not by having different numbers of operands, but rather by requiring operands of different types. The difference between overloading of / and overloading function names is that the compiler has already done the overloading of / and we program the overloading of the function name. We will see in a later chapter how to overload operators such as +, –, and so on.

> ## Polymorphism
> The use of the same function name to mean different things is called **polymorphism,** a term derived from some Greek words meaning "many forms." Overloading is our first example of polymorphism.

■)) PROGRAMMING EXAMPLE
Revised Pizza-Buying Program

The Pizza Consumers Union has been very successful with the program that we wrote for it in Display 3.9. In fact, now everybody always buys the pizza that is the best buy. One disreputable pizza parlor used to make money by fooling consumers into buying the more expensive pizza, but our program has put an end to their evil practices. However, the owners wish to continue their despicable behavior and have come up with a new way to fool consumers. They now offer both round pizzas and rectangular pizzas. They know that the program we wrote cannot deal with rectangularly shaped pizzas, so they hope they can again confuse consumers. We need to update our program so that we can foil their nefarious scheme. We want to change the program so that it can compare a round pizza and a rectangular pizza.

The changes we need to make to our pizza evaluation program are clear: We need to change the input and output a bit so that it deals with two different shapes of pizzas. We also need to add a new function that can compute the cost per square inch of a rectangular pizza. We could use the following function definition in our program so that we can compute the unit price for a rectangular pizza:

```
double unitprice_rectangular
        (int length, int width, double price)
{
    double area = length * width;
    return (price/area);
}
```

However, this is a rather long name for a function; in fact, it's so long that we needed to put the function heading on two lines. That is legal, but it would be nicer to use the same name, `unitprice`, for both the function that computes the unit price for a round pizza and for the function that computes the unit price for a rectangular pizza. Since C++ allows overloading of function names, we can do this. Having two definitions for the function `unitprice` will pose no problems to the compiler because the two functions will have different numbers of arguments. Display 3.16 shows the program we obtained when we modified our pizza evaluation program to allow us to compare round pizzas with rectangular pizzas.

Automatic Type Conversion

Suppose that the following function definition occurs in your program, and that you have *not* overloaded the function name mpg (so this is the only definition of a function called mpg).

```
double mpg(double miles, double gallons)
//Returns miles per gallon.
{
    return (miles/gallons);
}
```

If you call the function mpg with arguments of type *int*, then C++ will automatically convert any argument of type *int* to a value of type *double*. Hence, the following will output 22.5 miles per gallon to the screen:

```
cout << mpg(45, 2) << " miles per gallon";
```

C++ converts the 45 to 45.0 and the 2 to 2.0, then performs the division 45.0/2.0 to obtain the value returned which is 22.5.

interaction of overloading and type conversion

If a function requires an argument of type *double* and you give it an argument of type *int*, C++ will automatically convert the *int* argument to a value of type *double*. This is so useful and natural that we hardly give it a thought. However, overloading can interfere with this automatic type conversion. Let's look at an example.

Suppose you had (foolishly) overloaded the function name mpg so that your program also contained the following definition of mpg (as well as the one above):

```
int mpg(int goals, int misses)
//Returns the Measure of Perfect Goals
//which is computed as (goals - misses).
{
    return (goals - misses);
}
```

Display 3.16 Overloading a Function Name *(part 1 of 3)*

```
//Determines whether a round pizza or a rectangular pizza is the best buy.
#include <iostream>

double unitprice(int diameter, double price);
//Returns the price per square inch of a round pizza.
//The formal parameter named diameter is the diameter of the pizza
//in inches. The formal parameter named price is the price of the pizza.

double unitprice(int length, int width, double price);
//Returns the price per square inch of a rectangular pizza
//with dimensions length by width inches.
//The formal parameter price is the price of the pizza.

int main( )
{
    using namespace std;
    int diameter, length, width;
    double price_round, unit_price_round,
            price_rectangular, unitprice_rectangular;

    cout << "Welcome to the Pizza Consumers Union.\n";
    cout << "Enter the diameter in inches"
        << " of a round pizza: ";
    cin >> diameter;
    cout << "Enter the price of a round pizza: $";
    cin >> price_round;
    cout << "Enter length and width in inches\n"
        << "of a rectangular pizza: ";
    cin >> length >> width;
    cout << "Enter the price of a rectangular pizza: $";
    cin >> price_rectangular;

    unitprice_rectangular =
                unitprice(length, width, price_rectangular);
    unit_price_round = unitprice(diameter, price_round);

    cout.setf(ios::fixed);
    cout.setf(ios::showpoint);
    cout.precision(2);
```

Display 3.16 Overloading a Function Name *(part 2 of 3)*

```
    cout << endl
        << "Round pizza: Diameter = "
        << diameter << " inches\n"
        << "Price = $" << price_round
        << " Per square inch = $" << unit_price_round
        << endl
        << "Rectangular pizza: length = "
        << length << " inches\n"
        << "Rectangular pizza: Width = "
        << width << " inches\n"
        << "Price = $" << price_rectangular
        << " Per square inch = $" << unitprice_rectangular
        << endl;

    if (unit_price_round < unitprice_rectangular)
        cout << "The round one is the better buy.\n";
    else
        cout << "The rectangular one is the better buy.\n";
    cout << "Buon Appetito!\n";

    return 0;
}

double unitprice(int diameter, double price)
{
    const double PI = 3.14159;
    double radius, area;

    radius = diameter/double(2);
    area = PI * radius * radius;
    return (price/area);
}

double unitprice(int length, int width, double price)
{
    double area = length * width;
    return (price/area);
}
```

Display 3.16 Overloading a Function Name *(part 3 of 3)*

Sample Dialogue

```
Welcome to the Pizza Consumers Union.
Enter the diameter in inches of a round pizza: 10
Enter the price of a round pizza: $8.50
Enter length and width in inches
of a rectangular pizza: 6 4
Enter the price of a rectangular pizza: $7.55

Round pizza: Diameter = 10 inches
Price = $8.50 Per square inch = $0.11
Rectangular pizza: Length = 6 inches
Rectangular pizza: Width = 4 inches
Price = $7.55 Per square inch = $0.31
The round one is the better buy.
Buon Appetito!
```

In a program that contains both of these definitions for the function name mpg, the following will (unfortunately) output 43 miles per gallon (since 43 is 45 – 2):

```
cout << mpg(45, 2) << " miles per gallon";
```

When C++ sees the function call mpg(45, 2), which has two arguments of type *int*, C++ *first* looks for a function definition of mpg that has two formal parameters of type *int*. If it finds such a function definition, C++ uses that function definition. C++ does not convert an *int* argument to a value of type *double* unless that is the only way it can find a matching function definition.

The mpg example illustrates one more point about overloading. You should not use the same function name for two unrelated functions. Such careless use of function names is certain to eventually produce confusion.

SELF-TEST EXERCISES

18 Suppose you have two function definitions with the following prototypes:

```
double score(double time, double distance);
int score(double points);
```

Which function definition would be used in the following function call and why would it be the one used? (x is of type *double*.)

```
final_score = score(x);
```

19 Suppose you have two function definitions with the following prototypes:

```
double the_answer(double data1, double data2);
double the_answer(double time, int count);
```

Which function definition would be used in the following function call and why would it be the one used? (x and y are of type double.)

```
x = the_answer(y, 6.0);
```

20 This question has to do with the programming example "Revised Pizza-Buying Program." Suppose the evil pizza parlor that is always trying to fool customers introduces a square pizza. Can you overload the function `unitprice` so that it can compute the price per square inch of a square pizza as well as the price per square inch of a round pizza? Why or why not?

21 Look at the program in Display 3.16. The `main` function contains the *using* directive:

```
using namespace std;
```

Why doesn't the method `unitprice` contain this *using* directive?

CHAPTER SUMMARY

- A good plan of attack for designing the algorithm for a program is to break down the task to be accomplished into a few subtasks, then decompose each subtask into smaller subtasks, and so forth until the subtasks are simple enough that they can easily be implemented as C++ code. This approach is called **top-down design.**

- A function that returns a value is like a small program. The arguments to the function serve as the input to this "small program" and the value returned is like the output of the "small program."

■ When a subtask for a program takes some values as input and produces a single value as its only result, then that subtask can be implemented as a function.

■ A function should be defined so that it can be used as a black box. The programmer who uses the function should not need to know any details about how the function is coded. All the programmer should need to know is the function prototype and the accompanying comment that describes the value returned. This rule is sometimes called the **principle of procedural abstraction.**

■ A variable that is declared in a function definition is said to be **local to the function.**

■ Global named constants are declared using the `const` modifier. Declarations for global named constants are normally placed at the start of a program after the `include` directives and before the function prototypes.

■ Call-by-value formal parameters (which are the only kind of formal parameter discussed in this chapter) are variables that are local to the function. Occasionally, it is useful to use a formal parameter as a local variable.

■ When you have two or more function definitions for the same function name, that is called **overloading** the function name. When you overload a function name, the function definitions must have different numbers of formal parameters or some formal parameters of different types.

Answers to Self-Test Exercises

```
1 4.0      4.0      8.0
  8.0      8.0      1.21
  3        3        0
  3.0      3.5      3.5
  6.0      6.0      5.0
  5.0      4.5      4.5
  3        3.0      3.0
```

2

```
sqrt(x + y),   pow(x, y + 7),   sqrt(area + fudge),
sqrt(time+tide)/nobody,  (-b + sqrt(b*b - 4*a*c))/(2*a), abs(x - y) or
                                                    labs(x - y) or
                                                    fabs(x - y)
```

3

```
//Computes the square root of 3.14159.
#include <iostream>
#include <cmath>
using namespace std;
int main( )
{
    cout << "The square root of  " >> PI
        << sqrt(PI) << endl;
    return 0;
}
```

4 a. // to determine whether the compiler will tolerate spaces before the # in
       // the #include:

```
        #include <iostream>
    int main( )
    {
        cout << "hello world" << endl;
    }
```

   b. // to determine if the compiler will allow spaces between the # and
       // include in the #include:
```
    # include<iostream>
    using namespace std;
```
       // the rest of the program can be identical to the above.

5   Wow

6 The prototype is:

```
int sum(int n1, int n2, int n3);
//Returns the sum of n1, n2, and n3.
```

   The function definition is:

```
int sum(int n1, int n2, int n3)
{
    return (n1 + n2 + n3);
}
```

7 The prototype is:

```
char positive_test(double number);
//Returns 'P' if number is positive.
//Returns 'N' if number is negative or zero.
```

The function definition is:

```
char positive_test(double number)
{
    if (number > 0)
        return 'P';
    else
        return 'N';
}
```

8 Suppose the function is defined with arguments, say `param1` and `param2`. The function is then called with corresponding arguments `arg1` and `arg2`. The values of the arguments are "plugged in" for the corresponding formal parameters, `arg1` into `param1`, `arg2` into `param2`. The formal parameters are then used in the function.

9 Predefined (library) functions usually require that you `#include` a header file. For a programmer-defined function, the programmer puts the code for the function into either the file with the main part or in another file to be compiled and linked to the main program.

10 The comment explains what value the function returns and gives any other information that you need to know in order to use the function.

11 The principle of procedural abstraction says that a function should be written so that it can be used like a black box. This means that the programmer who uses the function need not look at the body of the function definition to see how the function works. The function prototype and accompanying comment should be all the programmer needs to know in order to use the function.

12 When we say that the programmer who uses a function should be able to treat the function like a black box, we mean the programmer should not need to look at the body of the function definition to see how the function works. The function prototype and accompanying comment should be all the programmer needs to know in order to use the function.

13 In order to increase your confidence in your program, you should test it on input values for which you know the correct answers. Perhaps you can calculate the answers by some other means, such as pencil and paper, or hand calculator. Limiting cases (e.g., the two-inch pizza of the text's example) or other simple cases are good starting points.

14 Yes, the function would return the same value in either case, so the two definitions are black-box equivalent.

15   If you use a variable in a function definition, you should declare the variable in the body of the function definition.

16   Everything will be fine. The program will compile (assuming everything else is correct). The program will run (assuming that everything else is correct). The program will not generate an error message when run (assuming everything else is correct). The program will give the correct output (assuming everything else is correct).

17   The function will work fine. That is the entire answer, but here is some additional information: The formal parameter `inches` is a call-by-value parameter and, as discussed in the text, it is therefore a local variable. Thus, the value of the argument will not be changed.

18   The function call has only one argument, so it would use the function definition that has only one formal parameter.

19   The function call has two arguments of type *double*, so it would use the function corresponding to the prototype with two arguments of type *double* (i.e., the first prototype).

20   This cannot be done (at least not in any nice way). The natural ways to represent a square and a round pizza are the same. Each is naturally represented as one number, which is the radius for a round pizza and the length of a side for a square pizza. In either case the function `unitprice` would need to have one formal parameter of type *double* for the price and one formal parameter of type *int* for the size (either radius or side). Thus, the two prototypes would have the same number and types of formal parameters. (Specifically, they would both have one formal parameter of type *double* and one formal parameter of type *int*.) Thus, the compiler would not be able to decide which definition to use. You can still defeat this evil pizza parlor's strategy by defining two functions, but they will need to have different names.

21   The definition of `unitprice` does not do any input or output and so does not use the library `iostream`. In `main` we needed the *using* directive because `cin` and `cout` are defined in `iostream` and those definitions place `cin` and `cout` in the `std` namespace.

Programming Projects

1   A liter is 0.264179 gallons. Write a program that will read in the number of liters of gasoline consumed by the user's car and the number of miles traveled by the car, and will then output the number of miles per gallon the car

delivered. Your program should allow the user to repeat this calculation as often as the user wishes. Define a function to compute the number of miles per gallon. Your program should use a globally defined constant for the number of liters per gallon.

2 The price of stocks is normally given to the nearest eighth of a dollar; for example, 29 7/8 or 89 1/2. Write a program that computes the value of the user's holding of one stock. The program asks for the number of shares of stock owned, the whole dollar portion of the price and the fraction portion. The fraction portion is to be input as two *int* values, one for the numerator and one for the denominator. The program then outputs the value of the user's holdings. Your program should allow the user to repeat this calculation as often as the user wishes. Your program will include a function definition that has three *int* arguments consisting of the whole dollar portion of the price and the two integers that make up the fraction part. The function returns the price of one share of stock as a single number of type *double*.

3 Write a program to gauge the rate of inflation for the past year. The program asks for the price of an item (such as a hot dog or a one carat diamond) both one year ago and today. It estimates the inflation rate as the difference in price divided by the year ago price. Your program should allow the user to repeat this calculation as often as the user wishes. Define a function to compute the rate of inflation. The inflation rate should be a value of type *double* giving the rate as a percent, for example 5.3 for 5.3%.

4 Enhance your program from the previous exercise by having it also print out the estimated price of the item in one and in two years from the time of the calculation. The increase in cost over one year is estimated as the inflation rate times the price at the start of the year. Define a second function to determine the estimated cost of an item in one year, given the current price of the item and the inflation rate as arguments.

5 Write a function declaration for a function that computes interest on a credit card account balance. The function takes arguments for the initial balance, the monthly interest rate, and the number of months for which interest must be paid. The value returned is the interest due. Do not forget to compound the interest—that is, to charge interest on the interest due. The interest due is added into the balance due, and the interest for the next month is computed using this larger balance. Use a *while*-loop that is similar to (but need not be identical to) the one shown in Display 2.14. Embed the function in a program that reads the values for the interest rate, initial account balance, and number of months, then outputs the interest due. Embed your function definition in a program that lets the user compute interest due on a credit account balance.

The program should allow the user to repeat the calculation until the user said he or she wants to end the program.

6   The gravitational attractive force between two bodies with masses m_1 and m_2 separated by a distance d is given by:

$$F = \frac{Gm_1 m_2}{d^2}$$

where G is the universal gravitational constant:

$G = 6.673 \times 10^{-8}$ cm^3/(g $\cdot$ sec^2)

Write a function definition that takes arguments for the masses of two bodies and the distance between them, and that returns the gravitational force between them. Since you will use the above formula, the gravitational force will be in dynes. One dyne equals a

g $\cdot$ cm/sec^2

You should use a globally defined constant for the universal gravitational constant. Embed your function definition in a complete program that computes the gravitational force between two objects given suitable inputs. Your program should allow the user to repeat this calculation as often as the user wishes.

7   Write a program that computes the annual after-tax cost of a new house for the first year of ownership. The cost is computed as the annual mortgage cost minus the tax savings. The input should be the price of the house and the down payment. The annual mortgage cost can be estimated as 3% of the initial loan balance credited toward paying off the loan principal plus 8% of the initial loan balance in interest. The initial loan balance is the price minus the down payment. Assume a 35% marginal tax rate and assume that interest payments are tax deductible. So, the tax savings is 35% of the interest payment. Your program should use at least two function definitions.   Your program should allow the user to repeat this calculation as often as the user wishes.

8   Write a program that asks for the user's height, weight, and age, and then computes clothing sizes according to the formulas:

• Hat size = weight in pounds divided by height in inches and all that multiplied by 2.9.

- Jacket size (chest in inches) = height times weight divided by 288 and then adjusted by adding 1/8 of an inch for each 10 years over age 30. (Note that the adjustment only takes place after a full 10 years. So, there is no adjustment for ages 30 through 39, but 1/8 of an inch is added for age 40.)
- Waist in inches = weight divided by 5.7 and then adjusted by adding 1/10 of an inch for each 2 years over age 28. (Note that the adjustment only takes place after a full 2 years. So, there is no adjustment for age 29, but 1/10 of an inch is added for age 30.)

Use functions for each calculation. Your program should allow the user to repeat this calculation as often as the user wishes.

9 That we are "blessed" with several absolute value functions is an accident of history. C libraries were already available when C++ arrived; they could be easily used, so they were not rewritten using function overloading. You are to find all the absolute value functions you can, and rewrite all of them overloading the `abs` function name. At a minimum you should have the `int`, `long`, `float`, and `double` types represented.

CHAPTER

4

Functions for All Subtasks

4 Functions for All Subtasks

Everything is possible.

COMMON MAXIM

Introduction

The top-down design strategy discussed in Chapter 3 is an effective way to design an algorithm for a program. You divide the program's task into subtasks and then implement the algorithms for these subtasks as functions. Thus far, we have seen how to define functions that start with the values of some arguments and return a single value as the result of the function call. A subtask that computes a single value is a very important kind of subtask, but it is not the only kind. In this chapter we will complete our description of C++ functions and present techniques for designing functions that perform other kinds of subtasks.

4.1 *void*-Functions

Subtasks are implemented as functions in C++. The functions discussed in Chapter 3 always return a single value, but there are other forms of subtasks. A subtask might produce several values or it might produce no values at all. In C++, a function must either return a single value or return no values at all. As we will see later in this chapter, a subtask that produces several different values is usually (and perhaps paradoxically) implemented as a function that returns no value. For the moment, however, let us avoid that complication and focus on subtasks that intuitively produce no values at all and let us see how these subtasks are implemented. A function that returns no value is called a *void*-**function.** For example, one typical subtask for a program is to output the results of some calculation. This subtask produces output on the screen, but it produces no values for the rest of the program to use. This kind of subtask would be implemented as a *void*-function.

void-functions return no value

Definitions of *void*-Functions

In C++ a *void*-function is defined in a way similar to the way that functions that return a value are defined. For example, the following is a *void*-function that outputs the result of a calculation that converts a temperature expressed in Fahrenheit degrees to a temperature expressed in Celsius degrees. The actual calculation would be done elsewhere in the program. This *void*-function implements only the subtask for outputting the results of the calculation. For now, we do not need to worry about how the calculation will be performed.

```
void show_results(double f_degrees, double c_degrees)
{
    using namespace std;
    cout.setf(ios::fixed);
    cout.setf(ios::showpoint);
    cout.precision(1);
    cout << f_degrees
         << " degrees Fahrenheit is equivalent to\n"
         << c_degrees << " degrees Celsius.\n";
    return;
}
```

As the above function definition illustrates, there are only two differences between a function definition for a *void*-function and the function definitions we discussed in Chapter 3. One difference is that we use the keyword *void* where we would normally specify the type of the value to be returned. This tells the compiler that this function will not return any value. The name *void* is used as a way of saying "no value is returned by this function." The second difference is that the *return*-statement does not contain an expression for a value to be returned, because, after all, there is no value returned. The syntax is summarized in Display 4.1.

function definition

A *void*-function call is an executable statement. For example, the above function show_results might be called as follows:

function call

```
show_results(32.5, 0.3);
```

If the above statement were executed in a program, it would cause the following to appear on the screen:

```
32.5 degrees Fahrenheit is equivalent to
0.3 degrees Celsius.
```

Notice that the function call ends with a semicolon, which tells the compiler that the function call is an executable statement.

When a *void*-function is called, the arguments are substituted for the formal parameters and the statements in the function body are executed. For example, a call to the *void*-function show_results, which we gave earlier in this section, will cause some output to be written to the screen. One way to think of a call to a

Display 4.1 Syntax for a *void*-Function Definition

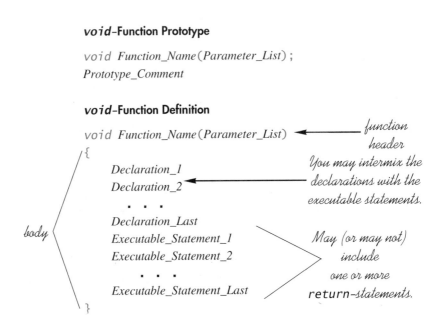

***void*-Function Prototype**

void Function_Name(Parameter_List);
Prototype_Comment

***void*-Function Definition**

void Function_Name(Parameter_List) ◀——— *function header*
{
    Declaration_1
    Declaration_2 ◀——— *You may intermix the declarations with the executable statements.*
    . . .
    Declaration_Last
    Executable_Statement_1
    Executable_Statement_2
    . . .
    Executable_Statement_Last
}

body

May (or may not) include one or more `return`*-statements.*

void-function is to imagine that the body of the function definition is copied into the program in place of the function call. When the function is called, the arguments are substituted for the formal parameters, and then it is just as if the body of the function were lines in the program.

functions with no arguments

It is perfectly legal, and sometimes useful, to have a function with no arguments. In that case there simply are no formal parameters listed in the function prototype and no arguments are used when the function is called. For example, the *void*-function `initialize_screen`, defined below, simply sends a new line command to the screen:

```
void initialize_screen()
{
    using namespace std;
    cout << endl;
    return;
}
```

If your program includes the following call to this function as its first executable statement, then the output from the previously run program will be separated from the output for your program:

```
initialize_screen( );
```

Be sure to notice that even when there are no parameters to a function, you still must include the parentheses in the function prototype and in a call to the function. The next programming example shows these two sample *void*-functions in a complete program.

▪)) *PROGRAMMING* *EXAMPLE*
Converting Temperatures from Fahrenheit to Celsius

The program in Display 4.2 takes a Fahrenheit temperature as input and outputs the equivalent Celsius temperature. A Fahrenheit temperature F can be converted to an equivalent Celsius temperature C as follows:

$$C = (5/9)(F - 32)$$

The function `celsius` shown in Display 4.2 uses this formula to do the temperature conversion.

return-**Statements in** *void*-**Functions**

Both *void*-functions and functions that return a value can have *return*-statements. In the case of a function that returns a value, the *return*-statement specifies the value returned. In the case of a *void*-function, the *return*-statement simply ends the function call. As we saw in the previous chapter, every function that returns a value must end by executing a *return*-statement. However, a *void*-function need not contain a *return*-statement. If it does not contain a *return*-statement, it will end after executing the code in the function body. It is as if there were an implicit *return*-statement just before the final closing brace } at the end of the function body. For example, the functions `initialize_screen` and `show_results` in Display 4.2 would perform exactly the same if we omitted the *return*-statements from their function definitions.

The fact that there is an implicit *return*-statement before the final closing brace in a function body does not mean that you never need a *return*-statement in a *void*-function. For example, the function definition in Display 4.3 might be used as part of a restaurant-management program. That function outputs instructions for dividing a given amount of ice cream among the people at a table. If there are no people at the table (i.e., if `number` equals 0), then the *return*-statement within the

void-functions and return-statements

Display 4.2 *void*-Functions *(part 1 of 2)*

```
//Program to convert a Fahrenheit temperature to a Celsius temperature.
#include <iostream>

void initialize_screen();
//Separates current output from
//the output of the previously run program.

double celsius(double fahrenheit);
//Converts a Fahrenheit temperature
//to a Celsius temperature.

void show_results(double f_degrees, double c_degrees);
//Displays output. Assumes that c_degrees
//Celsius is equivalent to f_degrees Fahrenheit.

int main()
{
    using namespace std;
    double f_temperature, c_temperature;

    initialize_screen();
    cout << "I will convert a Fahrenheit temperature"
         << " to Celsius.\n"
         << "Enter a temperature in Fahrenheit: ";
    cin >> f_temperature;

    c_temperature = celsius(f_temperature);

    show_results(f_temperature, c_temperature);
    return 0;
}

//Definition uses iostream:
void initialize_screen()
{
    using namespace std;
    cout << endl;
    return;            ◄─────────── This return is optional.
}
```

Display 4.2 *void*-**Functions** *(part 2 of 2)*

```
double celsius(double fahrenheit)
{
    return ((5.0/9.0)*(fahrenheit - 32));
}

//Definition uses iostream:
void show_results(double f_degrees, double c_degrees)
{
    using namespace std;
    cout.setf(ios::fixed);
    cout.setf(ios::showpoint);
    cout.precision(1);
    cout << f_degrees
        << " degrees Fahrenheit is equivalent to\n"
        << c_degrees << " degrees Celsius.\n";
    return;              ◄──────────── This return is optional.
}
```

Sample Dialogue

```
I will convert a Fahrenheit temperature to Celsius.
Enter a temperature in Fahrenheit: 32.5
32.5 degrees Fahrenheit is equivalent to
0.3 degrees Celsius.
```

if-statement terminates the function call and avoids a division by zero. If number is not 0, then the function call ends when the last cout-statement is executed at the end of the function body.

By now you may have guessed that the main part of a program is actually the definition of a function called main. When the program is run, the function main is automatically called and it, in turn, may call other functions. Although it may seem that the *return*-statement in the main part of a program should be optional, officially it is not. Technically, the main part of a program is a function that returns a value of type *int*, so it requires a *return*-statement. However, the function main is used as if it were a *void*-function. Treating the main part of your program as a function that returns an integer may sound crazy, but that's the tradition. It might be

The main *part of a program is a function.*

Display 4.3 Use of *return* in a *void*-Function

Prototype

```
void ice_cream_division(int number, double total_weight);
//Outputs instructions for dividing total_weight ounces of
//ice cream among number customers. If number is 0, nothing
//is done.
```

Function Definition

```
//Definition uses iostream:
void ice_cream_division(int number, double total_weight)
{
    using namespace std;
    double portion;

    if (number == 0)                        If number is 0, then the
        return;    ◄─────────────          function execution ends here.
    portion = total_weight/number;
    cout.setf(ios::fixed);
    cout.setf(ios::showpoint);
    cout.precision(2);
    cout << "Each one receives "
        << portion << " ounces of ice cream." << endl;
}
```

best to continue to think of the main part of the program as just "the main part of the program" and not worry about this minor detail.[1]

SELF-TEST EXERCISES

1 What is the output of the following program?

```
#include <iostream>

void friendly( );

void shy(int audience_count);
```

---

[1]The C++ Standard says that you can omit the *return* 0 in the main part, but many compilers still require it.

```
int main()
{
    using namespace std;
    friendly();
    shy(6);
    cout << "One more time:\n";
    shy(2);
    friendly();
    cout << "End of program.\n";
    return 0;
}
void friendly()
{
    using namespace std;
    cout << "Hello\n";

}
void shy(int audience_count)

{
    using namespace std;
    if (audience_count < 5)

        return;

    cout << "Goodbye\n";

}
```

2 Suppose you omitted the *return*-statement in the function definition for `initialize_screen` in Display 4.2. What effect would it have on the program? Would the program compile? Would it run? Would the program behave any differently? What about the *return*-statement in the function definition for `show_results` in that same program? What effect would it have on the program if you omitted the *return*-statement in the definition of `show_results`? What about the *return*-statement in the function definition for `celsius` in that same program? What effect would it have on the program if you omitted the *return*-statement in the definition of `celsius`?

3 Write a definition for a *void*-function that has three arguments of type *int* and that outputs to the screen the product of these three arguments. Put the definition in a complete program that reads in three numbers and then calls this function.

4 Does your compiler allow *void* main( ) and *int* main( )? What warnings are issued if you have *int* main( ) and do not supply a *return 0;*

statement? To find out, write several small test programs and perhaps ask your instructor or a local guru.

5   Is a correct call to a *void* function followed by a semicolon a statement in its own right? Or must we embed the function call in an expression?

4.2   Call-by-Reference Parameters

When a function is called its arguments are substituted for the formal parameters in the function definition, or to state it less formally, the arguments are "plugged in" for the formal parameters. There are different mechanisms used for this substitution process. The mechanism we used in Chapter 3, and thus far in this chapter, is known as the *call-by-value* mechanism. The second main mechanism for substituting arguments is known as the *call-by-reference* mechanism.

A First View of Call-by-Reference

The call-by-value mechanism that we used until now is not sufficient for certain subtasks. For example, one common subtask is to obtain one or more input values from the user. Look back at the program in Display 4.2. Its tasks are divided into four subtasks: initialize the screen, obtain the Fahrenheit temperature, compute the corresponding Celsius temperature, and output the results. Three of these four subtasks are implemented as the functions `initialize_screen`, `celsius`, and `show_results`. However, the subtask of obtaining the input is implemented as the following four lines of code (rather than as a function call):

```
cout << "I will convert a Fahrenheit temperature"
     << " to Celsius.\n"
     << "Enter a temperature in Fahrenheit: ";
cin >> f_temperature;
```

The subtask of obtaining the input should be accomplished by a function call. However, to do this with a function call, we need a call-by-reference parameter.

A function for obtaining input should set the values of one or more variables to values typed in at the keyboard, so the function call should have one or more variables as arguments and should change the values of these argument variables. With the call-by-value formal parameters that we have used until now, a corresponding argument in a function call can be a variable, but the function takes only the value of the variable and does not change the variable in any way. With a call-by-value formal parameter only *the value* of the argument is substituted for the formal parameter. For an input function, we want *the variable* (not the value of the variable) to be substituted for the formal parameter. The call-by-reference mechanism works in just this way. With a **call-by-reference** formal parameter, the corresponding argument in a function call must be a variable and this argument variable is substituted for the formal parameter. It is as if the argument variable were literally copied into the body of the function definition in place of the formal parameter. After the argument is substituted in, the code in the function body is executed and this code can change the value of the argument variable.

A call-by-reference parameter must be marked in some way so that the compiler will know it from a call-by-value parameter. The way that you indicate a **call-by-reference parameter** is to attach the **ampersand sign &** to the end of the type name in the formal parameter list in both the function prototype and the header of the function definition. For example, the following function definition has one formal parameter, f_variable, and that formal parameter is a call-by-reference parameter:

&

```
void get_input(double& f_variable)
{
    using namespace std;
    cout << "I will convert a Fahrenheit temperature"
         << " to Celsius.\n"
         << "Enter a temperature in Fahrenheit: ";
    cin >> f_variable;
}
```

In a program that contains this function definition, the following function call will set the variable f_temperature equal to a value read from the keyboard:

```
get_input(f_temperature);
```

Using this function definition, we could easily rewrite the program shown in Display 4.2 so that the subtask of reading the input is accomplished by this function call. However, rather than rewrite an old program, let's look at a completely new program.

Display 4.4 demonstrates call-by-reference parameters. The program doesn't do very much. It just reads in two numbers and writes the same numbers out, but in the reverse order. The parameters in the functions get_numbers and swap_values are call-by-reference parameters. The input is performed by the function call

```
get_numbers(first_num, second_num);
```

The values of the variables first_num and second_num are set by this function call. After that, the following function call reverses the values in the two variables first_num and second_num:

```
swap_values(first_num, second_num);
```

In the next few subsections we describe the call-by-reference mechanism in more detail and also explain the particular functions used in Display 4.4.

Display 4.4 Call-by-Reference Parameters *(part 1 of 2)*

```
//Program to demonstrate call-by-reference parameters.
#include <iostream>

void get_numbers(int& input1, int& input2);
//Reads two integers from the keyboard.

void swap_values(int& variable1, int& variable2);
//Interchanges the values of variable1 and variable2.

void show_results(int output1, int output2);
//Shows the values of variable1 and variable2, in that order.

int main( )
{
    int first_num, second_num;

    get_numbers(first_num, second_num);
    swap_values(first_num, second_num);
    show_results(first_num, second_num);
    return 0;
}

//Uses iostream:
void get_numbers(int& input1, int& input2)
{
    using namespace std;
    cout << "Enter two integers: ";
    cin >> input1
        >> input2;
}

void swap_values(int& variable1, int& variable2)
{
    int temp;

    temp = variable1;
    variable1 = variable2;
    variable2 = temp;
}
```

Display 4.4 Call-by-Reference Parameters (part 2 of 2)

```
//Uses iostream:
void show_results(int output1, int output2)
{
    using namespace std;
    cout << "In reverse order the numbers are: "
        << output1 << " " << output2 << endl;
}
```

Sample Dialogue

```
Enter two integers: 5 10
In reverse order the numbers are: 10 5
```

Call-by-Reference

To make a formal parameter a **call-by-reference** parameter append the **ampersand sign** & to its type name. The corresponding argument in a call to the function should then be a variable, not a constant or other expression. When the function is called, the corresponding variable argument (not its value) will be substituted for the formal parameter. Any change made to the formal parameter in the function body will be made to the argument variable when the function is called. The exact details of the substitution mechanisms are given in the text of this chapter.

Example (of call-by-reference parameters in a function prototype):

```
void get_data(int& first_in, double& second_in);
```

Call-by-Reference in Detail

In most situations the call-by-reference mechanism works as if the name of the variable given as the function argument were literally substituted for the call-by-reference formal parameter. However, the process is a bit more subtle than that. In some situations, this subtlety is important, so we need to examine more details of this call-by-reference substitution process.

Recall that program variables are implemented as memory locations. The compiler assigns one memory location to each variable. For example, when the program in Display 4.4 is compiled, the variable `first_num` might be assigned location 1010, and the variable `second_num` might be assigned 1012. For all practical purposes, these memory locations are the variables.

For example, consider the following function prototype from Display 4.4:

```
void get_numbers(int& input1, int& input2);
```

The call-by-reference formal parameters `input1` and `input2` are place holders for the actual arguments used in a function call.

Now consider a function call like the following from the same display:

```
get_numbers(first_num, second_num);
```

When the function call is executed, the function is not given the argument names `first_num` and `second_num`. Instead, it is given a list of the memory locations associated with each name. In this example, the list consists of the locations:

```
1010
1012
```

which are the locations assigned to the argument variables `first_num` and `second_num`, *in that order.* It is these memory locations that are associated with the formal parameters. The first memory location is associated with the first formal parameter, the second memory location is associated with the second formal parameter, and so forth. Diagrammatically, in this case the correspondence is

```
first_num   ──────► 1010 ──────► input1
second_num  ──────► 1012 ──────► input2
```

When the function statements are executed, whatever the function body says to do to a formal parameter is actually done to the variable in the memory location associated with that formal parameter. In this case, the instructions in the body of the function `get_numbers` say that a value should be stored in the formal parameter `input1` using a `cin`-statement, and so that value is stored in the variable in memory location 1010 (which happens to be the variable `first_num`). Similarly, the instructions in the body of the function `get_numbers` say that a value should then be stored in the formal parameter `input2` using a `cin`-statement, and so that value is stored in the variable in memory location 1012 (which happens to be the variable `second_num`). Thus, whatever the function instructs the computer to do to `input1` and `input2` is actually done to the variables `first_num` and `second_num`. These details of how the call-by-reference mechanism works in this function call to `get_numbers` are described in Display 4.5.

It may seem that there is an extra level of detail, or at least an extra level of verbiage. If `first_num` is the variable with memory location 1010, why do we insist on saying "the variable at memory location 1010" instead of simply saying "first_num"? This extra level of detail is needed if the arguments and formal parameters contain some confusing coincidence of names. For example, the function get_numbers has formal parameters named input1 and input2. Suppose you want to change the program in Display 4.4 so that it uses the function get_numbers with arguments that are also named input1 and input2, and suppose that you want to do something less than obvious. Suppose you want the first number typed in to be stored in a variable named input2, and the second number typed in to be stored in the variable named input1—perhaps because the second number will be processed first, or because it is the more important number. Now, let's suppose that the variables input1 and input2, which are declared in the main part of your program, have been assigned memory locations 1014 and 1016. The function call could be as follows:

```
int input1, input 2;
get_numbers(input2, input1);
```
Notice the order of the arguments

In this case if you say "input1," we do not know whether you mean the variable named input1 that is declared in the main part of your program or the formal parameter input1. However, if the variable input1 declared in the main part of your program is assigned memory location 1014, the phrase "the variable at memory location 1014" is unambiguous. Let's go over the details of the substitution mechanisms in this case.

In this call the argument corresponding to the formal parameter input1 is the variable input2, and the argument corresponding to the formal parameter input2 is the variable input1. This can be confusing to us, but it produces no problem at all for the computer, since the computer never does actually "substitute input2 for input1" or "substitute input1 for input2." The computer simply deals with memory locations. The computer substitutes "the variable at memory location 1016" for the formal parameter input1, and "the variable at memory location 1014" for the formal parameter input2.

■)) PROGRAMMING EXAMPLE
The swap_values *Function*

The function swap_values defined in Display 4.4 interchanges the values stored in two variables. The description of the function is given by the following prototype and accompanying comment:

```
void swap_values(int& variable1, int& variable2);
//Interchanges the values of variable1 and variable2.
```

Display 4.5 Behavior of Call-by-Reference Arguments *(part 1 of 2)*

Anatomy of a Function Call from Display 4.4
Using Call-by-Reference Arguments

0 Assume the variables `first_num` and `second_num` have been assigned the following memory address by the compiler:

first_num ⟶ 1010
second_num ⟶ 1012

(We do not know what addresses are assigned and the results will not depend on the actual addresses, but this will make the process very concrete and thus perhaps easier to follow.)

1 In the program in Display 4.4, the following function call begins executing:

```
get_numbers(first_num, second_num);
```

2 The function is told to use the memory location of the variable `first_num` in place of the formal parameter `input1` and the memory location of the `second_num` in place of the formal parameter `input2`. The effect is the same as if the function definition were rewritten to the following (which is not legal C++ code, but does have a clear meaning to us):

```
void get_numbers(int& <the variable at memory location 1010>,
                 int& <the variable at memory location 1012>)
{
    using namespace std;
    cout << "Enter two integers: ";
    cin >> <the variable at memory location 1010>
        >> <the variable at memory location 1012>;
}
```

Since the variables in locations 1010 and 1012 are `first_num` and `second_num`, the effect is thus the same as if the function definition were rewritten to the following:

```
void get_numbers(int& first_num, int& second_num)
{
    using namespace std;
    cout << "Enter two integers: ";
    cin >> first_num
        >> second_num;
}
```

To see how the function is supposed to work assume that the variable
`first_num` has the value 5 and the variable `second_num` has the value 10 and consider the function call:

```
swap_values(first_num, second_num);
```

After this function call, the value of `first_num` will be 10 and the value of
`second_num` will be 5.

As shown in Display 4.4, the definition of the function `swap_values` uses a
local variable called `temp`. This local variable is needed. You might be tempted to
think the function definition could be simplified to the following:

```
void swap_values(int& variable1, int& variable2)
{
    variable1 = variable2;                    This does not work!
    variable2 = variable1;
}
```

Display 4.5 Behavior of Call-by-Reference Arguments *(part 2 of 2)*

Anatomy of the Function Call in Display 4.4 *(concluded)*

3 The body of the function is executed. The effect is the same as if the following
were executed:

```
{
    using namespace std;
    cout << "Enter two integers: ";
    cin >> first_num
        >> second_num;
}
```

4 When the `cin`-statement is executed, the values of the variables `first_num`
and `second_num` are set to the values typed in at the keyboard. (If the dialogue
is as shown in Display 4.4, then the value of `first_num` is set to 5 and the value
of `second_num` is set to 10.)

5 When the function call ends, the variables `first_num` and `second_num` retain
the values that they were given by the `cin`-statement in the function body. (If the
dialogue is as shown in Display 4.4, then the value of `first_num` is 5 and the
value of `second_num` is 10 at the end of the function call.)

To see that this alternative definition cannot work, consider what would happen with this definition and the function call

```
swap_values(first_num, second_num);
```

The variables `first_num` and `second_num` are substituted for the formal parameters `variable1` and `variable2` so that, with this incorrect function definition, the function call is equivalent to the following:

```
first_num = second_num;
second_num = first_num;
```

This code does not produce the desired result. The value of `first_num` is set equal to the value of `second_num`, just as it should be. But then, the value of `second_num` is set equal to the changed value of `first_num`, which is now the original value of `second_num`. Thus the value of `second_num` is not changed at all. (If this is unclear go through the steps with specific values for the variables `first_num` and `second_num`.) What the function needs to do is to save the original value of `first_num` so that value is not lost. This is what the local variable `temp` in the correct function definition is used for. That correct definition is the one in Display 4.4. When that correct version is used and the function is called with the arguments `first_num` and `second_num`, the function call is equivalent to the following code, which works correctly:

```
temp = first_num;
first_num = second_num;
second_num = temp;
```

Mixed Parameter Lists

Whether a formal parameter is a call-by-value parameter or a call-by-reference parameter is determined by whether or not there is an ampersand attached to its type specification. If the ampersand is present, then the formal parameter is a call-by-reference parameter. If there is no ampersand associated with the formal parameter, then it is a call-by-value parameter.

mixing call-by-reference and call-by-value

It is perfectly legitimate to mix call-by-value and call-by-reference formal parameters in the same function. For example, the first and last of the formal parameters in the following function prototype are call-by-reference formal parameters and the middle one is a call-by-value parameter:

```
void good_stuff(int& par1, int par2, double& par3);
```

Call-by-reference parameters are not restricted to *void*-functions. You can also use them in functions that return a value. Thus, a function with a call-by-reference parameter could both change the value of a variable given as an argument and return a value.

Parameters and Arguments

All the different terms that have to do with parameters and arguments can be confusing. However, if you keep a few simple points in mind, you will be able to easily handle these terms.

1 The **formal parameters** for a function are listed in the function prototype and are used in the body of the function definition. A formal parameter (of any sort) is a kind of blank or place holder that is filled in with something when the function is called.

2 An **argument** is something that is used to fill in a formal parameter. When you write down a function call, the arguments are listed in parentheses after the function name. When the function call is executed, the arguments are "plugged in" for the formal parameters.

3 The terms *call-by-value* and *call-by-reference* refer to the mechanism that is used in the "plugging in" process. In the **call-by-value** method only the value of the argument is used. In this call-by-value mechanism, the formal parameter is a local variable that is initialized to the value of the corresponding argument. In the **call-by-reference** mechanism the argument is a variable and the entire variable is used. In the call-by-reference mechanism the argument variable is substituted for the formal parameter so that any change that is made to the formal parameter is actually made to the argument variable.

➤ *PROGRAMMING* TIP
What Kind of Parameter to Use

Display 4.6 illustrates the differences between how the compiler treats call-by-value and call-by-reference formal parameters. The parameters `par1_value` and `par2_ref` are both assigned a value inside the body of the function definition. But since they are different kinds of parameters, the effect is different in the two cases.

`par1_value` is a call-by-value parameter, so it is a local variable. When the function is called as follows

```
do_stuff(n1, n2);
```

the local variable `par1_value` is initialized to the value of `n1`. That is, the local variable `par1_value` is initialized to 1 and the variable `n1` is then ignored by the function. As you can see from the sample dialogue, the formal parameter

Display 4.6 Comparing Argument Mechanisms

```cpp
//Illustrates the difference between a call-by-value
//parameter and a call-by-reference parameter.
#include <iostream>

void do_stuff(int par1_value, int& par2_ref);
//par1_value is a call-by-value formal parameter and
//par2_ref is a call-by-reference formal parameter.

int main( )
{
    using namespace std;
    int n1, n2;

    n1 = 1;
    n2 = 2;
    do_stuff(n1, n2);
    cout << "n1 after function call = " << n1 << endl;
    cout << "n2 after function call = " << n2 << endl;
    return 0;
}

void do_stuff(int par1_value, int& par2_ref)
{
    using namespace std;
    par1_value = 111;
    cout << "par1_value in function call = "
        << par1_value << endl;
    par2_ref = 222;
    cout << "par2_ref in function call = "
        << par2_ref << endl;
}
```

Sample Dialogue

```
par1_value in function call = 111
par2_ref in function call = 222
n1 after function call = 1
n2 after function call = 222
```

par1_value (which is a local variable) is set to 111 in the function body and this value is output to the screen. However, the value of the argument n1 is not changed. As shown in the sample dialogue, n1 has retained its value of 1.

On the other hand, par2_ref is a call-by-reference parameter. When the function is called, the variable argument n2 (not just its value) is substituted for the formal parameter par2_ref. So that when the following code is executed:

```
par2_ref = 222;
```

it is the same as if the following were executed:

```
n2 = 222;
```

Thus, the value of the variable n2 is changed when the function body is executed, so, as the dialogue shows, the value of n2 is changed from 2 to 222 by the function call.

If you keep in mind the lesson of Display 4.6, it is easy to decide which parameter mechanism to use. If you want a function to change the value of a variable, then the corresponding formal parameter must be a call-by-reference formal parameter and so it must be marked with the ampersand sign &. In all other cases, you can use a call-by-value formal parameter.

◆ PITFALL   Inadvertent Local Variables

If you want a function to change the value of a variable, the corresponding formal parameter must be a call-by-reference parameter and so must have the ampersand & attached to its type. If you carelessly omit the ampersand, the function will have a call-by-value parameter where you meant to have a call-by-reference parameter, and when the program is run, you will discover that the function call does not change the value of the corresponding argument. This is because a formal call-by-value parameter is a local variable, so if it has its value changed in the function, then as with any local variable, that change has no effect outside of the function body. This is a logic error that can be very difficult to see because it *looks* right.

For example, the program in Display 4.7 is identical to the program in Display 4.4, except that the ampersands were mistakenly omitted from the function swap_values. As a result, the formal parameters variable1 and variable2 are local variables. The argument *variables* first_num and second_num are never substituted in for variable1 and variable2; variable1 and variable2 are instead initialized to *the values of* first_num and second_num. Then, the values of variable1 and variable2 are interchanged, but the values of first_num and second_num are left unchanged. The omission of two ampersands have made the

Display 4.7 Inadvertent Local Variable

```
//Program to demonstrate call-by-reference parameters.
#include <iostream>

void get_numbers(int& input1, int& input2);
//Reads two integers from the keyboard.

void swap_values(int variable1, int variable2);
//Interchanges the values of variable1 and variable2.

void show_results(int output1, int output2);
//Shows the values of variable1 and variable2, in that order.

int main()
{
    using namespace std;
    int first_num, second_num;

    get_numbers(first_num, second_num);
    swap_values(first_num, second_num);
    show_results(first_num, second_num);
    return 0;
}
void swap_values(int variable1, int variable2)
{
    int temp;

    temp = variable1;
    variable1 = variable2;
    variable2 = temp;
}
```

forgot the & here

forgot the & here

inadvertent local variables

```
        <The definitions of get_numbers and
             show_results are the same as in Display 4.4.>
```

Sample Dialogue

```
Enter two integers: 5 10
In reverse order the numbers are: 5 10
```

program completely wrong, yet it looks almost identical to the correct program and will compile and run without any error messages.

SELF-TEST EXERCISES

6 What is the output of the following program?

```cpp
#include <iostream>
void figure_me_out(int& x, int y, int& z);
int main( )
{
    using namespace std;
    int a, b, c;
    a = 10;
    b = 20;
    c = 30;
    figure_me_out(a, b, c);
    cout << a << " " << b << " " << c;
    return 0;
}
void figure_me_out(int& x, int y, int& z)
{
    using namespace std;
    cout << x << " " << y << " " << z << endl;
    x = 1;
    y = 2;
    z = 3;
    cout << x << " " << y << " " << z << endl;
}
```

7 What would be the output of the program in Display 4.4 if you omit the ampersands & from the first parameter in the prototype and function heading of swap_values? The ampersand is not removed from the second parameter.

8 What would be the output of the program in Display 4.6 if you change the prototype for the function do_stuff to the following and you change the function header to match, so that the formal parameter par2_ref is changed to a call-by-value parameter:

```cpp
void do_stuff(int par1_value, int par2_ref);
```

9 Write a void-function definition for a function called zero_both that has two reference parameters, both of which are variables of type int, and sets the values of both variables to 0.

10 Write a *void*-function definition for a function called `add_tax`. The function `add_tax` has two formal parameters: `tax_rate` which is the amount of sales tax expressed as a percentage and `cost` which is the cost of an item before tax. The function changes the value of `cost` so that it includes sales tax.

4.3 Using Procedural Abstraction

> *My memory is so bad,*
> *that many times I forget my own name!*
>
> MIGUEL DE CERVANTES SAAVEDRA, DON QUIXOTE

Recall that the principle of procedural abstraction says that functions should be designed so that they can be used as black boxes. For a programmer to use a function effectively, all the programmer should need to know is the function prototype and the accompanying comment that says what the function accomplishes. The programmer should not need to know any of the details contained in the function body. In this section we will discuss a number of topics that deal with this principle in more detail.

Functions Calling Functions

A function body may contain a call to another function. The situation for these sorts of function calls is exactly the same as it would be if the function call had occurred in the `main` function of the program; the only restriction is that the prototype should appear before the function is used. If you set up your programs as we have been doing, this will happen automatically, since all prototypes come before the `main` function and all function definitions come after the `main` function. Although you may include a function *call* within the definition of another function, you cannot place the *definition* of one function within the body of another function definition.

Display 4.8 shows an enhanced version of the program shown in Display 4.4. The program in Display 4.4 always reversed the values of the variables `first_num` and `second_num`. The program in Display 4.8 reverses these variables only some of the time. The program in Display 4.8 uses the function `order` to reorder the values in these variables so as to ensure that

    first_num <= second_num

Display 4.8 Function Calling Another Function *(part 1 of 2)*

```
//Program to demonstrate a function calling another function.
#include <iostream>

void get_input(int& input1, int& input2);
//Reads two integers from the keyboard.

void swap_values(int& variable1, int& variable2);
//Interchanges the values of variable1 and variable2.

void order(int& n1, int& n2);
//Orders the numbers in the variables n1 and n2
//so that after the function call n1 <= n2.

void give_results(int output1, int output2);
//Outputs the values in output1 and output2.
//Assumes that output1 <= output2


int main()
{
    int first_num, second_num;

    get_input(first_num, second_num);
    order(first_num, second_num);
    give_results(first_num, second_num);
    return 0;
}


//Uses iostream:
void get_input(int& input1, int& input2)
{
    using namespace std;
    cout << "Enter two integers: ";
    cin >> input1 >> input2;
}
```

Display 4.8 Function Calling Another Function (part 2 of 2)

```
void swap_values(int& variable1, int& variable2)
{
    int temp;

    temp = variable1;
    variable1 = variable2;
    variable2 = temp;
}
```

These function definitions can be in any order.

```
void order(int& n1, int& n2)
{
    if (n1 > n2)
        swap_values(n1, n2);
}
```

```
//Uses iostream:
void give_results(int output1, int output2)
{
    using namespace std;
    cout << "In increasing order the numbers are: "
        << output1 << " " << output2 << endl;
}
```

Sample Dialogue

```
Enter two integers: 10 5
In increasing order the numbers are: 5 10
```

If this condition is already true, then nothing is done to the variables first_num and second_num. If, however, first_num is greater than second_num, then the function swap_values is called to interchange the values of these two variables. This testing for order and exchanging of variable values all takes place within the body of the function order. Thus, the function swap_values is called within the body of the function order. This presents no special problems. Using the principle of procedural abstraction, we think of the function `swap_values` as performing an action (namely, interchanging the values of two variables); this action is the same no matter where it occurs.

Preconditions and Postconditions

One good way to write a function prototype comment is to break it down into two kinds of information called a *precondition* and a *postcondition*. The **precondition** states what is assumed to be true when the function is called. The function should not be used and cannot be expected to perform correctly unless the precondition holds. The **postcondition** describes the effect of the function call, that is, the postcondition tells what will be true after the function is executed in a situation in which the precondition holds. For a function that returns a value, the postcondition will describe the value returned by the function. For a function that changes the value of some argument variables, the postcondition will describe all the changes made to the values of the arguments.

precondition

postcondition

For example, the prototype comment for the function `swap_values` shown in Display 4.8 can be put into this format as follows:

```
void swap_values(int& variable1, int& variable2);
//Precondition: variable1 and variable2 have been given
//values.
//Postcondition: The values of variable1 and variable2
//have been interchanged.
```

The comment for the function `celsius` from Display 4.2 can be put into this format as follows:

```
double celsius(double fahrenheit);
//Precondition: fahrenheit is a temperature expressed
//in degrees Fahrenheit.
//Postcondition: Returns the equivalent temperature
//expressed in degrees Celsius.
```

When the only postcondition is a description of the value returned, programmers often omit the word *Postcondition*. A common and acceptable alternative form for the previous prototype comments is the following:

```
//Precondition: fahrenheit is a temperature expressed
//in degrees Fahrenheit.
//Returns the equivalent temperature expressed in degrees
//Celsius.
```

Another example of preconditions and postconditions is given by the following function prototype:

```
void post_interest(double& balance, double rate);
//Precondition: balance is a nonnegative savings account
//balance.
//rate is the interest rate expressed as a percent, such as 5
//for 5%.
//Postcondition: The value of balance has been increased by
//rate percent.
```

You do not need to know the definition of the function post_interest in order to use this function, so we have given only the prototype and accompanying comment.

Preconditions and postconditions are more than a way to summarize a function's actions. They should be the first step in designing and writing a function. When you design a program, you should specify what each function does before you start designing how the function will do it. In particular, the prototype comments and the function prototype should be designed and written down before starting to design the function body. If you later discover that your specification cannot be realized in a reasonable way, you may need to back up and rethink what the function should do, but by clearly specifying what you think the function should do you will minimize both design errors and wasted time writing code that does not fit the task at hand.

Case Study — Supermarket Pricing

This case study solves a very simple programming task. It may seem that it contains more detail than is needed for such a simple task. However, if you see the design elements in the context of a simple task, you can concentrate on learning them without the distraction of any side issues. Once you learn the techniques that are illustrated in this simple case study, you can apply these same techniques to much more complicated programming tasks.

PROBLEM DEFINITION

We have been commissioned by the Quick-Shop supermarket chain to write a program that will determine the retail price of an item given suitable input. Their pricing policy is that any item that is expected to sell in one week or less is marked up 5%, and any item that is expected to stay on the shelf for more than one week is marked up 10% over the wholesale price. Be sure to notice that the low markup of 5% is used for up to 7 days and that at 8 days the markup changes to 10%. It is important to be precise about exactly when a program should change from one form of calculation to a different one.

As always, we should be sure we have a clear statement of the input required and the output produced by the program.

INPUT:

The input will consist of the wholesale price of an item and the expected number of days until the item is sold.

OUTPUT:

The output will give the retail price of the item.

ANALYSIS OF THE PROBLEM

Like many simple programming tasks, this one breaks down into three main subtasks:

1 Input the data.

2 Compute the retail price of the item.

3 Output the results.

These three subtasks will be implemented by three functions. The three functions are described by their prototypes and accompanying comments, which are given below. Note that only those items that are changed by the functions are call-by-reference parameters. The remaining formal parameters are call-by-value parameters.

```
void get_input(double& cost, int& turnover);
//Precondition: User is ready to enter values correctly.
//Postcondition: The value of cost has been set to the
//wholesale cost of one item. The value of turnover has been
//set to the expected number of days until the item is sold.

double price(double cost, int turnover);
//Precondition: cost is the wholesale cost of one item.
//turnover is the expected number of days until sale of the item.
//Returns the retail price of the item.

void give_output(double cost, int turnover, double price);
//Precondition: cost is the wholesale cost of one item;
//turnover is the expected time until sale of the item;
//price is the retail price of the item.
//Postcondition: The values of cost, turnover, and price have
//been written to the screen.
```

Now that we have the function headings, it is trivial to write the main part of our program:

```
int main( )
{
    double wholesale_cost, retail_price;
    int shelf_time;

    get_input(wholesale_cost, shelf_time);
    retail_price = price(wholesale_cost, shelf_time);
    give_output(wholesale_cost, shelf_time, retail_price);
    return 0;
}
```

Even though we have not yet written the function bodies and have no idea of how the functions work, we can write the above code which uses the functions. That is what is meant by the principle of procedural abstraction. The functions are treated like black boxes.

ALGORITHM DESIGN

The implementations of the functions `get_input` and `give_output` are straightforward. They simply consist of a few `cin`- and `cout`-statements. The algorithm for the function `price` is given by the following pseudocode:

```
if turnover ≤ 7 days then
    return (cost + 5% of cost);
else
    return (cost + 10% of cost);
```

CODING

There are three constants used in this program: a low markup figure of 5%, a high markup figure of 10%, and an expected shelf stay of 7 days as the threshold above which the high markup is used. Since these constants might need to be changed to update the program should the company decide to change its pricing policy, we declare global named constants at the start of our program for each of these three numbers. The declarations with the *const* modifier are the following:

```
const double LOW_MARKUP = 0.05; //5%
const double HIGH_MARKUP = 0.10; //10%
const int THRESHOLD = 7; //Use HIGH_MARKUP if do not
                         //expect to sell in 7 days or less.
```

The body of the function `price` is a straightforward translation of our algorithm from pseudocode to C++ code:

```
    {
        if (turnover <= THRESHOLD)
            return ( cost + (LOW_MARKUP * cost) );
        else
            return ( cost + (HIGH_MARKUP * cost) );
    }
```

The complete program is shown in Display 4.9.

PROGRAM TESTING

An important technique in testing a program is to test all kinds of input. There is no precise definition of what we mean by a "kind" of input, but in practice, it is often easy to decide what kinds of input data a program deals with. In the case of our supermarket program, there are two main kinds of input: input that uses the low markup of 5% and input that uses the high markup of 10%. Thus, we should test at least one case in which the item is expected to remain on the shelf for less than 7 days and at least one case in which the item is expected to remain on the shelf for more than 7 days.

test all kinds of input

Another testing strategy is to test *boundary values*. Unfortunately, boundary value is another vague concept. An input (test) value is a **boundary value** if it is a value at which the program changes behavior. For example, in our supermarket program, the program's behavior changes at an expected shelf stay of 7 days. Thus, 7 is a boundary value; the program behaves differently for a number of days that is less than or equal to 7 than it does for a number of days that is greater than 7. Hence, we should test the program on at least one case in which the item is expected to remain on the shelf for exactly 7 days. Normally, you should also test input that is one step away from the boundary value as well, since you can easily be off by one in deciding where the boundary is. Hence, we should test our program on input for an item that is expected to remain on the shelf for 6 days, an item that is expected to remain on the shelf for 7 days, and an item that is expected to remain on the shelf for 8 days. (This is in addition to the test inputs described in the previous paragraph, which should be well below and well above 7 days.)

test boundary values

SELF-TEST EXERCISES

11   Can a function definition appear inside the body of another function definition?

12   Rewrite the prototype comment for the function `order` shown in Display 4.8 so that it is expressed in terms of preconditions and postconditions.

13   Give a precondition and a postcondition for the predefined function `sqrt`, which returns the square root of its argument.

Display 4.9 Supermarket Pricing (part 1 of 3)

```
//Determines the retail price of an item according to
//the pricing policies of the Quick-Shop supermarket chain.
#include <iostream>

const double LOW_MARKUP = 0.05; //5%
const double HIGH_MARKUP = 0.10; //10%
const int THRESHOLD = 7; //Use HIGH_MARKUP if do not
                         //expect to sell in 7 days or less.

void introduction( );
//Postcondition: Description of program is written on the screen.

void get_input(double& cost, int& turnover);
//Precondition: User is ready to enter values correctly.
//Postcondition: The value of cost has been set to the
//wholesale cost of one item. The value of turnover has been
//set to the expected number of days until the item is sold.

double price(double cost, int turnover);
//Precondition: cost is the wholesale cost of one item.
//turnover is the expected number of days until sale of the item.
//Returns the retail price of the item.

void give_output(double cost, int turnover, double price);
//Precondition: cost is the wholesale cost of one item; turnover is the
//expected time until sale of the item; price is the retail price of the item.
//Postcondition: The values of cost, turnover, and price have been
//written to the screen.

int main( )
{
    double wholesale_cost, retail_price;
    int shelf_time;

    introduction( );
    get_input(wholesale_cost, shelf_time);
    retail_price = price(wholesale_cost, shelf_time);
    give_output(wholesale_cost, shelf_time, retail_price);
    return 0;
}
```

Display 4.9 Supermarket Pricing *(part 2 of 3)*

```
//Uses iostream:
void introduction( )
{
    using namespace std;
    cout << "This program determines the retail price for\n"
        << "an item at a Quick-Shop supermarket store.\n";
}

//Uses iostream:
void get_input(double& cost, int& turnover)
{
    using namespace std;
    cout << "Enter the wholesale cost of item $";
    cin >> cost;
    cout << "Enter the expected number of days until sold: ";
    cin >> turnover;
}

//Uses iostream:
void give_output(double cost, int turnover, double price)
{
    using namespace std;
    cout.setf(ios::fixed);
    cout.setf(ios::showpoint);
    cout.precision(2);
    cout << "Wholesale cost = $" << cost << endl
        << "Expected time until sold = "
        << turnover << " days" << endl
        << "Retail price= $" << price << endl;
}

//Uses defined constants LOW_MARKUP, HIGH_MARKUP, and THRESHOLD:
double price(double cost, int turnover)
{
    if (turnover <= THRESHOLD)
        return ( cost + (LOW_MARKUP * cost) );
    else
        return ( cost + (HIGH_MARKUP * cost) );

}
```

Display 4.9 Supermarket Pricing *(part 3 of 3)*

Sample Dialogue

> This program determines the retail price for
> an item at a Quick-Shop supermarket store.
> Enter the wholesale cost of item: **$1.21**
> Enter the expected number of days until sold: **5**
> Wholesale cost = $1.21
> Expected time until sold = 5 days
> Retail price = $1.27

4.4 Testing and Debugging Functions

*"I beheld the wretch—the miserable monster
whom I had created."*

MARY WOLLSTONECRAFT SHELLEY, FRANKENSTEIN

Stubs and Drivers

drivers

Each function should be designed, coded, and tested as a separate unit from the rest of the program. This is the essence of the top-down design strategy. When you treat each function as a separate unit, you transform one big task into a series of smaller, more manageable tasks. But how do you test a function outside of the program for which it is intended? You write a special program to do the testing. For example, Display 4.10 shows a program to test the function get_input which was used in the program in Display 4.9. Programs like this one are called **driver programs.** These driver programs are temporary tools, and can be quite minimal. They need not have fancy input routines. They need not perform all the calculations the final program will perform. All they need do is obtain reasonable values for the function arguments in as simple a way as possible—typically from the user—then execute the function and show the result. A loop, as in the program shown in Display 4.10, will allow you to retest the function on different arguments without having to rerun the program.

Display 4.10 Driver Program *(part 1 of 2)*

```cpp
//Driver program for the function get_input.
#include <iostream>

void get_input(double& cost, int& turnover);
//Precondition: User is ready to enter values correctly.
//Postcondition: The value of cost has been set to the
//wholesale cost of one item. The value of turnover has been
//set to the expected number of days until the item is sold.

int main( )
{
    using namespace std;
    double wholesale_cost;
    int shelf_time;
    char ans;

    do
    {
        get_input(wholesale_cost, shelf_time);

        cout.setf(ios::fixed);
        cout.setf(ios::showpoint);
        cout.precision(2);
        cout << "Wholesale cost is now $"
             << wholesale_cost << endl;
        cout << "Days until sold is now "
             << shelf_time << endl;

        cout << "Test again?"
             << " (Type y for yes or n for no): ";
        cin >> ans;
        cout << endl;
    } while (ans == 'y' || ans == 'Y');

    return 0;
}
```

Display 4.10 Driver Program *(part 2 of 2)*

```
//Uses iostream:
void get_input(double& cost, int& turnover)
{
    using namespace std;
    cout << "Enter the wholesale cost of item $";
    cin >> cost;
    cout << "Enter the expected number of days until sold: ";
    cin >> turnover;
}
```

Sample Dialogue

```
Enter the wholesale cost of item: $123.45
Enter the expected number of days until sold: 67
Wholesale cost is now $123.45
Days until sold is now 67
Test again? (Type y for yes or n for no): y

Enter the wholesale cost of item: $9.05
Enter the expected number of days until sold: 3
Wholesale cost is now $9.05
Days until sold is now 3
Test again? (Type y for yes or n for no): n
```

If you test each function separately, you will find most of the mistakes in your program. Moreover, you will find out which functions contain the mistakes. If you were to test only the entire program, you would probably find out if there were a mistake, but may have no idea where the mistake is. Even worse, you may think you know where the mistake is, but be wrong.

Once you have fully tested a function, you can use it in the driver program for some other function. Each function should be tested in a program in which it is the only untested function. However, it's fine to use a fully tested function when testing some other function. If a bug is found, you know the bug is in the untested function. For example, after fully testing the function `get_input` with the driver program in Display 4.10, you can use `get_input` as the input routine in driver programs to test the remaining functions.

It is sometimes impossible or inconvenient to test a function without using some other function that has not yet been written or has not yet been tested. In this case, you can use a simplified version of the missing or untested function. These simplified functions are called **stubs.** These stubs will not necessarily perform the correct calculation, but they will deliver values that suffice for testing, and they are simple enough that you can have confidence in their performance. For example, the program in Display 4.11 is designed to test the function `give_output` from Display 4.9 as well as the basic layout of the program. This program uses the function `get_input`, which we already fully tested using the driver program shown in Display 4.10. This program also includes the function `initialize_screen`, which we assume has been tested in a driver program of its own, even though we have not bothered to show that simple driver program. Since we have not yet tested the function `price`, we have used a stub to stand in for it. Notice that we could use this program before we have even written the function `price`. This way we can test the basic program layout before we fill in the details of all the function definitions.

stubs

price

Using a program outline with stubs allows you to test and then "flesh out" the basic program outline, rather than write a completely new program to test each function. For this reason, a program outline with stubs is usually the most efficient method of testing. A common approach is to use driver programs to test some basic functions, like the input and output functions, and then use a program with stubs to test the remaining functions. The stubs are replaced by functions one at a time: One stub is replaced by a complete function and tested; once that function is fully tested and debugged, another stub is replaced by a full function definition, and so forth until the final program is produced.

The Fundamental Rule for Testing Functions

Every function should be tested in a program in which every other function in that program has already been fully tested and debugged.

SELF-TEST EXERCISES

14 What is the fundamental rule for testing functions? Why is this a good way to test functions?

15 What is a driver program?

16 Write a driver program for the function `introduction` shown in Display 4.11.

17 What is a stub?

Display 4.11 Program with a Stub (part 1 of 2)

```
//Determines the retail price of an item according to
//the pricing policies of the Quick-Shop supermarket chain.
#include <iostream>

void introduction();
//Postcondition: Description of program is written on the screen.

void get_input(double& cost, int& turnover);
//Precondition: User is ready to enter values correctly.
//Postcondition: The value of cost has been set to the
//wholesale cost of one item. The value of turnover has been
//set to the expected number of days until the item is sold.

double price(double cost, int turnover);
//Precondition: cost is the wholesale cost of one item.
//turnover is the expected number of days until sale of the item.
//Returns the retail price of the item.

void give_output(double cost, int turnover, double price);
//Precondition: cost is the wholesale cost of one item; turnover is the
//expected time until sale of the item; price is the retail price of the item.
//Postcondition: The values of cost, turnover, and price have been
//written to the screen.

int main()
{
    double wholesale_cost, retail_price;
    int shelf_time;

    introduction();
    get_input(wholesale_cost, shelf_time);
    retail_price = price(wholesale_cost, shelf_time);
    give_output(wholesale_cost, shelf_time, retail_price);
    return 0;
}

//Uses iostream:
void introduction()                            fully tested
{                                              function
    using namespace std;
    cout << "This program determines the retail price for\n"
         << "an item at a Quick-Shop supermarket store.\n";
}
```

Display 4.11 Program with a Stub *(part 2 of 2)*

```
//Uses iostream:
void get_input(double& cost, int& turnover)                          fully tested
{                                                                     function
    using namespace std;
    cout << "Enter the wholesale cost of item $";
    cin >> cost;
    cout << "Enter the expected number of days until sold: ";
    cin >> turnover;
}
                                                        function
//Uses iostream:                                        being tested
void give_output(double cost, int turnover, double price)
{
    using namespace std;
    cout.setf(ios::fixed);
    cout.setf(ios::showpoint);
    cout.precision(2);
    cout << "Wholesale cost = $" << cost << endl
         << "Expected time until sold = "
         << turnover << " days" << endl
         << "Retail price= $" << price << endl;
}

//This is only a stub:                                  stub
double price(double cost, int turnover)
{
    return 9.99; //Not correct, but good enough for some testing.
}
```

Sample Dialogue

```
This program determines the retail price for
an item at a Quick-Shop supermarket store.
Enter the wholesale cost of item: $1.21
Enter the expected number of days until sold: 5
Wholesale cost = $1.21
Expected time until sold = 5 days
Retail price = $9.99
```

18 Write a stub for the function whose prototype is given below. Do not write a whole program, only the stub that would go in a program. Hint: It will be very short.

```
double rain_prob(double pressure, double humidity, double temp);
//Precondition: pressure is the barometric pressure in inches of mercury,
//humidity is the relative humidity as a percent, and
//temp is the temperature in degrees Fahrenheit.
//Returns the probability of rain, which is a number between 0 and 1.
//0 means no chance of rain. 1 means rain is 100% certain.
```

CHAPTER SUMMARY

- All subtasks in a program can be implemented as functions, either as functions that return a value or as *void*-functions.

- A **formal parameter** is a kind of place holder that is filled in with a function **argument** when the function is called. There are two methods of performing this substitution, call-by-value and call-by-reference.

- In the **call-by-value** substitution mechanism, the value of an argument is substituted for its corresponding formal parameter. In the **call-by-reference** substitution mechanism, the argument should be a variable and the entire variable is substituted for the corresponding argument.

- The way to indicate a call-by-reference parameter in a function definition is to attach the ampersand sign & to the type of the formal parameter.

- An argument corresponding to a call-by-value parameter cannot be changed by a function call. An argument corresponding to a call-by-reference parameter can be changed by a function call. If you want a function to change the value of a variable, then you must use a call-by-reference parameter.

- A good way to write a function prototype comment is to use a precondition and a postcondition. The **precondition** states what is assumed to be true when the function is called. The **postcondition** describes the effect of the function call; that is, the postcondition tells what will be true after the function is executed in a situation in which the precondition holds.

- Every function should be tested in a program in which every other function in that program has already been fully tested and debugged.

- A **driver program** is a program that does nothing but test a function.

- A simplified version of a function is called a **stub.** A stub is used in place of a function definition that has not yet been tested (or possibly not even written) so that the rest of the program can be tested.

Answers to Self-Test Exercises

1
```
Hello
Goodbye
One more time:
Hello
End of program.
```

2 Omitting the *return*-statement in the function definition for initialize_screen in Display 4.2 would have absolutely no effect on how the program behaves. The program will compile, run, and behave exactly the same. Similarly, omitting the *return*-statement in the function definition for show_results also will have no effect on how the program behaves. However, if you omit the *return*-statement in the function definition for celsius that will be a serious error that will keep the program from running. The difference is that the functions initialize_screen and show_results are *void*-functions, but celsius is not a *void*-function.

3
```
#include <iostream>
void product_out(int n1, int n2, int n3);
int main( )
{
    using namespace std;
    int num1, num2, num3;
    cout << "Enter three integers: ";
    cin >> num1 >> num2 >> num3;
    product_out(num1, num2, num3);
    return 0;
}
```

```
void product_out(int n1, int n2, int n3)
{
    cout << "The product of the three numbers "
         << n1 << ", " << n2 << ", and "
         << n3 << " is " << (n1*n2*n3) << endl;
}
```

4 These answers are system dependent.

5 A call to a void function followed by a semicolon is a valid statement. Such a call may not be embedded in an expression.

6
```
10 20 30
1 2 3
1 20 3
```

7
```
Enter two integers: 5 10
In reverse order the numbers are: 5 5
```
← *different*

8
```
par1_value in function call = 111
par2_ref in function call = 222
n1 after function call = 1
n2 after function call = 2
```
← *different*

9

```
void zero_both(int& n1, int& n2)
{
    n1 = 0;
    n2 = 0;
}
```

10

```
void add_tax(double tax_rate, double& cost)
{
    cost = cost + ( tax_rate/100.0 )*cost;
}
```

The division by 100 is to convert a percent to a fraction. For example, 10 percent is 10/100.0 or 1/10th of the cost.

11 No, a function definition cannot appear inside the body of another function definition.

12

```
void order(int& n1, int& n2);
//Precondition: The variables n1 and n2 have values.
//Postcondition: The values in n1 and n2 have been ordered
//so that n1 <= n2.
```

13

```
double sqrt(double n);
//Precondition: n >= 0.
//Returns the squareroot of n.
```

You can rewrite the second comment line to the following if you prefer, but the version above is the usual form used for a function that returns a value:

```
//Postcondition: Returns the squareroot of n.
```

14 The fundamental rule for testing functions is that every function should be tested in a program in which every other function in that program has already been fully tested and debugged. This is a good way to test a function because if you follow this rule, then when you find a bug, you will know which function contains the bug.

15 A driver program is a program written for the sole purpose of testing a function.

16

```
#include <iostream>

void introduction();
//Postcondition: Description of program is written on the screen.
int main()
{
    using namespace std;
    introduction();
    cout << "End of test.\n";
    return 0;
}
//Uses iostream:
void introduction()
```

```
{
    using namespace std;
    cout << "This program determines the retail price for\n"
         << "an item at a Quick-Shop supermarket store.\n";
}
```

17 A stub is a simplified version of a function that is used in place of the function so that other functions can be tested.

18

```
//THIS IS JUST A STUB.
double rain_prob(double pressure, double humidity, double temp)
{
    return 0.25; //Not correct, but good enough for some testing.
}
```

Programming Projects

1 Write a program that converts from twenty-four-hour notation to twelve-hour notation. For example, it should convert 14:25 to 2:25 PM. The input is given as two integers. There should be at least three functions, one for input, one to do the conversion, and one for output. Record the AM/PM information as a value of type char, 'A' for AM and 'P' for PM. Thus, the function for doing the conversions will have a call-by-reference formal parameter of type *char* to record whether it is AM or PM. (The function will have other parameters as well.) Include a loop that lets the user repeat this computation for new input values again and again until the user says he or she wants to end the program.

2 Write a function that computes the average and standard deviation of four scores. The standard deviation is defined to be the square root of the average of the four values: $(s_i - a)^2$ where a is average of the four scores s_1, s_2, s_3, and s_4. The function will have six parameters and will call two other functions. Embed the function in a driver program that allows you to test the function again and again until you tell the program you are finished.

3 Write a program that tells what coins to give out for any amount of change from 1 cent to 99 cents. For example, if the amount is 86 cents, the output would be something like the following:

```
86 cents can be given as
3 quarter(s) 1 dime(s) and 1 penny(pennies)
```

Use coin denominations of 25 cents (quarters), 10 cents (dimes), and 1 cent (pennies). Do not use nickel and half-dollar coins. Your program will use the following function (among others):

```
void compute_coin(int coin_value, int& number, int& amount_left);
//Precondition: 0 < coin_value < 100; 0 <= amount_left < 100.
//Postcondition: number has been set equal to the maximum number of coins of
//denomination coin_value cents that can be obtained from amount_left cents.
//amount_left  has been decreased by the value of the coins, i.e.,
//decreased by number*coin_value.
```

For example, suppose the value of the variable amount_left is 86. Then, after the following call, the value of number will be 3 and the value of amount_left will be 11 (because if you take 3 quarters from 86 cents, that leaves 11 cents):

```
 compute_coins(25, number, amount_left);
```

Include a loop that lets the user repeat this computation for new input values until the user says he or she wants to end the program. Hint: Use integer division and the % operator to implement this function.

4   Write a program that will read in a length in feet and inches and will output the equivalent length in meters and centimeters. Use at least three functions: one for input, one or more for calculating, and one for output. Include a loop that lets the user repeat this computation for new input values until the user says he or she wants to end the program. There are 0.3048 meters in a foot, 100 centimeters in a meter, and 12 inches in a foot.

5   Write a program like that of the previous exercise that converts from meters and centimeters into feet and inches. Use functions for the subtasks.

6   (You should do the previous two programming projects before doing this one.) Write a program that combines the functions in the previous two programming projects. The program asks the user if he or she wants to convert from feet and inches to meters and centimeters or from meters and centimeters to feet and inches. The program then performs the desired conversion. Have the user respond by typing the integer 1 for one type of conversion and 2 for the other conversion. The program reads the user's answer and then executes an *if-else*-statement. Each branch of the *if-else*-statements will be a function call. The two functions called in the *if-else*-statement will have function definitions that are very similar to the programs for the

previous two programming projects. Thus, they will be fairly complicated function definitions that call other functions in their function bodies. Include a loop that lets the user repeat this computation for new input values until the user says he or she wants to end the program.

7   Write a program that will read in a weight in pounds and ounces and will output the equivalent weight in kilograms and grams. Use at least three functions: one for input, one or more for calculating, and one for output. Include a loop that lets the user repeat this computation for new input values until the user says he or she wants to end the program. There are 2.2046 pounds in a kilogram, 1000 grams in a kilogram, and 16 ounces in a pound.

8   Write a program like that of the previous exercise that converts from kilograms and grams into pounds and ounces. Use functions for the subtasks.

9   (You should do the previous two programming projects before doing this one.) Write a program that combines the functions of the previous two programming projects. The program asks the user if he or she wants to convert from pounds and ounces to kilograms and grams or from kilograms and grams to pounds and ounces. The program then performs the desired conversion. Have the user respond by typing the integer 1 for one type of conversion and 2 for the other. The program reads the user's answer and then executes an *if-else*-statement. Each branch of the *if-else*-statement will be a function call. The two functions called in the *if-else*-statement will have function definitions that are very similar to the programs for the previous two programming projects. Thus, they will be fairly complicated function definitions that call other functions in their function bodies. Include a loop that lets the user repeat this computation for new input values until the user says he or she wants to end the program.

10   (You need to do programming projects 6 and 9 before doing this programming project.) Write a program that combines the functions of programming projects 6 and 9. The program asks the user if he or she wants to convert lengths or weights. If the user chooses lengths, then the program asks the user if he or she wants to convert from feet and inches to meters and centimeters or from meters and centimeters to feet and inches. If the user chooses weights, a similar question about pounds, ounces, kilograms, and grams is asked. The program then performs the desired conversion. Have the user respond by typing the integer 1 for one type of conversion and 2 for the other. The program reads the user's answer and then executes an *if-else*-statement. Each branch of the *if-else*-statement will be a function call. The two functions called in the *if-else*-statement will have function defi-

nitions that are very similar to the programs for programming projects 6 and 9. Thus, these functions will be fairly complicated function definitions that call other functions in their function bodies; however, they will be very easy to write by adapting the programs you wrote for programming projects 6 and 9. Notice that your program will have *if-else*-statements embedded inside of *if-else*-statements, but only in an indirect way. The outer *if-else*-statement will include two function calls as its two branches. These two function calls will each in turn include an *if-else*-statement, but you need not think about that. They are just function calls and the details are in a black box that you create when you define these functions. If you try to create a four-way branch, you are probably on the wrong track. You should only need to think about two-way branches (even though the entire program does ultimately branch into four cases). Include a loop that lets the user repeat this computation for new input values until the user says he or she wants to end the program.

11　The area of an arbitrary triangle can be computed using the formula

$$area = \sqrt{s(s-a)(s-b)(s-c)}$$

where *a*, *b*, and *c* are the lengths of the sides, and *s* is the semiperimeter.

$$s = (a+b+c)/2$$

Write a *void* function that uses five parameters: three value parameters that provide the lengths of the edges, and computes the area and perimeter *(not the semiperimeter)* via reference parameters. Make your function robust. Note that not all combinations of *a*, *b*, and *c* produce a triangle. Your function should produce correct results for legal data and reasonable results for illegal combinations.

12　In cold weather, meteorologists report an index called the *wind chill factor,* that takes into account the wind speed and the temperature. The index provides a measure of the chilling effect of wind at a given air temperature. Wind chill may be approximated by the formula:

$$W = 33 - \frac{(10\sqrt{v} - v + 10.5)(33 - t)}{23.1}$$

where

v = wind speed in m/sec
t = temperature in degrees Celsius: $t <= 10$
W = wind chill index (in degrees Celsius)

Write a function that returns the wind chill index. Your code should ensure that the restriction on the temperature is not violated. Look up some weather reports in back issues of a newspaper in your university library and compare the wind chill index you calculate with the result reported in the newspaper.

CHAPTER 5

I/O Streams as an Introduction to Objects and Classes

5 I/O Streams as an Introduction to Objects and Classes

Fish say, they have their stream and pond;
  But is there anything beyond?

RUPERT BROOKE, HEAVEN (1913)

As a leaf is carried by a stream, whether the stream ends in a lake or in the sea, so
  too is the output of your program carried by a stream not knowing if the stream
  goes to the screen or to a file.

WASHROOM WALL OF A
COMPUTER SCIENCE DEPARTMENT (1995)

I/O refers to program input and output. Input can be taken from the keyboard or from a file. Similarly, output can be sent to the screen or to a file. In this chapter we explain how you can write your programs to take input from a file and send output to another file.

Input is delivered to your program via a C++ construct known as a *stream*, and output from your program is delivered to the output device via a stream. Streams are our first examples of *objects*. An object is a special kind of variable that has its own special-purpose functions that are, in a sense, attached to the variable. The ability to handle objects is one of the language features that sets C++ apart from earlier programming languages. In this chapter we tell you what streams are and explain how to use them for program I/O. In the process of explaining streams we will introduce you to the basic ideas about what objects are and about how objects are used in a program.

5.1 Streams and Basic File I/O

Good Heavens! For more than forty years I have been speaking prose without
  knowing it.

MOLIÈRE, LE BOURGEOIS GENTILHOMME

files

You are already using files to store your programs. You can also use files to store input for a program or to receive output from a program. The files used for program

I/O are the same kind of files as you use to store your programs. Streams, which we discuss next, allow you to write programs that handle file input and keyboard input in a unified way and that handle file output and screen output in a unified way.

A **stream** is a flow of characters (or other kind of data). If the flow is into your program, the stream is called an **input stream.** If the flow is out of your program, the stream is called an **output stream.** If the input stream flows from the keyboard, then your program will take input from the keyboard. If the input stream flows from a file, then your program will take its input from that file. Similarly, an output stream can go to the screen or to a file.

stream
input stream
output stream

Although you may not realize it, you have already been using streams in your programs. The `cin` that you have already used is an input stream connected to the keyboard and `cout` is an output stream connected to the screen. These two streams are automatically available to your program, as long as it has an `include` directive that names the header file `iostream`. You can define other streams that come from or go to files; once you have defined them, you can use them in your program in the same way you use the streams `cin` and `cout`. For example, suppose your program defines a stream called `in_stream` that comes from some file. (We'll tell you how to define it shortly.) You can then fill an `int` variable named `the_number` with a number from this file by using the following in your program:

`cin` *and* `cout`
are streams.

```
int the_number;
in_stream >> the_number;
```

Similarly, if your program defines an output stream, named `out_stream`, that goes to another file, then you can output the value of this variable to this other file. The following will output the string `"the_number is "` followed by the contents of the variable `the_number` to the output file that is connected to the stream `out_stream`.

```
out_stream << "the_number is " << the_number << endl;
```

Once the streams are connected to the desired files, your program can do file I/O the same way it does I/O using the keyboard and screen.

Why Use Files for I/O?

The keyboard input and screen output we have used so far deal with temporary data. When the program ends, the data typed in at the keyboard and the data left on the screen go away. Files provide you with a way to store data permanently. The contents of a file remain until a person or program changes the file. If your program sends its output to a file, the output file will remain after the program has finished running. An input file can be used over and over again by many programs without the need to type in the data separately for each program.

permanent storage

The input and output files used by your program are the same kind of files that you read and write with an editor, such as the editor you use to write your programs. This means you can create an input file for your program or read an output file produced by your program whenever it's convenient for you, as opposed to having to do all your reading and writing while the program is running.

Files also provide you with a convenient way to deal with large quantities of data. When your program takes its input from a large input file, your program receives a lot of data without making the user do a lot of typing.

File I/O

reading and writing

When your program takes input from a file it is said to be **reading** from the file and when your program sends output to a file it is said to be **writing** to the file. There are other ways of reading input from a file, but the method we will use reads the file from the beginning to the end (or as far as the program gets before ending). Using this method, your program is not allowed to back up and read anything in the file a second time. This is exactly what happens when your program takes input from the keyboard so this should not seem new or strange. (As we will see, your program can reread a file starting from the beginning of the file, but this is "starting over," not "backing up.") Similarly, for the method we present here, your program writes output into a file starting at the beginning of the file and proceeding forward. Your program is not allowed to backup and change any output that it has previously written to the file. This is exactly what happens when your program sends output to the screen; you can send more output to the screen, but you cannot backup and change the screen output. The way that you get input from a file into your program or send output from your program into a file is to connect your program to the file by means of a stream.

A stream is a variable

In C++, a **stream** is a special kind of variable known as an *object*. We will discuss objects in the next section, but we will first describe how your program can use stream objects to do simple file I/O. If you want to use a stream to get input from a file (or give output to a file) you must declare the stream, and you must connect the stream to the file.

You can think of the file that a stream is connected to as the value of the stream. You can disconnect a stream from one file and connect it to another file, so you can change the value of these stream variables. However, you must use special functions that apply only to streams in order to perform these changes. You *cannot* use a stream variable in an assignment statement the way that you can use a variable of type *int* or *char*. Although streams are variables, they are unusual sorts of variables.

declaring streams

The streams `cin` and `cout` are already declared for you, but if you want a stream to connect to a file, you must declare it just as you would declare any other variable. The type for input-file stream variables is named `ifstream` (for "input-file stream"). The type for output-file stream variables is named `ofstream` (for "output-file stream"). Thus, you can declare `in_stream` to be an input stream for a file and `out_stream` to be an output stream for another file as follows:

`ifstream` *and* `ofstream`

```
ifstream in_stream;
ofstream out_stream;
```

The types `ifstream` and `ofstream` are defined in the library with the header file `fstream` and so any program that declares stream variables in this way must contain the following directive:

`fstream`

```
#include <fstream>
```

Stream variables, such as `in_stream` and `out_stream` declared above, must each be **connected to** a file. This is called **opening the file** and is done with a function named `open`. For example, suppose you want the input stream `in_stream` connected to the file named `infile.dat`. Your program must then contain the following before it reads any input from this file:

connecting a stream to a file

open

```
in_stream.open("infile.dat");
```

This may seem like rather strange syntax for a function call. We will have more to say about this peculiar syntax in the next section. For now, just notice a couple of details about how this call to `open` is written. First, the stream variable name and a dot (i.e., a period) is placed before the function named `open`, and the file name is given as an argument to `open`. Also notice that the file name is given in quotes. The file name that is given as an argument is the same as the name you would use for the file if you wanted to write in it using the editor. If the input file is in the same directory as your program, you probably can simply give the name of the file in the manner we described. In some situations you might also need to specify the directory that contains the file. The details about specifying directories varies from one system to another. If you need to specify a directory, ask your instructor or some other local expert to explain the details.

file name

Once you have declared an input stream variable and connected it to a file using the `open` function, your program can take input from the file using the extraction operator `>>`. For example, the following reads two input numbers from the file connected to `in_stream`, and places them in the variables `one_number` and `another_number`:

```
int one_number, another_number;
in_stream >> one_number >> another_number;
```

An output stream is opened (i.e., connected to a file) in the same way as what we just described for input streams. For example, the following declares the output stream `out_stream` and connects it to the file name `outfile.dat`:

```
ofstream out_stream;
out_stream.open("outfile.dat");
```

When used with a stream of type `ofstream`, the member function `open` will create the output file if it does not already exist. If the output file does already exist, the member function `open` will discard the contents of the file, so that the output file is empty after the call to `open`. (There are other ways to open a file, but we will not discuss them in this book.)

After a file is connected to the stream `out_stream` with a call to `open`, the program can send output to that file using the insertion operator `<<`. For example, the following writes two strings and the contents of the variables `one_number` and `another_number` to the file which is connected to the stream `out_stream` (which in this example is the file named `outfile.dat`):

```
out_stream << "one_number = " << one_number
           << " another_number = " << another_number;
```

external file name

Notice that when your program is dealing with a file, it is as if the file had two names. One is the usual name for the file that is used by the operating system. This name is called the **external file name.** In our sample code the external file names were `infile.dat` and `outfile.dat`. The external file name is in some sense the "real name" for the file.[1] The conventions for spelling these external file names vary from one system to another; you will need to learn these conventions from your instructor or from some other local expert. The names `infile.dat` and `outfile.dat` which we used in our examples may or may not look like file names on your system. You should name your files following whatever conventions are used on your system. Although the external file name is the real name for the file, it is typ-

external file name only used once

ically used only once in a program. The external file name is given as an argument to the function `open`, but *after the file is opened, the file is always referred to by naming the stream that is connected to the file.* Thus, within your program, the stream name serves as a second name for the file.

The sample program in Display 5.1 reads three numbers from one file and writes their sum, as well as some text, to another file.

---

[1] The external file name is "real" in the sense that this name, and the file, may exist preceding the start of the program and may continue after the program terminates. The program's stream name must follow rules for C++ identifiers. That is why C++ does not use the external name in the program; the use of dot and extension in names would conflict with the use of dot to call object member functions.

A File Has Two Names

Every input and every output file used by your program has two names. The **external file** name is the real name of the file, but it is used only in the call to the function open, which connects the file to a stream. After the call to open, you always use the stream name as the name of the file.

Every file should be **closed** when your program is finished getting input from the file or sending output to the file. Closing a file disconnects the stream from the file. A file is closed with a call to the function close. The following lines from the program in Display 5.1 illustrate how to use the function close:

close

```
in_stream.close( );
out_stream.close( );
```

Notice that the function close takes no arguments. If your program ends normally but without closing a file, the system will automatically close the file for you. However, it is good to get in the habit of closing files for at least two reasons. First, the system will only close files for you if your program ends in a normal fashion. If your program ends abnormally due to an error, the file will not be closed and may be left in a corrupted state. If your program closes files as soon as it is finished with them, file corruption is less likely. A second reason for closing a file is that you may want your program to send output to a file and later read that output back into the program. To do this, your program should close the file after it is finished writing to the file, and then your program should connect the file to an input stream using the function open. (It is possible to open a file for both input and output, but this is done in a slightly different way and we will not be discussing this alternative.)

Introduction to Classes and Objects

The streams in_stream and out_stream discussed in the last section and the predefined streams cin and cout are objects. An **object** is a variable that has functions as well as data associated with it. For example, the streams in_stream and out_stream both have a function named open associated with them. Two sample calls of these functions, along with the declarations of the objects in_stream and out_stream, are given below:

object

```
ifstream in_stream;
ofstream out_stream;
in_stream.open("infile.dat");
out_stream.open("outfile.dat");
```

Display 5.1 Simple File Input/Output

```
//Reads three numbers from the file infile.dat, sums the numbers,
//and writes the sum to the file outfile.dat.
//(A better version of this program will be given in Display 5.2.)
#include <fstream>

int main( )
{
    using namespace std;
    ifstream in_stream;
    ofstream out_stream;

    in_stream.open("infile.dat");
    out_stream.open("outfile.dat");

    int first, second, third;
    in_stream >> first >> second >> third;
    out_stream << "The sum of the first 3\n"
               << "numbers in infile.dat\n"
               << "is " << (first + second + third)
               << endl;

    in_stream.close( );
    out_stream.close( );

    return 0;
}
```

infile.dat (Not changed by program.)	**outfile.dat** (After program is run.)
1 2 3 4	The sum of the first 3 numbers in infile.dat is 6

Sample Dialogue

There is no output to the screen
and no input from the keyboard.

There is a reason for this peculiar notation. The function named `open` that is associated with the object `in_stream` is a different function from the function named `open` that is associated with the object `out_stream`. One function opens a file for input and the other opens a file for output. Of course these two functions are similar. They both "open files." When we give two functions the same name it is because the two functions have some intuitive similarity. However, these two functions named `open` are different functions, even if they may be only slightly different. When the compiler sees a call to a function named `open`, it must decide which of these two functions named `open` you mean. The compiler determines which of these two functions you mean by looking at the name of the object that precedes the dot, in this case, either `in_stream` or `out_stream`. A function that is associated with an object is called a **member function.** So, for example, `open` is a member function of the object `in_stream` and another function named `open` is a member of the object `out_stream`.

member function

As we have just seen, different objects can have different member functions. These functions may have the same names, as was true of the functions named `open`, or they may have completely different names. The type of an object determines which member functions the object has. If two objects are of the same type, they may have different values, but they will have the same member functions. For example, suppose you declare the following stream objects:

```
ifstream in_stream, in_stream2;
ofstream out_stream, out_stream2;
```

The functions `in_stream.open` and `in_stream2.open` are the same function. Similarly, `out_stream.open` and `out_stream2.open` are the same function (but they are different from the functions `in_stream.open` and `in_stream2.open`). A type whose variables are objects—such as `ifstream` and `ofstream`—is called a **class.** Since the member functions for an object are completely determined by its class (i.e., by its type), these functions are called *member functions of the class* (as well as being called *members of the object*). For example, the class `ifstream` has a member function called `open` and the class `ofstream` has a different member function called `open`. The class `ofstream` also has a member function named `precision`, but the class `ifstream` has no member function named `precision`. You have already been using the member function `precision` with the stream `cout`, but we will discuss it in more detail later.

class

When you call a member function in a program, you always specify an object, usually by writing the object name and a dot before the function name, as in the following example:

calling a member function

```
in_stream.open("infile.dat");
```

One reason for naming the object is that the function can have some effect on the object. In the preceding example, the call to the function `open` connects the file `infile.dat` to the stream `in_stream`, so it needs to know the name of this stream.

In a function call, such as

```
in_stream.open("infile.dat");
```

dot operator
calling object

the dot is called the **dot operator** and the object named before the dot is referred to as the **calling object.** In some ways the calling object is like an additional argument to the function—the function can change the calling object as if it were an argument—but the calling object plays an even larger role in the function call. The calling object determines the meaning of the function name. The compiler uses the type of the calling object to determine the meaning of the function name. For example, in the above call to `open`, the type of the object `in_stream` determines the meaning of the function name `open`.

Classes and Objects

An **object** is a variable that has functions associated with it. These functions are called **member functions.** A **class** is a type whose variables are objects. The object's class (i.e., the type of the object) determines which member functions the object has.

Calling a Member Function

Syntax: *dot operator*

Calling_Object . Member_Function_Name (Argument_List) ;

Examples:

```
in_stream.open("infile.dat");
out_stream.open("outfile.dat");
out_stream.precision(2);
```

The meaning of the *Member_Function_Name* is determined by the class of (i.e., the type of) the *Calling_Object*.

The function name `close` is analogous to `open`. The classes `ifstream` and `ofstream` each have a member function named `close`. They both "close files" but they close them in different ways, because the files were opened in different ways and because the files were manipulated in different ways. We will be discussing more member functions for the classes `ifstream` and `ofstream` later in this chapter.

Polymorphism

As we noted in Chapter 3, the use of the same function name to mean different things is called **polymorphism.** Overloading a function name was our first example of polymorphism. We will see other examples in Chapter 13 on Templates and in Chapter 15 on Inheritance.

⤳ *PROGRAMMING* TIP
Check that a File Was
Opened Successfully

A call to `open` can be unsuccessful for a number of reasons. For example, if you open an input file and there is no file with the external name that you specify, then the call to `open` will fail. When this happens, you may not receive an error message and your program may simply proceed to do something unexpected. Thus, you should always follow a call to `open` with a test to see whether the call to `open` was successful, and to end the program (or take some other appropriate action) if the call to `open` was unsuccessful.

You can use the member function named `fail` to test whether or not a stream operation has failed. There is a member function named `fail` for each of the classes `ifstream` and `ofstream`. The `fail` function takes no arguments and returns a `bool` value. A call to the function `fail` for a stream named `in_stream` would be as follows:

the member function `fail`

```
in_stream.fail( )
```

This is a Boolean expression that can be used to control a *while*-loop or an *if-else*-statement.

You should place a call to `fail` immediately after each call to `open`; if the call to `open` fails, the function `fail` will return *true* (i.e., the Boolean expression will be satisfied). For example, if the following call to `open` fails, then the program will output an error message and end; if the call succeeds, the `fail` function returns `false`, so the program will continue.

```
in_stream.open("stuff.dat");
if (in_stream.fail( ))
{
    cout << "Input file opening failed.\n";
    exit(1);  ◄─────────  Ends the program
}
```

`fail` is a member function, so it is called using the stream name and a dot. Of
course, the call to `in_stream.fail` refers only to a call to `open` of the form
`in_stream.open`, and not to any call to the function `open` made with any other
stream as the calling object.

exit

The `exit`-statement shown above has nothing to do with classes and has nothing directly to do with streams, but it is often used in this context. The `exit`-state-
ment causes your program to end immediately. The `exit` function returns its
argument to the operating system. To use the `exit`-statement, your program must
contain the following `include` directive:

```
#include <cstdlib>
```

`exit` is a predefined function that takes a single integer argument. By convention, 1
is used as the argument if the call to `exit` was due to an error and 0 is used otherwise.[2] For our purposes, it makes no difference what integer you use, but it pays to
follow this convention since it is important in more advanced programming.

The `exit`-Statement

The `exit`-statement is written

```
exit(Integer_Value);
```

When the `exit`-statement is executed, the program ends immediately. Any
Integer_Value may be used, but by convention, 1 is used for a call to `exit` that is
caused by an error, and 0 is used in other cases. The `exit`-statement is a call to
the function `exit`, which is in the library with header file named `cstdlib`.
Therefore, any program that uses the `exit`-statement must contain the following
`include` directive:

```
#include <cstdlib>
```

Display 5.2 contains the program from Display 5.1 rewritten to include tests to
see if the input and output files were opened successfully. It processes files in exactly
the same way as the program in Display 5.1. In particular, assuming that the file

---

[2]Unix, MSDOS, and Windows use 1 for error, and 0 for success, whereas Digital's VMS reverses
this convention. You should ask your instructor what values to use.

Display 5.2 File I/O with Checks on open

```cpp
//Reads three numbers from the file infile.dat, sums the numbers,
//and writes the sum to the file outfile.dat.
#include <fstream>
#include <iostream>
#include <cstdlib>

int main( )
{
    using namespace std;
    ifstream in_stream;
    ofstream out_stream;

    in_stream.open("infile.dat");
    if (in_stream.fail( ))
    {
        cout << "Input file opening failed.\n";
        exit(1);
    }

    out_stream.open("outfile.dat");
    if (out_stream.fail( ))
    {
        cout << "Output file opening failed.\n";
        exit(1);
    }

    int first, second, third;
    in_stream >> first >> second >> third;
    out_stream << "The sum of the first 3\n"
               << "numbers in infile.dat\n"
               << "is " << (first + second + third)
               << endl;

    in_stream.close( );
    out_stream.close( );

    return 0;
}
```

Screen Output (If the file infile.dat **does not exist)**

```
Input file opening failed.
```

infile.dat exists and has the contents shown in Display 5.1, the program in Display 5.2 will create the file outfile.dat that is shown in Display 5.1. However, if there were something wrong and one of the calls to open failed, then the program in Display 5.2 would end and send an appropriate error message to the screen. For example, if there were no file named infile.dat, then the call to in_stream.open would fail, the program would end, and an error message would be written to the screen. Notice that we used cout to output the error message; this is because we want the error message to go to the screen, as opposed to going to a file. Since this program uses cout to output to the screen (as well as doing file I/O), we have added an include directive for the header file iostream. (Actually, your program does not need to have #include <iostream> when your program has #include <fstream>, but it causes no problems to include it, and it reminds you that the program is using screen output in addition to file I/O.)

Techniques for File I/O

As we already noted, the operators >> and << work the same for streams connected to files as they do for cin and cout. However, the programming style for file I/O is different from that for I/O using the screen and keyboard. When reading input from the keyboard you should prompt for input and echo the input, like thus:

```
cout << "Enter the number: ";
cin >> the_number;
cout << "The number you entered is " << the_number;
```

When your program takes its input from a file, you should not include such prompt lines or echoing of input, because there is nobody there to read and respond to the prompt and echo. When reading input from a file, you must be certain the data in the file is exactly the kind of data the program expects. Your program then simply reads the input file assuming that the data it needs will be there when it is requested. If in_file is a stream variable that is connected to an input file and you wish to replace the above keyboard/screen I/O with input from the file connected to in_file, then the above three lines would be replaced by the following line:

```
in_file >> the_number;
```

You may have any number of streams opened for input or for output. Thus, a single program can take input from the keyboard and also take input from one or more files. The same program could send output to the screen and to one or more files. Alternatively, a program could take all of its input from the keyboard and send output to both the screen and a file. Any combination of input and output streams is allowed. Most of the examples in this book will use cin and cout to do I/O using the keyboard and screen, but it is easy to modify these programs so that the program takes its input from a file and/or sends its output to a file.

Summary of File I/O Statements

In this sample the input comes from a file with the directory name `infile.dat` and the output goes to a file with the directory name `outfile.dat`.

- Place the following `include` directives in your program file:

  ```
  #include <fstream>   ←——————— for file I/O
  #include <iostream>  ←——————— for cout
  #include <cstdlib>   ←——— for exit
  ```

- Choose a stream name for the input stream, for example `in_stream`, and declare it to be a variable of type `ifstream`. Choose a stream name for the output file, for example `out_stream`, and declare it to be of type `ofstream`:

  ```
  using namespace std;
  ifstream in_stream;
  ofstream out_stream;
  ```

- Connect each stream to a file using the member function `open` with the external file name as an argument. Remember to use the member function `fail` to test that the call to open was successful:

  ```
  in_stream.open("infile.dat");
  if (in_stream.fail( ))
  {
      cout << "Input file opening failed.\n";
      exit(1);
  }

  out_stream.open("outfile.dat");
  if (out_stream.fail( ))
  {
      cout << "Output file opening failed.\n";
      exit(1);
  }
  ```

- Use the stream `in_stream` to get input from the file `infile.dat` just like you use `cin` to get input from the keyboard. For example:

  ```
  in_stream >> some_variable >> some_other_variable;
  ```

- Use the stream `out_stream` to send output to the file `outfile.dat` just like you use `cout` to send output to the screen. For example:

  ```
  out_stream << "some_variable = "
             << some_variable << endl;
  ```

- Close the streams using the function `close`:

  ```
  in_stream.close( );
  out_stream.close( );
  ```

SELF-TEST EXERCISES

1   Suppose you are writing a program that uses a stream called fin which will be connected to an input file and a stream called fout which will be connected to an output file. How do you declare fin and fout? What include directive, if any, do you need to place in your program file?

2   Suppose you are continuing to write the program discussed in the previous exercise and you want your program to take its input from the file stuff1.dat and send its output to the file stuff2.dat. What statements do you need to place in your program in order to connect the stream fin to the file stuff1.dat and to connect the stream fout to the file stuff2.dat? Be sure to include checks to make sure that the openings were successful.

3   Suppose that you are still writing the same program that we discussed in the previous two exercises and you reach the point that you no longer need to get input from the file stuff1.dat and no longer need to send output to the file stuff2.dat. How do you close these files?

4   Suppose you want to change the program in Display 5.1 so that it sends its output to the screen instead of the file outfile.dat. (The input should still come from the file infile1.dat.) What changes do you need to make to the program?

5   What include directive do you need to place in your program file if your program uses the function exit?

6   Suppose bla is an object, dobedo is a member function of the object bla, and dobedo takes one argument of type *int*. How do you write a call to the member function dobedo of the object bla using the argument 7?

7   Continuing question 5, what does exit(1) do with its argument?

8   What characteristics of files do ordinary program variables share? What characteristics of files are different from ordinary variables in a program?

9   Name at least three member functions associated with an iostream object, and give examples of usage of each.

10 A programmer has read half of the lines in a file. What must the programmer do to the file to enable reading the first line a second time?

File Names as Input *(Optional)*

Thus far, we have written the literal file names for our input and output files into the code of our programs. We did this by giving the file name as the argument to a call to the function `open`, as in the following example:

```
in_stream.open("infile.dat");
```

This can sometimes be inconvenient. For example, the program in Display 5.2 reads numbers from the file `infile.dat` and outputs their sum to the file `outfile.dat`. If you want to perform the same calculation on the numbers in another file named `infile2.dat` and write the sum of these numbers to another file named `outfile2.dat`, then you must change the file names in the two calls to the member function `open` and then recompile your program. A preferable alternative is to write your program so that it asks the user to type in the names of the input and/or output files. This way your program can use different files each time it is run.

A file name is a *string* and we will not discuss string handling in detail until Chapter 10. However, it is easy to learn enough about strings so that you can write programs that accept a file name as input. A **string** is just a sequence of characters. We have already used string values in output statements such as the following:

string

```
cout << "This is a string.";
```

We have also used string values as arguments to the member function `open`. Whenever you write a literal string, as in the `cout`-statement above, you must place the string in double quotes.

In order to read a file name into your program, you will need a variable that is capable of holding a string. A variable to hold a string value is declared as in the following example:

string variable

```
char file_name[16];
```

This declaration is the same as if you had declared the variable to be of type *char*, except that the variable name is followed by an integer in square brackets that specifies the maximum number of characters you can have in a string stored in the variable. As it turns out, this number must be *one larger than the maximum number of characters in the string value*. So, in our example, the variable `file_name` can contain any string that contains 15 or fewer characters. The name `file_name` can be replaced by any other identifier (that is not a keyword), and the number 16 can be replaced by any other positive integer.

You can input a string value to a string variable the same way that you input values of other types. For example, consider the following piece of code:

string input

```
cout << "Enter the file name (maximum of 15 characters):\n";
cin >> file_name;
cout << "OK, I will edit the file " << file_name << endl;
```

A possible dialogue for this code is:

```
Enter the file name (maximum of 15 characters):
myfile.dat
OK, I will edit the file myfile.dat
```

string variables as arguments to open

Once your program has read the name of a file into a string variable, such as the variable `file_name`, it can use this string variable as the argument to the member function `open`. For example, the following will connect the input-file stream `in_stream` to the file whose name is stored in the variable `file_name` (and will use the member function `fail` to check that the opening was successful):

```
ifstream in_stream;
in_stream.open(file_name);
if (in_stream.fail( ))
{
    cout << "Input file opening failed.\n";
    exit(1);
}
```

Note that when you use a string variable as an argument to the member function `open`, you do not use any quotes.

In Display 5.3 we have rewritten the program in Display 5.2 so that it takes its input from and sends its output to whatever files the user specifies. The input and output file names are read into the string variables `in_file_name` and `out_file_name` and then these variables are used as the arguments in calls to the member function `open`. Notice the declaration of the string variables. You must include a number in square brackets after each string variable name, as we did in Display 5.3.

Warning!

String variables are not ordinary variables and cannot be used in all the ways you can use ordinary variables. In particular, you cannot use an assignment statement to change the value of a string variable.[3]

5.2 Tools for Stream I/O

> *You shall see them on a beautiful quarto page, where a neat rivulet of text shall meander through a meadow of margin.*
>
> RICHARD BRINSLEY SHERIDAN, THE SCHOOL FOR SCANDAL

---

[3]There are two generalizations of these strings: arrays of any type, which we will study in Chapter 9, and the string class which we will study in Chapter 10.

Display 5.3 Inputting a File Name (Optional) *(part 1 of 2)*

```cpp
//Reads three numbers from the file specified by the user, sums the numbers,
//and writes the sum to another file specified by the user.
#include <fstream>
#include <iostream>
#include <cstdlib>

int main( )
{
    using namespace std;
    char in_file_name[16], out_file_name[16];
    ifstream in_stream;
    ofstream out_stream;

    cout << "I will sum three numbers taken from an input\n"
         << "file and write the sum to an output file.\n";
    cout << "Enter the input file name (maximum of 15 characters):\n";
    cin >> in_file_name;
    cout << "Enter the output file name (maximum of 15 characters):\n";
    cin >> out_file_name;
    cout << "I will read numbers from the file "
         << in_file_name << " and\n"
         << "place the sum in the file "
         << out_file_name << endl;

    in_stream.open(in_file_name);
    if (in_stream.fail( ))
    {
        cout << "Input file opening failed.\n";
        exit(1);
    }

    out_stream.open(out_file_name);
    if (out_stream.fail( ))
    {
        cout << "Output file opening failed.\n";
        exit(1);
    }
```

Display 5.3 Inputting a File Name (Optional) *(part 2 of 2)*

```
    int first, second, third;
    in_stream >> first >> second >> third;
    out_stream << "The sum of the first 3\n"
               << "numbers in " << in_file_name << endl
               << "is " << (first + second + third)
               << endl;

    in_stream.close( );
    out_stream.close( );

    cout << "End of Program.\n";
    return 0;
}
```

numbers.dat
(Not changed by program.)

```
1
2
3
4
```

sum.dat
(After program is run.)

```
The sum of the first 3
numbers in numbers.dat
is 6
```

Sample Dialogue

```
I will sum three numbers taken from an input
file and write the sum to an output file.
Enter the input file name (maximum of 15 characters):
numbers.dat
Enter the output file name (maximum of 15 characters):
sum.dat
I will read numbers from the file numbers.dat and
place the sum in the file sum.dat
End of Program.
```

Formatting Output with Stream Functions

The layout of a program's output is called the **format** of the output. In C++ you can
control the format with commands that determine such details as the number of
spaces between items and the number of digits after the decimal point. You already
used three output formatting instructions when you learned the formula for outputting dollar amounts of money in the usual way with two digits after the decimal
point (and not in e-notation). Before outputting amounts of money, you inserted the
following "magic formula" into your program:

```
cout.setf(ios::fixed);
cout.setf(ios::showpoint);
cout.precision(2);
```

format

Now that we know about object notation for streams we can explain this magic formula and a few other formatting commands.

The first thing to note is that you can use these formatting commands on any
output stream. If your program is sending output to a file that is connected to an output stream called out_stream, you can use these same commands to ensure that
numbers with a decimal point will be written in the way we normally write amounts
of money. Just insert the following in your program:

```
out_stream.setf(ios::fixed);
out_stream.setf(ios::showpoint);
out_stream.precision(2);
```

To explain this magic formula, we will consider the instructions in reverse order.

Every output stream has a member function named precision. When your program executes a call to precision such as the one above for the stream out_stream,
then from that point on in your program, any number with a decimal point that is output to that stream will be written with a total of two significant figures, or with two digits after the decimal point depending on when your compiler was written. The
following is some possible output from a compiler that sets two significant digits:

precision

    23.   2.2e7   2.2   6.9e-1   0.00069

The following is some possible output from a compiler that sets two digits after the
decimal point:

    23.56   2.26e7   2.21   0.69   0.69e-4

In this book, we assume the compiler sets two digits after the decimal point.

A call to precision applies only to the stream named in the call. If your program has another output stream named out_stream_two, then the call to
out_stream.precision affects the output to the stream out_stream, but has no
effect on the stream out_stream_two. Of course, you can also call precision with

the stream `out_stream_two`; you can even specify a different number of digits for the numbers output to the stream `out_stream_two`, as in the following:

```
out_stream_two.precision(3);
```

The other formatting instructions in our magic formula are a bit more complicated than the member function `precision`, and are necessary to guarantee that our desired two digits will appear after the decimal place on all systems. Below are two calls to the member function `setf` with the stream `out_stream` as the calling object:

```
out_stream.setf(ios::fixed);
out_stream.setf(ios::showpoint);
```

setf   `setf` is an abbreviation for *set flags*. A **flag** is an instruction to do something in one of two possible ways. If a flag is given as an argument to `setf`, then the flag tells the computer to write output to that stream in some specific way. What it causes the stream to do depends on the flag.

In the above example, there are two calls to the function `setf` and these two calls set the two flags `ios::fixed` and `ios::showpoint`. The flag `ios::fixed` causes the stream to output numbers of type *double* in what is called **fixed-point notation,** which is a fancy phrase for the way we normally write numbers. If the flag `ios::fixed` is set (by a call to `setf`), then all floating point numbers (such as numbers of type *double*) that are output to that stream will be written in ordinary everyday notation, rather than e-notation.

ios::showpoint   The flag `ios::showpoint` tells the stream to always include a decimal point in floating point numbers, such as numbers of type *double*. So if the number to be output has a value of 2.0, then it will be output as 2.0 and not simply as 2; that is, the output will include the decimal point even if all the digits after the decimal point are 0. Some common flags and the actions they cause are described in Display 5.4.

ios::showpos   Another useful flag is `ios::showpos`. If this flag is set for a stream, then positive numbers output to that stream will be written with the plus sign in front of them. If you want a plus sign to appear before positive numbers, insert the following:

```
cout.setf(ios::showpos);
```

Minus signs appear before negative numbers without setting any flags.

width   One very commonly used formatting function is `width`. For example, consider the following call to `width` made by the stream `cout`:

```
cout << "Start Now";
cout.width(4);
cout << 7 << endl;
```

This code will cause the following line to appear on the screen

```
Start Now    7
```

This output has exactly three spaces between the letter 'w' and the number 7. The width function tells the stream how many spaces to use when giving an item as output. In this case the item, namely the number 7, occupies only one space and width said to use 4 spaces, so 3 of the spaces are blank. If the output requires more space than you specified in the argument to width, then as much additional space as is needed will be used. The entire item is always output, no matter what argument you give to width.

A call to width applies only to the next item that is output. If you want to output twelve numbers, using 4 spaces to output each number, then you must call width twelve times. If this becomes a nuisance, you may prefer to use the manipulator setw that is described in the next subsection.

Display 5.4 Formatting Flags for setf

Flag	Meaning	Default
ios::fixed	If this flag is set, floating point numbers are not written in e-notation. (Setting this flag automatically unsets the flag ios::scientific.)	not set
ios::scientific	If this flag is set, floating point numbers are written in e-notation. (Setting this flag automatically unsets the flag ios::fixed.) If neither ios::fixed nor ios::scientific is set, then the system decides how to output each number.	not set
ios::showpoint	If this flag is set, a decimal point and trailing zeros are always shown for floating-point numbers. If it is not set, a number with all zeros after the decimal point might be output without the decimal point and following zeros.	not set
ios::showpos	If this flag is set, a plus sign is output before positive integer values.	not set

Display 5.4 Formatting Flags for `setf`

`ios::right`	If this flag is set and some field-width value is given with a call to the member function `width`, then the next item output will be at the right end of the space specified by `width`. In other words, any extra blanks are placed before the item output. (Setting this flag automatically unsets the flag `ios::left`.)	set
`ios::left`	If this flag is set and some field-width value is given with a call to the member function `width`, then the next item output will be at the left end of the space specified by `width`. In other words, any extra blanks are placed after the item output. (Setting this flag automatically unsets the flag `ios::right`.)	not set

`unsetf`

Any flag that is set may be unset. To unset a flag you use the function `unsetf`. For example, the following will cause your program to stop including plus signs on positive integers that are output to the streams `cout`:

```
cout.unsetf(ios::showpos);
```

Manipulators

manipulator

A **manipulator** is a function that is called in a nontraditional way. In turn, the manipulator function calls a member function. Manipulators are placed after the insertion operator <<, just as if the manipulator function call were an item to be output. Like traditional functions, manipulators may or may not have arguments. We have already seen one manipulator, `endl`. In this subsection we will discuss two manipulators called `setw` and `setprecision`.

`setw`

The manipulator `setw` and the member function `width` (which you have already seen) do exactly the same thing. You call the `setw` manipulator by writing it after the insertion operator <<, as if it were to be sent to the output `stream`, and this in turn calls the member function `width`. For example, the following will output the numbers 10, 20, and 30, using the field widths specified:

```
cout << "Start" << setw(4) << 10
        << setw(4) << 20 << setw(6) << 30;
```

> ### Flag Terminology
>
> Why are the arguments to `setf`, such as `ios::showpoint`, called *flags*? And what is meant by the strange notation `ios::`?
>
> The word **flag** is used for something that can be turned on or off. The origin of the term apparently comes from some phrase similar to "When the flag is up, do it." Or perhaps the term was "when the flag is down, do it." Moreover, apparently nobody can recall what the exact originating phrase was because programmers now say "when the flag is set" and that does not conjure up any picture. In any event, when the flag `ios::showpoint` is set (that is, when it is an argument to `setf`), the stream that called the `setf` function will behave as described in Display 5.4; when any other flag is set (that is, is given as an argument to `setf`), that signals the stream to behave as Display 5.4 specifies for that flag.
>
> The explanation for the notation `ios::` is rather mundane for such exotic notation. The `ios` indicates that the meaning of terms such as `fixed` or `showpoint` is the meaning that they have when used with an **i**nput or **o**utput **s**tream. The notation `::` means "use the meaning of what follows the `::` in the context of what comes before the `::`." We will say more about this `::` notation later in this book.

The preceding statement will produce the following output

```
Start  10  20    30
```

(There are two spaces before the 10, two spaces before the 20, and four spaces before the 30.)

The manipulator `setprecision` does exactly the same thing as the member function `precision` (which you have already seen). However, a call to `setprecision` is written after the insertion operator `<<`, in a manner similar to how you call the `setw` manipulator. For example, the following will output the numbers listed using the number of digits after the decimal point that are indicated by the call to `setprecision`:

`setprecision`

```
cout.setf(ios::fixed);
cout.setf(ios::showpoint);
cout << "$" << setprecision(2) << 10.3 << endl
     << "$" << 20.5 << endl;
```

The above statement will produce the following output:

```
$10.30
$20.50
```

When you set the number of digits after the decimal point using the manipulator setprecision, then just as was the case with the member function precision, the setting stays in effect until you reset it to some other number by another call to either setprecision or precision.

iomanip

In order to use either of the manipulators setw or setprecision you must include the following directive in your program:

```
#include <iomanip>
```

SELF-TEST EXERCISES

11   What output will be produced when the following lines are executed (assuming the lines are embedded in a complete and correct program with the proper include directives)?

```
cout << "*";
cout.width(5);
cout << 123
     << "*" << 123 << "*" << endl;
cout << "*" << setw(5) << 123
     << "*" << 123 << "*" << endl;
```

12   What output will be produced when the following lines are executed (assuming the lines are embedded in a complete and correct program with the proper include directives)?

```
cout << "*" << setw(5) << 123;
cout.setf(ios::left);
cout << "*" << setw(5) << 123;
cout.setf(ios::right);
cout << "*" << setw(5) << 123 << "*" << endl;
```

13   What output will be produced when the following lines are executed (assuming the lines are embedded in a complete and correct program with the proper include directives)?

```
cout << "*" << setw(5) << 123 << "*"
     << 123 << "*" << endl;
cout.setf(ios::showpos);
cout << "*" << setw(5) << 123 << "*"
     << 123 << "*" << endl;
cout.unsetf(ios::showpos);
cout.setf(ios::left);
```

```
cout << "*" << setw(5) << 123 << "*"
     << setw(5) << 123 << "*" << endl;
```

14 What output will be sent to the file `stuff.dat` when the following lines are
executed (assuming the lines are embedded in a complete and correct program with the proper `include` directives)?

```
ofstream fout;
fout.open("stuff.dat");
fout << "*" << setw(5) << 123 << "*"
     << 123 << "*" << endl;
fout.setf(ios::showpos);
fout << "*" << setw(5) << 123 << "*"
     << 123 << "*" << endl;
fout.unsetf(ios::showpos);
fout.setf(ios::left);
fout << "*" << setw(5) << 123 << "*"
     << setw(5) << 123 << "*" << endl;
```

15 What output will be produced when the following line is executed (assuming
the line is embedded in a complete and correct program with the proper
`include` directives)?

```
cout << "*" << setw(3) << 12345 << "*" << endl;
```

16 In formatting output, the following flag constants are used with the `stream`
member function `setf`. What effect does each have?

   a. `ios::fixed`
   b. `ios::scientific`
   c. `ios::showpoint`
   d. `ios::showpos`
   e. `ios::right`
   f. `ios::left`

17 Here is a code segment that copies three integers from `infile.dat` to
`outfile.dat`. What changes are necessary to make the output go to the
screen? (The input is still to come from `infile.dat`.)

```
// Problem for Self Test. Copies three int numbers
// between files.
#include <fstream>
int main( )
{
```

```
using namespace std;
ifstream instream;
ofstream outstream;

instream.open("infile.dat");
outstream.open("outfile.dat");
int first, second, third;
instream >> first >> second >> third;
outstream << "The sum of the first 3" << endl
          << "number in infile.dat is " << endl
          << (first + second + third) << endl;

instream.close( );
outstream.close( );
return 0;
}
```

Streams as Arguments to Functions

Stream parameters must be call-by-reference

A stream can be an argument to a function. The only restriction is that the function formal parameter must be call-by-reference. A stream parameter cannot be a call-by-value parameter.[4] For example, the function make_neat in Display 5.5 has two stream parameters: one is of type ifstream and is for a stream connected to an input file; another is of type ofstream and is for a stream connected to an output file. We will discuss the other features of the program in Display 5.5 in the next two subsections.

~ PROGRAMMING TIP
Checking for the End of a File

That's all there is, there isn't any more.

ETHEL BARRYMORE

When you write a program that takes its input from a file you will often want the program to read all the data in the file. For example, if the file contains numbers, you might want your program to calculate the average of all the numbers in the file. Since you might run the program with different data files at different times, the program cannot assume it knows how many numbers are in the file. You would like to write your program so that it keeps reading numbers from the file until there are no

---

[4]We change the stream by reading or writing the stream, so call-by-reference is reasonable.

Display 5.5 Formatting Output (part 1 of 3)

```
//Illustrates output formatting instructions.
//Reads all the numbers in the file rawdata.dat and writes the numbers
//to the screen and to the file neat.dat in a neatly formatted way.
#include <iostream>
#include <fstream>
#include <cstdlib>
#include <iomanip>
using namespace std;

void make_neat(ifstream& messy_file, ofstream& neat_file,
               int number_after_decimalpoint, int field_width);
//Precondition: The streams messy_file and neat_file have been connected
//to files using the function open.
//Postcondition: The numbers in the file connected to messy_file have been
//written to the screen and to the file connected to the stream neat_file.
//The numbers are written one per line, in fixed point notation (i.e., not in
//e-notation), with number_after_decimalpoint digits after the decimal point;
//each number is preceded by a plus or minus sign and each number is in a field of
//width field_width. (This function does not close the file.)

int main( )
{
    ifstream fin;
    ofstream fout;

    fin.open("rawdata.dat");
    if (fin.fail( ))
    {
        cout << "Input file opening failed.\n";
        exit(1);
    }

    fout.open("neat.dat");
    if (fout.fail( ))
    {
        cout << "Output file opening failed.\n";
        exit(1);
    }
```

needed for setw

Stream parameters must be call-by-reference.

Display 5.5 Formatting Output *(part 2 of 3)*

```
    make_neat(fin, fout, 5, 12);

    fin.close( );
    fout.close( );

    cout << "End of program.\n";
    return 0;
}


//Uses iostream, fstream, and iomanip:
void make_neat(ifstream& messy_file, ofstream& neat_file,
               int number_after_decimalpoint, int field_width)
{
    neat_file.setf(ios::fixed);            not in e-notation
    neat_file.setf(ios::showpoint);        show decimal point
    neat_file.setf(ios::showpos);          show + sign
    neat_file.precision(number_after_decimalpoint);
    cout.setf(ios::fixed);
    cout.setf(ios::showpoint);
    cout.setf(ios::showpos);
    cout.precision(number_after_decimalpoint);

    double next;
    while (messy_file >> next)             Satisfied if there is a
    {                                      next number to read.
        cout << setw(field_width) << next << endl;
        neat_file << setw(field_width) << next << endl;
    }
}
```

more numbers left to be read. If `in_stream` is a stream connected to the input file, then the algorithm for computing this average can be stated as follows:

```
double next, sum = 0;
int count = 0;
while (There are still numbers to be read)
{
    in_stream >> next;
    sum = sum + next;
    count++;
}
```

The average is `sum/count`.

This algorithm is already almost all C++ code, but we still must express the following test in C++:

(There are still numbers to be read)

Display 5.5 Formatting Output *(part 3 of 3)*

---

rawdata.dat

(Not changed by program.)

```
10.37       -9.89897
2.313    -8.950   15.0

    7.33333     92.8765
-1.237568432e2
```

neat.dat	**Screen Output**
(After program is run.)	
+10.37000	+10.37000
-9.89897	-9.89897
+2.31300	+2.31300
-8.95000	-8.95000
+15.00000	+15.00000
+7.33333	+7.33333
+92.87650	+92.87650
-123.75684	-123.75684
	End of program.

Even though it may not look correct at first, one way to express the above test is the following:

```
(in_stream >> next)
```

So the above algorithm can be rewritten as the following C++ code (plus one last line in pseudocode that is not the issue here):

```
double next, sum = 0;
int count = 0;
while (in_stream >> next)
{
    sum = sum + next;
    count++;
}
The average is sum/count.
```

Notice that the loop body is not identical to what it was in our pseudocode. Since in_stream >> next is now in the Boolean expression, it is no longer in the loop body.

The above loop may look a bit peculiar, because in_stream >> next is both the way you input a number from the stream in_stream and the controlling Boolean expression for the *while*-loop. An expression involving the extraction operator >> is simultaneously both an action and a Boolean condition.[5] It is an instruction to take one input number from the input stream and it is also a Boolean expression that is either satisfied or not. If there is another number to be input, then the number is read and the Boolean expression is satisfied, so the body of the loop is executed one more time. If there are no more numbers to be read in, then nothing is input and the Boolean expression is not satisfied, so the loop ends. In this example the type of the input variable next was *double*, but this method of checking for the end of the file works the same way for other data types, such as *int* and *char*.

A Note on Namespaces

We have tried to keep our *using* directives local to a function definition. This is an admirable goal, but now we have a problem—functions whose parameter type is in a

---

[5]Technically, the Boolean condition works this way: The overloading of operator>> for the input stream classes is done with functions associated with the stream. This function is named operator>>. (Surprisingly, this function is not a member of the istream class. We will see in detail how operator overloading works in Chapter 8.) The return value of this operator function is an input stream reference (istream& or ifstream&). A function is provided to convert the stream reference to a bool value. The resulting value is true if the stream is able to extract data, and false otherwise.

namespace. In our immediate examples we need the stream type names that are in the namespace `std`. Thus, we need a *using* directive (or something) outside of the function definition body so that C++ will understand the parameter type names, such as `ifstream`. The easiest fix is to simply place one *using* directive at the start of the file (after the `include` directives). We have done this in Display 5.5.

Placing a single *using* directive at the start of a file is the easiest solution to our problem, but many experts would not consider it the best solution, since it would not allow the use of two namespaces that have names in common, and this is the whole purpose of namespaces. At this point we are only using the namespace `std`[6], so there is no problem. In Chapter 8, we will teach you another way around this problem with parameters and namespaces. This other approach will allow you to use any kinds of multiple namespaces.

Many programmers prefer to place *using* directives at the start of the program file. For example, consider the following *using* directive:

```
using namespace std;
```

Many of the programs in this book do not place this *using* directive at the start of the program file. Instead, this *using* directive is placed at the start of each function definition that needs the namespace `std` (immediately after the opening curly bracket). An example of this is shown in Display 5.3. An even better example is shown in Display 4.11. All of the programs that have appeared so far in this book, and almost all programs that follow, would behave exactly the same if there were just one *using* directive for the namespace `std` and that one *using* directive were placed immediately after the `include` directives, as in Display 5.5. For the namespace `std`, the placement of the *using* directive can safely be placed at the start of the file (in almost all cases). For some other namespaces, a single *using* directive will not always suffice, but you will not see any of these cases for some time.

We advocate placing the *using* directives inside of function definition (or inside of some other small unit of code), so that it does not interfere with any other possible *using* directives. This is to train you to use namespaces correctly in preparation for when you write more complicated code later in your programming career. In the meantime, we sometimes violate this rule ourselves when following the rule becomes too burdensome to the other issues we are discussing. If you are taking a course, do whatever your instructor requires. Otherwise, you have some latitude in where you place your *using* directives.

---

[6]We are actually using two namespaces: the namespace `std` and a namespace called the **global namespace,** which is a namespace that consists of all names that are not in some other namespace. But this technical detail is not a big issue to us now.

■)) *PROGRAMMING EXAMPLE*
Cleaning Up a File Format

The program in Display 5.5 (on page 249) takes its input from the file rawdata.dat and writes its output, in a neat format, both to the screen and to the file neat.dat. The program copies numbers from the file rawdata.dat to the file neat.dat, but it uses formatting instructions to write them in a neat way. The numbers are written one per line in a field of width 12, which means that each number is preceded by enough blanks so that the blanks plus the number occupy 12 spaces. The numbers are written in ordinary notation; that is, they are not written in e-notation. Each number is written with 5 digits after the decimal point and with a plus or minus sign. The output to the screen is the same as the output to the file neat.dat, except that the screen output has one extra line that announces that the program is ending. The program uses a function, named make_neat, that has formal parameters for the input-file stream and the output-file stream.

SELF-TEST EXERCISES

18 What output will be produced when the following lines are executed, assuming the file list.dat contains the data shown (and assuming the lines are embedded in a complete and correct program with the proper include directives)?

```
ifstream ins;
ins.open("list.dat");
int count = 0, next;
while (ins >> next)
{
    count++;
    cout << next << endl;
}
ins.close( );
cout << count;
```

The file list.dat contains the following three numbers (and nothing more):

```
1 2
3
```

19 Write the definition for a *void*-function called to_screen. The function to_screen has one formal parameter called file_stream, which is of type

ifstream. The precondition and postcondition for the function are given below:

```
//Precondition: The stream file_stream has been connected
//to a file with a call to the member function open. The
//file contains a list of integers (and nothing else).
//Postcondition: The numbers in the file connected to
//file_stream have been written to the screen one per line.
//(This function does not close the file.)
```

20 (This exercise is for those who have studied the optional section on **File Names as Input**.) Suppose you are given the following string variable declaration and input statement.

```
#include <iostream>
using namespace std;
// ...
char name[21];
cout >> name;
```

Suppose this code segment is embedded in a correct program. What is the longest name that can be entered into the string variable name?

5.3 Character I/O

Polonius: What do you read, my lord?
Hamlet: Words, words, words.

WILLIAM SHAKESPEARE, HAMLET

All data is input and output as character data. When your program outputs the number 10, it is really the two characters '1' and '0' that are output. Similarly, when the user wants to type in the number 10, he or she types in the character '1' followed by the character '0'. Whether the computer interprets this 10 as two characters or as the number ten depends on how your program is written. But, however your program is written, the computer hardware is always reading the characters '1' and '0', not the number ten. This conversion between characters and numbers is usually done automatically, so you need not think about such detail—but, sometimes all this automatic help gets in the way. Therefore, C++ provides some low-level facilities for input and output of character data. These low-level facilities include no automatic conversions. This allows you to bypass the automatic facilities and do input/output in absolutely anyway you want. You could even write input and output functions that can read and write numbers in Roman numeral notation, if you wanted to be so perverse.

The Member Functions get and put

The function get allows your program to read in one character of input and store it in a variable of type *char*. Every input stream, whether it is an input-file stream or the stream cin, has get as a member function. We will describe get as a member function of the stream cin, but it behaves exactly the same for input-file streams as it does for cin, so you can apply all that we say about get to input-file streams, as well as to the stream cin.

Before now, we have used cin with the extraction operator >> in order to read a character of input (or any other input for that matter). When you use the extraction operator >>, as we have been doing, some things are done for you automatically, such as skipping blanks. With the member function get, nothing is done automatically. If you want, for example, to skip over blanks using cin.get, you must write code to read and discard the blanks.

Stream_Name.get

The member function get takes one argument, which should be a variable of type *char*. That argument receives the input character that is read from the input stream. For example, the following will read in the next input character from the keyboard and store it in the variable next_symbol:

```
char next_symbol;
cin.get(next_symbol);
```

reading blanks and '\n'

It is important to note that your program can read any character in this way. If the next input character is a blank, this code will not skip over the blank, but will read the blank and set the value of next_symbol equal to the blank character. If the next character is the new-line character '\n', that is, if the program has just reached the end of an input line, then the above call to cin.get will set the value of next_symbol equal to '\n'. Although we write it as two symbols, '\n' is just a single character in C++. With the member function get, the character '\n' can be input and output just like any other character. For example, suppose your program contains the following code:

```
char c1, c2, c3;
cin.get(c1);
cin.get(c2);
cin.get(c3);
```

and suppose you type in the following two lines of input to be read by this code:

```
AB
CD
```

That is, suppose you type AB followed by return and then CD followed by return. As you would expect, the value of c1 is set to 'A' and the value of c2 is set to 'B'. That's nothing new. But when this code fills the variable c3 things are different from what they would be if you had used the extraction operator >> instead of the member function `get`. When the above code is executed on the input we showed, the value of c3 is set to '\n', that is, the value of c3 is set equal to the new-line character. The variable c3 is not set equal to 'C'.

One thing you can do with the member function `get` is to have your program detect the end of a line. The following loop will read a line of input and stop after passing the new-line character '\n'. Then, any subsequent input will be read from the beginning of the next line. For this first example, we have simply echoed the input, but the same technique would allow you to do whatever you want with the input:

detecting the end of an input line

```
cout << "Enter a line of input and I will echo it:\n";
char symbol;
do
{
    cin.get(symbol);
    cout << symbol;
} while (symbol != '\n');
cout << "That's all for this demonstration.";
```

This loop will read any line of input and echo it exactly, including blanks. The following is a sample dialogue produced by this code:

```
Enter a line of input and I will echo it:
Do Be Do 1 2    34
Do Be Do 1 2    34
That's all for this demonstration.
```

Notice that the new-line character '\n' is both read and output. Since '\n' is output, the string that begins with the word "That's" is on a new line.

'\n' and "\n"

'\n' and "\n" sometimes seem like the same thing. In a `cout`-statement, they produce the same effect, but they cannot be used interchangeably in all situations. '\n' is a value of type *char* and can be stored in a variable of type *char*. On the other hand, "\n" is a string, that happens to be made up of exactly one character. Thus, "\n" is not of type *char* and cannot be stored in a variable of type *char*.

The member function `put` is analogous to the member function `get` except that it is used for output rather than input. `put` allows your program to output one character. The member function `put` takes one argument which should be an expression of type *char*, such as a constant or a variable of type *char*. The value of the argument

Stream_Name.put

The Member Function get

Every input stream has a member function named get that can be used to read one character of input. Unlike the extraction operator >>, get reads the next input character, no matter what that character is. In particular, get will read a blank or the new-line character '\n', if either of these are the next input character. The function get takes one argument, which should be a variable of type *char*. When get is called, the next input character is read and the argument variable (called *Char_Variable* below) has its value set equal to this input character.

Syntax:

Input_Stream . get (*Char_Variable*) ;

Example:

```
char next_symbol;
cin.get(next_symbol);
```

If you wish to use get to read from a file, you use an input-file stream in place of the stream cin. For example, if in_stream is an input stream for a file, then the following will read one character from the input file and place the character in the *char* variable next_symbol:

```
in_stream.get(next_symbol);
```

Before you can use get with an input-file stream such as in_stream, your program must first connect the stream to the input file with a call to open.

---

is output to the stream when the function is called. For example, the following will output the letter 'a' to the screen:

```
cout.put('a');
```

The function cout.put does not allow you to do anything you could not do by the methods we discussed before, but we include it for completeness.

If your program uses cin.get and/or cout.put, then just as with other uses of cin and cout, your program should include the following directive:

```
#include <iostream>
```

Similarly, if your program uses get for an input-file stream or put for an output-file stream, then just as with any other file I/O, your program should contain the following directive:

```
#include <fstream>
```

The putback **Member Function** *(Optional)*

Sometimes your program needs to know the next character in the input stream. However, after reading the next character, it might turn out that you do not want to process that character and so would like to simply put it back in the input stream. For example, if you want your program to read up to *but not including* the first blank it encounters in an input stream, then your program must read that first blank in order to know when to stop reading—but then that blank is no longer in the stream. Some other part of your program might need to read and process this blank. There are a number of ways to deal with this sort of situation, but the easiest is to use the member function putback. The function putback is a member of every input stream. It takes one argument of type *char* and it places the value of that argument back in the input stream. The argument can be any expression that evaluates to a value of type *char*.

For example, the following will read characters from the file connected to the input stream fin and write them to the file connected to the output stream fout. The code reads characters up to, but not including, the first blank it encounters.

The Member Function put

Every output stream has a member function named put. The member function put takes one argument which should be an expression of type *char*. When the member function put is called, the value of its argument (called *Char_Expression* below) is output to the output stream.

Syntax:

Output_Stream . put (*Char_Expression*) ;

Examples:

```
cout.put(next_symbol);
cout.put('a');
```

If you wish to use put to output to a file, you use an output-file stream in place of the stream cout. For example, if out_stream is an output stream for a file, then the following will output the character 'Z' to the file connected to out_stream:

```
out_stream.put('Z');
```

Before you can use put with an output-file stream, such as out_stream, your program must first connect the stream to the output file with a call to the member function open.

```
fin.get(next);
while (next != ' ')
{
    fout.put(next);
    fin.get(next);
}
fin.putback(next);
```

Notice that after this code is executed, the blank that was read is still in the input stream `fin`, because the code puts it back after reading it.

Notice that `putback` places a character in an *input* stream, while `put` places a character in an *output* stream.

The character that is put back into the input stream with the member function `putback` need not be the last character read; it can be any character you wish. If you put back a character other than the last character read, the text in the input file will not be changed by `putback`, although your program will behave as if the text in the input file had been changed.

■)) PROGRAMMING EXAMPLE
Checking Input

If a user enters incorrect input, the entire run of the program can become worthless. To ensure that your program is not hampered by incorrect input, you should use input functions that allow the user to reenter input until the input is correct. The function `get_int` in Display 5.6 asks the user if the input is correct and asks for a new value if the user says the input is incorrect. The program in Display 5.6 is just a driver program to test the function `get_int`, but the function, or one very similar to it, can be used in just about any kind of program that takes its input from the keyboard.

Notice the call to the function `new_line( )`. The function `new_line` reads all the characters on the remainder of the current line but does nothing with them. This amounts to discarding the remainder of the line. Thus, if the user types in **No,** then the program reads the first letter, which is **N,** and then calls the function `new_line`, which discards the rest of the input line. This means that if the user types **75** on the next input line, as shown in the sample dialogue, the program will read the number **75** and will not attempt to read the letter **o** in the word **No.** If the program did not include a call to the function `new_line`, then the next item read would be the **o** in the line containing **No** instead of the number **75** on the following line.

Notice the Boolean expression that ends the *do-while*-loop in the function `get_int`. If the input is not correct, the user is supposed to type **No** (or some variant such as **no**) and this will cause one more iteration of the loop. However, rather than

get_int

new_line( )

When in doubt, enter the input again

checking to see if the user types a word that starts with 'N', the *do-while*-loop checks to see if the first letter of the user's response is *not* equal to 'Y' (and not equal to the lowercase version of 'Y'). As long as the user makes no mistakes and responds with some form of **Yes** or **No,** but never with anything else, then checking for **No** or checking for not being **Yes** are the same thing. However, since the user might respond in some other way, checking for not being **Yes** is safer. To see why this is safer, suppose the user makes a mistake in entering the input number. The computer echos the number and asks if it is correct. The user should type in **No,** but suppose the user makes a mistake and types in **Bo,** which is not unlikely since 'B' is right next to 'N' on the keyboard. Since 'B' is not equal to 'Y', the body of the *do-while*-loop will be executed, and the user will be given a chance to reenter the input.

But, what happens if the correct response is **Yes** and the user mistakenly enters something that begins with a letter other than 'Y' or 'y'? In that case, the loop should not iterate, but it does iterate one extra time. This is a mistake, but not nearly as bad a mistake as the one discussed in the last paragraph. It means the user must type in the input number one extra time, but it does not waste the entire run of the program. When checking input, it is better to risk an extra loop iteration than to risk proceeding with incorrect input.

◆ PITFALL   Unexpected '\n' in Input

When using the member function `get` you must account for every character of input, even the characters you do not think of as being symbols, such as blanks and the new-line character '\n'. A common problem when using `get` is forgetting to dispose of the '\n' that ends every input line. If there is a new-line character in the input stream that is not read (and usually discarded), then when your program next expects to read a "real" symbol using the member function `get`, it will instead read the character '\n'. To clear the input stream of any leftover '\n', you can use the function `new_line`, which we defined in Display 5.6. Let's look at a concrete example.

It is legal to mix the different forms of `cin`. For example, the following is legal:

```
cout << "Enter a number:\n";
int number;
cin >> number;
cout << "Now enter a letter:\n";
char symbol;
cin.get(symbol);
```

Display 5.6 Checking Input *(part 1 of 2)*

```
//Program to demonstrate the functions new_line and get_input.
#include <iostream>
using namespace std;

void new_line( );
//Discards all the input remaining on the current input line.
//Also discards the '\n' at the end of the line.
//This version only works for input from the keyboard.

void get_int(int& number);
//Postcondition: The variable number has been
//given a value that the user approves of.


int main( )
{
    int n;

    get_int(n);
    cout << "Final value read in = " << n << endl
         << "End of demonstration.\n";
    return 0;
}


//Uses iostream:
void new_line( )
{
    char symbol;
    do
    {
        cin.get(symbol);
    } while (symbol != '\n');
}
```

Display 5.6 Checking Input *(part 2 of 2)*

```
//Uses iostream:
void get_int(int& number)
{
    char ans;
    do
    {
        cout << "Enter input number: ";
        cin >> number;
        cout << "You entered " << number
            << " Is that correct? (yes/no): ";
        cin >> ans;
        new_line( );
    } while ((ans != 'Y') && (ans != 'y'));
}
```

Sample Dialogue

```
Enter input number: 57
You entered 57 Is that correct? (yes/no): No
Enter input number: 75
You entered 75 Is that correct? (yes/no): yes
Final value read in = 75
End of demonstration.
```

However, this can produce problems, as illustrated by the following dialogue:

```
Enter a number:
21
Now enter a letter:
A
```

With this dialogue, the value of number will be 21 as you expect. However, if you expect the value of the variable symbol to be 'A', you will be disappointed. The value given to symbol is '\n'. After reading the number 21, the next character in the input stream is the new-line character, '\n', and so that is read next. Remember, get does not skip over line breaks and spaces. (In fact, depending on what is in the rest of the program, you may not even get a chance to type in the A. Once the variable `symbol` is filled with the character `'\n'`, the program proceeds to whatever statement is next in the program. If the next statement sends output to the screen, the screen will be filled with output before you get a chance to type in the A.)

Either of the following rewritings of the above code will cause the above dialogue to fill the variable `number` with `21` and fill the variable `symbol` with `'A'`:

```
cout << "Enter a number:\n";
int number;
cin >> number;
cout << "Now enter a letter:\n";
char symbol;
cin >> symbol;
```

Alternatively, you can use the function `new_line`, defined in Display 5.6, as follows:

```
cout << "Enter a number:\n";
int number;
cin >> number;
new_line( );
cout << "Now enter a letter:\n";
char symbol;
cin.get(symbol);
```

As this second rewrite indicates, you can mix the two forms of `cin` and have your program work correctly, but it does require some extra care.

The `eof` Member Function

Every input-file stream has a member function, called `eof`, that can be used to determine when all of the file has been read and there is no more input left for the program. This is the second technique we have presented for determining when a program has read everything in a file. The previous method works best for input that consists of numeric data; the `eof` function works best for input that is text.

The letters `eof` stand for *end of file* and `eof` is normally pronounced by saying the three letters e-o-f. The function `eof` takes no arguments, so if the input stream is called `fin`, then a call to the function `eof` is written

```
fin.eof( )
```

This is a Boolean expression that can be used to control a *while*-loop, *do-while*-loop, or an *if-else*-statement. This expression is satisfied (that is, is *true*), if the program has read past the end of the input file, otherwise the above expression is not satisfied (that is, is *false*).

Since we usually want to test that we are *not* at the end of a file, a call to the member function eof is typically used with a *not* in front of it. Recall that in C++ the symbol ! is used to express *not*. For example, consider the following statement:

eof is usually used with "not."

```
if (! fin.eof( ))
    cout << "Not done yet.";
else
    cout << "End of the file.";
```

The Boolean expression after the *if* means "not at the end of the file connected to fin." Thus, the above *if-else*-statement will output the following to the screen:

```
Not done yet.
```

provided the program has not yet read past the end of the file that is connected to the stream fin. The *if-else*-statement will output the following, if the program has read beyond the end of the file:

```
End of the file.
```

As another example of using the eof member function, suppose that the input stream in_stream has been connected to an input file with a call to open. Then the entire contents of the file can be written to the screen with the following *while*-loop:

ending an input loop with the eof function

```
in_stream.get(next);
while (! in_stream.eof( ))
{
    cout << next;              If you prefer, you can
    in_stream.get(next);       use cout.put(next) here.
}
```

The above *while*-loop reads each character from the input file into the *char* variable next using the member function get, and then it writes the character to the screen. After the program has passed the end of the file, the value of in_stream.eof( ) changes from *false* to *true*. So,

```
(! in_stream.eof( ))
```

changes from *true* to *false* and the loop ends.

Notice that `in_stream.eof( )` does not become *true* until the program attempts to read one character beyond the end of the file. For example, suppose the file contains the following (without any new-line after the c):

ab
c

This is actually the following list of four characters:

ab<the new-line character '\n'>c

The above loop will read an `'a'` and write it to the screen, then read a `'b'` and write it to the screen, then read the new-line character `'\n'` and write it to the screen, then read a `'c'` and write it to the screen. At that point the loop will have read all the characters in the file. However, `in_stream.eof( )` will still be *false*. The value of `in_stream.eof( )` will not change from *false* to *true* until the program tries to read one more character. That is why the above *while*-loop ends with `in_stream.get(next)`. The loop needs to read one extra character in order to end the loop.

There is a special end-of-file marker at the end of a file. The member function `eof` does not change from *false* to *true* until this end-of-file marker is read. That's why the above *while*-loop could read one character beyond what you think of as the last character in the file. However, this end-of-file marker is not an ordinary character and should not be manipulated like an ordinary character. You can read this end-of-file marker, but you should not write it out again. If you write out the end-of-file marker, the result is unpredictable. The system automatically places this end-of-file marker at the end of each file for you.

The next Programming Example uses the `eof` member function to determine when the program has read the entire input file.

deciding how to test for the end of an input file

You now have two methods for detecting the end of a file. You can use the `eof` member function or you can use the method we described in the Programming Tip on page 242 entitled "Checking for the End of a File." In most situations you can use either method, but many programmers use the two different methods in different situations. If you do not have any other reason to prefer one of these two methods, then use the following general rule: use the `eof` member function when you are treating the input as text and reading the input with the `get` member function; use the other method when you are processing numeric data.

SELF-TEST EXERCISES

21 Consider the following code (and assume that it is embedded in a complete and correct program and then run):

```
char c1, c2, c3, c4;
```

```
cout << "Enter a line of input:\n";
cin.get(c1);
cin.get(c2);
cin.get(c3);
cin.get(c4);
cout << c1 << c2 << c3 << c4 << "END OF OUTPUT";
```

If the dialogue begins as follows, what will be the next line of output?

```
Enter a line of input:
a b c d e f g
```

22 Consider the following code (and assume that it is embedded in a complete and correct program and then run):

```
char next;
int count = 0;
cout << "Enter a line of input:\n";
cin.get(next);
while (next != '\n')
{
    if ((count%2) == 0)      ← True if count is even.
        cout << next;
    count++;
    cin.get(next);
}
```

If the dialogue begins as follows, what will be the next line of output?

```
Enter a line of input:
abcdef gh
```

23 Suppose that the program described in Self-Test Exercise 22 is run and the dialogue begins as follows (instead of beginning as shown in Self-Test Exercise 22). What will be the next line of output?

```
Enter a line of input:
0 1 2 3 4 5 6 7 8 9 10 11
```

24 Consider the following code (and assume that it is embedded in a complete and correct program and then run):

```
char next;
int count = 0;
cout << "Enter a line of input:\n";
cin >> next;
while (next != '\n')
{
    if ((count%2) == 0)
        cout << next;
    count++;
    cin >> next;
}
```

If the dialogue begins as follows, what will be the next line of output?

```
Enter a line of input:
0 1 2 3 4 5 6 7 8 9 10 11
```

25 Write the definition for a *void*-function called `text_to_screen` which has one formal parameter called `file_stream` that is of type `ifstream`. The precondition and postcondition for the function are:

```
//Precondition: The stream file_stream has been connected
//to a file with a call to the member function open.
//Postcondition: The contents of the file connected to
//file_stream have been copied to the screen character by
//character so that the screen output is the same as the
//contents of the text in the file.
//(This function does not close the file.)
```

◼)) PROGRAMMING EXAMPLE
Editing a Text File

The program discussed here is a very simple example of text editing applied to files. It might be used by a software firm to update its advertising literature. The firm has been marketing compilers for the C programming language and has recently introduced a line of C++ compilers. This program can be used to automatically generate C++ advertising material from the existing C advertising material. The program takes its input from a file that contains advertising copy that says good things about C and writes similar advertising copy about C++ in another file. The file that contains the C advertising copy is called `cad.dat`, and the new file that receives the C++ advertising copy is called `cplusad.dat`. The program is shown in Display 5.7. The program simply reads every character in the file `cad.dat` and copies the characters to the file `cplusad.dat`. Every character is copied unchanged, except that when the uppercase letter `'C'` is read from the input file, the program writes the string `"C++"` to the output file. This program assumes that whenever the letter `'C'` occurs in the input file, it names the C programming language; so this change is exactly what is needed to produce the updated advertising copy.

Notice that the line breaks are preserved when the program reads characters from the input file and writes the characters to the output file. The new-line character `'\n'` is treated just like any other character. It is read from the input file with the member function `get`, and it is written to the output file using the insertion operator `<<`. We must use the member function `get` to read the input. If we instead use the extraction operator `>>` to read the input, the program would skip over all the whitespace, which means that none of the blanks and none of the new-line characters `'\n'` would be read from the input file, so they would not be copied to the output file.

Also notice that the member function `eof` is used to detect the end of the input file and end the *while*-loop.

Predefined Character Functions

In text processing you often want to convert lowercase letters to uppercase or vice versa. The predefined function `toupper` can be used to convert a lowercase letter to an uppercase letter. For example, `toupper('a')` returns `'A'`. If the argument to the function `toupper` is anything other than a lowercase letter, then `toupper` simply returns the argument unchanged. So `toupper('A')` also returns `'A'`. The function `tolower` is similar except that it converts an uppercase letter to its lowercase version.

The functions `toupper` and `tolower` are in the library with the header file `cctype`, so any program that uses these functions, or any other functions in this library, must contain the following `include` directive:

```
#include <cctype>
```

Display 5.8 contains descriptions of some of the most commonly used functions in the library `cctype`.

The function `isspace` returns *true* if its argument is a *whitespace* character. **Whitespace** characters are all the characters that are displayed as blank space on the

whitespace

Display 5.7 Editing a File of Text *(part 1 of 2)*

```
//Program to create a file called cplusad.dat which is identical to the file
//cad.dat, except that all occurrences of 'C' are replaced by "C++".
//Assumes that the uppercase letter 'C' does not occur in cad.dat, except
//as the name of the C programming language.

#include <fstream>
#include <iostream>
#include <cstdlib>
using namespace std;

void add_plus_plus(ifstream& in_stream, ofstream& out_stream);
//Precondition: in_stream has been connected to an input file with open.
//out_stream has been connected to an output file with open.
//Postcondition: The contents of the file connected to in_stream have been
//copied into the file connected to out_stream, but with each 'C' replaced
//by "C++". (The files are not closed by this function.)

int main( )
{
    ifstream fin;
    ofstream fout;

    cout << "Begin editing files.\n";

    fin.open("cad.dat");
    if (fin.fail( ))
    {
        cout << "Input file opening failed.\n";
        exit(1);
    }

    fout.open("cplusad.dat");
    if (fout.fail( ))
    {
        cout << "Output file opening failed.\n";
        exit(1);
    }

    add_plus_plus(fin, fout);
```

Display 5.7 Editing a File of Text *(part 2 of 2)*

```
    fin.close( );
    fout.close( );

    cout << "End of editing files.\n";
    return 0;
}

void add_plus_plus(ifstream& in_stream, ofstream& out_stream)
{
    char next;

    in_stream.get(next);
    while (! in_stream.eof( ))
    {
        if (next == 'C')
            out_stream << "C++";
        else
            out_stream << next;

        in_stream.get(next);
    }
}
```

cad.dat

(Not changed by program.)

```
C is one of the world's most modern
programming languages. There is no
language as versatile as C, and C
is fun to use.
```

cplusad.dat

(After program is run.)

```
C++ is one of the world's most modern
programming languages. There is no
language as versatile as C++, and C++
is fun to use.
```

Screen Output

```
Begin editing files.
End of editing files.
```

screen, including the blank character, the tab character, and the new-line character '\n'. If the argument to isspace is not a whitespace character, then isspace returns *false*. Thus, isspace(' ') returns *true* and isspace('a') returns *false*.

For example, the following will read a sentence terminated with a period and echo the string with all whitespace characters replaced with the symbol '-':

```
char next;
do
{
    cin.get(next);
    if (isspace(next))          True if the character
        cout << '-';            in next is whitespace.
    else
        cout << next;
} while (next != '.');
```

For example, if the above code is given the following input:

Ahh   do be do.

then it will produce the following output:

```
Ahh---do-be-do.
```

◆ PITFALL   toupper **and** tolower **Return** *int* **Values**

In many ways C++ considers characters to be whole numbers, similar to the numbers of type *int*. Each character is assigned a number and when the character is stored in a variable of type *char* it is this number that is placed in the computer's memory. In C++ you can use a value of type *char* as a number, for example, by placing it in a variable of type *int*. You can also store a number of type *int* in a variable of type *char* (provided the number is not too large). Thus, the type *char* can be used as the type for characters or as a type for small whole numbers. Usually you need not be concerned with this detail, and can simply think of values of type *char* as being characters and not worry about their use as numbers. However, when using the functions in cctype, this detail can be important. The functions toupper and tolower actually return values of type *int* rather than values of type *char*; that is, they return the number corresponding to the character we think of them as returning, rather than the character itself. Thus, the following will not output the letter 'A', but will instead output the number that is assigned to 'A'.

```
cout << toupper('a');
```

Display 5.8 Some Predefined Character Functions in `cctype` *(part 1 of 2)*

Function	Description	Example
`toupper`(*Char_Exp*)	Returns the upper-case version of *Char_Exp*.	*char* c = toupper('a'); cout << c; **Outputs:** A
`tolower`(*Char_Exp*)	Returns the lower-case version of *Char_Exp*.	*char* c = tolower('A'); cout << c; **Outputs:** a

`isupper`(*Char_Exp*)	Returns *true* pro-vided *Char_Exp* is an uppercase let-ter; otherwise returns *false*.	*if* (isupper(c))
		     cout << c << " is uppercase.";
		else
		     cout << c
		          << " is not uppercase.";

`islower`(*Char_Exp*)	Returns *true* pro-vided *Char_Exp* is a lowercase letter; otherwise returns *false*.	*char* c = 'a'; *if* (islower(c)) cout << c << " is lowercase."; **Outputs:** a is lowercase.

`isalpha`(*Char_Exp*)	Returns *true* pro-vided *Char_Exp* is a letter of the alpha-bet; otherwise returns *false*.	*char* c = '$';
		if (isalpha(c))
		     cout << c << " is a letter.";
		else
		     cout << c
		          << " is not a letter.";
		Outputs: $ is not a letter.

`isdigit`(*Char_Exp*)	Returns *true* pro-vided *Char_Exp* is one of the digits '0' through '9'; otherwise returns *false*.	*if* (isdigit('3'))
		     cout << "It's a digit.";
		else
		     cout << "It's not a digit.";
		Outputs: It's a digit.

Display 5.8 Some Predefined Character Functions in `cctype` *(part 2 of 2)*

Function	Description	Example

isspace(*Char_Exp*)	Returns *true* provided *Char_Exp* is a whitespace character, such as the blank or newline symbol; otherwise returns *false*.	`//Skips over one "word" and`
		`//sets c equal to the first`
		`//whitespace character after`
		`//the "word":`
		`do`
		`{`
		`   cin.get(c);`
		`} while (! isspace(c));`

In order to get the computer to treat the value returned by `toupper` or `tolower` as a value of type *char* (as opposed to a value of type *int*), you need to indicate that you want a value of type *char*. One way to do this is to place the value returned in a variable of type *char*. The following will output the character 'A', which is usually what we want:

```
char c = toupper('a');  ◄──────    Places 'A' in the
cout << c;                          variable c.
```

Another way to get the computer to treat the value returned by `toupper` or `tolower` as a value of type *char* is to use a type cast as follows:

```
cout << char(toupper('a'));   ◄──────   Outputs the
                                         character 'A'.
```

(Type casts were discussed in Chapter 3 in the section "Type Changing Functions.")

SELF-TEST EXERCISES

26 Consider the following code (and assume that it is embedded in a complete and correct program and then run):

```
cout << "Enter a line of input:\n";
char next;
do
{
   cin.get(next);
   cout << next;
} while ( (! isdigit(next)) && (next != '\n') );
cout << "<END OF OUTPUT";
```

If the dialogue begins as follows, what will be the next line of output?

```
Enter a line of input:
I'll see you at 10:30 AM.
```

27 Write some C++ code that will read a line of text and echo the line with all uppercase letters deleted.

5.4 Inheritance

One of the most powerful features of C++ is the use of *derived classes*. When we say that one class was derived from another class we mean that the derived class was obtained from the other class by adding features. For example, the class of input-*file* streams is derived from the class of *all* input streams by adding additional member functions such as open and close. The stream cin belongs to the class of *all* input streams, but does *not* belong to the class of input-*file* streams because cin has no member functions named open and close. A stream that you declared to be of type ifstream is an input-*file* stream because it has added member functions such as open and close. In this section we will introduce you to the notion of a derived class as it applies to streams. The word *inheritance* is just another name for the topic of derived classes. It may take a while before you are completely comfortable with the idea of a derived class, but you can easily learn enough about derived classes to start using them in some simple, and very useful, ways.

Inheritance Among Stream Classes

In order to get some of the simpler terminology straight, recall that an **object** is a variable that has member functions, and that a **class** is a type whose variables are objects. Streams (such as cin, cout, input-file streams, and output-file streams) are objects, so stream types, such as ifstream and ofstream, are classes. With that brief review in mind, let us consider some examples of streams and stream classes.

Both the predefined stream cin and an input-file stream are input streams, so in some sense they are similar. For example, you can use the extraction operator >> with either kind of stream. On the other hand, an input-file stream can be connected to a file using the member function open, but the stream cin has no member function named open. An input-file stream is a similar but different kind of stream than cin. An input-file stream is of type ifstream. As we will see shortly, cin is of type istream (spelled without the 'f'). The classes ifstream and istream are different but closely related types. The class ifstream is a *derived class* of the class istream. In this subsection we explain what it means for one class to be a derived class of another class.

Consider the following function, which reads two integers from the input stream source_file and writes their sum to the screen:

```
void two_sum(ifstream& source_file)
{
    int n1, n2;
    source_file >> n1 >> n2;
    cout << n1 << " + " << n2 << " = " << (n1 + n2) << endl;
}
```

Suppose your program contains the above function definition and the following stream declaration:

```
ifstream fin;
```

If fin is connected to a file with a call to open, you can use the function two_sum to read two integers from that file and write their sum to the screen. The call would be the following:

```
two_sum(fin);
```

Now, suppose that later on in the same program, you want your program to read two numbers from the keyboard and write their sum to the screen. Since all input streams are similar, you might think you can use cin as the argument in a second call to two_sum, as shown below:

```
two_sum(cin); //WILL NOT WORK
```

istream
ifstream

As the comment indicates, this will produce an error message when you compile your program. cin is not of type ifstream; cin is of type istream (without an 'f'). If you want to use cin as an argument to a function, then the corresponding function parameter should be of type istream (not of type ifstream). The following rewritten version of two_sum will accept cin as its argument:

```
void better_two_sum(istream& source_file)
{
    int n1, n2;
    source_file >> n1 >> n2;
    cout << n1 << " + " << n2 << " = " << (n1 + n2) << endl;
}
```

Aside from changing the types of the parameter, this function better_two_sum is identical to the function two_sum. Since the parameter in the function `better_two_sum` matches the type of `cin`, the following function call can be used in place of the above illegal call to `two_sum`:

    better_two_sum(cin);

Now we have some good, and perhaps surprising, news. The function `better_two_sum` can be used with any kind of input stream, not just with the input stream `cin`. The following is also legal:

    better_two_sum(fin);

This is perhaps surprising because `fin` is of type `ifstream` and the argument to `better_two_sum` must be of type `istream`. It appears that the stream `fin` is of type `ifstream` and also of type `istream`. Not only does this appear to be true. It is true! The stream `fin` has two types. How can this be true? The types in questions have a special relationship. The type `ifstream` is a derived class of the class `istream`.

When we say that some class A is a **derived class** of some other class B, it means that class A has all the features of class B but it also has *extra added features*. For example, any stream of type `istream` (without the `'f'`) can be used with the extraction operator >>. The class `ifstream` (with the `'f'`) is a derived class of the class `istream`, so an object of type `ifstream` can be used with the extraction operator >>. But, `ifstream` has added features so that you can do more with an object of type `ifstream`. For example, one added feature is that a stream of type `ifstream` can be used with the function `open`. The stream `cin` is only of type `istream` and not of type `ifstream`, so you cannot use `cin` with the function `open`.

derived class

Any stream that is of type `ifstream` is also of type `istream`, so a formal parameter of type `istream` can be replaced by an argument of type `ifstream` in a function call. If you are defining a function with a formal parameter for an input stream and you give the input stream parameter the type `istream`, then your function will be more versatile. With a formal parameter of type `istream`, the argument used in a function call can be either an input stream connected to a file or the stream `cin`.

what type to use for a stream parameter

If you define a function with a parameter of type `istream`, then that parameter can only use `istream` member functions. In particular, it cannot use the functions `open` and `close`. Similarly, a parameter of type `ostream` can only use `ostream` member functions. With parameters of type `istream` or `ostream`, all opening of files must be done before the function call and all closing must be done after the function call.

Inheritance can seem strange at first, but the idea of a derived class is really quite common. An example from everyday life may help to make the idea clearer. The class of all convertibles, for instance, is a derived class of the class of all automobiles. Every convertible is an automobile, but a convertible is not just an automobile. A convertible is a special kind of automobile with special properties that other kinds of automobiles do not have. If you have a convertible, you can lower the top so that the car is open. (You might say that a convertible has an "open" function as an added feature.) Similarly, the class ifstream of input-*file* streams is a derived class of the class istream, which consists of *all* input streams. Every input-file stream is an input stream, but an input-file stream has extra properties (for example, the function open) that other kinds of input streams (such as cin) do not have.

inheritance

Derived classes are often discussed using the metaphor of inheritance and family relationships. If class B is a derived class of class A, then class B is called a **child** of class A and class A is called a **parent** of class B. The derived class is said to **inherit** the member functions of its parent class. For example, every convertible inherits the fact that it has four wheels from the class of all automobiles, and every input-file stream inherits the extraction operator >> from the class of all input streams. This is why the topic of derived classes is often called *inheritance*.

If you are not yet completely comfortable with the idea of a derived class, you will become more comfortable with the idea as you use it. The box entitled "Making Stream Parameters Versatile" tells you all that you absolutely must know in order to use the derived classes discussed in this subsection.

ostream and
ofstream

So far we have discussed two classes for input streams, istream and its derived class ifstream. The situation with output streams is similar. The class ostream is the class of all output streams. The stream cout is of type ostream. In contrast to cout, an output-file stream is declared to be of type ofstream. The class ofstream of output-file streams is a derived class of the class ostream. For example, the following function writes the word "Hello" to the output stream given as its argument.

```
void say_hello(ostream& any_out_stream)
{
    any_out_stream << "Hello";
}
```

Making Stream Parameters Versatile

If you want to define a function that takes an input stream as an argument and you want that argument to be cin in some cases and an input-file stream in other cases, then use a formal parameter of type istream (without an 'f'). However, an input-file stream, even if used as an argument of type istream, must still be declared to be of type ifstream (with an 'f').

Similarly, if you want to define a function that takes an output stream as an argument and you want that argument to be cout in some cases and an output-file stream in other cases, then use a formal parameter of type ostream. However, an output-file stream, even if used as an argument of type ostream, must still be declared to be of type ofstream. You cannot open or close a stream parameter of type istream or ostream. Open these objects before passing them to your function and close them after the call.

The first of the following calls writes "Hello" to the screen; the second writes "Hello" to the file with the external file name `afile.dat`:

```
ofstream fout;
fout.open("afile.dat");
say_hello(cout);
say_hello(fout);
```

Note that an output-file stream is of type `ofstream` *and also* of type `ostream`.

■)) *PROGRAMMING EXAMPLE*
Another new_line *Function*

As another example of how you can make a stream function more versatile, consider the function `new_line` in Display 5.6 (on page 262). That function works only for input from the keyboard, which is input from the predefined stream `cin`. The function `new_line` in Display 5.6 has no arguments. Below we have rewritten the function `new_line` so that it has a formal parameter of type `istream` for the input stream:

```
//Uses iostream:
void new_line(istream& in_stream)
{
    char symbol;
    do
    {
        in_stream.get(symbol);
    } while (symbol != '\n');
}
```

Now, suppose your program contains this new version of the function `new_line`. If your program is taking input from an input stream called `fin` (which is connected to an input file), the following will discard all the input left on the line currently being read from the input file:

```
new_line(fin);
```

On the other hand, if your program is also reading some input from the keyboard, the following will discard the remainder of the input line that was typed in at the keyboard:

```
new_line(cin);
```

using both versions
of new_line

If your program has only the above rewritten version of new_line, which takes a stream argument such as fin or cin, you must always give the stream name, even if the stream name is cin. But thanks to overloading, you can have both versions of the function new_line in the same program: the version with no arguments that is given in Display 5.6 and the version with one argument of type istream, which we just defined. In a program with both definitions of new_line, the following two calls are equivalent

```
new_line(cin);
```

and the equivalent

```
new_line( );
```

You do not really need two versions of the function new_line. The version with one argument of type istream can serve all your needs. However, many programmers find it convenient to have a version with no arguments for keyboard input, since keyboard input is used so frequently.

Default Arguments for Functions (*Optional*)

An alternative to having two versions of the new_line function is to use **default arguments.** In the following code, we have rewritten the new_line function a third time:

```
//Uses iostream:
void new_line(istream& in_stream = cin)
{
    char symbol;
    do
    {
        in_stream.get(symbol);
    } while (symbol != '\n');
}
```

If we call this function as

```
new_line( );
```

the formal parameter takes the default argument cin. If we call this as

```
new_line(fin);
```

the formal parameter takes the argument provided in the call fin. This facility is available to us with any argument type and any number of arguments.

If some parameters are provided default arguments and some not, the formal parameters with default arguments must all be together at the end of the argument list. If you provide several defaults and several nondefault arguments, the call may provide as few arguments as there are nondefault arguments, up to the number of parameters. The arguments will be applied to the parameters without default arguments in order, then the parameters with default arguments up to the number of parameters.

Here is an example:

```
//To test default argument behavior
//Uses iostream
void default_args(int arg1, int arg2, int arg3 = -3,
                int arg4 = -4)
{
    cout << arg1 << ' ' << arg2 << ' ' << arg3 << ' ' << arg4
        << endl;
}
```

Calls to this may be made with two, three, or four arguments:

```
default_args(5, 6);
```

This call supplies the nondefault arguments and uses the two default arguments. The output is

```
5 6 -3 -4
```

Next, consider

```
default_args(6, 7, 8);
```

This call supplies the nondefault arguments and the first default argument, and the last argument uses the default. This call gives output

```
6 7 8 -4
```

The call

```
default_args(5, 6, 7, 8);
```

assigns all the arguments from the argument list, and gives output

```
5 6 7 8
```

SELF-TEST EXERCISES

28   What is the type of the stream `cin`? What is the type of the stream `cout`?

29 Define a function called `copy_char` that takes one argument that is an input stream. When called, `copy_char` will read one character of input from the input stream given as its argument, and will write that character to the screen. You should be able to call your function using either `cin` or an input-file stream as the argument to your function `copy_char`. (If the argument is an input-file stream, then the stream is connected to a file before the function is called, so `copy_char` will not open or close any files.) For example, the first of the following two calls to `copy_char` will copy a character from the file `stuff.dat` to the screen, and the second will copy a character from the keyboard to the screen:

```
ifstream fin;
fin.open("stuff.dat");
copy_char(fin);
copy_char(cin);
```

30 Define a function called `copy_line` that takes one argument that is an input stream. When called, `copy_line` reads one line of input from the input stream given as its argument and writes that line to the screen. You should be able to call your function using either `cin` or an input-file stream as the argument to your function `copy_line`. (If the argument is an input-file stream, then the stream is connected to a file before the function is called, so `copy_line` will not open or close any files.) For example, the first of the following two calls to `copy_line` will copy a line from the file `stuff.dat` to the screen, and the second will copy a line from the keyboard to the screen:

```
ifstream fin;
fin.open("stuff.dat");
copy_line(fin);
copy_line(cin);
```

31 Define a function called `send_line` that takes one argument that is an output stream. When called, `send_line` reads one line of input from the keyboard and outputs the line to the output stream given as its argument. You should be able to call your function using either `cout` or an output-file stream as the argument to your function `send_line`. (If the argument is an output-file stream, then the stream is connected to a file before the function is called, so `send_line` will not open or close any files.) For example, the first of the following calls to `send_line` will copy a line from the keyboard to the file `morestuf.dat`, and the second will copy a line from the keyboard to the screen:

```
ofstream fout;
fout.open("morestuf.dat");
cout << "Enter 2 lines of input:\n";
```

```
send_line(fout);
send_line(cout);
```

32 (This exercise is for those who have studied the optional section on Default Arguments.) What output does the following function provide in response to the following calls?

```
void func(double x, double y = 1.1, double z = 2.3)
{
    cout << x << " " << y << " " << z << endl;
}
Calls:
a) func(2.0);
b) func(2.0, 3.0);
c) func(2.0, 3.0, 4.0);
```

33 (This exercise is for those who have studied the optional section on Default Arguments.) Write several functions that overload the function name to get the same effect as all the calls in the default function arguments in the previous Self-Test exercise.

34 Is the following `true` or `false`? If it is `false`, correct it, and in either event, explain carefully.

A function written using parameter of class `fstream`, `ifstream` or `ofstream` can be called with `istream` or `ostream` arguments.

CHAPTER SUMMARY

- A stream of type `ifstream` can be connected to a file with a call to the member function `open`. Your program can then take input from that file.

- A stream of type `ofstream` can be connected to a file with a call to the member function `open`. Your program can then send output to that file.

- You should use the member function `fail` to check whether a call to `open` was successful.

- An **object** is a variable that has functions associated with it. These functions are called **member functions**. A **class** is a type whose variables are objects. A stream is an example of an object. The types `ifstream` and `ofstream` are examples of classes.

- The following is the syntax you use when you write a call to a member function of an object:

  Calling_Object. *Member_Function_Name*(*Argument_List*) ;

  An example with the stream `cout` as the calling object and `precision` as the member function is the following:

  ```
  cout.precision(2);
  ```

- Stream member functions, such as `width`, `setf`, and `precision`, can be used to format output. These output functions work the same for the stream `cout`, which is connected to the screen, and for output streams connected to files.

- A function may have formal parameters of a stream type, but they must be call-by-reference parameters. They cannot be call-by-value parameters. The type `ifstream` can be used for an input-file stream and the type `ofstream` can be used for an output-file stream. (See the next summary point for other type possibilities.)

- If you use `istream` (spelled without the `'f'`) as the type for an input stream parameter, then the argument corresponding to that formal parameter can be either the stream `cin` or an input-file stream of type `ifstream` (spelled with the `'f'`). If you use `ostream` (spelled without the `'f'`) as the type for an output stream parameter, then the argument corresponding to that formal parameter can be either the stream `cout` or an output-file stream of type `ofstream` (spelled with the `'f'`).

- Every input stream has a member function named `get` that can be used to read one character of input. The member function `get` will not skip over whitespace. Every output stream also has a member function named `put` that can be used to write one character to the output stream.

- The member function `eof` can be used to test when a program has reached the end of an input file. The member function `eof` works well for text processing. However, when processing numeric data, you might prefer to test for the end of a file by using the other method we discussed in this chapter.

- Function parameters can have default arguments that provide values for the parameters if the corresponding argument is omitted in the call. These arguments must follow any parameters that are not provided default arguments. Calls to such a function must supply arguments for parameters without default arguments first. Arguments beyond this are used instead of defaults, up to the number of parameters the function has.

Answers to Self-Test Exercises

1 The streams fin and fout are declared as follows:

```
ifstream fin;
ofstream fout;
```

The include directive that goes at the top of your file is:

```
#include <fstream>
```

2

```
fin.open("stuff1.dat");
if (fin.fail( ))
{
    cout << "Input file opening failed.\n";
    exit(1);
}

fout.open("stuff2.dat");
if (fout.fail( ))
{
    cout << "Output file opening failed.\n";
    exit(1);
}
```

3

```
fin.close( );
fout.close( );
```

4 You need to replace the stream out_stream with the stream cout. Note that you do not need to declare cout, you do not need to call open with cout, and you do not need to close cout.

5

```
#include <cstdlib>
```

6

```
bla.dobedo(7);
```

7 The exit(1) function returns the argument to the operating system. By convention the operating system uses a 1 as an indication of error status, and 0 as an indication of success. What is actually done is system dependent.

8 Both files and program variables store values and can have values retrieved from them. Program variables exist only while the program runs, whereas files may exist before a program is run, and may continue to exist after a program stops. In short, files may be permanent, variables are not. Files provide the ability to store large quantities of data whereas program variables do not provide quite so large a store.

9 We have seen the: `open`, `close`, and `fail` member functions at this point. The following illustrate their use.

```
int c;
ifstream in;
ofstream out;
in.open("in.dat");
in >> c;
out.open("out.dat");
out << c
out.close( );
in.close( );
```

10 This is the "starting over" the text describes at the beginning of this chapter. The file must be closed and opened again. This action puts the read position at the start of the file, ready to be read again.

11
```
*   123*123*
*   123*123*
```

Each of the spaces contain exactly two blank characters. Notice that a call to `width` or call to `setw` only lasts for one output item.

12
```
*   123*123   *   123*
```

Each of the spaces consists of exactly two blank characters.

13
```
*   123*123*
*  +123*+123*
*123   *123    *
```

There is just one space between the '`*`' and the '`+`' on the second line. Each of the other spaces contain exactly two blank characters.

14 The output to the file `stuff.dat` will be exactly the same as the output given in the answer to Exercise 13.

15
```
*12345*
```

Notice that the entire integer is output even though this requires more space than was specified by `setw`.

16 a. `ios::fixed` Setting this flag causes floating point numbers not to be displayed in e-notation, i.e., not in 'scientific notation.' Setting this unsets `ios::scientific`.

b. `ios::scientific` Setting this flag causes floating point numbers to be displayed in e-notation, i.e., 'scientific notation.' Setting this unsets `ios::fixed`.

c. `ios::showpoint` Setting this flag causes the decimal point and trailing zeros always to be displayed.

d. `ios::showpos` Setting this flag causes a plus sign to be output before positive integer values.

e. `ios::right` Setting this flag causes the next output to be placed at the right end of any field that is set with the width member function. That is, any extra blanks are put before the output. Setting this flag clears `ios::left`.

f. `ios::left` Setting this flag causes the next output to be placed at the left end of any field that is set with the width member function. That is, any extra blanks are put after the output. Setting this flag clears `ios::right`.

17 You need to replace `outstream` with `cout`, and delete the `open` and `close` calls for `outstream`. You do not need to declare `cout`, open `cout`, nor close `cout`. The `#include <fstream>` has all the `iostream` members you need for screen I/O, though it does no harm, and may make the program clearer to `#include <iostream>`.

18
```
1
2
3
3
```

19

```
void to_screen(ifstream& file_stream)
{
    int next;
    while (file_stream >> next)
        cout << next << endl;
}
```

20   The maximum number of characters that can be typed in for a string variable is one less than the declared size. Here the value is 20.

21   The complete dialogue is:

```
Enter a line of input:
a b c d e f g
a b END OF OUTPUT
```

22   The complete dialogue is:

```
Enter a line of input:
abcdef gh
ace h
```

Note that the output is simply every other character of the input, and note that the blank is treated just like any other character.

23   The complete dialogue is:

```
Enter a line of input:
0 1 2 3 4 5 6 7 8 9 10 11
01234567891 1
```

Be sure to note that only the '1' in the input string 10 is output. This is because cin.get is reading characters, not numbers, and so it reads the input 10 as the two characters '1' and '0'. Since this code is written to echo only every other character, the '0' is not output. Since the '0' is not output, the next character, which is a blank, is output, and so there is one blank in the output. Similarly, only one of the two '1' characters in 11 is output. If this is unclear, write the input on a sheet of paper and use a small square for the blank character. Then, cross out every other character; the output shown above is what is left.

24 This code contains an infinite loop and will continue as long as the user continues to give it input. The Boolean expression (next != '\n') is always true because next is filled via the statement

```
cin >> next;
```

and this statement always skips the new-line character '\n' (as well as any blanks). The code will run and if the user gives no additional input, the dialogue will be as follows:

```
Enter a line of input:
0 1 2 3 4 5 6 7 8 9 10 11
0246811
```

Notice that the code in Self-Test Exercise 23 used cin.get, so it reads every character, *whether the character is the blank or not*, and then it outputs every other character. So the code in Self-Test Exercise 23 outputs every other character even if the character is the blank. On the other hand, the code in this Self-Test Exercise uses cin and >>, so it *skips over all blanks* and considers only nonblank characters (which in this case are the digits '0' through '9'). Thus, this code outputs every other *nonblank* character. The two '1' characters in the output are the first character in the input **10** and the first character in the input **11.**

25

```
void text_to_screen(ifstream& file_stream)
{
    char next;
    file_stream.get(next);
    while (! file_stream.eof( ))
    {
        cout << next;
        file_stream.get(next);
    }
}
```

If you prefer, you can use cout.put(next); instead of cout << next;

26 The complete dialogue is as follows:

```
Enter a line of input:
I'll see you at 10:30 AM.
I'll see you at 1<END OF OUTPUT
```

27

```
cout << "Enter a line of input:\n";
char next;
do
{
    cin.get(next);
    if (!isupper(next))
        cout << next;
} while (next != '\n');
```

Note that you should use !isupper(next) and not use islower(next). This is because islower(next) is *false* if next contains a character that is not a letter (such as the blank or comma symbol).

28   cin is of type istream; cout is of type ostream.

29

```
void copy_char(istream& source_file)
{
    char next;
    source_file.get(next);
    cout << next;
}
```

30

```
void copy_line(istream& source_file)
{
    char next;
    do
    {
        source_file.get(next);
        cout << next;
    }while (next != '\n');
}
```

31

```
void send_line(ostream& target_stream)
{
    char next;
```

```
    do
    {
        cin.get(next);
        target_stream << next;
    }while (next != '\n');
}
```

32 a. 2.0 1.1 2.3

    b. 2.0 3.0 2.3

    c. 2.0 3.0 4.0

33 One set of functions follows:

```
void func(double x)
{
    double y = 1.1;
    double z = 2.3;
    cout << x << " " << y << " " << z << endl;
}
void func(double x, double y)
{
    double z = 2.3;
    cout << x << " " << y << " " << z << endl;
}
void func(double x, double y, double z)
{
    cout << x << " " << y << " " << z << endl;
}
```

34 False. The situation stated here is the reverse of the correct situation. Any stream that is of type ifstream is also of type istream, so a formal parameter of type istream can be replaced by an argument of type ifstream in a function call, and similarly for the streams ostream and ofstream.

Programming Projects

1 Write a program that will search a file of numbers of type *int* and write the largest and the smallest numbers to the screen. The file contains nothing but numbers of type *int* separated by blanks or line breaks. If this is being done as a class assignment, obtain the file name from your instructor.

2 Write a program that takes its input from a file of numbers of type *double* and outputs the average of the numbers in the file to the screen. The file contains nothing but numbers of type *double* separated by blanks and/or line breaks. If this is being done as a class assignment, obtain the file name from your instructor.

3 a. Compute the median of a data file. The median is the number that has the same number of data elements greater than the number as there are less than the number. For purposes of this problem, you are to assume that the data is sorted (i.e., is in increasing order). The median is the middle element of the file if there are an odd number of elements, or the average of the two middle elements if the file has an even number of elements. You will need to open the file, count the members, close the file and calculate the location of the middle of the file, open the file again (recall the 'start over' discussion at the beginning of this chapter), count up to the file entries you need, and calculate the middle.

   If your instructor has assigned this problem, ask for a data file to test your program with. Otherwise, construct several files on your own, one with an even number of data points, increasing, and an odd number, also increasing.

   b. For a sorted file, a quartile is one of three numbers; the first has 1/4 the data values less than it, 1/4 the data values between the first and second numbers, 1/4 the data points between the second and the third, and 1/4 above the third quartile. Find the three quartiles for the datafile you used for part (a).

   Hint: You should recognize that having done part (a) you have one-third of your job done. (You have the second quartile already.) You also should recognize that you have done almost all the work toward finding the other two quartiles as well.

4 Write a program that takes its input from a file of numbers of type *double*. The program outputs to the screen the average and standard deviation of the numbers in the file. The file contains nothing but numbers of type *double* separated by blanks and/or line breaks. The standard deviation of a list of numbers n_1, n_2, n_3, and so forth is defined as the square root of the average of the following numbers:

$$(n_1 - a)^2, (n_2 - a)^2, (n_3 - a)^2, \text{ and so forth.}$$

The number a is the average of the numbers n_1, n_2, n_3, and so forth. If this is being done as a class assignment, obtain the file name from your instructor. Hint: Write your program so that it first reads the entire file and computes the average of all the numbers, then closes the file, then reopens the file and computes the standard deviation. You will find it helpful to first do Programming Project 2 and then modify that program to obtain the program for this Project.

5   Write a program that gives and takes advice on program writing. The program starts by writing a piece of advice to the screen and asking the user to type in a different piece of advice. The program then ends. The next person to run the program receives the advice given by the person who last ran the program. The advice is kept in a file and the contents of the file changes after each run of the program. You can use your editor to enter the initial piece of advice in the file so that the first person who runs the program receives some advice. Allow the user to type in advice of any length so that it can be any number of lines long. The user is told to end his or her advice by pressing the return key two times. Your program can then test to see that it has reached the end of the input by checking to see when it reads two consecutive occurrences of the character '\n'.

6   Write a program that reads text from one file and writes an edited version of the same text to another file. The edited version is identical to the unedited version except that every string of two or more consecutive blanks is replaced by a single blank. Thus, the text is edited to remove any extra blank characters. Your program should define a function that is called with the input and output-file streams as arguments. If this is being done as a class assignment, obtain the file names from your instructor.

7   Write a program that merges the numbers in two files and writes all the numbers into a third file. Your program takes input from two different files and writes its output to a third file. Each input file contains a list of numbers of type *int* in sorted order from the smallest to the largest. After the program is run, the output file will contain all the numbers in the two input files in one longer list in sorted order from smallest to largest. Your program should define a function that is called with the two input-file streams and the output-file stream as three arguments. If this is being done as a class assignment, obtain the file names from your instructor.

8   Write a program to generate personalized junk mail. The program takes input both from an input file and from the keyboard. The input file contains the text of a letter, except that the name of the recipient is indicated by the three characters #N#. The program asks the user for a name and then writes the letter to a second file but with the three letters #N# replaced by the name. The three-letter string #N# will occur exactly once in the letter. Hint: Have your program read from the input file until it encounters the three characters #N#, and have it copy what it reads to the output file as it goes. When it encounters

the three letters #N#, it then sends output to the screen asking for the name from the keyboard. You should be able to figure out the rest of the details. Your program should define a function that is called with the input and output-file streams as arguments. If this is being done as a class assignment, obtain the file names from your instructor.

Harder version (using material in the section "File Names as Input (Optional))": Allow the string #N# to occur any number of times in the file. In this case the name is stored in two string variables. For this version assume that there is a first name and last name but no middle names or initials.

9   Write a program to compute numeric grades for a course. The course records are in a file that will serve as the input file. The input file is in exactly the following format: Each line contains a student's last name, then one space, then the student's first name, then one space, then ten quiz scores all on one line. The quiz scores are whole numbers and are separated by one space. Your program will take its input from this file and send its output to a second file. The data in the output file will be exactly the same as the data in the input file except that there will be one additional number (of type *double*) at the end of each line. This number will be the average of the student's ten quiz scores. If this is being done as a class assignment, obtain the file names from your instructor. Use at least one function that has file streams as all or some of its arguments.

10   Enhance the program you wrote for Programming Project 9 in all of the following ways.

1) The list of quiz scores on each line will contain ten or fewer quiz scores. (If there are fewer than ten quiz scores that means that the student missed one or more quizzes.) The average score is still the sum of the quiz scores divided by 10. This amounts to giving the student a 0 for any missed quiz.

2) The output file will contain a line (or lines) at the beginning of the file explaining the output. Use formatting instructions to make the layout neat and easy to read.

3) After placing the desired output in an output file, your program will close all files and then copy the contents of the "output" file to the "input" file so the net effect is to change the contents of the input file.

Use at least two functions that have file streams as all or some of their arguments. If this is being done as a class assignment, obtain the file names from your instructor.

11 Write a program that will compute the average word length (average number of characters per word) for a file that contains some text. A word is defined to be any string of symbols that is preceded and followed by one of the following at each end: a blank, a comma, a period, the beginning of a line, or the end of a line. Your program should define a function that is called with the input-file stream as an argument. This function should also work with the stream `cin` as the input stream, although the function will not be called with `cin` as an argument in this program. If this is being done as a class assignment, obtain the file names from your instructor.

12 Write a program that will correct a C++ program that has errors in which operator, << or >>, it uses with `cin` and `cout`. The program replaces each (incorrect) occurrence of

    cin <<

with the corrected version

    cin >>

and each (incorrect) occurrence of

    cout >>

with the corrected version

    cout <<

For an easier version assume that there is always exactly one blank symbol between any occurrence of `cin` and a following <<, and similarly assume that there is always exactly one blank space between each occurrence of `cout` and a following >>. For a harder version allow for the possibility that there may be any number of blanks, even zero blanks, between `cin` and << and between `cout` and >>; in this harder case, the replacement corrected version has only one blank between the `cin` or `cout` and the following operator. The program to be corrected is in one file and the corrected version is output to a second file. Your program should define a function that is called with the input and output-file streams as arguments. If this is being done as a class assignment, obtain the file names from your instructor and ask your instructor whether you should do the easier version or the harder version. Hint: Even if you are doing the harder version, you will probably find it easier and quicker to first do the easier version and then modify your program so that it performs the harder task.

13 Write a program that allows the user to type in any one line question and that answers that question. The program will not really pay any attention to the question, but will simply read the question line and discard all that it reads. It always gives one of the following answers:

```
I'm not sure but I think you will find the answer in Chapter #N.
That's a good question.
If I were you, I would not worry about such things.
That question has puzzled philosophers for centuries.
I don't know. I'm just a machine.
Think about it and the answer will come to you.
I used to know the answer to that question, but I've forgotten it.
The answer can be found in a secret place in the woods.
```

These answers are stored in a file (one answer per line), and your program simply reads the next answer from the file and writes it out as the answer to the question. After your program has read the entire file, it simply closes the file, reopens the file, and starts down the list of answers again. Whenever your program outputs the first answer it should replace the two symbols #N with a number between 1 and 14 (including the possibility of 1 and 14). In order to choose a number between 1 and 14, your program should initialize a variable to 14 and decrease the variable's value by 1 each time it outputs a number so that the chapter numbers count backward from 14 to 1. When the variable reaches the value 0, your program should change its value back to 14. Give the number 14 the name NUMBER_OF_CHAPTERS with a global named constant declaration using the *const* modifier. Hint: Use the function new_line defined in this chapter.

14 This project is the same as Programming Project 13 except that in this project your program will use a more sophisticated method for choosing the answer to a question. When your program reads a question, it counts the number of characters in the question and stores the number in a variable named count. It then responds with answer number count%ANSWERS. The first answer in the file is answer number 0, the next is answer number 1, then 2, and so forth. ANSWERS is defined in a constant declaration, as shown below, so that it is equal to the number of answers in the answer file:

```
const int ANSWERS = 8;
```

This way you can change the answer file so that it contains more or fewer answers and you need change only the constant declaration to make your program work correctly for a different number of possible answers. Assume that the answer listed first in the file will always be the following, even if the answer file is changed:

```
I'm not sure but I think you will find the answer in Chapter #N.
```

When replacing the two characters #N with a number, use the number (count%NUMBER_OF_CHAPTERS + 1), where count is the variable discussed above, and NUMBER_OF_CHAPTERS is a global named constant defined to be equal to the number of chapters in this book.

15 This program numbers the lines found in a text file.

Write a program that reads text from a file and outputs each line preceded by a line number. Print the line number right-adjusted in a field of 3 spaces. Follow the line number with a colon, then one space, then the text of the line. You should get a character at a time, and write code to ignore leading blanks on each line. You may assume that the lines are short enough to fit within a line on the screen. Otherwise, allow default printer or screen output behavior if the line is too long (i.e., wrap or truncate).

A somewhat harder version determines the number of spaces needed in the field for the line numbers by counting lines before processing the lines of the file. This version of the program should insert a new line after the last complete word that will fit within a 72-character line.

CHAPTER

6

Defining Classes and Abstract Data Types

6 Defining Classes and Abstract Data Types

The Time has come the walrus said
  to talk of many things
of shoes and ships and sealing wax
  of cabbages and kings.

LEWIS CARROLL, THROUGH THE LOOKING GLASS

Introduction

In Chapter 5 you learned how to use classes and objects, but not how to define classes. In this chapter we will show you how to define your own classes. A class is a data type. You can use the classes you define in the same way you use the predefined data types, such as *int*, *char*, and ifstream. However, unless you define your classes the right way, they will not be as well behaved as the predefined data types. An *abstract data type* is a programmer-defined data type that is as well behaved as the predefined data types. In this chapter we will define what it means for a data type to be an abstract data type and show you how to define your classes in a way that will make them abstract data types.

6.1 Structures

As we said in Chapter 5, an object is a variable that has member functions and a class is a data type whose variables are objects. Thus, the definition of a class should be a data type definition that describes two things: 1) what kinds of values the variables can hold and 2) what the member functions are. We will do this in two steps. We will first tell you how to give a type definition for a *structure*. A structure (of the kind discussed here) can be thought of as an object without any member functions. After you learn about structures it will be a natural extension to define classes.

Structures for Diverse Data

Sometimes it is useful to have a collection of values of different types and to treat the collection as a single item. For example, consider a bank certificate of deposit, which is often called a CD. A CD is a bank account that does not allow withdrawals for a specified number of months. A CD naturally has three pieces of data associated with it: the account balance, the interest rate for the account, and the term, which is the number of months until maturity. The first two items can be represented as values of type *double*, and the number of months can be represented as a value of type *int*. Display 6.1 shows the definition of a structure called CDAccount which can be used for this kind of account. The definition is embedded in a complete program that demonstrates this structure type definition. As you can see from the sample dialogue, this particular bank specializes in short-term CDs so the term will always be 12 or fewer months. Let's look at how this sample structure is defined and used.

The structure definition is as follows:

struct

```
struct CDAccount
{
    double balance;
    double interest_rate;
    int term;//months until maturity
};
```

The keyword *struct* announces that this is a structure type definition. The identifier CDAccount is the name of the structure type. The name of a structure type is called the **structure tag.** The structure tag can be any legal identifier (but not a keyword). Although this is not required by the C++ language, structure tags are usually spelled with a mix of uppercase and lowercase letters. The identifiers declared inside the braces {} are called **member names.** As illustrated in this example, a structure type definition ends with both a brace } *and a semicolon.*

structure tag

member names

A structure definition is usually placed outside of any function definition (in the same way that globally defined constant declarations are placed outside of all function definitions). The structure type is then available to all the code that follows the structure definition.

where to place a structure definition

Once a structure type definition has been given, the structure type can be used just like the predefined types *int*, *char*, and so forth. For example, the following will declare two variables, named my_account and your_account, both of type CDAccount:

structure variables

```
CDAccount my_account, your_account;
```

A structure variable can hold values just like any other variable can hold values. A **structure value** is a collection of smaller values called **member values.** There is one member value for each member name declared in the structure definition. For example, a value of the type CDAccount is a collection of three member values, two of type *double* and one of type *int*. The member values that together make up the structure value are stored in *member variables*, which we discuss next.

structure value member values

Each structure type specifies a list of member names. In Display 6.1 the structure CDAccount has the three member names: balance, interest_rate, and term. Each of these member names can be used to pick out one smaller variable that is a

Display 6.1 A Structure Definition (part 1 of 2)

```
//Program to demonstrate the CDAccount structure type.
#include <iostream>
using namespace std;

//Structure for a bank certificate of deposit:
struct CDAccount
{
    double balance;
    double interest_rate;
    int term;//months until maturity
};


void get_data(CDAccount& the_account);
//Postcondition: the_account.balance and the_account.interest_rate
//have been given values that the user entered at the keyboard.


int main( )
{
    CDAccount account;
    get_data(account);

    double rate_fraction, interest;
    rate_fraction = account.interest_rate/100.0;
    interest = account.balance*rate_fraction*(account.term/12.0);
    account.balance = account.balance + interest;

    cout.setf(ios::fixed);
    cout.setf(ios::showpoint);
    cout.precision(2);
    cout << "When your CD matures in "
         << account.term << " months,\n"
         << "it will have a balance of $"
         << account.balance << endl;
    return 0;
}
```

Display 6.1 A Structure Definition *(part 2 of 2)*

```
//Uses iostream:
void get_data(CDAccount& the_account)
{
    cout << "Enter account balance: $";
    cin >> the_account.balance;
    cout << "Enter account interest rate: ";
    cin >> the_account.interest_rate;
    cout << "Enter the number of months until maturity\n"
         << "(must be 12 or fewer months): ";
    cin >> the_account.term;
}
```

Sample Dialogue

```
Enter account balance: $100.00
Enter account interest rate: 10.0
Enter the number of months until maturity
(must be 12 or fewer months): 6
When your CD matures in 6 months,
it will have a balance of $105.00
```

part of the larger structure variable. These smaller variables are called **member variables.** Member variables are specified by giving the name of the structure variable followed by a dot (that is, followed by a period) and then the member name. For example, if account is a structure variable of type CDAccount (as declared in Display 6.1), then the structure variable account has the following three member variables:

member variables

```
account.balance
account.interest_rate
account.term
```

The first two member variables are of type *double* and the last is of type *int*. These member variables can be used just like any other variables of those types. For example, the above member variables can be given values with the following three assignment statements:

```
account.balance = 1000.00;
account.interest_rate = 4.7;
account.term = 11;
```

The result of these three statements is diagrammed in Display 6.2. Member variables can be used in all the ways that ordinary variables can be used. For example, the following line from the program in Display 6.1 will add the value contained in the member variable `account.balance` and the value contained in the ordinary variable `interest` and will then place the result in the member variable `account.balance`:

```
account.balance = account.balance + interest;
```

dot operator

Notice that you specify a member variable for a structure variable by using the dot operator in exactly the same way you used it in Chapter 5, where the dot operator was used to specify a member function of a class. The only difference is that in the case of structures, the members are variables rather than functions.

reusing member names

Two or more structure types may use the same member names. For example, it is perfectly legal to have the following two type definitions in the same program:

```
struct FertilizerStock
{
    double quantity;
    double nitrogen_content;
};
```

and

```
struct CropYield
{
    int quantity;
    double size;
};
```

This coincidence of names will produce no problems. For example, if you declare the following two structure variables:

```
FertilizerStock super_grow;
CropYield apples;
```

then the quantity of `super_grow` fertilizer is stored in the member variable `super_grow.quantity` and the quantity of apples produced is stored in the member variable `apples.quantity`. The dot operator and the structure variable specify which `quantity` is meant in each instance.

Display 6.2 Member Values

```
struct CDAccount
{
    double balance;
    double interest_rate;
    int term;//months until maturity
};
int main()
{
    CDAccount account;
        . . .
```

```
                                    balance        │    ?    │ ⎫
                                    interest_rate  │    ?    │ ⎬ account
                                    term           │    ?    │ ⎭
account.balance = 1000.00;
                                    balance        │ 1000.00 │ ⎫
                                    interest_rate  │    ?    │ ⎬ account
                                    term           │    ?    │ ⎭
account.interest_rate = 4.7;
                                    balance        │ 1000.00 │ ⎫
                                    interest_rate  │   4.7   │ ⎬ account
                                    term           │    ?    │ ⎭
account.term = 11;
                                    balance        │ 1000.00 │ ⎫
                                    interest_rate  │   4.7   │ ⎬ account
                                    term           │   11    │ ⎭
```

A structure value can be viewed as a collection of member values. Viewed this way a structure value is many different values. A structure value can also be viewed as a single (complex) value (that just happens to be made up of member values). Since a structure value can be viewed as a single value, structure values and structure variables can be used in the same ways that you use simple values and simple variables of the predefined types such as *int*. In particular, you can assign structure values using the equal sign. For example, if apples and oranges are structure variables of the type CropYield defined on page 304, then the following is perfectly legal:

structure variables in assignment statements

```
apples = oranges;
```

The above assignment statement is equivalent to:

```
apples.quantity = oranges.quantity;
apples.size = oranges.size;
```

The Dot Operator

The **dot operator** is used to specify a member variable of a structure variable.

Syntax:

dot operator

Structure_Variable_Name . *Member_Variable_Name*

Examples:

```
struct StudentRecord
{
    int student_number;
    char grade;
};

int main( )
{
    StudentRecord your_record;
    your_record.student_number = 2001;
    your_record.grade = 'A';
```

Some writers call the dot operator the "structure member access operator," although we will not use that term.

◆ **PITFALL**   **Forgetting a Semicolon in a Structure Definition**

When you add the final brace } to a structure definition it feels like the structure definition is finished, but it is not. You must also place a semicolon after that final brace. There is a reason for this, even though the reason is a feature that we will have no occasion to use. A structure definition is more than a definition. It can also be used to declare structure variables. You are allowed to list structure variable names between that final brace and that final semicolon. For example, the following defines a structure called WeatherData and declares two structure variables, data_point1 and data_point2, both of type WeatherData:

```
struct WeatherData
{
    double temperature;
    double wind_velocity;
} data_point1, data_point2;
```

However, as we said, we will always separate a structure definition and the declaration of variables of that structure type, so our structure definitions will always have a semicolon immediately after the final brace.

Structures as Function Arguments

A function can have call-by-value parameters of a structure type and/or call-by-reference parameters of a structure type. The program in Display 6.1, for example, includes a function named get_data that has a call-by-reference parameter with the structure type CDAccount.

structure arguments

A structure type can also be the type for the value returned by a function. For example, the following defines a function that takes three appropriate arguments and returns a value of type CDAccount:

Functions can return structures

```
CDAccount shrink_wrap(double the_balance,
                      double the_rate, int the_term)
{
    CDAccount temp;
    temp.balance = the_balance;
    temp.interest_rate = the_rate;
    temp.term = the_term;
    return temp;
}
```

Notice the local variable temp of type CDAccount; temp is used to build up a complete structure value, which is then returned by the function. Once you have defined the function shrink_wrap, you can give a value to a variable of type CDAccount as illustrated below:

```
CDAccount new_account;
new_account = shrink_wrap(10000.00, 5.1, 11);
```

Simple Structure Types

You define a **structure type** as shown below. The *Structure_Tag* is the name of the structure type.

Syntax:

```
struct Structure_Tag
{
      Type_1  Member_Variable_Name_1;
      Type_2  Member_Variable_Name_2;
                    ⋮
      Type_Last  Member_Variable_Name_Last;
};  ←——————— Do not forget this semicolon.
```

Example:

```
struct Automobile
{
      int year;
      int doors;
      double horse_power;
      char model;
};
```

Although we will not use this feature, you can combine member names of the same type into a single list separated by commas. For example, the following is equivalent to the above structure definition:

```
struct Automobile
{
    int year, doors;
    double horse_power;
    char model;
};
```

Variables of a structure type can be declared in the same way as variables of other types. For example:

```
Automobile my_car, your_car;
```

The member variables are specified using the **dot operator.** For example: `my_car.year`, `my_car.doors`, `my_car.horse_power`, and `my_car.model`.

→ *PROGRAMMING* TIP
Use Hierarchical Structures

Sometimes it makes sense to have structures whose members are themselves smaller structures. For example, a structure type called `PersonInfo` which can be used to store a person's height, weight, and birth date, can be defined as follows:

structures within structures

```
struct Date
{
    int month;
    int day;
    int year;
};

struct PersonInfo
{
    double height;//in inches
    int weight;//in pounds
    Date birthday;
};
```

A structure variable of type `PersonInfo` is declared in the usual way:

```
PersonInfo person1;
```

If the structure variable `person1` has had its value set to record a person's birth date, then the year the person was born can be output to the screen as follows:

```
cout << person1.birthday.year;
```

The way to read such expressions is left to right, and very carefully. Starting at the left end, `person1` is a structure variable of type `PersonInfo`. To obtain the member variable with the name `birthday`, you use the dot operator as follows:

```
person1.birthday
```

This member variable is itself a structure variable of type `Date`. Thus, this member variable itself has member variables. A member variable of the structure variable `person1.birthday` is obtained by adding a dot and the member variable name, such as `year`, which produces the expression `person1.birthday.year` shown above.

Initializing Structures

You can initialize a structure at the time that it is declared. To give a structure variable a value you follow it by an equal sign and a list of the member values enclosed in braces. For example, the following definition of a structure type for a date was given in the previous subsection:

```
struct Date
{
    int month;
    int day;
    int year;
};
```

Once the type Date is defined, you can declare and initialize a structure variable called due_date as follows:

```
Date due_date = {12, 31, 1999};
```

Be sure to notice that the initializing values must be given in the order that corresponds to the order of member variables in the structure type definition. In this example, due_date.month receives the first initializing value of 12, due_date.day receives the second value of 31, and due_date.year receives the third value of 1999.

It is an error if there are more initializers than struct members. If there are fewer initializer values than struct members, the provided values are used to initialize data members, in order. Each data member without an initializer is initialized to a zero value of an appropriate type for the variable.

SELF-TEST EXERCISES

1   Given the structure and structure variable declaration:

```
struct CDAccount
{
    double balance;
    double interest_rate;
    int term;
    char initial1;
    char initial2;
};

CDAccount account;
```

what is the type of each of the following? Mark any that are not correct.

a. `account.balance`
b. `account.interest_rate`
c. `CDAccount.term`
d. `savings_account.initial1`
e. `account.initial2`
f. `account`

2 Consider the following type definition:

```
struct ShoeType
{
    char style;
    double price;
};
```

Given the above structure type definitions, what will be the output produced by the following code:

```
ShoeType shoe1, shoe2;
shoe1.style ='A';
shoe1.price = 9.99;
cout << shoe1.style << " $" << shoe1.price << endl;
shoe2 = shoe1;

shoe2.price = shoe2.price/9;
cout << shoe2.style << " $" << shoe2.price << endl;
```

3 What is the error in the following structure definition? What is the message your compiler gives for this error? State what the error is, in your own words.

```
struct Stuff
{
    int b;
    int c;
}
int main( )
{
    Stuff x;
    // other code
}
```

4 Given the following `struct` definition:

```
struct A
{
    int member b;
    int member c;
};
```

Declare x to have this structure type. Initialize the members of x, member a and member b, to the values 1 and 2, respectively.

Note: This requests an initialization, not an assignment of the members. This distinction is important and will be made in the text in a later chapter.

5 Here is an initialization of a structure type. Tell what happens with each initialization. Note any problems with these initializations.

```
struct Date
{
    int month;
    int day;
    int year;
};
```
a. `Date due_date = {12, 21};`
b. `Date due_date = {12, 21, 1995};`
c. `Date due_date = {12, 21, 19, 95};`
d. `Date due_date = {12, 21, 95};`

6 Write a definition for a structure type for records consisting of a person's wage rate, accrued vacation (which is some whole number of days), and status (which is either hourly or salaried). Represent the status as one of the two *char* values 'H' and 'S'. Call the type `EmployeeRecord`.

7 Give a function definition corresponding to the following function prototype. (The type `ShoeType` is given in Self-Test Exercise 2.)

```
void read_shoe_record(ShoeType& new_shoe);
//Fills new_shoe with values read from the keyboard.
```

8 Give a function definition corresponding to the following function prototype. (The type `ShoeType` is given in Self-Test Exercise 2.)

```
ShoeType discount(ShoeType old_record);
//Returns a structure that is the same as its argument,
//but with the price reduced by 10%.
```

6.2 Classes

I don't care to belong to any club that will accept me as a member.

GROUCHO MARX, THE GROUCHO LETTERS

Defining Classes and Member Functions

A **class** is a data type whose variables are objects. In Chapter 5 we described an **object** as a variable that has member functions as well as the ability to hold data values. Thus, within a C++ program, the definition of a class should be a data type definition that describes what kinds of values the variables can hold and also what the member functions are. A structure definition describes some of these things. A structure is a defined type that allows you to define values of the structure type by defining member variables. To obtain a class from a structure, all you need to do is add some member functions. A sample class definition is given in the program shown in Display 6.3. The type DayOfYear defined there is a class definition for objects whose values are dates, such as January 1 or July 4. These values can be used to record holidays, birthdays, and other special dates. In this definition of DayOfYear the month is recorded as an *int* value with 1 standing for January, 2 standing for February, and so forth. The day of the month is recorded in a second *int* member variable. The class DayOfYear has one member function called output, which has no arguments and outputs the month and day values to the screen. Let's look at the definition for the class DayOfYear in detail.

class
object

The definition of the class DayOfYear is shown near the top of Display 6.3. For the moment, ignore the line that contains the keyword *public*. This line simply says that the member variables and functions have no restriction on them. We will explain this line later in this chapter. The rest of the definition of the class DayOfYear is very much like a structure definition, except that it uses the keyword *class* instead of *struct* and it lists the member function output (as well as the member variables month and day). Notice that the member function output is listed by giving its prototype. A class definition contains only the prototypes for its member functions. The definitions for the member functions are given elsewhere. (In a C++ class definition, you can intermix the ordering of the member variables and member functions in any way you wish, but the style we will follow has a tendency to list the member functions before the member variables.) Objects (that is, variables) of a class type are declared in the same way as variables of the predefined types and in the same way as structure variables.

a member function

Member functions for classes that you define are called in the same way as we described in Chapter 5 for predefined classes. For example, the program in Display 6.3

calling member functions

Display 6.3 Class with a Member Function (part 1 of 2)

```
//Program to demonstrate a very simple example of a class.
//A better version of the class DayOfYear will be given in Display 6.4.
#include <iostream>
using namespace std;

class DayOfYear
{
public:
    void output( );                    member function prototype
    int month;
    int day;
};

int main( )
{
    DayOfYear today, birthday;

    cout << "Enter today's date:\n";
    cout << "Enter month as a number: ";
    cin >> today.month;
    cout << "Enter the day of the month: ";
    cin >> today.day;
    cout << "Enter your birthday:\n";
    cout << "Enter month as a number: ";
    cin >> birthday.month;
    cout << "Enter the day of the month: ";
    cin >> birthday.day;

    cout << "Today's date is ";
    today.output( );
    cout << "Your birthday is ";                calls to the member
    birthday.output( );                         function output

    if (today.month == birthday.month
        && today.day == birthday.day)
        cout << "Happy Birthday!\n";
    else
        cout << "Happy Unbirthday!\n";

    return 0;
}
```

Display 6.3 Class with a Member Function *(part 2 of 2)*

```
//Uses iostream:
void DayOfYear::output( )
{
    cout << "month = " << month
         << ", day = " << day << endl;
}
```

member function definition

Sample Dialogue

```
Enter today's date:
Enter month as a number: 10
Enter the day of the month: 15
Enter your birthday:
Enter month as a number: 2
Enter the day of the month: 21
Today's date is month = 10, day = 15
Your birthday is month = 2, day = 21
Happy Unbirthday!
```

declares two objects of type DayOfYear in the following way:

```
DayOfYear today, birthday;
```

The member function output is called with the object today as follows:

```
today.output( );
```

and the member function output is called with the object birthday as follows:

```
birthday.output( );
```

Encapsulation

Combining a number of items, such as variables and functions, into a single package, such as an object of some class, is called **encapsulation.**

When a member function is defined, the definition must include the class name, because there may be two or more classes that have member functions with the same name. In Display 6.3 there is only one class definition, but in other situations you may have many class definitions, and each class may have a member function called output. The definition for the member function output of the class DayOfYear is shown in part 2 of Display 6.3. The definition is similar to an ordinary function definition but there are some differences.

The heading of the function definition for the member function output is as follows:

```
void DayOfYear::output( )
```

The operator :: is called the **scope resolution operator,** and it serves a purpose similar to that of the dot operator. Both the dot operator and the scope resolution operator are used to tell what a member function is a member of. However, the scope resolution operator :: is used with a class name, while the dot operator is used with objects (that is, with class variables). The scope resolution operator consists of two colons with no space between them. The class name that precedes the scope resolution operator is often called a **type qualifier,** because it specializes ("qualifies") the function name to one particular type.

Look at the definition of the member function DayOfYear::output given in Display 6.3. Notice that in the function definition of DayOfYear::output, we used the member names month and day by themselves without first giving the object and dot operator. That is not as strange as it may at first appear. At this point we are simply defining the member function output. This definition of output will apply to all objects of type DayOfYear, but at this point we do not know the names of the objects of type DayOfYear that we will use, so we cannot give their names. When the member function is called, as in

```
today.output( );
```

all the member names in the function definition are specialized to the name of the calling object. So the above function call is equivalent to the following:

```
{
    cout << "month = " << today.month
         << ", day = " << today.day << endl;
}
```

In the function definition for a member function you can use the names of all members of that class (both the data members and the function members) without using the dot operator.

Member Function Definition

A member function is defined the same way as any other function except that the *Class_Name* and the scope resolution operator : : are given in the function heading.

Syntax:

Returned_Type Class_Name : : *Function_Name* (*Parameter_List*)
{
    Function_Body_Statements
}

Example:

```
//Uses iostream:
void DayOfYear::output( )
{
    cout << "month = " << month
        << ", day = " << day << endl;
}
```

The class definition for the above example class DayOfYear is given in Display 6.3, where month and day are defined as the names of member variables for the class DayOfYear. Note that month and day are not preceded by an object name and dot.

SELF-TEST EXERCISES

9   Below we have redefined the class DayOfYear from Display 6.3 so that it now has one additional member function called input. Write an appropriate definition for the member function input.

```
class DayOfYear
{
public:
    void input( );
    void output( );
    int month;
    int day;
};
```

The Dot Operator and the Scope Resolution Operator

Both the dot operator and the scope resolution operator are used with member names to specify what thing they are a member of. For example, suppose you have declared a class called DayOfYear and you declare an object called today as follows:

    DayOfYear today;

You use the **dot operator** to specify a member of the object today. For example, output is a member function for the class DayOfYear (defined in Display 6.3) and the following function call will output the data values stored in the object today:

    today.output( );

You use the **scope resolution operator** : : to specify the class name when giving the function definition for a member function. For example, the heading of the function definition for the member function output would be as follows:

    void DayOfYear::output( )

Remember, the scope resolution operator : : is used with a class name, while the dot operator is used with an object of that class.

10 Given the following class definition, write an appropriate definition for the member function set:

```
class Temperature
{
public:
    void set(double new_degrees, char new_scale);
    //Sets the member variables to the values given as
    //arguments.

    double degrees;
    char scale; //'F' for Fahrenheit or 'C' for Celsius.
};
```

11 Carefully distinguish between the meaning and use of the dot operator and the scope resolution operator : :.

Public and Private Members

The predefined types such as *double* are not implemented as C++ classes, but the people who wrote your C++ compiler did design some way to represent values of type *double* in your computer. It is possible to implement the type *double* in many different ways. In fact different versions of C++ do implement the type *double* in slightly different ways, but if you move your C++ program from one computer to another with a different implementation of the type *double*, your program should still work correctly.[1] Classes are types that you define and the types that you define should behave as well as the predefined types. You can build a library of your own class type definitions and use your types as if they were predefined types. For example, you could place each class definition in a separate file and copy it into any program that uses the type. Your class definitions should separate the rules for using the class and the details of the class implementation in as strong a way as was done for the predefined types. If you change the implementation of a class (for example, by changing some details in the definition of a member function in order to make function calls run faster), then you should not need to change any of the other parts of your programs. In order to realize this ideal, we need to describe one more feature of class definitions.

Look back at the definition of the type DayOfYear given in Display 6.3. The type DayOfYear is designed to hold values that represent dates such as birthdays and holidays. We chose to represent these dates as two integers, one for the month and one for the day of the month. We might later decide to change the representation of the month from one variable of type *int* to three variables of type *char*. In this changed version, the three characters would be an abbreviation of the month's name. For example, the three *char* values 'J', 'a', and 'n' would represent the month January. However, whether you use a single member variable of type *int* to record the month or three member variables of type *char* is an implementation detail that need not concern a programmer who uses the type DayOfYear. Of course, if you change the way the class DayOfYear represents the month, then you must change the implementation of the member function output—but that is all you should need to change. You should not need to change any other part of a program that uses your class definition for DayOfYear. Unfortunately, the program in Display 6.3 does not meet this ideal. For example, if you replace the one member variable named month with three member variables of type *char*, then there will be no member variable named month, so you must change those parts of the program that perform input and also change the *if-else*-statement.

---

[1]Sometimes this ideal is not quite realized, but in the ideal world it should be realized, and at least for simple programs, it is realized even in the imperfect world that we live in.

With an ideal class definition, you should be able to change the details of how the class is implemented and the only things you should need to change in any program that uses the class are the definitions of the member functions. In order to realize this ideal you must have enough member functions that you never need to access the member variables directly, but access them only through the member functions. Then, if you change the member variables, you need only change the definitions of the member functions to match your changes to the member variables, and nothing else in your programs need change. In Display 6.4 we have redefined the class DayOfYear so that it has enough member functions to do everything we want our programs to do, and so the program does not need to directly reference any member variables. If you look carefully at the program in Display 6.4, you will see that the only place the member variable names month and day are used is in the definitions of the member functions. There is no reference to today.month, today.day, bach_birthday.month, nor bach_birthday.day anyplace outside of the definitions of member functions.

The program in Display 6.4 has one new feature that is designed to ensure that no programmer who uses the class DayOfYear will ever directly reference any of its member variables. Notice the line in the definition of the class DayOfYear that contains the keyword *private*. All the member variable names that are listed after this line are **private members,** which means that they cannot be directly accessed in the program except within the definition of a member function. If you try to access one of these member variables in the main part of your program or in the definition of some function that is not a member function of this particular class, the compiler will give you an error message. If you insert the keyword *private* and a colon in the list of member variables and member functions, all the members that follow the label *private*: will be **private members.** The variables that follow the label *private*: will be **private member variables,** and the functions that follow it will be **private member functions.**

All the private members for the class DayOfYear defined in Display 6.4 are variables. A private member variable may be used in the definition of any of the member functions, but nowhere else. For example, with this changed definition of the class DayOfYear, the following two assignments are no longer permitted in the main part of the program:

private:

private member variables

```
DayOfYear today; //This line is OK.
today.month = 12;//ILLEGAL
today.day = 25;//ILLEGAL
```

Any reference to these private variables is illegal (except in the definition of member functions). Since this new definition makes month and day private member

Display 6.4 Class with Private Members *(part 1 of 2)*

```
//Program to demonstrate the class DayOfYear.
#include <iostream>
using namespace std;

class DayOfYear
{
public:
    void input();
    void output();

    void set(int new_month, int new_day);
    //Precondition: new_month and new_day form a possible date.
    //Postcondition: The date is reset according to the arguments.

    int get_month();
    //Returns the month, 1 for January, 2 for February, etc.

    int get_day();
    //Returns the day of the month.
private:
    int month;
    int day;
};

int main()
{
    DayOfYear today, bach_birthday;
    cout << "Enter today's date:\n";
    today.input();
    cout << "Today's date is ";
    today.output();

    bach_birthday.set(3, 21);
    cout << "J. S. Bach's birthday is ";
    bach_birthday.output();

    if ( today.get_month() == bach_birthday.get_month() &&
            today.get_day() == bach_birthday.get_day() )
        cout << "Happy Birthday Johann Sebastian!\n";
    else
        cout << "Happy Unbirthday Johann Sebastian!\n";
    return 0;
}
```

This is an improved version of the class DayOfYear *which we gave in Display 6.3.*

private members

Display 6.4 Class with Private Members *(part 2 of 2)*

```
//Uses iostream:
void DayOfYear::input()
{
    cout << "Enter the month as a number: ";
    cin >> month;
    cout << "Enter the day of the month: ";
    cin >> day;
}

void DayOfYear::output()
    <The rest of the definition of DayOfYear::output is given in Display 6.3.>

void DayOfYear::set(int new_month, int new_day)
{
    month = new_month;
    day = new_day;
}

int DayOfYear::get_month()
{
    return month;
}

int DayOfYear::get_day()
{
    return day;
}
```

Private members may be used in member function definitions (but not elsewhere).

Sample Dialogue

```
Enter today's date:
Enter the month as a number: 3
Enter the day of the month: 21
Today's date is month = 3, day = 21
J. S. Bach's birthday is month = 3, day = 21
Happy Birthday Johann Sebastian!
```

variables, the following are also illegal in the main part of any program that declares today to be of type DayOfYear:

```
cout << today.month;//ILLEGAL
cout << today.day;//ILLEGAL
if (today.month == 1) //ILLEGAL
    cout << "January";
```

Once you make a member variable a private member variable, there is then no way to change its value (nor to reference the member variable in any other way), except by using one of the member functions. This is a severe restriction, but, it is usually a wise restriction to impose. Programmers find that it usually makes their code easier to understand and easier to update if they make all member variables private.

It may seem that the program in Display 6.4 does not really disallow direct access to the private member variables, since they can be changed using the member function DayOfYear::set, and their values can be discovered using the member functions DayOfYear::get_month and DayOfYear::get_day. While that is true for the program in Display 6.4, it might not be true if we changed the implementation of how we represented the month and/or day in our dates. For example, suppose we change the type definition of DayOfYear to the following:

```
class DayOfYear
{
public:
    void input( );
    void output( );

    void set(int new_month, int new_day);
    //Precondition: new_month and new_day form a possible date.
    //Postcondition: The date is reset according to the
    //arguments.

    int get_month( );
    //Returns the month, 1 for January, 2 for February, etc.

    int get_day( );
    //Returns the day of the month.
private:
    char first_letter;//of month
    char second_letter;//of month
    char third_letter;//of month
    int day;
};
```

It would then be slightly more difficult to define the member functions, but they could be redefined so that they would behave *exactly* as they did before. For example, the definition of the function get_month might start as follows:

```
int DayOfYear::get_month( )
{
    if (first_letter == 'J' && second_letter == 'a'
            && third_letter == 'n')
        return 1;
    if (first_letter == 'F' && second_letter == 'e'
            && third_letter == 'b')
        return 2;
        . . .
```

This would be rather tedious, but not difficult.

private member functions

It is also possible to make a member function private. Like a private member variable, a private member function can be used in the definition of any other member function, but nowhere else, such as in the main part of a program that uses the class type. The next Programming Example includes a class with a private member function.

public:

The keyword *public* is used to indicate **public members** the same way that the *private* is used to indicate private members. For example, for the class DayOfYear defined in Display 6.4, all the member functions are public members (and all the member variables are private members). A public member can be used in the main body of your program or in the definition of any function, even a nonmember function.

You can have any number of occurrences of *public* and *private* in a class definition. Every time you insert the label

    public:

the list of members changes from private to public. Every time you insert the label

    private:

the list of members changes back to being private members. For example, the member function do_something_else and the member variable more_stuff in the following structure definition are private members, while the other four members are all public:

```
class SampleClass
{
public:
    void do_something( );
```

```
    int stuff;
private:
    void do_something_else( );
    char more_stuff;
public:
    double do_yet_another_thing( );
    double even_more_stuff;
};
```

(If you list members at the start of your class definition and do not insert either
public: or *private*: before these first members, then they will be private members. However, it is a good idea to always explicitly label each group of members as
either *public* or *private*.)

↷ *PROGRAMMING* `TIP`
Make All Member Variables Private

When defining a class, the normal practice is to make all member variables private.
This means that the member variables can only be accessed or changed using the
member functions. Much of this chapter is dedicated to explaining how and why you
should define classes in this way.

↷ *PROGRAMMING* `TIP`
Define Accessor Functions

The operator == can be used to test two values of a simple type to see if they are equal.
Unfortunately, the predefined operator == does not automatically apply to objects. In
Chapter 8 we will show you how you can make the operator == apply to the objects of
the classes you define. Until then, you will not be able to use the equality operator ==
with objects (nor can you use it with structures). This can produce some complications. When defining a class, the preferred style is to make all member variables private. Thus, in order to test two objects to see if they represent the same value, you need
some way to access the values of the member variables (or something equivalent to the
values of the member variables). This allows you to test for equality by testing the values of each pair of corresponding member variables. To do this in Display 6.4 we used
the member functions get_month and get_day in the *if-else*-statement.

Member functions, such as get_month and get_day, that give you access to the
values of the private member variables, are called **accessor functions.** Given the
techniques you have learned to date, it is important to always include a complete set
of accessor functions with each class definition so that you can test objects for equality. The accessor functions need not literally return the values of each member

accessor functions

Classes and Objects

A **class** is a type whose variables are **objects.** These objects can have both member variables and member functions. The syntax for a class definition is:

Syntax:

```
class Class_Name
{
public:
        Member_Specification_1
        Member_Specification_2
                ⋮
        Member_Specification_n
private:
        Member_Specification_n+1
        Member_Specification_n+2
                ⋮
};
```

public members

private members

Do not forget this semicolon.

Each *Member_Specification_i* is either a member variable declaration or a member function prototype. (Additional `public` and `private` sections are permitted.)

Example:

```
class Bicycle
{
public:
    char get_color();
    int number_of_speeds();
    void set(int the_speeds, char the_color);
private:
    int speeds;
    char color;
};
```

Once a class is defined, an **object** (which is just a variable of the class type) can be declared in the same way as variables of any other type. For example, the following declares two objects of type `Bicycle`:

```
Bicycle my_bike, your_bike;
```

variable, but they must return something equivalent to those values. In Chapter 8 we will develop a more elegant method to test two objects for equality, but even after you learn that technique, it will still be handy to have accessor functions.

➤ PROGRAMMING TIP
Use the Assignment Operator
with Objects

It is perfectly legal to use the assignment operator = with objects or with structures. For example, suppose the class DayOfYear is defined as shown in Display 6.4 so that it has two private member variables named month and day, and suppose that the objects due_date and tomorrow are declared as follows:

```
DayOfYear due_date, tomorrow;
```

then the following is perfectly legal (provided the member variables of the object tomorrow have already been given values):

```
due_date = tomorrow;
```

The above assignment is equivalent to the following:

```
due_date.month = tomorrow.month;
due_date.day = tomorrow.day;
```

Moreover, this is true even though the member variables named month and day are private members of the class DayOfYear.[2]

SELF-TEST EXERCISES

12 Suppose your program contains the following class definition:

```
class Automobile
{
public:
    void set_price(double new_price);
    void set_profit(double new_profit);
    double get_price();
```

---

[2]In Chapter 11 we will see situations in which the assignment operator = should be overloaded by a class, but you need not worry about that now.

```
private:
    double price;
    double profit;
    double get_profit( );
};
```

and suppose the `main` part of your program contains the following declaration and that the program somehow sets the values of all the member variables to some values:

```
Automobile hyundai, jaguar;
```

Which of the following statements are then allowed in the `main` part of your program?

```
hyundai.price = 4999.99;
jaguar.set_price(30000.97);
double a_price, a_profit;
a_price = jaguar.get_price( );
a_profit = jaguar.get_profit( );
a_profit = hyundai.get_profit( );
if (hyundai == jaguar)
    cout << "Want to swap cars?";
hyundai = jaguar;
```

13 Suppose you change Self-Test Exercise 12 so that the definition of the class `Automobile` omits the line that contains the keyword *private*. How would this change your answer to the question in Self-Test Exercise 12?

14 Explain what *public:* and *private:* do in a class definition. In particular, explain why we do not just make everything *public:* and save difficulty in access.

15 a. How many *public:* sections are required in a class for the class to be useful?

   b. How many *private:* sections are required in a class?

   c. What kind of section do you have between the opening { and the first *public:* section of a class?

   d. What kind of section do you have between the opening { and the first *public:* section of a structure?

■)) *PROGRAMMING* *EXAMPLE*
Bank Account Class—Version 1

Display 6.5 contains a class definition for a bank account that illustrates all of the points about class definitions you have seen thus far. This type of bank account allows you to withdraw your money at any time, so it has no term as did the type CDAccount which you saw earlier. A more important difference is the fact that the class BankAccount has member functions for all the operations you would expect to use in a program. Objects of the class BankAccount have two private member variables: one to record the account balance and one to record the interest rate. A number of features of the class BankAccount are new. Let's discuss them one at a time.

First, notice that the class BankAccount has a private member function called fraction. Since fraction is a private member function, it cannot be called in the body of main or in the body of any function that is not a member function of the class BankAccount. The function fraction can only be called in the definitions of other member functions of the class BankAccount. The only reason we have this (or any) private member function is to aid us in defining other member functions for the same class. In our definition of the class BankAccount, we included the member function fraction so that we could use it in the definition of the function update. The function fraction takes one argument that is a percentage figure, like 10.0 for 10.0%, and converts it to a fraction, like 0.10. That allows us to compute the amount of interest on the account at the given percent. If the account contains $100.00 and the interest rate is 10%, then the interest is equal to $100 times 0.10, which is $10.00.

private member function

When you call a public member function, such as update, in the main body of your program, you must include an object name and a dot as in the following line from Display 6.5:

```
account1.update();
```

However, when you call a private member function (or any other member functions) within the definition of another member function, you use only the member function name without any calling object or dot operator. For example, the following definition of the member function BankAccount::update includes a call to BankAccount::fraction (as shown in Display 6.5):

one member function calling another

```
void BankAccount::update()
{
    balance = balance + fraction(interest_rate)*balance;
}
```

Display 6.5 The BankAccount Class (part 1 of 3)

```
//Program to demonstrate the class BankAccount.
#include <iostream>
using namespace std;

//Class for a bank account:
class BankAccount
{
public:
    void set(int dollars, int cents, double rate);
    //Postcondition: The account balance has been set to $dollars.cents;
    //The interest rate has been set to rate percent.

    void set(int dollars, double rate);
    //Postcondition: The account balance has been set to $dollars.00.
    //The interest rate has been set to rate percent.

    void update();
    //Postcondition: One year of simple interest has been
    //added to the account balance.

    double get_balance();
    //Returns the current account balance.

    double get_rate();
    //Returns the current account interest rate as a percent.

    void output(ostream& outs);
    //Precondition: If outs is a file output stream, then
    //outs has already been connected to a file.
    //Postcondition: Account balance and interest rate have been written to the
    //stream outs.
private:
    double balance;
    double interest_rate;

    double fraction(double percent);
    //Converts a percent to a fraction. For example, fraction(50.3) returns 0.503.
};

int main()
{
    BankAccount account1, account2;
    cout << "Start of Test:\n";
```

The member function set is overloaded.

Display 6.5 The BankAccount Class *(part 2 of 3)*

```
        account1.set(123, 99, 3.0);
        cout << "account1 initial statement:\n";
        account1.output(cout);

        account1.set(100, 5.0);
        cout << "account1 with new setup:\n";
        account1.output(cout);

        account1.update();
        cout << "account1 after update:\n";
        account1.output(cout);

        account2 = account1;
        cout << "account2:\n";
        account2.output(cout);
        return 0;
}

void BankAccount::set(int dollars, int cents, double rate)
{
        balance = dollars + 0.01*cents;
        interest_rate = rate;
}

void BankAccount::set(int dollars, double rate)
{
        balance = dollars;
        interest_rate = rate;
}

void BankAccount::update()
{
        balance = balance + fraction(interest_rate)*balance;
}

double BankAccount::fraction(double percent)
{
        return (percent/100.0);
}
```

calls to the overloaded member function set

definitions of overloaded member function set

In the definition of a member function you call another member function like this.

Display 6.5 The BankAccount Class *(part 3 of 3)*

```
double BankAccount::get_balance()
{
    return balance;
}

double BankAccount::get_rate()
{
    return interest_rate;
}

//Uses iostream:
void BankAccount::output(ostream& outs)
{
    outs.setf(ios::fixed);
    outs.setf(ios::showpoint);
    outs.precision(2);
    outs << "Account balance $" << balance << endl;
    outs << "Interest rate " << interest_rate << "%" << endl;
}
```

stream parameter that can be replaced with either cout *or with a file output stream*

Sample Dialogue

```
Start of Test:
account1 initial statement:
Account balance $123.99
Interest rate 3.00%
account1 with new setup:
Account balance $100.00
Interest rate 5.00%
account1 after update:
Account balance $105.00
Interest rate 5.00%
account2:
Account balance $105.00
Interest rate 5.00%
```

The calling object for the member function `fraction` and for the member variables `balance` and `interest_rate` are determined when the function `update` is called. For example, the meaning of

```
account1.update();
```

is the following:

```
{
    account1.balance = account1.balance +
        account1.fraction(account1.interest_rate)*account1.balance;
}
```

Notice that the call to the member function `fraction` is handled in the same way in this regard as the references to the member variables.

Like the classes we discussed earlier, the class `BankAccount` has a member function that outputs the data information stored in the object. In this program we are sending output to the screen. However, we want to write this class definition so that it can be copied into other programs and used unchanged in those other programs. Since some other program may want to send output to a file, we have given the member function `output` a formal parameter of type `ostream` so that the function `output` can be called with an argument that is either the stream `cout` or a file output stream. In the sample program we want the output to go to the screen, so the first function call to the member function `output` has the form

input/output stream arguments

```
account1.output(cout);
```

Other calls to `output` also use `cout` as the argument, so all output is sent to the screen. If you want the output to go to a file instead, then you must first connect the file to an output stream as we discussed in Chapter 5. If the file output stream is called `fout` and is connected to a file, then the following would write the data information for the object `account1` to this file rather than to the screen:

```
account1.output(fout);
```

The value of an object of type `BankAccount` represents a bank account that has some balance and pays some interest rate. The balance and interest rate can be set with the member function `set`. Notice that we have overloaded the member function named `set` so that there are two versions of `set`. One version has three formal parameters and the other has only two formal parameters. Both versions have a formal parameter of type *double* for the interest rate, but the two versions of `set` use different formal parameters to set the account balance. One version has two formal parameters to set the balance, one for the dollars and one for the cents in the account balance. The other version has only a single formal parameter, which gives the

overloading member functions

number of dollars in the account and assumes that the number of cents is zero. This second version of set is handy, since most people open an account with some "even" amount of money, such as $1,000 and no cents. Notice that this overloading is nothing new. A member function is overloaded in the same way as an ordinary function is overloaded.

Structures versus Classes

Structures are normally used with all member variables public and with no member functions. However, in C++ a structure can have private member variables and both public and private member functions. Aside from some notational differences, a C++ structure can do anything a class can do. Having said this and satisfied the "truth in advertising" requirement, we advocate that you forget this technical detail about structures. If you take this technical detail seriously and use structures in the same way that you use classes, then you have two names (with different syntax rules) for the same concept. On the other hand, if you use structures as we described them, then you will have a meaningful difference between structures (as you use them) and classes; and your usage will be the same as that of most other programmers.

Summary of Some Properties of Classes

Classes have all of the properties that we described for structures plus all the properties associated with member functions. Below is a list of some points to keep in mind when using classes:

1 Classes have both member variables and member functions.

2 A member (either a member variable or a member function) may be either public or private.

3 Normally, all the member variables of a class are labeled as private members.

4 A private member of a class cannot be used except within the definition of another member function of the same class.

5 The name of a member function for a class may be overloaded just like the name of an ordinary function.

6 A class may use another class as the type for a member variable.

7 A function may have formal parameters whose types are classes. (See Self-Test Exercises 16 and 17.)

8 A function may return an object; that is, a class may be the type for the value returned by a function. (See Self-Test Exercise 18.)

SELF-TEST EXERCISES

16 Give a definition for the function with the following prototype. The class
    BankAccount is defined in Display 6.5.

```
double difference(BankAccount account1, BankAccount account2);
//Precondition: account1 and account2 have been given values
// (that is, their member variables have been given values).
//Returns the balance in account1 minus the balance in account2.
```

17 Give a definition for the function with the following prototype. The class
    BankAccount is defined in Display 6.5. (Hint: It's easy if you use a member
    function.)

```
void double_update(BankAccount& the_account);
//Precondition: the_account has previously been given a value
// (that is, its member variables have been given values).
//Postcondition: The account balance has been changed so that
//two years' interest has been posted to the account.
```

18 Give a definition for the function with the following prototype. The class
    BankAccount is defined in Display 6.5.

```
BankAccount new_account(BankAccount old_account);
//Precondition: old_account has previously been given a value
// (that is, its member variables have been given values).
//Returns the value for a new account that has a balance of zero
//and the same interest rate as the old_account.
```

For example, after this function is defined, a program could contain the
following:

```
BankAccount account3, account4;
account3.set(999, 99, 5.5);
account4 = new_account(account3);
account4.output(cout);
```

This would produce the following output:

```
Account balance $0.00
Interest rate 5.50%
```

Constructors for Initialization

You often want to initialize some or all the member variables for an object when you declare the object. As we will see later in this book, there are other initializing actions you might also want to take, but initializing member variables is the most common sort of initialization. C++ includes special provisions for such initializations. When you define a class you can define a special kind of member function known as a **constructor.** A constructor is a member function that is automatically called when an object of that class is declared. A constructor is used to initialize the values of some or all member variables and to do any other sort of initialization that may be needed. You define a constructor the same way that you define any other member function, except for two points:

1 A constructor must have the same name as the class. For example, if the class is named BankAccount, then any constructor for this class must be named BankAccount.

2 A constructor definition cannot return a value. Moreover, no type, not even *void*, can be given at the start of the function prototype or in the function header.

For example, suppose we wanted to add a constructor for initializing the balance and interest rate for objects of type BankAccount shown in Display 6.5. The class definition could be as follows. (We have omitted some of the comments to save space, but they should be included.)

```
class BankAccount
{
public:
    BankAccount(int dollars, int cents, double rate);
    //Initializes the account balance to $dollars.cents and
    //initializes the interest rate to rate percent.

    void set(int dollars, int cents, double rate);
    void set(int dollars, double rate);
    void update( );

    double get_balance( );
    double get_rate( );
    void output(ostream& outs);
private:
    double balance;
    double interest_rate;
    double fraction(double percent);
};
```

Notice that the constructor is named BankAccount, which is the name of the class. Also notice that the prototype for the constructor BankAccount does not start with *void* or with any other type name. Finally, notice that the constructor is placed in the public section of the class definition. Normally, you should make your constructors public member functions. If you were to make all your constructors private members, then you would not be able to declare any objects of that class type, which would make the class completely useless.

With the redefined class BankAccount, two objects of type BankAccount can be declared and initialized as follows:

```
BankAccount account1(10, 50, 2.0), account2(500, 0, 4.5);
```

Assuming that the definition of the constructor performs the initializing action that we promised, the above declaration will declare the object account1, set the value of account1.balance to 10.50, and set the value of account1.interest_rate to 2.0. Thus, the object account1 is initialized so that it represents a bank account with a balance of $10.50 and an interest rate of 2.0%. Similarly, account2 is initialized so that it represents a bank account with a balance of $500.00 and an interest rate of 4.5%. What happens is that the object account1 is declared and then the constructor BankAccount is called with the three arguments 10, 50, and 2.0. Similarly, account2 is declared and then the constructor BankAccount is called with the arguments 500, 0, and 4.5. The result is conceptually equivalent to the following (although you cannot write it this way in C++):

```
BankAccount account1, account2; //PROBLEMS--BUT FIXABLE
account1.BankAccount(10, 50, 2.0); //VERY ILLEGAL
account2.BankAccount(500, 0, 4.5); //VERY ILLEGAL
```

As the comments indicate, you cannot place the above three lines in your program. The first line can be made to be acceptable, but the two calls to the constructor BankAccount are illegal. A constructor cannot be called in the same way as an ordinary member function is called. Still, it is clear what we want to happen when we write the above three lines, and that happens automatically when you declare the objects account1 and account2 as follows:

```
BankAccount account1(10, 50, 2.0), account2(500, 0, 4.5);
```

The definition of a constructor is given in the same way as any other member function. For example, if you revise the definition of the class BankAccount by adding the constructor just described, you need to also add the following definition of the constructor:

```
BankAccount::BankAccount(int dollars, int cents, double rate)
{
    balance = dollars + 0.01*cents;
    interest_rate = rate;
}
```

Since the class and the constructor function have the same name, the name BankAccount occurs twice in the function heading; the BankAccount before the scope resolution operator :: is the name of the class and the BankAccount after the scope resolution operator is the name of the constructor function. Also notice that no return type is specified in the heading of the constructor definition, not even the type *void*. Aside from these points, a constructor is defined in the same way as an ordinary member function.

You can overload a constructor name like BankAccount::BankAccount, just as you can overload any other member function name, such as we did with Bank-Account::set in Display 6.5. In fact, constructors usually are overloaded, so that objects can be initialized in more than one way. For example, in Display 6.6 we have redefined the class BankAccount so that it has three versions of its constructor. This redefinition overloads the constructor name BankAccount so that it may have three arguments (as we just discussed), two arguments, or no arguments.

For example, suppose you give only two arguments when you declare an object of type BankAccount, as in the following example:

```
BankAccount account1(100, 2.3);
```

Then the object account1 is initialized so that it represents an account with a balance of $100.00 and an interest rate of 2.3%.

On the other hand, if no arguments are given, as in the following example,

```
BankAccount account2;
```

then the object is initialized to represent an account with a balance of $0.00 and an interest rate of 0.0%. Notice that when the constructor has no arguments, you do not include any parentheses in the object declaration. The following is incorrect:

```
BankAccount account2( );//WRONG! DO NOT DO THIS!
```

We have omitted the (overloaded) member function set from this revised class definition of BankAccount (given in Display 6.6). Once you have a good set of constructor definitions, there is no need for any other member functions to set the member variables of the class. You can use the overloaded constructor BankAccount in Display 6.6 for the same purposes that you would use the overloaded member function set (which we included in the old version of the class shown in Display 6.5).

Constructor

A **constructor** is a member function of a class that has the same name as the class. A constructor is called automatically when an object of the class is declared. Constructors are used to initialize objects. A constructor must have the same name as the class of which it is a member.

Display 6.6 Class with Constructors (part 1 of 2)

```
//Program to demonstrate the class BankAccount.
#include <iostream>
using namespace std;

//Class for a bank account:
class BankAccount
{
public:
    BankAccount(int dollars, int cents, double rate);
    //Initializes the account balance to $dollars.cents and
    //initializes the interest rate to rate percent.

    BankAccount(int dollars, double rate);
    //Initializes the account balance to $dollars.00 and
    //initializes the interest rate to rate percent.

    BankAccount( );
    //Initializes the account balance to $0.00 and the interest rate to 0.0%.

    void update( );
    //Postcondition: One year of simple interest has been added to the account
    //balance.

    double get_balance( );
    //Returns the current account balance.

    double get_rate( );
    //Returns the current account interest rate as a percent.

    void output(ostream& outs);
    //Precondition: If outs is a file output stream, then
    //outs has already been connected to a file.
    //Postcondition: Account balance and interest rate have been written to the
    //stream outs.
private:
    double balance;
    double interest_rate;

    double fraction(double percent);
    //Converts a percent to a fraction. For example, fraction(50.3) returns 0.503.
};

int main( )
{
    BankAccount account1(100, 2.3), account2;
```

This definition of BankAccount is an improved version of the class BankAccount given in Display 6.5.

— *default constructor*

This declaration causes a call to the default constructor. Notice that there are no parentheses.

Display 6.6 Class with Constructors *(part 2 of 2)*

```
    cout << "account1 initialized as follows:\n";
    account1.output(cout);
    cout << "account2 initialized as follows:\n";
    account2.output(cout);

    account1 = BankAccount(999, 99, 5.5);
    cout << "account1 reset to the following:\n";
    account1.output(cout);
    return 0;
}


BankAccount::BankAccount(int dollars, int cents, double rate)
{
    balance = dollars + 0.01*cents;
    interest_rate = rate;
}


BankAccount::BankAccount(int dollars, double rate)
{
    balance = dollars;
    interest_rate = rate;
}


BankAccount::BankAccount( )
{
    balance = 0;
    interest_rate = 0.0;
}
```

an explicit call to the constructor
BankAccount::BankAccount

<Definitions of the other member functions
are the same as in Display 6.5.>

Screen Output

```
account1 initialized as follows
Account balance $100.00
Interest rate 2.30%
account2 initialized as follows:
Account balance $0.00
Interest rate 0.00%
account1 reset to the following:
Account balance $999.99
Interest rate 5.50%
```

Calling a Constructor

A constructor is called automatically when an object is declared, but you must give the arguments for the constructor when you declare the object. A constructor can also be called explicitly in order to create a new object.

Syntax (for an object declaration when you have constructors):

>   *Class_Name Object_Name(Arguments_for_Constructor);*

Example:

```
BankAccount account1(100, 2.3);
```

Syntax (for an explicit constructor call):

>   *Object = Constructor_Name(Arguments_For_Constructor);*

Example:

```
account1 = BankAccount(200, 3.5);
```

A constructor must have the same name as the class of which it is a member. Thus, in the above syntax descriptions, *Class_Name* and *Constructor_Name* are the same identifier.

A constructor is called automatically whenever you declare an object of the class type, but it can also be called again after the object has been declared. This allows you to conveniently set all the members of an object. The technical details are as follows. Calling the constructor creates an anonymous object with new values. An anonymous object is an object that is not named (as yet) by any variable. The anonymous object can be assigned to the named object. For example, the following is a call to the constructor `BankAccount` that creates an anonymous object with a balance of $999.99 and interest rate of 5.5%. This anonymous object is assigned to object `account1` so that it too represents an account with a balance of $999.99 and an interest rate of 5.5%:

explicit constructor call

```
account1 = BankAccount(999, 99, 5.5);
```

(As you might guess from the notation, a constructor behaves like a function that returns an object of its class type.)

➤ PROGRAMMING TIP
Always Include a Default Constructor

Using constructors is an all or nothing situation. If you give no constructor, the compiler will generate a default constructor that does nothing. This constructor will be called if class objects are declared. If you give at least one constructor definition for a class, then the C++ compiler will generate no other constructors. Every time you declare an object of that type, C++ will look for an appropriate constructor definition to use. If you declare an object without using arguments for the constructor, C++ will look for a default constructor, and if you have not defined a default constructor, none will be there for it to find.

For example, suppose you define a class as follows:

```
class SampleClass
{
public:
    SampleClass(int parameter1, double parameter2);
    void do_stuff( );
private:
    int data1;
    double data2;
};
```

constructor that requires two arguments (pointing to `SampleClass(int parameter1, double parameter2);`)

You should recognize the following as a legal way to declare an object of type `SampleClass` and call the constructor for that class:

```
SampleClass my_object(7, 7.77);
```

However, you may be surprised to learn that the following is illegal:

```
SampleClass your_object;
```

Since the class `SampleClass` has a constructor, the compiler interprets the above declaration as including a call to a constructor with no arguments, but there is no definition for a constructor with zero arguments. You must either add two arguments to the declaration of `your_object` or else you must add a constructor definition for a constructor with no arguments.

A constructor that can be called with no arguments is called a **default constructor,** since it applies in the default case where you declare an object without specifying any arguments. Since it is likely that you will sometimes want to declare an object without giving any constructor arguments, you should always include a default constructor. The following redefined version of `SampleClass` includes a default constructor:

If you redefine the class `SampleClass` as follows, then the above declaration of `your_object` would be legal:

```
class SampleClass
{
public:
    SampleClass(int parameter1, double parameter2);
    SampleClass( );
```

default constructor (pointing to `SampleClass( );`)

```
    void do_stuff( );
private:
    int data1;
    double data2;
};
```

If you do not want the default constructor to initialize any member variables, you can simply give it an empty body when you implement it. The following constructor definition is perfectly legal. It does nothing when called except make the compiler happy:

```
SampleClass::SampleClass( )
{
    //Do nothing.
}
```

⬡ PITFALL   **Constructors with No Arguments**

If a constructor for a class called BankAccount has two formal parameters, you declare an object and give the arguments to the constructor as follows:

```
BankAccount account1(100, 2.3);
```

To call the constructor with no arguments, you would naturally think that you would declare the object as follows:

```
BankAccount account2( ); //THIS WILL CAUSE PROBLEMS.
```

After all, when you call a function that has no arguments, you include a pair of empty parentheses. However, this is wrong for a constructor. Moreover, it may not produce an error message, since it does have an unintended meaning. The compiler will think that the above is the prototype for a function called account2 that takes no arguments and returns a value of type BankAccount.

You do not include parentheses when you declare an object and want C++ to use the constructor with no arguments. The correct way to declare account2 using the constructor with no arguments is:

```
BankAccount account2;
```

However, if you explicitly call a constructor in an assignment statement, you do use the parentheses. If the definitions and declarations are as in Display 6.6, then the following will set the account balance for account1 to $0.00 and set the interest rate to 0.0%:

```
account1 = BankAccount( );
```

Constructors with No Arguments

When you declare an object and want the constructor with zero arguments to be called, you do not include any parentheses. For example, to declare an object and pass two arguments to the constructor, you might do the following:

    BankAccount account1(100, 2.3);

However, if you want the constructor with zero arguments to be used, you declare the object as follows:

    BankAccount account1;

You do *not* declare the object as follows:

    BankAccount account1( );//INCORRECT DECLARATION

(The problem is that this syntax delcares a function that returns a BankAccount object and has no parameters.)

SELF-TEST EXERCISES

19 Suppose your program contains the following class definition (along with definitions of the member functions):

```
class YourClass
{
public:
    YourClass(int new_info, char more_new_info);
    YourClass( );
    void do_stuff( );
private:
    int information;
    char more_information;
};
```

Which of the following are legal?

```
YourClass an_object(42, 'A');
YourClass another_object;
YourClass yet_another_object( );
an_object = YourClass(99, 'B');
an_object = YourClass( );
an_object = YourClass;
```

20   How would you change the definition of the class DayOfYear in Display 6.4 so that it has two versions of an (overloaded) constructor? One version should have two *int* formal parameters (one for the month and one for the day) and will set the private member variables to represent that month and day. The other will have no formal parameters and will set the date represented to January 1.

6.3   Abstract Data Types

We all know—the Times *knows—*
but we pretend we don't.

Virginia Woolf, Monday or Tuesday

A data type, such as the type *int*, has certain specified values, such as 0, 1, –1, 2, and so forth. You tend to think of the data type as being these values, but the operations on these values are just as important as the values. Without the operations, you could do nothing of interest with the values. The operations for the type *int* consist of +, –, *, /, %, and a few other operators and predefined library functions. You should not think of a data type as being simply a collection of values. A **data type** consists of a collection of values *together with* a set of basic operations defined on these values. A data type is called an **abstract data type** (abbreviated **ADT**) if the programmers who use the type do not have access to the details of how the values and operations are implemented. The predefined types, such as *int*, are abstract data types (ADTs). You do not know how the operations, such as + and *, are implemented for the type *int*. Even if you did know, you would not use this information in any C++ program. Programmer-defined types, such as the structure types and class types, are not automatically ADTs. Unless they are defined and used with care, programmer-defined types can be used in unintuitive ways that make a program difficult to understand and difficult to modify. The best way to avoid these problems is to make sure all the data types that you define are ADTs. The way that you do this in C++ is to use classes, but not every class is an ADT. To make it an ADT you must define the class in a certain way, and that is the topic of the next subsection.

data types and abstract data types

Classes to Produce ADTs

A class is a type that you define, as opposed to the types, such as *int* and *char*, that are already defined for you. A value for a class type is the set of values of the member variables. For example, a value for the type BankAccount in Display 6.6

consists of two numbers of type *double*. For easy reference, we repeat the class definition below (omitting only the comments):

```
class BankAccount
{
public:
    BankAccount(int dollars, int cents, double rate);
    BankAccount(int dollars, double rate);
    BankAccount( );
    void update( );
    double get_balance( );
    double get_rate( );
    void output(ostream& outs);
private:
    double balance;
    double interest_rate;
    double fraction(double percent);
};
```

The programmer who uses the type BankAccount need not know how you implement the definition of BankAccount::update or any of the other member functions. The function definition for the member function BankAccount::update that we used is as follows:

```
void BankAccount::update( )
{
    balance = balance + fraction(interest_rate)*balance;
}
```

However, we could have dispensed with the private function `fraction` and implemented the member function `update` with the following slightly more complicated formula:

```
void BankAccount::update( )
{
    balance = balance + (interest_rate/100.0)*balance;
}
```

The programmer who uses the class BankAccount need not be concerned with which implementation of update we use, since both implementations have the exact same effect.

Similarly, the programmer who uses the class BankAccount need not be concerned about how the values of the class are implemented. We chose to implement the values as two values of type *double*. If vacation_savings is an object of type

BankAccount, the value of `vacation_savings` consists of the two values of type *double* stored in the two member variables

    `vacation_savings.balance` and
    `vacation_savings.interest_rate.`

However, you do not want to think of the value of the object `vacation_savings` as two numbers of type *double*, such as `1.3546e+2` and `4.5`. You want to think of the value of `vacation_savings` as the single entry

    Account balance $135.46

    Interest rate 4.50%

That is why our implementation of `BankAccount::output` writes the class value in this format.

The fact that we chose to implement this `BankAccount` value as the two *double* values `1.3546e+2` and `4.5` is an implementation detail. We could instead have implemented this `BankAccount` value as the two *int* values 135 and 46 (for the dollars and cents part of the balance) and the single value `0.045` of type *double*. The value `0.045` is simply the percent 4.5% converted to a fraction, which might be a more useful way to implement a percentage figure. After all, in order to compute interest on the account we convert a percentage to just such a fraction. With this alternative implementation of the class `BankAccount`, the public members would remain unchanged but the private members would change to the following:

```
class BankAccount
{
public:
      <This part is exactly the same as before>
private:
      int dollars_part;
      int cents_part;
      double interest_rate;
      double fraction(double percent);
};
```

We would need to change the member function definitions to match this change, but that is easy to do. For example, the function definitions for `get_balance` and one version of the constructor could be changed to the following:

```
double BankAccount::get_balance( )
{
      return (dollars_part + 0.01*cents_part);
}
```

```
BankAccount::BankAccount(int dollars, int cents, double rate)
{
    dollars_part = dollars;
    cents_part = cents;
    interest_rate = rate;
}
```

Similarly, each of the other member functions could be redefined to accommodate this new way of storing the account balance and the interest rate.

Notice that even though the user may think of the account balance as a single number, that does not mean the implementation has to be a single number of type *double*. You have just seen that it could, for example, be two numbers of type *int*. The programmer who uses the type BankAccount need not know any of this detail about how the values of the type BankAccount are implemented.

*how to write
an ADT*

These comments about the type BankAccount illustrate the basic technique for defining a class so that it will be an abstract data type. In order to define a class so that it is an abstract data type, you need to separate the specification of how the type is *used* by a programmer from the details of how the type is *implemented*. The separation should be so complete that you can change the implementation of the class, and any program that uses the class ADT should not need any additional changes. One way to ensure this separation is to:

1 Make all the member variables private members of the class.

2 Make each of the basic operations that the programmer needs a public member function of the class, and fully specify how to use each such public member function.

3 Make any helping functions private member functions.

In Chapter 8 you will learn some alternative approaches to defining ADTs, but these three rules are one common way to ensure that a class is an abstract data type.

interface

The **interface** of an ADT tells you how to use the ADT in your program. When you define an ADT as a C++ class, the **interface** consists of the public member functions of the class along with the comments that tell you how to use these public member functions. *The interface of the ADT should be all you need to know in order to use the ADT in your program.* The **implementation** of the ADT tells how this interface is realized as C++ code. The **implementation** of the ADT consists of the private members of the class and the definitions of both the public and private member functions. Although you need the implementation in order to run a program that uses the ADT, you should not need to know anything about the implementation in order to write the rest of a program that uses the ADT; that is, you should not need to know anything about the implementation in order to write the main part of the program and to write any nonmember functions used by the main part of the program. The situation is similar to what we advocated for ordinary function definitions in Chapters 3 and 4. The

implementation

implementation of an ADT, like the implementation of an ordinary function, should be thought of as being in a black box that you cannot see inside of.

In Chapter 8 you will learn how to place the interface and implementation of an ADT in files separate from each other and separate from the programs that use the ADT. That way a programmer who uses the ADT literally does not see the implementation. Until then, we will place all of the details about our ADT classes in the same file as the `main` part of our program, but we still think of the *interface* (given in the public section of the class definitions) and the *implementation* (the private section and the member function definitions) as separate parts of the ADT. We will strive to write our ADTs so that the user of the ADT need only know about the interface of the ADT and need not know anything about the implementation. To be sure you are defining your ADTs this way, simply make sure that if you change the implementation of your ADT, then your program will still work without your needing to change any other part of the program. This is illustrated in the next Programming Example.

The most obvious benefit you derive from making your classes ADTs is that you can change the implementation, and you will not have to change the other parts of your program. But ADTs provide more benefits than that. If you make your classes ADTs, you can divide work among different programmers, one programmer designing and writing the ADT and other programmers using the ADT. Even if you are the only programmer working on a project, you have divided one larger task into two smaller tasks, which makes your program easier to design and easier to debug.

Separate interface and implementation

■)) *PROGRAMMING* \ *EXAMPLE*
Alternative Implementation of a Class

Display 6.7 contains the alternative implementation of the ADT `BankAccount` discussed in the previous subsection. In this version the data for a bank account is implemented as three member values: one for the dollars part of the account balance, one for the cents part of the account balance, and one for the interest rate.

Notice that, although both the implementation in Display 6.6 and the implementation in Display 6.7 each have a member variable called `interest_rate`, the value stored is slightly different in the two implementations. If the account pays interest at a rate of 4.7%, then in the implementation in Display 6.6 (which is basically the same as the one in Display 6.5), the value of `interest_rate` is 4.7. However, in the implementation in Display 6.7, the value of `interest_rate` would be 0.047. This alternative implementation, shown in Display 6.7, stores the interest rate as a fraction rather than as a percentage figure. The basic difference in this new implementation is that when an interest rate is set, the function `fraction` is used to

different member variables

`interest_rate`

Display 6.7 Alternative BankAccount Class Implementation (part 1 of 3)

```
//Demonstrates an alternative implementation of the class BankAccount.
#include <iostream>
#include <cmath>
using namespace std;

//Class for a bank account:
class BankAccount
{
public:
    BankAccount(int dollars, int cents, double rate);
    //Initializes the account balance to $dollars.cents and
    //initializes the interest rate to rate percent.

    BankAccount(int dollars, double rate);
    //Initializes the account balance to $dollars.00 and
    //initializes the interest rate to rate percent.

    BankAccount( );
    //Initializes the account balance to $0.00 and the interest rate to 0.0%.

    void update( );
    //Postcondition: One year of simple interest has been added to the account
    //balance.

    double get_balance( );
    //Returns the current account balance.

    double get_rate( );
    //Returns the current account interest rate as a percent.

    void output(ostream& outs);
    //Precondition: If outs is a file output stream, then
    //outs has already been connected to a file.
    //Postcondition: Account balance and interest rate have been written to the stream
    //outs.
private:
    int dollars_part;
    int cents_part;
    double interest_rate;//expressed as a fraction, e.g., 0.057 for 5.7%

    double fraction(double percent);
    //Converts a percent to a fraction. For example, fraction(50.3) returns 0.503.

    double percent(double fraction_value);    ←————————————  new
    //Converts a fraction to a percent. For example, percent(0.503) returns 50.3.
};
```

Notice that the public members of BankAccount *look and behave exactly the same as in Display 6.6.*

Display 6.7 Alternative BankAccount Class Implementation (part 2 of 3)

```
int main( )
{
    BankAccount account1(100, 2.3), account2;

    cout << "account1 initialized as follows:\n";
    account1.output(cout);
    cout << "account2 initialized as follows:\n";
    account2.output(cout);

    account1 = BankAccount(999, 99, 5.5);
    cout << "account1 reset to the following:\n";
    account1.output(cout);
    return 0;
}
```

Since the body of main *is identical to what it is in Display 6.6, the screen output is also identical to that in Display 6.6.*

```
BankAccount::BankAccount(int dollars, int cents, double rate)
{
    dollars_part = dollars;
    cents_part = cents;
    interest_rate = fraction(rate);
}
```

In the old implementation of this ADT, the private member function fraction *was used in the definition of* update*. In this implementation,* fraction *is instead used in the definition of constructors.*

```
BankAccount::BankAccount(int dollars, double rate)
{
    dollars_part = dollars;
    cents_part = 0;
    interest_rate = fraction(rate);
}

BankAccount::BankAccount( )
{
    dollars_part = 0;
    cents_part = 0;
    interest_rate = 0.0;
}
```

Display 6.7 Alternative BankAccount Class Implementation *(part 3 of 3)*

```
double BankAccount::fraction(double percent)
{
    return (percent/100.0);
}

//Uses cmath:
void BankAccount::update( )
{
    double balance = get_balance( );
    balance = balance + interest_rate*balance;
    dollars_part = floor(balance);
    cents_part = floor((balance - dollars_part)*100);
}

double BankAccount::get_balance( )
{
    return (dollars_part + 0.01*cents_part);
}

double BankAccount::percent(double fraction_value)
{
    return (fraction_value*100);
}

double BankAccount::get_rate( )
{
    return percent(interest_rate);
}

//Uses iostream:
void BankAccount::output(ostream& outs)
{
    outs.setf(ios::fixed);
    outs.setf(ios::showpoint);
    outs.precision(2);
    outs << "Account balance $" << get_balance( ) << endl;
    outs << "Interest rate " << get_rate( ) << "%" << endl;
}
```

The new definitions of get_balance and get_rate ensure that the output will still be in the correct units.

immediately convert the interest rate to a fraction. Hence, in this new implementation the private member function `fraction` is used in the definitions of constructors, but is not needed in the definition of the member function `update`, because the value in the member variable `interest_rate` has already been converted to a fraction. In the old implementation (shown in Display 6.5 and Display 6.6), the situation was just the reverse. In the old implementation the private member function `fraction` was not used in the definition of constructors but was used in the definition of `update`.

Although we have changed the private members of the class `BankAccount`, we have not changed anything in the public section of the class definition. The public member functions have the exact same prototypes and they behave exactly as they did in the old version of the ADT given in Display 6.6. For example, although this new implementation stores a percentage such as 4.7% as the fraction `0.047`, the member function `get_rate` still returns the value `4.7`, just as it would for the old implementation in Display 6.5. Similarly, the member function `get_balance` returns a single value of type *double*, which gives the balance as a number with a decimal point, just as it did in the old implementation in Display 6.5. This is true even though the balance is now stored in two member variables of type *int*, rather than in a single member variable of type *double* (as in the old versions).

The public interface is not changed

Notice that there is an important difference between how you treat the public member functions and how you treat the private member functions. If you want to preserve the interface of an ADT so that any programs that use it need not change (other than changing the definitions of the class and its member functions), then you must leave the public member function prototypes unchanged. However, you are

changing private member functions

Information Hiding[3]

We discussed information hiding when we introduced functions in Chapter 3. We said that **information hiding,** as applied to functions, means that you should write your functions so that they could be used as black boxes, that is, so that the programmer who uses the function need not know any details about how the function is implemented. This principle means that all the programmer who uses a function needs to know is the function prototype and the accompanying comment that explains how to use the function. The use of private member variables and private member functions in the definition of an abstract data type is another way to implement information hiding, but now we apply the principle to data values as well as to functions.

[3]The very important notion of **information hiding** originated in the early 1970s with the work of David Parnas. To read more about this and other important ideas, see D. W. Parnas's paper, "On the Criteria to Be Used in Decomposing Systems into Modules." Communications of the ACM, Vol. 5, No. 12 (December 1972), pp. 1053–58. This paper is reprinted, along with other important papers, in *Classics in Software Engineering*, edited by E. Yourdon, Yourdon Press, 1979.

free to add, delete, or change any of the private member functions. In this example, we have added one additional private function called `percent`, which is the inverse of the function `fraction`. The function `fraction` converts a percentage figure to a fraction and the function `percent` converts a fraction back to a percentage. For example, `fraction(4.7)` returns `0.047` and `percent(0.047)` returns `4.7`.

SELF-TEST EXERCISES

21 When you define an ADT as a C++ class, should you make the member variables public or private? Should you make the member functions public or private?

22 When you define an ADT as a C++ class, what items are considered part of the interface for the ADT? What items are considered part of the implementation for the ADT?

23 Suppose your friend defines an ADT as a C++ class in the way we described in the section on ADTs (Section 6.3). You are given the task of writing a program that uses this ADT. That is, you must write the `main` part of the program as well as any nonmember functions that are used in the `main` part of the program. The ADT is very long and you do not have a lot of time to write this program. What parts of the ADT do you need to read and what parts can you safely ignore?

CHAPTER SUMMARY

- A structure can be used to combine data of different types into a single (compound) data value.

- A class can be used to combine data and functions into a single (compound) object.

- A member variable or a member function for a class may be either public or private. If it is public, it can be used outside of the class. If it is private it can be used only in the definition of another member function.

- A function may have formal parameters of a class or structure type. A function may return values of a class or structure type.

- A member function for a class can be overloaded in the same way as ordinary functions are overloaded.

■ A **constructor** is a member function of a class that is called automatically when an object of the class is declared. A constructor must have the same name as the class of which it is a member.

■ A **data type** consists of a collection of values *together with* a set of basic operations defined on these values.

■ A data type is called an **abstract data type** (abbreviated **ADT**) if a programmer who uses the type does not need to know any of the details about how the values and operations for that type are implemented.

■ One way to implement an abstract data type in C++ is to define a class with all member variables private and with the operations implemented as public member functions.

Answers to Self-Test Exercises

1 a. *double*

   b. *double*

   c. illegal—cannot use `struct` tag instead of a structure variable

   d. illegal—savings account undeclared.

   e. *char*

   f. CDAccount

2
```
A $9.99
A $1.11
```

3 Many compilers give poor error messages. Surprisingly, the error message from g++ is quite informative.

```
g++ -fsyntax-only c6testg1.cc
prob1.cc:8: semicolon missing after declaration of
'Stuff'
prob1.cc:8: extraneous 'int' ignored
prob1.cc:8: semicolon missing after declaration of
'struct Stuff'
```

4 `A x = {1,2};`

5 *struct* Date;

   a. Too few initializers, not a syntax error. After initialization, month==12, day==21, year==0. Member variables not provided an initializer are initialized to a zero of appropriate type.

   b. Correct after initialization. 12==month, 21==day, 1998==year.

   c. Error: too many initializers.

   d. May be a design error, i.e., an error in intent. The author of the code provides only two digits for the date initializer. There should be four digits used for the year because a program using two-digit dates could fail in ways that vary from amusing to disastrous at the turn of the century.

6

```
struct EmployeeRecord
{
    double wage_rate;
    int vacation;
    char status;
};
```

7

```
void read_shoe_record(ShoeType& new_shoe)
{
    cout << "Enter shoe style (one letter): ";
    cin >> new_shoe.style;
    cout << "Enter shoe price $";
    cin >> new_shoe.price;
}
```

8

```
ShoeType discount(ShoeType old_record)
{
    ShoeType temp;
    temp.style = old_record.style;
    temp.price = 0.90*old_record.price;
    return temp;
}
```

9

```
void DayOfYear::input()
{
    cout << "Enter month as a number: ";
    cin >> month;
    cout << "Enter the day of the month: ";
    cin >> day;
}
```

10

```
void Temperature::set(double new_degrees, char new_scale)
{
    degrees = new_degrees;
    scale = new_scale;
}
```

11 Both the dot operator and the scope resolution operator are used with member names to specify what class or struct the member name is a member of. If class DayOfYear is as defined in Display 6.3 and today is an object of the class DayOfYear, then the member month may be accessed with the dot operator: today.month. When we give the definition of a member function, the scope resolution operator is used to tell the compiler that this function is the one declared in the class.

12

```
hyundai.price = 4999.99; //ILLEGAL. price is private.
jaguar.set_price(30000.97); //LEGAL
double a_price, a_profit;//LEGAL
a_price = jaguar.get_price();//LEGAL
a_profit = jaguar.get_profit();//ILLEGAL. get_profit is private.
a_profit = hyundai.get_profit();//ILLEGAL. get_profit is private.
if (hyundai == jaguar) //ILLEGAL. Cannot use == with classes.
    cout << "Want to swap cars?";
hyundai = jaguar;//LEGAL
```

13 After the change, they would all be legal except for the following, which is still illegal:

```
if (hyundai == jaguar) //ILLEGAL. Cannot use == with classes.
    cout << "Want to swap cars?";
```

14 *private* restricts access to function definitions for member functions of the same class. This restricts any change of `private` variables to functions provided by the class author. The class author is then in control of these changes to the private data, preventing inadvertent corruption of the class data.

15 a. Only one. The compiler warns if you have no *public:* members in a `class` (or *struct* for that matter).

b. None; we normally expect to find at least one *private:* section in a `class` or a *struct*.

c. A class is *private:* by default; such a section is a *private:* section.

d. A struct is *public:* by default; such a section is a *public:* section.

16 A correct answer is:

```
double difference(BankAccount account1, BankAccount account2)
{
    return (account1.get_balance() - account2.get_balance());
}
```

Note that the following is *not correct*, because `balance` is a private member:

```
double difference(BankAccount account1, BankAccount account2)
{
    return (account1.balance - account2.balance);//ILLEGAL
}
```

17

```
void double_update(BankAccount& the_account)
{
    the_account.update();
    the_account.update();
}
```

Note that since this is not a member function, you must give the object name and dot operator when you call `update`.

18

```
BankAccount new_account(BankAccount old_account)
{
    BankAccount temp;
    temp.set(0, old_account.get_rate());
    return temp;
}
```

19

```
YourClass an_object(42, 'A'); //LEGAL
YourClass another_object; //LEGAL
YourClass yet_another_object( ); //PROBLEM
an_object = YourClass(99, 'B'); //LEGAL
an_object = YourClass( ); //LEGAL
an_object = YourClass; //ILLEGAL
```

The statement marked //PROBLEM is not strictly speaking illegal, but it does not mean what you might think it means. If you mean this to be a declaration of an object called yet_another_object, then it is wrong. It is a correct prototype for a function called yet_another_object that takes zero arguments and that returns a value of type YourClass, but that is not the intended meaning. As a practical matter, you can probably consider it illegal. The correct way to declare an object called yet_another_object, so that it will be initialized with the default constructor, is as follows:

```
YourClass yet_another_object;
```

20 The modified class definition is as follows:

```
class DayOfYear
{
public:
    DayOfYear(int the_month, int the_day);
    //Precondition: the_month and the_day form a possible date.
    //Initializes the date according to the arguments.

    DayOfYear( );
    //Initializes the date to January first.

    void input( );

    void output( );

    int get_month( );
    //Returns the month, 1 for January, 2 for February, etc.

    int get_day( );
    //Returns the day of the month.
private:
    int month;
    int day;
};
```

Notice that we have omitted the member function `set`, since the constructors make `set` unnecessary. You must also add the following function definitions (and delete the function definition for `DayOfYear::set`):

```
DayOfYear::DayOfYear(int the_month, int the_day)
{
    month = the_month;
    day = the_day;
}
DayOfYear::DayOfYear( )
{
    month = 1;
    day = 1;
}
```

21 The member variables should all be private. The member functions that are part of the interface for the ADT (that is, the member functions that are operations for the ADT) should be public. You may also have auxiliary helping functions that are only used in the definitions of other member functions. These auxiliary functions should be private.

22 All the declarations of private member variables are part of the implementation. (There should be no public member variables.) All the prototypes for public member functions of the class (which are listed in the class definitions) as well as the explanatory comments for these prototypes are parts of the interface. All the prototypes for private member functions are parts of the implementation. All member function definitions (whether the function is public or private) are parts of the implementation.

23 You need to read only the interface parts. That is, you need to read only the prototypes for public members of the class (which are listed in the class definitions) as well as the explanatory comments for these prototypes. You need not read any of the prototypes of the private member functions, the declarations of the private member variables, the definitions of the public member functions, nor the definitions of the private member functions.

Programming Projects

1 Write a grading program for a class with the following grading policies:

a There are two quizzes each graded on the basis of ten points.

b There is one midterm exam and one final exam each graded on the basis of 100 points.

c The final exam counts for 50% of the grade, the midterm counts for 25% and the two quizzes together count for a total of 25%. (Do not forget to normalize the quiz scores. They should be converted to a percent before they are averaged in.)

Any grade of 90 or more is an A, any grade of 80 or more (but less than 90) is a B, any grade of 70 or more (but less than 80) is a C, any grade of 60 or more (but less than 70) is a D, and any grade below 60 is an F. The program will read in the student's scores and output the student's record, which consists of two quiz and two exam scores as well as the student's average numeric score for the entire course and final letter grade. Define and use a structure for the student record. If this is a class assignment, ask your instructor if input/output should be done with the keyboard and screen or if it should be done with files. If it is to be done with files, ask your instructor for instructions on file names.

2 Redefine CDAccount from Display 6.1 so that it is a class rather than a structure. Use the same member variables as in Display 6.1 but make them private. Include member functions for each of the following: one to return the initial balance, one to return the balance at maturity, one to return the interest rate, and one to return the term. Include a constructor that sets all of the member variables to any specified values as well as a default constructor. Also, include an input member function with one formal parameter of type istream and an output member function with one formal parameter of type ostream. Embed your class definition in a test program.

3 Redo your definition of the class CDAccount from Project 2 so that it has the same interface but a different implementation. The new implementation is in many ways similar to the second implementation for the class BankAccount given in Display 6.7. Your new implementation for the class CDAccount will record the balance as two values of type *int*: one for the dollars and one for the cents. The member variable for the interest rate will store the interest rate as a fraction rather than as a percentage figure. For example, an interest rate of 4.3% will be stored as the value 0.043 of type *double*. Store the term in the same way as in Display 6.1 and in Project 2.

4 Define a class for a type called CounterType. An object of this type is used to count things, so it records a count that is a nonnegative whole number. Include a default constructor that sets the counter to zero and a constructor with one argument that sets the counter to the value specified by its argument. Include member functions to increase the count by one and to decrease the count by one. Be sure that no member function allows the value of the counter to become negative. Also, include a member function that returns the

current count value and one that outputs the count to a stream. The member function for doing output will have one formal parameter of type `ostream` for the output stream that receives the output. Embed your class definition in a test program.

5 Define a class called `Month` that is an abstract data type for a month. Your class will have one member variable of type *int* to represent a month (1 for January, 2 for February, and so forth). Include all the following member functions: a constructor to set the month using the first three letters in the name of the month as three arguments, a constructor to set the month using an integer as an argument (1 for January, 2 for February, and so forth), a default constructor, an input function that reads the month as an integer, an input function that reads the month as the first three letters in the name of the month, an output function that outputs the month as an integer, an output function that outputs the month as the first three letters in the name of the month, and a member function that returns the next month as a value of type `Month`. The input and output functions will each have one formal parameter for the stream. Embed your class definition in a test program.

6 Redefine the implementation of the class `Month` described in Project 5 (or do the definition for the first time, but do the implementation as described here). This time the month is implemented as three member variables of type *char* that store the first three letters in the name of the month. Embed your definition in a test program.

7 (In order to do this project you must have first done either Project 5 or Project 6.) Rewrite the program in Display 6.4, but use the class `Month` that you defined in Project 5 or Project 6 as the type for the member variable to record the month. (You may define the class `Month` either as described in Project 5 or as described in Project 6.) Redefine the member function `output` so that it has one formal parameter of type `ostream` for the output stream. Also, modify the program so that everything that is output to the screen is *also* output to a file. This means that all output statements will occur twice: once with the argument `cout` and once with an output stream argument. If you are in a class, obtain the file name from your instructor. The input will still come from the keyboard. Only the output will be sent to a file.

8 My mother always took a little red counter to the grocery store. The counter was used to keep tally of the amount of money she would have spent so far on that visit to the store, if she bought all in the basket. There was a four-digit display and increment buttons for each digit, and a reset button. There was an overflow indicator that came up red if more money was entered than the $99.99 it would register. (This was a *long* time ago.)

Write and implement the member functions of a class `Counter` that simulates and slightly generalizes the behavior of this grocery store counter. The constructor should create a `Counter` object that can count up to the constructor's argument. That is, `Counter(9999)` should provide a counter that can count up to 9999. A newly constructed counter displays a reading of 0. The member function `void reset( );` sets the counter's number to 0. The member functions `void incr1( );` increments the units digits by 1, `void incr10( );` increments the tens digit by 1, and `void incr100( );`, and `void incr1000( );` increment the next two digits, respectively. Accounting for any carry when you increment should require no further action than adding an appropriate number to the private data member. A member function `bool overflow( );` detects overflow. (Overflow is the result of incrementing the counter's private data member beyond the maximum entered at counter construction.)

Use this class to provide a simulation of my mother's little red clicker. Even though the display is an integer, in the simulation, the rightmost (lower order) two digits are always thought of as cents, tens of cents, the next digit is dollars, and the fourth digit is tens of dollars.

Provide keys for cents, dimes, dollars, and tens of dollars. Unfortunately no choice of keys seems particularly mnemonic. One choice is to use one of the keys: asdfo: **a** for cents, followed by a digit 1-9, **s** for dimes, followed by digits 1-9, **d** for dollars followed by a digit 1-9, and **f** for tens of dollars again followed by a digit 1-9. Each entry (one of **asdf** followed by 1-9) is followed by pressing the return key. Any overflow is reported after each operation. Overflow can be requested by pressing the **o** key.

9 Write a rational number class. This problem will be revisited in Chapter 8 where operator overloading will make the problem much nicer. For now we will use member functions `add`, `sub`, `mul`, `div`, and, `less` that each carry out the operations +, -, *, ., and <. For example, a + b will be written `a.add(b)` and a < b will be written `a.less(b)`.

Define a class for rational numbers. A rational number is a "ratio-nal" number, composed of two integers with division indicated. The division is not carried out, it is only indicated, as in 1/2, 2/3, 15/32, 65/4, 16/5. You should represent rational numbers by two *int* values, numerator and denominator.

A principle of abstract data type construction is that constructors must be present to create objects with any legal values. You should provide constructors to make objects out of pairs of int values; this is a two *int* parameter constructor. Since every *int* is also a rational, as in 2/1 or 17/1, you should provide a single *int* parameter constructor.

Provide member functions input and output that take an istream and ostream argument, respectively, and fetch or write rational numbers in the form 2/3 or 37/51 to or from the keyboard (and to or from a file).

Provide member functions add, sub, mul, and div that return a rational value. Provide a function less that returns a *bool* value. These functions should do the operation suggested by the name. Provide a member function neg that has no parameters and returns the negative of the calling object.

Provide a main function that thoroughly tests your class implementation. The following formulas will be useful in defining functions:

```
a/b + c/d = (a*d + b*c) / (b*d)
a/b - c/d = (a*d - b*c) / (b*d)
(a/b) * (c/d) = (a*c) / (b*d)
(a/b) / (c/d) = (a*d) / (c*b)
-(a/b) = (-a/b)
(a/b) < (c/d) means (a*d) < (c*b)
(a/b) == (c/d) means (a*d) == (c*b)
```

Let any sign be carried by the numerator; keep the denominator positive.

CHAPTER

7

More Flow of Control

7 More Flow of Control

When you come to a fork in the road,
   take it.

ATTRIBUTED TO YOGI BERRA

Introduction

flow of control

The order in which the statements in your program are performed is called **flow of control.** The *if-else*-statement, the *while*-statement, and the *do-while*-statement are three ways to specify flow of control. In this chapter we explore some new ways to use these statements and introduce two new statements called the *switch*-statement and the *for*-statement, which are also used for flow of control. The actions of an *if-else*-statement, a *while*-statement, or a *do-while*-statement are controlled by Boolean expressions. We begin by discussing Boolean expressions in more detail.

7.1 Using Boolean Expressions

"Contrariwise," continued Tweedledee.
   "If it was so, it might be;
   and if it were so, it would be;
   but as it isn't, it ain't. That's logic."

LEWIS CARROLL, THROUGH THE LOOKING GLASS

Evaluating Boolean Expressions

A **Boolean expression** is an expression that can be thought of as being *true* or *false* (that is, *true* if satisfied or *false* if not satisfied). Thus far you have used Boolean expressions as the test condition in *if-else*-statements and as the controlling expression in loops, such as a *while*-loop. However, a Boolean expression has an independent identity apart from any *if-else*-statement or loop statement you might use it in. The C++ type ***bool*** provides us the ability to declare variables that can carry the values *true* and *false*. A Boolean expression can be evaluated in the same way that an arithmetic expression is evaluated. The only difference is that an arithmetic expression uses operations such as +, *, and /, and produces a number as the final result, while a Boolean expression uses relational operations such as ==, <, and Boolean operations such as &&, ||, and !, and produces one of the two values *true* and *false* as the final result. Note that =, !=, <, <=, and so forth operate on pairs of any built-in type to produce a Boolean value *true* or *false*. If you understand the way Boolean expressions are evaluated, you will be able to write and understand complex Boolean expressions and be able to use Boolean expressions for the value returned by a function.

First let's review evaluating an arithmetic expression. The same technique will work in the same way to evaluate Boolean expressions. Consider the following arithmetic expression:

```
(x + 1) * (x + 3)
```

Assume that the variable x has the value 2. To evaluate this arithmetic expression, you evaluate the two sums to obtain the numbers 3 and 5, then you combine these two numbers 3 and 5 using the * operator to obtain 15 as the final value. Notice that in performing this evaluation, you do not multiply the expressions (x + 1) and (x + 3). Instead, you multiply the values of these expressions. You use 3; you do not use (x + 1). You use 5; you do not use (x + 3).

The computer evaluates Boolean expressions the same way. Subexpressions are evaluated to obtain values, each of which is either *true* or *false*. These individual values of *true* or *false* are then combined according to the rules in the tables shown in Display 7.1. For example, consider the Boolean expression

```
!( ( y < 3) || (y > 7) )
```

which might be the controlling expression for an *if-else*-statement or a *while*-statement. Suppose the value of y is 8. In this case (y < 3) evaluates to *false* and (y > 7) evaluates to *true*, so the above Boolean expression is equivalent to

```
!( false || true )
```

Consulting the tables for || (which is labeled **OR**), the computer sees that the expression inside the parentheses evaluates to *true*. Thus, the computer sees that the entire expression is equivalent to

```
!(true)
```

Consulting the tables again, the computer sees that !(*true*) evaluates to *false*, and so it concludes that *false* is the value of the original Boolean expression.

Almost all the examples we have constructed thus far have been fully parenthesized to show exactly what expressions each &&, ||, and ! applies to. This is not always required. If you omit parentheses, the default precedence is as follows: perform ! first, then perform relational operators such as <, then &&, and then ||. However, it is a good practice to include most parentheses in order to make the

parentheses

Display 7.1 Truth Tables

AND

Exp_1	Exp_2	Exp_1 && Exp_2
true	true	true
true	false	false
false	true	false
false	false	false

NOT

Exp	!(Exp)
true	false
false	true

OR

Exp_1	Exp_2	Exp_1 || Exp_2
true	true	true
true	false	true
false	true	true
false	false	false

expression easier to understand. One place where parentheses can safely be omitted is a simple string of &&'s or ||'s (but not a mixture of the two). The following expression is acceptable in terms of both the C++ compiler and readability:

```
(temperature > 90) && (humidity > 0.90) && (pool_gate == OPEN)
```

Since the relational operators > and == are performed before the && operator, you could omit the parentheses in the above expression and it would have the same meaning, but including some parentheses makes the expression easier to read.

precedence rules

When parentheses are omitted from an expression, the computer groups items according to rules known as **precedence rules.** Some of the precedence rules for C++ are given in Display 7.2. If one operator is performed before another, the operator that is performed first is said to have **higher precedence.** Binary operators of equal precedence are performed in left-to-right order. Unary operators of equal precedence are performed in right-to-left order. A complete set of precedence rules is given in Appendix 2.

Display 7.2 Precedence Rules

First: the unary operators: +, −, ++, −−, and !.

Next: the binary arithmetic operators: *, /, %

Next: the binary arithmetic operators: +, −

Next: the Boolean operators: <, >, <=, >=

Next: the Boolean operators: ==, !=

Next: the Boolean operator &&

Next: the Boolean operator ||

highest precedence (done first)

lowest precedence (done last)

Notice that the precedence rules include both arithmetic operators such as + and * as well as Boolean operators such as && and ||. This is because many expressions combine arithmetic and Boolean operations, as in the following simple example:

```
(x + 1) > 2 || (x + 1) < -3
```

If you check the precedence rules given in Display 7.2, you will see that this expression is equivalent to:

```
((x + 1) > 2) || ((x + 1) < -3)
```

because > and < have higher precedence than ||. In fact, you could omit all the parentheses in the above expression and it would have the same meaning, although it would be harder to read. Although we do not advocate omitting all the parentheses, it might be instructive to see how such an expression is interpreted using the precedence rules. Here is the expression without any parentheses:

```
x + 1 > 2 || x + 1 < -3
```

The precedences rules say first apply the unary −, then apply the +'s, then do the > and the <, and finally do the ||, which is exactly what the fully parenthesized version says to do.

The above description of how a Boolean expression is evaluated is basically correct, but in C++, the computer actually takes an occasional shortcut when evaluating a Boolean expression. Notice that in many cases you need to evaluate only the first of two subexpressions in a Boolean expression. For example, consider the following:

```
(x >= 0) && (y > 1)
```

If x is negative, then (x >= 0) is *false*, and as you can see in the tables in Display 7.1, when one subexpression in an && expression is *false*, then the whole expression is *false*, no matter whether the other expression is *true* or *false*. Thus, if we know that the first expression is *false*, there is no need to evaluate the second expression. A similar thing happens with || expressions. If the first of two expressions joined with the || operator is *true*, then you know the entire expression is *true*, no matter whether the second expression is *true* or *false*. The C++ language uses this fact to sometimes save itself the trouble of evaluating the second subexpression in a logical expression connected with an && or an ||. C++ first evaluates the leftmost of the two expressions joined by an && or an ||. If that gives it enough information to determine the final value of the expression (independent of the value of the second expression), then C++ does not bother to evaluate the second expression. This method of evaluation is called **short-circuit evaluation.**

Some languages, other than C++, use **complete evaluation.** In complete evaluation, when two expressions are joined by an && or an ||, both subexpressions are always evaluated and then the truth tables are used to obtain the value of the final expression.

Both short-circuit evaluation and complete evaluation give the same answer, so why should you care that C++ uses short-circuit evaluation? Most of the time you need not care. As long as both subexpressions joined by the && or the || have a value, the two methods yield the same result. However, if the second subexpression is undefined, you might be happy to know that C++ uses short-circuit evaluation. Let's look at an example that illustrates this point. Consider the following statement:

```
if ( (kids != 0) && ((pieces/kids) >= 2) )
    cout << "Each child may have two pieces!";
```

If the value of kids is not zero, this statement involves no subtleties. However, suppose the value of kids is zero and consider how short-circuit evaluation handles this case. The expression (kids != 0) evaluates to *false*, so there would be no need to evaluate the second expression. Using short-circuit evaluation, C++ says that the entire expression is *false*, *without bothering to evaluate the second expression.* This prevents a run-time error, since evaluating the second expression would involve dividing by zero.

C++ sometimes uses integers as if they were Boolean values. In particular, C++ converts the integer 1 to *true* and converts the integer 0 to *false*. The situation is even a bit more complicated than simply using 1 for *true* and 0 for *false*. The compiler will treat any nonzero number as if it were the value *true* and will treat 0 as if it were the value *false*. As long as you make no mistakes in writing Boolean expressions, this conversion causes no problems. As long as you make no mistakes in writing

Boolean expressions, you usually need not even be aware of the fact that *true* and *false* may be converted to or from 1 and 0. However, when you are debugging, it might help to know that the compiler is happy to combine integers using the Boolean operators &&, | |, and !.

Boolean (bool) values are true and false

In C++, a Boolean expression evaluates to the *bool* value *true* when it is satisfied and to the *bool* value *false* when it is not satisfied.

⬢ *PITFALL*   Boolean Expressions Convert to *int* Values

Suppose you want to use a Boolean expression in an *if-else*-statement, and you want it to be *true* provided that time has not yet run out (in some game or process). To phrase it a bit more precisely, suppose you want a Boolean expression to use in an *if-else*-statement and you want it to be *true* provided the value of a variable time of type *int* is not greater than the value of a variable called limit. You might write the following (where *Something* and *Something_Else* are some C++ statements):

```
if (!time > limit)          Wrong for what we want.
        Something
else
        Something_Else
```

This sounds right if you read it out loud: "not time greater than limit." The Boolean expression is wrong, however, and unfortunately, the compiler will not give you an error message. We have been bitten by the precedence rules of C++. The compiler will instead apply the precedence rules from Display 7.2 and interpret your Boolean expression as the following:

```
(!time) > limit
```

This looks like nonsense, and intuitively it is nonsense. If the value of time is, for example, 36, what could possibly be the meaning of (!time)? After all, that is equivalent to "not 36." But in C++, any nonzero integer converts to *true* and 0 is converted to *false*. Thus, !36 is interpreted as "not *true*" and so it evaluates to *false*, which is in turn converted back to 0 because we are comparing to an *int*.

What we want as the value of this Boolean expression and what C++ gives us are not the same. If `time` has a value of 36 and `limit` has a value of 60, you want the above displayed Boolean expression to evaluate to *true* (because it is *not true* that `time > limit`). Unfortunately, the Boolean expression instead evaluates as follows: (`!time`) evaluates to *false,* which is converted to 0, so the entire Boolean expression is equivalent to

```
0 > limit
```

and that in turn is equivalent to 0 > 60, because 60 is the value of `limit`, and that evaluates to *false*. Thus, the above logical expression evaluates to *false*, when you want it to evaluate to *true*.

There are two ways to correct this problem. One way is to use the ! operator correctly. When using the operator !, be sure to include parentheses around the argument. The correct way to write the above Boolean expression is:

```
if (!(time > limit))
    Something
else
    Something_Else
```

Another way to correct this problem is to completely avoid using the ! operator. For example, the following is also correct and easier to read:

```
if (time <= limit)
    Something
else
    Something_Else
```

Avoid using "not"

You can almost always avoid using the ! operator, and some programmers advocate avoiding it as much as possible. They say that just as *not* in English can make things not undifficult to read, so too can the "not" operator ! make C++ programs difficult to read. There is no need to be obsessive in avoiding the ! operator, but before using it, you should see if you can express the same thing more clearly without using the ! operator.

The Type *bool* Is New

Older versions of C++ have no type *bool*, but instead used the integers 1 and 0 for *true* and *false*. If you have an older version of C++ that does not have the type *bool*, Appendix 10 tells you how to simulate the type *bool* on your system.

SELF-TEST EXERCISES

1 Determine the value, *true* or *false*, of each of the following Boolean expressions, assuming that the value of the variable count is 0 and the value of the variable limit is 10. Give your answer as one of the values *true* or *false*.

a. (count == 0) && (limit < 20)

b. count == 0 && limit < 20

c. (limit > 20) || (count < 5)

d. !(count == 12)

e. (count == 1) && (x < y)

f. (count < 10) || (x < y)

g. !(((count < 10) || (x < y)) && (count >= 0))

h. ((limit/count) > 7) || (limit < 20)

i. (limit < 20) || ((limit/count) > 7)

j. ((limit/count) > 7) && (limit < 0)

k. (limit < 0) && ((limit/count) > 7)

l. (5 && 7) + (!6)

2 Name two kinds of statements in C++ that alter the order in which actions are performed. Give some examples.

3 In College algebra we see numeric intervals given as

   2 < x < 3

   In C++ this interval does not have the meaning you may expect. Explain and give the correct C++ Boolean expression that specifies that x lies between 2 and 3.

4 Does the following sequence produce division by zero?

```
j = -1;
if ((j > 0) && (1/(j+1) > 10))
    cout << i << endl;
```

Functions That Return a Boolean Value

A function may return a *bool* value just like any other built-in type, and can be used in a Boolean expression to control an *if-else*-statement, to control a loop statement, or can be used anywhere else that a Boolean expression is allowed. The returned type for such a function should be the type *bool*.

A call to a function that returns a Boolean value of *true* or *false* can be used anywhere that a Boolean expression is allowed. This can often make a program easier to read. By means of a function declaration, you can associate a complex Boolean expression with a meaningful name and use the name as a Boolean expression in an *if-else*-statement or anywhere else that a Boolean expression is allowed. For example, the statement

```
if (((rate >= 10) && (rate < 20)) || (rate == 0))
{
    ...
}
```

can be made to read

```
if (appropriate(rate))
{
    ...
}
```

provided that the following function has been defined:

```
bool appropriate(int rate)
{
    return (((rate >= 10) && (rate < 20)) || (rate == 0));
}
```

SELF-TEST EXERCISES

5 Write a function definition for a function called in_order that takes three arguments of type *int*. The function returns *true* if the three arguments are in ascending order; otherwise, it returns *false*. For example, in_order(1, 2, 3) and in_order(1, 2, 2) both return *true*, while in_order(1, 3, 2) returns *false*.

6 Write a function definition for a function called even that takes one argument of type *int* and returns a *bool* value. The function returns *true* if its one argument is an even number; otherwise, it returns *false*.

7 Write a function definition for a function isDigit that takes one argument of type *char* and returns a *bool* value. The function returns *true* if the argument is a decimal digit; otherwise, it returns *false*.

Enumeration Types *(Optional)*

An **enumeration type** is a type whose values are defined by a list of constants of type *int*. An enumeration type is very much like a list of declared constants.

When defining an enumeration type, you can use any *int* values, and you can have any number of constants defined in an enumeration type. For example, the following enumeration type defines a constant for the length of each month:

```
enum MonthLength { JAN_LENGTH = 31, FEB_LENGTH = 28,
    MAR_LENGTH = 31, APR_LENGTH = 30, MAY_LENGTH = 31,
    JUN_LENGTH = 30, JUL_LENGTH = 31, AUG_LENGTH = 31,
    SEP_LENGTH = 30, OCT_LENGTH = 31, NOV_LENGTH = 30,
    DEC_LENGTH = 31 };
```

As this example shows, two or more named constants in an enumeration type can receive the same *int* value.

If you do not specify any numeric values, the identifiers in an enumeration type definition are assigned consecutive values beginning with 0. For example, the type definition:

```
enum Direction { NORTH = 0, SOUTH = 1, EAST = 2, WEST = 3 };
```

is equivalent to

```
enum Direction { NORTH, SOUTH, EAST, WEST };
```

The form that does not explicitly list the *int* values is normally used when you just want a list of names and do not care about what values they have.

If you initialize an enumeration constant to some value, say

```
enum MyEnum { ONE = 17, TWO, THREE, FOUR = -3, FIVE };
```

then ONE takes the value 17, TWO takes the next *int* value 18, THREE takes the next value 19, FOUR takes -3, and FIVE takes the next value, -2.

In short, the default for the first enumeration constant is 0. The rest increase by 1 unless you set one or more of the enumeration contstants.

7.2 Multiway Branches

> *"Would you tell me, please, which*
> *way I ought to go from here?"*
> *"That depends a good deal on where*
> *you want to get to," said the Cat.*
>
> LEWIS CARROLL, ALICE IN WONDERLAND

Any programming construct that chooses one out of a number of alternative actions is called a **branching mechanism.** The *if-else*-statement chooses between two alternatives. In this section we will discuss methods for choosing from among more than two alternatives.

Nested Statements

As you have seen, *if-else*-statements and *if*-statements contain smaller statements within them. Thus far we have used compound statements and simple statements such as assignment statements as these smaller substatements, but there are other possibilities. In fact, any statement at all can be used as a subpart of an *if-else*-statement, of an *if*-statement, of a *while*-statement, or of a *do-while*-statement. This is illustrated in Display 7.3. The statement in that display has three levels of nesting, as indicated by the boxes. There are two cout-statements nested within an *if-else*-statement and then that *if-else*-statement is nested within an *if*-statement.

indenting

When nesting statements, you normally indent each level of nested substatements. In Display 7.3 there are three levels of nesting, so there are three levels of indenting. Both cout-statements are indented the same amount because they are both at the same level of nesting. Later in this chapter, you will see some specific cases where it makes sense to use other indenting patterns, but unless there is some rule to the contrary, you should indent each level of nesting as illustrated in Display 7.3.

↝ PROGRAMMING TIP
Use Braces in Nested Statements

Suppose we want to write an *if-else*-statement to use in an onboard computer monitoring system for a racing car. This part of the program warns the driver when fuel is low, but tells the driver to bypass pit stops if the fuel is close to full. In all

Display 7.3 An *if-else*-Statement within An *if*-Statement

```
if (count > 0)

    if (score > 5)

        cout << "count > 0 and score > 5\n";

    else

        cout << "count > 0 and score <= 5\n";
```

other situations the program gives no output so as not to distract the driver. We design the following pseudocode:

> If the fuel gauge is below $\frac{3}{4}$ full, then:
>> Check if the fuel gauge is below $\frac{1}{4}$ full and issue a low fuel warning if it is.
> Otherwise (i.e., if fuel gauge is over $\frac{3}{4}$ full):
>> Output a statement telling the driver not to stop.

If we are not being too careful, we might implement the pseudocode as follows:

```
if (fuel_gauge_reading < 0.75)            Read text to see what
    if (fuel_gauge_reading < 0.25)        is wrong with this.
        cout << "Fuel very low. Caution!\n";
else
    cout << "Fuel over 3/4. Don't stop now!\n";
```

This implementation looks fine, and it is indeed a correctly formed C++ statement that the compiler will accept and that will run with no error messages. However, it does not implement the pseudocode. Notice that this statement has two occurrences of `if` and only one `else`. The compiler must decide which `if` gets paired with the one `else`. We have nicely indented this nested statement to show that the `else` should be paired with the first `if`, but the compiler does not care about indenting. To the compiler, the preceding nested statement is the same as the following version, which differs only in how it is indented:

```
if (fuel_gauge_reading < 0.75)
    if (fuel_gauge_reading < 0.25)
        cout << "Fuel very low. Caution!\n";
    else
        cout << "Fuel over 3/4. Don't stop now!\n";
```

Unfortunately for us, the compiler will use the second interpretation and will pair the one `else` with the second `if`, rather than the first `if`. This is sometimes called the **dangling else problem,** and is illustrated by the program in Display 7.4.

dangling else

The compiler always pairs an `else` with the nearest previous `if` that is not already paired with some `else`. But, do not try to work within this rule. Ignore the rule! Change the rules! You are the boss! Always tell the compiler what you want it to do and the compiler will then do what you want. How do you tell the compiler what you want? You use braces. Braces in nested statements are like parentheses in arithmetic expressions. The braces tell the compiler how to group things, rather than leaving them to be grouped according to default conventions, which may or may not be what you want. To avoid problems and to make your programs easier to read, place braces, { and }, around substatements in `if-else`-statements, as we have

rule for pairing else*'s with* if*'s*

Display 7.4 The Importance of Braces

```
//Illustrates the importance of using braces in if-else-statements.
#include <iostream>
using namespace std;
int main( )
{
    double fuel_gauge_reading;

    cout << "Enter fuel gauge reading: ";
    cin >> fuel_gauge_reading;

    cout << "First with braces:\n";
    if (fuel_gauge_reading < 0.75)
    {
        if (fuel_gauge_reading < 0.25)
            cout << "Fuel very low. Caution!\n";
    }
    else
    {
        cout << "Fuel over 3/4. Don't stop now!\n";
    }

    cout << "Now without braces:\n";
    if (fuel_gauge_reading < 0.75)
        if (fuel_gauge_reading < 0.25)
            cout << "Fuel very low. Caution!\n";
    else
        cout << "Fuel over 3/4. Don't stop now!\n";

    return 0;
}
```

This indenting is nice, but is not what the computer follows.

Sample Dialogue 1

```
Enter fuel gauge reading: 0.1
First with braces:
Fuel very low. Caution!
Now without braces:
Fuel very low. Caution!
```

Braces make no difference in this case, but see Dialogue 2.

Sample Dialogue 2

```
Enter fuel gauge reading: 0.5
First with braces:
Now without braces:
Fuel over 3/4. Don't stop now!
```

There should be no output here, and thanks to braces, there is none. Incorrect output from the version without braces.

done in the first *if-else*-statement in Display 7.4. For very simple substatements, such as a single assignment statement or a single `cout`-statement, you can safely omit the braces. In Display 7.4, the braces around the following substatement (within the first *if-else*-statement) are not needed:

```
cout << "Fuel over 3/4. Don't stop now!\n";
```

However, even in these simple cases, the braces can sometimes aid readability. Some programmers advocate using braces around even the simplest substatements when they occur within *if-else*-statements, and that is what we have done in the first *if-else*-statement in Display 7.4.

Multiway *if-else*-Statements

An *if-else*-statement is a two-way branch. It allows a program to choose one of two possible actions. Often you will want to have a three- or four-way branch so that your program can choose between more than two alternative actions. You can implement such multiway branches by nesting *if-else*-statements. By way of example, suppose you are designing a game-playing program in which the user must guess the value of some number. The number can be in a variable named `number`, and the guess can be in a variable named `guess`. If you wish to give a hint after each guess, you might design the following pseudocode:

Output "Too high." when `guess` > `number`.
Output "Too low." when `guess` < `number`.
Output "Correct!" when `guess` == `number`.

Any time a branching action is described as a list of mutually exclusive conditions and corresponding actions, as in this example, it can be implemented by using a nested *if-else*-statement. For example, the above pseudocode translates to:

```
if (guess > number)
    cout << "Too high.";
else if (guess < number)
    cout << "Too low.";
else if (guess == number)
    cout << "Correct!";
```

The indenting pattern used here is slightly different from what we have advocated previously. If we followed our indenting rules, we would produce something like the following:

indenting

```
if (guess > number)
    cout << "Too high.";
else
    if (guess < number)
        cout << "Too low.";

    else
        if (guess == number)
            cout << "Correct!";
```

Use the previous indenting pattern rather than this one.

This is one of those rare cases in which you should not follow our general guidelines for indenting nested statements. The reason is that by lining up all the *else*'s, you also line up all the condition/action pairs and so make the layout of the program reflect your reasoning. Another reason is that, even for not-too-deeply nested *if-else*-statements, you can quickly run out of space on your page!

Since the conditions are mutually exclusive, the last *if* in the above nested *if-else*-statement is superfluous and can be omitted, but it is sometimes best to include it in a comment as follows:

```
if (guess > number)
    cout << "Too high.";
else if (guess < number)
    cout << "Too low.";
else // (guess == number)
    cout << "Correct!";
```

You can use this form of multiple branch *if-else*-statement even if the conditions are not mutually exclusive. Whether the conditions are mutually exclusive or not, the computer will evaluate the conditions in the order in which they appear until it finds the first condition that is *true* and then it executes the action corresponding to this condition. If no condition is *true*, no action is taken. If the statement ends with a plain *else* without any *if*, then the last statement is executed when all the conditions are *false*.

▪)) *PROGRAMMING* EXAMPLE
State Income Tax

Display 7.5 contains a function definition that uses a multiway *if-else*-statement. The function takes one argument, which is the tax payer's net income rounded to a whole number of dollars and computes the state income tax due on this net income. This state computes tax according to the rate schedule below:

1 No tax is paid on the first $15,000 of net income.

2 A tax of 5% is assessed on each dollar of net income from $15,001 to $25,000.

3 A tax of 10% is assessed on each dollar of net income over $25,000.

Display 7.5 Multiway *if-else*-Statement *(part 1 of 2)*

```
//Program to compute state income tax.
#include <iostream>
using namespace std;


double tax(int net_income);
//Precondition: The formal parameter net_income is net income, rounded
//to a whole number of dollars.
//Returns the amount of state income tax due computed as follows:
//no tax on income up to $15,000; 5% on income between $15,001
//and $25,000 plus 10% on income over $25,000.


int main()
{
    int net_income;
    double tax_bill;

    cout << "Enter net income (rounded to whole dollars) $";
    cin >> net_income;

    tax_bill = tax(net_income);

    cout.setf(ios::fixed);
    cout.setf(ios::showpoint);
    cout.precision(2);
    cout << "Net income = $" << net_income << endl
         << "Tax bill = $" << tax_bill << endl;

    return 0;
}


double tax(int net_income)
{
    double five_percent_tax, ten_percent_tax;
```

Display 7.5 Multiway *if-else-***Statement** *(part 2 of 2)*

```
if (net_income <= 15000)
    return 0;
else if ((net_income > 15000) && (net_income <= 25000))
    //return 5% of amount over $15,000
    return (0.05*(net_income - 15000));
else //net_income > $25,000
{
    //five_percent_tax = 5% of income from $15,000 to $25,000.
    five_percent_tax = 0.05*10000;
    //ten_percent_tax = 10% of income over $25,000.
    ten_percent_tax = 0.10*(net_income - 25000);
    return (five_percent_tax + ten_percent_tax);
}
}
```

Sample Dialogue

```
Enter net income (rounded to whole dollars) $25100
Net income = $25100.00
Tax bill = $510.00
```

The function defined in Display 7.5 uses a multiway *if-else*-statement with one action for each of the above three cases. The condition for the second case is actually more complicated than it needs to be. The computer will not get to the second condition unless it has already tried the first condition and found it to be *false*. Thus, you know that whenever the computer tries the second condition, it will know that net_income is greater than 15000. Hence, you can replace the line

```
else if ((net_income > 15000) && (net_income <= 25000))
```

with the following, and the program will perform exactly the same:

```
else if (net_income <= 25000)
```

Multiway *if-else*-**Statement**

Syntax:

```
if (Boolean_Expression_1)
    Statement_1
else if (Boolean_Expression_2)
    Statement_2
        .
        .
        .
else if (Boolean_Expression_n)
    Statement_n
else
    Statement_For_All_Other_Possibilities
```

Example:

```
if ((temperature < -10) && (day == SUNDAY))
    cout << "Stay home.";
else if (temperature < -10) //and day != SUNDAY
    cout << "Stay home, but call work.";
else if (temperature <= 0) //and temperature >= -10
    cout << "Dress warm.";
else //temperature > 0
    cout << "Work hard and play hard.";
```

The Boolean expressions are checked in order until the first *true* Boolean expression is encountered and then the corresponding statement is executed. If none of the Boolean expressions is *true*, then the *Statement_For_All_Other_Possibilities* is executed.

SELF-TEST EXERCISES

8 What output will be produced by the following code, when embedded in a complete program?

```
int x = 2;
cout << "Start\n";
if (x <= 3)
    if (x != 0)
        cout << "Hello from the second if.\n";
```

```
            else
                cout << "Hello from the else.\n";
        cout << "End\n";

        cout << "Start again\n";
        if (x > 3)
            if (x != 0)
                cout << "Hello from the second if.\n";
            else
                cout << "Hello from the else.\n";
        cout << "End again\n";
```

9 What output will be produced by the following code, when embedded in a complete program?

```
    int extra = 2;
    if (extra < 0)
        cout << "small";
    else if (extra == 0)
        cout << "medium";
    else
        cout << "large";
```

10 What would be the output in Self-Test Exercise 9 if the assignment were changed to the following?

```
    int extra = -37;
```

11 What would be the output in Self-Test Exercise 9 if the assignment were changed to the following?

```
    int extra = 0;
```

12 Write a multiway *if-else*-statement that classifies the value of an *int* variable n into one of the following categories and writes out an appropriate message:

```
    n < 0 or 0 ≤ n ≤ 100 or n > 100
```

13 Given the following declaration and output statement, assume that this has been embedded in a correct program and is run. What is the output?

```
    enum Direction { N, S, E, W };
    //...
    cout << W << " " << E << " " << S << " " << N << endl;
```

14 Given the following declaration and output statement, assume that this has
    been embedded in a correct program and is run. What is the output?

```
enum Direction { N = 5, S = 7, E = 1, W };
// ...
cout << W << " " << E << " " << S << " " N << endl;
```

The *switch*-Statement

You have seen *if-else*-statements used to construct multiway branches. The
switch-statement is another kind of C++ statement that also implements multiway
branches. A sample *switch*-statement is shown in Display 7.6. This particular
switch-statement has four regular branches and a fifth branch for illegal input. The
variable grade determines which branch is executed. There is one branch for each of
the grades of 'A', 'B', and 'C'. The grades 'D' and 'F' cause the same branch to
be taken, rather than having a separate action for each of 'D' and 'F'. If the value of
grade is any character other than 'A', 'B', 'C', 'D', or 'F', then the cout-statement after the identifier *default* is executed.

The syntax and preferred indenting pattern for the *switch*-statement are shown
in the sample *switch*-statement in Display 7.6 and in the box on page 388.

When a *switch*-statement is executed, one of a number of different branches is
executed. The choice of which branch to execute is determined by a **controlling
expression** given in parentheses after the keyword *switch*. The controlling expression
in the sample *switch*-statement shown in Display 7.6 is of type *char*. The controlling
expression for a *switch*-statement must always return either a *bool* value, an *enum*
constant, one of the integer types, or a character. When the *switch*-statement is executed, this controlling expression is evaluated and the computer looks at the constant
values given after the various occurrences of the identifiers *case*. If it finds a constant
that equals the value of the controlling expression, it executes the code for that *case*.
For example, if the expression evaluates to 'B', then it looks for the following and executes the statements that follow this line:

*controlling
expression*

```
case 'B':
```

Notice that the constant is followed by a colon. Also note that you cannot have two
occurrences of *case* with the same constant value after them, since that would be an
ambiguous instruction.

A *break*-statement consists of the keyword *break* followed by a semicolon.
When the computer executes the statements after a *case* label, it continues until it
reaches a *break*-statement. When the computer encounters a *break*-statement, the
switch-statement ends. If you omit the *break*-statements, then after executing the
code for one *case*, the computer will go on to execute the code for the next *case*.

break

Display 7.6 A *switch*-**Statement** *(part 1 of 2)*

```
//Program to illustrate the switch-statement.
#include <iostream>
using namespace std;

int main( )
{
    char grade;

    cout << "Enter your midterm grade and press return: ";
    cin >> grade;

    switch (grade)
    {
        case 'A':
            cout << "Excellent. "
                 << "You need not take the final.\n";
            break;
        case 'B':
            cout << "Very good. ";
            grade = 'A';
            cout << "Your midterm grade now is "
                 << grade << endl;
            break;
        case 'C':
            cout << "Passing.\n";
            break;
        case 'D':
        case 'F':
            cout << "Not good. "
                 << "Go study.\n";
            break;
        default:
            cout << "That is not a possible grade.\n";
    }

    cout << "End of program.\n";
    return 0;
}
```

Display 7.6 A *switch*-**Statement** *(part 2 of 2)*

Sample Dialogue 1

```
Enter your midterm grade and press return: A
Excellent. You need not take the final.
End of program.
```

Sample Dialogue 2

```
Enter your midterm grade and press return: B
Very good. Your midterm grade is now A.
End of program.
```

Sample Dialogue 3

```
Enter your midterm grade and press return: D
Not good. Go study.
End of program.
```

Sample Dialogue 4

```
Enter your midterm grade and press return: E
That is not a possible grade.
End of program.
```

Note that you can have two *case* labels for the same section of code. In the *switch*-statement in Display 7.6, the same action is taken for the values 'D' and 'F'. This technique can also be used to allow for both upper- and lowercase letters. For example, to allow both lowercase 'a' and uppercase 'A' in the program in Display 7.6, you can replace

```
case 'A':
    cout << "Excellent. "
         << "You need not take the final.\n";
    break;
```

switch-Statement

Syntax:

```
switch (Controlling_Expression)
{
    case Constant_1:
        Statement_Sequence_1
        break;
    case Constant_2:
        Statement_Sequence_2
        break;

            ⋮

    case Constant_n:
        Statement_Sequence_n
        break;
    default:
        Default_Statement_Sequence
}
```

Example:

```
int vehicle_class;
cout << "Enter vehicle class: ";
cin >> vehicle_class;

switch (vehicle_class)
{
    case 1:
        cout << "Passenger car.";
        toll = 0.50;
        break;
    case 2:
        cout << "Bus.";
        toll = 1.50;
        break;
    case 3:
        cout << "Truck.";
        toll = 2.00;
        break;
    default:
        cout << "Unknown vehicle class!";
}
```

*If you forget this **break**, then passenger cars will pay $1.50.*

with the following:

```
case 'A':
case 'a':
    cout << "Excellent. "
        << "You need not take the final.\n";
    break;
```

Of course, the same can be done for all the other letters.

If no *case* label has a constant that matches the value of the controlling expression, then the statements following the *default* label are executed. You need not have a *default* section. If there is no *default* section and no match is found for the value of the controlling expression, then nothing happens when the *switch*-statement is executed. However, it is safest to always have a *default* section. If you think your *case* labels list all possible outcomes, then you can put an error message in the *default* section. This is what we did in Display 7.6.

default

◆ PITFALL   Forgetting a *break* in a *switch*-Statement

If you forget a *break* in a *switch*-statement, the compiler will not issue an error message. You will have written a syntactically correct *switch*-statement, but it will not do what you intended it to do. Consider the *switch*-statement in the box labeled "*switch*-Statement." If a *break*-statement were omitted, as indicated by the arrow, then when the variable vehicle_class has the value 1, the *case* labeled

```
case 1:
```

will be executed as desired, but then the computer will go on to also execute the next *case*. This will produce a puzzling output that says the vehicle is a passenger car and then later says it is a bus; moreover the final value of toll will be 1.50, not 0.50 as it should be. When the computer starts to execute a *case*, it does not stop until it encounters either a *break* or the end of the *switch*-statement.

Using *switch*-Statements for Menus

The multiway *if-else*-statement is more versatile than the *switch*-statement, and you can use a multiway *if-else*-statement anywhere you can use a *switch*-statement. However, sometimes the *switch*-statement is clearer. For example, the *switch*-statement is perfect for implementing *menus*.

A *menu* in a restaurant presents a list of alternatives for a customer to choose from. A **menu** in a computer program does the same thing; it presents a list of alternatives on the screen for the user to choose from. Display 7.7 shows the outline of a

Display 7.7 A Menu (part 1 of 2)

```
//Program to give out homework assignment information.
#include <iostream>
using namespace std;

void show_assignment();
//Displays next assignment on screen.

void show_grade();
//Asks for a student number and gives the corresponding grade.

void give_hints();
//Displays a hint for the current assignment.

int main()
{
    int choice;
    do
    {
        cout << endl
             << "Choose 1 to see the next homework assignment.\n"
             << "Choose 2 for your grade on the last assignment.\n"
             << "Choose 3 for assignment hints.\n"
             << "Choose 4 to exit this program.\n"
             << "Enter your choice and press return: ";
        cin >> choice;

        switch (choice)
        {
            case 1:
                show_assignment();
                break;
            case 2:
                show_grade();
                break;
            case 3:
                give_hints();
                break;
```

Display 7.7 A Menu *(part 2 of 2)*

```
        case 4:
            cout << "End of Program.\n";
            break;
        default:
            cout << "Not a valid choice.\n"
                 << "Choose again.\n";
    }
}while (choice != 4);

    return 0;
}
```

<The definitions for the functions show_assignment,
        show_grade, and give_hints are inserted here.>

Sample Dialogue

```
Choose 1 to see the next homework assignment.
Choose 2 for your grade on the last assignment.
Choose 3 for assignment hints.
Choose 4 to exit this program.
Enter your choice and press return: 3

Assignment hints:
Analyze the problem.
Write an algorithm in pseudocode.
Translate the pseudocode into a C++ program.

Choose 1 to see the next homework assignment.
Choose 2 for your grade on the last assignment.
Choose 3 for assignment hints.
Choose 4 to exit this program.
Enter your choice and press return: 4
End of Program.
```

The exact output will depend on the definition of the function give_hints.

program designed to give students information on homework assignments. The program uses a menu to let the student choose which information she or he wants. (If you want to see the menu part of this program in action before designing the functions it uses, simply use stubs for the function definitions. Stubs are discussed in Chapter 4.)

↝ *PROGRAMMING* TIP
Use Function Calls in Branching Statements

The *switch*-statement and the multiway *if-else*-statement allow you to place several different statements in each branch. However, doing so can make the *switch*-statement or *if-else*-statement difficult to read. Look at the *switch*-statement in Display 7.7. Each of the branches for choices 1, 2, and 3 is a single function call. This makes the layout of the *switch*-statement and the overall structure of the program clear. If we had instead placed all the code for each branch in the *switch*-statement, instead of in the function definitions, then the *switch*-statement would be an incomprehensible sea of C++ statements. In fact, the *switch*-statement would not even fit on one screen.

Blocks

Each branch of a *switch*-statement or of an *if-else*-statement is a separate subtask. As indicated in the previous Programming Tip, it is often best to make the action of each branch a function call. That way the subtask for each branch can be designed, written, and tested separately. On the other hand, sometimes the action of one branch is so simple that you can just make it a compound statement. Occasionally, you may want to give this compound statement its own local variables. For example, consider the program in Display 7.8. It calculates the final bill for a specified number of items at a given price. If the sale is a wholesale transaction, then no sales tax is charged (presumably because the tax will be paid when the items are resold to retail buyers). If, however, the sale is a retail transaction, then sales tax must be added. An *if-else*-statement is used to produce different calculations for wholesale and retail purchases. For the retail purchase, the calculation uses a temporary variable called subtotal and so that variable is declared within the compound statement for that branch of the *if-else*-statement.

local variables   As shown in Display 7.8, the variable subtotal is declared within a compound statement. If we wanted to, we could have used the variable name subtotal for something else outside of the compound statement in which it is declared. A variable

Display 7.8 Block with a Local Variable (part 1 of 2)

```
//Program to compute bill for either a wholesale or a retail purchase.
#include <iostream>
using namespace std;
const double TAX_RATE = 0.05; //5% sales tax.

int main( )
{
    char sale_type;
    int number;
    double price, total;

    cout << "Enter price $";
    cin >> price;
    cout << "Enter number purchased: ";
    cin >> number;
    cout << "Type W if this is a wholesale purchase.\n"
         << "Type R if this is a retail purchase.\n"
         << "Then press return.\n";
    cin >> sale_type;

    if ((sale_type == 'W') || (sale_type == 'w'))
    {
        total = price * number;
    }
    else if ((sale_type == 'R') || (sale_type == 'r'))
    {
        double subtotal;          ⟵————————————  local to the block
        subtotal = price * number;
        total = subtotal + subtotal * TAX_RATE;
    }
    else
    {
        cout << "Error in input.\n";
    }
```

Display 7.8 Block with a Local Variable *(part 2 of 2)*

```
        cout.setf(ios::fixed);
        cout.setf(ios::showpoint);
        cout.precision(2);
        cout << number << " items at $" << price << endl;
        cout << "Total Bill = $" << total;
        if ((sale_type == 'R') || (sale_type == 'r'))
            cout << " including sales tax.\n";

        return 0;
    }
```

Sample Dialogue

```
    Enter price: $10.00
    Enter number purchased: 2
    Type W if this is a wholesale purchase.
    Type R if this is a retail purchase.
    Then press return.
    R
    2 items at $10.00
    Total Bill = $21.00 including sales tax.
```

that is declared inside a compound statement is local to the compound statement. It is the same as if you made the compound statement the body of a function definition so that the variable declaration was inside a function definition. The compound statement does, however, have one advantage over a function definition: Within a compound statement, you can use all the variables declared outside of the compound statement, as well as the local variables declared inside the compound statement.

block

A compound statement with declarations is more than a simple compound statement, so it has a special name. A compound statement that contains variable declarations is usually called a **block,** and the variables declared within the block are said to

scope

be **local to the block** or to **have the block as their scope.** (A plain old compound statement that does not contain any variable declarations is also called a *block.* Any code enclosed in braces is called a *block.*)

Notice that the body of a function definition is a block. There is no standard name for a block that is not the body of a function; but we want to talk about these kinds of blocks, so let us create a name for them. Let's call a block a **statement block** when it is not the body of a function (and not the body of the main part of a program).

Blocks

A **block** is some C++ code enclosed in braces. The variables declared in a block are local to the block and so the variable names can be used outside of the block for something else (such as being reused as the name for a different variable).

Statement blocks can be nested within other statement blocks, and basically the same rules about local variable names applies to these nested statement blocks as what we have already discussed, but applying the rules can be tricky when statement blocks are nested. A better rule is to not nest statement blocks. Nested statement blocks make a program hard to read. If you feel the need to nest statement blocks, instead make some of the statement blocks into function definitions and use function calls rather than nested statement blocks. In fact, statement blocks of any kind should be used sparingly. In most situations, a function call is preferable to a statement block. For completeness, we include the scope rule for nested blocks in the next summary box.

nested blocks

Scope Rule for Nested Blocks

If an identifier is declared as a variable in each of two blocks, one within the other, then these are two different variables with the same name. One variable exists only within the inner block and cannot be accessed outside of the inner block. The other variable exists only in the outer block and cannot be accessed in the inner block. The two variables are distinct, so changes made to one of these variables will have no effect on the other of these two variables.

◆ PITFALL   Inadvertent Local Variables

When you declare a variable within a pair of braces { } that variable becomes a local variable for the block enclosed in the pair { }. This is *true* whether you wanted the variable to be local or not. If you want a variable to be available outside of the braces { }, then you must declare it outside of the braces.

SELF-TEST EXERCISES

15   What output will be produced by the following code, when embedded in a complete program?

```
int first_choice = 1;
switch (first_choice + 1)
{
    case 1:
        cout << "Roast beef\n";
        break;
    case 2:
        cout << "Roast worms\n";
        break;
    case 3:
        cout << "Chocolate ice cream\n";
    case 4:
        cout << "Onion ice cream\n";
        break;
    default:
        cout << "Bon appetit!\n";
}
```

16   What would be the output in Self-Test Exercise 15 if the first line were changed to the following:

```
int first_choice = 3;
```

17   What would be the output in Self-Test Exercise 15 if the first line were changed to the following:

```
int first_choice = 2;
```

18   What would be the output in Self-Test Exercise 15 if the first line were changed to the following:

```
int first_choice = 4;
```

19   What output will be produced by the following code, when embedded in a complete program?

```
int number = 22;
{
    int number = 42;
    cout << number << " ";
```

```
        }
        cout << number;
```

20 Though we urge you not to program using this style, we are providing an
    exercise that uses nested blocks to help you understand the scope rules. Give
    the output that this code fragment would produce if embedded in an other-
    wise complete, correct program.

```
    {
        int x = 1;
        cout << x << endl;
        {
            cout << x << endl;
            int x = 2;
            cout << x << endl;
            {
                cout << x << endl;
                int x = 3;
                cout << x << endl;
            }
            cout << x << endl;
        }
        cout << x << endl;
    }
```

7.3 More About C++ Loop Statements

It is not true that life is one damn thing after another—
It's one damn thing over and over.

EDNA ST. VINCENT MILLAY,
    LETTER TO ARTHUR DARISON FICKE, OCTOBER 24, 1930

A **loop** is any program construction that repeats a statement or sequence of statements a number of times. The simple *while*-loops and *do-while*-loops that we
have already seen are examples of loops. The statement (or group of statements) to
be repeated in a loop is called the **body** of the loop, and each repetition of the loop
body is called an **iteration** of the loop. The two main design questions when con-
structing loops are: What should the loop body be? How many times should the loop
body be iterated?

loop body
loop iteration

while and do-while compared

The *while*-Statements Reviewed

The syntax for the *while*-statement and its variant, the *do-while*-statement, are reviewed in Display 7.9. The important difference between the two types of loops involves *when* the controlling Boolean expression is checked. With a *while*-statement the Boolean expression is checked *before* the loop body is executed. If the Boolean expression evaluates to *false*, then the body is not executed at all. With a *do-while*-statement, the body of the loop is executed first and the Boolean expression is checked *after* the loop body is executed. Thus, the *do-while*-statement always executes the loop body at least once. After this start-up, the *while*-loop and the *do-while*-loop behave very much the same. After each iteration of the loop body, the Boolean expression is again checked and if it is *true*, then the loop is iterated again. If it has changed from *true* to *false*, then the loop statement ends.

executing the body zero times

   The first thing that happens when a *while*-loop is executed is that the controlling Boolean expression is evaluated. If the Boolean expression evaluates to *false* at that point, then the body of the loop is never executed. It may seem pointless to execute the body of a loop zero times, but that is sometimes the desired action. For example, a *while*-loop is often used to sum a list of numbers, but the list could be empty. To be more specific, a checkbook balancing program might use a *while*-loop to sum the values of all the checks you have written in a month—but you might take a month's vacation and write no checks at all. In that case, there are zero numbers to sum and so the loop is iterated zero times.

Increment and Decrement Operators Revisited

You have used the increment operator as a statement that increments the value of a variable by one. For example, the following will output 42 to the screen:

```
int number = 41;
number++;
cout << number;
```

increment operator in expressions

Thus far we have always used the increment operator as a statement. But, the increment operator is also an operator, just like the + and – operators. An expression like number++ also returns a value, so number++ can be used in an arithmetic expression such as:

```
2*(number++)
```

Display 7.9 Syntax of the *while*-Statement and *do-while*-Statement

A *while*-statement with a single statement body:

while (*Boolean_Expression*)
    Statement   ←   *body*

A *while*-statement with a multi-statement body:

while (*Boolean_Expression*)
{
    Statement_1
    Statement_2
       .
       .   >   *body*
       .
    Statement_Last
}

A *do-while*-statement with a single statement body:

do   *body*
    Statement   ←
while (*Boolean_Expression*);

A *do-while*-statement with a multi-statement body:

do
{
    Statement_1
    Statement_2
       .
       .   >   *body*
       .
    Statement_Last
}*while* (*Boolean_Expression*);

The expression number++ first returns the value of the variable number, and *then* the value of number is increased by one. For example, consider the following code:

```
int number = 2;
int value_produced = 2*(number++);
cout << value_produced << endl;
cout << number << endl;
```

This code will produce the output:

```
4
3
```

Notice the expression 2*(number++). When C++ evaluates this expression it uses the value that number has *before* it is incremented, not the value that it has after it is incremented. Thus, the value produced by the expression number++ is 2, even though the increment operator changes the value of number to 3. This may seem strange, but sometimes it is just what you want. And, as you are about to see, if you want an expression that behaves differently, you can have it.

v++ *versus*
++v

The expression v++ evaluates to the value of the variable v and *then* the value of the variable v is incremented by one. If you reverse the order and place the ++ in front of the variable, the order of these two actions is reversed. The expression ++v first increments the value of the variable v and then returns this increased value of v. For example, consider the following code:

```
int number = 2;
int value_produced = 2*(++number);
cout << value_produced << endl;
cout << number << endl;
```

This code is the same as the previous piece of code except that the ++ is before the variable, so this code will produce the following output:

```
6
3
```

Notice that the two increment operators number++ and ++number have the exact same effect on a variable number: They both increase the value of number by one. But the two expressions evaluate to different values. Remember, if the ++ is *before* the variable, then the incrementing is done *before* the value is returned; if the ++ is *after* the variable, then the incrementing is done *after* the value is returned.

The program in Display 7.10 uses the increment operator in a *while*-loop to count the number of times the loop body is repeated. One of the main uses of the increment operator is to control the iteration of loops in ways similar to what is done in Display 7.10.

Display 7.10 The Increment Operator as an Expression

```cpp
//Calorie-counting program.
#include <iostream>
using namespace std;

int main( )
{
    int number_of_items, count,
        calories_for_item, total_calories;

    cout << "How many items did you eat today? ";
    cin >> number_of_items;

    total_calories = 0;
    count = 1;
    cout << "Enter the number of calories in each of the\n"
        << number_of_items << " items eaten:\n";

    while (count++ <= number_of_items)
    {
        cin >> calories_for_item;
        total_calories = total_calories
                        + calories_for_item;
    }

    cout << "Total calories eaten today = "
        << total_calories << endl;
    return 0;
}
```

Sample Dialogue

```
How many items did you eat today? 7
Enter the number of calories in each of the
7 items eaten:
300 60 1200 600 150 1 120
Total calories eaten today = 2431
```

decrement operator

Everything we said about the increment operator applies to the decrement operator as well, except that the value of the variable is decreased by one rather than increased by one. For example, consider the following code:

```
int number = 8;
int value_produced = number--;
cout << value_produced << endl;
cout << number << endl;
```

This produces the output:

```
8
7
```

On the other hand, the code

```
int number = 8;
int value_produced = --number;
cout << value_produced << endl;
cout << number << endl;
```

produces the output:

```
7
7
```

`number--` returns the value of `number` and then decrements `number`; on the other hand, `--number` first decrements `number` and then returns the value of `number`.

++ and -- can only be used with variables

You cannot apply the increment and decrement operators to anything other than a single variable. Expressions such as `(x + y)++`, `--(x + y)`, `5++`, and so forth are all illegal in C++.

SELF-TEST EXERCISES

21 What is the output of the following (when embedded in a complete program)?

```
int count = 3;
while (count-- > 0)
    cout << count << " ";
```

22 What is the output of the following (when embedded in a complete program)?

```
int count = 3;
while (--count > 0)
    cout << count << " ";
```

23 What is the output of the following (when embedded in a complete program)?

```
int n = 1;
do
    cout << n << " ";
while (n++ <= 3);
```

24 What is the output of the following (when embedded in a complete program)?

```
int n = 1;
do
    cout << n << " ";
while (++n <= 3);
```

The *for*-Statement

The *while*-statement and the *do-while*-statement are all the loop mechanisms you absolutely need. In fact, the *while*-statement alone is enough. However, there is one sort of loop that is so common that C++ includes a special statement for this kind of loop. In performing numeric calculations, it is common to do a calculation with the number one, then with the number two, then with three, and so forth, until some last value is reached. For example, to add one through ten, you want the computer to perform the following statement ten times, with the value of n equal to 1 the first time and with n increased by one each subsequent time:

```
sum = sum + n;
```

The following is one way to accomplish this with a *while*-statement:

```
sum = 0;
n = 1;
while (n <= 10)
{
    sum = sum + n;
    n++;
}
```

Although a *while*-loop will do here, this sort of situation is just what the *for*-statement (also called the *for*-**loop**) was designed for. The following *for*-statement will neatly accomplish the same task:

```
sum = 0;
for (n = 1; n <= 10; n++)
    sum = sum + n;
```

Let's look at this *for*-statement piece by piece.

First, notice that the *while*-loop version and the *for*-loop version are made by putting together the same pieces: They both start with an assignment statement that sets the variable sum equal to 0. In both cases this assignment statement for sum is placed before the loop statement itself begins. The loop statements themselves are both made from the pieces

```
n = 1; n <= 10; n++ and sum = sum + n;
```

These pieces serve the same function in the *for*-statement as they do in the *while*-statement. The *for*-statement is simply a more compact way of saying the same thing. Although other things are possible, we will only use *for*-statements to perform loops controlled by one variable. In our example, that would be the variable n. With the equivalence of the above two loops to guide us, let's go over the rules for writing a *for*-statement.

A *for*-statement begins with the keyword *for* followed by three things in parentheses that tell the computer what to do with the controlling variable. The beginning of a *for*-statement looks like the following:

```
for (Initialization_Action; Boolean_Expression; Update_Action)
```

The first expression tells how the variable is initialized, the second gives a Boolean expression that is used to check for when the loop should end, and the last expression tells how the loop control variable is updated after each iteration of the loop body. For example, the above *for*-loop begins

```
for (n = 1; n <= 10; n++)
```

The n = 1 says that n is initialized to 1. The n <= 10 says the loop will continue to iterate the body as long as n is less than or equal to 10. The last expression, n++, says that n is incremented by one after each time the loop body is executed.

The three expressions at the start of a *for*-statement are separated by two, and only two, semicolons. Do not succumb to the temptation to place a semicolon after the third expression. (The technical explanation is that these three things are expressions, not statements, and so do not require a semicolon at the end.)

Display 7.11 shows the syntax of a *for*-statement and also describes the action of the *for*-statement by showing how it translates into an equivalent *while*-statement. Notice that in a *for*-statement, as in the corresponding *while*-statement, the stopping condition is tested before the first loop iteration. Thus, it is possible to have a *for*-loop whose body is executed zero times.

Display 7.11 The *for*-Statement

for-Statement:

Syntax:

```
for (Initialization_Action; Boolean_Expression; Update_Action)
    Body_Statement
```

Example:

```
for (number = 100; number >= 0; number--)
    cout << number
        << " bottles of beer on the shelf.\n";
```

Equivalent *while*-loop:

Equivalent Syntax:

```
Initialization_Action;
while (Boolean_Expression)
{
    Body_Statement
    Update_Action;
}
```

Equivalent Example:

```
number = 100;
while (number >= 0)
{
    cout << number
        << " bottles of beer on the shelf.\n";
    number--;
}
```

Output

```
100 bottles of beer on the shelf.
99 bottles of beer on the shelf.
            .
            .
            .
0 bottles of beer on the shelf.
```

*declaring variables
within a for-statement*

Display 7.12 shows a sample *for*-statement embedded in a complete (although very simple) program. The *for*-statement in Display 7.12 is similar to the one discussed above, but it has one new feature. The variable n is declared when it is initialized to 1. So, the declaration of n is inside the *for*-statement. The initializing action in a *for*-statement can include a variable declaration. When a variable is used only within the *for*-statement, this can be the best place to declare the variable. However, if the variable is also used outside of the *for*-statement, then it is best to declare the variable outside of the *for*-statement.

The ANSI C++ Standard requires that a C++ compiler that claims compliance with the Standard treat any declaration in a *for*-loop initializer as if it were local to the body of the loop. Earlier C++ compilers did not do this. You should determine how your compiler treats variables declared in a *for*-loop initializer. In the interests of portability you should not write code that depends on this behavior. The ANSI C++ Standard requires that variables declared in the initialization expression of a *for*-loop be local to the block of the *for*-loop. The next generation of C++ compilers will likely comply with this rule, but compilers presently available may or may not comply.

Our description of a *for*-statement was a bit less general than what is allowed. The three expressions at the start of a *for*-statement may be any C++ expressions and, so, they may involve more (or even fewer!) than one variable. However, our *for*-statements will always use only a single variable in these expressions.

In the *for*-statement in Display 7.12 the body was the simple assignment statement

```
sum = sum + n;
```

The body may be any statement at all. In particular, the body may be a compound statement. This allows us to place several statements in the body of a *for*-loop, as shown in Display 7.13.

*more possible
update actions*

Thus far, you have seen *for*-loops that increase the loop control variable by one after each loop iteration, and you have seen *for*-loops that decrease the loop control variable by one after each loop iteration. There are many more possible kinds of variable updates. The variable can be incremented or decremented by 2 or 3 or any number. If the variable is of type *double*, it can be incremented or decremented by a fractional amount. All of the following are legitimate *for*-loops:

```
int n;
for (n = 1; n <= 10; n = n + 2)
    cout << "n is now equal to " << n << endl;

for (n = 0; n > -100; n = n - 7)
    cout << "n is now equal to " << n << endl;

for (double size = 0.75; size <= 5; size = size + 0.05)
    cout << "size is now equal to " << size << endl;
```

Display 7.12 A *for*-Statement

```
//Illustrates a for-loop.
#include <iostream>
using namespace std;

int main()
{
    int sum = 0;

    for (int n = 1; n <= 10; n++)   //Note that the variable n is a local
        sum = sum + n;              //variable of the body of the for loop!

    cout << "The sum of the numbers 1 to 10 is "
         << sum << endl;
    return 0;
}
```

Initializing action

Repeat the loop as long as this is true.

Done after each loop body iteration.

Output

```
The sum of the numbers 1 to 10 is 55
```

The update need not even be an addition or subtraction. Moreover, the initialization need not simply set a variable equal to a constant. You can initialize and change a loop control variable in just about any way you wish. For example, the following demonstrates one more way to start a *for*-loop:

```
for (double x = pow(y, 3.0); x > 2.0; x = sqrt(x))
    cout << "x is now equal to " << x << endl;
```

⬡ PITFALL   **Extra Semicolon in a *for*-Statement**

Do not place a semicolon after the parentheses at the beginning of a *for*-loop. To see what can happen, consider the following *for*-loop:

```
for (int count = 1; count <= 10; count++);
    cout << "Hello\n";
```

Problem semicolon

Display 7.13 *for*-**Loop with a Multi-Statement Body**

Syntax:

> *for* (*Initialization_Action* ; *Boolean_Expression* ; *Update_Action*)
> {
>   *Statement_1*
>   *Statement_2*
>   ⋮
>   *Statement_Last*
> }

(annotation) *body*

Example:

```
for (int number = 100; number >= 0; number--)
{
    cout << number
        << " bottles of beer on the shelf.\n";
    if (number > 0)
        cout << "Take one down and pass it around.\n";
}
```

If you did not notice the extra semicolon, you might expect this *for*-loop to write
`Hello` to the screen ten times. If you do notice the semicolon, you might expect the
compiler to issue an error message. Neither of those things happens. If you embed
this *for*-loop in a complete program, the compiler will not complain. If you run the
program, only one `Hello` will be output instead of ten `Hello`s. What is happening?
To answer that question, we need a little background.

One way to create a statement in C++ is to put a semicolon after something. If
you put a semicolon after x++, you change the expression

    x++

into the statement

    x++;

empty statement

If you place a semicolon after nothing, you still create a statement. Thus, the
semicolon by itself is a statement, which is called the **empty statement** or the **null
statement.** The empty statement performs no action, but still, it is a statement.

Therefore, the following is a complete and legitimate *for*-loop, whose body is the empty statement:

```
for (int count = 1; count <= 10; count++);
```

This *for*-loop is indeed iterated ten times, but since the body is the empty statement, nothing happens when the body is iterated. This loop does nothing, and it does nothing ten times!

Now let's go back and consider the *for*-loop code labeled *problem semicolon*. Because of the extra semicolon, that code begins with a *for*-loop that has an empty body, and as we just discussed, that *for*-loop accomplishes nothing. After the *for*-loop is completed, the following cout-statement is executed and it writes Hello to the screen one time:

```
cout << "Hello\n";
```

You will eventually see some uses for *for*-loops with empty bodies, but at this stage, such a *for*-loop is likely to be just a careless mistake.

What Kind of Loop to Use

When designing a loop, the choice of which C++ loop statement to use is best postponed to the end of the design process. First design the loop using pseudocode, then translate the pseudocode into C++ code. At that point it will be easy to decide what type of C++ loop statement to use.

If the loop involves a numeric calculation using a variable that is changed by equal amounts each time through the loop, use a *for*-loop. In fact, whenever you have a loop for a numeric calculation, you should consider using a *for*-loop. It will not always be suitable, but it is often the clearest and easiest loop to use for numeric calculations.

In most other cases, you should use a *while*-loop or a *do-while*-loop; it is fairly easy to decide which of these two to use. If you want to insist that the loop body will be executed at least once, you may use a *do-while*-loop. If there are circumstances for which the loop body should not be executed at all, then you must use a *while*-loop. A common situation that demands a *while*-loop is reading input when there is a possibility of no data at all. For example, if the program reads in a list of exam scores, there may be cases of students who have taken no exams, and hence the input loop may be faced with an empty list. This calls for a *while*-loop.

SELF-TEST EXERCISES

25 What is the output of the following (when embedded in a complete program)?

```
for (int count = 1; count < 5; count++)
    cout << (2 * count) << " ";
```

26 What is the output of the following (when embedded in a complete program)?

```
for (int n = 10; n > 0; n = n - 2)
{
    cout << "Hello ";
    cout << n << endl;
}
```

27 What is the output of the following (when embedded in a complete program)?

```
for (double sample = 2; sample > 0; sample = sample - 0.5)
    cout << sample << " ";
```

28 For each of the following situations, tell which type of loop (*while*, *do-while*, or *for*) would work best:

a Summing a series, such as 1/2 + 1/3 + 1/4 + 1/5 + ... + 1/10.

b Reading in the list of exam scores for one student.

c Reading in the number of days of sick leave taken by employees in a department.

d Testing a function to see how it performs for different values of its arguments.

29 Rewrite the following loops as *for*-loops:

```
a. int i = 1;
   while(i <= 10)
   {
       if (i < 5 && i != 2)
           cout << 'X';
       i++;
   }
b. int i = 1;
   while(i <=10)
   {
       cout << 'X';
```

```
            i = i + 3;
        }
    c. long m = 100;
       do
       {
           cout << 'X';
           m = m + 100;
       } while(m < 1000);
```

30 What is the output of this loop? Identify the connection between the value of
    n and the value of the variable log.

```
    int n = 1024;
    int log = 0;
    for (int i = 1; i < n; i = i * 2)
        log++;
    cout << n << " " << log << endl;
```

31 What is the output of this loop? Comment on the code.

```
    int n = 1024;
    int log = 0;
    for (int i = 1; i < n; i = i * 2);
        log++;
    cout << n << " " << log << endl;
```

32 What is the output of this loop? Comment on the code.

```
    int n = 1024;
    int log = 0;
    for (int i = 0; i < n; i = i * 2)
        log++;
    cout << n << " " << log << endl;
```

◆ PITFALL   Uninitialized Variables and Infinite Loops

When we first introduced simple *while*- and *do-while*-loops in Chapter 2, we
warned you of two pitfalls associated with loops. We said that you should be sure all
variables that need to have a value in the loop are initialized (that is, given a value)
before the loop is executed. This seems obvious when stated in the abstract, but in
practice it is easy to become so concerned with designing a loop that you forget to
initialize variables before the loop. We also said that you should be careful to avoid
infinite loops. Both of these cautions apply equally well to *for*-loops.

The *break*-Statement

break;

You have already used the *break*-statement as a way of ending a *switch*-statement. This same *break*-statement can be used to exit a loop. Sometimes you want to exit a loop before it ends in the normal way. For example, the loop might contain a check for improper input and if some improper input is encountered, then you may want to simply end the loop. The code in Display 7.14 reads a list of negative numbers and computes their sum as the value of the variable sum. The loop ends normally provided the user types in 10 negative numbers. If the user forgets a minus sign, the computation is ruined and the loop ends immediately when the *break*-statement is executed.

The *break*-Statement

The *break*-statement can be used to exit a loop statement. When the *break*-statement is executed, the loop statement ends immediately and execution continues with the statement following the loop statement. The *break*-statement may be used in any form of loop, in a *while*-loop, in a *do-while*-loop, or in a *for*-loop. This is the same *break*-statement that we have already used in *switch*-statements.

◆ PITFALL   The *break*-Statement in Nested Loops

A *break*-statement ends only the innermost loop that contains it. If you have a loop within a loop and a *break*-statement in the inner loop, then the *break*-statement will only end the inner loop.

SELF-TEST EXERCISES

33 What is the output of the following (when embedded in a complete program)?

```
int n = 5;
while (--n > 0)
{
    if (n == 2)
        break;
    cout << n << " ";
}
cout << "End of Loop.";
```

Display 7.14 A *break*-Statement in a Loop

```
//Sums a list of 10 negative numbers.
#include <iostream>
using namespace std;

int main()
{
    int number, sum = 0, count = 0;
    cout << "Enter 10 negative numbers:\n";

    while (++count <= 10)
    {
        cin >> number;

        if (number >= 0)
        {
            cout << "ERROR: positive number"
                 << " or zero was entered as the\n"
                 << count << "th number! Input ends "
                 << "with the " << count << "th number.\n"
                 << count << "th number was not added in.\n";
            break;
        }
        sum = sum + number;
    }
    cout << sum << " is the sum of the first "
         << (count - 1) << " numbers.\n";

    return 0;
}
```

Sample Dialogue

```
Enter 10 negative numbers:
-1 -2 -3 4 -5 -6 -7 -8 -9 -10
ERROR: positive number or zero was entered as the
4th number! Input ends with the 4th number.
4th number was not added in
-6 is the sum of the first 3 numbers.
```

34 What is the output of the following (when embedded in a complete program)?

```
int n = 5;
while (--n > 0)
{
    if (n == 2)
        exit(0);
    cout << n << " ";
}
cout << "End of Loop.";
```

35 What does a *break*; statement do? Where is it legal to put a *break*; statement?

7.4 Designing Loops

Round and round she goes,
and where she stops nobody knows.

TRADITIONAL CARNIVAL BARKER'S CALL

When designing a loop, you need to design three things:

1 the body of the loop,
2 the initializing statements, and
3 the conditions for ending the loop.

We begin with a section on two common loop tasks and show how to design these three elements for each of the two tasks.

Loops for Sums and Products

sums

Many common tasks involve reading in a list of numbers and computing their sum. If you know how many numbers there will be, such a task can easily be accomplished by the following pseudocode. The value of the variable this_many is the number of numbers to be added. The sum is accumulated in the variable sum.

```
sum = 0;
repeat the following this_many times:
    cin >> next;
    sum = sum + next;
end of loop.
```

This pseudocode is easily implemented as the *for*-loop shown below:

```
int sum = 0;
for (int count = 1; count <= this_many; count++)
{
    cin >> next;
    sum = sum + next;
}
```

Notice that the variable sum is expected to have a value when the following loop body statement is executed:

```
sum = sum + next;
```

Since sum must have a value the very first time this statement is executed, sum must be initialized to some value before the loop is executed. In order to determine the correct initializing value for sum think about what you want to happen after one loop iteration. After adding in the first number, the value of sum should be that number. That is, the first time through the loop the value of sum + next should equal next. To make this *true*, the value of sum must be initialized to 0.

Repeat "This Many Times"

A *for*-statement can be used to produce a loop that repeats the loop body a predetermined number of times:

Pseudocode:

Repeat the following *This_Many* times:
    Loop_Body

Equivalent *for*-Statement:

```
for (int count = 1; count <= This_Many; count++)
    Loop_Body
```

Example:

```
for (int count = 1; count <= 3; count++)
    cout << "Hip, Hip, Hurray\n";
```

products

You can form the product of a list of numbers in a way that is similar to how we formed the sum of a list of numbers. The technique is illustrated by the following code:

```
int product = 1;
for (int count = 1; count <= this_many; count++)
{
    cin >> next;
    product = product * next;
}
```

The variable `product` must be given an initial value. Do not assume that all variables should be initialized to zero. If `product` were initialized to 0, then it would still be zero after the above loop has finished. As indicated in the C++ code above, the correct initializing value for `product` is 1. To see that 1 is the correct initial value, notice that the first time through the loop this will leave the `product` equal to the first number read in, which is what you want.

Ending a Loop

input loops

There are four commonly used methods for terminating an input loop. We will discuss them in order.

1 List headed by size.

2 Ask before iterating.

3 List ended with a sentinel value.

4 Running out of input.

list headed by size

If your program can determine the size of an input list beforehand, either by asking the user or by some other method, you can use a "repeat n times" loop to read input exactly n times, where n is the size of the list. This method is called **list headed by size.**

ask before iterating

The second method for ending an input loop is simply to ask the user, after each loop iteration, whether or not the loop should be iterated again. For example:

```
sum = 0;
cout << "Are there any numbers in the list? (Type\n"
     << "Y and return for Yes, N and return for No): ";
char ans;
cin >> ans;
while ((ans == 'Y') || (ans == 'y'))
{
    cout << "Enter number: ";
    cin >> number;
```

```
    sum = sum + number;
    cout << "Are there any more numbers? (Type\n"
         << "Y for Yes, N for No. End with return.): ";
    cin >> ans;
}
```

However, for reading in a long list this is very tiresome to the user. Imagine typing in a list of 100 numbers this way. The user is likely to progress from happy, to sarcastic, to angry and frustrated. When reading in a long list it is preferable to include only one stopping signal, which is the method we discuss next.

Perhaps the nicest way to terminate a loop that reads a list of values from the keyboard is with a *sentinel value*. A **sentinel value** is one that is somehow distinct from all the possible values on the list being read in and so can be used to signal the end of the list. For example, if the loop reads in a list of positive numbers, then a negative number can be used as a sentinel value to indicate the end of the list. A loop such as the following can be used to add a list of nonnegative numbers:

sentinel value

```
cout << "Enter a list of nonnegative integers.\n"
     << "Place a negative integer after the list.\n";
sum = 0;
cin >> number;
while (number >= 0)
{
    sum = sum + number;
    cin >> number;
}
```

Notice that the last number in the list is read but is not added into sum. To add the numbers 1, 2, and 3, the user appends a negative number to the end of the list like so:

```
   1 2 3 -1
```

The final –1 is read in but not added into the sum.

To use a sentinel value this way, you must be certain there is at least one value of the data type in question that definitely will not appear on the list of input values, and so can be used as the sentinel value. If the list consists of integers that might be any value whatsoever, then there is no value left to serve as the sentinel value. In this situation, you must use some other method to terminate the loop.

When reading input from a file, you can use a sentinel value, but a more common method is to simply check to see if all the input in the file has been read and to end the loop when there is no more input left to be read. This method of ending an input loop was discussed in Chapter 5 in the programming tip section entitled "Checking for the End of a File" and in the section entitled "The eof Member Function."

running out of input

The techniques we gave for ending an input loop are all special cases of more general techniques that can be used to end loops of any kind. The more general techniques are:

1 Count controlled loops.
2 Ask before iterating.
3 Exit on a flag condition.

A **count controlled loop** is any loop that determines the number of iterations before the loop begins and then iterates the loop body that many times. The list headed by size technique that we discussed for input loops is an example of a count controlled loop. All of our "repeat this many times" loops are count controlled loops.

We already discussed the **ask before iterating** technique. You can use it for loops other than input loops, but the most common use for this technique is for processing input.

exit on a flag

Earlier in this section we discussed input loops that end when a sentinel value is read. In our example, the program read nonnegative integers into a variable called number. When number received a negative value, that indicated the end of the input; the negative value was the sentinel value. This is an example of a more general technique known as **exit on a flag condition.** A variable that changes value to indicate that some event has taken place is often called a **flag.** In our example input loop, the flag was the variable number and when it becomes negative that indicates that the input list has ended.

Ending a file input loop by running out of input is another example of the exit on a flag technique. In this case the flag condition is determined by the system. The system keeps track of whether or not input reading has reached the end of a file.

A flag can also be used to terminate loops other than input loops. For example, the following sample loop can be used to find a tutor for a student. Students in the class are numbered starting with 1. The loop checks each student number to see if that student received a high grade and stops the loop as soon as a student with a high grade is found. For this example, a grade of 90 or more is considered high. We assume that the function compute_grade has already been defined.

```
int n = 1;
grade = compute_grade(n);
while (grade < 90)
{
    n++;
    grade = compute_grade(n);
}
cout << "Student number " << n << " may be a tutor.\n"
     << "This student has a score of " << grade << endl;
```

In this example, the variable grade serves as the flag.

The previous loop indicates a problem that can arise when designing loops. *runaway loops* What happens if no student has a score of 90 or better? The answer depends on the definition for the function compute_grade. If grade is defined for all positive integers, it could be an infinite loop. Even worse, if grade is defined to be, say, 100 for all arguments n that are not students, then it may try to make a tutor out of a nonexistent student. In any event, something will go wrong. If there is a danger of a loop turning into an infinite loop or even a danger of it iterating more times than is sensible, then you should include a check to see that the loop is not iterated too many times. For example, a better condition for the loop above would be the following, where the variable number_of_students has been set equal to the number of students in the class.

```
int n = 1;
grade = compute_grade(n);
while ((grade < 90) && (n < number_of_students))
{
    n++;
    grade = compute_grade(n);
}
if (grade >= 90)
    cout << "Student number " << n << " may be a tutor.\n"
            << "This student has a score of " << grade << endl;
else
    cout << "No student has a high score.";
```

Nested Loops

The program in Display 7.15 was designed to help track the reproduction rate of the green-necked vulture, an endangered species. In the district where this vulture survives, conservationists annually perform a count of the number of eggs in green-necked vulture nests. The program in Display 7.15 takes the reports of each of the conservations in the district and calculates the total number of eggs contained in all the nests observed by all the conservationists.

Each conservationist's report consists of a list of numbers. Each number is the count of the number of eggs observed in one green-necked vulture nest. The *void*-function named get_one_total reads in the report of one conservationist and calculates the total number of eggs found by this conservationist. The list of numbers for each conservationist has a negative number added to the end of the list. This serves as a sentinel value. The function call to get_one_total is included in a *for*-loop so that this function is called once for each conservationist report.

Display 7.15 Nicely Nested Loops *(part 1 of 3)*

```
//Determines the total number of green-necked vulture eggs
//counted by all conservationists in the conservation district.
#include <iostream>
using namespace std;

void instructions();

void get_one_total(int& total);
//Precondition: User will enter a list of egg counts
//followed by a negative number.
//Postcondition: total is equal to the sum of all the egg counts.

int main()
{
    instructions();

    int number_of_reports;
    cout << "How many conservationist reports are there? ";
    cin >> number_of_reports;

    int grand_total = 0, subtotal, count;
    for (count = 1; count <= number_of_reports; count++)
    {
        cout << endl << "Enter the report of "
             << "conservationist number " << count << endl;
        get_one_total(subtotal);
        cout << "Total egg count for conservationist "
             << " number " << count << " is "
             << subtotal << endl;
        grand_total = grand_total + subtotal;
    }

    cout << endl << "Total egg count for all reports = "
         << grand_total << endl;

    return 0;
}
```

Display 7.15 Nicely Nested Loops *(part 2 of 3)*

```
//Uses iostream:
void instructions( )
{
    cout << "This program tallies conservationist reports\n"
         << "on the green-necked vulture.\n"
         << "Each conservationist's report consists of\n"
         << "a list of numbers. Each number is the count of\n"
         << "the eggs observed in one"
         << " green-necked vulture nest.\n"
         << "This program then tallies"
         << " the total number of eggs.\n";
}

//Uses iostream:
void get_one_total(int& total)
{
    cout << "Enter the number of eggs in each nest.\n"
         << "Place a negative integer"
         << " at the end of your list.\n";

    total = 0;
    int next;
    cin >> next;
    while (next >= 0)
    {
        total = total + next;
        cin >> next;
    }
}
```

The body of a loop may contain any kind of statement, so it is possible to have loops nested within loops (as well as eggs nested within nests). The program in Display 7.15 contains a loop within a loop. Normally, you do not think of code such as this as containing a nested loop because the inner loop is contained within a function and it is the function call that is contained in the outer loop. There is a lesson to be learned from these unobtrusively nested loops—namely, that nested loops are no different than any other loops. The program in Display 7.16 is a rewritten version of the

Display 7.15 Nicely Nested Loops *(part 3 of 3)*

Sample Dialogue

```
This program tallies conservationist reports
on the green-necked vulture.
Each conservationist's report consists of
a list of numbers. Each number is the count of
the eggs observed in one green-necked vulture nest.
This program then tallies the total number of eggs.
How many conservationist reports are there? 3

Enter the report of conservationist number 1
Enter the number of eggs in each nest.
Place a negative integer at the end of your list.
1 0 0 2 -1
Total egg count for conservationist number 1 is 3

Enter the report of conservationist number 2
Enter the number of eggs in each nest.
Place a negative integer at the end of your list.
0 3 1 -1
Total egg count for conservationist number 2 is 4

Enter the report of conservationist number 3
Enter the number of eggs in each nest.
Place a negative integer at the end of your list.
-1
Total egg count for conservationist number 3 is 0

Total egg count for all reports = 7
```

program in Display 7.15, but with the nested loop explicitly displayed. The nested loop in Display 7.16 is executed once for each value of count from 1 to number_of_reports. For each such iteration of the outer *for*-loop there is one complete execution of the inner *while*-loop.

The two versions of our program for totaling green-necked vulture eggs are equivalent. Both programs produce the same dialogue with the user. However, most people find the version in Display 7.15 easier to understand because the loop body is a function call. When considering the outer loop, you should think of computing the subtotal for one conservationist's report as a single operation and not think of it as a loop.

Display 7.16 Explicitly Nested Loops

```
//Determines the total number of green-necked vulture eggs
//counted by all conservationists in the conservation district.
#include <iostream>
using namespace std;

void instructions( );

int main( )
{
    instructions( );

    int number_of_reports;
    cout << "How many conservationist reports are there? ";
    cin >> number_of_reports;

    int grand_total = 0, subtotal, count;
    for (count = 1; count <= number_of_reports; count++)
    {
        cout << endl << "Enter the report of "
             << "conservationist number " << count << endl;
        cout << "Enter the number of eggs in each nest.\n"
             << "Place a negative integer"
             << " at the end of your list.\n";
        subtotal = 0;
        int next;
        cin >> next;
        while (next >= 0)
        {
            subtotal = subtotal + next;
            cin >> next;
        }
        cout << "Total egg count for conservationist "
             << " number " << count << " is "
             << subtotal << endl;
        grand_total = grand_total + subtotal;
    }
    cout << endl << "Total egg count for all reports = "
         << grand_total << endl;
    return 0;
}
```

<The definition of instructions is the same as in Display 7.15.>

> **Make a Loop Body a Function Call**
>
> Whenever you have a loop nested within a loop, or any other complex computation included in a loop body, make the loop body a function call. This way you can separate the design of the loop body from the design of the rest of the program. This divides your programming task into two smaller subtasks.

SELF-TEST EXERCISES

36 Write a loop that will write the word Hello to the screen 10 times (when embedded in a complete program).

37 Write a loop that will read in a list of even numbers (such as **2**, **−4**, **8**, **6**) and compute the total of the numbers on the list. The list is ended with a sentinel value. Among other things, you must decide what would be a good sentinel value(s) to use.

38 Predict the output of the following nested loops:

```
int n, m;
for (n = 1; n <= 10; n++)
    for (m = 10; m >= 1; m--)
        cout << n << " times " << m
             << " = " << n*m << endl;
```

Debugging Loops

off-by-one errors

No matter how carefully a program is designed, mistakes will still sometimes occur. In the case of loops, there is a pattern to the kinds of mistakes programmers most often make. Most loop errors involve the first or last iteration of the loop. If you find that your loop does not perform as expected, check to see if the loop is iterated one too many or one too few times. Loops that iterate one too many or one too few times are said to have an **off-by-one error,** and these errors are among the most common loop bugs. Be sure you are not confusing less-than with less-than-or-equal-to. Be sure you have initialized the loop correctly. Remember that a loop may sometimes need to be iterated zero times and check that your loop handles that possibility correctly.

infinite loops

Infinite loops usually result from a mistake in the Boolean expression that controls the stopping of the loop. Check to see that you have not reversed an inequality, confusing less-than with greater-than. Another common source of infinite loops is terminating a loop with a test for equality, rather than something involving greater-than or less-than. With values of type *double*, testing for equality does not give meaningful answers, since the quantities being compared are only approximate values. Even for values of type *int*, equality can be a dangerous test to use for ending a loop, since there is only one way that it can be satisfied.

If you check and recheck your loop and can find no error, but your program still misbehaves, then you will need to do some more sophisticated testing. First, make sure that the mistake is indeed in the loop. Just because the program is performing incorrectly does not mean the bug is where you think it is. If your program is divided into functions, it should be easy to determine the approximate location of the bug or bugs.

First, localize the problem

Once you have decided that the bug is in a particular loop, you should watch the loop change the value of variables while the program is running. This way you can see what the loop is doing and thus see what it is doing wrong. Watching the value of a variable change while the program is running is called **tracing** the variable. Many systems have debugging utilities that allow you to easily trace variables without making any changes to your program. If your system has such a debugging utility, it would be well worth your effort to learn how to use it. If your system does not have a debugging utility, you can trace a variable by placing a temporary cout-statement in the loop body; that way the value of the variable will be written to the screen on each loop iteration.

tracing variables

For example, consider the following piece of program code, which needs to be debugged:

```
int next = 2, product = 1;
while (next < 5)
{
    next++;
    product = product * next;
}
//The variable product contains
//the product of the numbers 2 through 5.
```

code with a bug

The comment at the end of the loop tells what the loop is supposed to do, but we have tested it and know that it gives the variable product an incorrect value. We need to find out what is wrong. To help us debug this loop, we trace the variables next and product. If you have a debugging utility you could use it. If you do not have a debugging facility, you can trace the variables by inserting a cout-statement as follows:

```
int next = 2, product = 1;
while (next < 5)
{
    next++;
    product = product * next;
    cout << "next = " << next
         << " product = " << product << endl;
}
```

second try

When we trace the variables product and next, we find that after the first loop iteration, the values of product and next are both 3. It is then clear to us that we have multiplied only the numbers 3 through 5 and have missed multiplying by 2.

There are at least two good ways to fix this bug. The easiest fix is to initialize the variable next to 1, rather than 2. That way, when next is incremented the first time through the loop, it will receive the value 2 rather than 3. Another way to fix the loop is to place the increment after the multiplication, as follows:

```
int next = 2, product = 1;
while (next < 5)
{
    product = product * next;
    next++;
}
```

Let's assume we fix the bug by moving the statement next++ as indicated above. After we add this fix, we are not yet done. We must test this revised code. When we test this revised code, we will see that it still gives an incorrect result. If we again trace variables, we will discover that the loop stops after multiplying by 4, and never multiplies by 5. This tells us that the Boolean expression should now use a less-than-or-equal sign, rather than a less-than sign. Thus, the correct code is:

```
int next = 2, product = 1;
while (next <= 5)
{
    product = product * next;
    next++;
}
```

Every change requires retesting

Every time you change a program, you should retest the program. Never assume that your change will make the program correct. Just because you found one thing to correct does not mean you have found all the things that need to be corrected. Also, as illustrated by this example, when you change one part of your program to make it correct, that change may require you to change some other part of the program as well.

Testing a Loop

Every loop should be tested with inputs that cause each of the following loop behaviors (or as many as are possible): zero iterations of the loop body, one iteration of the loop body, the maximum number of iterations of the loop body, and one less than the maximum number of iterations of the loop body. (This is only a minimal set of test situations. You should also conduct other tests that are particular to the loop you are testing.)

The techniques we have developed will help you find the few bugs that may find their way into a well-designed program. However, no amount of debugging can convert a poorly designed program into a reliable and readable one. If a program or algorithm is very difficult to understand or performs very poorly, do not try to fix it. Instead, throw it away and start over. This will result in a program that is easier to read and that is less likely to contain hidden errors. What may not be so obvious is that by throwing out the poorly designed code and starting over, you will produce a working program faster than if you try to repair the old code. It may seem like wasted effort to throw out all the code that you worked so hard on, but that is the most efficient way to proceed. The work that went into the discarded code is not wasted. The lessons you learned by writing it will help you to design a better program faster than if you started with no experience. The bad code itself is unlikely to help at all.

Debugging a Very Bad Program

If your program is very bad, do not try to debug it. Instead, throw it out and start over.

SELF-TEST EXERCISES

39   What does it mean to trace a variable? How do you trace a variable?

40   What is an off-by-one loop error?

41   You have a fence that is to be 100 meters long. Your fence posts are to be placed every 10 feet. How many fence posts do you need? Why is the presence of this problem in a programming book not as silly as it might seem? What problem that programmers have does this question address?

CHAPTER SUMMARY

- Boolean expressions are evaluated similar to the way arithmetic expressions are evaluated.

- Most modern compilers have a *bool* type having the values *true* and *false*. There are still compilers in use that do not implement the full ANSI

Standard C++. With these older compilers, *true* is represented as 1 and *false* is represented as 0. Appendix 10 describes one way to simulate the type *bool* on these older compilers.

■ You can write a function so that it returns a value of *true* or *false*. A call to such a function can be used as a Boolean expression in an *if-else*-statement or anywhere else that a Boolean expression is permitted.

■ One approach to solving a task or subtask is to write down conditions and corresponding actions that need to be taken under each condition. This can be implemented in C++ as a multiway *if-else*-statement.

■ A *switch*-statement is a good way to implement a menu for the user of your program.

■ Use function calls in multiway branch statements, such as *switch*-statements and multiway *if-else*-statements.

■ A **block** is a compound statement that contains variable declarations. The variables declared in a block are local to the block. Among other uses, blocks can be used for the action in one branch of a multiway branch statement, such as a multiway *if-else*-statement.

■ A *for*-loop can be used to obtain the equivalent of the instruction "repeat the loop body n times."

■ There are four commonly used methods for terminating an input loop: list headed by size, ask before iterating, list ended with a sentinel value, and running out of input.

■ It is usually best to design loops in pseudocode that does not specify a choice of C++ looping mechanism. Once the algorithm has been designed, the choice of which C++ loop statement to use is usually clear.

■ One way to simplify your reasoning about nested loops is to make the loop body a function call.

■ Always check loops to be sure that the variables used by the loop are properly initialized before the loop begins.

■ Always check loops to be certain they are not iterated one too many or one too few times.

■ When debugging loops, it helps to trace key variables in the loop body.

■ If a program or algorithm is very difficult to understand or performs very poorly, do not try to fix it. Instead, throw it away and start over.

Answers to Self-Test Exercises

1

a   *true*.

b   *true*. Note that expressions a and b mean exactly the same thing. Because the operators == and < have higher precedence than &&, you do not need to include the parentheses. The parentheses do, however, make it easier to read. Most people find the expression in a easier to read than the expression in b, even though they mean the same thing.

c   *true*.

d   *true*.

e   *false*. Since the value of the first subexpression (count == 1) is *false*, you know that the entire expression is *false* without bothering to evaluate the second subexpression. Thus, it does not matter what the values of x and y are. This is called *short-circuit evaluation*, which is what C++ does.

f   *true*. Since the value of the first subexpression (count < 10) is *true*, you know that the entire expression is *true* without bothering to evaluate the second subexpression. Thus, it does not matter what the values of x and y are. This is called *short-circuit evaluation*, which is what C++ does.

g   *false*. Notice that the expression in g includes the expression in f as a subexpression. This subexpression is evaluated using short-circuit evaluation as we described for f. The entire expression in g is equivalent to

   `!( (true || (x < y)) && true )`

   which in turn is equivalent to ! (*true* && *true*), and that is equivalent to ! (*true*) which is equivalent to the final value of *false*.

h   This expression produces an error when it is evaluated because the first subexpression ((limit/count) > 7) involves a division by zero.

i   *true*. Since the value of the first subexpression (limit < 20) is *true*, you know that the entire expression is *true* without bothering to evaluate the second subexpression. Thus, the second subexpression

   `((limit/count) > 7)`

   is never evaluated and so the fact that it involves a division by zero is never noticed by the computer. This is short-circuit evaluation, which is what C++ does.

j   This expression produces an error when it is evaluated because the first subexpression ((limit/count) > 7) involves a division by zero.

k *false*. Since the value of the first subexpression (`limit < 0`) is *false*, you know that the entire expression is *false* without bothering to evaluate the second subexpression. Thus, the second subexpression

```
((limit/count) > 7)
```

is never evaluated and so the fact that it involves a division by zero is never noticed by the computer. This is short-circuit evaluation, which is what C++ does.

l If you think this expression is nonsense, you are correct. The expression has no intuitive meaning, but C++ converts the `int` values to `bool` then evaluates the `&&` and `!` operations and so C++ will evaluate this mess. Recall that in C++, any nonzero integer converts to *true* and 0 converts to *false* and so C++ will evaluate

```
(5 && 7) + (!6) as follows:
```

in the expression (5 `&&` 7) the 5 and 7 convert to *true*, *true&&true* evaluates to *true*, which C++ converts to 1; in (`!6`) the 6 is converted to *true*, so !(*true*) evaluates to *false*, which C++ converts to 0; so the entire expression evaluates to 1 + 0, which is 1. The final value is thus 1. C++ will convert the number 1 to *true*, but the answer has little intuitive meaning as *true*; it is perhaps better to just say the answer is 1. There is no need to become proficient at evaluating these nonsense expressions, but doing a few will help you to understand why the compiler does not give you an error message when you make the mistake of incorrectly mixing numeric and Boolean operators in a single expression.

2 To this point we have studied branching statements, iteration statements, and function call statements.

Examples of branching statements we have studied are *if* and *if-else* statements. Examples of iteration statements are *while* and *do-while* statements.

3 The expression 2 < x < 3 is legal. It does not mean (2 < x)&&(x < 3) as many would wish. It means (2 < x) < 3. Since (2 < x) is a Boolean expression, its value is either *true* or *false*, so that 2 < x < 3 is always *true*. The output is "true" regardless of the value of x.

4 No. In the Boolean expression > 0 is *false* (j was just assigned –1). The && uses short-circuit evaluation, which does not evaluate the second expression if the truth value can be determined from the first expression. The first is false, the second does not matter.

5

```cpp
bool in_order(int n1, int n2, int n3)
{
    return ((n1 <= n2) && (n2 <= n3));
}
```

6

```cpp
bool even(int n)
{
    return ((n % 2) == 0);
}
```

7

```cpp
bool isDigit(char ch)
{
   return ('0' <= ch) && (ch <= '9');
}
```

8
```
Start
Hello from the second if.
End
Start again
End again
```

9
```
large
```

10
```
small
```

11
```
medium
```

12 Both of the following are correct:

```
if (n < 0)
    cout << n << " is less than zero.\n";
else if ((0 <= n) && (n <= 100))
    cout << n << " is between 0 and 100 (inclusive).\n";
else if (n >100)
    cout << n << " is larger than 100.\n";
```

and

```
if (n < 0)
    cout << n << " is less than zero.\n";
else if (n <= 100)
    cout << n << " is between 0 and 100 (inclusive).\n";
else
    cout << n << " is larger than 100.\n";
```

13 *enum* constants are given default values starting at 0, unless otherwise assigned. The constants increment by 1. The output is 3 2 1 0

14 *enum* constants are given values as assigned. Unassigned constants increment the previous value by 1. The output is 2 1 7 5

15   ```
Roast worms
```

16      ```
Onion ice cream
```

17   ```
Chocolate ice cream
Onion ice cream
```

(This is because there is no *break*-statement in *case* 3.)

18      ```
Bon appetit!
```

19   ```
42 22
```
```

20 It helps to slightly change the code fragment to understand to which declaration each usage resolves.

```
{
    int x1 = 1;                 // output in this column
    cout << x1 << endl;         // 1<cr>
    {
        cout << x1 << endl;     // 1<cr>
        int x2 = 2;
        cout << x2 << endl;     // 2<cr>
        {
            cout << x2 << endl;     // 2<cr>
            int x3 = 3;
            cout << x3 << endl;     // 3<cr>
        }
        cout << x2 << endl;     // 2<cr>
    }
    cout << x1 << endl;         // 1<cr>
}
```

Here <cr> indicates that the output starts a new line.

21
```
2 1 0
```

22
```
2 1
```

23
```
1 2 3 4
```

24
```
1 2 3
```

25
```
2 4 6 8
```

26
```
Hello 10
Hello 8
Hello 6
Hello 4
Hello 2
```

27   2.000000 1.500000 1.000000 0.500000

28

    a A *for*-loop

    b and c   both require a *while*-loop since the input list might be empty.

    d A *do-while* loop can be used since at least one test will be performed.

29 a. *for* (int i = 1; i <= 10; i++)
        if (i < 5 && i != 2)
           cout << 'X';

    b. *for* (i = 1; i <= 10; i = i + 3)
       cout << 'X';

    c. cout << 'X'   *// necessary to keep output the same. Note*
                    // also the change in initialization of m
     for (long m = 200; m < 1000; m = m + 100)
       cout << 'X';

30 The output is: 1024 10. The second number is the base 2 log of the first number.

31 The output is: 1024 1. The ';' after the *for* is probably a pitfall error.

32 This is an infinite loop. Consider the update expression, i = i * 2. It cannot change i because its initial value is 0, so it leaves i at its initial value, 0.

33   4 3 End of Loop

34   4 3

Notice that since the exit-statement ends the program, the phrase End of Loop is not output.

35 A *break;* statement is used to exit a loop: a *while*, *do-while*, or *for* statement, or to terminate a case in a *switch*-statement. A *break;* is not legal anywhere else in a C++ program. Note that if the loops are nested, a *break;* only terminates one level of the loop.

36

```
for (int count = 1; count <= 10; count++)
    cout << "Hello\n";
```

37 You can use any odd number as a sentinel value.

```
int sum = 0, next;
cout << "Enter a list of even numbers. Place an\n"
     << "odd number at the end of the list.\n";
cin >> next;
while ((next % 2) == 0)
{
    sum = sum + next;
    cin >> next;
}
```

38 The output is too long to reproduce here. The pattern is as follows:

```
1 times 10 = 10
1 times 9 = 9

    .

    .

    .

1 times 1 = 1
2 times 10 = 20
2 times 9 = 18

    .

    .

    .

2 times 1 = 2
3 times 10 = 30

    .

    .

    .
```

39 *Tracing a variable* means watching a program variable change value while the program is running. This can be done with special debugging facilities or by inserting temporary output statements in the program.

40 Loops which iterate the loop body one too many or one too few times are said to have an **off-by-one error.**

41 Off-by-one errors abound in problem solving, not just writing loops. Typical reasoning from those who do not think carefully is

10 posts = 100 feet of fence / 10 feet between posts.

This, of course, will leave the last 10 feet of fence without a post. You need 11 posts to provide 10 between-the-post 10-foot intervals to get 100 feet of fence.

Programming Projects

1   Write a program to score the paper-rock-scissor game. Each of two users types in either **P, R,** or **S** and the program then announces the winner as well as the basis for determining the winner: Paper covers rock, Rock breaks scissors, Scissors cut paper, or Nobody wins. Be sure to allow the users to use lowercase as well as uppercase letters. Your program should include a loop that lets the user play again until the user says she or he is done.

2   Write a program to compute the interest due, total amount due, and the minimum payment for a revolving credit account. The program accepts the account balance as input, then adds on the interest to get the total amount due. The rate schedules are the following: The interest is 1.5% on the first $1,000 and 1% on any amount over that. The minimum payment is the total amount due if that is $10 or less; otherwise it is $10 or 10% of the total amount owed, whichever is larger. Your program should include a loop that lets the user repeat this calculation until the user says she or he is done.

3   Write an astrology program. The user types in a birthday and the program responds with the sign and horoscope for that birthday. The month may be entered as a number from one to twelve. Use a newspaper horoscope section for the horoscopes and dates of each sign. Then enhance your program so that if the birthday is only one or two days away from an adjacent sign, then the program announces that the birthday is on a "cusp" and also outputs the horoscope for that nearest adjacent sign. This program will have a long multiway branch. Store the horoscopes in a file. If you are doing this as a class assignment, ask your instructor if there are any special instructions about the file name or location. Your program should include a loop that lets the user repeat this calculation until the user says she or he is done.

4   Write a program that computes the cost of a long-distance call. The cost of the call is determined according to the following rate schedule:

a Any call started between 8:00 AM and 6:00 PM, Monday through Friday, is billed at a rate of $0.40 per minute.

b Any call starting before 8:00 AM or after 6:00 PM, Monday through Friday, is charged at a rate of $0.25 per minute.

c Any call started on a Saturday or Sunday is charged at a rate of $0.15 per minute.

The input will consist of the day of the week, the time the call started, and the length of the call in minutes. The output will be the cost of the call. The time is to be input in 24-hour notation, so the time 1:30 PM is input as

13:30

The day of the week will be read as one of the following pairs of character values, which are stored in two variables of type *char*:

Mo   Tu   We   Th   Fr   Sa   Su

Be sure to allow the user to use either uppercase or lowercase letters or a combination of the two. The number of minutes will be input as a value of type *int*. (You can assume that the user rounds the input to a whole number of minutes.) Your program should include a loop that lets the user repeat this calculation until the user says she or he is done. After you have completely debugged your program, produce a variant on this program that reads the information for all the phone calls in one week from a file and then writes a phone bill to another file. The phone bill should show each call and the charge for each call as well as the total bill for all the calls. List the phone calls in the output file in the same order as they appear in the input file. If you are doing this as a class assignment, ask your instructor if there are any special instructions about the file names.

5 Write a program that accepts a year written as a four-digit Arabic (ordinary) numeral and outputs the year written in Roman numerals. Important Roman numerals are: V for 5, X for 10, L for 50, C for 100, D for 500 and M for 1000. Recall that some numbers are formed by using a kind of subtraction of one Roman "digit"; e.g., IV is 4 produced as V minus I, XL is 40, CM is 900, etc. A few sample years: MCM is 1900, MCML is 1950, MCMLX is 1960, MCMXL is 1940, MCMLXXXIX is 1989. Assume the year is between 1000 and 3000. Your program should include a loop that lets the user repeat this calculation until the user says she or he is done.

6 Write a program that scores a blackjack hand. In blackjack, a player receives from two to five cards. (The player decides how many, but that has no effect on this exercise.) The cards 2 through 10 are scored as 2 through 10 points

each. The face cards—jack, queen, and king—are scored as 10 points. The goal is to come as close to a score of 21 as possible without going over 21. Hence, any score over 21 is called "busted." The ace can count as either 1 or 11, whichever is better for the user. For example, an ace and a 10 can be scored as either 11 or 21. Since 21 is a better score, this hand is scored as 21. An ace and two 8's can be scored as either 17 or 27. Since 27 is a "busted" score, this hand is scored as 17. The user is asked how many cards she or he has and the user responds with one of the integers 2, 3, 4, or 5. The user is then asked for the card values. Card values are 2 through 10, jack, queen, king, and ace. A good way to handle input is to use the type *char* so that the card input 2, for example, is read as the character '2', rather than as the number 2. Input the values 2 through 9 as the characters '2' through '9'. Input the values ten, jack, queen, king, and ace as the characters 't', 'j', 'q', 'k', and 'a'. (Of course, the user does not type in the single quotes.) Be sure to allow upper- as well as lowercase letters as input. After reading in the values, the program should convert them from character values to numeric card scores, taking special care for aces. The output is either a number between 2 and 21 (inclusive) or the word Busted. Use lots of functions. You are likely to have one or more long multiway branches that uses a *switch*-statement or nested *if-else*-statement. Your program should include a loop that lets the user repeat this calculation until the user says she or he is done.

7 Interest on a loan is paid on a declining balance, and hence a loan with an interest rate of, say, 14% can cost significantly less than 14% of the balance. Write a program that takes a loan amount and interest rate as input and then outputs the monthly payments and balance of the loan until the loan is paid off. Assume that the monthly payments are one twentieth of the original loan amount, and that any amount in excess of the interest is credited toward decreasing the balance due. Thus, on a loan of $20,000, the payments would be $1000 a month. If the interest rate is 10%, then each month the interest is one twelfth of 10% of the remaining balance. The first month (10% of $20,000)/12 or $166.67 would be paid in interest, and the remaining $833.33 would decrease the balance to $19,166.67. The following month the interest would be (10% of $19,166.67)/12, and so forth. Also have the program output the total interest paid over the life of the loan. Finally, determine what simple annualized percentage of the original loan balance was paid in interest. For example, if $1,000 was paid in interest on a $10,000 loan and it took two years to pay off, then the annualized interest is $500, which is 5% of the $10,000 loan amount. If this is a class assignment, ask your instructor if the input and output should be done with the keyboard and screen or should be

done with files. If input and output is via keyboard and screen, then your program should allow the user to repeat this calculation as often as desired.

8 The **Fibonacci numbers** F_n are defined as follows. F_0 is 1, F_1 is 1, and

$$F_{i+2} = F_i + F_{i+1}$$

$i = 0, 1, 2, \dots$. In other words, each number is the sum of the previous two numbers. The first few Fibonacci numbers are 1, 1, 2, 3, 5, and 8. One place where these numbers occur is as certain population growth rates. If a population has no deaths, then the series shows the size of the population after each time period. It takes an organism two time periods to mature to reproducing age, and then the organism reproduces once every time period. The formula applies most straightforwardly to asexual reproduction at a rate of one offspring per time period. In any event, the green crud population grows at this rate and has a time period of five days. Hence, if a green crud population starts out as 10 pounds of crud, then in five days there is still 10 pounds of crud; in ten days there is 20 pounds of crud, in fifteen days 30 pounds, in twenty days 50 pounds, and so forth. Write a program that takes both the initial size of a green crud population (in pounds) and a number of days as input, and that outputs the number of pounds of green crud after that many days. Assume that the population size is the same for four days and then increases every fifth day. Your program should allow the user to repeat this calculation as often as desired.

Alternative Version Using Files: An alternative version reads its input from a file and writes its output to another file. In this version your program reads initial population size and number of days from the input file and writes the initial population size, the number of days, and the size of the population after that many days to the output file. The input file should contain two numbers per line giving the initial population size and number of days. Your program will contain a loop that processes all the data in the input file. If you are doing this as a class assignment, ask your instructor if there are any special instructions about the file names or the format of the files.

9 The value e^x can be approximated by the sum:

$$1 + x + x^2/2! + x^3/3! + \dots + x^n/n!$$

Write a program that takes a value x as input and outputs this sum for n taken to be each of the values 1 to 100. The program should also output e^x calculated using the predefined function exp. The function exp is a predefined function such that exp(x) returns an approximation to the value

e^x. The function exp is in the library with the header file math.h. Your program should repeat the calculation for new values of x until the user says she or he is through. Use variables of type *double* to store the factorials or you are likely to produce integer overflow (or arrange your calculation to avoid any direct calculation of factorials). Your program should take its input from the keyboard (or from a file if told to do so by your instructor) and it should send its output to a file. If you are doing this as a class assignment, ask your instructor for the name of the output file, and if the input is to come from a file, then also ask for the name of the input file.

CHAPTER

8

Tools for Defining ADTs

8 Tools for Defining ADTs

Give us the tools, and we'll finish the job.

WINSTON CHURCHILL, RADIO BROADCAST, FEBRUARY 9, 1941

Introduction

In this chapter we teach you more techniques for defining abstract data types (ADTs). We begin by discussing new ways of adding operations to your ADT class, including overloading common operators such as +, *, and / so that they can be used with the classes you define in the same way that they are used with the predefined types such as *int* and *double*. We then show you how to compile your ADTs into libraries so that you can use them in your programs the same way you use the predefined libraries.

8.1 Defining ADT Operations

Until now we have implemented ADT operations as member functions of the class ADT, but for some operations, it is more natural to implement the operations as ordinary (nonmember) functions. In this section, we discuss techniques for defining operations on objects as nonmember functions. We begin with a simple example.

■)) PROGRAMMING EXAMPLE
An Equality Function

In Chapter 6, we developed a class called DayOfYear that records a date, such as January 1 or July 4, that might be a holiday or birthday or some other annual event. We gave progressively better versions of the class. The final version was produced in Self-Test Exercise 9 of Chapter 6. In Display 8.1 we repeat this final version of the class DayOfYear. In Display 8.1 we have enhanced the class one more time by adding a function called equal that can test two objects of type DayOfYear to see if their values represent the same date.

Display 8.1 Equality Function *(part 1 of 3)*

```
//Program to demonstrate the function equal. The class DayOfYear
//is the same as in Self-Test Exercise 9 in Chapter 6.
#include <iostream>
using namespace std;

class DayOfYear
{
public:
    DayOfYear(int the_month, int the_day);
    //Precondition: the_month and the_day form a possible date.
    //Initializes the date according to the arguments.

    DayOfYear();
    //Initializes the date to January first.

    void input();

    void output();

    int get_month();
    //Returns the month, 1 for January, 2 for February, etc.

    int get_day();
    //Returns the day of the month.
private:
    int month;
    int day;
};

bool equal(DayOfYear date1, DayOfYear date2);
//Precondition: date1 and date2 have values.
//Returns true if date1 and date2 represent the same date,
//otherwise returns false.

int main()
{
    DayOfYear today, bach_birthday(3, 21);

    cout << "Enter today's date:\n";
    today.input();
    cout << "Today's date is ";
    today.output();
```

Display 8.1 Equality Function *(part 2 of 3)*

```
        cout << "J. S. Bach's birthday is ";
        bach_birthday.output( );

        if ( equal(today, bach_birthday))
            cout << "Happy Birthday Johann Sebastian!\n";
        else
            cout << "Happy Unbirthday Johann Sebastian!\n";
        return 0;
}

bool equal(DayOfYear date1, DayOfYear date2)
{
        return ( date1.get_month( ) == date2.get_month( ) &&
                    date1.get_day( ) == date2.get_day( ) );
}

DayOfYear::DayOfYear(int the_month, int the_day)
{
    month = the_month;
    day = the_day;
}
DayOfYear::DayOfYear( )
{
    month = 1;
    day = 1;
}

int DayOfYear::get_month( )
{
    return month;
}

int DayOfYear::get_day( )
{
    return day;
}
```

Display 8.1 Equality Function *(part 3 of 3)*

```
//Uses iostream:
void DayOfYear::input( )
{
    cout << "Enter the month as a number: ";
    cin >> month;
    cout << "Enter the day of the month: ";
    cin >> day;
}

//Uses iostream:
void DayOfYear::output( )
{
    cout << "month = " << month
         << ", day = " << day << endl;
}
```

Sample Dialogue

```
Enter today's date:
Enter the month as a number: 3
Enter the day of the month: 21
Today's date is month = 3, day = 21
J. S. Bach's birthday is month = 3, day = 21
Happy Birthday Johann Sebastian!
```

Suppose `today` and `bach_birthday` are two objects of type `DayOfYear` that have been given values representing some dates. You can test to see if they represent the same date with the following Boolean expression:

```
equal(today, bach_birthday)
```

This call to the function `equal` returns *true* if `today` and `bach_birthday` represent the same date. In Display 8.1 this Boolean expression is used to control an *if-else*-statement.

The definition of the function `equal` is straightforward. Two dates are equal if they represent the same month and the same day of the month. The definition of `equal` uses accessor functions `get_month` and `get_day` to compare the months and the days represented by the two objects.

Notice that we did not make the function `equal` a member function. It would be possible to make `equal` a member function of the class `DayOfYear`, but `equal` compares *two* objects of type `DayOfYear`. If you make `equal` a member function, you must decide whether the calling object should be the first date or the second date. Rather than arbitrarily choosing one of the two dates as the calling object, we instead treated the two dates in the same way. We made `equal` an ordinary (nonmember) function that takes two dates as its arguments.

SELF-TEST EXERCISE

1 Write a function definition for a function called `before` that takes two arguments of the type `DayOfYear`, which is defined in Display 8.1. The function returns a *bool* value and returns *true* if the first argument represents a date that comes before the date represented by the second argument; otherwise, the function returns *false*. For example, January 5 comes before February 2.

Friend Functions

If your class has a full set of accessor functions, you can use the accessor functions to define a function to test for equality or to do any other kind of computing that depends on the private member variables. However, although this may give you access to the private member variables, it may not give you efficient access to them. Look again at the definition of the function `equal` given in Display 8.1. To read the month, it must make a call to the accessor function `get_month`. To read the day it must make a call to the accessor function `get_day`. This works, but the code would be simpler and more efficient if we could just access the member variables. A simpler and more efficient definition of the function `equal` given in Display 8.1 would be:

```
bool equal(DayOfYear date1, DayOfYear date2)
{
    return ( date1.month == date2.month &&
                date1.day == date2.day );
}
```

There is just one problem with this definition: It's illegal! It's illegal because the member variables `month` and `day` are private members of the class `DayOfYear`. Private member variables (and private member functions) cannot normally be referenced in the body of a function unless the function is a member function, and `equal` is not a member function of the class `DayOfYear`. But there is a way to give a nonmember function the same access privileges as a member function. If we make the function `equal` a *friend* of the class `DayOfYear`, then the above definition of `equal` will be legal.

A **friend function** of a class is not a member function of the class, but a friend function has access to the private members of that class just as a member function does. To make a function a friend function, you must name it as a friend in the class definition. For example, in Display 8.2 we have rewritten the definition of the class DayOfYear so that the function equal is a friend of the class. You make a function a friend of a class by listing the function prototype in the definition of the class and placing the keyword *friend* in front of the function prototype.

*Friends can access
private members*

A friend function is added to a class definition by listing its prototype, just as you would list the prototype of a member function, except that you precede the prototype by the keyword *friend*. However, a friend is not a member function; rather, it really is an ordinary function with extraordinary access to the data numbers of the class, granted by the class. The friend is called exactly like the ordinary function it is. In particular, the function definition for equal shown in Display 8.2 does not include the qualifier DayOfYear:: in the function heading. Also, the equal function is not called by using the dot operator. The function equal takes objects of type DayOfYear as arguments the same way that any other nonmember function would take arguments of any other type.

*A friend is NOT
a member*

↝ PROGRAMMING TIP
Define Both Accessor Functions and Friend Functions

It may seem that if you make all your basic functions friends of a class, then there is no need to include accessor functions in the class. After all, friend functions have access to the private member variables and so do not need accessor functions. This is not entirely wrong. It is true that if you made all the functions in the world friends of a class, you would not need accessor functions. However, making all functions friends is not practical.

In order to see why you still need accessor functions, consider the example of the class DayOfYear given in Display 8.2. You might use this class in another program, and that other program might very well want to do something with the month part of a DayOfYear object. For example, the program might want to calculate how many months there are remaining in the year. Specifically, the main part of the program might contain the following:

```
DayOfYear today;
cout << "enter today's date: \n";
today.input();
cout << "There are " << (12 - today.get_month())
     << " months left in this year.\n";
```

Display 8.2 Equality Function as a Friend

```
//Demonstrate the function equal. In this version equal is a friend of the class
//DayOfYear.
#include <iostream>
using namespace std;

class DayOfYear
{
public:
    friend bool equal(DayOfYear date1, DayOfYear date2);
    //Precondition: date1 and date2 have values.
    //Returns true if date1 and date2 represent the same date;
    //otherwise returns false.

    DayOfYear(int the_month, int the_day);
    //Precondition: the_month and the_day form a possible date.
    //Initializes the date according to the arguments.

    DayOfYear( );
    //Initializes the date to January first.

    void input( );

    void output( );

    int get_month( );
    //Returns the month, 1 for January, 2 for February, etc.

    int get_day( );
    //Returns the day of the month.
private:
    int month;
    int day;
};

int main( )
{
            <The main part of the program is the same as in Display 8.1.>
}

bool equal(DayOfYear date1, DayOfYear date2)
{
    return ( date1.month == date2.month &&
                     date1.day == date2.day );
}
```

```
<The rest of this display, including the Sample Dialogue, is the same as Display 8.1.>
```

Friend Functions

A **friend function** of a class is an ordinary function except that it has access to the private members of objects of that class. To make a function a friend of a class, you must list the function prototype for the friend function in the class definition. The prototype is preceded by the keyword *friend*. The prototype may be placed in either the private section or the public section, but it will be a public function in either case, so it is clearer to list it in the public section.

Syntax (of a class definition with friend functions):

```
class Class_Name
{
public:
        friend Prototype_for_Friend_Function_1
        friend Prototype_for_Friend_Function_2
                                :
                                :
        Member_Function_Prototypes
private:
        Private_Member_Declarations_and_Prototypes
};
```

You need not list the friend functions first. You can intermix the order of these prototypes.

Example:

```
class FuelTank
{
public:
        friend double need_to_fill(FuelTank the_tank);
        //Precondition: The member variables of the_tank have
        //values.
        //Returns the number of liters needed to fill the tank.

        FuelTank(double the_capacity, double the_level);
        FuelTank( );
        void input( );
        void output( );
private:
        double capacity;//in liters
        double level;
};
```

A friend function is *not* a member function. A friend function is defined and called the same way as an ordinary function. You do not use the dot operator in a call to a friend function and you do not use a type qualifier in the definition of a friend function.

You cannot replace `today.get_month( )` with `today.month` because `month` is a private member of the class. You need the accessor function `get_month`.

You have just seen that you definitely need to include accessor functions in your class ADTs. You may think that, since you usually need accessor functions, you do not need friends. In a sense, that is true. Notice that you could define the function `equal` either as a friend without using accessor functions (Display 8.2) or not make it a friend and use accessor functions (as in Display 8.1). In most situations, the only reason to make a function a friend is to make the definition of the function simpler and more efficient; but sometimes, that is reason enough.

~ PROGRAMMING TIP
Use Both Member and Nonmember Functions

Member functions and friend functions serve a very similar role. In fact, sometimes it is not clear whether you should make a particular function a friend of your class or a member function of the class. In most cases, you can make a function either a member function or a friend and have it perform the same task in the same way. There are, however, places where it is better to use a member function and places where it is better to use friend (or even a plain old function that isn't a friend, like the version of `equal` in Display 8.1). A simple rule to help you decide between member functions and nonmember functions is the following:

- Use a member function if the task being performed by the function involves only one object.
- Use a nonmember function if the task being performed involves more than one object. For example, the function `equal` in Display 8.1 (and Display 8.2) involves two objects, so we made it a a nonmember (friend) function.

Whether you make a nonmember function a friend function or use accessor functions is a matter of efficiency and personal taste. As long as you have enough accessor functions, either approach will work.

The choice of whether to use a member or nonmember function is not as simple as the above two rules. With more experience, you will discover situations in which it pays to violate those rules. A more accurate but harder to understand rule is to use member functions if the task is intimately related to a single object; use a nonmember function when the task involves more than one object and the objects are used symmetrically. However, this more accurate rule is not clear-cut, and the two simple rules given above will serve as a reliable guide until you become more sophisticated in handling objects. Clarity and readability of the code should always be a consideration in every situation.

PITFALL   **Compilers without Friends**

In the process of updating compilers to meet the new C++ standard, some compilers introduced problems with friend functions. On some newer compilers, friend functions simply do work as they are supposed to work. On these compilers friend functions do not have access to private members of the class. Presumably, this will be fixed in later releases of the compilers. In the meantime, you will have to work around this problem. If you have one of these compilers, for which friend functions do not work, you have at least four ways to work around the problem:

1. You can make private members public. This is a very poor technique, but might be okay for a quick check of some code.

2. You can use all member functions and member overloaded operations and no friend functions or friend overloaded operations. However, this solution is not without its problems. When overloading binary operators as member operators you lose automatic type conversions of the first argument and, more generally, you lose the sense of symmetry between the two arguments. Still, for some compilers, this is a price you may have to pay until they update the compilers. Overloading operators as member operators is covered in Appendix 12.

3. Instead of using friend functions, use nonmember, nonfriend functions (and operators) and use accessor functions, like the functions `get_month` and `get_date` in Display 8.1. This is probably the best solution if you cannot change your compiler.

4. Get a different compiler that allows friends. This is the best solution, if it is practical for you.

When overloading << and >> alternative 2 will not work (since the first argument, such as `cin` or `cout`, is not an object of the class). When overloading << and >>, your best bets are alternatives 3 and 4.

▮)) *PROGRAMMING EXAMPLE*
Money ADT (Version 1)

Display 8.3 contains the definition of a class called `Money`, which is an ADT for amounts of U.S. currency. The value is implemented as a single integer value that represents the amount of money as if it were converted to all pennies. For example, $9.95 would be stored as the value 995. Since we use an integer to represent the amount of money, the amount is represented as an exact quantity. We did not use a value of type *double* because values of type *double* are stored as approximate values and we want our money amounts to be exact quantities. This integer for the amount of money (expressed as all cents) is stored in a member variable named `all_cents`. We could use *int* for the type of the member variable `all_cents`, but with some compilers that would severely limit the amounts of money we could represent. In some implementations of C++, only two bytes are used to store the *int* type.[1] The result of the two-byte implementation is that the largest value of type *int* is only slightly larger than 32000, but 32000 cents represents only $320, which is a fairly small amount of money. Since we may want to deal with amounts of money much larger than $320, we have used *long* for the type of the member variable all_cents. C++ compilers that implement the *int* type in two bytes usually implement the type *long* in four bytes. Values of type *long* are integers just like the values of the type *int*, except that the four-byte *long* implementation enables the largest allowable value of type *long* to be much larger than the largest allowable value of type *int*. On most systems the largest allowable value of type *long* is 2 billion or larger. (The type *long* is also called *long int*. The two names *long* and *long int* refer to the same type.)

long

A full ADT might contain other operations besides the ones we have included in Display 8.3, such as a subtraction function. However, the operations shown illustrate all the main points about defining an ADT as a class.

The ADT Money has two operations that are friend functions: namely equal and add (which are defined in Display 8.3). The function add returns an object whose value is the sum of the values of its two arguments. A function call of the form equal(amount1, amount2) returns *true* if the two objects amount1 and amount2 have values that represent equal amounts of money.

input

Notice that the class Money reads and writes amounts of money as we normally write amounts of money, such as **$9.95** or –**$9.95**. First, consider the member function input (also defined in Display 8.3). That function first reads a single character, which should be either the dollar sign '$' or the minus sign '–'. If this first character is the minus sign, '–', then the function remembers that the amount is negative by setting the value of the variable negative to *true,* and then it reads an addition character, which should be the dollar sign. On the other hand, if the first symbol is not '–', then negative is set equal to *false.* At this point the negative sign (if any) and the dollar sign have been read. The function input then reads the number of dollars as a value of type *long* and places the number of dollars in the local variable named dollars. After reading the dollars part of the input, the function input reads the remainder of the input as values of type *char*; it reads in three characters, which should be a decimal point and two digits.

(You might be tempted to define the member function input so that it reads the decimal point as a value of type *char* and then reads the number of cents as a value of type *int*. This is not done in a straightforward way because of the way that many C++ compilers treat leading zeros. As explained in the PITFALL section that follows soon after this subsection, many compilers still in use do not read numbers with

[1]See Chapter 2 for details. Display 2.2 has a description of data types, as most recent compilers implement them.

Display 8.3 Money ADT—Version 1 *(part 1 of 5)*

```
//Program to demonstrate the class Money.
#include <iostream>
#include <cstdlib>
#include <cctype>
using namespace std;

//Class for amounts of money in U.S. currency.
class Money
{
public:
    friend Money add(Money amount1, Money amount2);
    //Precondition: amount1 and amount2 have been given values.
    //Returns the sum of the values of amount1 and amount2.

    friend bool equal(Money amount1, Money amount2);
    //Precondition: amount1 and amount2 have been given values.
    //Returns true if the amount1 and amount2 have the same value;
    //otherwise, returns false.

    Money(long dollars, int cents);
    //Initializes the object so its value represents an amount with the dollars and cents
    //given by the arguments. If the amount is negative, then both dollars and cents
    //should be negative.

    Money(long dollars);
    //Initializes the object so its value represents $dollars.00.

    Money();
    //Initializes the object so its value represents $0.00.

    double get_value();
    //Precondition: The calling object has been given a value.
    //Returns the amount of money recorded in the data portion of the calling object.

    void input(istream& ins);
    //Precondition: If ins is a file input stream, then ins has already been connected to a
    //file. An amount of money, including a dollar sign, has been entered in the input
    //stream ins. Notation for negative amounts is as in –$100.00.
    //Postcondition: The value of the calling object has been set to
    //the amount of money read from the input stream ins.

    void output(ostream& outs);
    //Precondition: If outs is a file output stream, then outs has already been
    //connected to a file.
    //Postcondition: A dollar sign and the amount of money recorded
    //in the calling object have been sent to the output stream outs.
```

Display 8.3 Money ADT—Version 1 *(part 2 of 5)*

```
private:
    long all_cents;
};

//Prototype for use in the definition of Money::input:
int digit_to_int(char c);
//Precondition: c is one of the digits '0' through '9'.
//Returns the integer for the digit; e.g., digit_to_int('3') returns 3.

int main( )
{
    Money your_amount, my_amount(10, 9), our_amount;
    cout << "Enter an amount of money: ";
    your_amount.input(cin);
    cout << "Your amount is ";
    your_amount.output(cout);
    cout << endl;
    cout << "My amount is ";
    my_amount.output(cout);
    cout << endl;

    if (equal(your_amount, my_amount))
        cout << "We have the same amounts.\n";
    else
        cout << "One of us is richer.\n";
    our_amount = add(your_amount, my_amount);
    your_amount.output(cout);
    cout << " + ";
    my_amount.output(cout);
    cout << " equals ";
    our_amount.output(cout);
    cout << endl;
    return 0;
}

Money add(Money amount1, Money amount2)
{
    Money temp;
```

Display 8.3 Money ADT—Version 1 *(part 3 of 5)*

```
        temp.all_cents = amount1.all_cents + amount2.all_cents;
        return temp;
}

bool equal(Money amount1, Money amount2)
{
        return (amount1.all_cents == amount2.all_cents);
}

Money::Money(long dollars, int cents)
{
        all_cents = dollars*100 + cents;
}

Money::Money(long dollars)
{
        all_cents = dollars*100;
}

Money::Money()
{
        all_cents = 0;
}

double Money::get_value()
{
        return (all_cents * 0.01);
}

//Uses iostream, cctype, cstdlib:
void Money::input(istream& ins)
{
        char one_char, decimal_point,
             digit1, digit2; //digits for the amount of cents
        long dollars;
        int cents;
        bool negative;//set to true if input is negative.
```

Display 8.3 Money ADT—Version 1 *(part 4 of 5)*

```
        ins >> one_char;
        if (one_char == '-')
        {
            negative = true;
            ins >> one_char; //read '$'
        }
        else
            negative = false;
        //if input is legal, then one_char == '$'

        ins >> dollars >> decimal_point >> digit1 >> digit2;

        if ( one_char != '$' || decimal_point != '.'
            || !isdigit(digit1) || !isdigit(digit2) )
        {
            cout << "Error illegal form for money input\n";
            exit(1);
        }
        cents = digit_to_int(digit1)*10 + digit_to_int(digit2);

        all_cents = dollars*100 + cents;
        if (negative)
            all_cents = -all_cents;
}

//Uses cstdlib and iostream:
void Money::output(ostream& outs)
{
    long positive_cents, dollars, cents;
    positive_cents = labs(all_cents);
    dollars = positive_cents/100;
    cents = positive_cents%100;

    if (all_cents < 0)
        outs << "-$" << dollars << '.';
    else
        outs << "$" << dollars << '.';

    if (cents < 10)
        outs << '0';
    outs << cents;
}
```

Display 8.3 Money ADT—Version 1 *(part 5 of 5)*

```
int digit_to_int(char c)
{
    return ( int(c) - int('0') );
}
```

Sample Dialogue

```
Enter an amount of money: $123.45
Your amount is $123.45
My amount is $10.09.
One of us is richer.
$123.45 + $10.09 equals $133.54
```

leading zeros as you would like them to, so an amount like $7.09 may be read incorrectly if your C++ code were to read the 09 as a value of type *int*.)

The following assignment statement converts the two digits that make up the cents part of the input amount to a single integer, which is stored in the local variable cents:

```
cents = digit_to_int(digit1)*10 + digit_to_int(digit2);
```

After this assignment statement is executed, the value of cents is the number of cents in the input amount.

The helping function digit_to_int takes an argument that is a digit, such as '3', and converts it to the corresponding *int* value, such as 3. We need this helping function because the member function input reads the two digits for the number of cents as two values of type *char* which are stored in the local variables digit1 and digit2. However, once the digits are read into the computer, we want to use them as numbers. Therefore, we use the function digit_to_int to convert a digit, such as '3' to a number such as 3. The definition of the function digit_to_int is given in Display 8.3. You can simply take it on faith that this definition does what it is supposed to do, and treat the function as a black box. All you need to know is that digit_to_int('0') returns 0, digit_to_int('1') returns 1, and so forth. However, it is not too difficult to see how this function works, so you may want to read the optional section which follows this one. It explains the implementation of digit_to_int.

digit_to_int

Once the local variables dollars and cents are set to the number of dollars and the number of cents in the input amount, it is easy to set the member variable all_cents. The following assignment statement sets all_cents to the correct number of cents:

```
all_cents = dollars*100 + cents;
```

However, this always sets all_cents to a positive amount. If the amount of money is negative, then the value of all_cents must be changed from positive to negative. This is done with the following statement:

```
if (negative)
    all_cents = -all_cents;
```

The member function output (Display 8.3) calculates the number of dollars and the number of cents from the value of the member variable all_cents. It computes the number of dollars and the number of cents using integer division by 100. For example, if all_cents has a value of 995 (cents), then the number of dollars is 995/100, which is 9, and the number of cents is 995%100, which is 95. Thus, $9.95 would be the value output when the value of all_cents is 995 (cents).

The definition for the member function output needs to make special provisions for outputting negative amounts of money. The result of integer division with negative numbers does not have a standard definition and can vary from one implementation to another. To avoid this problem, we have taken the absolute value of the number in all_cents before performing division. To compute the absolute value we use the pre-defined function labs. The function labs returns the absolute value of its argument, just like the function abs, but labs takes an argument of type *long* and returns a value of type *long*. The function labs is in the library with header file cstdlib, just like the function abs. (Some older versions of C++ do not include labs. If your implementation of C++ does not include labs, you can easily define the function for yourself.)

Implementation of digit_to_int *(Optional)*

The definition of the function digit_to_int from Display 8.3 is reproduced below:

```
int digit_to_int(char c)
{
    return ( int(c) - int('0') );
}
```

At first glance the formula for the value returned may seem a bit strange, but the details are not too complicated. The digit to be converted, for example '3', is the parameter c, and the returned value will turn out to be the corresponding *int* value, in this example 3. As we pointed out in Chapters 2 and 5, values of type *char* are implemented as numbers. Unfortunately, the number implementing the digit '3', for example, is not the number 3. The type cast *int*(c) produces the number that implements the character c and converts this number to the type *int*. This changes c from the type *char* to a number of type *int* but, unfortunately, not to the number we want. For example, *int*('3') is not 3, but is some other number. We need to convert *int*(c) to the number corresponding to c (e.g., '3' to 3). So let's see how we must adjust *int*(c) to get the number we want.

We know that the digits are in order. So *int*('0') + 1 is equal to *int*('1'); *int*('1') + 1 is equal to *int*('2'); *int*('2') + 1 is equal to *int*('3'), and so forth. Knowing that the digits are in this order is all we need to know in order to see that digit_to_int returns the correct value. If c is '0', the value returned is

$$int(c) - int('0'), \text{which is } int('0') - int('0').$$

So digit_to_int('0') returns 0.

Now let's consider what happens when c has the value '1'. The value returned is then

$$int(c) - int('0'), \text{which is } int('1') - int('0'), \text{and}$$
that is $(int('0') + 1) - int('0')$, and that, in turn, is
$$int('0') - int('0') + 1.$$

Since $int('0') - int('0')$ is 0, this result is 0 + 1 or 1. You can check the other digits, '2' through '9', for yourself; each digit produces a number one larger than the previous digit.

⬧ PITFALL   Leading Zeros in Number Constants

Below we have reproduced the object declarations given in the main part of the program in Display 8.3:

```
Money your_amount, my_amount(10, 9), our_amount;
```

The two arguments to the constructor call for my_amount represent $10.09. Since we normally write the cents in this format (that is, ".09")—you might be tempted to write the object declaration as my_amount(10, 09). However, this will cause problems. In mathematics the numerals 9 and 09 represent the same number. However, some C++ compilers use a leading zero to signal a different kind of numeral, so in C++ the constants 9 and 09 are not the same number. With some compilers a leading zero means that the number is written in base 8 rather than base 10. Since base 8 numerals do not use the digit 9, the constant 09 does not make sense in C++. The constants 00 through 07 should work correctly, since they mean the same thing in base 8 and in base 10, but some systems in some contexts will have trouble even with 00 through 07.

ANSI C++ Standard provides that input should default to interpreting input as decimal, regardless of the leading 0, The GNU project C++ compiler, g++, and Microsoft's VC++ compilers do not have the "feature"[2] we discussed above, i.e., they comply with the Standard. Most compiler vendors track the ANSI standard, so should be compliant with the ANSI C++ Standard. You should write a small program to test this on your compiler.

---

[2]The 1981 Apple II hardware reference manual defined a "feature" as a "bug" described by the marketing department.

SELF-TEST EXERCISES

2   What is the difference between a friend function for a class and a member function for the class?

3   Suppose you wish to add a friend function to the class `DayOfYear` defined in Display 8.2. This friend function will be called `after` and will take two arguments of the type `DayOfYear`. The function returns *true* if the first argument represents a date that comes after the date represented by the second argument; otherwise, the function returns *false*. For example, February 2 comes after January 5. What do you need to add to the definition of the class `DayOfYear` in Display 8.2?

4   Suppose you wish to add a friend function for subtraction to the class `Money` defined in Display 8.3. What do you need to add to the description of the class `Money` that we gave in Display 8.3? The subtraction function should take two arguments of type `Money` and return a value of type `Money` whose value is the value of the first argument minus the value of the second argument.

5   Notice the member function `output` in the class definition of `Money` given in Display 8.3. In order to write a value of type `Money` to the screen, you call `output` with `cout` as an argument. For example, if `purse` is an object of type `Money`, then to output the amount of money in `purse` to the screen, you write the following in your program

```
purse.output(cout);
```

It might be nicer not to have to list the stream `cout` when you send output to the screen. Rewrite the class definition for the type `Money` given in Display 8.3. The only change is that this rewritten version overloads the function name `output` so that there are two versions of `output`. One version is just like the one shown in Display 8.3; the other version of `output` takes no arguments and sends its output to the screen. With this rewritten version of the type `Money`, the following two calls are equivalent:

```
purse.output(cout);
```

and the equivalent

```
purse.output( );
```

but the second is simpler. Note that since there will be two versions of the function `output`, you can still send output to a file. If `outs` is an output file stream that is connected to a file, then the following will output the money in the object `purse` to the file connected to `outs`:

```
purse.output(outs);
```

6   Notice the definition of the member function input of the class Money given in Display 8.3. If the user enters certain kinds of incorrect input, the function issues an error message and ends the program. For example, if the user omits a dollar sign, the function issues an error message. However, the checks given there do not catch all kinds of incorrect input. For example, negative amounts of money are supposed to be entered in the form –**$9.95,** but if the user mistakenly enters the amount in the form **$–9.95,** then the input will not issue an error message and the value of the Money object will be set to an incorrect value. What amount will the member function input read, if the user mistakenly enters **$–9.95**? How might you add addition checks to catch most errors caused by such a misplaced minus sign?

7   The immediately preceding PITFALL section suggests that you write a short program to test whether a leading 0 will cause your compiler to interpret input numbers as base-eight numerals. Write such a program.

The *const* Parameter Modifier

A call-by-reference parameter is more efficient than a call-by-value parameter. A call-by-value parameter is a local variable that is initialized to the value of its argument, so when the function is called there are two copies of the argument. With a call-by-reference parameter, the parameter is just a place holder that is replaced by the argument, so there is only one copy of the argument. For parameters of simple types, such as *int* or *double*, the difference in efficiency is negligible, but for class parameters the difference in efficiency can sometimes be important. Thus, it can make sense to use a call-by-reference parameter rather than a call-by-value parameter for a class, even if the function does not change the parameter.

If you are using a call-by-reference parameter and your function does not change the value of the parameter, you can mark the parameter so that the compiler knows that the parameter should not be changed. To do so place the modifier *const* before the parameter type. The parameter is then called a **constant parameter.** For example, consider the class Money defined in Display 8.3. The Money parameters for the friend function add can be made into constant parameters as follows:

constant parameter

```
class Money
{
public:
    friend Money add(const Money& amount1, const Money& amount2);
    //Precondition: amount1 and amount2 have been given values.
    //Returns the sum of the values of amount1 and amount2.
        ...
```

When you use constant parameters, the modifier *const* must be used in both the function prototype and in the heading of the function definition, so with the above change in the class definition, the function definition for add would begin as follows:

```
Money add(const Money& amount1, const Money& amount2)
{
    . . .
```

The remainder of the function definition would be the same as in Display 8.3.

Constant parameters are a form of automatic error checking. If your function definition contains a mistake that causes an inadvertent change to the constant parameter, then the computer will issue an error message.

The parameter modifier *const* can be used with any kind of parameter; however, it is normally used only for call-by-reference parameters for classes (and occasionally for certain other parameters whose corresponding arguments are large).

const with member functions

Call-by-reference parameters are replaced with arguments when a function is called, and the function call may (or may not) change the value of the argument. When you have a call to a member function, the calling object behaves very much like a call-by-reference parameter. When you have a call to a member function, that function call can change the value of the calling object. For example, consider the following, where the class Money is as in Display 8.3:

```
Money m;
m.input(cin);
```

When the object m is declared, the value of the member variable all_cents is initialized to 0. The call to the member function input changes the value of the member variable all_cents to a new value determined by what the user types in. Thus, the call m.input(cin) changes the value of m, just as if m were a call-by-reference argument.

The modifier *const* applies to calling objects in the same way that it applies to parameters. If you have a member function that should not change the value of a calling object, you can mark the function with the *const* modifier; then the computer will issue an error message if your function code does inadvertently change the value of the calling object. In the case of a member function, the *const* goes at the end of the prototype, just before the final semicolon, as shown below:

```
class Money
{
public:
        . . .
    void output(ostream& outs) const;
        . . .
```

The modifier *const* should be used in both the function prototype and the function definition, so the function definition for output would begin:

```
void Money::output(ostream& outs) const
{
    ...
```

The remainder of the function definition would be the same as in Display 8.3.

---

const **Parameter Modifier**

If you place the modifier *const* before the type for a call-by-reference parameter, the parameter is called a **constant parameter.** When you add the *const* you are telling the compiler that this parameter should not be changed. If you make a mistake in your definition of the function so that it does change the constant parameter, then the computer will give an error message. Parameters of a class type that are not changed by the function ordinarily should be constant call-by-reference parameters, rather than call-by-value parameters.

   If a member function does not change the value of its calling object, then you can mark the function by adding the *const* modifier to the function prototype. If you make a mistake in your definition of the function so that it does change the calling object and the function is marked with *const*, then the computer will give an error message. The *const* is placed at the end of the prototype, just before the final semicolon. The heading of the function definition should also have a *const*, so that it matches the prototype.

Example:

```
class Sample
{
public:
    Sample();
    friend int compare(const Sample& s1, const Sample& s2);
    void input();
    void output() const;
private:
    int stuff;
    double more_stuff;
};
```

Use of the *const* modifier is an all or nothing proposition. You should use the *const* modifier whenever it is appropriate for a class parameter and whenever it is appropriate for a member function of the class. If you do not use *const* every time that it is appropriate for a class, then you should never use it for that class.

◆ *PITFALL*   **Inconsistent Use of** *const*

Use of the *const* modifier is an all or nothing proposition. If you use *const* for one parameter of a particular type, then you should use it for every other parameter that has that type and that is not changed by the function call; moreover, if the type is a class type, then you should also use the *const* modifier for every member function that does not change the value of its calling object. The reason has to do with function calls within function calls. For example, consider the following definition of the function guarantee:

```
void guarantee(const Money& price)
{
    cout << "If not satisfied, we will pay you\n"
        << "double your money back.\n"
        << "That's a refund of $"
        << (2*price.get_value()) << endl;
}
```

If you do *not* add the *const* modifier to the prototype for the member function get_value, then the function guarantee will give an error message on most compilers. The member function get_value does not change the calling object price. However, when the compiler processes the function definition for guarantee it will think that get_value does (or at least might) change the value of price. This is because, when it is translating the function definition for guarantee all that the compiler knows about the member function get_value is the prototype for get_value; if the prototype does not contain a *const* that tells the compiler that the calling object will not be changed, then the compiler assumes that the calling object will be changed. Thus, if you use the modifier *const* with parameters of type Money, then you should also use *const* with all Money member functions that do not change the value of their calling object. In particular, the prototype for the member function get_value should include a *const*.

In Display 8.4 we have rewritten the definition of the class Money given in Display 8.3, but this time we have used the *const* modifier where appropriate. The definitions of the member and friend functions would be the same as they are in Display 8.3, except that the modifier *const* must be used in function headings so that the headings match the prototypes shown in Display 8.4.

SELF-TEST EXERCISES

8 Give the complete definition of the member function get_value that you would use with the definition of Money given in Display 8.4.

Display 8.4 Class Definition for Money ADT with Constant Parameters

```
//Class for amounts of money in U.S. currency.
class Money
{
public:
    friend Money add(const Money& amount1, const Money& amount2);
    //Precondition: amount1 and amount2 have been given values.
    //Returns the sum of the values of amount1 and amount2.

    friend bool equal(const Money& amount1, const Money& amount2);
    //Precondition: amount1 and amount2 have been given values.
    //Returns true if amount1 and amount2 have the same value;
    //otherwise, returns false.

    Money(long dollars, int cents);
    //Initializes the object so its value represents an amount with the dollars and
    //cents given by the arguments. If the amount is negative, then both dollars and
    //cents should be negative.

    Money(long dollars);
    //Initializes the object so its value represents $dollars.00.

    Money( );
    //Initializes the object so its value represents $0.00.

    double get_value( ) const;
    //Precondition: The calling object has been given a value.
    //Returns the amount of money recorded in the data portion of the calling object.

    void input(istream& ins);
    //Precondition: If ins is a file input stream, then ins has already been connected
    //to a file. An amount of money, including a dollar sign, has been entered in the
    //input stream ins. Notation for negative amounts is as in -$100.00.
    //Postcondition: The value of the calling object has been set to
    //the amount of money read from the input stream ins.

    void output(ostream& outs) const;
    //Precondition: If outs is a file output stream, then outs has already been
    //connected to a file.
    //Postcondition: A dollar sign and the amount of money recorded
    //in the calling object have been sent to the output stream outs.
private:
    long all_cents;
};
```

9 Why would it be incorrect to add the modifier *const*, as shown below, to the
   prototype for the member function `input` of the class `Money` given in Display 8.4?

```
class Money
{
     . . .
public:
    void input(istream& ins) const;
     . . .
```

10 What are the differences and the similarities between a call-by-value parameter and a call-by-*const*-reference parameter? Prototypes that illustrate these
   follow:

```
void call_by_value(int x);
void call_by_const_reference(const int & x);
```

11 Given the definitions:

```
const int x = 17;
class A
{
public:
    A( );
    A(int);
    int f( )const;
    int g(const A& x);
private:
    int i;
};
```

Each of the three *const* keywords is a promise to the compiler that the
compiler will enforce. What is the promise in each case?

Overloading Operators

Earlier in this chapter, we showed you how to make the function add a friend of the
class `Money` and use it to add two objects of type `Money` (Display 8.3). The function
add is adequate for adding objects, but it would be nicer if you could simply use the
usual + operator to add values of type `Money`, as in the last line of the following code:

```
Money total, cost, tax;
cout << "Enter cost and tax: ";
```

```
cost.input(cin);
tax.input(cin);
total = cost + tax;
```

instead of having to use the slightly more awkward

```
total = add(cost, tax);
```

Recall that an operator, such as +, is really just a function except that the syntax for how it is used is slightly different from that of a function. In a function call the arguments are placed in parentheses after the function name as in:

operators and functions

```
add(cost, tax)
```

With a (binary) operator, the arguments are placed on either side of the operator, as shown below:

```
cost + tax
```

A function can be overloaded to take arguments of different types and an operator is really a function, so an operator can be overloaded. The way you overload an operator, such as +, is very similar to the way you overload a function name.

You can overload the operator + (and many other operators) so that it will accept arguments of a class type. The difference between overloading the + operator and defining the function add involves only a slight difference in syntax. The definition of the overloaded operator + is basically the same as the definition of the function add. The only differences are that you use the name + instead of the name add and you precede the + with the keyword *operator*. In Display 8.5 we have rewritten the type Money to include the overloaded operator + and we have embedded the definition in a small demonstration program.

how to overload an operator

The class Money, as defined in Display 8.5, also overloads the == operator so that == can be used to compare two objects of type Money. If amount1 and amount2 are two objects of type Money, we want the expression

```
amount1 == amount2
```

to return the same value as the following Boolean expression

```
amount1.all_cents == amount2.all_cents
```

As shown in Display 8.5, this is the value returned by the overloaded operator ==.

(In the version of the class Money given in Display 8.5 we have also added the *const* parameter modifier where appropriate.)

Display 8.5 Overloading Operators *(part 1 of 2)*

```
//Program to demonstrate the class Money. (This is an improved version of
//the class Money which we gave in Display 8.3 and rewrote in Display 8.4.)
#include <iostream>
#include <cstdlib>
#include <cctype>
using namespace std;


//Class for amounts of money in U.S. currency.
class Money
{
public:
    friend Money operator +(const Money& amount1, const Money& amount2);
    //Precondition: amount1 and amount2 have been given values.
    //Returns the sum of the values of amount1 and amount2.

    friend bool operator ==(const Money& amount1, const Money& amount2);
    //Precondition: amount1 and amount2 have been given values.
    //Returns true if amount1 and amount2 have the same value;
    //otherwise, returns false.

    Money(long dollars, int cents);

    Money(long dollars);

    Money( );

    double get_value( ) const;

    void input(istream& ins);

    void output(ostream& outs) const;
private:
    long all_cents;
};
            <Any extra prototypes from Display 8.3 go here. >
int main( )
{
    Money cost(1, 50), tax(0, 15), total;
    total = cost + tax;
    cout << "cost = ";
    cost.output(cout);
    cout << endl;
```

Some comments from Display 8.4 have been omitted to save space in this book, but they should be included in a real program.

Display 8.5 Overloading Operators *(part 2 of 2)*

```
        cout << "tax = ";
        tax.output(cout);
        cout << endl;
        cout << "total bill = ";
        total.output(cout);
        cout << endl;
        if (cost == tax)
            cout << "Move to another state.\n";
        else
            cout << "Things seem normal.\n";
        return 0;
}


Money operator +(const Money& amount1, const Money& amount2)
{
    Money temp;
    temp.all_cents = amount1.all_cents + amount2.all_cents;
    return temp;
}

bool operator ==(const Money& amount1, const Money& amount2)
{
    return (amount1.all_cents == amount2.all_cents);
}
```

        <The definitions of the member functions are the same as in Display 8.3
            except that *const* is added to the function headings in various places so
            that the function headings match the prototypes in the above class definition.
            No other changes are needed in the member function definitions. The bodies
            of the member function definitions are identical to those in Display 8.3.>

Output

```
cost = $1.50
tax = $0.15
total bill = $1.65
Things seem normal.
```

You can overload most but not all operators. The operator need not be a friend of a class, but you will often want it to be a friend. Check the box entitled "Rules on Overloading Operators" (on page 471) for some technical details on when and how you can overload an operator.

Operator Overloading

A (binary) operator, such as +, −, /, %, and so forth, is simply a function that is called using a different syntax for listing its arguments. With an operator, the arguments are listed before and after the operator; with a function the arguments are listed in parentheses after the function name. An operator definition is written in the same way as a function definition, except that the operator definition includes the reserved word *operator* before the operator name. The predefined operators, such as + and so forth, can be overloaded by giving them a new definition for a class type.

An operator may be a friend of a class although this is not required. An example of overloading the + operator as a friend is given in Display 8.5.

SELF-TEST EXERCISES

12 What is the difference between a (binary) operator and a function?

13 Suppose you wish to overload the operator < so that it applies to the type Money defined in Display 8.5. What do you need to add to the description of Money given in Display 8.5?

14 Is it possible using operator overloading to change the behavior of + on integers? Why or why not?

Constructors for Automatic Type Conversion

If your class definition contains the appropriate constructors, the system will perform certain type conversions automatically. For example, if your program contains the definition of the class Money given in Display 8.5, you could use the following in your program:

```
Money base_amount(100, 60), full_amount;
full_amount = base_amount + 25;
full_amount.output(cout);
```

Rules on Overloading Operators

- When overloading an operator, at least one argument of the resulting overloaded operator must be of a class type.

- An overloaded operator can be, but does not have to be, a friend of a class, i.e., the operator function may be a member of the class.

- You cannot create a new operator. All you can do is overload existing operators such as +, −, *, /, %, and so forth.

- You cannot change the number of arguments that an operator takes. For example, you cannot change % from a binary to a unary operator when you overload %; you cannot change ++ from a unary to a binary operator when you overload it.

- You cannot change the precedence of an operator. An overloaded operator has the same precedence as the ordinary version of the operator. For example, x*y + z always means (x*y) + z, even if x, y, and z are objects and the operators + and * have been overloaded for the appropriate classes.

- The following operators cannot be overloaded:
  the dot operator (.), the scope resolution operator (::), and the operators .* and ?:, which are not discussed in this book.

- Although the assignment operator = can be overloaded so that the default meaning of = is replaced by a new meaning, this must be done in a different way from what is described here. Overloading = is discussed in Chapter 11. Some other operators, including [] and ->, also must be overloaded in a way that is different from what is described in this chapter. The operators [] and -> are discussed later in this book.

The output will be

```
$125.60
```

The code above may look simple and natural enough, but there is one subtle point. The 25 (in the expression base_amount + 25) is not of the appropriate type. In Display 8.5 we only overloaded the operator + so that it could be used with two values of type Money. We did not overload + so that it could be used with a value of type Money and an integer. The constant 25 is an integer and is not of type Money. The constant 25 can be considered to be of type *int* or of type *long*, but 25 cannot be used as a value of type Money, unless the class definition somehow tells the system how to convert an integer to a value of type Money. The only way that the system knows that 25 means $25.00 is that we included a constructor that takes a single argument of type *long*. When the system sees the expression

```
base_amount + 25
```

the system first checks to see if the operator + has been overloaded for the combination of a value of type Money and an integer. Since there is no such overloading, the system next looks to see if there is a constructor that takes a single argument that is an integer. If it finds a constructor that takes a single integer argument, it uses that constructor to convert the integer 25 to a value of type Money. The constructor with one argument of type *long* tells the system how to convert an integer, such as 25, to a value of type Money. The one argument constructor says that 25 should be converted to an object of type Money whose member variable all_cents is equal to 2500; in other words, the constructor converts 25 to an object of type Money that represents $25.00. (The definition of the constructor is in Display 8.3.)

Note that this type conversion will not work unless there is a suitable constructor. For example, the type Money (Display 8.5) has no constructor that takes an argument of type *double*, so the following is illegal and would produce an error message if you were to put it in a program that declares base_amount and full_amount to be of type Money:

```
full_amount = base_amount + 25.67;
```

To make the above use of + legal you must change the definition of the class Money by adding another constructor. The prototype for the constructor you need to add is the following:

```
class Money
{
public:
        . . .
    Money(double amount);
    //Initializes the object so its value represents $amount.
        . . .
```

Writing a definition of this new constructor is Self-Test Exercise 15.

These automatic type conversions (produced by constructors) seem most common and compelling with overloaded numeric operators such as + and –. However, these automatic conversions apply in exactly the same way to arguments for ordinary functions, arguments for member functions, and arguments for other overloaded operators.

SELF-TEST EXERCISES

15 Give the definition for the constructor discussed at the end of the previous section. The constructor is to be added to the class Money in Display 8.5. The definition begins as follows:

```
Money::Money(double amount)
{
```

16 Here is a definition of a class called Pairs. Objects of type Pairs can be used in any situation where ordered pairs are needed. Your task is to write implementations of the overloaded operator>> and operator<< so that objects of class Pairs are to be input and output in the form (5,6) (5,-4) (-5,4) or (-5,-6). You need not implement any constructor or other member, and you need not do any input format checking.

```
#include <iostream>
using namespace std;
class Pairs
{
public:
    Pairs( );
    Pairs(int first, int second);
    //other members and friends
    friend istream& operator>> (istream& ins, Pairs& second);
    friend ostream& operator<< (ostream& outs,
                                    const Pairs& second);
private:
    int f;
    int s;
};
```

Overloading Unary Operators

In addition to the binary operators, such as + in x + y, there are also unary operators, such as the *operator* - when it is used to mean negation. In the statement below, the unary *operator* - is used to set the value of a variable x equal to the negative of the value of the variable y:

```
x = -y;
```

The increment and decrement operators ++ and -- are other examples of unary operators.

You can overload unary operators as well as binary operators. For example, you can redefine the type Money given in Display 8.5 so that it has both a unary and a binary operator version of the subtraction/negation *operator* -. The redone class definition is given in Display 8.6. Suppose your program contains this class definition and the following code:

```
Money amount1(10), amount2(6), amount3;
```

Then the following sets the value of amount3 to amount1 minus amount2:

```
amount3 = amount1 - amount2;
```

The following will, then, output $4.00 to the screen:

```
amount3.output(cout);
```

On the other hand, the following will set amount3 equal to the negative of amount1:

```
amount3 = -amount1;
```

so the following will, then, output -$10.00 to the screen:

```
amount3.output(cout);
```

++ and --

You can overload the ++ and -- operators in ways similar to how we overloaded the negation operator in Display 8.6. The overloading definition will apply to the operator when it is used in prefix position, as in ++x and --x. The postfix versions of ++ and --, as in x++ and x--, are handled in a different manner, but we will not discuss the postfix versions of ++ and --. (Hey, you can't learn everything in a first course!)

Overloading >> and <<

<< is an operator

The insertion operator << that we used with cout is an operator like + or -. For example, consider the following:

```
cout << "Hello out there.\n";
```

The operator is <<, the first operand is the output stream cout, and the second operand is the string value "Hello out there.\n". You can change either of these operands. If fout is an output stream of type ofstream and fout has been connected to a file with a call to open, then you can replace cout with fout and the string will instead be written to the file connected to fout. Of course, you can also replace the string "Hello out there.\n" with another string, a variable, or a number. Since the insertion operator << is an operator you should be able to overload

Display 8.6 Overloading a Unary Operator

```
//Class for amounts of money in U.S. currency.
class Money
{
public:
    friend Money operator +(const Money& amount1, const Money& amount2);

    friend Money operator -(const Money& amount1, const Money& amount2);
    //Precondition: amount1 and amount2 have been given values.
    //Returns amount 1 minus amount2.

    friend Money operator -(const Money& amount);
    //Precondition: amount has been given a value.
    //Returns the negative of the value of amount.

    friend bool operator ==(const Money& amount1, const Money& amount2);

    Money(long dollars, int cents);

    Money(long dollars);

    Money();

    double get_value() const;

    void input(istream& ins);
    void output(ostream& outs) const;
private:
    long all_cents;
};
```

This is an improved version of the class Money given in Display 8.5.

We have omitted the include directives and some of the comments, but you should include them in your programs.

<Any additional prototypes as well as the main part of the program go here.>

```
Money operator -(const Money& amount1, const Money& amount2)
{
    Money temp;
    temp.all_cents = amount1.all_cents - amount2.all_cents;
    return temp;
}
Money operator -(const Money& amount)
{
    Money temp;
    temp.all_cents = -amount.all_cents;
    return temp;
}
```

<The other function definitions are the same as in Display 8.5.>

it just as you overload operators such as + and −. This is true, but there are a few more details to worry about when you overload the input and output operators >> and <<.

In our previous definitions of the class `Money` we used the member function `output` to output values of type `Money` (Display 8.3 through Display 8.6). This is adequate, but it would be nicer if we could simply use the insertion operator << to output values of type `Money` as in the following:

```
Money amount(100);
cout << "I have " << amount << " in my purse.\n";
```

instead of having to use the member function `output` as shown below:

```
Money amount(100);
cout << "I have ";
amount.output(cout);
cout << " in my purse.\n";
```

One problem in overloading the operator << is deciding what value should be returned when << is used in an expression like the following:

```
cout << amount
```

The two operands in the above expression are `cout` and `amount`, and evaluating the expression should cause the value of `amount` to be written to the screen. But, if << is an operator like + or *, then the above expression should also return some value. After all, expressions with other operands, such as n1 + n2, return values. But, what does `cout  <<  amount` return? In order to obtain the answer to that question, we need to look at a more complicated expression involving <<.

Let's consider the following expression, which involves evaluating a chain of expressions using <<:

```
cout << "I have " << amount << " in my purse.\n";
```

If you think of the operator << as being analogous to other operators, such as +, then the above should be (and in fact it is) equivalent to the following:

```
((cout << "I have ") << amount) << " in my purse.\n";
```

What value should << return in order to make sense out of the above expression? The first thing evaluated is the subexpression:

```
(cout << "I have ")
```

If things are to work out, then the above subexpression had better return `cout` so that the computation can continue as follows:

```
(cout << amount) << " in my purse.\n";
```

And if things are to continue to work out, (cout << amount) had better also return cout so that the computation can continue as follows:

```
cout << " in my purse.\n";
```

This is illustrated in Display 8.7. The operator << should return its first argument, which is a stream of type ostream.   *<< returns a stream*

Thus, the prototype for the overloaded operator << (to use with the class Money) should be as follows:

```
class Money
{
public:
     ...
    friend ostream& operator <<(ostream& outs, const Money& amount);
    //Precondition: If outs is a file output stream, then outs
    //has already been connected to a file.
    //Postcondition: A dollar sign and the amount of money recorded
    //in the calling object have been sent to the output stream outs.
     . . .
```

Once we have overloaded the insertion (output) operator <<, we will no longer need the member function output, and will delete output from our definition of the class Money. The definition of the overloaded operator << is very similar to the member function output. In outline form, the definition for the overloaded operator is as follows:

```
ostream& operator <<(ostream& outs, const Money& amount)
{
        <This part is the same as the body of
         Money::output which is given in Display 8.3 (except that
          all_cents is replaced with amount.all_cents)>

        return outs;
}
```

There is one thing left to explain in the above prototype and definition for the overloaded operator <<. What is the meaning of the & in the returned type ostream&? The easiest answer is that *whenever an operator (or a function) returns a stream, you must add an & to the end of the name for the returned type.* That simple rule will allow you to overload the operators << and >>. However,   *<< and >> return a reference*

Display 8.7 << as an Operator

```
cout << "I have " << amount << " in my purse.\n";
```

means the same as

```
((cout << "I have ") << amount) << " in my purse.\n";
```

and is evaluated as follows:

First evaluate (cout << "I have "), which returns cout:
```
((cout << "I have ") << amount) << " in my purse.\n";
```

and the string "I have" *is output.*

```
(cout << amount) << " in my purse.\n";
```

Then evaluate (cout << amount), which returns cout:

```
(cout << amount) << " in my purse.\n";
```

and the value of amount *is output.*

```
cout << " in my purse.\n";
```

Then evaluate cout << " in my purse.\n", which returns cout:

```
cout << " in my purse.\n";
```

and the string " in my purse.\n" *is output.*

```
cout;
```

Since there are no more <<
operators, the process ends.

while that is a good working rule that will allow you to write your class definitions and programs, it is not very satisfying. You do not need to know what that & really means, but if we explain it, that will remove some of the mystery from the rule that tells you to add an &.

When you add an & to the name of a returned type, you are saying that the oper- *returning* ator (or function) returns a *reference*. All the functions and operators we have seen *a reference* thus far return values. However, if the returned type is a stream, you cannot simply return the value of the stream. In the case of a stream, the value of the stream is an entire file or the keyboard or the screen, and it may not make sense to return those things. Thus, you want to return only the stream itself rather than the value of the stream. When you add an & to the name of a returned type, you are saying that the operator (or function) returns a **reference,** which means that you are returning the object itself, as opposed to the value of the object.

The extraction operator >> is overloaded in a way that is analogous to what we described for the insertion operator <<. However, with the extraction (input) operator >>, the second argument will be the object that receives the input value, so the second parameter must be an ordinary call-by-reference parameter. In outline form the definition for the overloaded extraction operator >> is:

```
istream& operator >>(istream& ins, Money& amount)
{

        <This part is the same as the body of
         Money::input given in Display 8.3 (except that
         all_cents is replaced with amount.all_cents)>

        return ins;
}
```

The complete definitions of the overloaded operators << and >> are given in Display 8.8, where we have rewritten the class Money yet again. This time we have rewritten the class so that the operators << and >> are overloaded to allow us to use these operators with values of type Money.

Overloading >> and <<

The input and output operators >> and << can be overloaded just like any other operators. The value returned must be the stream. The type for the value returned must have the & symbol added to the end of the type name. The prototypes and beginnings of the function definitions are as shown below. See Display 8.8 for an example.

Prototypes:

```
class Class_Name
{
public:
    . . .
    friend istream& operator >>(istream& Parameter_1,
                                Class_Name& Parameter_2);

    friend ostream& operator <<(ostream& Parameter_3,
                                const Class_Name& Parameter_4);
    . . .
```

Parameter for the stream.

Parameter for the object to receive the input.

Definitions:

```
istream& operator >>(istream& Parameter_1,
                     Class_Name& Parameter_2)
{
    . . .
}

ostream& operator <<(ostream& Parameter_3,
                     const Class_Name& Parameter_4)
{
    . . .
```

Display 8.8 Overloading << and >> *(part 1 of 4)*

```
//Program to demonstrate the class Money.
#include <iostream>
#include <fstream>
#include <cstdlib>
#include <cctype>
using namespace std;

//Class for amounts of money in U.S. currency.
class Money
{
public:
    friend Money operator +(const Money& amount1, const Money& amount2);

    friend Money operator -(const Money& amount1, const Money& amount2);

    friend Money operator -(const Money& amount);

    friend bool operator ==(const Money& amount1, const Money& amount2);

    Money(long dollars, int cents);

    Money(long dollars);

    Money();

    double get_value() const;

    friend istream& operator >>(istream& ins, Money& amount);
    //Overloads the >> operator so it can be used to input values of type Money.
    //Notation for inputting negative amounts is as in -$100.00.
    //Precondition: If ins is a file input stream, then ins has already been
    //connected to a file.

    friend ostream& operator <<(ostream& outs, const Money& amount);
    //Overloads the << operator so it can be used to output values of type Money.
    //Precedes each output value of type Money with a dollar sign.
    //Precondition: If outs is a file output stream,
    //then outs has already been connected to a file.
private:
    long all_cents;
};
```

This is an improved version of the class Money which we gave in Display 8.6.

Although we have omitted some of the comments from Displays 8.5 and 8.6, you should include them.

Display 8.8 Overloading << and >> *(part 2 of 4)*

```
//Prototype for use in the definition of the overloaded input operator >>:
int digit_to_int(char c);
//Precondition: c is one of the digits '0' through '9'.
//Returns the integer for the digit; e.g., digit_to_int('3') returns 3.

int main( )
{
    Money amount;
    ifstream in_stream;
    ofstream out_stream;

     in_stream.open("infile.dat");
     if (in_stream.fail( ))
     {
         cout << "Input file opening failed.\n";
         exit(1);
     }

     out_stream.open("outfile.dat");
     if (out_stream.fail( ))
     {
         cout << "Output file opening failed.\n";
         exit(1);
     }

    in_stream >> amount;
    out_stream << amount
               << " copied from the file infile.dat.\n";
    cout << amount
         << " copied from the file infile.dat.\n";

    in_stream.close( );
    out_stream.close( );

    return 0;
}
```

Display 8.8 Overloading << and >> *(part 3 of 4)*

```
//Uses iostream, cctype, cstdlib:
istream& operator >>(istream& ins, Money& amount)
{
    char one_char, decimal_point,
        digit1, digit2; //digits for the amount of cents
    long dollars;
    int cents;
    bool negative;//set to true if input is negative.

    ins >> one_char;
    if (one_char == '-')
    {
        negative = true;
        ins >> one_char; //read '$'
    }
    else
        negative = false;
    //if input is legal, then one_char == '$'

    ins >> dollars >> decimal_point >> digit1 >> digit2;

    if ( one_char != '$' || decimal_point != '.'
         || !isdigit(digit1) || !isdigit(digit2) )
    {
        cout << "Error illegal form for money input\n";
        exit(1);
    }
    cents = digit_to_int(digit1)*10 + digit_to_int(digit2);

    amount.all_cents = dollars*100 + cents;
    if (negative)
        amount.all_cents = -amount.all_cents;

    return ins;
}

int digit_to_int(char c)
{
    return ( int(c) - int('0') );
}
```

Display 8.8 Overloading << and >> *(part 4 of 4)*

```
//Uses cstdlib and iostream:
ostream& operator <<(ostream& outs, const Money& amount)
{
    long positive_cents, dollars, cents;
    positive_cents = labs(amount.all_cents);
    dollars = positive_cents/100;
    cents = positive_cents%100;

    if (amount.all_cents < 0)
        outs << "-$" << dollars << '.';
    else
        outs << "$" << dollars << '.';

    if (cents < 10)
        outs << '0';
    outs << cents;

    return outs;
}
```

<The definitions of the member functions and other overloaded operators go here.
See Displays 8.3, 8.4, 8.5, and 8.6 for the definitions.>

infile.dat (Not changed by program.)	**outfile.dat** (After program is run.)
$1.11 $2.22 $3.33	$1.11 copied from the file infile.dat.

Screen Output

$1.11 copied from the file infile.dat.

SELF-TEST EXERCISE

17 Below is the definition for a class called `Percent`. Objects of type `Percent`
represent percentages such as 10% or 99%. Give the definitions of the overloaded operators `>>` and `<<` so that they can be used for input and output with
objects of the class `Percent`. Assume that input always consists of an integer
followed by the character '**%**', such as **25%**. All percentages are whole numbers and are stored in the *int* member variable named `value`. You do not need
to define the other overloaded operators and do not need to define the constructor. You only have to define the overloaded operators `>>` and `<<`.

```
#include <iostream>
using namespace std;

class Percent
{
public:
    friend bool operator ==(const Percent& first,
                            const Percent& second);

    friend bool operator <(const Percent& first,
                           const Percent& second);

    Percent();

    friend istream& operator >>(istream& ins,
                               Percent& the_object);
    //Overloads the >> operator to input values of type
    //Percent.
    //Precondition: If ins is a file input stream, then ins
    //has already
    //been connected to a file.

    friend ostream& operator <<(ostream& outs,
                               const Percent& a_percent);
    //Overloads the << operator for output values of type
    //Percent.
    //Precondition: If outs is a file output stream, then
    //outs has already been connected to a file.
private:
    int value;
};
```

8.2 Separate Compilation

From mine own library with volumes that
I prize above my dukedom.

WILLIAM SHAKESPEARE, THE TEMPEST

C++ has facilities for dividing a program into parts that are kept in separate files, compiled separately, and then linked together when (or just before) the program is run. You can place the definition for an ADT class (and its associated function definitions) in files that are separate from the programs that use the ADT. That way you can build up a library of ADTs so that many programs can use the same ADT. You can compile the ADT once and then use it in many different programs, just like you use the predefined libraries such as those with header files `iostream` and `cstdlib`. Moreover, you can define the ADT itself in two files so that the specification of what the ADT does is separate from how the ADT is implemented. If you only change the implementation of the ADT, then you need only recompile the file with the ADT implementation. The other files, including the files with the programs that use the ADT, need not be changed or even recompiled. In this section we tell you how to carry out this separate compilation of ADTs.

ADTs Reviewed

In order to define a class so that it is an abstract data type, you need to separate the specification of how the class is used by a programmer from the details of how the class is implemented. The separation should be so complete that you can change the implementation and any program that uses the abstract data type should not need to be changed at all. The way to ensure this separation can be summarized in three rules:

1 Make all the member variables private members of the class.

2 Make each of the basic operations for the ADT either a public member function of the class, a friend function, an ordinary function, or an overloaded operator. Group the class definition and the function and operator prototypes together. This group, along with its accompanying comments, is called the **interface** for the ADT. Fully specify how to use each such function or operator in a comment given with the class or with the function or operator prototype.

3 Make the implementation of the basic operations unavailable to the programmer who uses the abstract data type. The **implementation** consists of the function definitions and overloaded operator definitions (along with any helping functions or other additional items these definitions require).

In C++, the best way to ensure that you follow these rules is to place the interface and the implementation of the ADT class in separate files. As you might guess, the file that contains the interface is often called the **interface file,** and the file that contains the implementation is called the **implementation file.** The exact details of how to set up, compile, and use these files will vary slightly from one version of C++ to another, but the basic scheme is the same in all versions of C++. In particular, the details of what goes into the files is the same in all systems. The only things that vary are what commands you use to compile and link these files. The details about what goes into these files are illustrated in the next Case Study.

An ADT has private member variables. Private member variables (and private member functions) present a problem to our basic philosophy of placing the interface and the implementation of an ADT in separate files. The public part of the class definition for an ADT is part of the interface for the ADT, but the private part is part of the implementation. This is a problem because C++ will not allow you to split the class definition across two files. Thus, some sort of compromise is needed. The only sensible compromise, and the one we will use, is to place the entire class definition in the interface file. Since a programmer who is using the ADT cannot use any of the private members of the class, the private members will, in effect, still be hidden from the programmer.

interface file and implementation files

Private members are part of the implementation.

Case Study	DigitalTime**—An ADT Compiled Separately**

Display 8.9 contains the interface file for an ADT called DigitalTime. DigitalTime is a class whose values are times of day, such as 9:30. Only the public members of the class are part of the interface. The private members are part of the implementation, even though they are in the interface file. The label *private:* warns you that these private members are not part of the public interface. Everything that a programmer needs to know in order to use the ADT DigitalTime is explained in the comment at the start of the file and in the comments in the public section of the class definition. This interface tells the programmer how to use the two versions of the member function named advance, the constructors, and the overloaded operators ==, >>, and <<. The member functions named advance, the overloaded operators, and the assignment statement are the only ways that a programmer can manipulate objects and values of this class. As noted in the comment at the top of the interface file, this ADT uses 24-hour notation, so, for instance, 1:30 PM is input and output as 13:30. This and the other details you must know in order to effectively use the class DigitalTime are included in the comments given with the member functions.

interface file

Display 8.9 Interface File for the DigitalTime **ADT**

```
//This is the HEADER FILE dtime.h. This is the INTERFACE for the class DigitalTime.
//Values of this type are times of day. The values are input and output in
//24 hour notation as in 9:30 for 9:30 AM and 14:45 for 2:45 PM.
#include <iostream>
using namespace std;
```

For the definition of the types istream and ostream which are used as parameter types.

```
class DigitalTime
{
public:
    friend bool operator ==(const DigitalTime& time1, const DigitalTime& time2);
    //Returns true if time1 and time2 represent the same time;
    //otherwise, returns false.

    DigitalTime(int the_hour, int the_minute);
    //Precondition: 0 <= the_hour <= 23 and 0 <= the_minute <= 59.
    //Initializes the time value to the_hour and the_minute.

    DigitalTime();
    //Initializes the time value to 0:00 (which is midnight).

    void advance(int minutes_added);
    //Precondition: The object has a time value.
    //Postcondition: The time value has been changed to minutes_added minutes later.

    void advance(int hours_added, int minutes_added);
    //Precondition: The object has a time value.
    //Postcondition: The time value has been advanced
    //hours_added hours plus minutes_added minutes.

    friend istream& operator >>(istream& ins, DigitalTime& the_object);
    //Overloads the >> operator for input values of type DigitalTime.
    //Precondition: If ins is a file input stream, then ins has already been
    //connected to a file.

    friend ostream& operator <<(ostream& outs, const DigitalTime& the_object);
    //Overloads the << operator for output values of type DigitalTime.
    //Precondition: If outs is a file output stream, then outs has already been
    //connected to a file.
private:
    int hour;
    int minute;
};
```

This is part of the implementation. It is not part of the interface. The word private *indicates that this is not part of the public interface.*

We have placed the interface in a file named dtime.h. The suffix .h indicates
that this is a header file. An interface file is always a header file and so always ends
with the suffix .h. Any program that uses the class DigitalTime must contain an
include directive like the following, which names this file:

header files

```
#include "dtime.h"
```

When you write an include directive, you must indicate whether the header file is a
predefined header file that is provided for you or is a header file that you wrote. If the
header file is predefined, you write the header file name in angular brackets, like
<iostream>. If the header file is one that you wrote, then you write the header file
name in quotes, like "dtime.h". This distinction tells the compiler where to look
for the header file. If the header file name is in angular brackets, the compiler looks
wherever the predefined header files are kept in your implementation of C++. If the
header file name is in quotes, the compiler looks in the current directory or wherever
programmer-defined header files are kept on your system.

include

Any program that uses our DigitalTime ADT must contain the above include
directive that names the header file dtime.h. That is enough to allow you to compile
the program, but is not enough to allow you to run the program. In order to run the
program you must write (and compile) the definitions of the member functions and
the overloaded operators. We have placed these function and operator definitions in
another file, which is called the **implementation file.** Although it is not required by
most compilers, it is tradition to give the interface file and the implementation file
the same name. The two files do, however, end in different suffixes. We have placed
the interface for our ADT in the file named dtime.h and the implementation for our
ADT in a file named dtime.cxx. The suffix you use on the implementation file
depends on your version of C++. Use the same suffix on the implementation file as
you normally use on files that contain C++ programs. If your program files end in
.c, then you would use .c in place of .cxx. If your program files end in .CPP, then
your implementation files will end in .CPP instead of .cxx. If your program files
end in .hxx, then you would use .hxx in place of .cxx. If your program files end in
.hpp, then your implementation files will end in .hpp instead of .cxx. We are using
.cxx to stand in for whatever it is that your system uses as the suffix for a file that
contains a C++ program. The implementation file for our DigitalTime ADT is
given in Display 8.10. After we explain how the various files for our ADT interact
with each other, we will return to Display 8.10 and discuss the details of the definitions in this implementation file.

implementation file

file names

In order to use the ADT DigitalTime in a program, the program must contain
the include directive

```
#include "dtime.h"
```

Display 8.10 Implementation File (part 1 of 4)

```
//This is the IMPLEMENTATION FILE: dtime.cxx (Your system may require some
//suffix other than .cxx). This is the IMPLEMENTATION of the ADT DigitalTime.
//The interface for the class DigitalTime is in the header file dtime.h.
#include <iostream>
#include <cctype>
#include <cstdlib>
#include "dtime.h"
using namespace std;

//These PROTOTYPES are for the definition of the overloaded input operator >>:

void read_hour(istream& ins, int& the_hour);
//Precondition: Next input in the stream ins is a time in notation, like 9:45 or
//14:45.
//Postcondition: the_hour has been set to the hour part of the time.
//The colon has been discarded and the next input to be read is the minute.

void read_minute(istream& ins, int& the_minute);
//Reads the minute from the stream ins after read_hour has read the hour.

int digit_to_int(char c);
//Precondition: c is one of the digits '0' through '9'.
//Returns the integer for the digit; e.g., digit_to_int('3') returns 3.

bool operator ==(const DigitalTime& time1, const DigitalTime& time2)
{
    return (time1.hour == time2.hour && time1.minute == time2.minute);
}

//Uses iostream and cstdlib:
DigitalTime::DigitalTime(int the_hour, int the_minute)
{
    if (the_hour < 0 || the_hour > 23 || the_minute < 0 || the_minute > 59)
    {
        cout << "Illegal argument to DigitalTime constructor.";
        exit(1);
    }
    else
    {
        hour = the_hour;
        minute = the_minute;
    }
}
```

Display 8.10 Implementation File *(part 2 of 4)*

```
DigitalTime::DigitalTime( )
{
    hour = 0;
    minute = 0;
}

void DigitalTime::advance(int minutes_added)
{
    int gross_minutes = minute + minutes_added;
    minute = gross_minutes%60;

    int hour_adjustment = gross_minutes/60;
    hour = (hour + hour_adjustment)%24;
}

void DigitalTime::advance(int hours_added, int minutes_added)
{
    hour = (hour + hours_added)%24;
    advance(minutes_added);
}

//Uses iostream:
istream& operator >>(istream& ins, DigitalTime& the_object)
{
    read_hour(ins, the_object.hour);
    read_minute(ins, the_object.minute);
    return ins;
}

//Uses iostream:
ostream& operator <<(ostream& outs, const DigitalTime& the_object)
{
    outs << the_object.hour << ':';
    if (the_object.minute < 10)
        outs << '0';
    outs << the_object.minute;
    return outs;
}
```

Display 8.10 Implementation File *(part 3 of 4)*

```
int digit_to_int(char c)
{
    return ( int(c) - int('0') );
}


//Uses iostream, cctype, and cstdlib:
void read_hour(istream& ins, int& the_hour)
{
    char c1, c2;
    ins >> c1 >> c2;
    if ( !( isdigit(c1) && (isdigit(c2) || c2 == ':' ) ) )
    {
        cout << "Error illegal input to read_hour\n";
        exit(1);
    }

    if (isdigit(c1) && c2 == ':')
    {
        the_hour = digit_to_int(c1);
    }
    else //(isdigit(c1) && isdigit(c2))
    {
        the_hour = digit_to_int(c1)*10 + digit_to_int(c2);
        ins >> c2;//discard ':'
        if (c2 != ':')
        {
            cout << "Error illegal input to read_hour\n";
            exit(1);
        }
    }

    if ( the_hour < 0 || the_hour > 23 )
    {
        cout << "Error illegal input to read_hour\n";
        exit(1);
    }
}
```

Display 8.10 Implementation File *(part 4 of 4)*

```
//Uses iostream, cctype, and cstdlib:
void read_minute(istream& ins, int& the_minute)
{
    char c1, c2;
    ins >> c1 >> c2;

    if (!(isdigit(c1) && isdigit(c2)))
    {
        cout << "Error illegal input to read_minute\n";
        exit(1);
    }

    the_minute = digit_to_int(c1)*10 + digit_to_int(c2);

    if (the_minute < 0 || the_minute > 59)
    {
        cout << "Error illegal input to read_minute\n";
        exit(1);
    }
}
```

Notice that both the implementation file and the program file must contain this `include` directive that names the interface file. The file that contains the program (that is, the file that contains the `main` part of the program) is often called the **application file.** Display 8.11 contains an application file with a very simple program that uses and demonstrates the `DigitalTime` ADT.

application file

The exact details on how you run this complete program, which is contained in three files, depend on what system you are using. However, the basic details are the same for all systems. You must compile the implementation file and you must compile the application file that contains the `main` part of your program. You do not compile the interface file, which in this example is the file `dtime.h` given in Display 8.9. You do not need to compile the interface file because the compiler thinks the contents of this interface file are already contained in each of the other two files. Recall that both the implementation file and the application file contain the directive

compiling and running the program

```
#include "dtime.h"
```

Display 8.11 Application File Using `DigitalTime` **ADT**

```
//This is the APPLICATION FILE: timedemo.cxx. (Your system may require some
//suffix other than .cxx). This program demonstrates use of the class
//DigitalTime.
#include <iostream>
#include "dtime.h"
using namespace std;

int main()
{
    DigitalTime clock, old_clock;

    cout << "Enter the time in 24 hour notation: ";
    cin >> clock;

    old_clock = clock;
    clock.advance(15);
    if (clock == old_clock)
        cout << "Something is wrong.";
    cout << "You entered " << old_clock << endl;
    cout << "15 minutes later the time will be "
         << clock << endl;

    clock.advance(2, 15);
    cout << "2 hours and 15 minutes after that\n"
         << "the time will be "
         << clock << endl;

    return 0;
}
```

Sample Dialogue

```
Enter the time in 24 hour notation: 11:15
You entered 11:15
15 minutes later the time will be 11:30
2 hours and 15 minutes after that
the time will be 13:45
```

Compiling your program automatically invokes a preprocessor that reads this include directive and replaces this include directive with the text in the file dtime.h. Thus, the compiler sees the contents of dtime.h, and so the file dtime.h does not need to be compiled separately. (In fact, the compiler sees the contents of dtime.h twice: once when you compile the implementation file and once when you compile the application file.) This copying of the file dtime.h is only a conceptual copying. The compiler acts as if the contents of dtime.h were copied into each file that has the include directive. However, if you look in that file after it is compiled, you will only find the include directive; you will not find the contents of the file dtime.h.

Once the implementation file and the application file are compiled, you still need to connect these files so that they can work together. This is called **linking** the files, and is done by a separate utility called a **linker.** The details for how you call the linker depends on what system you are using. After the files are linked, you can run your program.

linking

This sounds like a complicated process, but many systems have facilities that manage much of this detail for you automatically or semiautomatically. On any system, the details quickly become routine.

Displays 8.9, 8.10, and 8.11 contain one complete program divided into pieces and placed in three different files. You could instead combine the contents of these three files into one file, and then compile and run this one file without all this fuss about include directives and linking separate files. Why bother with three separate files? There are several advantages to dividing your program into separate files. Since you have the definition and the implementation of the class DigitalTime in files separate from the application file, you can use this class in many different programs without needing to rewrite the definition of the class in each of the programs. Moreover, you need to compile the implementation file only once, no matter how many programs use the class DigitalTime. But there are more advantages than that. Since you have separated the interface from the implementation of your DigitalTime ADT, you can change the implementation file and will not need to change any program that uses the ADT. In fact, you will not even need to recompile the program. If you change the implementation file, you only need to recompile the implementation file and to relink the files. Saving a bit of recompiling time is nice, but the big advantage is not having to rewrite code. You can use the ADT in many programs without writing the ADT code into each program. You can change the implementation of the ADT and you need not rewrite any part of any program that uses the ADT.

Why separate files?

Now that we have explained how the various files in our ADT and program are used, let's discuss the implementation of our ADT (Display 8.10) in more detail. Most of the implementation details are straightforward, but there are two things that merit comment. Notice that the member function name advance is overloaded so

implementation details

Defining an ADT Class in Separate Files
A Summary

You can define an ADT as a class and place the definition of the class and the implementation of its member functions in separate files. You can then compile the ADT separately from any program that uses the ADT and you can use this same ADT in any number of different programs. The ADT is placed in three files as follows:

1 Put the definition of the class in a header file called the **interface file.** The name of this header file ends in `.h`. The interface file also contains the prototypes for any functions and overloaded operators that define basic ADT operations but that are not listed in the class definition. Include comments that explain how all these functions and operators are used.

2 The definitions of all the functions and overloaded operators mentioned in 1 (whether they are members or friends or neither) are placed in another file called the **implementation file.** This file must contain an `include` directive that names the interface file described above. This `include` directive uses quotes around the file name as in the following example:

```
#include "dtime.h"
```

The interface file and the implementation file traditionally have the same name, but end in different suffixes. The interface file ends in `.h`. The implementation file ends in the same suffix that you use for files that contain a complete C++ program. The implementation file is compiled separately before it is used in any program.

3 When you want to use the ADT in a program, you place the `main` part of the program (and any additional function definitions, constant declarations, and such) in another file called an **application file.** This file also must contain an `include` directive naming the interface file, as in the following example:

```
#include "dtime.h"
```

The application file is compiled separately from the implementation file. You can write any number of these application files to use with one pair of interface and implementation files. To run an entire program, you must first link the object code produced by compiling the application file and the object code produced by compiling the implementation file. (On some systems the linking may be done automatically or semiautomatically.)

that it has two function definitions. Also notice that the definition for the overloaded extraction (input) operator >> uses two "helping functions" called read_hour and read_minute and these two helping functions themselves use a third helping function called digit_to_int. Let's discuss these points.

The class DigitalTime (Display 8.9 and Display 8.10) has two member functions called advance. One version takes a single argument, that is an integer giving the number of minutes to advance the time. The other version takes two arguments, one for a number of hours and one for a number of minutes, and advances the time by that number of hours plus that number of minutes. Notice that the definition of the two-argument version of advance includes a call to the one-argument version of advance. Look at the definition of the two-argument version that is given in Display 8.10. First the time is advanced by hours_added hours and then the single argument version of advance is used to advance the time by an additional minutes_added minutes. At first this may seem strange, but it is perfectly legal. The two functions named advance are two different functions that, as far as the compiler is concerned, just coincidentally happen to have the same name. The situation is no different in this regard than it would be if one of the two versions of the overloaded function advance had been called another_advance.

advance

Now let's discuss the helping functions. The helping functions read_hour and read_minute read the input one character at a time and then convert the input to integer values that are placed in the member variables hour and minute. The functions read_hour and read_minute read the hour and minute one digit at a time, so they are reading values of type *char*. This is more complicated than reading the input as *int* values, but it allows us to perform error checking to see whether the input is correctly formed and to issue an error message if the input is not well formed. These helping functions read_hour and read_minute use another helping function named digit_to_int, which is the same as the digit_to_int function we used in our definition of the class Money. The function digit_to_int converts a digit, such as '3', to a number, such as 3.

↪ *PROGRAMMING* ⟩ *TIP*
Hiding the Helping Functions

When you define the member functions for a class you may need to define some helping functions that you use in the body of one or more member function definitions. For example, look at the definition of the overloaded operator >> in Display 8.10. That definition uses the helping functions read_hour and read_minute, which in turn use the helping function digit_to_int. When you divide a class

Reusable Components

An ADT developed and coded into separate files is a software component that can be used again and again in a number of different programs. **Reusability,** such as the reusability of these ADTs, is an important goal to strive for when designing software components. A reusable component saves effort because it does not need to be redesigned, recoded, and retested for every application. A reusable component is also likely to be more reliable than a component that is used only once. It is likely to be more reliable for two reasons. First, you can afford to spend more time and effort on a component if it will be used many times. Second, if the component is used again and again, it is tested again and again. Every use of a software component is a test of that component. Using a software component many times in a variety of contexts is one of the best ways to discover any remaining bugs in the software.

ADT description into an interface file and an implementation file, you normally place all these helping functions in the implementation file. When you place them in the implementation file, the helping functions will not be available to any program that uses the ADT. Moreover, this allows you to revise the implementation of the ADT, including changing or removing or adding helping functions, and any program that uses the ADT will not need to be changed.

Using #ifndef

We have given you a method for placing a program in three files: two for the interface and implementation of a class and one for the application part of the program. A program can be kept in more than three files. For example, a program might use several classes and each class might be kept in a separate pair of files. Suppose you have a program spread across a number of files and more than one file has an `include` directive for a class interface file such as the following

```
#include "dtime.h"
```

Under these circumstances you can have files that include other files and these other files may in turn include yet other files. This can easily lead to a situation in which a file, in effect, contains the definitions in `dtime.h` more than once. C++ does not allow you to define a class more than once, even if the repeated definitions are identical. Moreover, if you are using the same header file in many different projects, it becomes close to impossible to keep track of whether or not you included the class definition more than once. To avoid this problem, C++ provides a way of marking a section of code to say "if you have already included this stuff once before, do not include it again." The way this is done is quite intuitive, although the notation may look a bit weird until you get used to it. We will go through an example, explaining the details as we go.

The following directive **defines** DTIME_H:

```
#define DTIME_H
```

What this means is that the compiler's preprocessor puts DTIME_H on a list to indicate that DTIME_H has been seen. *Defined* is perhaps not the best word for this, since DTIME_H is not defined to mean anything but merely put on a list. The important point is that you can use another directive to test whether or not DTIME_H has been defined and so test whether or not a section of code has already been processed. You can use any (nonkeyword) identifier in place of DTIME_H, but you will see that there are standard conventions for which identifier you should use.

The following directive tests to see whether or not DTIME_H has been defined:

```
#ifndef DTIME_H
```

If DTIME_H has already been defined, then everything between this directive and the first occurrence of the following directive is skipped:

```
#endif
```

(An equivalent way to state this, which may clarify the way the directives are spelled, is the following: If DTIME_H is *not* defined, then the compiler processes everything up to the next #endif. That *not* is why there is an n in #ifndef. This may lead you to wonder whether there is a #ifdef directive as well as a #ifndef directive. There is and it has the obvious meaning, but we will have no occasion to use #ifdef.)

Now consider the code:

```
#ifndef DTIME_H
#define DTIME_H
<a class definition>
#endif
```

If this code is in a file named dtime.h, then no matter how many times your program contains

```
#include "dtime.h"
```

the class will be defined only one time.

The first time

```
#include "dtime.h"
```

is processed, the flag DTIME_H is defined and the class is defined. Now, suppose the compiler again encounters

```
#include "dtime.h"
```

When the include directive is processed this second time, the directive

```
#ifndef DTIME_H
```

says to skip everything up to

```
#endif
```

and so the class is not defined again.

In Display 8.12 we have rewritten the header file dtime.h shown in Display 8.9, but this time we used these directives to prevent multiple definitions. With the ver-

Display 8.12 Avoiding Multiple Definitions of a Class

```
//This is the HEADER FILE dtime.h. This is the INTERFACE for the class
//DigitalTime.
//Values of this type are times of day. The values are input and output in
//24 hour notation as in 9:30 for 9:30 AM and 14:45 for 2:45 PM.

#ifndef DTIME_H
#define DTIME_H

#include <iostream>
using namespace std;

class DigitalTime
{

        <The definition of the class DigitalTime is the same as in Display 8.9.>

};

#endif //DTIME_H
```

sion of dtime.h shown in Display 8.12, if a file contains the following include directive more than once, the class DigitalTime will still be defined only once:

```
#include "dtime.h"
```

You may use some other identifier in place of DTIME_H, but the normal convention is to use the name of the file written in all uppercase letters with the underscore used in place of the period. You should follow this convention so that others can more easily read your code and so that you do not have to remember the flag name. This way the flag name is determined automatically and there is nothing arbitrary to remember.

These same directives can be used to skip over code in files other than header files, but we will not have occasion to use these directives except in header files.

➥ *PROGRAMMING* TIP
Choosing ADT Operations

When you define the interface for an ADT you should think of yourself as adding a new data type to the C++ language. If you later discover that you need to change a member function or add another member function to your ADT, you can go back and change the definition of the ADT, just as the designers of the C++ language can and sometimes do go back to add or change features in C++. However, you should try to avoid having to make such changes. If the C++ language is changed, some or all of the programs written in C++ might need to be rewritten. If you change the definition of an ADT that you have previously defined, then some or all of the programs that use the ADT might need to be rewritten. In order to avoid this rewriting, you should choose the member functions for your ADTs with care.

When you define an ADT, you should make every attempt to include all the member functions, nonmember functions, and overloaded operators that you might later need as basic ADT operations. You need not include every function you might later use in a program. Many of the functions you would use in a program can be defined using these basic functions as building blocks, but you do want to ensure that you have an adequate repertoire of building blocks. For example, you usually need to overload the >> operator or else add some other basic input function so that you can input values of the ADT type. However, you need not include input functions that give prompt lines for each possible situation. The prompt line may depend on the particular program in which it is used and may change from program to program. The situation for ADTs is the same as the situation for predefined types like *int*. The C++ language provides the programmer with the ability to read a value of type *int*, but the programmer provides the details, such as the prompt lines, that are peculiar to one particular program. At a minimum, an ADT would normally contain functions (or overloaded operators) for each of the following tasks:

1. Constructors for setting and changing the data value(s) of an object of the ADT, including a default constructor.
2. Some way to test two objects to see whether or not they represent the same data value(s). Typically this is done by overloading the == operator.
3. A method for inputting data for the value(s) of an object of the ADT type. Often, the best way to do this is by overloading the extraction operator >>.
4. A method for outputting the data value(s) of an object of the ADT type. Often, the best way to do this is by overloading the insertion operator <<.
5. Some functions to perform *basic* operations. For example, the (overloaded) function to advance the time in the `DigitalTime` ADT is an example of such basic functions. Which functions you include will depend on the particular ADT.

When defining an ADT, it is important to include all the basic functions you are likely to need. However, it is even more important that you carefully design the function prototypes and rules for using the functions that you do choose to include in your ADT. If you later discover that you need another basic function, you can add it to the ADT; the older programs that have no need for this new function will not need to be rewritten (though you may need to recompile and relink the old programs). However, if you change the prototype for a function or the instructions for how to use the function, then you will need to rewrite some or even all of the old programs that use the ADT. If you do not change any of the old functions or overloaded operators, but only add new functions and overloaded operators to your ADT, then your new ADT is said to be **backward-compatible.** It is important to try to keep any revised software component backward-compatible, but unless the original component was carefully designed, this can be difficult to do. Thus, you should take the time to carefully design the interface for ADT operations.

PROGRAMMING TIP
Defining Other Libraries

You need not define an ADT in order to use separate compilation. If you have a collection of related functions that you want to make into a library of your own design, you can place the function prototypes and accompanying comments in a header file and the function definitions in an implementation file, just as we outlined for ADTs. After that, you can use this library in your programs the same way you would use a class ADT that you placed in separate files.

SELF-TEST EXERCISES

18 Suppose that you are defining an ADT as a class and that you then use this ADT in a program. You want to separate the ADT and program parts into separate files as described in this chapter. Tell whether each of the following should be placed in the interface file, implementation file, or application file.

   a The class definition.

   b The prototype for a function that is to serve as an ADT operation, but that is neither a member nor a friend of the class.

   c The prototype for an overloaded operator that is to serve as an ADT operation, but that is neither a member nor a friend of the class.

   d The definition for a function that is to serve as an ADT operation, but that is neither a member nor a friend of the class.

   e The definition for a friend function that is to serve as an ADT operation.

   f The definition for a member function.

   g The definition for an overloaded operator that is to serve as an ADT operation, but that is neither a member nor a friend of the class.

   h The definition for an overloaded operator that is to serve as an ADT operation and that is a friend of the class.

   i The main part of your program.

19 Which of the following files has a name that ends in .h: the interface file for an ADT, the implementation file for the ADT, or the application file that uses the ADT?

20 When you define an ADT in separate files, there is an interface file and an implementation file. Which of these files need to be compiled? (Both? Neither? Only one? If so, which one?)

21 Suppose you define an ADT in separate files and use the ADT in a program. Now suppose you change the ADT implementation file. Which of the following files, if any, need to be recompiled: the interface file, the implementation file, and/or the application file?

22 Suppose you want to change the implementation of the ADT DigitalTime given in Display 8.9 and Display 8.10. Specifically, you want to change the way the time is recorded. Instead of using the two private variables hour and minute, you want to use a single (private) *int* variable, which will be called minutes. In this new implementation the private variable minutes will record the time as the number of minutes since the time 0:00 (that is, since midnight). So 1:30 is recorded as 90 minutes, since it is 90 minutes past

midnight. Describe how you need to change the interface and implementation files shown in Display 8.9 and Display 8.10. You need not write out the files in their entirety; just indicate what items you need to change and how, in a very general way, you would change them.

8.3 Namespaces

namespace

When a program uses different classes and functions written by different programmers there is a possibility that two programmers will use the same name for two different things. Namespaces are a way to deal with this problem. A **namespace** is a collection of name definitions, such as class definitions and variable declarations.

Namespaces and Using Directives

We have already been using the namespace that is named `std`. The `std` namespace contains all the names defined in the standard library files (such as `iostream` and `cstdlib`) that you use. For example, when you place the following at the start of a file

```
#include <iostream>
```

that places all of the name definitions (for names like `cin` and `cout`) into the `std` namespace. Your program does not know about names in the `std` namespace unless you specify that it is using the `std` namespace. So far, the only way we know how to specify the `std` namespace (or any namespace) is with the following sort of *using* directive:

```
using namespace std;
```

A good way to see why you might want to include this *using* directive is to think about why you might want to *not* include it. *If you do not include this using directive for the namespace* `std`, then you can define `cin` and `cout` to have some meaning other than their standard meaning. (Perhaps you want to redefine `cin` and `cout` because you want them to behave a bit differently from the standard versions.) Their standard meaning is in the `std` namespace, and without the *using* directive (or something like it), your code knows nothing about the `std` namespace, and so, as far as your code is concerned, the only definitions of `cin` and `cout` are whatever definition you give them.

*global
namespace*

Every bit of code you write is in some namespace. If you do not place the code in some specific namespace, then the code is in a namespace known as the **global namespace**. So far we have not placed any code we wrote in any namespace, so all of our code has been in the global namespace. The global namespace does not have a *using* directive because you are always using the global namespace. You could say that there is always an implicit automatic *using* directive that says you are using the global namespace.

Note that you can be using more than one namespace at the same time. For example, we are always using the global namespace and we are usually using the std namespace. What happens if a name is defined in two namespaces and you are using both namespaces? This results in an error (either a compiler error or a run-time error depending on the exact details). You can have the same name defined in two different namespaces, but if that is true, then you can only use one of those namespaces at a time. However, this does not mean you cannot use the two namespaces in the same program. You can use them each at different times in the same program.

For example, suppose ns1 and ns2 are two namespaces and suppose my_function is a *void* function with no arguments that is defined in both namespaces but defined in different ways in the two namespaces, then the following is legal:

```
{
    using namespace ns1;
    my_function( );
}
{
    using namespace ns2;
    my_function( );
}
```

The first invocation would use the definition of my_function given in the namespace ns1 and the second invocation would use the definition of the my_function given in the namespace ns2.

Recall that a block is a list of statements, declarations, and possible other code, enclosed in braces {}. A *using* directive at the start of a block applies only to that block. So the first *using* directive applies only in the first block and the second *using* directive applies only in the second block. The usual way of phrasing this is to say that the **scope** of the ns1 namespace is the first block, while the scope of the ns2 namespace is the second block. Note that because of this scope rule, we are able to use two conflicting namespaces in the same program (such as in a program that contains the two blocks we discussed in the previous paragraph).

scope

When you use a *using* directive in a block, it is typically the block consisting of the body of a function definition. If you place a *using* directive at the start of a file (as we have usually done so far), then the *using* directive applies to the entire file. (A *using* directive should normally be placed near the start of a file or the start of a block.)

Creating a Namespace

In order to place some code in a namespace, you simply place it in a **namespace grouping** of the following form:

```
namespace Name_Space_Name
{
    Some_Code
}
```

When you include one of these groupings in your code, you are said to place the names defined in *Some_Code* into the namespace *Name_Space_Name*. These names (really the definitions of these names) can be made available with the *using* directive

```
using namespace Name_Space_Name;
```

For example, the following, taken from Display 8.13, places a function prototype in the namespace savitch1:

```
namespace savitch1
{
    void greeting( );
}
```

If you look again at Display 8.13, you see that the definition of the function greeting is also placed in namespace savitch1. That is done with the following additional namespace grouping:

```
namespace savitch1
{
    void greeting( )
    {
        cout << "Hello from namespace savitch1.\n";
    }
}
```

Note that you can have any number of these namespace groupings for a single namespace. In Display 8.13, we used two namespace groupings for namespace savitch1 and two other groupings for namespace savitch2.

Every name defined in a namespace is available inside the namespace groupings, but the names can be also be made available to code outside of the namespace. That prototype and function definition in the namespace savitch1 can be made available with the *using* directive

```
using namespace savitch1
```

as illustrated in Display 8.13.

Display 8.13 Namespace Demonstration *(part 1 of 2)*

```
#include <iostream>
using namespace std;

namespace savitch1
{
    void greeting( );
}

namespace savitch2
{
    void greeting( );
}

void big_greeting( );

int main( )
{
    {
        using namespace savitch2;
        greeting( );
    }

    {
        using namespace savitch1;
        greeting( );
    }

    big_greeting( );

    return 0;
}
```

Names in this block use definitions in namespaces savitch2, std, and the global namespace

Names in this block use definitions in namespaces savitch1, std, and the global namespace

Names out here only use definitions in namespaces std, and the global namespace

Display 8.13 Namespace Demonstration *(part 2 of 2)*

```
namespace savitch1
{
    void greeting( )
    {
        cout << "Hello from namespace savitch1.\n";
    }
}

namespace savitch2
{
    void greeting( )
    {
        cout << "Greetings from namespace savitch2.\n";
    }
}

void big_greeting( )
{
    cout << "A Big Global Hello!\n";
}
```

Sample Dialogue

```
Greetings from namespace savitch2.
Hello from namespace savitch1.
A Big Global Hello!
```

Scope Rule for *using* Directives

The scope of a *using* directive is the block in which it appears (more precisely from the location of the *using* directive to the end of the block). If the *using* directive is outside of all blocks, then it applies to all of the file that follows the *using* directive.

SELF-TEST EXERCISES

23 Consider the program shown in Display 8.13. Could we use the name greeting in place of big_greeting?

24 In Exercise 23, we saw that you could *not* add a definition for the following function (to the global namespace):

```
void greeting( );
```

Can you add a definition for the following function prototype to the global namespace?

```
void greeting(int how_many );
```

Qualifying Names

Suppose you are faced with the following situation: You have two namespaces ns1 and ns2. You want to use the function fun1 defined in ns1 and the function fun2 defined in namespace ns2. The complication is that both ns1 and ns2 define a function my_function. (Assume all functions in this discussion take no arguments, so overloading does not apply). You cannot use;

```
using namespace ns1;
using namespace ns2;
```

This would provide confliction definitions for my_function.

What you need is a way to say you are using fun1 in namespace ns1 and fun2 in namespace ns2 and nothing else in the namespaces ns1 and ns2. The following is your answer:

```
using ns1::fun1;
using ns2::fun2;
```

A directive of the form

```
using Name_Space::One_Name
```

makes (definition of) the name *One_Name* from the namespace *Name_Space* available, but does not make any other names in *Name_Space* available.

Note that you have seen the scope resolution operator : : before. For example, in Display 8.10 we had the following function definition:

```
void DigitalTime::advance(int hours_added, int minutes_added)
{
    hour = (hour + hours_added)%24;
    advance(minutes_added);
}
```

In this case the : : means that we are defining the function `advance` for the class `DigitalTime`, as opposed to any other function named `advance` in any other class. Similarly,

```
using ns1::fun1;
```

means we are using the named `fun1` as defined in the namespace `ns1`, as opposed to any other definition of `fun1` in any other namespace.

Now suppose that you intend to use the name `fun1` as defined in the namespace `ns1`, but you intend to use it only one time (or a small number of times), then you can name the function (or other item) using the name of the namespace and the scope resolution operator, as in:

```
ns1::fun1( );
```

This form is often used when specifying a parameter type. For example, consider

```
int get_number(std::istream input_stream)
    . . .
```

In the function `get_number`, the parameter `input_stream` is of type `istream` where `istream` is defined as in the `std` namespace. If this use of the type name `istream` is the only name you need from the `std` namespace (or if all the names you need are similarly qualified with `std::`), then you do *not* need

```
using namespace std;
```

SELF-TEST EXERCISES

25 Write the prototype for a *void* function named wow. The function wow has two parameters, the first of type `speed` as defined in the `speedway` namespace and the second of type `speed` as defined in the `indy500` namespace.

26 Consider the following function prototypes from the definition of the class Money in Display 8.6.

```
void input(istream& ins);
void output(ostream& outs) const;
```

Rewrite these prototypes so that they do not need to be preceded by

```
using namespace std;
```

▪)) *PROGRAMMING EXAMPLE*
A Class Definition in a Namespace

In Displays 8.14 and 8.15 we have again rewritten both the header file dtime.h for the class DigitalTime and the implementation file for the class DigitalTime. This time (no pun intended), we have placed the definition in a namespace called savitchdtime. (It is a good idea to include your name or some other unique string in the names of your namespaces, so as to reduce the chance that somebody else will use the same namespace name as you do.)

Display 8.14 Placing a Class in a Namespace (Header File)

```
//This is the HEADER FILE dtime.h. This is the INTERFACE for the class
//DigitalTime.
//Values of this type are times of day. The values are input and output in
//24-hour notation, as in 9:30 for 9:30 AM and 14:45 for 2:45 PM.

#ifndef DTIME_H
#define DTIME_H

#include <iostream>
using namespace std;

namespace savitchdtime
{

    class DigitalTime
    {

     <The definition of the class DigitalTime is the same as in Display 8.9.>
    };
}//end savitchdtime

#endif //DTIME_H
```

If you rewrite the definition of the class DigitalTime as shown in Displays 8.14 and 8.15, then the application program in Display 8.11 needs to be rewritten to give access to the namespace savitchdtime. We do this in Display 8.16.

Display 8.15 Placing a Class in a Namespace (Implementation File)

```
//This is the IMPLEMENTATION FILE: dtime.cxx (your system may require some
//suffix other than .cxx). This is the IMPLEMENTATION of the ADT DigitalTime.
//The interface for the class DigitalTime is in the header file dtime.h.
#include <iostream>
#include <cctype>
#include <cstdlib>
#include "dtime.h"
using namespace std;

namespace savitchdtime
{

    <All the prototypes and function definitions from Display 8.10 go here.>

}//end savitchdtime
```

Display 8.16 Application Program Using a Namespace (part 1 of 2)

```
//This is the APPLICATION FILE: timedemo.cxx. (Your system may require some
//suffix other than .cxx). This program demonstrates use of the class
//DigitalTime.
#include <iostream>
#include "dtime.h"

int main()
{
    using namespace std;
    using namespace savitchdtime;

    DigitalTime clock, old_clock;
```

If you place the using directives here, then the program behavior will be the same. However, it is a good practice to make the scope of each using directive as small as you can.

Display 8.16 Application Program Using a Namespace *(part 2 of 2)*

```
    cout << "Enter the time in 24 hour notation: ";
    cin >> clock;

    old_clock = clock;
    clock.advance(15);
    if (clock == old_clock)
        cout << "Something is wrong.";
    cout << "You entered " << old_clock << endl;
    cout << "15 minutes later the time will be "
        << clock << endl;

    clock.advance(2, 15);
    cout << "2 hours and 15 minutes after that\n"
        << "the time will be "
        << clock << endl;

    return 0;
}
```

The sample dialog is the same as in Display 8.11.

CHAPTER SUMMARY

- A **friend** function of a class is an ordinary function except that it has access to the private members of the class, just like the member functions do.

- If your classes each have a full set of accessor functions, then the only reason to make a function a friend is to make the definition of the friend function simpler and more efficient, but that is often reason enough.

- A parameter of a class type that is not changed by the function should normally be a constant parameter.

- Operators, such as + and ==, can be overloaded so they can be used with objects of a class type that you define.

- When overloading the >> or << operators, the type returned should be a stream type and the type returned must be a reference, which is indicated by appending an & to the name of the returned type.

- In C++, abstract data types (ADTs) are implemented as classes with all member variables private, and with the operations implemented as public member and nonmember functions and overloaded operators.

- You can define an ADT as a class and place the definition of the class and the implementation of its member functions in separate files. You can then compile the ADT separately from any program that uses it and you can use this same ADT in any number of different programs.

Answers to Self-Test Exercises

1

```
bool before(DayOfYear date1, DayOfYear date2)
{
    return ( (date1.get_month( ) < date2.get_month( ))
          || (date1.get_month( ) == date2.get_month( )
                  && date1.get_day( ) < date2.get_day( )) );
}
```

The above Boolean expression says that date1 is before date2, provided the month of date1 is before the month of date2 or else the months are the same and the day of date1 is before the day of date2.

2 A friend function and a member function are alike in that they both can use any member of the class (either public or private) in their function definition. However, a friend function is defined and used just like an ordinary function; the dot operator is not used when you call a friend function and no type qualifier is used when you define a friend function. A member function, on the other hand, is called using an object name and the dot operator. Also, a member function definition includes a type qualifier consisting of the class name and the scope resolution operator::.

3 The modified definition of the class DayOfYear is shown below. The part in color is new. We have omitted some comments to save space, but all the comments shown in Display 8.2 should be included in this definition.

```
class DayOfYear
{
public:
    friend bool equal(DayOfYear date1, DayOfYear date2);

    friend bool after(DayOfYear date1, DayOfYear date2);
    //Precondition: date1 and date2 have values.
```

```
     //Returns true if date1 follows date2 on the calendar,
     //otherwise returns false.
     DayOfYear(int the_month, int the_day);
     DayOfYear();
     void input();
     void output();
     int get_month();
     int get_day();
private:
     int month;
     int day;
};
```

You also must add the following definition of the function `after`:

```
bool after(DayOfYear date1, DayOfYear date2)
{
     return ( (date1.month > date2.month) ||
              ((date1.month == date2.month) && (date1.day > date2.day) ) );
}
```

4 The modified definition of the class Money is shown below. The part in color
is new. We have omitted some comments to save space, but all the comments
shown in Display 8.3 should be included in this definition.

```
class Money
{
public:
     friend Money add(Money amount1, Money amount2);

     friend Money subtract(Money amount1, Money amount2);
     //Precondition: amount1 and amount2 have been given
     //values.
     //Returns amount1 minus amount2.

     friend bool equal(Money amount1, Money amount2);
     Money(long dollars, int cents);
     Money(long dollars);
     Money();
     double get_value();

     void input(istream& ins);
     void output(ostream& outs);
```

```
private:
    long all_cents;
};
```

You also must add the following definition of the function `subtract`:

```
Money subtract(Money amount1, Money amount2)
{
    Money temp;
    temp.all_cents = amount1.all_cents
                            - amount2.all_cents;
    return temp;
}
```

5 The modified definition of the class Money is shown below. The part in color is new. We have omitted some comments to save space, but all the comments shown in Display 8.3 should be included in this definition.

```
class Money
{
public:
    friend Money add(Money amount1, Money amount2);
    friend int equal(Money amount1, Money amount2);
    Money(long dollars, int cents);
    Money(long dollars);
    Money();
    double get_value();
    void input(istream& ins);

    void output(ostream& outs);
    //Precondition: If outs is a file output stream, then
    //outs has already been connected to a file.
    //Postcondition: A dollar sign and the amount of money
    //recorded in the calling object has been sent to the
    //output stream outs.

    void output();
    //Postcondition: A dollar sign and the amount of money
    //recorded in the calling object has been output to the
    //screen.
private:
    long all_cents;
};
```

You also must add the following definition of the function name `output`. (The old definition of `output` stays so that there are two definitions of `output`.)

```
void Money::output( )
{
    output(cout);
}
```

The following longer version of the function definition also works:

```
//Uses cstdlib and iostream
void Money::output( )
{
    long positive_cents, dollars, cents;
    positive_cents = labs(all_cents);
    dollars = positive_cents/100;
    cents = positive_cents%100;

    if (all_cents < 0)
        cout << "-$" << dollars << '.';
    else
        cout << "$" << dollars << '.';

    if (cents < 10)
        cout << '0';
    cout << cents;
}
```

You can also overload the member function `input` so that a call like

```
purse.input( );
```

means the same as

```
purse.input(cin);
```

And, of course, you can combine this enhancement with the enhancements from previous Self-Test Exercises to produce one highly improved class `Money`.

6 If the user enters **$-9.95** (instead of –**$9.95**), the function `input` will read the `'$'` as the value of `one_char`, the –9 as the value of `dollars`, the `'.'` as the value of `decimal_point`, and the `'9'` and `'5'` as the values of `digit1` and `digit2`. That means it will set `dollars` equal to –9 and `cents` equal to

95 and so set the amount equal to a value that represents –**$9.00** plus **0.95** which is –**$8.05**. One way to catch this problem is to test if the value of `dollars` is negative (since the value of `dollars` should be an absolute value). To do this rewrite the error message portion to the following:

```
if ( one_char != '$' || decimal_point != '.'
        || !isdigit(digit1) || !isdigit(digit2)
        || dollars < 0 )  ◄──────── New
{
    cout << "Error illegal form for money input\n";
    exit(1);
}
```

This still will not give an error message for incorrect input with zero dollars as in $–0.95. However, with the material we have learned thus far, a test for this case, while certainly possible, would significantly complicate the code and make it harder to read.

7

```
#include <iostream>
using namespace std;
int main( )
{
    int x;
    cin >> x;
    cout << x << endl;
    return 0;
}
```

If the compiler interprets input with leading 0 as a base-eight numeral, then with input data 077, the output should be 63. The output should be 77 if the compiler does not interpret data with leading 0 as indicating base eight.

8 The only change from the version given in Display 8.3 is that the modifier *const* is added to the function heading, so the definition is:

```
double Money::get_value( ) const
{
    return (all_cents * 0.01);
}
```

9 The member function `input` changes the value of its calling object and so the compiler will issue an error message if you add the *const* modifier.

10 Similarities: Each parameter call method protects the caller's argument from change. Differences: If the type is a large `struct` or `class` object, the call-by-value makes a copy of the caller's argument, so uses much more memory than call-by-constant-reference. The value parameter acts like a modifiable local variable, whereas the call-by-const-reference parameter cannot be modified.

11 In the *const int* x = 17; the const keyword promises the compiler that code written by the author will not change the value of x.

In the `int f() const`; declaration, the *const* keyword is a promise to the compiler that code written by the author to implement function f will not change anything in the calling object.

In the *int g(const A& x)*; the *const* keyword is a promise to the compiler that code written by the class author will not change the argument plugged in for x.

12 The difference between a (binary) operator (such as +, *, /, and so forth) and a function involves the syntax of how they are called. In a function call, the arguments are given in parentheses after the function name. With an operator the arguments are given before and after the operator. Also, you must use the reserved word *operator* in the prototype and in the definition of an over-loaded operator.

13 The modified definition of the class Money is shown below. The part in color is new. We have omitted some comments to save space, but all the comments shown in Display 8.5 should be included in this definition.

```
class Money
{
public:
    friend Money operator +(const Money& amount1,
                            const Money& amount2);
    friend bool operator ==(const Money& amount1,
                            const Money& amount2);

    friend bool operator < (const Money& amount1,
                            const Money& amount2);
    //Precondition: amount1 and amount2 have been given
    //values.
    //Returns true if amount1 is less than amount2;
    //otherwise, returns false.

    Money(long dollars, int cents);
```

```
    Money(long dollars);
    Money( );
    double get_value( ) const;
    void input(istream& ins);
    void output(ostream& outs) const;
private:
    long all_cents;
};
```

You also must add the following definition of the overloaded operator <:

```
bool operator < (const Money& amount1,
                              const Money& amount2)
{
    return (amount1.all_cents < amount2.all_cents);
}
```

14 When overloading an operator, at least one of the arguments to the operator
must be of a class type. This prevents changing the behavior of + for integers.
Actually, this requirement prevents changing the effect of any operator on
any built-in type.

15

```
//Uses cmath (for floor):
Money::Money(double amount)
{
    all_cents = floor(amount*100);
}
```

The definition above simply discards any amount that is less than one cent.
For example, it converts 12.34999 to the integer 1234 which represents the
amount $12.34. It is possible to define the constructor to instead do other
things with any fraction of a cent.

16

```
istream& operator>>(istream& ins, Pairs& second)
{
    char ch;
    ins>>ch;          //discard initial '('
    ins>>second.f;
    ins>>ch;          //discard comma ','
    ins>>second.s;
```

```
    ins>>ch;          //discard final ')'
    return ins;
}
ostream& operator<<(ostream& outs, const Pairs& second)
{
    outs<<'(';
    outs<<second.f;
    outs<<',';
    outs<<second.s;
    outs<<')';
    return outs;
}
```

17

```
//Uses iostream:
istream& operator >>(istream& ins, Percent& the_object)
{
    char percent_sign;
    ins >> the_object.value;
    ins >> percent_sign;//Discards the % sign.
    return ins;
}
//Uses iostream:
ostream& operator <<(ostream& outs,
                             const Percent& a_percent)
{
    outs << a_percent.value << '%';
    return outs;
}
```

18 Parts a, b, and c go in the interface file; d through h go in the implementation
    file. (All the definitions of ADT operations of any sort go in the implementa-
    tion file.) Part i (i.e., the main part of your program) goes in the application
    file.

19 The name of the interface file ends in .h.

20 Only the implementation file needs to be compiled. The interface file does
    not need to be compiled.

21 Only the implementation file needs to be recompiled. You do, however, need to relink the files.

22 You need to delete the private member variables hour and minute from the interface file shown in Display 8.9 and replace them with the member variable minutes (with an s). You do not need to make any other changes in the interface file. In the implementation file, you need to change the definitions of all the constructors and other member functions, as well as the definitions of the overloaded operators, so they work for this new way of recording time. (In this case, you do not need to change any of the helping functions read_hour, read_minute, or digit_to_int, but that might not be true for some other ADT or even some other reimplementation of this ADT.) For example, the definition of the overloaded operator >> could be changed to the following:

```
istream& operator >>(istream& ins, DigitalTime& the_object)
{
    int input_hour, input_minute;
    read_hour(ins, input_hour);
    read_minute(ins, input_minute);
    the_object.minutes = input_minute + 60*input_hour;
    return ins;
}
```

You need not change any application files for programs that use the ADT. However, since the interface file is changed (as well as the implementation file), you will need to recompile any application files, and of course you will need to recompile the implementation file.

23 No. If you replace big_greeting with greeting, then you will have a definition for the name greeting in the global namespace. There are parts of the program where all the names definitions in the namespace savitch1 and all the name definitions in the global namespace are simultaneously available. In those parts of the program, there would be two distinct definitions for

```
void greeting( );
```

24 Yes, the additional definition would cause no problems. This is because overloading is always allowed. When, for example, the namespaces savitch1 and the global namespace are available, the function name greeting would be overloaded. The problem in Exercise 23 was that there

would sometimes be two definitions of the function name `greeting` with the exact same parameter lists.

```
25  void wow(speedway::speed s1, indy500::speed s2);

26

    void input(std::istream& ins);
       void output(std::ostream& outs) const;
```

Programming Projects

1 Add the following member function to the ADT `DigitalTime` defined in Display 8.9 and Display 8.10:

```
void DigitalTime::interval_since(const DigitalTime& a_previous_time,
                int& hours_in_interval, int& minutes_in_interval) const
```

This function computes the time interval between two values of type `DigitalTime`. One of the values of type `DigitalTime` is the object that calls the member function `interval_since` and the other value of type `DigitalTime` is given as the first argument. For example, consider the following code:

```
DigitalTime current(5, 45), previous(2, 30);
int hours, minutes;
current.interval_since(previous, hours, minutes);
cout << "The time interval between " << previous
     << " and " << current << endl
     << "is " << hours << " hours and "
     << minutes << " minutes.\n";
```

In a program that uses your revised version of the `DigitalTime` ADT, the above code should produce the output:

```
The time interval between 2:30 and 5:45
is 3 hours and 15 minutes.
```

Allow the time given by the first argument to be later in the day than the time of the calling object. In this case, the time given as the first argument is assumed to be on the previous day. You should also write a program to test this revised ADT.

2 Modify the definition of the class Money shown in Display 8.8 so that all of the following are added:

   a The operators <, <=, >, and >= have each been overloaded to apply to the type Money. (Hint: See Self-Test Exercise 13)

   b The following member function has been added to the class definition. (We show the prototype as it should appear in the class definition. The definition of the function itself will include the qualifier Money::.)

```
Money percent(int percent_figure) const;
//Returns a percentage of the money amount in the calling object.
//For example, if percent_figure is 10, then the value returned is
//10% of the amount of money represented by the calling object.
```

   For example, if purse is an object of type Money whose value represents the amount $100.10, then the call

```
      purse.percent(10);
```

   returns 10% of $100.10, that is, it returns a value of type Money that represents the amount $10.01.

3 Do Self-Test Exercise 22 in full detail. Write out the complete ADT including interface and implementation files. Also write a program to test your ADT.

4 The program for this project uses the revised ADT DigitalTime from Programming Project 1 and uses the ADT Money from Programming Project 2. (You can do this exercise using the definition of DigitalTime given in Display 8.9 and Display 8.10 and using the definition of Money given in Display 8.8, but you will find that the extra operations added in Programming Projects 1 and 2 will come in handy.) In this project you will write a program to compute the gross pay for one week for an hourly employee. The program asks for the basic hourly rate of pay and then it asks for the start and stop times for the worker for a day. There may be multiple start and stop times in a day. For example, the worker would normally stop for lunch and then restart after lunch. Assume that the start and stop times are the same for every day from Monday through Friday. Assume the worker only works on the five days Monday through Friday. After gathering the input data, the program displays the total number of hours worked and the gross pay for that number of hours. (The *gross pay* is the number of dollars earned. We call it *gross pay* because, in this program, we do not compute deductions for income tax and other such items.) Your program should use the basic hourly rate of pay for all hours up to 40 hours and use 1.5 times the basic pay rate

for all hours after the first 40 hours worked. If this is a class assignment, ask your instructor if input/output should be done with the keyboard and screen or if it should be done with files. If it is to be done with files, ask your instructor for instructions on file names.

5 Define an ADT for rational numbers. A rational number is a number that can be represented as the quotient of two integers. For example, 1/2, 3/4, 64/2, and so forth are all rational numbers. (By 1/2 etc. we mean the everyday meaning of the fraction, not the integer division this expression would produce in a C++ program.) Represent rational numbers as two values of type *int*, one for the numerator and one for the denominator. Call the class Rational. Include a constructor with two arguments that can be used to set the member variables of an object to any legitimate values. Also, include a constructor that has only a single parameter of type *int*; call this single parameter whole_number and define the constructor so that the object will be initialized to the rational number whole_number/1. Also, include a default constructor that initializes an object to 0 (i.e., to 0/1). Overload the input and output operators >> and <<. Numbers are to be input and output in the form 1/2, 15/32, 300/401, and so forth. Note that the numerator, the denominator, or both may contain a minus sign, so –1/2, 15/–32, and –300/–401 are also possible inputs. Overload all of the following operators so that they correctly apply to the type Rational: ==, <, <=, >, >=, +, –, *, and /. Define your ADT in separate files so that it can be compiled separately. Also write a test program to test your ADT. Hints: Two rational numbers *a/b* and *c/d* are equal if *a*d* equals *c*b*. If *b* and *d* are *positive* rational numbers, *a/b* is less than *c/d* provided *a*d* is less than *c*b*. You should include a function to normalize the values stored so that, after normalization, the denominator is positive and the numerator and denominator are as small as possible. For example, after normalization 4/–8 would be represented the same as –1/2. You should also write a test program to test your ADT.

6 Define an ADT for complex numbers. A complex number is a number of the form

   a + b*i

where for our purposes, *a* and *b* are numbers of type *double*, and *i* is a number that represents the quantity $\sqrt{-1}$. Represent a complex number as two values of type *double*. Name the member variables real and imaginary. (The variable for the number that is multiplied by *i* is the one called imaginary.) Call the class Complex. Include a constructor with two parameters of type *double* that can be used to set the member variables of an object to any values. Also, include a constructor that has only a single parameter of type *double*; call this parameter `real_part` and define the constructor so that the object will be initialized to `real_part + 0*i`. Also, include a default constructor that initializes an object to 0 (i.e., to 0 + 0*i). Overload all of the following operators so that they correctly apply to the type `Complex`: ==, +, −, *, >>, and <<. Define your ADT in a pair of files so that it can be compiled separately. You should also write a test program to test your ADT. Hints: To add or subtract two complex numbers, you add or subtract the two member variables of type *double*. The product of two complex numbers is given by the following formula:

$$(a + b*i)*(c + d*i) == (a*c - b*d) + (a*d + b*c)*i$$

In the interface file, you should define a constant i as follows:

const Complex i(0, 1);

This defined constant i will be the same as the *i* discussed above.

7 Self-Test Exercise 16 asked you to implement `operator>>` and `operator<<` overloading for a `class Pairs`. Complete and test this exercise. Implement a default constructor, and a one and a two `int` parameter constructor. The one parameter constructor should initialize the first member of the pair, the second member of the pair is to be 0.

Overload binary `operator +` to add pairs according to the rule

$$(a, b) + (c, d) = (a + c, b + d)$$

Overload `operator -` analogously.

Overload `operator*` on pairs and *int* according to the rule

$$(a, b) * c = (a * c, b * c)$$

8 This is a detailed extension of an exercise we saw first in Stroustrup. *The C++ Programming Language* 2nd edition, Addison Wesley, 1991, page 254, Exercise 8. If you do this exercise carefully and reflectively, you will gain an understanding of Abstract Data Types, classes and operator overloading that otherwise would take you a long time to gain.

Implement and test a `class INT` that mimics the built-in *int* type.

Details:

Use a single `private` *int* data member.

Implement a default constructor that mimics the fact that the standard *int* type does not initialize an *int*:

```
int x;  //x is left with a garbage value in it
INT xx; //xx is left with a garbage value in it.
```

Implement a constructor that mimics *int* behavior:

```
int x(5);
INT xx(5);
```

Overload binary operators +, -, *, /, ==, <, >, &&, ||, and unary operators !, +, and -. Notice that you can implement <=, >=, == in terms of other relational operators. Hint: Do these one at a time and test, test, test.

Overload each operator << and >> as a *friend* of the INT class.

You should overload operator *int*( ) to convert an INT value to an *int*.

We do not discuss overloading the cast-to-int, i.e., operator *int*( ), in the text so we provide some details. It is used like this:

```
INT Ix(7);
int x;
x = int(Ix);
```

Here is how the overloading is done:

```
class INT
{
   public:
      // ...
          operator int( )
          {
              return i;
          }
private:
   int i;
}
```

One last note: There are things you do not need to do. You are using a single *int* data member, so you do not need an operator assignment overload, nor a copy constructor, nor a destructor.

CHAPTER

9

Arrays

9 Arrays

It is a capital mistake to theorize
before one has data.

SIR ARTHUR CONAN DOYLE,
SCANDAL IN BOHEMIA (SHERLOCK HOLMES)

Introduction

An *array* is used to process a collection of data all of which is of the same type: such as a list of test scores, a list of temperatures, or a list of names. In this chapter we introduce you to the basics of defining and using arrays in C++ and present many of the basic techniques used when designing algorithms and programs that use arrays.

9.1 Introduction to Arrays

Suppose we wish to write a program that reads in five test scores and performs some manipulations on these scores. For instance, the program might compute the highest test score and then output the amount by which each score falls short of the highest. The highest score is not known until all five scores are read in. Hence, all five scores must be retained in storage so that after the highest score is computed each score can be compared to it. To retain the five scores we will need something equivalent to five variables of type *int*. We could use five individual variables of type *int*, but five variables are hard to keep track of. We could make the program more readable by giving the variables related names such as score1, score2, and so forth, but this solution becomes absurd if the number of scores is very large. Imagine doing this if there were one hundred scores instead of just five. The solution we will propose is similar to using a list of variables with related names, but will handle the details much more elegantly.

To solve this programming task we introduce a new C++ construct known as an **array.** An array is very much like a list of variables, each of which has a two-part name. One part of the name is the same for each of the variables that collectively constitute the array. The other part is different for each variable. For example, the names for the five individual variables we need might be score[1], score[2], score[3], score[4], and score[5]. The part that does not change, in this case score, is the name of the array. The part that can change is the integer in the square brackets []. In C++ there are, of course, precise rules for declaring and using arrays.

In particular, we will see that in C++ an array consisting of five numbered variables would be numbered 0 through 4, rather than 1 through 5.

Declaring and Referencing Arrays

In C++, an array consisting of five variables of type *int* can be declared as follows:

```
int score[5];
```

This declaration is like declaring the following five variables to all be of type *int*:

```
score[0], score[1], score[2], score[3], score[4]
```

These individual variables that together make up the array are referred to in a variety of different ways. We will call them **indexed variables,** though they are also sometimes called **subscripted variables** or **elements** of the array. The number in square brackets is called an **index** or a **subscript.** *Indexes are numbered starting with 0, not starting with 1 or any other number except 0.* The number of indexed variables in an array is called the **declared size** of the array, or sometimes simply the **size** of the array. When an array is declared, the size of the array is given in square brackets after the array name. The indexed variables are then numbered (also using square brackets) starting with 0 and ending with the integer that is *one less than the size of the array.*

In our example, the indexed variables were of type *int,* but an array can have indexed variables of any type. For example, to declare an array with indexed variables of type *double,* simply use the type name *double* instead of *int* in the declaration of the array. All the indexed variables for one array are, however, of the same type. This type is called the **base type** of the array. Thus, in our example of the array score, the base type is *int.*

You can declare arrays and regular variables together. For example, instead of using the above declaration for the array score, we could have instead used the following, which declares the two *int* variables next and max in addition to the array score:

```
int next, score[5], max;[1]
```

indexed variable
subscripted variable
element

index, subscript

declared size

base type

---

[1]Though we often honor this advice in the breach, for maximum readability, we encourage you to declare each variable on a separate line. Here this one line might be written as

```
int next;
int score[5];
int max;
```

An indexed variable like `score[3]` can be used anyplace that an ordinary variable of type *int* can be used. For example, with the array `score` declared as above, the following are all legal C++ statements:

```
cin >> score[4] >> score[2];
cout << score[2] << " " << score[4];
cin >> score[3] >> score[0];
max = score[3] + score[0];
cin >> next;
score[1] = next;
score[3] = 42;
```

Do not confuse the two ways to use the square brackets [] with an array name. When used in a declaration, such as

```
int score[5];
```

the number enclosed in the square brackets specifies how many indexed variables the array has. When used anywhere else, the number enclosed in the square brackets tells which indexed variable is meant. For example, `score[0]` through `score[4]` are indexed variables.

The index inside the square brackets need not be given as an integer constant. You can use any expression in the square brackets so long as the expression evaluates to one of the integers 0 through the integer one less than the size of the array. For example, the following will set the value of `score[2]` equal to 99 and write 99 to the screen two times:

```
int student;
student = 2;
score[student] = 99;
cout << score[student] << " " << score[2];
```

Although they may look different, `score[student]` and `score[2]` are the same indexed variable in the above code. That is because in the above code, `student` evaluates to 2. Similarly, when the value of n is 2, the indexed variable `score[n + 1]` is the same variable as `score[3]`.

The identity of an indexed variable, such as `score[i]`, is determined by the value of its index, which in this instance is i. Thus, you can write programs that say things like "do such and such to the ith indexed variable," where the value of i is computed by the program. For example, the program in Display 9.1 reads in scores and processes them in the way we described at the start of this chapter. The first *for*-loop in the program executes the following code four times; once with the index i equal to each of the values 1, 2, 3, and 4. (The index 0 is handled before the loop begins.)

Display 9.1 Program Using an Array

```
//Reads in 5 scores and shows how much each
//score differs from the highest score.
#include <iostream>

int main( )
{
    using namespace std;
    int i, score[5], max;

    cout << "Enter 5 scores:\n";
    cin >> score[0];
    max = score[0];
    for (i = 1; i < 5; i++)
    {
        cin >> score[i];
        if (score[i] > max)
            max = score[i];
        //max is the largest of the values score[0],..., score[i].
    }
    cout << "The highest score is " << max << endl
         << "The scores and their\n"
         << "differences from the highest are:\n";
    for (i = 0; i < 5; i++)
        cout << score[i] << " off by "
             << (max - score[i]) << endl;

    return 0;
}
```

Sample Dialogue

```
Enter 5 scores:
5 9 2 10 6
The highest score is 10
The scores and their
differences from the highest are:
5 off by 5
9 off by 1
2 off by 8
10 off by 0
6 off by 4
```

Display 9.2 Array Terminology

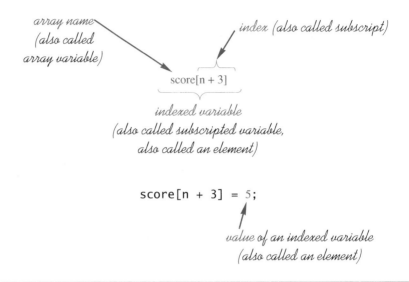

```
cin >> score[i];
if (score[i] > max)
    max = score[i];
```

There is a lot of terminology associated with arrays, and people do not always use the terms consistently, but you quickly adapt to the usage. Display 9.2 summarizes some of the terminology commonly used. Notice that the term **element** can be used to mean an indexed variable and it can also be used to mean the value of an indexed variable. That ambiguity may be unfortunate, but that is common usage and so you are stuck with it.

element

↝ PROGRAMMING TIP
Use for-Loops with Arrays

The second *for*-loop in Display 9.1 illustrates a common way to step through an array using a *for*-loop:

```
for (i = 0; i < 5; i++)
    cout << score[i] << " off by "
        << (max - score[i]) << endl;
```

The *for*-statement is ideally suited to array manipulations. You can step through all the indexed variables of an array called your_array as follows:

> *for* (*int* index = 0; index < *Declared_Size_Of_Array*; index++)
>   Do something to your_array[index]

Array Declaration

Syntax:

Type_Name Array_Name[*Declared_Size*];

Examples:

```
int big_array[100];
double a[3];
double b[5];
char grade[10], one_grade;
```

An array declaration, of the form shown above, will define *Declared_Size* index variables, namely the indexed variables *Array_Name*[0] through *Array_Name*[*Declared_Size*–1]. Each index variable is a variable of type *Type_Name*.

The array a consists of the indexed variables a[0], a[1], and a[2], all of type *double*. The array b consists of the indexed variables b[0], b[1], b[2], b[3], and b[4], also all of type *double*. You can combine array declarations with the declaration of simple variables such as the variable one_grade shown above.

Arrays in Memory

Before we discuss how arrays are represented in a computer's memory, let's review how ordinary variables are represented in memory. Recall that a computer's memory consists of a list of numbered locations called *bytes* and that a variable is represented as a portion of this memory. This portion of memory will consist of some number of bytes; the number of bytes is determined by the type of the variable. Thus, a variable in memory is described by two pieces of information: an address in memory (giving the location of the first byte for that variable) and the type of the variable, which tells how many bytes of memory the variable requires. When we speak of the *address of a variable*, it is this address we are talking about. When your program stores a value in the variable, what really happens is that the value (coded as zeros and ones) is placed in those bytes of memory that are assigned to that variable. Similarly, when a variable is given as a (call-by-reference) argument to a function, it is the address of the variable that is actually given to the calling function. Now that we have reviewed how ordinary variables are stored in memory, let's move on to discuss how arrays are stored in memory. (If this review has not given you a clear picture of how ordinary variables are represented in the computer's memory, you may want to reread the section of Chapter 1 entitled "Hardware.")

arrays in memory

Array indexed variables are represented in memory the same way as ordinary variables, but with arrays there is a little more to the story. The locations of the various array indexed variables are always placed next to one another in memory. For example, consider the following:

```
int a[6];
```

When you declare this array, the computer reserves enough memory to hold six variables of type `int`. Moreover, the computer always places these variables one after the other in memory. The computer then remembers the address of indexed variable a[0], but it does not remember the address of any other indexed variable. When your program needs the address of some other indexed variable, the computer calculates the address for this other indexed variable from the address of a[0]. For example, if you start at the address of a[0] and count past enough memory for three variables of type `int`, then you will be at the address of a[3]. To obtain the address of a[3], the computer starts with the address of a[0] (which is a number). The computer then adds the number of bytes needed to hold three variables of type `int` to the number for the address of a[0]. The result is the address of a[3]. This implementation is diagrammed in Display 9.3. Many of the peculiarities of arrays in C++ can only be understood in terms of these details about memory. For example, in the next pitfall section, we use these details to explain what happens when your program uses an illegal array index.

◆ PITFALL   Array Index Out of Range

The most common programming error made when using arrays is attempting to reference a nonexistent array index. For example, consider the following array declaration:

```
int a[6];
```

illegal
array index

When using the array a, every index expression must evaluate to one of the integers 0 through 5. For example, if your program contains the indexed variable a[i], the i must evaluate to one of the six integers 0, 1, 2, 3, 4, or 5. If i evaluates to anything else that is an error. When an index expression evaluates to some value other than those allowed by the array declaration, the index is said to be **out of range** or simply

Display 9.3 An Array in Memory

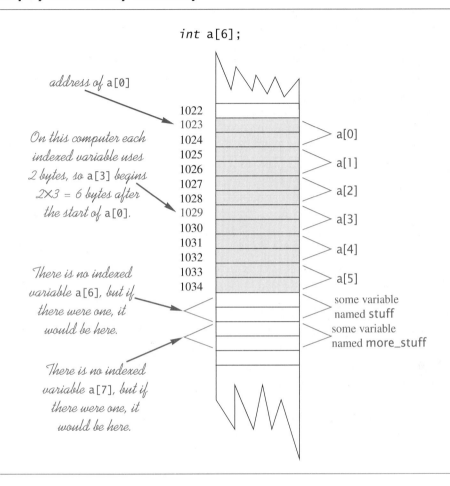

int a[6];

address of a[0]

On this computer each indexed variable uses 2 bytes, so a[3] begins 2×3 = 6 bytes after the start of a[0].

1022
1023
1024
1025
1026
1027
1028
1029
1030
1031
1032
1033
1034

a[0]
a[1]
a[2]
a[3]
a[4]
a[5]

some variable named stuff
some variable named more_stuff

There is no indexed variable a[6], but if there were one, it would be here.

There is no indexed variable a[7], but if there were one, it would be here.

illegal. If your system has a very nice implementation of C++ and this happens, you might receive an error message. Unfortunately, most implementations of C++ do not give such error messages. On most systems, the result of an illegal array index is that your program will simply do something wrong, possibly disastrously wrong, and it will do so without giving you any warning.

For example, suppose your system is typical, the array a is declared as above, and your program contains the following:

```
a[i] = 238;
```

Now, suppose the value of i, unfortunately, happens to be 7. The computer proceeds as if a[7] were a legal indexed variable. The computer calculates the address where a[7] would be (if only there were an a[7]), and places the value 238 in that location in memory. However, there is no indexed variable a[7], and the memory that receives this 238 probably belongs to some other variable, maybe a variable named more_stuff. So the value of more_stuff has been unintentionally changed. The situation is illustrated in Display 9.3.[2]

Array indexes get out of range most commonly at the first or last iteration of a loop that processes the array. Be sure to carefully check all array processing loops to be certain that they begin and end with legal array indexes.

Another common situation that can cause your program to use an illegal array index is when you are filling an array with input to the program. When reading input into an array with a loop, it is easy to attempt to read more values than there are array elements. One way to guard against this sort of error is to test to see if the last array index has been used and to terminate the loop if it has.

Initializing Arrays

A simple variable can be initialized when it is declared, as in the following example:

```
int sum = 0;
```

An array can be initialized in a similar way. When initializing an array in this way, the values for the various indexed variables are enclosed in braces and separated with commas. For example, the following will initialize all three of the indexed variables of the array children:

```
int children[3] = {2, 12, 1};
```

The above declaration is equivalent to the following code:

```
int children[3];
children[0] = 2;
children[1] = 12;
children[2] = 1;
```

If you list fewer values than there are indexed variables, those values will be used to initialize the first few indexed variables, and the remaining indexed variables will be initialized to a zero of the array base type. In this situation, indexed variables not provided with initializers are initialized to 0. However, arrays with no initializers and other variables declared within a function definition or declared within the main part of a program are not initialized. Although array indexed variables (and other

---

[2]This author has seen various effects of an array written with an out-of-range index—from no detectable effect, to the abnormal end of the program, to the operating system crashing, to the next application crashing on startup.

variables) may sometimes be automatically initialized to 0, you cannot and should not count on it.

If you initialize an array when it is declared, you can omit the size of the array, and the array will automatically be declared to have the minimum size needed for the initialization values. For example, the following declaration

```
int b[] = {5, 12, 11};
```

is equivalent to

```
int b[3] = {5, 12, 11};
```

SELF-TEST EXERCISES

1 Describe the difference in the meaning of `int x[5];` and the meaning of `x[4]`. What is the meaning of the `[5]` and `[4]` in each case?

2 In the array declaration

```
double score[5];
```

what is

a. the array name

b. the base type

c. the declared size of the array

d. the range of values an index accessing this array can have

e. one of the indexed variables (or elements) of this array

3 Identify any errors in the following array declarations. This code is assumed to be embedded in an otherwise correct C++ program.

a. `int x[4] = { 8, 7, 6, 4, 3 };`

b. `int x[] = { 8, 7, 6, 4 };`

c. `const int SIZE = 4;`

   `int x[SIZE];`

d. `const int SIZE = 4;`

   `int x[SIZE - 4];`

4 What is the output of the following code (when embedded in a complete and correct program)?

```
char symbol[3] = {'a', 'b', 'c'};
for (int index = 0; index < 3; index++)
    cout << symbol[index];
```

5 What is the output of the following code (when embedded in a complete and correct program)?

```
double a[3] = {1.1, 2.2, 3.3};
cout << a[0] << " " << a[1] << " " << a[2] << endl;
a[1] = a[2];
cout << a[0] << " " << a[1] << " " << a[2] << endl;
```

6 What is the output of the following code (when embedded in a complete and correct program)?

```
int i, temp[10];
for (i = 0; i < 10; i++)
    temp[i] = 2*i;
for (i = 0; i < 10; i++)
    cout << temp[i] << " ";
cout << endl;
for (i = 0; i < 10; i = i + 2)
    cout << temp[i] << " ";
```

7 What is wrong with the following piece of code?

```
int sample_array[10];
for (int index = 1; index <= 10; index++)
    sample_array[index] = 3*index;
```

8 Suppose we expect the elements of the array a to be ordered so that

a[0] ≤ a[1] ≤a[2]≤...

However, to be safe we want our program to test the array and issue a warning in case it turns out that some elements are out of order. The following code is supposed to output such a warning, but it contains a bug; what is it?

```
double a[10];
    <Some code to fill the array a goes here.>
for (int index = 0; index < 10; index++)
    if (a[index] > a[index + 1])
        cout << "Array elements " << index << " and "
            << (index + 1) << " are out of order.";
```

9   Write some C++ code that will fill an array a with 20 values of type *int* read
    in from the keyboard. You need not write a full program, just the code to do
    this, but do give the declarations for the array and for all variables.

10   Suppose you have the following array declaration in your program:

```
int your_array[7];
```

Also, suppose that in your implementation of C++ variables of type *int* use
two bytes of memory. When you run your program, how much memory will
this array consume? Suppose that, when you run your program, the system
assigns the memory address 1000 to the indexed variable your_array[0].
What will be the address of the indexed variable your_array[3]?

9.2 Arrays in Functions

You can use both array indexed variables and entire arrays as arguments to functions. We first discuss array indexed variables as arguments to functions.

Indexed Variables as Function Arguments

An indexed variable can be an argument to a function in exactly the same way that
any variable can be an argument. For example, suppose a program contains the following declarations:

```
int i, n, a[10];
```

If my_function takes one argument of type *int*, then the following is legal:

```
my_function(n);
```

Since an indexed variable of the array a is also a variable of type *int*, just like n, the
following is equally legal:

```
my_function(a[3]);
```

There is one subtlety that does apply to indexed variables used as arguments.
For example, consider the following function call:

```
my_function(a[i]);
```

If the value of i is 3, then the argument is a[3]. On the other hand, if the value of i
is 0, then this call is equivalent to the following:

```
my_function(a[0]);
```

The indexed expression is evaluated in order to determine exactly which indexed variable is given as the argument.

Display 9.4 contains a simple example of indexed variables used as function arguments. The program shown there gives five additional vacation days to each of three employees in a small business. The program is extremely simple, but it does illustrate how indexed variables are used as arguments to functions. Notice the function `adjust_days`. This function has a formal parameter called `old_days` which is of type *int*. In the main body of the program, this function is called with the argument `vacation[number]` for various values of `number`. Notice that there was nothing special about the formal parameter `old_days`. It is just an ordinary formal parameter of type *int*, which is the base type of the array `vacation`. In Display 9.4 the indexed variables are call-by-value arguments. The same remarks apply to call-by-reference arguments. An indexed variable can be a call-by-value argument or a call-by-reference argument.

⬢ PITFALL   Array Indexes Always Start with Zero

The indexes of an array always start with 0 and end with the integer that is one less than the size of the array. Sometimes it is more natural to think in terms of some other numbering scheme. For example, in the program in Display 9.4 the employees are numbered 1, 2, and 3. But the indexes for the array `vacation` are numbered 0, 1, and 2. This means we need to do some manipulation of the employee number to get the correct index for the employee. The number of vacation days for employee `number` is stored in the indexed variable `vacation[number–1]`, not in `vacation[number]`. If you forget that array indexes start with 0 and attempt to use indexed variables `vacation[1]` through `vacation[3]`, instead of `vacation[0]` through `vacation[2]`, then you will be using an illegal index, because there is no such indexed variable as `vacation[3]`. If your program attempts to use `vacation[3]`, it will be reading and/or making changes to random places in memory.

↝ PROGRAMMING TIP
Use a Defined Constant for the Size of an Array

Look again at the program in Display 9.4. It only works for businesses that have exactly three employees. Most businesses do not have exactly three employees. One way to make a program more versatile is to use a defined constant for the size of each array. In Display 9.4 we used the defined constant NUMBER_OF_EMPLOYEES as the size of our array. In order to use this program for a business with 50 employees,

Display 9.4 Indexed Variable as an Argument

```cpp
//Illustrates the use of an indexed variable as an argument.
//Adds 5 to each employee's allowed number of vacation days.
#include <iostream>

const int NUMBER_OF_EMPLOYEES = 3;

int adjust_days(int old_days);
//Returns old_days plus 5.

int main( )
{
    using namespace std;
    int vacation[NUMBER_OF_EMPLOYEES], number;

    cout << "Enter allowed vacation days for employees 1"
         << " through " << NUMBER_OF_EMPLOYEES << ":\n";
    for (number = 1; number <= NUMBER_OF_EMPLOYEES; number++)
        cin >> vacation[number-1];

    for (number = 0; number < NUMBER_OF_EMPLOYEES; number++)
        vacation[number] = adjust_days(vacation[number]);

    cout << "The revised number of vacation days are:\n";
    for (number = 1; number <= NUMBER_OF_EMPLOYEES; number++)
        cout << "Employee number " << number
             << " vacation days = " << vacation[number-1] << endl;

    return 0;
}
int adjust_days(int old_days)
{
    return (old_days + 5);
}
```

Sample Dialogue

```
Enter allowed vacation days for employees 1 through 3:
10 20 5
The revised number of vacation days are:
Employee number 1 vacation days = 15
Employee number 2 vacation days = 25
Employee number 3 vacation days = 10
```

you would only need to change the constant declaration to the following and you need not even look at the rest of the program:

```
const int NUMBER_OF_EMPLOYEES = 50;
```

SELF-TEST EXERCISES

11 Consider the following function definition:

```
void tripler(int& n)
{
    n = 3*n;
}
```

Which of the following are acceptable function calls?

```
int a[3] = {4, 5, 6}, number = 2;
tripler(number);
tripler(a[2]);
tripler(a[3]);
tripler(a[number]);
tripler(a);
```

12 What (if anything) is wrong with the following code? The definition of `tripler` is given in Self-Test Exercise 11.

```
int b[5] = {1, 2, 3, 4, 5};
for (int i = 1; i <= 5; i++)
    tripler(b[i]);
```

Entire Arrays as Function Arguments

review of formal parameters and arguments

You have seen that an indexed variable of an array can be used as an argument to a function. It is also possible to use an entire array as an argument to a function, but the way that is done in C++ requires a bit of explanation. Before we explain these entire array parameters, let's review the terminology we have learned for describing other kinds of function parameters. Recall that a **formal parameter** is a kind of place holder that occurs in a function definition and that is filled in with an argument when the function is called. An **argument** is given in parentheses when the function is called. When the function is called, each argument is *plugged in* for its corresponding formal parameter and then the code in the function body (with the arguments plugged in) is executed. For example, suppose a function definition begins as follows:

```
void sample_function(int n1, int& n2)
{
    ...
```

Then n1 and n2 are formal parameters, and the two *int* variables v1 and v2, in the following function call, are arguments:

```
sample_function(v1, v2);
```

The formal parameter n1 in the above example is a call-by-value parameter. This means that n1 is actually a local variable for the function sample_function. When the function is called this local variable n1 is initialized to the value of v1. Since n1 is a call-by-value parameter, only the value of v1 is used. Thus, no matter what changes are made to n1 in the function body, the value of v1 is not changed by the function call. On the other hand, the formal parameter n2, in the above example, is a call-by-reference parameter. This means that when the function sample_function is called, the argument v2 itself (not just its value) is plugged in

Display 9.5 Function with an Array Parameter

Function Prototype:

```
void fill_up(int a[], int size);
//Precondition: size is the declared size of the array a.
//The user will type in size integers.
//Postcondition: The array a is filled with size integers
//from the keyboard.
```

Function Definition:

```
//Uses iostream:
void fill_up(int a[], int size)
{
    using namespace std;
    cout << "Enter " << size << " numbers:\n";
    for (int i = 0; i < size; i++)
        cin >> a[i];
    size--;
    cout << "The last array index used is " << size << endl;
}
```

for the formal parameter n2. To phrase it more precisely, the function `sample_function` uses the memory location assigned to v2 in place of the formal parameter n2, so any change that is made to n2 in the function body will actually be made to v2. Thus, the function call can change the value of v2.

array parameters

A function can have a formal parameter for an entire array so that when the function is called, the argument that is plugged in for this formal parameter is an entire array. However, a formal parameter for an entire array is neither a call-by-value parameter nor a call-by-reference parameter; it is a new kind of formal parameter referred to as an **array parameter.** Let's start with an example.

The function defined in Display 9.5 has one array parameter a, which will be replaced by an entire array when the function is called. It also has one ordinary call-by-value parameter (`size`) that is assumed to be an integer value equal to the size of the array. This function fills its array argument (that is, fills all the array's indexed variables) with values typed in from the keyboard, and then the function outputs a message to the screen telling the index of the last array index used.

The formal parameter *int* a[] is an array parameter. The square brackets, with no index expression inside, are what C++ uses to indicate an array parameter. An array parameter is *not* quite a call-by-reference parameter, but for most practical purposes it behaves very much like a call-by-reference parameter. Let's go through this example in detail to see how an array argument works in this case. (An **array argument** is, of course, an array that is plugged in for an array parameter, such as a[].)

When the function `fill_up` is called it must have two arguments: the first gives an array of integers and the second should give the declared size of the array. For example, the following is an acceptable function call:

```
int score[5], number_of_scores = 5;
fill_up(score, number_of_scores);
```

when to use []

This call to `fill_up` will fill the array `score` with five integers typed in at the keyboard. Notice that the formal parameter a[] (which is used in the function prototype and the heading of the function definition) is given with square brackets, but no index expression. (You may insert a number inside the square brackets for an array parameter, but the compiler will simply ignore the number, so we will not use such numbers in this book.) On the other hand, the argument given in the function call (`score` in this example) is given without any square brackets or any index expression.

What happens to the array argument `score` in this function call? Very loosely speaking, the argument `score` is *plugged in* for the formal array parameter a in the body of the function, and then the function body is executed. Thus, the function call

```
fill_up(score, number_of_scores);
```

is equivalent to the code:

```
{
     size = 5;          ← 5 is the value of
                          number_of_scores
     cout << "Enter " << size << " numbers:\n";
     for (int i = 0; i < size; i++)
          cin >> score[i];
     size--;
     cout << "The last array index used is " << size << endl;
}
```

Note that `size` is a call-by-value parameter and so is a local variable that is initialized with the value of the corresponding argument `number_of_scores`; the argument `number_of_scores` is not changed even though the value of the formal parameter `size` is changed by the decrement operator `size--`. However, the formal parameter `a` is not a local variable; the formal parameter `a` is merely a placeholder for the argument `score`. When the function `fill_up` is called with `score` as the array argument, the computer behaves as if `a` were replaced with the corresponding argument `score`. *When an array is used as an argument in a function call, any action that is performed on the array parameter is performed on the array argument, so the values of the indexed variables of the array argument can be changed by the function.* If the formal parameter in the function body is changed (for example, with a `cin`-statement), then the array argument will be changed.

So far it looks like an array parameter is simply a call-by-reference parameter for an array. That is close to being true, but an array parameter is slightly different from a call-by-reference parameter. To help explain the difference, let's review some details about arrays.

Recall that an array is stored as a contiguous chunk of memory. For example, consider the following declaration for the array `score`:

arrays in memory

```
int score[5];
```

When you declare this array, the computer reserves enough memory to hold five variables of type `int`, which are stored one after the other in the computer's memory. The computer does not remember the addresses of each of these five indexed variables; it remembers only the address of indexed variable `score[0]`. The computer also remembers that `score` has a total of five indexed variables, all of type `int`. It does not remember the address in memory of any indexed variable other than `score[0]`. For example, when your program needs `score[3]`, the computer calculates the address of `score[3]` from the address of `score[0]`. The computer knows that `score[3]` is located three `int` variables past `score[0]`. Thus, to obtain the address of `score[3]` the computer takes the address of `score[0]` and adds a number that represents the amount of memory used by three *int* variables; the result is the address of score[3].

array argument

Viewed this way, an array has three parts: the address (location in memory) of the first indexed variable, the base type of the array (which determines how much memory each indexed variable uses), and the size of the array (i.e., the number of indexed variables). When an array is used as an array argument to a function, only the first of these three parts is given to the function. When an array argument is plugged in for its corresponding formal parameter, all that is plugged in is the address of the array's first indexed variable. The base type of the array argument must match the base type of the formal parameter, so the function also knows the base type of the array. *However, the array argument does not tell the function the size of the array.* When the code in the function body is executed, the computer knows where the array starts in memory and how much memory each indexed variable uses, but (unless you make special provisions) *it does not know how many indexed variables the array has.* That is why it is critical that you always have another *int* argument telling the function the size of the array. (That is also why an array parameter is *not* the same as a call-by-reference parameter. You can think of an array parameter as a weak form of call-by-reference parameter in which everything about the array is told to the function *except for the size of the array.*)

Different size array arguments can be plugged in for the same array parameter

These array parameters may seem a little strange, but these array parameters have at least one very nice property as a direct result of their seemingly strange definition. This advantage is best illustrated by again looking at our example of the function fill_up given in Display 9.5. *That same function can be used to fill an array of any size,* as long as the base type of the array is *int*. For example, suppose you have the following array declarations:

```
int score[5], time[10];
```

The first of the following calls to fill_up fills the array score with five values and the second fills the array time with ten values:

```
fill_up(score, 5);
fill_up(time, 10);
```

You can use the same function for array arguments of different sizes, because the size is a separate argument.

The *const* Parameter Modifier

When you use an array argument in a function call, the function can change the values stored in the array. This is usually fine. However, in a complicated function definition you might write code that inadvertently changes one or more of the values stored in an array, even though the array should not be changed at all. As a check, you can tell the compiler that you do not intend to change the array argument, and the computer will then check to make sure your code does not inadvertently change

---

Array Formal Parameters and Arguments

An argument to a function may be an entire array, but an argument for an entire array is neither a call-by-value argument nor a call-by-reference argument. It is a new kind of argument known as an **array argument.** When an array argument is plugged in for an **array parameter,** all that is given to the function is the address in memory of the first indexed variable of the array argument (the one indexed by 0). The array argument does not tell the function the size of the array. Therefore, when you have an array parameter to a function, *you normally must also have another formal parameter of type int that gives the size of the array* (as in the example below).

An array argument is like a call-by-reference argument in the following way: if the function body changes the array parameter, then when the function is called, that change is actually made to the array argument. Thus, a function can change the values of an array argument (that is, can change the values of its indexed variables).

The syntax for a function prototype with an array parameter is:

Syntax:

Type_Returned Function_Name(..., *Base_Type Array_Name*[],...);

Example:

```
void sum_array(double& sum, double a[], int size);
```

---

any of the values in the array. To tell the compiler that an array argument should not be changed by your function, you insert the modifier *const* before the array parameter for that argument position. An array parameter that is modified with a *const* is called a **constant array parameter.**

For example, the following function outputs the values in an array, but does not change the values in the array:

```
void show_the_world(int a[], int size_of_a)
//Precondition: size_of_a is the declared size of the array a.
//All indexed variables of a have been given values.
//Postcondition: The values in a have been written to the
//screen.
{
    using namespace std;
    cout << "The array contains the following values:\n";
    for (int i = 0; i < size_of_a; i++)
        cout << a[i] << " ";
    cout << endl;
}
```

This function will work fine. However, as an added safety measure you can add the modifier *const* to the function heading as follows:

```
void show_the_world(const int a[], int size_of_a)
```

With the addition of this modifier *const*, the computer will issue an error message if your function definition contains a mistake that changes any of the values in the array argument.

For example, the following is a version of the function show_the_world that contains a mistake that inadvertently changes the value of the array argument. Fortunately, this version of the function definition includes the modifier *const*, so that an error message will tell us that the array a is changed. This error message will help to explain the mistake:

```
void show_the_world(const int a[], int size_of_a)
//Precondition: size_of_a is the declared size of the array a.
//All indexed variables of a have been given values.
//Postcondition: The values in a have been written to the
//screen.
{
    using namespace std;
    cout << "The array contains the following values:\n";
    for (int i = 0; i < size_of_a; a[i]++)
        cout << a[i] << " ";
    cout << endl;
}
```

Mistake, but the compiler will not catch it unless you use the const *modifier.*

If we had not used the *const* modifier in the above function definition and if we made the mistake shown, the function would compile and run with no error messages. However, the code would contain an infinite loop which continually increments a[0] and writes its new value to the screen.

The problem with this incorrect version of show_the_world is that the wrong item is incremented in the *for*-loop. The indexed variable a[i] is incremented, but it should be the index i that is incremented. In this incorrect version, the index i starts with the value 0 and that value is never changed. But a[i], which is the same as a[0], is incremented. When the indexed variable a[i] is incremented, that changes a value in the array, and since we included the modifier *const*, the computer will issue a warning message. That error message should serve as a clue to what is wrong.

Use const in both the function heading and the function prototype.

You normally have a function prototype in your program in addition to the function definition. When you use the *const* modifier in a function definition, you must also use it in the function prototype so that the function heading and the function prototype are consistent.

The modifier *const* can be used with any kind of parameter, but it is normally used only with array parameters and call-by-reference parameters for classes.

Warning!

The *const* parameter modifier is an all or nothing proposition. If you use it for one array parameter of a particular type, then you should use it for every other array parameter that has that type and that is not changed by the function. The reason has to do with function calls within function calls. Consider the definition of the function show_difference, which is given below along with the prototype of a function used in the definition:

```
double compute_average(int a[], int number_used);
//Returns the average of the elements in the first number_used
//elements of the array a. The array a is unchanged.

void show_difference(const int a[], int number_used)
{
    using namespace std;
    double average = compute_average(a, number_used);
    cout << "Average of the " << number_used
         << " numbers = " << average << endl
         << "The numbers are:\n";
    for (int index = 0; index < number_used; index++)
        cout << a[index] << " differs from average by "
             << (a[index] - average) << endl;
}
```

The above will give an error message or warning message with some compilers. The function compute_average does not change its parameter a. However, when the compiler processes the function definition for show_difference it will think that compute_average does (or at least might) change the value of its parameter a. This is because, when it is translating the function definition for show_difference, all the compiler knows about the function compute_average is the prototype for compute_average, and the prototype does not contain a *const* to tell the compiler that the parameter a will not be changed. Thus, if you use *const* with the parameter a in the function show_difference, then you should also use the modifier *const* with the parameter a in the function compute_average. The prototype for compute_average should be as follows:

```
double compute_average(const int a[], int number_used);
```

SELF-TEST EXERCISES

13 Write a function definition for a function called one_more, which has a formal parameter for an array of integers and increases the value of each array element by one. Add any other formal parameters that are needed.

14 Consider the following function definition:

```
void too2(int a[], int how_many)
{
    for (int index = 0; index < how_many; index++)
        a[index] = 2;
}
```

Which of the following are acceptable function calls?

```
int my_array[29];
too2(my_array, 29);
too2(my_array, 10);
too2(my_array, 55);
"Hey too2. Please, come over here."
int your_array[100];
too2(your_array, 100);
too2(my_array[3], 29);
```

15 Insert *const* before any of the following array parameters that can be changed to constant array parameters:

```
void output(double a[], int size);
//Precondition: a[0] through a[size - 1] have values.
//Postcondition: a[0] through a[size - 1] have been written
//out.

void drop_odd(int a[], int size);
//Precondition: a[0] through a[size - 1] have values.
//Postcondition: All odd numbers in a[0] through a[size - 1]
//have been changed to 0.
```

16 Write an *int* function named outOfOrder that takes as parameters an array of *double* and an *int*, size. This function will test this array for being out of order, meaning that the array violates the condition:

```
a[0] <= a[1] <= a[2] <= ...
```

The function returns –1 if the elements are not out of order; otherwise, it will return the index of the first element of the array that is out of order. For example, consider the declaration

```
double a[10] = { 1.2, 2.1, 3.3, 2.5, 4.5, 7.9, 5.4, 8.7,
                 9.9, 1.0 };
```

in the array above, a[2] and a[3] are the first pair out of order, a[3] is the first element out of order, so the function returns 3. If the array were sorted, the function would return –1.

9.3 Programming with Arrays

Never trust to general impressions, my boy
but concentrate yourself upon details.

SIR ARTHUR CONAN DOYLE,
         A CASE OF IDENTITY (SHERLOCK HOLMES)

Case Study   Production Graph

In this case study we use arrays in the top-down design of a program. We use both
indexed variables and entire arrays as arguments to the functions for subtasks.

PROBLEM DEFINITION

The Apex Plastic Spoon Manufacturing Company has commissioned us to write a
program that will display a bar graph showing the productivity of each of their four
manufacturing plants for any given week. Plants keep separate production figures for
each department, such as the teaspoon department, soup spoon department, plain
cocktail spoon department, colored cocktail spoon department, and so forth. Moreover, each plant has a different number of departments. For example, only one plant
manufactures colored cocktail spoons. The input is entered plant-by-plant and consists of a list of numbers giving the production for each department in that plant. The
output will consist of a bar graph in the following form:

```
Plant #1 **********
Plant #2 *************
Plant #3 ********************
Plant #4 *****
```

Each asterisk represents 1,000 units of output.

We decide to read in the input separately for each department in a plant. Since
departments cannot produce a negative number of spoons, we know that the production figure for each department will be nonnegative. Hence, we can use a negative
number as a sentinel value to mark the end of the production numbers for each plant.

Since output is in units of 1,000, it must be scaled by dividing it by 1,000. This
presents a problem since the computer must display a whole number of asterisks. It
cannot display 1.6 asterisks for 1,600 units. We will thus round to the nearest
1,000th. Thus, 1,600 will be the same as 2,000 and will produce two asterisks. A precise statement of the program's input and output is as follows:

INPUT:

There are four manufacturing plants numbered 1 through 4. The following input is
given for each of the four plants.

A list of numbers giving the production for each department in that plant. The list is
terminated with a negative number that serves as a sentinel value.

OUTPUT:

A bar graph showing the total production for each plant. Each asterisk in the bar graph equals 1,000 units. The production of each plant is rounded to the nearest 1,000 units.

ANALYSIS OF THE PROBLEM

We will use an array called `production`, which will hold the total production for each of the four plants. In C++ array indexes always start with 0. But since the plants are numbered 1 through 4, rather than 0 through 3, we will not use the plant number as the array index. Instead we will place the total production for plant number n in indexed variable `production[n–1]`. The total output for plant number 1 will be held in `production[0]`, the figures for plant 2 will be held in `production[1]`, and so forth.

Since the output is in 1,000s of units, the program will scale the values of the array elements. If the total output for plant number 3 is 4,040 units, then the value of `production[2]` will initially be set to `4040`. This value of `4040` will then be scaled to 4 so that the value of `production[2]` is changed to 4 and four asterisks will be output in the graph to represent the output for plant number 3.

subtasks

The task for our program can be divided into the following subtasks:

1 `input_data`: Read the input data for each plant and set the value of the indexed variable `production[plant_number–1]` equal to the total production for that plant, where `plant_number` is the number of the plant.

2 `scale`: For each `plant_number`, change the value of the indexed variable `production[plant_number–1]` to the correct number of asterisks.

3 `graph`: Output the bar graph.

The entire array `production` will be an argument for the functions that carry out these subtasks. As is usual with an array parameter, this means we must have an additional formal parameter for the size of the array, which in this case is the same as the number of plants. We will use a defined constant for the number of plants, and this constant will serve as the size of the array `production`. The `main` part of our program, together with the prototypes for the functions that perform the subtasks and the defined constant for the number of plants, are shown in Display 9.6. Notice that, since there is no reason to change the array parameter to the function `graph`, we have made that array parameter a constant parameter by adding the *const* parameter modifier. The material in Display 9.6 is the outline for our program, and if it is in a separate file, that file can be compiled so that we can check for any syntax errors in this outline before we go on to define the functions corresponding to the prototypes shown.

Having compiled the file shown in Display 9.6, we are ready to design the implementation of the functions for the three subtasks. For each of these three functions, we will design an algorithm, write the code for the function, and test the function before we go on to design the next function.

Display 9.6 Prototypes for the main Part of the Graph Program

```
//Reads data and displays a bar graph showing productivity for each plant.
#include <iostream>
const int NUMBER_OF_PLANTS = 4;


void input_data(int a[], int last_plant_number);
//Precondition: last_plant_number is the declared size of the array a.
//Postcondition: For plant_number = 1 through last_plant_number:
//a[plant_number-1] equals the total production for plant number plant_number.


void scale(int a[], int size);
//Precondition: a[0] through a[size-1] each have a nonnegative value.
//Postcondition: a[i] has been changed to the number of 1000s (rounded to
//an integer) that were originally in a[i], for all i such that 0 <= i <= size-1.


void graph(const int asterisk_count[], int last_plant_number);
//Precondition: asterisk_count[0] through asterisk_count[last_plant_number-1]
//have nonnegative values.
//Postcondition: A bar graph has been displayed saying that plant
//number N has produced asterisk_count[N-1] 1000s of units, for each N such that
//1 <= N <= last_plant_number

int main( )
{
    using namespace std;
    int production[NUMBER_OF_PLANTS];

    cout << "This program displays a graph showing\n"
         << "production for each plant in the company.\n";

    input_data(production, NUMBER_OF_PLANTS);
    scale(production, NUMBER_OF_PLANTS);
    graph(production, NUMBER_OF_PLANTS);

    return 0;
}
```

ALGORITHM DESIGN FOR input_data

The prototype and descriptive comment for the function input_data is shown in Display 9.6. As indicated in the body of the main part of our program (also shown in Display 9.6), when input_data is called, the formal array parameter a will be replaced with the array production, and since the last plant number is the same as the number of plants, the formal parameter last_plant_number will be replaced by NUMBER_OF_PLANTS. The algorithm for input_data is straightforward:

> For plant_number equal to each of 1, 2, through last_plant_number
> do the following:
>> Read in all the data for plant whose number is plant_number.
>> Sum the numbers.
>> Set production[plant_number–1] equal to that total.

CODING FOR input_data

The algorithm for the function input_data translates to the following code:

```
//Uses iostream:
void input_data(int a[], int last_plant_number)
{
    using namespace std;
    for (int plant_number = 1;
        plant_number <= last_plant_number; plant_number++)
    {
        cout << endl
            << "Enter production data for plant number "
            << plant_number << endl;
        get_total(a[plant_number - 1]);
    }
}
```

The code is routine since all the work is done by the function get_total, which we still need to design. But before we move on to discuss the function get_total, let's observe a few things about the above function input_data. Notice that we store the figures for plant number plant_number in the indexed variable with index plant_number–1; this is because arrays always start with index 0, while the plant numbers start with 1. Also, notice that we use an indexed variable for the argument to the function get_total. The function get_total really does all the work for the function input_data, and we next consider get_total.

get_total

The function get_total does all the input work for one plant. It reads the production figures for that plant, sums the figures, and stores the total in the indexed variable for that plant. But, get_total does not need to know that its argument is an indexed variable. To a function like get_total an indexed variable is just like any other variable of type *int*. Thus, `get_total` will have an ordinary call-by-reference parameter of type *int*. That means that `get_total` is just an ordinary input function like others that we have seen before we discussed arrays. The function `get_total` reads in a list of numbers ended with a sentinel value, sums the numbers as it reads them in, and sets the value of its argument, which is a variable of type *int*, equal to this sum. There is nothing new to us in the function `get_total`. Display 9.7 shows the function definitions for both `get_total` and `input_data`. The functions are embedded in a simple test program.

TESTING `input_data`

Every function should be tested in a program in which it is the only untested function. The function `input_data` includes a call to the function `get_total`. Therefore we should test `get_total` in a driver program of its own. Once `get_total` has been completely tested, we can use it in a program, like the one in Display 9.7, to test the function `input_data`.

When testing the function `input_data`, we should include tests with all possible kinds of production figures for a plant. We should include a plant that has no production figures (as we did for plant 4 in Display 9.7), we should include a test for a plant with only one production figure (as we did for plant 3 in Display 9.7) and we should include a test for a plant with more than one production figure (as we did for plants 1 and 2 in Display 9.7). We should test for both nonzero and zero production figures, which is why we included a 0 in the input list for plant 2 in Display 9.7.

ALGORITHM DESIGN FOR `scale`

The function `scale` changes the value of each indexed variable in the array `production` so that it shows the number of asterisks to print out. Since there should be one asterisk for every 1,000 units of production, the value of each indexed variable must be divided by `1000.0`. Then to get a whole number of asterisks, this number is rounded to the nearest integer. This method can be used to scale the values in any array a of any size, so the prototype for `scale`, shown in Display 9.6 and repeated below, is stated in terms of an arbitrary array a of some arbitrary size:

```
void scale(int a[], int size);
//Precondition: a[0] through a[size-1] each have a
//nonnegative value.
//Postcondition: a[i] has been changed to the number of 1000s
//(rounded to an integer) that were originally in a[i], for
//all i such that 0 <= i <= size-1.
```

When the function `scale` is called, the array parameter a will be replaced by the array `production`, and the formal parameter `size` will be replaced by `NUMBER_OF_PLANTS` so that the function call looks like the following:

```
scale(production, NUMBER_OF_PLANTS);
```

Display 9.7 Test of Function `input_data` *(part 1 of 3)*

```
//Tests the function input_data.
#include <iostream>
const int NUMBER_OF_PLANTS = 4;

void input_data(int a[], int last_plant_number);
//Precondition: last_plant_number is the declared size of the array a.
//Postcondition: For plant_number = 1 through last_plant_number:
//a[plant_number–1] equals the total production for plant number plant_number.

void get_total(int& sum);
//Reads nonnegative integers from the keyboard and
//places their total in sum.

int main( )
{
    using namespace std;
    int production[NUMBER_OF_PLANTS];
    char ans;

    do
    {
        input_data(production, NUMBER_OF_PLANTS);
        cout << endl
            << "Total production for each"
            << " of plants 1 through 4:\n";
        for (int number = 1; number <= NUMBER_OF_PLANTS; number++)
        cout << production[number - 1] << " ";

        cout << endl
            << "Test Again?(Type y or n and return): ";
        cin >> ans;
    }while ( (ans != 'N') && (ans != 'n') );

    cout << endl;

    return 0;
}
```

Display 9.7 Test of Function input_data *(part 2 of 3)*

```
//Uses iostream:
void input_data(int a[], int last_plant_number)
{
    using namespace std;
    for (int plant_number = 1;
                    plant_number <= last_plant_number; plant_number++)
    {
        cout << endl
            << "Enter production data for plant number "
            << plant_number << endl;
        get_total(a[plant_number - 1]);
    }
}



//Uses iostream:
void get_total(int& sum)
{
    using namespace std;
    cout << "Enter number of units produced by each department.\n"
        << "Append a negative number to the end of the list.\n";

    sum = 0;
    int next;
    cin >> next;
    while (next >= 0)
    {
        sum = sum + next;
        cin >> next;
    }

    cout << "Total = " << sum << endl;
}
```

Display 9.7 Test of Function `input_data` *(part 3 of 3)*

Sample Dialogue

```
Enter production data for plant number 1
Enter number of units produced by each department.
Append a negative number to the end of the list.
1 2 3 -1
Total = 6

Enter production data for plant number 2
Enter number of units produced by each department.
Append a negative number to the end of the list.
0 2 3 -1
Total = 5

Enter production data for plant number 3
Enter number of units produced by each department.
Append a negative number to the end of the list.
2 -1
Total = 2

Enter production data for plant number 4
Enter number of units produced by each department.
Append a negative number to the end of the list.
-1
Total = 0

Total production for each of plants 1 through 4:
6 5 2 0
Test Again?(Type y or n and return): n
```

The algorithm for the function `scale` is as follows:

for (*int* index = 0; index < size; index++)
    Divide the value of a[index] by one thousand and round the result to
    the nearest whole number; the result is the new value of a[index].

CODING FOR scale

The algorithm for scale translates into the C++ code given below, where round is a function we still need to define. The function round takes one argument of type *double* and returns a type *int* value that is the integer nearest to its argument, that is, the function round will round its argument to the nearest whole number:

```
void scale(int a[], int size)
{
    for (int index = 0; index < size; index++)
        a[index] = round(a[index]/1000.0 );
}
```

Notice that we divided by 1000.0, not by 1000 (without the decimal point). If we had divided by 1000, we would have performed integer division. For example, 2600/1000 would give the answer 2, but 2600/1000.0 gives the answer 2.6. It is true that we want an integer for the final answer after rounding, but we want 2600 divided by 1000 to produce 3, not 2, when it is rounded to a whole number.

We now turn to the definition of the function round, which rounds its argument to the nearest integer. For example, round(2.3) returns 2 and round(2.6) returns 3. The code for the function round, as well as that for scale, is given in Display 9.8. The code for round may require a bit of explanation.

round

The function round uses the predefined function floor from the library with the header file cmath. The function floor returns the whole numbers just below its argument. For example, floor(2.1) and floor(2.9) both return 2. To see that round works correctly, let's look at some examples. Consider round(2.4). The value returned is

floor(2.4 + 0.5)

which is floor(2.9) and that is 2.0. In fact, for any number that is greater-than-or-equal to 2.0 and strictly less than 2.5, that number plus 0.5 will be less than 3.0, and so floor applied to that number plus 0.5 will return 2.0. Thus, round applied to any number that is greater-than-or-equal to 2.0 and strictly less than 2.5 will return 2. (Since the prototype for round specifies that the type for the value returned is *int*, the computed value of 2.0 will be converted to the integer value 2 without a decimal point and 2 will be returned.)

Now consider numbers greater-than-or-equal to 2.5; for example, 2.6. The value returned by the call round(2.6) is

floor(2.6 + 0.5)

which is floor(3.1) and that is 3.0. In fact, for any number that is greater-than-or-equal to 2.5 and less-than-or-equal to 3.0, that number plus 0.5 will be greater than 3.0. Thus, round called with any number that is greater-than-or-equal to 2.5 and less-than-or-equal to 3.0 will return 3.

Display 9.8 The Function scale *(part 1 of 2)*

```
//Demonstration program for the function scale.
#include <iostream>
#include <cmath>

void scale(int a[], int size);
//Precondition: a[0] through a[size-1] each has a nonnegative value.
//Postcondition: a[i] has been changed to the number of 1000s (rounded to
//an integer) that were originally in a[i], for all i such that 0 <= i <= size-1.

int round(double number);
//Precondition: number >= 0.
//Returns number rounded to the nearest integer.

int main( )
{
    using namespace std;
    int some_array[4], index;

    cout << "Enter 4 numbers to scale: ";
    for (index = 0; index < 4; index++)
        cin >> some_array[index];

    scale(some_array, 4);

    cout << "Values scaled to the number of 1000s are: ";
    for (index = 0; index < 4; index++)
        cout << some_array[index] << " ";
    cout << endl;

    return 0;
}

void scale(int a[], int size)
{
    for (int index = 0; index < size; index++)
        a[index] = round(a[index]/1000.0);
}
```

Display 9.8 The Function scale *(part 2 of 2)*

```
//Uses cmath:
int round(double number)
{
    using namespace std;
    return floor(number + 0.5);
}
```

Sample Dialogue

```
Enter 4 numbers to scale: 2600 999 465 3501
Values scaled to the number of 1000s are: 3 1 0 4
```

Thus, round works correctly for all arguments between 2.0 and 3.0. Clearly, there is nothing special about arguments between 2.0 and 3.0. A similar argument applies to all nonnegative numbers. So, round works correctly for all nonnegative arguments.

TESTING scale

Display 9.8 contains a demonstration program for the function scale, but the testing programs for the functions round and scale should be more elaborate than this simple program. In particular, they should allow you to retest the tested function several times rather than just once. We will not give the complete testing programs, but you should first test round (which is used by scale) in a driver program of its own, and then test scale in a driver program. The program to test round should test arguments that are 0, arguments that round up like 2.6, and arguments that round down like 2.3. The program to test scale should test a similar variety of values for the elements of the array.

THE FUNCTION graph

The complete program for producing the desired bar graph is shown in Display 9.9. We have not taken you step-by-step through the design of the function graph because it is quite straightforward.

Partially Filled Arrays

Often the exact size needed for an array is not known when a program is written or the size may vary from one run of the program to another. One common and easy way to handle this situation is to declare the array to be of the largest size the

Display 9.9 Production Graph Program *(part 1 of 3)*

```
//Reads data and displays a bar graph showing productivity for each plant.
#include <iostream>
#include <cmath>
const int NUMBER_OF_PLANTS = 4;

void input_data(int a[], int last_plant_number);
//Precondition: last_plant_number is the declared size of the array a.
//Postcondition: For plant_number = 1 through last_plant_number:
//a[plant_number-1] equals the total production for plant number plant_number.

void scale(int a[], int size);
//Precondition: a[0] through a[size-1] each have a nonnegative value.
//Postcondition: a[i] has been changed to the number of 1000s (rounded to
//an integer) that were originally in a[i], for all i such that 0 <= i <= size-1.

void graph(const int asterisk_count[], int last_plant_number);
//Precondition: asterisk_count[0] through asterisk_count[last_plant_number-1]
//have nonnegative values.
//Postcondition: A bar graph has been displayed saying that plant
//number N has produced asterisk_count[N-1] 1000s of units, for each N such that
//1 <= N <= last_plant_number

void get_total(int& sum);
//Reads nonnegative integers from the keyboard and
//places their total in sum.

int round(double number);
//Precondition: number >= 0.
//Returns number rounded to the nearest integer.

void print_asterisks(int n);
//Prints n asterisks to the screen.

int main( )
{
    using namespace std;
    int production[NUMBER_OF_PLANTS];

    cout << "This program displays a graph showing\n"
         << "production for each plant in the company.\n";
```

Display 9.9 Production Graph Program *(part 2 of 3)*

```
        input_data(production, NUMBER_OF_PLANTS);
        scale(production, NUMBER_OF_PLANTS);
        graph(production, NUMBER_OF_PLANTS);
        return 0;
}

//Uses iostream:
void input_data(int a[], int last_plant_number)
        <The rest of the definition of input_data is given in Display 9.7. >

//Uses iostream:
void get_total(int& sum)
        <The rest of the definition of get_total is given in Display 9.7. >

void scale(int a[], int size)
        <The rest of the definition of scale is given in Display 9.8. >

//Uses cmath:
int round(double number)
        <The rest of the definition of round is given in Display 9.8. >

//Uses iostream:
void graph(const int asterisk_count[], int last_plant_number)
{
    using namespace std;
    cout << "\nUnits produced in thousands of units:\n";
    for (int plant_number = 1;
              plant_number <= last_plant_number; plant_number++)
    {
        cout << "Plant #" << plant_number << " ";
        print_asterisks(asterisk_count[plant_number - 1]);
        cout << endl;
    }
}

//Uses iostream:
void print_asterisks(int n)
{
    using namespace std;
    for (int count = 1; count <= n; count++)
        cout << "*";
}
```

Display 9.9 Production Graph Program *(part 3 of 3)*

Sample Dialogue

```
This program displays a graph showing
production for each plant in the company.

Enter production data for plant number 1
Enter number of units produced by each department.
Append a negative number to the end of the list.
2000 3000 1000 -1
Total = 6000

Enter production data for plant number 2
Enter number of units produced by each department.
Append a negative number to the end of the list.
2050 3002 1300 -1
Total = 6352

Enter production data for plant number 3
Enter number of units produced by each department.
Append a negative number to the end of the list.
5000 4020 500 4348 -1
Total = 13868

Enter production data for plant number 4
Enter number of units produced by each department.
Append a negative number to the end of the list.
2507 6050 1809 -1
Total = 10366

Units produced in thousands of units:

Plant #1 ******
Plant #2 ******
Plant #3 **************
Plant #4 **********
```

program could possibly need. The program is then free to use as much or as little of the array as is needed.

Partially filled arrays require some care. The program must keep track of how much of the array is used and must not reference any indexed variable that has not been given a value. The program in Display 9.10 illustrates this point. The program reads in a list of golf scores and shows how much each score differs from the average. This program will work for lists as short as one score, as long as ten scores, and of any length in between. The scores are stored in the array `score`, which has ten indexed variables, but the program uses only as much of the array as it needs. The variable `number_used` keeps track of how many elements are stored in the array. The elements (i.e., the scores) are stored in positions `score[0]` through `score[number_used – 1]`. The details are very similar to what they would be if `number_used` were the declared size of the array and the entire array were used. In particular, the variable `number_used` must always be an argument to any function that manipulates the partially filled array. Since the argument `number_used` (when used properly) can often ensure that the function will not reference an illegal array index, this sometimes (but not always) eliminates the need for an argument that gives the declared size of the array. For example, the functions `show_difference` and `compute_average` use the argument `number_used` to ensure that only legal array indexes are used. However, the function `fill_array` needs to know the maximum declared size for the array so that it does not overfill the array.

■)) *PROGRAMMING* EXAMPLE
Searching an Array

A common programming task is to search an array for a given value. For example, the array may contain the student numbers for all students in a given course. To tell whether a particular student is enrolled, the array is searched to see if it contains the student's number. The simple program in Display 9.11 fills an array and then searches the array for values specified by the user. A real application program would be much more elaborate, but this shows all the essentials of the *sequential search* algorithm. The **sequential search** algorithm is the most straightforward searching algorithm you could imagine: The program looks at the array elements in the order first to last to see if the target number is equal to any of the array elements.

sequential search

In Display 9.11 the array is filled in the same way, in fact using the same input function, as in Display 9.10. The function `search` is then used to search the array. When searching an array, you often want to know more than simply whether or not the target value is in the array. If the target value is in the array, you often want to know the index of the indexed variable holding that target value, since the index may serve as a guide to some additional information about the target value. Therefore, we

Display 9.10 Partially Filled Array *(part 1 of 3)*

```
//Shows the difference between each of a list of golf scores and their average.
#include <iostream>
const int MAX_NUMBER_SCORES = 10;

void fill_array(int a[], int size, int& number_used);
//Precondition: size is the declared size of the array a.
//Postcondition: number_used is the number of values stored in a.
//a[0] through a[number_used-1] have been filled with
//nonnegative integers read from the keyboard.

double compute_average(const int a[], int number_used);
//Precondition: a[0] through a[number_used-1] have values; number_used > 0.
//Returns the average of numbers a[0] through a[number_used-1].

void show_difference(const int a[], int number_used);
//Precondition: The first number_used indexed variables of a have values.
//Postcondition: Gives screen output showing how much each of the first
//number_used
//elements of a differ from their average.

int main( )
{
    using namespace std;
    int score[MAX_NUMBER_SCORES], number_used;

    cout << "This program reads golf scores and shows\n"
         << "how much each differs from the average.\n";

    cout << "Enter golf scores:\n";
    fill_array(score, MAX_NUMBER_SCORES, number_used);
    show_difference(score, number_used);

    return 0;
}

//Uses iostream:
void fill_array(int a[], int size, int& number_used)
{
    using namespace std;
    cout << "Enter up to " << size << " nonnegative whole numbers.\n"
         << "Mark the end of the list with a negative number.\n";
```

Display 9.10 Partially Filled Array (part 2 of 3)

```cpp
    int next, index = 0;
    cin >> next;
    while ((next >= 0) && (index < size))
    {
        a[index] = next;
        index++;
        cin >> next;
    }

    number_used = index;
}

double compute_average(const int a[], int number_used)
{
    double total = 0;
    for (int index = 0; index < number_used; index++)
        total = total + a[index];
    if (number_used > 0)
    {
        return (total/number_used);
    }
    else
    {
        using namespace std;
        cout << "ERROR: number of elements is 0 in compute_average.\n"
             << "compute_average returns 0.\n";
        return 0;
    }
}

void show_difference(const int a[], int number_used)
{
    using namespace std;
    double average = compute_average(a, number_used);
    cout << "Average of the " << number_used
         << " scores = " << average << endl
         << "The scores are:\n";
    for (int index = 0; index < number_used; index++)
    cout << a[index] << " differs from average by "
         << (a[index] - average) << endl;
}
```

Display 9.10 Partially Filled Array *(part 3 of 3)*

Sample Dialogue

```
This program reads golf scores and shows
how much each differs from the average.
Enter golf scores:
Enter up to 10 nonnegative whole numbers.
Mark the end of the list with a negative number.
69 74 68 -1
Average of the 3 scores = 70.3333
The scores are:
69 differs from average by -1.33333
74 differs from average by 3.66667
68 differs from average by -2.33333
```

designed the function `search` to return an index giving the location of the target value in the array, provided the target value is, in fact, in the array. If the target value is not in the array, `search` returns –1. Let's look at the function `search` in a little more detail.

The function `search` uses a *while*-loop to check the array elements one after the other to see whether any of them equals the target value. The variable `found` is used as a flag to record whether or not the target element has been found. If the target element is found in the array, `found` is set to *true*, which in turn ends the *while*-loop. (When `found` is *true*, !`found`—that is, "not found"—is *false* and so the Boolean expression that controls the *while*-loop is *false* and the loop ends.)

↝ *PROGRAMMING* **TIP**
Do Not Skimp on Formal Parameters

Notice the function `fill_array` in Display 9.10. When `fill_array` is called, the declared array size `MAX_NUMBER_SCORES` is given as one of the arguments, as shown in the following function call from Display 9.10:

```
fill_array(score, MAX_NUMBER_SCORES, number_used);
```

You might protest that `MAX_NUMBER_SCORES` is a globally defined constant and so it could be used in the definition of `fill_array` without the need to make it an argument. You would be correct, and if we did not use `fill_array` in any program

Display 9.11 Searching an Array *(part 1 of 2)*

```
//Searches a partially filled array of nonnegative integers.
#include <iostream>
const int DECLARED_SIZE = 20;

void fill_array(int a[], int size, int& number_used);
//Precondition: size is the declared size of the array a.
//Postcondition: number_used is the number of values stored in a.
//a[0] through a[number_used-1] have been filled with
//nonnegative integers read from the keyboard.

int search(const int a[], int number_used, int target);
//Precondition: number_used is <= the declared size of a.
//Also, a[0] through a[number_used -1] have values.
//Returns the first index such that a[index] == target,
//provided there is such an index, otherwise returns -1.

int main( )
{
    using namespace std;
    int arr[DECLARED_SIZE], list_size, target;

    fill_array(arr, DECLARED_SIZE, list_size);

    char ans;
    int result;
    do
    {
        cout << "Enter a number to search for: ";
        cin >> target;

        result = search(arr, list_size, target);
        if (result == -1)
            cout << target << " is not on the list.\n";
        else
            cout << target << " is stored in array position "
                 << result << endl
                 << "(Remember: The first position is 0.)\n";

        cout << "Search again?(y/n followed by return): ";
        cin >> ans;
    }while ((ans != 'n') && (ans != 'N'));

    cout << "End of program.\n";
    return 0;
}
```

Display 9.11 Searching an Array (part 2 of 2)

```
//Uses iostream:
void fill_array(int a[], int size, int& number_used)
            <The rest of the definition of fill_array is given in Display 9.10. >

int search(const int a[], int number_used, int target)
{

    int index = 0;
    bool found = false;
    while ((!found) && (index < number_used))
        if (target == a[index])
            found = true;
        else
            index++;

    if (found)
        return index;
    else
        return -1;
}
```

Sample Dialogue

```
Enter up to 20 nonnegative whole numbers.
Mark the end of the list with a negative number.
10 20 30 40 50 60 70 80 -1
Enter a number to search for: 10
10 is stored in array position 0
(Remember: The first position is 0.)
Search again?(y/n followed by return): y
Enter a number to search for: 40
40 is stored in array position 3
(Remember: The first position is 0.)
Search again?(y/n followed by return): y
Enter a number to search for: 42
42 is not on the list.
Search again?(y/n followed by return): n
End of program.
```

other than the one in Display 9.10, we could get by without making MAX_NUMBER_SCORES an argument to `fill_array`. But, `fill_array` is a generally useful function that you may want to use in several different programs. We do in fact also use the function `fill_array` in the program in Display 9.11. In the program in Display 9.11 the argument for the declared array size is a different named global constant. If we had written the global constant MAX_NUMBER_SCORES into the body of the function `fill_array`, we would not have been able to reuse the function in the program in Display 9.11. It would be a good idea to make a library of general-purpose array-manipulating functions such as `fill_array` and to compile this library so it could be used in any program that needs the functions. If you do that, then your functions must have a formal parameter for the declared array size.

Even if we used `fill_array` in only one program, it can still be a good idea to make the declared array size an argument to `fill_array`. Displaying the declared size of the array as an argument reminds us that the function needs this information in a critically important way.

■)) PROGRAMMING EXAMPLE
Sorting an Array

One of the most widely encountered programming tasks, and certainly the most thoroughly studied, is sorting a list of values, such as a list of sales figures that must be sorted from lowest to highest or from highest to lowest, or a list of words that must be sorted into alphabetical order. In this section we will describe a function called `sort` that will sort a partially filled array of numbers so that they are ordered from smallest to largest.

The procedure `sort` has one array parameter a. The array a will be partially filled so there is an additional formal parameter called `number_used`, which tells how many array positions are used. Thus, the prototype and precondition for the function `sort` will be:

```
void sort(int a[], int number_used);
//Precondition: number_used <= declared size of the array a.
//The array elements a[0] through a[number_used–1] have
//values.
```

The function `sort` rearranges the elements in array a so that after the function call is completed the elements are sorted as follows:

```
a[0] ≤ a[1] ≤ a[2] ≤ ... ≤ a[number_used – 1]
```

The algorithm we use to do the sorting is called *selection sort*. It is one of the easiest of the sorting algorithms to understand.

selection sort

One way to design an algorithm is to rely on the definition of the problem. In this case the problem is to sort an array a from smallest to largest. That means rearranging the values so that a[0] is the smallest, a[1] the next smallest, and so forth. That definition yields an outline for the **selection sort** algorithm:

for (*int* index = 0; index < number_used; index++)
    Place the index^th smallest element in a[index]

There are many ways to realize this general approach. The details could be developed using two arrays and copying the elements from one array to the other in sorted order, but one array should be both adequate and economical. Therefore, the function sort uses only the one array containing the values to be sorted. The function sort rearranges the values in the array a by interchanging pairs of values. Let us go through a concrete example so that you can see how the algorithm works.

Consider the array shown in Display 9.12. The algorithm will place the smallest value in a[0]. The smallest value is the value in a[3]. So the algorithm interchanges the values of a[0] and a[3]. The algorithm then looks for the next smallest element. The value in a[0] is now the smallest element and so the next smallest element is the smallest of the remaining elements a[1], a[2], a[3], ..., a[9]. In the example in Display 9.12 the next smallest element is in a[5] so the algorithm interchanges

Display 9.12 Selection Sort

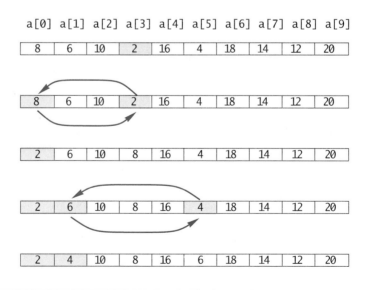

the values of a[1] and a[5]. This positioning of the second smallest element is illustrated in the fourth and fifth array pictures in Display 9.12. The algorithm then positions the third smallest element, and so forth. As the sorting proceeds, the beginning array elements are set equal to the correct sorted values. The sorted portion of the array grows by adding elements one after the other from the elements in the unsorted end of the array. Notice that the algorithm need not do anything with the value in the last indexed variable a[9]. That is because once the other elements are positioned correctly, a[9] must also have the correct value. After all, the correct value for a[9] is the smallest value left to be moved, and the only value left to be moved is the value that is already in a[9].

The definition of the function sort, included in a demonstration program, is given in Display 9.13. sort uses the function index_of_smallest to find the index of the smallest element in the unsorted end of the array, then it does an interchange to move this next smallest element down into the sorted part of the array.

The function swap_values, shown in Display 9.13, is used to interchange the values of indexed variables. For example, the following call will interchange the values of a[0] and a[3]:

```
swap_values(a[0], a[3])
```

The function swap_values was explained in Chapter 4.

index_of_smallest

swap_values

SELF-TEST EXERCISES

17 Write a program that will read up to 10 nonnegative integers into an array called number_array and then write the integers back to the screen. For this exercise you need not use any functions. This is just a toy program and can be very minimal.

18 Write a program that will read up to 10 letters into an array and write the letters back to the screen in the reverse order. For example, if the input is

   abcd.

   then the output should be

   dcba

   Use a period as a sentinel value to mark the end of the input. Call the array letter_box. For this exercise you need not use any functions. This is just a toy program and can be very minimal.

(text continues on page 578)

Display 9.13 Sorting an Array (part 1 of 3)

```
//Tests the procedure sort.
#include <iostream>

void fill_array(int a[], int size, int& number_used);
//Precondition: size is the declared size of the array a.
//Postcondition: number_used is the number of values stored in a.
//a[0] through a[number_used - 1] have been filled with
//nonnegative integers read from the keyboard.

void sort(int a[], int number_used);
//Precondition: number_used <= declared size of the array a.
//The array elements a[0] through a[number_used - 1] have values.
//Postcondition: The values of a[0] through a[number_used - 1] have
//been rearranged so that a[0] <= a[1] <= ... <= a[number_used - 1].

void swap_values(int& v1, int& v2);
//Interchanges the values of v1 and v2.

int index_of_smallest(const int a[], int start_index, int number_used);
//Precondition: 0 <= start_index < number_used. References array elements have
//values.
//Returns the index i such that a[i] is the smallest of the values
//a[start_index], a[start_index + 1], ..., a[number_used - 1].

int main()
{
    using namespace std;
    cout << "This program sorts numbers from lowest to highest.\n";

    int sample_array[10], number_used;
    fill_array(sample_array, 10, number_used);
    sort(sample_array, number_used);

    cout << "In sorted order the numbers are:\n";
    for (int index = 0; index < number_used; index++)
        cout << sample_array[index] << " ";
    cout << endl;

    return 0;
}

//Uses iostream:
void fill_array(int a[], int size, int& number_used)
```

                <The rest of the definition of fill_array is given in Display 9.10. >

Display 9.13 Sorting an Array *(part 2 of 3)*

```
void sort(int a[], int number_used)
{
    int index_of_next_smallest;
    for (int index = 0; index < number_used - 1; index++)
    {//Place the correct value in a[index]:
        index_of_next_smallest =
                    index_of_smallest(a, index, number_used);
        swap_values(a[index], a[index_of_next_smallest]);
        //a[0] <= a[1] <=...<= a[index] are the smallest of the original array
        //elements. The rest of the elements are in the remaining positions.
    }
}


void swap_values(int& v1, int& v2)
{
    int temp;
    temp = v1;
    v1 = v2;
    v2 = temp;
}


int index_of_smallest(const int a[], int start_index, int number_used)
{
    int min = a[start_index],
        index_of_min = start_index;
    for (int index = start_index + 1; index < number_used; index++)
        if (a[index] < min)
        {
            min = a[index];
            index_of_min = index;
            //min is the smallest of a[start_index] through a[index]
        }

    return index_of_min;
}
```

Display 9.13 Sorting an Array *(part 3 of 3)*

Sample Dialogue

```
This program sorts numbers from lowest to highest.
Enter up to 10 nonnegative whole numbers.
Mark the end of the list with a negative number.
80 30 50 70 60 90 20 30 40 -1
In sorted order the numbers are:
20 30 30 40 50 60 70 80 90
```

19 Below is the prototype for an alternative version of the function search defined in Display 9.11. In order to use this alternative version of the search function we would need to rewrite the program slightly, but for this exercise all you need to do is to write the function definition for this alternative version of search.

```
bool search(const int a[], int number_used,
                           int target, int& where);
//Precondition: number_used is <= the declared size of the
//array a. Also, a[0] through a[number_used -1] have
//values.
//Postcondition: If target is one of the elements a[0]
//through a[number_used - 1], then this function returns
//true and sets the value of where so that a[where] ==
//target; otherwise this function returns false and the
//value of where is unchanged.
```

9.4 Arrays and Classes

You can combine arrays, structures, and classes to form intricately structured types such as arrays of structures, arrays of classes, and classes with arrays as member variables. In this section we discuss a few simple examples to give you an idea of the possibilities.

Arrays of Classes

The base type of an array may be any type, including types that you define, such as structure and class types. If you want each array element to contain items of different types, make the array an array of structures. For example, suppose you want an array to hold 10 weather data points, where each data point is a wind velocity and a wind direction (north, south, east, or west). You might use the following type definition and array declaration:

```
struct WindInfo
{
    double velocity; //in miles per hour
    char direction; //'N', 'S', 'E', or 'W'
};
```

```
WindInfo data_point[10];
```

To fill the array `data_point`, you could use the following *for*-loop:

```
int i;
for (i = 0; i < 10; i++)
{
    cout << "Enter velocity for "
         << i << " numbered data point: ";
    cin >> data_point[i].velocity;
    cout << "Enter direction for that data point"
         << " (N, S, E, or W): ";
    cin >> data_point[i].direction;
}
```

The way to read an expression such as `data_point[i].velocity` is left-to-right and very carefully. First, `data_point` is an array. So, `data_point[i]` is the `i`th indexed variable of this array. An indexed variable of this array is of type `WindInfo`, which is a structure with two member variables named `velocity` and `direction`. So, `data_point[i].velocity` is the member variable named `velocity` for the `i`th array element. Less formally, `data_point[i].velocity` is the wind velocity for the `i`th data point. Similarly, `data_point[i].direction` is the wind direction for the `i`th data point.

The 10 data points in the array `data_point` can be written to the screen with the following *for*-loop:

```
for (i = 0; i < 10; i++)
    cout << "Wind data point number " << i << ": \n"
         << data_point[i].velocity
         << " miles per hour\n"
         << "direction " << data_point[i].direction
         << endl;
```

Display 9.14 contains the interface file for a class called Money. Objects of the class Money are used to represent amounts of money in U.S. currency. The definitions of the member functions, member operations, and friend functions for this class can be found in Display 8.3 through Display 8.8 and in the answer to Self-Test Exercise 13 of Chapter 8. These definitions should be collected into an implementation file. However, we will not show the implementation file, since all you need to know in order to use the class Money is given in the interface file.

You can have arrays whose base type is the type Money. A simple example is given in Display 9.15. That program reads in a list of five amounts of money and computes how much each amount differs from the largest of the five amounts. Notice that an array whose base type is a class is treated basically the same as any other array. In fact, the program in Display 9.15 is very similar to the program in Display 9.1 except that in Display 9.15 the base type is a class.

constructor call

When an array of classes is declared, the default constructor is called to initialize the indexed variables, so it is important to have a default constructor for any class that will be the base type of an array.

An array of classes is manipulated just like an array with a simple base type like *int* or *double*. For example, the difference between each amount and the largest amount is stored in an array named difference, as follows:

```
Money difference[5];
for (i = 0; i < 5; i++)
    difference[i] = max - amount[i];
```

SELF-TEST EXERCISES

20 Give a type definition for a structure called Score that has two member variables called home_team and opponent. Both member variables are of type *int*. Declare an array called game that is an array with 10 elements of type Score. The array game might be used to record the scores of each of 10 games for a sports team.

21 Write a program that reads in five amounts of money, doubles each amount, and then writes out the doubled values to the screen. Use one array with Money as the base type. Hint: Use Display 9.15 as a guide, but this program will be simpler than the one in Display 9.15.

Arrays as Class Members

You can have a structure or class that has an array as a member variable. For example, suppose you are a speed swimmer and want a program to keep track of your

Display 9.14 Header File for the Class Money *(part 1 of 2)*

```
//This is the HEADER FILE money.h. This is the INTERFACE for the class Money.
//Values of this type are amounts of money in U.S. currency.
#ifndef MONEY_H
#define MONEY_H
#include <iostream>
using namespace std;
namespace savitchmoney
{

    class Money
    {
    public:
        friend Money operator +(const Money& amount1, const Money& amount2);
        //Returns the sum of the values of amount 1 and amount2.

        friend Money operator -(const Money& amount1, const Money& amount2);
        //Returns amount 1 minus amount2.

        friend Money operator -(const Money& amount);
        //Returns the negative of the value of amount.

        friend bool operator ==(const Money& amount1, const Money& amount2);
        //Returns true if the amount1 and amount2 have the same value, false otherwise.

        friend bool operator < (const Money& amount1, const Money& amount2);
        //Returns true if amount1 is less than amount2, false otherwise.

        Money(long dollars, int cents);
        //Initializes the object so its value represents an amount with
        //the dollars and cents given by the arguments. If the amount
        //is negative, then both dollars and cents should be negative.

        Money(long dollars);
        //Initializes the object so its value represents $dollars.00.

        Money( );
        //Initializes the object so its value represents $0.00.

        double get_value( ) const;
        //Returns the amount of money recorded in the data portion of the calling
        //object.

        friend istream& operator >>(istream& ins, Money& amount);
        //Overloads the >> operator so it can be used to input values of type
        //Money. Notation for inputting negative amounts is as in -$100.00.
        //Precondition: If ins is a file input stream, then ins has already been
        //connected to a file.
```

Display 9.14 Header File for the Class Money (*part 2 of 2*)

```
    friend ostream& operator <<(ostream& outs, const Money& amount);
    //Overloads the << operator so it can be used to output values of type
    //Money. Precedes each output value of type Money with a dollar sign.
    //Precondition: If outs is a file output stream, then outs has already been
    //connected to a file.
  private:
    long all_cents;
  };
}//namespace savitchmoney
#endif //MONEY_H
```

practice times for various distances. You can use the structure my_best (of the type Data given below) to record a distance (in meters) and the times (in seconds) for each of ten practice tries swimming that distance:

```
    struct Data
    {
        double time[10];
        int distance;
    };
```

```
    Data my_best;
```

The structure my_best, declared above, has two member variables: one, named distance, is a variable of type *int* (to record a distance); the other, named time, is an array of ten values of type *double* (to hold times for ten practice tries at the specified distance). To set the distance equal to 20 (meters), you can use the following:

```
    my_best.distance = 20;
```

You can set the 10 array elements with values from the keyboard as follows:

```
    cout << "Enter ten times (in seconds):\n";
    for (int i = 0; i < 10; i++)
        cin >> my_best.time[i];
```

The expression my_best.time[i] is read left to right: my_best is a structure. my_best.time is the member variable named time. Since my_best.time is an array, it makes sense to add an index. So, the expression my_best.time[i] is the ith indexed variable of the array my_best.time. If you use a class rather than a

Display 9.15 Program Using an Array of Objects *(part 1 of 2)*

```cpp
//Reads in 5 amounts of money and shows how much each
//amount differs from the largest amount.
#include <iostream>
#include "money.h"

int main()
{
    using namespace std;
    using namespace savitchmoney;
    Money amount[5], max;
    int i;

    cout << "Enter 5 amounts of money:\n";
    cin >> amount[0];
    max = amount[0];
    for (i = 1; i < 5; i++)
    {
        cin >> amount[i];
        if (max < amount[i])
            max = amount[i];
        //max is the largest of amount[0],..., amount[i].
    }

    Money difference[5];
    for (i = 0; i < 5; i++)
        difference[i] = max - amount[i];

    cout << "The highest amount is " << max << endl;
    cout << "The amounts and their\n"
         << "differences from the largest are:\n";
    for (i = 0; i < 5; i++)
    {
        cout << amount[i] << " off by "
             << difference[i] << endl;
    }

    return 0;
}
```

Display 9.15 Program Using an Array of Objects (part 2 of 2)

Sample Dialogue

```
Enter 5 amounts of money:
$5.00 $10.00 $19.99 $20.00 $12.79
The highest amount is $20.00
The amounts and their
differences from the largest are:
$5.00 off by $15.00
$10.00 off by $10.00
$19.99 off by $0.01
$20.00 off by $0.00
$12.79 off by $7.21
```

structure type, then you can do all your array manipulations with member functions and avoid such confusing expressions. This is illustrated in the following Programming Example. Additional material on using classes with arrays as member variables is given in Chapter 10.

■)) *PROGRAMMING EXAMPLE*
A Class for a Partially Filled Array

Displays 9.16 and 9.17 show the definition for a class called TemperatureList, whose objects are lists of temperatures. You might use an object of type TemperatureList in a program that does weather analysis. The list of temperatures is kept in the member variable list, which is an array. Since this array will typically be only partially filled, a second member variable, called size, is used to keep track of how much of the array is used. The value of size is the number of indexed variables of the array list that are being used to store values.

In a program that uses this class, the header file must be mentioned in an include directive, just like any other class that is placed in a separate file. Thus, any program that uses the class TemperatureList must contain the following include directive:

```
#include "templist.h"
```

Display 9.16 Interface for a Class with an Array Member

```
//This is the HEADER FILE templist.h. This is the INTERFACE for the class
//TemperatureList. Values of this type are lists of Fahrenheit temperatures.

#ifndef TEMPLIST_H
#define TEMPLIST_H
#include <iostream>
using namespace std;
namespace savitchtlist
{
    const int MAX_LIST_SIZE = 50;

    class TemperatureList
    {
    public:
        TemperatureList( );
        //Initializes the object to an empty list.

        void add_temperature(double temperature);
        //Precondition: The list is not full.
        //Postcondition: The temperature has been added to the list.

        bool full( ) const;
        //Returns true if the list is full, false otherwise.

        friend ostream& operator <<(ostream& outs,
                                const TemperatureList& the_object);
        //Overloads the << operator so it can be used to output values of
        //type TemperatureList. Temperatures are output one per line.
        //Precondition: If outs is a file output stream, then outs
        //has already been connected to a file.
    private:
        double list[MAX_LIST_SIZE]; //of temperatures in Fahrenheit
        int size; //number of array positions filled
    };
}//namespace savitchtlist
#endif //TEMPLIST_H
```

Display 9.17 Implementation for a Class with an Array Member

```
//This is the IMPLEMENTATION FILE: templist.cxx for the class TemperatureList.
//The interface for the class TemperatureList is in the file templist.h.
#include <iostream>
#include <cstdlib>
#include "templist.h"
using namespace std;
namespace savitchtlist
{
    TemperatureList::TemperatureList( )
    {
        size = 0;
    }

    void TemperatureList::add_temperature(double temperature)
    {//Uses iostream and cstdlib:
        if ( full( ) )
        {
            cout << "Error: adding to a full list.\n";
            exit(1);
        }
        else
        {
            list[size] = temperature;
            size = size + 1;
        }
    }

    bool TemperatureList::full( ) const
    {
        return (size == MAX_LIST_SIZE);
    }

    //Uses iostream:
    ostream& operator <<(ostream& outs, const TemperatureList& the_object)
    {
        for (int i = 0; i < the_object.size; i++)
            outs << the_object.list[i] << " F\n";
        return outs;
    }
}//namespace savitchtlist
```

An object of type `TemperatureList` is declared, like an object of any other type. For example, the following declares `my_data` to be an object of type `TemperatureList`:

```
TemperatureList my_data;
```

This declaration calls the default constructor with the new object `my_data`, and so the object `my_data` is initialized so that the member variable `size` has the value `0`, indicating an empty list.

Once you have declared an object such as `my_data`, you can add an item to the list of temperatures (that is, to the member array `list`) with a call to the member function `add_temperature` as follows:

```
my_data.add_temperature(77);
```

In fact, this is the only way you can add a temperature to the list `my_data`, since the array `list` is a private member variable. Notice that when you add an item with a call to the member function `add_temperature`, the function call first tests to see if the array list is full and only adds the value if the array is not full.

The class `TemperatureList` is very specialized. The only things you can do with an object of the class `TemperatureList` are to initialize the list so it is empty, add items to the list, check if the list is full, and output the list. To output the temperatures stored in the object `my_data` (declared above), the call would be as follows:

```
cout << my_data;
```

With the class `TemperatureList` you cannot delete a temperature from the list (array) of temperatures. You can, however, erase the entire list and start over with an empty list by calling the default constructor, as follows:

```
my_data = TemperatureList( );
```

The type `TemperatureList` uses almost no properties of temperatures. You could define a similar class for lists of pressures or list of distances or list of any other data expressed as values of type *double*. To save yourself the trouble of defining all these different classes you could define a single class that represents an arbitrary list of values of type *double* without specifying what the values represent. You are asked to define just such a list class in Programming Project 11.

SELF-TEST EXERCISES

22 Change the class `TemperatureList` given in Displays 9.16 and 9.17 by adding a member function called `get_size`, which takes no arguments and returns the number of temperatures on the list.

23 Change the type `TemperatureList` given in Displays 9.16 and 9.17 by adding a member function called `get_temperature`, which takes one *int* argument that is an integer greater than or equal to 0 and strictly less than `MAX_LIST_SIZE`. The function returns a value of type *double*, which is the temperature in that position on the list. So, with an argument of 0, `get_temperature` returns the first temperature; with an argument of 1, it returns the second temperature, and so forth. Assume that `get_temperature` will not be called with an argument that specifies a location on the list that does not currently contain a temperature.

CHAPTER SUMMARY

- An array can be used to store and manipulate a collection of data that is all of the same type.

- The indexed variables of an array can be used just like any other variables of the base type of the array.

- A *for*-loop is a good way to step through the elements of an array and perform some program action on each indexed variable.

- The most common programming error made when using arrays is attempting to access a nonexistent array index. Always check the first and last iterations of a loop that manipulates an array to make sure it does not use an index that is illegally small or illegally large.

- An array formal parameter is neither a call-by-value parameter nor a call-by-reference parameter, but a new kind of parameter. An array parameter is similar to a call-by-reference parameter in that any change that is made to the formal parameter in the body of the function will be made to the array argument when the function is called.

- The indexed variables for an array are stored next to each other in the computer's memory so that the array occupies a contiguous portion of memory. When the array is passed as an argument to a function, only the address of the first indexed variable (the one numbered 0) is given to the calling function. Therefore, a function with an array parameter usually needs another formal parameter of type *int* to give the size of the array.

- When using a partially filled array your program needs an additional variable of type *int* to keep track of how much of the array is being used.

- To tell the compiler that an array argument should not be changed by your function, you can insert the modifier *const* before the array parameter for that argument position. An array parameter that is modified with a *const* is called a **constant array parameter.**

- The base type of an array can be a structure or class type. A structure or class can have an array as a member variable.

Answers to Self-Test Exercises

1 The statement, *int* x[5]; is a declaration, where 5 is the number of array elements. The expression x[4] is an access into the array defined by the previous statement. The access is to the element having index 4, which is the fifth (and last) array element.

2 a. score

  b. *double*

  c. 5

  d. 0 through 4

  e. any of score[0], score[1], score[2], score[3], score[4]

3 a. One too many initializers

  b. Correct. The array size is 4

  c. Correct. The array size is 4

  d. Attempt to specify array size 0

4
```
abc
```

5
```
1.1 2.2 3.3
1.1 3.3 3.3
```

(Remember that the indexes start with 0, not 1.)

6
```
0 2 4 6 8 10 12 14 16 18
0 4 8 12 16
```

7 The indexed variables of `sample_array` are `sample_array[0]` through `sample_array[9]`, but this piece of code tries to fill `sample_array[1]` through `sample_array[10]`. The index 10 in `sample_array[10]` is out of range.

8 There is an index out of range. When `index` is equal to 9, `index + 1` is equal to 10, so `a[index + 1]`, which is the same as `a[10]`, has an illegal index. The loop should stop with one fewer iteration. To correct the code, change the first line of the *for*-loop to:

```
for (int index = 0; index < 9; index++)
```

9
```
int i, a[20];
cout << "Enter 20 numbers:\n";
for (i = 0; i < 20; i++)
    cin >> a[i];
```

10 The array will consume 14 bytes of memory. The address of the indexed variable `your_array[3]` is 1006.

11 The following function calls are acceptable:

```
tripler(number);
tripler(a[2]);
tripler(a[number]);
```

The following function calls are incorrect. The first one has an illegal index. The second has no indexed expression at all. You cannot use an entire array as an argument to `tripler`, as in the second call below. The section "Entire Arrays as Function Arguments" discusses a different situation in which you can use an entire array as an argument.

```
tripler(a[3]);
tripler(a);
```

12 The loop steps through indexed variables `b[1]` through `b[5]`, but 5 is an illegal index for the array b. The indexes are 0, 1, 2, 3, and 4. The correct version of the code is given below:

```
int b[5] = {1, 2, 3, 4, 5};
for (int i = 0; i < 5; i++)
    tripler(b[i]);
```

13

```
void one_more(int a[], int size)
//Precondition: size is the declared size of the array a.
//a[0] through a[size-1] have been given values.
//Postcondition: a[index] has been increased by 1
//for all indexed variables of a.
{
    for (int index = 0; index < size; index++)
        a[index] = a[index] + 1;
}
```

14 The following function calls are all acceptable:

```
too2(my_array, 29);
too2(my_array, 10);
too2(your_array, 100);
```

The call

```
too2(my_array, 10);
```

is legal, but will fill only the first 10 indexed variables of my_array. If that is what is desired the call is acceptable.

The following function calls are all incorrect:

```
too2(my_array, 55);
"Hey too2. Please, come over here."
too2(my_array[3], 29);
```

The first of these is incorrect because the second argument is too large. The second because it is missing a final semicolon (and for other reasons). The third one because it uses an indexed variable for an argument where it should use the entire array.

15 You can make the array parameter in output a constant parameter, since there is no need to change the values of any indexed variables of the array parameter. You cannot make the parameter in drop_odd a constant parameter because it may have the values of some of its indexed variables changed.

```
void output(const double a[], int size);
//Precondition: a[0] through a[size - 1] have values.
//Postcondition: a[0] through a[size - 1] have been
//written out.
```

```
void drop_odd(int a[], int size);
//Precondition: a[0] through a[size - 1] have values.
//Postcondition: All odd numbers in a[0] through a[size - 1]
//have been changed to 0.
```

16

```
int outOfOrder ( double array[], int size )
{
    for( int i = 0; i < size - 1; i++) // This is (size - 1) because
        if ( array[i] > array[i+1] )    // we fetch a[i+1] for each i.
            return i+1;                 // Continuing up to size would
    return -1;                          // cause the element at index
}                                       // size to be fetched. This can
                                        // cause erroneous results since
                                        // it is an illegal location.
```

17

```
#include <iostream>
const int DECLARED_SIZE = 10;
int main( )
{
    using namespace std;
    cout << "Enter up to ten nonnegative integers.\n"
        << "Place a negative number at the end.\n";
    int number_array[DECLARED_SIZE], next, index = 0;
    cin >> next;
    while ( (next >= 0) && (index < DECLARED_SIZE) )
    {
        number_array[index] = next;
        index++;
        cin >> next;
    }
    int number_used = index;
    cout << "Here they are back at you:";
    for (index = 0; index < number_used; index++)
        cout << number_array[index] << " ";
    cout << endl;
    return 0;
}
```

18

```cpp
#include <iostream>
const int DECLARED_SIZE = 10;
int main()
{
    using namespace std;
    cout << "Enter up to ten letters"
         << " followed by a period:\n";
    char letter_box[DECLARED_SIZE], next;
    int index = 0;
    cin >> next;
    while ( (next != '.') && (index < DECLARED_SIZE) )
    {
        letter_box[index] = next;
        index++;
        cin >> next;
    }
    int number_used = index;
    cout << "Here they are backwards:\n";
    for (index = number_used-1; index >= 0; index--)
        cout << letter_box[index];
    cout << endl;
    return 0;
}
```

19

```cpp
bool search(const int a[], int number_used,
                           int target, int& where)
{
    int index = 0;
    bool found = false;
    while ((!found) && (index < number_used))
    if (target == a[index])
        found = true;
    else
        index++;
    //If target was found, then
    //found == true and a[index] == target.

    if (found)
        where = index;
    return found;
}
```

20

```
struct Score
{
    int home_team;
    int opponent;
};
Score game[10];
```

21

```
//Reads in 5 amounts of money, doubles each amount,
//and outputs the results.
#include <iostream>
#include "money.h"

int main( )
{
    using namespace std;
    Money amount[5];
    int i;
    cout << "Enter 5 amounts of money:\n";
    for (i = 0; i < 5; i++)
        cin >> amount[i];
    for (i = 0; i < 5; i++)
    amount[i] = amount[i] + amount[i];
    cout << "After doubling, the amounts are:\n";
    for (i = 0; i < 5; i++)
        cout << amount[i] << " ";
    cout << endl;

    return 0;
}
```

(You cannot use 2*amount[i], since * has not been overloaded for operands of type Money.)

22 See answer 23.

23 This answer combines the answers to this and the previous Self-Test Exercise. The class definition would change to the following. We have deleted some comments from Display 9.16 to save space, but you should include them in your answer.

```
namespace savitchtlist
{
    class TemperatureList
    {
    public:
        TemperatureList( );

        int get_size( ) const;
        //Returns the number of temperatures on the list.

        void add_temperature(double temperature);

        double get_temperature(int position) const;
        //Precondition: 0 <= position < get_size( ).
        //Returns the temperature that was added in position
        //specified. The first temperature that was added is in
        //position 0.

        bool full( ) const;

        friend ostream& operator <<(ostream& outs,
                        const TemperatureList& the_object);
    private:
        double list[MAX_LIST_SIZE];//of temperatures in
                                   //Fahrenheit
        int size; //number of array positions filled
    };
}//namespace savitchtlist
```

You also need to add the following member function definitions:

```
int TemperatureList::get_size( ) const
{
    return size;
}
//Uses iostream and cstdlib:
double TemperatureList::get_temperature (int position) const
{
    if ( (position >= size) || (position < 0) )
    {
        cout << "Error:"
            << " reading an empty list position.\n";
        exit(1);
    }
```

```
        else
        {
            return (list[position]);
        }
    }
```

Programming Projects

Projects 1 through 7 do not require the use of structures or classes (although Project 7 can be done more elegantly by using structures). Projects 8 through the end are meant to be done using structures or classes.

1 A palindrome is a word that is spelled the same forward and backward, such as "radar." Write a program that will accept a string of letters terminated by a period and will determine whether or not the word (without the period) is a palindrome. You may assume that the input contains only lowercase letters and that the input word is at most twenty letters long. Your program need not check that the words are actually English words. The word "aabbcbbaa" will be considered a palindrome by your program. Include a loop that allows the user to check additional words until the user requests that the program end.

2 There are three versions of this project.

Version 1 (all interactive): Write a program that reads in the average monthly rainfall for a city for each month of the year and then reads in the actual monthly rainfall for each of the previous twelve months. The program then prints out a nicely formatted table showing the rainfall for each of the previous twelve months as well as how much above or below average the rainfall was for each month. The average monthly rainfall is given for the months January, February, and so forth, in order. To obtain the actual rainfall for the previous twelve months, the program first asks what the current month is and then asks for the rainfall figures for the previous twelve months. The output should correctly label the months. There are a variety of ways to deal with the month names. One straightforward method is to code the months as integers and then do a conversion before doing the output. A large *switch*-statement is acceptable in an output function. The month input can be handled in any manner you wish so long as it is relatively easy and pleasant for the user. After you have completed the above program, produce an enhanced version that also outputs a graph showing the average rainfall and the actual rainfall for each of the previous twelve months. The graph should be similar to the one shown in Display 9.9, except that there should be two bar graphs for each month and they should be labeled as the average rainfall and the rainfall for the most recent month. Your program should ask the user whether she or he wants to see the table or the bar graph and then displays whichever format is requested. Include a loop that allows the user to see either format as often as the user wishes until the user requests that the program end.

Version 2 (combines interactive and file output): For a more elaborate version also allow the user to request that the table and graph be output to a file. The file name is entered by the user. This program does everything that the Version 1 program does, but has this added feature. To read a file name you must use material presented in the optional section of Chapter 5 entitled "File Names as Input."

Version 3 (all I/O with files): This version is like Version 1 except that input is taken from a file and the output is sent to a file. Since there is no user to interact with, there is no loop to allow repeating the display; both the table and the graph are output to the same file. If this is a class assignment ask your instructor for instructions on what file names to use.

3 Write a function called `delete_repeats` that has a partially filled array of characters as a formal parameter and that deletes all repeated letters from the array. Since a partially filled array requires two arguments, the function will actually have two formal parameters: an array parameter and a formal parameter of type *int* that gives the number of array positions used. When a letter is deleted, the remaining letters are moved forward to fill in the gap. This will create empty positions at the end of the array so that less of the array is used. Since the formal parameter is a partially filled array, a second formal parameter of type *int* will tell how many array positions are filled. This second formal parameter will be a call-by-reference parameter and will be changed to show how much of the array is used after the repeated letters are deleted. For example, consider the following code:

```
char a[10];
a[0] = 'a';
a[1] = 'b';
a[2] = 'a';
a[3] = 'c';
int size = 4;
delete_repeats(a, size);
```

After this code is executed, the value of a[0] is 'a', the value of a[1] is 'b', the value of a[2] is 'c', and the value of size is 3. (The value of a[3] is no longer of any concern, since the partially filled array no longer uses this indexed variable.) You may assume that the partially filled array contains only lowercase letters. Embed your function in a suitable test program.

4 The standard deviation of a list of numbers is a measure of how much the numbers deviate from the average. If the standard deviation is small, the numbers are clustered close to the average. If the standard deviation is large, the numbers are scattered far from the average. The **standard deviation, S,** of a list of N numbers x_i is defined as follows:

$$S = \sqrt{\frac{\sum_{i=1}^{N} (x_i - \bar{x})^2}{N}}$$

where $\bar{x}$ is the average of the N numbers x_1, x_2,... Define a function that takes a partially filled array of numbers as its arguments and returns the standard deviation of the numbers in the partially filled array. Since a partially filled array requires two arguments, the function will actually have two formal parameters, an array parameter and a formal parameter of type *int* that gives the number of array positions used. The numbers in the array will be of type *double*. Embed your function in a suitable test program.

5 Write a program that reads in an array of type *int*. Provide facility to either read this array from the keyboard or from a file, at the user's option. If the user chooses file input, the program should request a file name. You may assume that there are fewer than 50 entries in the array. Your program determines how many entries there are. The output is to be a two-column list. The first column is a list of the distinct array elements; the second column is the count of the number of occurrences of each element. The list should be sorted on entries in the first column, largest to smallest.

For the array

-12 3 -12 4 1 1 -12 1 -1 1 2 3 4 2 3 -12

the output should be

N	Count
4	2
3	3
2	2
1	4
-1	1
-12	4

6 The text discusses the selection sort. We propose a different 'sort' routine, the **insertion sort.** This routine is in a sense the opposite of the selection sort in that it picks up successive elements from the array and *inserts* each of these into the correct position in an already sorted subarray (at one end of the array we are sorting).

The array to be sorted is divided into a sorted subarray and an unexamined subarray. Initially, the sorted subarray is empty. Each element of the unexamined subarray is picked and inserted into its correct position in the sorted subarray.

Write a function and a test program to implement the selection sort. Thoroughly test your program.

Example and Hints:

The implementation involves an outside loop that selects successive elements in the unsorted subarray and a nested loop that inserts each element in its proper position in the sorted subarray.

Initially, the sorted subarray is empty, and the unsorted subarray is all of the array:

The sorted subarray is empty:

The unsorted subarray is the entire array

a[0]	a[1]	a[2]	a[3]	a[4]	a[5]	a[6]	a[7]	a[8]	a[9]
8	6	10	2	16	4	18	14	12	10

The sorted subarray is of size 0, and the unsorted subarray is all of the array. Pick the first element, a[0], i.e., 8, and place it in the first position. The inside loop has nothing to do in this first case. The array and subarrays look like this:

sorted   unsorted

a[0]	a[1]	a[2]	a[3]	a[4]	a[5]	a[6]	a[7]	a[8]	a[9]
8	6	10	2	16	4	18	14	12	10

The first element from the unsorted subarray (a[2], which has value 6). Insert this into the sorted subarray in its proper position. These are out of order, so the inside loop must swap values in position 0 and position 1. The result is:

sorted		unsorted							
a[0]	a[1]	a[2]	a[3]	a[4]	a[5]	a[6]	a[7]	a[8]	a[9]
6	8	10	2	16	4	18	14	10	12

Note that the sorted subarray has grown by one entry. Do this for the first unsorted subarray entry, a[2], finding a place where a[2] can be placed so the subarray remains sorted. Since a[2] is already in place, i.e., it is larger than the largest element in the sorted subarray, the inside loop has nothing to do.

sorted			unsorted						
a[0]	a[1]	a[2]	a[3]	a[4]	a[5]	a[6]	a[7]	a[8]	a[9]
6	8	10	2	16	4	18	14	10	12

Again, pick the first unsorted array element, a[3], but this time the inside loop has to swap values until the value of a[3] is in its proper position. This involves some swapping:

sorted				unsorted					
a[0]	a[1]	a[2]	a[3]	a[4]	a[5]	a[6]	a[7]	a[8]	a[9]
6	8	10<-->2		16	4	18	14	10	12

sorted				unsorted					
a[0]	a[1]	a[2]	a[3]	a[4]	a[5]	a[6]	a[7]	a[8]	a[9]
6	8<--->2		10	16	4	18	14	10	12

sorted				unsorted					
a[0]	a[1]	a[2]	a[3]	a[4]	a[5]	a[6]	a[7]	a[8]	a[9]
6<--->2		8	10	16	4	18	14	10	12

The result of placing the 2 in the sorted subarray is

sorted				unsorted					
a[0]	a[1]	a[2]	a[3]	a[4]	a[5]	a[6]	a[7]	a[8]	a[9]
2	6	8	10	16	4	18	14	10	12

The algorithm continues in this fashion until the unsorted array is empty, and the sorted array has all the original array's elements.

7 An array can be used to store large integers one digit at a time. For example, the integer 1234 could be stored in the array a by setting a[0] to 1, a[1] to 2, a[2] to 3, and a[3] to 4. However, for this exercise you might find it more useful to store the digits backward, that is, place 4 in a[0], 3 in a[1], 2 in a[2], and 1 in a[3]. In this exercise you will write a program that reads in two positive integers that are 20 or fewer digits in length and then outputs the sum of the two numbers. Your program will read the digits as values of type *char* so that the number 1234 is read as the four characters '1', '2', '3', and '4'. After they are read into the program, the characters are changed to values of type *int*. The digits will be read into a partially filled array, and you might find it useful to reverse the order of the elements in the array after the array is filled with data from the keyboard. (Whether or not you reverse the order of the elements in the array is up to you. It can be done either way and each way has its advantages and disadvantages.) Your program will perform the addition by implementing the usual paper-and-pencil addition algorithm. The result of the addition is stored in an array of size 20 and the result is then written to the screen. If the result of the addition is an integer with more than the maximum number of digits (i.e., more than 20 digits), then your program should issue a message saying that it has encountered "integer overflow." You should be able to change the maximum length of the integers by changing only one globally defined constant. Include a loop that allows the user to continue to do more additions until the user says the program should end.

8 Write a program that will read a line of text and output a list of all the letters that occur in the text together with the number of times each letter occurs in the line. End the line with a period that serves as a sentinel value. The letters should be listed in the order: the most frequently occurring letter, the next

most frequently occurring letter, and so forth. Use an array with a *struct* type as its base type so that each array element can hold both a letter and an integer. You may assume that the input uses all lowercase letters. For example, the input

do be do bo.

should produce output similar to the following:

```
Letter:   Number of Occurrences
    o     3
    d     2
    b     2
    e     1
```

Your program will need to sort the array according to the integer members of the *struct*s in the array. This will require that you modify the function sort given in Display 9.13. You cannot use sort to solve this problem without changing the function. If this is a class assignment, ask your instructor if input/output should be done with the keyboard and screen or if it should be done with files. If it is to be done with files, ask your instructor for instructions on file names.

9   Write a program to score five-card poker hands into one of the following categories: nothing, one pair, two pairs, three of a kind, straight (in order with no gaps), flush (all the same suit, e.g., all spades), full house (one pair and three of a kind), four of a kind, straight flush (both a straight and a flush). Use an array of structures to store the hand. The structure will have two member variables: one for the value of the card and one for the suit. Include a loop that allows the user to continue to score more hands until the user says the program should end.

10 Write a checkbook balancing program. The program will read in the following for all checks that were not cashed as of the last time you balanced your checkbook: the number of each check, the amount of the check, and whether or not it has been cashed yet. Use an array with a class base type. The class should be a class for a check. There should be three member variables to record the check number, the check amount, and whether or not the check was cashed. The class for a check will have a member variable of type Money (as defined in Display 9.14) to record the check amount. So, you will have a class used within a class. The class for a check should have accessor functions as well as constructors and functions for both input and output of a check. In addition to the checks, the program also reads all the deposits, as

well as the old and the new account balance. You may want another array to hold the deposits. The new account balance should be the old balance plus all deposits, minus all checks that have been cashed. The program outputs the total of the checks cashed, the total of the deposits, what the new balance should be, and how much this figure differs from what the bank says the new balance is. It also outputs two lists of checks: the checks cashed since the last time you balanced your checkbook and the checks still not cashed. Display both lists of checks in sorted order from lowest to highest check number. If this is a class assignment, ask your instructor if input/output should be done with the keyboard and screen or if it should be done with files. If it is to be done with files, ask your instructor for instructions on file names.

11 Define a class called `List` that can hold a list of values of type *double*. Model your class definition after the class `TemperatureList` given in Displays 9.16 and 9.17, but your class `List` will make no reference to temperatures when it outputs values. The values may represent any sort of data items as long as they are of type *double*. Include the additional features specified in Self-Test Exercises 22 and 23. Change the member function names so that they do not refer to `temperature`. Add a member function called `get_last` that takes no arguments and returns the last item on the list. The member function `get_last` does not change the list. The member function `get_last` should not be called if the list is empty. Add another member function called `delete_last` that deletes the last element on the list. The member function `delete_last` is a *void*-function. Note that when the last element is deleted, the member variable `size` must be adjusted. If `delete_last` is called with an empty list as the calling object, the function call has no effect. You should place your class definition in an interface file and an implementation file as we did with the type `TemperatureList` in Displays 9.16 and 9.17. Design a program to thoroughly test your definition for the class `List`.

CHAPTER 10

Strings and Multidimensional Arrays

10 Strings and Multidimensional Arrays

Polonius: What do you read, my lord?
Hamlet: Words, words, words.

WILLIAM SHAKESPEARE, HAMLET

Introduction

In this chapter we continue our study of arrays by presenting more material on the kinds of strings we have already seen, material on multidimensional arrays, and material on the relatively new ANSI C++ string class. Since we will now be discussing two kinds of strings, we call the sort of strings we have seen before **cstrings** and the new kind of strings that we introduce in this chapter simply strings. The quoted strings we have seen before, like `"Enter the input:"` are what we call *cstrings*. The ANSI C++ string class is a new kind of representation for strings which we have not discussed before this chapter.

A multidimensional array is an array with more than one index. Multidimensional arrays can be used, among other things, to create arrays of strings. If you wish, you may skip the material on multidimensional arrays in Section 10.2 and read the material on the new ANSI C++ string class in Section 10.3 before you read Section 10.2.

10.1 String Basics

In this section we describe the facilities for processing strings that are automatically provided by C++. Later in this chapter we will discuss how you might create additional string-processing facilities, concluding with the ANSI Standard string class.

Cstring Values and Cstring Variables

string values

We have already used **string values.** The string `"Hi Mom!"` in the following `cout`-statement is a string value:

```
cout << "Hi Mom!";
```

In C++, you can store string values in variables and manipulate string values in ways that are similar to how you manipulate data of other types.

In C++ there is also the class `string` from the Standard Library, whose members are declared in the `<string>` header. We will discuss the class `string` and objects of this class in Section 10.4. To distinguish between these two varieties of string, we will refer to the earlier strings as **cstrings**. The reason we call these cstrings is that this is the string type that C++ automatically gets through its C language heritage.

A **cstring variable** is exactly the same thing as an array of characters. If you think about it, this is very natural. A cstring is a list of characters and an array of characters is just what you need to store a list of characters. Thus, the following array declaration provides us with a cstring variable capable of storing a cstring value with 9 or fewer characters:

cstring variables

```
char s[10];
```

That is not a mistake. We said that this cstring variable `s` can hold a cstring with 9 or fewer characters. The cstring variable `s` cannot hold a cstring with 10 characters. That is because a cstring variable is used in a slightly different way than an ordinary array of characters.

A cstring variable is a partially filled array of characters. Like any other partially filled array, a cstring variable uses positions starting at indexed variable 0 through as many as are needed. But, a cstring variable uses a different technique to remember how much of the partially filled array is used. With a cstring variable, we do not necessarily have another variable of type *int* to record how much of the array has been filled. *Instead, a string variable places the special symbol '\0' in the array immediately after the last character of the cstring.* Thus, if `s` contains the string "Hi Mom!", then the array elements are filled as shown below:

```
s[0] s[1] s[2] s[3] s[4] s[5] s[6] s[7] s[8] s[9]
```

H	i		M	o	m	!	\0	?	?

The character '\0' is used as a sentinel value to mark the end of the cstring. If you read the characters in the cstring starting at indexed variable `s[0]`, proceed to `s[1]`, then to `s[2]`, and so forth, you know that when you encounter the symbol '\0', then you have reached the end of the cstring. Since the symbol '\0' always occupies one element of the array, the length of the longest string that the array can hold is one less than the size of the array.

The Null Character, '\0'

The null character, '\0', is used to mark the end of a cstring that is stored in an array of characters. When an array of characters is used in this way, the array is often called a cstring variable. Although the null character '\0' is written using two symbols, it is a single character that fits in one variable of type *char* or one indexed variable of an array of characters.

Cstring Variable Declaration

A **cstring variable** is the exact same thing as an array of characters, but it is used differently. A cstring variable is declared to be an array of characters in the usual way:

Syntax:

```
char Array_Name[Maximum_Cstring_Size + 1];
```

Example:

```
char my_cstring[11];
```

The + 1 allows for the null character '\0', which terminates any cstring stored in the array. For example, the cstring variable my_cstring in the above example can hold cstrings that are 10 or fewer characters long.

---

the null character '\0'

The character '\0' is called the **null character.** The null character is a special character, just like the new line character '\n' is a special character. Just like '\n', we spell '\0' with two symbols when we write it in a program, but just like '\n', the character '\0' is really only a single character value. Like any other character value, '\0' can be stored in one variable of type *char* or one indexed variable of an array of characters. Because '\0' is different from all ordinary characters, we can use '\0' as a sentinel value to mark the end of a string of ordinary characters.

cstring variables vs. arrays of characters

The thing that distinguishes a cstring variable from an ordinary array of characters is that a cstring variable must contain the null character '\0' at the end of the cstring value. This is a distinction in how the array is used rather than a distinction about what the array is. *A cstring variable is an array of characters, but it is used in a different way.*

You can initialize a cstring variable when you declare it, as illustrated by the following example:

initializing
cstring variables

```
char my_message[20] = "Hi there.";
```

Notice that the cstring assigned to the cstring variable need not fill the entire array.

When you initialize a cstring variable, you can omit the array size and C++ will automatically make the size of the cstring variable one more than the length of the cstring. (The one extra indexed variable is for '\0'.) For example,

```
char short_string[] = "abc";
```

is equivalent to

```
char short_string[4] = "abc";
```

Be sure you do not confuse the following initializations:

```
char short_string[] = "abc";
        and
char short_string[] = {'a', 'b', 'c'};
```

They are *not equivalent*. The first of these two possible initializations places the null character '\0' in the array after the characters 'a', 'b', and 'c'. The second one does not put a '\0' anyplace in the array.

Initializing a Cstring Variable

A cstring variable can be initialized when it is declared, as illustrated by the following example:

```
char your_string[11] = "Do Be Do";
```

Initializing in this way automatically places the null character, '\0', in the array at the end of the cstring specified.

If you omit the number inside the square brackets [], then the cstring variable will be given a size one character longer than the length of the cstring. For example, the following declares my_string to have nine indexed variables (eight for the characters of the cstring "Do Be Do" and one for the null character '\0'):

```
char my_string[] = "Do Be Do";
```

A cstring variable is an array, so it has indexed variables that can be used just like those of any other array. For example, suppose your program contains the following cstring variable declarations:

```
char our_string[5] = "Hi";
```

With `our_string` declared as above, your program has the following indexed variables: `our_string[0]`, `our_string[1]`, `our_string[2]`, `our_string[3]`, and `our_string[4]`. For example, the following will change the cstring value in `our_string` to a cstring of the same length consisting of all `'X'` characters:

```
int index = 0;
while (our_string[index] != '\0')
{
    our_string[index] = 'X';
    index++;
}
```

When manipulating these indexed variables you should be very careful not to replace the null character `'\0'` with some other value. If the array loses the value `'\0'` it will no longer behave like a `cstring` variable. For example, the following will change the array `happy_string` so that it no longer contains a string:

```
char happy_string[7] = "DoBeDo";
happy_string[6] = 'Z';
```

After the above code is executed, the array `happy_string` will still contain the six letters in the `cstring` "DoBeDo", but `happy_string` will no longer contain the null character `'\0'` to mark the end of the cstring. Many string-manipulating functions depend critically on the presence of `'\0'` to mark the end of the cstring value.

As another example, consider the above *while*-loop that changes characters in the `cstring` variable `our_string`. That *while*-loop changes characters until it encounters a `'\0'`. If the loop never encounters a `'\0'`, then it could change a large chunk of memory to some unwanted values, and that could make your program do strange things. As a safety feature, it would be wise to rewrite the above *while*-loop as follows, so that if the null character `'\0'` is lost, the loop will not inadvertently change memory locations beyond the end of the array:

```
int index = 0;
while ( (our_string[index] != '\0') && (index < SIZE) )
{
    our_string[index] = 'X';
    index++;
}
```

SIZE is a defined constant equal to the declared size of the array `our_string`.

● PITFALL   Using = and == with cstrings

Cstring values and cstring variables are not like values and variables of other data types, and many of the usual operations do not work for cstrings. You cannot use a cstring variable in an assignment statement using =. If you use == to test cstrings for equality, you will not get the result you expect. The reason for these problems is that cstrings and cstring variables are arrays rather than simple values and simple variables.

Assigning a value to a cstring variable is not as simple as it is for other kinds of variables. The following is illegal:

assigning a cstring value

```
char a_string[10];
a_string = "Hello";  ←——————  Illegal!
```

Although you can use the equal sign to assign a value to a cstring variable when the variable is declared, you cannot do it anywhere else in your program. Technically, a use of the equal sign in a declaration, as in

```
char happy_string[7] = "DoBeDo";
```

is an initialization not an assignment. As we will see in Chapter 11, assignment and initialization are two very different things. If you want to assign a value to a cstring variable, you must do something else. There are a number of different ways to assign a value to a cstring variable. The easiest way is to use the predefined function `strcpy` as shown below

```
strcpy(a_string, "Hello");
```

This will set the value of `a_string` equal to `"Hello"`.

You also cannot use the operator == in an expression to test whether two cstrings are the same. (Things are actually much worse than that. You can use == with cstrings, but it does not test for the cstrings being equal. So if you use == to test two cstrings for equality, you will get incorrect results!) To test whether two cstrings are the same, you can use the predefined function `strcmp`. For example:

testing cstrings fpr equality

```
if (strcmp(cstring1, cstring2))
    cout << "The strings are NOT the same.";
else
    cout << "The strings are the same.";
```

Note that the function `strcmp` works differently than you might guess. The function `strcmp` compares the characters in the `cstring` arguments a character at a time. If at any point the numeric encoding of the character from `cstring1` is less than the numeric encoding of the corresponding character from `cstring2`, at that point the testing stops, and a negative number is returned. If the character from `cstring1` is greater than the character from `cstring2`, then a positive number is returned. (Some implementations of `strcmp` return the difference of the character encodings, but you should not depend on that!) If the cstrings are the same, a 0 is returned. An order relation based on the order of the first characters that are different is called **lexicographic** order. Note that if both strings are all in uppercase or all in lowercase, then lexicographic order is just alphabetic order.

We see that `strcmp` returns negative value, a positive value, or zero, depending on whether the cstrings compare lexicographically less, greater, or equal. If you use `strcmp` as a Boolean expression in an *if* or a looping statement to test cstrings for equality, then the nonzero value will be converted to *true* if the strings are different, and the zero will be converted to *false*. Be sure that you remember this inverted logic in your testing for cstring equality.

The functions `strcpy` and `strcmp` are in the library with the header file `<cstring>`. So, any program that uses these functions must have an `include` directive like the following:[1]

```
#include <cstring>
```

There are some problems associated with `strcpy` and some of the other functions in the library with the header file `cstring` (or `string.h`); these are discussed in the Pitfall section "Dangers in Using Functions from `cstring`."

Predefined Cstring Functions

Display 10.1 contains a few of the most commonly used functions from the library with the header file `cstring`. When you use any of these functions, your program must contain an `include` directive for the header file `cstring`, as described at the end of the previous section.

---

[1] <cstring> is the name that the ANSI C++ Standard requires. However, some compilers may not yet have such a header file. The interim solution is to use the <string.h>, or perhaps <cstring.h>, header file in place of <cstring>. If you find that <cstring> does not work properly, consult your compiler documentation or consult a guru for local details. Eventually all up-to-date compilers will have the <cstring> header.

Display 10.1 Some Predefined Cstring Functions in cstring

Function	Description	Cautions
strcpy(*Target_String_Var*, *Src_String*)	Copies the cstring value *Src_String* into the cstring variable *Target_String_Var*.	Does not check to make sure *Target_String_Var* is large enough to hold the value *Src_String*.
strcat(*Target_String_Var*, *Src_String*)	Concatenates the cstring value *Src_String* onto the end of the cstring in the cstring variable *Target_String_Var*.	Does not check to see that *Target_String_Var* is large enough to hold the result of the concatenation.
strlen(*Src_String*)	Returns an integer equal to the length of *Src_String*. (The null character, '\0', is not counted in the length.)	
strcmp(*String_1*, *String_2*)	Returns 0 if *String_1* and *String_2* are the same. Returns a value < 0 if *String_1* is less than *String_2*. Returns a value > 0 if *String_1* is greater than *String_2* (i.e., returns a nonzero value if *String_1* and *String_2* are different). The order is lexicographic.	If *String_1* equals *String_2*, this function returns 0, which converts to *false*. Check to make sure you do not need to add a ! (i.e., add a *not*).

We have already discussed strcpy and strcmp. The function strlen is easy to understand and use. For example, strlen("dobedo") returns 6 because there are 6 characters in "dobedo".

The function strcat is used to concatenate two cstrings; that is, to form a longer string by placing the two shorter cstrings end-to-end. The first argument must be a cstring variable; the second argument can be anything that evaluates to a cstring value, such as a quoted string. The result is placed in the cstring variable that is the first argument. For example, consider the following:

```
char string_var[20] = "The rain";
strcat(string_var, "in Spain");
```

This code will change the value of `string_var` to `"The rainin Spain"`. As this example illustrates, you need to be careful to account for blanks when concatenating cstrings.

◆ PITFALL   Dangers in Using Functions from <cstring>

There is one danger associated with the functions `strcpy` and `strcat`. In most implementations of C++, these functions will let you assign a string that is too large for the `cstring` variable receiving the value. The following is unlikely to produce an error message, although it will still cause problems:

```
char short_string[3];
strcpy(short_string, "Now, here is a long string.");
```

With this call the function `strcpy` will fill the three indexed variables for the array `short_string`; then rather than stopping, it will continue to fill whatever memory follows the last indexed variable of `short_string`, even though this memory is being used for something else and should not be changed.

The function `strcat` similarly does not check to see if the concatenated cstring will fit in the cstring variable used as its first argument. When using either `strcpy` or `strcat` you must make sure the lengths of cstrings are not too long for their destination. These functions use the null terminator in the source cstring to decide when to stop copying, not the size of the target.

SELF-TEST EXERCISES

1   Which of the following declarations are equivalent?

```
char string_var[10] = "Hello";
char string_var[10] = {'H', 'e', 'l', 'l', 'o', '\0'};
char string_var[10] = {'H', 'e', 'l', 'l', 'o'};
char string_var[6] = "Hello";
char string_var[] = "Hello";
```

2   What cstring will be stored in `singing_string` after the following code is run?

```
char singing_string[20] = "DoBeDo";
strcat(singing_string, " to you");
```

Assume that the code is embedded in a complete and correct program and that an `include` directive for `cstring` is in the program file.

3 What (if anything) is wrong with the following code?

```
char string_var[] = "Hello";
strcat(string_var, " and Good-bye.");
cout << string_var;
```

Assume that the code is embedded in a complete program and that an `include` directive for `cstring` is in the program file.

4 Suppose the function `strlen` (which returns the length of its string argument) was not already defined for you. Give a function definition for `strlen`. Note that `strlen` has only one argument, which is a cstring. Do not add additional arguments; they are not needed.

5 What is the length (maximum) of a string that can be placed in the string variable declared by the following declaration? Explain.

```
char s[6];
```

6 How many characters are in each of the following character and string constants:

  c. `'\n'`
  d. `'n'`
  e. `"Mary"`
  f. `"M"`
  g. `"Mary\n"`

7 Since character strings are just arrays of *char*, why does the text caution you not to confuse the following declaration and initialization?

```
char short_string[] = "abc";
char short_string[] = { 'a', 'b', 'c'};
```

8 Given the following declaration and initialization of the string variable, write a loop to assign `'X'` to all positions of this string variable, keeping the length the same.

```
char our_string[5] = "Hi there!";
```

9 Given the declaration of a `cstring` variable, where `SIZE` is a defined constant:

```
char our_string[SIZE];
```

The `cstring` variable `our_string` has been assigned in code not shown here. For correct `cstring` variables, the following loop reassigns all positions of `our_string` the value `'X'`, leaving the length the same as before. Assume this code fragment is embedded in an otherwise complete and correct program. Answer the questions following this code fragment:

```
index = 0;
while (our_string[index] != '\0')
{
    our_string[index] = 'X';
    index++;
}
```

a. Explain how this code can destroy the contents of memory beyond the end of the array.

b. Modify this loop to protect against inadvertently changing memory beyond the end of the array.

10 Write code using a library function to copy the string constant `"Hello"` into the string variable declared below. Be sure to `#include` the necessary header file to get the declaration of the function you use.

```
char a_string[10];
```

11 What string will be output when this code is run? (Assume, as always, that this code is embedded in a complete, correct program.)

```
char song[10] = "I did it ";
char franks_song[20];
strcpy ( franks_song, song );
strcat ( franks_song, "my way!");
cout << franks_song << endl;
```

12 What is the problem (if any) with this code?

```
char to_Barbara[] = "Frank sang, \"";
strcat(to_Barbara, "Come Fly with me.");
```

Defining Cstring Functions

The problem with the function `strcpy` that we discussed in the previous pitfall section has to do with the arguments given to it. In a sense, `strcpy` does not have enough arguments. Let's review what happens when a cstring variable, which is an array, is passed as an argument to a function. Recall that when an array is passed as an argument to a function, the calling function is only told the location in memory of the first indexed variable of the array. Unless there is an additional *int* argument giving the size of the array, the function has no way of knowing the declared size of the array. Since a cstring variable is an array variable, the same is true when a cstring variable is passed as an argument to a function. Unless there is an additional *int* argument giving the size of the cstring variable, the function has no way of knowing the declared size of the array. Therefore, whenever you define a function that can change the value of a cstring variable, you should include an additional *int* argument giving the declared size of the array. The situation is similar to what we discussed in the section "Partially Filled Arrays" of Chapter 9. This technique is illustrated in the function shown in Display 10.2, which is a safer version of the function strcpy. We called this safer version string_copy to distinguish it from the function strcpy.[2] The function string_copy has an extra *int* argument that gives the declared size of the cstring variable. The function string_copy copies only as much of the second cstring as will fit in the cstring variable.

Notice that the function string_copy does not need an argument giving the declared size of the second argument, even though that argument can be a cstring variable (as in the second call to string_copy in Display 10.2). This is because the second argument is never changed by the function string_copy. As long as the function only needs to read the value in a cstring variable, it does not need to know the declared size of that cstring variable. As long as the function only needs to read the value in the cstring variable, it can use the null symbol '\0' to tell it when to stop reading.

Cstring Arguments and Parameters

A cstring variable is an array, so a **cstring parameter** to a function is simply an array parameter.

As with any array parameter, whenever a function changes the value of a cstring parameter, it is safest to include an additional *int* parameter giving the declared size of the cstring variable.

On the other hand, if a function only uses the value in a cstring argument, but does not change that value, then there is no need to include another parameter to give either the declared size of the cstring variable or the amount of the cstring variable array that is filled. The null character '\0' can be used to detect the end of the cstring value that is stored in the cstring variable.

---

[2]There are versions of strcpy and strcat with the added parameter already defined in the cstring library, called strncat and strncpy. See Appendix 4, String Functions.

Display 10.2 The Function `string_copy`

```
//Program to demonstrate the function string_copy
#include <iostream>
#include <cstring>

void string_copy(char target[], const char source[], int target_size);
//Precondition: target_size is the declared size of the cstring variable target.
//The array source contains a cstring value terminated with '\0'.
//Postcondition: The value of target has been set to the cstring value in source,
//provided the declared size of target is large enough. If target is not large
//enough to hold the entire cstring, a cstring equal to as much of the value of
//source as will fit is stored in target.

int main( )
{
    using namespace std;
    char short_string[11]; //Can hold cstrings of up to 10 characters.
    string_copy(short_string, "Hello", 11);
    cout << short_string << "STRING ENDS HERE.\n";

    char long_string[] = "This is rather long.";
    string_copy(short_string, long_string, 11);
    cout << short_string << "STRING ENDS HERE.\n";
    return 0;
}

//Uses header file cstring:
void string_copy(char target[], const char source[], int target_size)
{
    using namespace std;
    int new_length = strlen(source);
    if (new_length > (target_size - 1))
        new_length = target_size - 1; //That is all that will fit.
    int index;
    for (index = 0; index < new_length; index++)
        target[index] = source[index];
    target[index] = '\0';
}
```

Output

```
HelloSTRING ENDS HERE
This is raSTRING ENDS HERE
```

Cstring Input and Output

Cstrings can be output using the insertion operator <<. For example, the program in Display 10.2 contains the following statement, which outputs the value of the cstring variable short_string (followed by a quoted cstring):

```
cout << short_string << "STRING ENDS HERE.\n";
```

It is possible to fill a cstring variable using the input operator >>, but there is one thing to keep in mind. As for all other types of data, all whitespace (blanks and line breaks) are skipped when cstrings are read this way. Moreover, each reading of input stops at the next space or line break. For example, consider the following code:

```
char a[80], b[80];
cout << "Enter some input:\n";
cin >> a >> b;
cout << a << b << "END OF OUTPUT\n";
```

When embedded in a complete program, this code produces a dialogue like the following:

```
Enter some input:
Do be do to you!
DobeEND OF OUTPUT
```

The cstring variables a and b each receive only one word of the input: a receives the cstring value "Do" because the input character following **Do** is a blank; b receives "be" because the input character following **be** is a blank.

If you want your program to read an entire line of input, you can use the extraction operator >> to read the line one word at a time. This can be tedious and it still will not read the blanks in the line. There is an easy way to read an entire line of input and place the resulting cstring into a cstring variable: Just use the predefined member function getline, which is a member function of every input stream (such as cin or a file input stream). The function getline has two arguments. The first argument is a cstring variable to receive the input and the second is an integer that typically is the declared size of the cstring variable. This second argument serves the same purpose as the second argument in our function string_copy in Display 10.2. (To be precise, the second argument tells the maximum number of array elements in the cstring variable that getline will be allowed to fill with characters.) For example, consider the following code:

getline

```
char a[80];
cout << "Enter some input:\n";
cin.getline(a, 80);
cout << a << "END OF OUTPUT\n";
```

When embedded in a complete program, this code produces a dialogue like the following:

```
Enter some input:
Do be do to you!
Do be do to you!END OF OUTPUT
```

With the function `cin.getline`, the entire line is read. The reading ends when the line ends, even though the resulting cstring may be shorter than the maximum number of characters specified by the second argument.

When `getline` is executed, the reading stops after the number of characters given by the second argument have been filled in the cstring array, even if the end of the line has not been reached. For example, consider the following code:

```
char short_string[5];
cout << "Enter some input:\n";
cin.getline(short_string, 5);
cout << short_string << "END OF OUTPUT\n";
```

When embedded in a complete program, this code produces a dialogue like the following:

```
Enter some input:
dobedowap
dobeEND OF OUTPUT
```

Notice that four, not five, characters are read into the cstring variable `short_string`, even though the second argument is 5. This is because the null character `'\0'` fills one array position. Every cstring is terminated with the null character when it is stored in a cstring variable and this always consumes one array position.

input/output with files   The cstring input and output techniques we illustrated for `cout` and `cin` work the same way for input and output with files. The input stream `cin` can be replaced by any input stream that is connected to a file. The output stream `cout` can be replaced by any output stream that is connected to a file. For example, if the stream `in_stream` has been connected to the file `infile.dat` with a call to the member function `open`, then the following will read one line (or as much as will fit in the array `one_line`) from the file `infile.dat`, and store the resulting cstring in the array `one_line`:

```
char one_line[80];
in_stream.getline(one_line, 80);
```

---

getline

The member function `getline` can be used to read a line of input and place the cstring of characters on that line into a cstring variable.

Syntax:

Input_Stream.`getline`(*String_Var*, *Max_Characters* + 1);

One line of input is read from the stream *Input_Stream* and the resulting cstring is placed in *String_Var*. If the line is more than *Max_Characters* long, then only the first *Max_Characters* on the line are read. (The +1 is needed because every cstring has the null character '\0' added to the end of the cstring and so the string stored in *String_Var* is one longer than the number of characters read in.)

Example:

```
char one_line[80];
cin.getline(one_line, 80);
```

Cstring-to-Number Conversions and Robust Input

The cstring "1234" and the number 1234 are not the same things. The first is a sequence of characters; the second is a number. In everyday life, we write them the same way and blur this distinction—but, in a C++ program this distinction cannot be ignored. If you want to do arithmetic, you need 1234, not "1234". If you want to add a comma to the numeral for one thousand two hundred thirty four, then you want to change the *cstring* "1234" to the *cstring* "1,234". When designing numeric input, it is often useful to read the input as a string of characters, edit the string, and then convert the string to a number. For example, if you want your program to read an amount of money, the input may or may not begin with a dollar sign. If your program is reading percentages, the input may or may not have a percent sign at the end. If your program reads the input as a string of characters, it can store the string in a cstring variable and remove any unwanted characters, leaving only a cstring of digits. Your program then needs to convert this cstring of digits to a number, and that can easily be done with the predefined function `atoi`.

The function `atoi` takes one argument that is a cstring and returns the *int* value that corresponds to that cstring. For example, `atoi`("1234") returns the integer 1234. If the argument does not correspond to an *int* value, then `atoi` returns 0. For example, `atoi`("#37") returns 0, because the character '#' is not a digit. You pronounce `atoi` as "A to I," which is an abbreviation of "alphabetic to integer." The

atoi

function `atoi` is in the library with header file `cstdlib`, so any program that uses it must contain the following directive:

```
#include <cstdlib>
```

`atol`

If your numbers are too large to be values of type *int*, you can convert them from cstrings to values of type *long*. The function `atol` performs the same conversion as the function `atoi` except that `atol` returns values of type *long* and so can accommodate larger integer values (on systems where this is a concern).

`read_and_clean`

Display 10.3 contains the definition of a function called `read_and_clean` that reads a line of input and discards all characters other than the digits '0' through '9'. The function then uses the function `atoi` to convert the "cleaned up" cstring of digits to an integer value. As the demonstration program indicates, you can use this function to read money amounts and it will not matter whether the user included a dollar sign or not. Similarly, you can read percentages and it will not matter whether the user types in a percent sign or not. Although the output makes it look as if the function `read_and_clean` simply removes some symbols, more than that is happening. The value produced is a true *int* value that can be used in a program as a number; it is not a cstring of characters.

`get_int`

The function `read_and_clean` shown in Display 10.3 will delete any nondigits from the string typed in, but it cannot check that the remaining digits will yield the number the user has in mind. The user should be given a chance to look at the final value and see whether it is correct. If the value is not correct, the user should be given a chance to reenter the input. In Display 10.4 we have used the function `read_and_clean` in another function called `get_int`, which will accept anything the user types and it will allow the user to reenter the input until she or he is satisfied with the number that is computed from the input string. It is a very robust input procedure. (The function `get_int` is an improved version of the function of the same name given in Display 5.6.)

`atof`

The functions `read_and_clean` in Display 10.3 and `get_int` in Display 10.4 are samples of the various input functions you can design by reading numeric input as a string value. Programming Project 3 at the end of this chapter asks you to define a function similar to `get_int` that reads in a number of type *double*, as opposed to a number of type *int*. To write that function, it would be nice to have a predefined function that converts a string value to a number of type *double*. Fortunately, the predefined function `atof`, which is also in the library with header file `cstdlib`, does just that. For example, `atof("9.99")` returns the value 9.99 of type *double*. If the argument does not correspond to a number of type *double*, then `atof` returns 0.0. You pronounce `atof` as "A to F," which is an abbreviation of "alphabetic to floating point." Recall that numbers with a decimal point are often called *floating-point* numbers because of the way the computer handles the decimal point when storing these numbers in memory.

Display 10.3 Cstrings to Integers (part 1 of 2)

```
//Demonstrates the function read_and_clean.
#include <iostream>
#include <cstdlib>
#include <cctype>

void read_and_clean(int& n);
//Reads a line of input. Discards all symbols except the digits. Converts
//the cstring to an integer and sets n equal to the value of this integer.

void new_line();
//Discards all the input remaining on the current input line.
//Also discards the '\n' at the end of the line.

int main()
{
    using namespace std;
    int n;
    char ans;
    do
    {
        cout << "Enter an integer and press return: ";
        read_and_clean(n);
        cout << "That string converts to the integer " << n << endl;
        cout << "Again? (yes/no): ";
        cin >> ans;
        new_line();
    } while ( (ans != 'n') && (ans != 'N') );
    return 0;
}
```

Display 10.3 Cstrings to Integers *(part 2 of 2)*

```
//Uses iostream, cstdlib, and cctype:
void read_and_clean(int& n)
{
    using namespace std;
    const int ARRAY_SIZE = 6;
    char digit_string[ARRAY_SIZE];

    char next;
    cin.get(next);
    int index = 0;
    while (next != '\n')
    {
        if ( (isdigit(next)) && (index < ARRAY_SIZE - 1) )
        {
            digit_string[index] = next;
            index++;
        }
        cin.get(next);
    }
    digit_string[index] = '\0';

    n = atoi(digit_string);
}

//Uses iostream:
void new_line( )
        <The rest of the definition of new_line is given in Display 5.6. >
```

Sample Dialogue

```
Enter an integer and press return: $ 100
That string converts to the integer 100
Again? (yes/no): yes
Enter an integer and press return: 100
That string converts to the integer 100
Again? (yes/no): yes
Enter an integer and press return: 99%
That string converts to the integer 99
Again? (yes/no): yes
Enter an integer and press return: 23% &&5 *12
That string converts to the integer 23512
Again? (yes/no): no
```

Display 10.4 Robust Input Function *(part 1 of 2)*

```
//Demonstration program for improved version of get_int.
#include <iostream>
#include <cstdlib>
#include <cctype>

void read_and_clean(int& n);
//Reads a line of input. Discards all symbols except the digits. Converts
//the cstring to an integer and sets n equal to the value of this integer.

void new_line();
//Discards all the input remaining on the current input line.
//Also discards the '\n' at the end of the line.

void get_int(int& input_number);
//Gives input_number a value that the user approves of.

int main()
{
    using namespace std;
    int input_number;
    get_int(input_number);
    cout << "Final value read in = " << input_number << endl;
    return 0;
}

//Uses iostream and read_and_clean:
void get_int(int& input_number)
{
    using namespace std;
    char ans;
    do
    {
        cout << "Enter input number: ";
        read_and_clean(input_number);
        cout << "You entered " << input_number
             << " Is that correct? (yes/no): ";
        cin >> ans;
        new_line();
    } while ((ans != 'y') && (ans != 'Y'));
}
```

Display 10.4 Robust Input Function *(part 2 of 2)*

```
//Uses iostream, cstdlib, and cctype:
void read_and_clean(int& n)
        <The rest of the definition of read_and_clean is given in Display 10.3.>

//Uses iostream:
void new_line( )
        <The rest of the definition of new_line is given in Display 5.6.>
```

Sample Dialogue

```
Enter input number: $57
You entered 57 Is that correct? (yes/no): no
Enter input number: $77*5xa
You entered 775 Is that correct? (yes/no): no
Enter input number: 77
You entered 77 Is that correct? (yes/no): no
Enter input number: $75
You entered 75 Is that correct? (yes/no): yes
Final value read in = 75
```

Cstring-to-Number Functions

The functions atoi, atol, and atof can be used to convert a cstring of digits to the corresponding numeric value. The functions atoi and atol convert cstrings to integers. The only difference between atoi and atol is that atoi returns a value of type *int* while atol returns a value of type *long*. The function atof converts a cstring to a value of type *double*. If the cstring argument (to either function) is such that the conversion cannot be made, then the function returns zero. For example

```
int x = atoi("657");
```

sets the value of x to 657 and

```
double y = atof("12.37");
```

sets the value of y to 12.37.

Any program that uses atoi or atof must contain the following directive:

```
#include <cstdlib>
```

SELF-TEST EXERCISES

13 Consider the following code (and assume it is embedded in a complete and correct program and then run):

```
char my_string[80];
cout << "Enter a line of input:\n";
cin.getline(my_string, 6);
cout << my_string << "<END OF OUTPUT";
```

If the dialogue begins as follows, what will be the next line of output?

Enter a line of input:
May the hair on your toes grow long and curly.

14 Give the function definition for the function whose prototype is given below. This is a safer version of the predefined function strcat. Do not use strcat in your code. You may, however, use strlen in your code.

```
void append(char str_var[], int size_str_var, const char to_add[]);
//Precondition: size_str_var is the declared size of the cstring variable str_var.
//Both str_var and to_add have cstring values properly terminated with '\0'.
//Postcondition: The cstring value in to_add has been appended to the end of
//the value in str_var and this longer cstring is the new value of str_var.
//If this would result in a cstring that is too long for str_var, then only as much
//of to_add as will fit has been appended to the end of the cstring in str_var.
```

15 Given the declarations:

```
char number1[] = "3456";
char number2[] = "3.456e-7";
int n1;
double n2;
```

Give a code fragment to translate these strings to numbers as indicated. You may use predefined (library) routines. Provide any necessary header #include.

a. number1 into an *int* value and assign it to n1,

b. number2 into a *double* value and assign it to n2.

10.2 Multidimensional Arrays

Multidimensional Array Basics

array declarations
indexed variables

It is sometimes useful to have an array with more than one index, and this is allowed in C++. The following declares an array of characters called page. The array page has two indexes: the first index ranging from 0 to 29 and the second from 0 to 99.

```
char page[30][100];
```

The indexed variables for this array are:

```
page[0][0], page[0][1], ..., page[0][99]
page[1][0], page[1][1], ..., page[1][99]
page[2][0], page[2][1], ..., page[2][99]
       .
       .
       .
page[29][0], page[29][1], ..., page[29][99]
```

Note that each index must be enclosed in its own set of square brackets. As was true of the one-dimensional arrays we have already seen, each indexed variable for a multidimensional array is a variable of the base type. So, each indexed variable of the array page is a variable of type *char*. You might use the array page to store all

---

Multidimensional Array Declaration

Syntax:

Type Array_Name[*Size_Dim_1*][*Size_Dim_2*]...[*Size_Dim_Last*];

Examples:
```
char page[30][100];
int matrix[2][3];
double three_d_picture[10][20][30];
```

An array declaration, of the form shown above, will define one indexed variable for each combination of array indexes. For example, the second of the above sample declarations defines the following six indexed variables for the array matrix:

```
matrix[0][0], matrix[0][1], matrix[0][2],
matrix[1][0], matrix[1][1], matrix[1][2]
```

the characters on a page of text that has thirty lines (numbered 0 through 29) and 100 characters on each line (numbered 0 through 99). In this example, the array page had two indexes. A multidimensional array can have any number of indexes, but we will concentrate on the case of two-dimensional arrays, i.e., arrays with two indexes.

A multidimensional array is an array of arrays

In C++, a two-dimensional array, such as page, is actually an array of arrays. The above array page is actually a one-dimensional array of size 30, whose base type is a one-dimensional array of characters of size 100. Normally, this need not concern you, and you can usually act as if the array page is actually an array with two indexes (rather than an array of arrays, which is harder to keep track of). There is, however, at least one situation where a two-dimensional array looks very much like an array of arrays, namely when you have a function with an array parameter for a two-dimensional array. For example, the following is a function that takes an array, like page, and prints it to the screen:

multidimensional array parameters

```
void display_page(const char p[][100], int size_dimension_1)
{
    for (int index1 = 0; index1 < size_dimension_1; index1++)
    {//Printing one line:
        for (int index2 = 0; index2 < 100; index2++)
            cout << p[index1][index2];
        cout << endl;
    }
}
```

Notice that with a two-dimensional array parameter, the size of the first dimension is not given, so we must include an *int* parameter to give the size of this first dimension. (As with ordinary arrays, the compiler will allow you to specify the first dimension by placing a number within the first pair of square brackets. However, such a number is only a comment; the compiler ignores any such number.) The size of the second dimension (and all other dimensions if there are more than two) is given after the array parameter, as shown for the parameter

```
const char p[][100]
```

You can simply memorize this rule: for multidimensional array parameters, all the dimension sizes except the first must be listed in square brackets after the parameter name in a function heading. However, if you realize that a multidimensional array is an array of arrays, then this rule begins to make sense. Since the two-dimensional array parameter *const char* p[][100] is a parameter for an array of arrays, the first dimension is really the index of the array and is treated just like an array index for an ordinary, one-dimensional array. The second dimension is part of the description of the base type, which is an array of characters of size 100.

> **Multidimensional Array Parameters**
> When a multidimensional array parameter is given in a function heading or prototype, the size of the first dimension is not given, but the remaining dimension sizes must be given in square brackets. Since the first dimension size is not given, you usually need an additional parameter of type *int* that gives the size of this first dimension. Below is an example of a function prototype with a two-dimensional array parameter p:
>
>   void get_page(char p[][100], int size_dimension_1);

■)) PROGRAMMING EXAMPLE
Two-Dimensional Grading Program

grade

Display 10.5 contains a program that uses a two-dimensional array, named grade, to store and then display the grade records for a small class. The class has four students, and includes three quizzes. Display 10.6 illustrates how the array grade is used to store data. The first array index is used to designate a student and the second array index is used to designate a quiz. Since the students and quizzes are numbered starting with 1 rather than 0, we must subtract one from the student number and subtract one from the quiz number to obtain the indexed variable that stores a particular quiz score. For example, the score that student number 4 received on quiz number 1 is recorded in grade[3][0].

st_ave *and* quiz_ave

Our program also uses two ordinary one-dimensional arrays. The array st_ave will be used to record the average quiz score for each of the students. For example, the program will set st_ave[0] equal to the average of the quiz scores received by student 1, st_ave[1] equal to the average of the quiz scores received by student 2, and so forth. The array quiz_ave will be used to record the average score for each quiz. For example, the program will set quiz_ave[0] equal to the average of all the student scores for quiz 1, quiz_ave[1] will record the average score for quiz 2, and so forth. Display 10.6 illustrates the relationship between the arrays grade, st_ave, and quiz_ave. In that display, we have shown some sample data for the array grade. These data, in turn, determine the values that the program stores in st_ave and in quiz_ave. Display 10.6 also shows these values, which the program computes for st_ave and quiz_ave.

The complete program for filling the array grade and then computing and displaying both the student averages and the quiz averages is shown in Display 10.5. In that program we have declared array dimensions as global named constants. Since the procedures are particular to this program and could not be reused elsewhere, we

Display 10.5 Two-dimensional Array *(part 1 of 3)*

```
//Reads quiz scores for each student into the two-dimensional array grade (but the input
//code is not shown in this display). Computes the average score for each student and
//the average score for each quiz. Displays the quiz scores and the averages.
#include <iostream>
#include <iomanip>
const int NUMBER_STUDENTS = 4, NUMBER_QUIZZES = 3;


void compute_st_ave(const int grade[][NUMBER_QUIZZES], double st_ave[]);
//Precondition: Global constant NUMBER_STUDENTS and NUMBER_QUIZZES
//are the dimensions of the array grade. Each of the indexed variables
//grade[st_num-1, quiz_num-1] contains the score for student st_num on quiz quiz_num.
//Postcondition: Each st_ave[st_num-1] contains the average for student number stu_num.


void compute_quiz_ave(const int grade[][NUMBER_QUIZZES], double quiz_ave[]);
//Precondition: Global constant NUMBER_STUDENTS and NUMBER_QUIZZES
//are the dimensions of the array grade. Each of the indexed variables
//grade[st_num-1, quiz_num-1] contains the score for student st_num on quiz quiz_num.
//Postcondition: Each quiz_ave[quiz_num-1] contains the average for quiz numbered
//quiz_num.


void display(const int grade[][NUMBER_QUIZZES],
                        const double st_ave[], const double quiz_ave[]);
//Precondition: Global constant NUMBER_STUDENTS and NUMBER_QUIZZES are the
//dimensions of the array grade. Each of the indexed variables grade[st_num-1,
//quiz_num-1] contains the score for student st_num on quiz quiz_num. Each
//st_ave[st_num-1] contains the average for student stu_num. Each quiz_ave[quiz_num-1]
//contains the average for quiz numbered quiz_num.
//Postcondition: All the data in grade, st_ave, and quiz_ave have been output.


int main()
{
    using namespace std;
    int grade[NUMBER_STUDENTS][NUMBER_QUIZZES];
    double st_ave[NUMBER_STUDENTS];
    double quiz_ave[NUMBER_QUIZZES];

    <The code for filling the array grade goes here, but is not shown.>
```

Display 10.5 Two-dimensional Array *(part 2 of 3)*

```
        compute_st_ave(grade, st_ave);
        compute_quiz_ave(grade, quiz_ave);
        display(grade, st_ave, quiz_ave);
        return 0;
}


void compute_st_ave(const int grade[][NUMBER_QUIZZES], double st_ave[])
{
    for (int st_num = 1; st_num <= NUMBER_STUDENTS; st_num++)
    {//Process one st_num:
        double sum = 0;
        for (int quiz_num = 1; quiz_num <= NUMBER_QUIZZES; quiz_num++)
            sum = sum + grade[st_num-1][quiz_num-1];
        //sum contains the sum of the quiz scores for student number st_num.
        st_ave[st_num-1] = sum/NUMBER_QUIZZES;
        //Average for student st_num is the value of st_ave[st_num-1]
    }
}


void compute_quiz_ave(const int grade[][NUMBER_QUIZZES], double quiz_ave[])
{
    for (int quiz_num = 1; quiz_num <= NUMBER_QUIZZES; quiz_num++)
    {//Process one quiz (for all students):
        double sum = 0;
        for (int st_num = 1; st_num <= NUMBER_STUDENTS; st_num++)
            sum = sum + grade[st_num-1][quiz_num-1];
        //sum contains the sum of all student scores on quiz number quiz_num.
        quiz_ave[quiz_num-1] = sum/NUMBER_STUDENTS;
        //Average for quiz quiz_num is the value of quiz_ave[quiz_num-1]
    }
}
```

Display 10.5 Two-dimensional Array *(part 3 of 3)*

```
//Uses iostream and iomanip:
void display(const int grade[][NUMBER_QUIZZES],
                        const double st_ave[], const double quiz_ave[])
{
    using namespace std;
    cout.setf(ios::fixed);
    cout.setf(ios::showpoint);
    cout.precision(1);

    cout << setw(10) << "Student"
         << setw(5) << "Ave"
         << setw(15) << "Quizzes\n";
    for (int st_num = 1; st_num <= NUMBER_STUDENTS; st_num++)
    {//Display for one st_num:
        cout << setw(10) << st_num
             << setw(5) << st_ave[st_num-1] << " ";
        for (int quiz_num = 1; quiz_num <= NUMBER_QUIZZES; quiz_num++)
            cout << setw(5) << grade[st_num-1][quiz_num-1];
        cout << endl;
    }

    cout << "Quiz averages = ";
    for (int quiz_num = 1; quiz_num <= NUMBER_QUIZZES; quiz_num++)
        cout << setw(5) << quiz_ave[quiz_num-1];
    cout << endl;
}
```

Sample Dialogue

```
<The dialogue for filling the array grade is not shown.>
Student      Ave           Quizzes
        1    10.0       10   10   10
        2     1.0        2    0    1
        3     7.7        8    6    9
        4     7.3        8    4   10
Quiz Average =          7.0  5.0  7.5
```

Display 10.6 The Two-dimensional Array grade

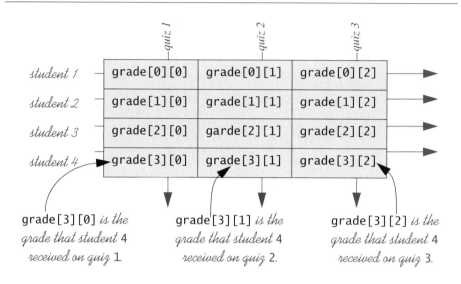

Display 10.7 The Two-dimensional Array grade

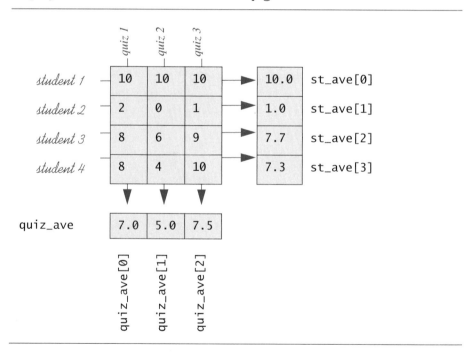

have used these globally defined constants in the procedure bodies, rather than having parameters for the size of the array dimensions. Since it is routine, the display does not show the code that fills the array.

Arrays of Cstrings

In C++ an array of cstrings is represented as a two-dimensional array of characters. For example, the following declares an array called `name` which can hold a list of five names, with at most 19 characters in each name. (Recall that cstring arrays need one indexed variable to hold the null character `'\0'`. That is why the names can only contain 19 characters.)

```
char name[5][20];
```

The indexed variable `name[4][3]`, for example, would contain letter number 3 in name number 4. Since the first index is normally considered a row index and the second a column index, this corresponds to the normal way of writing a list of names on paper. This is illustrated in Display 10.8.

An array of cstrings can be manipulated by using both indexes simultaneously, just like any other two-dimensional array. However, it is often nicer to manipulate an array of cstrings by considering only one index at a time. A list of cstrings can be manipulated by a loop that steps through values of the first index and treats each indexed variable—such as `name[0]`, `name[1]`, and so forth—as a single cstring variable that is manipulated by some cstring function. For example, the following code will fill the above-declared array `name` with names typed in at the keyboard, one per line:

```
cout << "Enter 5 names, one per line:\n";
int index;
for (index = 0; index < 5; index++)
    cin.getline(name[index], 20);
```

Similarly, once the array of cstrings is filled with names, the names can be written back out to the screen with the following simple loop:

```
for (index = 0; index < 5; index++)
    cout << name[index] << endl;
```

SELF-TEST EXERCISES

16 Declare a `void` function `my_func` that accepts an array declared as

```
int arr[10][25];
```

Display 10.8 An Array of Strings

	0	1	2	3	4	5	6	7	8	9	10	11	12	13	14	15	16	17	18	19
name[0]	O	l	g	a		R	h	y	t	h	m	\0	?	?	?	?	?	?	?	?
name[1]	D	u	s	t	y		R	h	o	d	e	s	\0	?	?	?	?	?	?	?
name[2]	C	h	a	r	l	e	s		S	t	e	a	k	\0	?	?	?	?	?	?
name[3]	F	l	a	c	o		F	r	e	d	d	y	\0	?	?	?	?	?	?	?
name[4]	J	o	s	e	p	h	i	n	e		S	t	u	d	e	n	t	\0	?	?

name[4][3]

as one parameter. One other parameter is necessary. Give a function declaration (prototype) for this function. (Do not define it, you don't have enough information.)

17   Suppose you have a complete and correct program that includes the following code. This code will fill the array list with 10 names typed in at the keyboard.

```
char list[10][20];
int index;
cout << "Enter 10 names, one per line:\n";
for (index = 0; index < 10; index++)
    cin.getline(list[index], 20);
```

What code could be added to your program so that it will output the first letter of each name to the screen? The letters should be output one per line.

18   What is the output produced by the following code (when embedded in a complete and correct program)?

```
int my_array[4][4], index1, index2;
for (index1 = 0; index1 < 4; index1++)
    for (index2 = 0; index2 < 4; index2++)
        my_array[index1][index2] = index2;
for (index1 = 0; index1 < 4; index1++)
{
    for (index2 = 0; index2 < 4; index2++)
        cout << my_array[index1][index2] << " ";
    cout << endl;
}
```

19 Write code that will fill the array a (declared below) with numbers typed in at the keyboard. The numbers will be input five per line, on four lines (although your solution need not depend on how the input numbers are divided into lines):

```
int a[4][5];
```

20 Write a function definition for a *void* function called echo such that the following function call will echo the input described in Self-Test Exercise 19, and will echo it in the same format as we specified for the input (that is, four lines of five numbers per line):

```
echo(a, 4);
```

21 Write a function definition for a *void* function called get_names that reads in a list of names and fills an array of strings with names typed in at the keyboard. The array of strings will be an argument to get_names. Add parameters for any other arguments the function should have. Assume that the names contain at most 25 characters.

10.3 The C++ Standard `string` Class

The predefined string operations described in Display 10.1 are not as safe as they should be. For example, the following unfortunate situation might be allowed to pass without an error message:

```
char string1[] = "A wet bird never flies at night.";
char string2[30];
strcpy(string2, string1);
```

The problem with this code is that the string in string1 has 32 characters and the array string2 has room for only 29 characters (plus the end marker '\0'). In most implementations of C++ this will result in some random portion of memory being overwritten with the extra three characters. To avoid such problems and to provide additional string operations, you can use the ANSI C++ Standard `string` library. The ANSI C++ Standard requires C++ compilers that claim to comply with the Standard to supply the standard `string` class.

Interface for the Standard Class string

The class `string` allows you to perform the same operations you can with `cstrings` and more. (A lot more! There are well over 100 members and other functions associated with the Standard `string` class.) With cstrings, we used the `strcpy` function to copy strings, and `strcat` to concatenate them. The Standard `string` class overloads the = operator to copy one string into another, and overloads the + operator to concatenate strings. (Recall that the concatenation of two strings is the string obtained by writing one string after the other to form a longer string.) Suppose s1, s2, and s3 are objects of type `string` and both s1 and s2 have string values. Then s3 can be set equal to the concatenation of the string value in s1 followed by the string value in s2 as follows:

+ does concatenation

```
s3 = s1 + s2;
```

These operations take care of some of the concern about safety mentioned earlier. If the sum of the lengths of s1 and s2 exceeds the capacity of s3, then more space is allocated for s3 automatically.

constructors

The class `string` has a default constructor that initializes a `string` object to the empty string. The class `string` also has a second constructor that takes one argument that is a standard C++ string (of the form discussed in Section 10.1). This second constructor initializes the `string` object to a value that represents the same string as its `cstring` argument. This second constructor makes the new class `string` compatible with the standard C++ strings discussed in Section 10.1. For example, consider the following:

```
string phrase, word1("hot"), word2("dog");
phrase = word1 + word2;
cout << phrase;
```

This declares `phrase` to be an object of type `string` and initializes it to the empty string. The object word1 is declared and given an initial value that represents the `cstring` "hot". (What actually happens is that the characters 'h', 'o', 't', and the number 3 are stored in private variables, but it is preferable to simply think of this as the string we normally write as *hot*.) Similarly, the object word2 is initialized to a value that represents the string "dog". The output produced by the above code is thus:

```
hotdog
```

The above output raises a problem that often occurs when doing string processing. When you concatenate two words, no extra space is inserted between the words
unless your code specifies that a space is to be added. You can rewrite the above
assignment statement as follows, and it will insert a space between the two words:

```
phrase = word1 + " " + word2;
```

With this new assignment statement, the output would instead be:

```
hot dog
```

C++ must do a lot of work to allow you to concatenate strings in this simple and
natural fashion. The string constant " " is not a value of type string. A string constant like " " is stored as an array of characters in C++ and so is a cstring. The
constant " " is a cstring of the kind we discussed in Section 10.1. When C++ sees
" " as an argument to +, it finds the definition (or overloading) of + that applies to a
value such as " ". There are overloadings of the + operator that have a cstring on
the left and a string on the right, as well as the reverse of this positioning. There is,
of course, the overloading you expect, with type string for both arguments.

converting cstring *constants to the type* string

If these overloadings were not provided, C++ would look for a constructor that
can perform a type conversion to convert the cstring " " to a value for which + did
apply. In this case, the constructor with the one cstring parameter would perform
just such a conversion.

Also note that we did not need parentheses when concatenating three (or more)
things with the + operator. If you omit parentheses with the + operator, the operations are performed left to right, and this is true whether the + applies to numbers or
has been overloaded for some class, such as the class string.

The behavior of the overloaded operators >> and << is very natural. They perform input and output in much the same way as input and output is performed with
cstrings. A program that demonstrates the use of the standard class string,
including the use of >> and <<, is given in Display 10.9. Notice that the overloaded
extraction operator >> skips over whitespace, just as was true when we used >> with
the standard types such as *int*. The overloaded operator >> reads up to the next
whitespace (and discards that whitespace) so that when you perform input using >>,
your program reads *words*, not lines. In this context a **word** is any string of non-
whitespace characters. With the cstrings we saw earlier, to read an entire line you
used the istream member function getline. The corresponding function to use for
class string objects is also called getline, but this getline is not a member of
either class iostream or class string. It is a standalone function whose first argument is an istream object, second argument is a string object, and third argument
(if present) is a character whose presence on the input terminates input. This termi-

overloading >> and <<

Display 10.9 Program Using the Class string (part 1 of 2)

```
//Demonstrates the class string.

#include <iostream>
#include <string>  //Required for the class string.

void new_line();

int main()
{
    using namespace std;
    string first_name, last_name, record_name;

    cout << "Enter your first and last name:\n";
    cin >> first_name >> last_name;
    new_line();
    record_name = last_name + ", " + first_name;

    cout << "Your name in our records is: ";
    cout << record_name << endl;

    cout << "Your last name is spelled: ";
    for (int i = 0; i < last_name.length(); i++)
        cout << last_name[i] << " ";
    cout << endl;

    string motto("Your records are our records.");
    cout << "Our motto is\n";
    cout << motto << endl;

    cout << "Please suggest a better (one line) motto:\n";
    getline(cin, motto);
    cout << "Our new motto will be:\n";
    cout << motto << endl;

    return 0;
}

void new_line()
<The definition of new_line(); is given in Display 5.6.>
```

Display 10.9 Program Using the Class string *(part 2 of 2)*

Sample Dialogue

```
Enter your first and last name:
  B'Elanna Torres
Your name in our records is: Torres, B'Elanna
Your last name is spelled: T o r r e s
Our motto is
Your records are our records.
Please suggest a better (one line) motto:
Our records go where no records dared to go before.
Our new motto will be:
Our records go where no records dared to go before.
```

---

nating character defaults to '\n'. Display 10.9 shows an example of using the function getline.

Characteristic uses of the getline function follow. Note that both the iostream and the string headers must be included.

```
#include <iostream>
#include <string>
using namespace std;
//  . . .
string str1; //declares empty strings
getline(cin, str1);
          //inserts into str1 all that is typed
          //into the line up to '\n' The '\n' is
          //removed from the input and discarded.
```

Notice the following *for*-statement from Display 10.9:

```
for (int i = 0; i < last_name.length( ); i++)
    cout << last_name[i] << " ";
```

string objects can act like arrays

The class string overloads the square brackets [] that you are used to using with arrays so that they also work for objects of the class string. The indexed expression last_name[i] behaves exactly like indexing with cstrings: it picks out one character in the string value held by the string object last_name. Thus the expression last_name[i] can be used to retrieve characters much the same as you retrieve characters in an ordinary array of characters.

It is important to note that the indexing overloading in the `string` class does **not range-check index values,** that is, it does not check to see if you use an illegal index value. There is a member function named `at` that provides range-checked access to individual characters. The member function named `at` behaves basically the same as the square brackets, except for two points: You use function notation with `at`, so instead of `a[i]`, you use `a.at(i)`, and the `at` member function checks to see if `i` evaluates to an illegal index. In the following two example code fragments, the attempted access is out of range; yet, the first of these probably will not produce an error message, although it will be accessing a nonexistent indexed variable:

```
string str("Mary");
cout << str[6] << endl;
```

The second example, however, will cause the program to terminate abnormally, so you at least know that something is wrong:

```
string str("Mary");
cout << str.at(6) << endl;
```

You can change a single character in the string by assigning the indexed variable, `name[i]`. This may also be done with the member function `at(pos)`. (Neither assigning an indexed `string` variable nor assigning a string position using the `at` function is illustrated in Display 10.9.) For example, to change the third character in the string object `last_name` to `'X'`, you can use the following code fragment:

```
last_name.at(2)='X';
```

or

```
last_name[2]='X';
```

As in an ordinary array of characters, character positions for objects of type `string` are indexed starting with 0 so that the third character in a string is in index position 2.

---

getline for Class string Objects

The `getline` function for `string` objects has two prototypes:

```
string& getline(istream& ins, string& strVar,char delimiter);
```
and
```
string& getline(istream& ins, string& srVar);
```

The first version of this function reads characters from the `istream` object given as the first argument, inserting the characters into the `string` variable, until an instance of the `delimiter` character is encountered. The `delimiter` is removed from the input and discarded. The second version uses `'\n'` for the default value of `delimiter`; otherwise, it works the same.

◆ PITFALL   Code That Depends on Order of Evaluation Is Illegal

The ANSI-C++ Standard does not specify the order of evaluation for elements of an expression, and it prohibits writing code that depends on order of evaluation. For example, if subexpressions have side effects, the order of these side effects is not specified.

For example:

```
int i = 0;
cout << i << " " << i++ << endl; // many compilers give the
                                 // counter-intuitive output: 1 0
```

In spite of the fact that the above means:

```
((cout << i) << " ") << i++ << endl;
```

It appears that the `cout << i` should be "done first," then the `i` should be incremented. This seems to imply that the output should be `0 1`. In fact, on many compilers, the value of `i` for the `i++` is fetched, the value is used for the `cout` argument, `i` is incremented, then the value of `i` is fetched for the first `i`.

Instead, write code where you can guarantee the results:

```
int i = 0;
cout << i << " ";
i++;
cout << i << endl;
```

In short, though C and C++ programmers do use the `x++`, `++x`, `--x` and `x--` as expressions that return values, many professionals detest this practice. We discourage such usage as difficult to understand and error prone.

↝ PROGRAMMING TIP
The Ignore Member Function

With `cin >> intVar`, anything after the integer that is read in will still be available for the next input, including the return that you pressed to make the line of data available to your program. (This is true for any type of variable being extracted from an input `stream`.) This can cause `getline` to misbehave. One fix was the `new_line` function given in Chapter 5.

An alternative solution that is provided by the `iostream` library is the `cin` member function, whose prototype is:

    istream& ignore(*int* count, *char* delimiter);

This function will read up to `count` characters, or until the delimiter is reached, whichever is first, and discard these characters.

◆ *PITFALL* / **Mixing** `cin >> variable;` **and** `getline` **Can Lose Input**

Take care in mixing input using `cin >> variable;` with input using `getline`. Both the `istream` member version and the `string` version of `getline` can cause problems. Using `cin >> variable` skips leading whitespace on the input, and leaves the `'\n'` for the next input. A `getline` reads everything up to a `'\n'`, and stops there. Use of the `getline` after a `cin >> x` makes the `getline` see the `'\n'`, so `getline` gets an empty string. If you find your program appearing to skip input data, see if you have mixed these two kinds of input. You may need to use either the `new_line` function from the text, Chapter 5, Display 5.6 part 1, or the `istream` member function `ignore`, for example, `cin.ignore(10000,  '\n');`. With these arguments, a call to the `ignore` member function will read and discard (ignore, really) up to **10,000** characters that you may enter, or until you press `'\n'`, whichever occurs sooner.

■)) *PROGRAMMING EXAMPLE*
Palindrome Testing

In Chapter 9, Programming Project 1 we asked you to write a program that will determine whether a string is a palindrome. In this programming example we use strings to solve this problem.

A palindrome is a `string` that reads the same front to back as it does back to front. The programming project allowed the assumption that there are only lowercase letters and no punctuation in the input strings. We will not make these assumptions. Our code will simply disregard all spaces and punctuations and will consider upper- and lowercase versions of a letter to be the same when deciding if something is a palindrome.

Display 10.10 Palindrome Testing Program (*part 1 of 4*)

```
//test for palindrome property

#include <iostream>
#include <string>
#include <cctype>
using namespace std;

void swap(char& lhs, char& rhs);
//swaps char args corresponding to parameters lhs and rhs

string reverse(const string& str);
//returns a copy of arg corresponding to parameter
//str with characters in reverse order.

string removePunct(const string& src,
                          const string& punct);
//returns copy of string src with characters
//in string punct removed

string makeLower (const string& s);
//returns a copy of parameter s that has all upper case
//characters forced to lower case, other characters unchanged.
//Uses <string>, which provides tolower

bool isPal(const string& this_String);
//uses makeLower, removePunct.
//if  this_String is a palindrome,
//    return true;
//else
//    return false;
```

Display 10.10 Palindrome Testing Program (*part 2 of 4*)

```cpp
int main()
{
    string str;
    cout << "Enter a candidate for palindrome test "
         << "\nfollowed by pressing return.\n";
    getline(cin, str);
    if (isPal(str))
        cout << "\"" << str + "\" is a palindrome ";
    else
        cout << "\"" << str + "\" is not a palindrome ";
    cout << endl;
    return 0;
}

void swap(char& lhs, char& rhs)
{
    char tmp = lhs;
    lhs = rhs;
    rhs = tmp;
}

string reverse(const string& str)
{
    int start = 0;
    int end = str.length();
    string tmp(str);

    while (start < end)
    {
        end--;
        swap(tmp[start], tmp[end]);
        start++;
    }
    return tmp;
}
```

Display 10.10 Palindrome Testing Program (*part 3 of 4*)

```
//Returns arg that has all upper case characters forced to lower case,
//other characters unchanged. makeLower uses <string>, which provides
//tolower
string makeLower(const string& s)   //uses cctype
{
    string temp(s); //This creates a working copy of s
    for (int i = 0; i < s.length(); i++)
        temp[i] = tolower(s[i]);
    return temp;
}


//returns a copy of src with characters in punct removed
string removePunct(const string& src,
                                    const string& punct)
{

    string no_punct;
    int src_len = src.length();
    int punct_len = punct.length();
    for(int i = 0; i < src_len; i++)
    {
        string aChar = src.substr(i,1);
        int location = punct.find(aChar, 0);
        //find location of successive characters
        //of src in punct

      if (location < 0 || location >= punct_len)
          no_punct = no_punct + aChar; //aChar not in punct -- keep it
    }
    return no_punct;
}
```

Display 10.10 Palindrome Testing Program (*part 4 of 4*)

```
//uses functions makeLower, removePunct.
//Returned value:
//if this_String is a palindrome,
//    return true;
//else
//    return false;
bool isPal(const string& this_String)
{
    string punctuation(",;:.?!'\" ");   //includes a blank
    string str(this_String);
    str = makeLower(str);
    string lowerStr = removePunct(str, punctuation);
    return lowerStr == reverse(lowerStr);
}
```

Sample Dialogues:

```
Enter a candidate for palindrome test
followed by pressing return.
Madam, I'm Adam.
"Madam, I'm Adam." is a palindrome
```

```
Enter a candidate for palindrome test
followed by pressing return.
Radar
"Radar" is a palindrome
```

```
Enter a candidate for palindrome test
followed by pressing return.
Madam I'm
"Madam I'm" is not a palindrome
```

We will introduce some immediately useful features of the string class interface with code that tests for palindromes.

Some palindrome examples are:

Able was I 'ere I saw Elba.

I Love Me, Vol. I.

Madam, I'm Adam.

A man, a plan, a canal, Panama.

Rats live on no evil star.

radar

deed

mom

racecar

We begin the discussion of the `string` facilities used in Display 10.10 with the `main` function. The first line of the `main` function in part 2 of Display 10.10,

```
string str;
```

declares `str` to be an empty string. The next line prompts the user for input. The next line,

```
getline(cin, str);
```

takes a line of input, spaces and all, up to the next `'\n'` that is typed. The next lines,

```
if (isPal(str))
    cout << "\"" << str + "\" is a palindrome ";
else
    cout << "\"" << str + "\" is not a palindrome ";
```

use the `isPal` function (which we will discuss a bit later) to determine whether the string is a palindrome and reports the result. The `cout` statement is interesting because it uses the string overloading of the + operators.

The high points of this code are the declaration of the empty `string`, the use of the `getline` function, and the overloaded + operator for `strings`.

The `isPal` function defines a string, `punctuation`, that has the characters we want to remove from our palindrome before testing. There is a copy, `str`, made of the parameter, `this_string`, that contains our palindrome candidate. A call to `removePunct` removes the punctuation. The characters in the `string`, `punctuation`, are removed from `str` with a call to `removePunct`.

The `reverse` function makes use of the ++ and -- operators and the `swap` routine. You have seen the `swap` routine in an earlier chapter. You will be asked why this code does not swap the elements of the string twice.

Display 10.11 Typical Calls to Members of the Standard Class `string`

Members	Remarks
Constructors	
`string str;`	Default constructor creates empty string object s.
`string str("string");`	Creates a string object with data `"string"`.
`string str(aString);`	Creates a string object `str` that is a copy of `aString`, which is an object of the class `string`.
Element access	
`str[i]`	Read/write access to character at index i.
`str.substr(position, length)`	Returns substring of calling object starting at `position` for `length` characters (read-only access).
`str.c_str()`	Returns read-only access to the `cstring` of data in `string str`.
`str.at(i)`	Returns read/write reference to character in `str` at index i.
Assignment/modifiers	
`str1 = str2;`	Allocates space and initializes it to `str2`'s data, releases memory Allocated for `str1`, sets `str1`'s size to `str2`.
`str1 += str2;`	Character data of `str2` is concatenated to the end of `str1`; the size is set appropriately.
`s.empty()`	Returns *true* if s is an empty `string`, *false* if s is not empty.
`str1+str2`	Returns a `string` that has `str2`'s data concatenated onto the end of `str1`'s data. The size is set appropriately.
`str.insert(pos, str2)`	Inserts `str2` into `str` beginning at position *pos*.
`str.remove(pos, len)`	Removes substring of `len`, starting at position *pos*.
Comparisons	
`str1 == str2` `str1 != str2`	Compare for equality or inequality; returns a Boolean value.
`str1 < str2` `str1 > str2`	
`sst1 <= str2` `str1 >= str2`	All are lexicographical comparisons.
`str.find(str1)`	Returns index of the first occurrence of `str1` in `str`.
`str.find(str1, pos)`	Returns index of the first occurrence of string `str1` in `str`; the search starts at position pos.
`str.find_first_of(str1, pos)`	Finds first instance of any character in `str1` in `str`, starting the search at position pos.
`str.find_first_not_of(str1, pos)`	Finds first instance of any character *not* in `str1` in `str`, starting search at position pos.

The `makeLower` function runs through each character of the parameter `s`, returning a `string` that has each character that is an uppercase letter replaced by its lowercase equivalent.

The `removePunct` function is of interest in that it uses the `string` member functions `substr` and `find`. The member function `substr` extracts a substring of the calling object, given the position and length of the desired substring. The first three lines of `removePunct` declare variables for use in the function. The *for* loop runs through the characters of the parameter `src` one at a time, and tries to `find` them in the `punct` string. To do this, a `string` that is the substring of `src`, of length `1` at each character position, is extracted. The position of this substring in the `punct` is determined using the `find` member function (more on the specifics in the next section). If this one-character `string` is not in the `punct` string, then the one character `string` is concatenated to the `no_punct` string that is to be returned.

The function `isPal` makes use of each of the above helper functions in carrying out its task. The first line creates a `string` of punctuation to be excluded before testing the `string`. The second line makes a copy of the argument. (We could have passed the string by value and have used the parameter, but we chose to make a copy.) The `makeLower` function is called, then the `removePunct` function is called. Finally, the `lowerStr` (which has punctuation removed) is compared to the result of calling `reverse` on `lowerStr`. The Boolean value of this comparison is returned to the caller.

The important string members mentioned here are the member functions `substr` and `find`.

= and == Are Different for strings and cstrings

It should be noted that the operators =, ==, !=, <, >, <=, >= when used with the Standard C++ type `string`, produce results that correspond to our intuitive notion of how strings compare, so they do not misbehave as they do with the `cstrings` we saw before this chapter. When used with `cstring` objects, these operators do not produce syntax errors; nevertheless, what you are comparing is *not* the strings themselves. Consequently, these operations produce results that appear to be nonsense when used with `cstrings`. The `cstring` operations corresponding to =, <, >, ==, !=, etc. must be performed with great care by using `strcmp` and `strcpy`.

Arrays of strings Revisited

You can use the type string just like any other type. In particular, you can have arrays whose base type is string. For example, the array list declared below can be used to keep a list of 20 names:

```
string list[20];
```

You can fill the array list as follows:

```
cout << "Enter 20 names one per line:\n";
int i;
for (i = 0; i < 20; i++)
    getline(cin, list[i]);
```

You can write the names back out to the screen as follows:

```
cout << "Here come the 20 names:\n";
for (i = 0; i < 20; i++)
    cout << list[i] << endl;
```

SELF-TEST EXERCISES

22   Write a void function that has parameters that are an array of string objects and a count parameter. The function should fetch names from the keyboard and enter them into the array, and return the array to the caller. Part of your job is to decide how to stop entering names.

23   Do Exercise 22, then write a second function that displays the names that were entered.

Namespaces Revisited

In Display 10.12 we have redone the program from Display 10.10. The two programs are equivalent, but they differ in the details of how they deal with the namespace std. The program in Display 10.10 has a single global namespace directive like the following that applies to the entire file:

```
using namespace std;
```

The version in Display 10.12 keeps the scope of such *using* directives confined to single function definitions. In particular, note that there is no *using* directive for the namespace std that applies to the swap function (since none is needed).

Placing the *using* directives inside the body of function definitions leaves the function headings outside the scope of any *using* directives for namespace `std`. To make names such as `string`, which are in the `std` namespace, available in the function headings, we qualified the names, such as `std::string`.

Many programming authorities advocate the technique in Display 10.12 over the simpler technique in Display 10.10. Their reasoning is that by keeping the scope of a namespace directive small, you avoid any conflict of names between namespaces. You can have two namespaces that have two different definitions for the same name, and you can use both namespaces as long as you use them in different blocks, each with their own *using* directive. These authorities further advocate that you always use the technique in Display 10.12, even when it is not needed. In this way, you develop good programming habits.

So which technique should you use? Because it is unlikely that any namespace would have names in conflict with the `std` namespace, you can usually use either technique for the `std` namespace. Certainly if you are using only one namespace (besides the global namespace), then either technique can be used. However, when using your own namespaces, it would be a good idea to use the technique shown in Display 10.12. (And, of course, while it is unlikely that any namespace would have names in common with the `std` namespace, it is not impossible, and such a situation can force you to use the technique in Display 10.12.)

If you are in a course, you should use whichever technique your instructor specifies. If you are free to make your own choice, you should use the technique in Display 10.12 often enough to learn it. After that, you will have to make your own decision on which technique to use in which situations.

Location of *using* namespace std;

In order to simplify the presentation and to make our code easily adaptable to all compilers, from now on, we will place the following directive at the start of a file (rather than inside of smaller blocks):

   using namespace std;

However, if you have an up-to-date compiler, you should consider placing this *using* directive inside of smaller blocks or using qualified names, as we discussed in the subsection entitled "Namespace Revisited."

Display 10.12 Careful Namespace Usage (*part 1 of 4*)

```
//test for palindrome property

#include <iostream>
#include <string>
#include <cctype>

void swap(char& lhs, char& rhs);
//swaps char args corresponding to parameters lhs and rhs

std::string reverse(const std::string& str);
//returns a copy of arg corresponding to parameter
//str with characters in reverse order.

std::string removePunct(const std::string& src,
                        const std::string& punct);
//returns copy of string src with characters
//in string punct removed

std::string makeLower (const std::string& s);
//returns a copy of parameter s that has all uppercase
//characters forced to lowercase, other characters unchanged.
//Uses <string>, which provides tolower

bool isPal(const std::string& this_String);
//uses makeLower, removePunct.
//if this_String is a palindrome,
//    return true;
//else
//    return false;
```

This program is the same as the program in Display 10.10 except that the namespace directives are done differently.

Display 10.12 Careful Namespace Usage (*part 2 of 4*)

```cpp
int main()
{
    using namespace std;
    string str;
    cout << "Enter a candidate for palindrome test "
         << "\nfollowed by pressing return.\n";
    getline(cin, str);
    if (isPal(str))
        cout << "\"" << str + "\" is a palindrome ";
    else
        cout << "\"" << str + "\" is not a palindrome ";
    cout << endl;
    return 0;
}

void swap(char& lhs, char& rhs)
{
    char tmp = lhs;
    lhs = rhs;
    rhs = tmp;
}

std::string reverse(const std::string& str)
{
    using namespace std;
    int start = 0;
    int end = str.length();
    string tmp(str);

    while (start < end)
    {
        end--;
        swap(tmp[start], tmp[end]);
        start++;
    }
    return tmp;
}
```

Display 10.12 Careful Namespace Usage (*part 3 of 4*)

```cpp
//Returns arg that has all uppercase characters forced to lowercase,
//other characters unchanged. makeLower uses <string>, which provides
//tolower
std::string makeLower(const std::string& s)   //uses <cctype>
{
    using namespace std;
    string temp(s); //This creates a working copy of s
    for (int i = 0; i < s.length(); i++)
        temp[i] = tolower(s[i]);
    return temp;
}


//returns a copy of src with characters in punct removed
std::string removePunct(const std::string& src,
                                    const std::string& punct)
{
    using namespace std;
    string no_punct;
    int src_len = src.length();
    int punct_len = punct.length();
    for(int i = 0; i < src_len; i++)
    {
        string aChar = src.substr(i,1);
        int location = punct.find(aChar, 0);
        //find location of successive characters
        //of src in punct

      if (location < 0 || location >= punct_len)
        no_punct = no_punct + aChar; //aChar not in punct -- keep it
    }
    return no_punct;
}
```

Display 10.12 Careful Namespace Usage (*part 4 of 4*)

```
//uses functions makeLower, removePunct.
//Returned value:
//if this_String is a palindrome,
//   return true;
//else
//   return false;
bool isPal(const std::string& this_String)
{
    using namespace std;
    string punctuation(",;:.?!'\" ");  //includes a blank
    string str(this_String);
    str = makeLower(str);
    string lowerStr = removePunct(str, punctuation);
    return lowerStr == reverse(lowerStr);
}
```

The sample dialogue is the same as in Display 10.10.

CHAPTER SUMMARY

- A cstring variable is the same thing as an array of characters, but it is used in a slightly different way. A string variable uses the null character, `'\0'`, to mark the end of the string stored in the array.

- cstring variables usually must be treated like arrays, rather than simple variables of the kind we used for numbers and single characters. In particular, you cannot assign a cstring value to a cstring variable using the equal sign, `=`, and you cannot compare the values in two cstring variables using the `==` operator. Instead you must use special cstring functions to perform these tasks.

- When you define a function that changes the value in a cstring variable, your function should have an additional *int* parameter for the declared size of the cstring variable. That way the function can check to make sure it does not attempt to place more characters in the cstring variable than the cstring variable can hold. The predefined functions in the library with the header file `cstring` do not have such a parameter, so extra care must be exercised when using many of them.

- A very robust input function that will read anything the user types in must read the input as a string of characters. If numeric input is desired, the string of digits that is read in will need to be converted to a number.

- If you need an array with more than one index, you can use a multidimensional array, which is actually an array of arrays.

- An array of strings can be implemented as a two-dimensional array of characters.

- The ANSI Standard string library provides a fully featured `string` class. The use of the `string` class is illustrated in Display 10.9 and Display 10.10. Typical calls to many members of class `string` are shown in Display 10.11.

Answers to Self-Test Exercises

1   The following two are equivalent to each other (but not equivalent to any others):

```
char string_var[10] = "Hello";
char string_var[10] = {'H', 'e', 'l', 'l', 'o', '\0'};
```

The following two are equivalent to each other (but not equivalent to any others):

```
char string_var[6] = "Hello";
char string_var[] = "Hello";
```

The following is not equivalent to any of the others:

```
char string_var[10] = {'H', 'e', 'l', 'l', 'o'};
```

(In some situations, the following two declarations are equivalent, but you cannot count on their being equivalent in all, nor even most, situations:

```
char string_var[10] = "Hello";
char string_var[10] = {'H', 'e', 'l', 'l', 'o'};
```

The first of the above two declarations will insert the null character '\0' in the indexed variable `string_var[5]`; but in some situations, such as an array declaration within a function definition, the second will leave `string_var[5]` undefined. The exact details about when they are equivalent are beyond the scope of this book. As a practical matter, you can safely consider them to *not* be equivalent.)

2 "DoBeDo to you"

3 The declaration means that `string_var` has room for only six characters (including the null character `'\0'`). The function `strcat` does not check that there is room to add more characters to `string_var`, so `strcat` will write all the characters in the string `" and Good-bye."` into memory, even though that requires more memory than has been assigned to `string_var`. This means memory that should not be changed will be changed. The net effect is unpredictable, but bad.

4 If `strlen` were not already defined for you, you could use the following definition:

```
int strlen(const char str[])
//Precondition: str contains a string value terminated
//with '\0'.
//Returns the number of characters in the string str (not
//counting '\0').
{
    int index = 0;
    while (str[index] != '\0')
        index++;
    return index;
}
```

5 Maximum number of characters is 5 because the sixth position is needed for the `null` terminator (`'\0'`).

6 a. 1

  b. 1

  c. 5 (including the `'\0'`)

  d. 2 (including the `'\0'`)

  e. 6 (including the `'\0'`)

7   These are *not equivalent*. The first of these places the null character `'\0'` in
the array after the characters `'a'`, `'b'`, and `'c'`. The second only assigns the
successive positions `'a'`, `'b'`, and `'c'` but *does not put a* `'\0'` *anywhere.*

8
```
int index = 0;
while ( our_string[index] != '\0' )
{
    our_string[index] = 'X';
    index++;
}
```

9   a. If the `cstring` variable does not have a `null` terminator, the loop can run
beyond memory allocated for the `cstring`, destroying the contents of
memory there. To protect memory beyond the end of the array, change the
while condition as shown in b.

   b. `while( our_string[index] != '\0' && index < SIZE )`

10
```
#include <cstring>
//needed to get the declaration of strcpy
...
strcpy(a_string, "Hello");
```

11   `I did it my way!`

12   The string `"Come fly with me."` is too long for `to_Barbara`. A chunk of
memory that doesn't belong to the array `to_Barbara` will be overwritten.

13   The complete dialogue is as follows:

```
Enter a line of input:
May the hair on your toes grow long and curly.
May t<END OF OUTPUT
```

14
```
//Uses cstring:
void append(char str_var[], int size_str_var,
                                const char to_add[])
{
    using namespace std;
    int new_length = strlen(str_var) + strlen(to_add);
    if (new_length > (size_str_var - 1))
        new_length = size_str_var - 1;//All that will fit in
                                      //str_var.
```

```
    int start_add = strlen(str_var);

    int index;
    for (index = 0; start_add + index < new_length; index++)
        str_var[start_add + index] = to_add[index];
    str_var[start_add + index] = '\0';
}
```

15

```
#include <cstdlib>
using namespace std;
//. . .
char number1[] = "3456";
char number2[] = "3.456e-7";
int n1;
double n2;
n1 = atoi(number1);
n2 = atof(number2);
```

16 `void my_func(int a[][25], int dimension_1_size);`

17

```
for (index = 0; index < 10; index++)
    cout << list[index][0] << endl;
```

18

```
0 1 2 3
0 1 2 3
0 1 2 3
0 1 2 3
```

19

```
int a[4][5];
int index1, index2;
for (index1 = 0; index1 < 4; index1++)
    for (index2 = 0; index2 < 5; index2++)
        cin >> a[index1][index2];
```

20

```cpp
//Uses iostream:
void echo(const int a[][5], int size_of_a)
//Outputs the values in the array a on size_of_a lines
//with 5 numbers per line.
{
    using namespace std;
    for (int index1 = 0; index1 < size_of_a; index1++)
    {
        for (int index2 = 0; index2 < 5; index2++)
            cout << a[index1][index2] << " ";
        cout << endl;
    }
}
```

21

```cpp
//Uses iostream:
void get_names(char name[][25], int size)
{
    using namespace std;
    int index;
    cout << "Enter " << size
         << " names, one per line:\n";
    for (index = 0; index < size; index++)
        cin.getline(name[index], 25);
}
```

22

```
//Combined solution to Exercises 22 and 23, together with
//test code.
//
#include <string>
#include <iostream>
using namespace std;
//
//Exercise 22
//
//uses: iostream, string
//Precondition:
//       Argument for names parameter is an array of string
//       of fewer entries than argument for count
//Postcondition:
//     Returns an array of names in the string array names.
//     Fetches names until an empty name is entered (only a
//     '\n' was entered) or the number of lines
//     exceeds count.

void getStrings(string names[], const int count)
{
    bool last_line_empty = false;
    for (int i = 0; (i < count) && (!last_line_empty); i++)
    {
      getline(cin, names[i]);
      if (names[i].empty())
         last_line_empty = true;
    }
}


//
//Exercise 23:
//
//uses iostream, string
//
//Precondition:
//   argument for names is an empty string delimited
//   array of strings
```

```
//Postcondition:
//    list has been displayed as a numbered list of
//    lines.
void displayStrings(const string names[], const int count)
{
    int i = 0;
    while ( (i < count) && (!names[i].empty()) )
    {
        cout << i << ": \t";
        cout << names[i] << endl;
        i++;
    }
}

int main()
{
    const int MAX_COUNT = 60;
    string names[MAX_COUNT];
    cout << "before getStrings and displayStrings "
         << endl;
    getStrings(names, MAX_COUNT);
    cout << " between getStrings and displayStrings "
         << endl;
    displayStrings(names, MAX_COUNT);
}
//Following the principle that loop test data should cause
//   the loop not to execute, to execute one time, to
//   execute several times, and to execute the limit number
//   of times:
//Test this by typing a single return to give it a single
//   blank line,
//Test by typing one line followed by a blank line
//Test by typing in several lines ending with a blank line
//   at the end
//Finally, decrease MAXCOUNT, compile and enter more than
//   MAX_COUNT lines.
```

Programming Projects

Most of the projects that deal with strings can be done either with the material in Section 10.1 or with the material in Section 10.3.

1 Write a program that will read in a sentence of up to 100 characters and output the sentence with spacing corrected and with letters corrected for capitalization. In other words, in the output sentence all strings of two or more blanks should be compressed to a single blank. The sentence should start with an uppercase letter but should contain no other uppercase letters. Do not worry about proper names; if their first letter is changed to lowercase, that is acceptable. Treat a line break as if it were a blank in the sense that a line break and any number of blanks are compressed to a single blank. Assume that the sentence ends with a period and contains no other periods. For example, the input

   ```
   the      Answer to life, the Universe, and    everything
   IS 42.
   ```

   should produce the following output:

   ```
   The answer to life, the universe, and everything is 42.
   ```

2 Write a program that will read in a line of text and output the number of words in the line and the number of occurrences of each letter. Define a word to be any string of letters that is delimited at each end by either whitespace, a period, a comma, or the beginning or end of the line. You can assume that the input consists entirely of letters, whitespace, commas, and periods. When outputting the number of letters that occur in a line, be sure to count upper- and lowercase versions of a letter as the same letter. Output the letters in alphabetical order and list only those letters that do occur in the input line. For example, the input line

   ```
   I say Hi.
   ```

   should produce output similar to the following:

   ```
   3 words
   1 a
   1 h
   2 i
   1 s
   1 y
   ```

3   Give the function definition for the function with the following prototype. Embed your definition in a suitable test program.

```
void get_double(double& input_number);
//Postcondition:input_number is given a value
//that the user approves of.
```

You can assume that the user types in the input in normal everyday notation, such as **23.789**, and does not use e notation to type in the number. Model your definition after the definition of the function get_int given in Display 10.4 so that your function reads the input as characters, edits the string of characters, and converts the resulting string to a number of type *double*. You will need to define a function like read_and_clean that is more sophisticated than the one in Display 10.3, since it must cope with the decimal point. This is a fairly easy project. For a more difficult project, allow the user to enter the number in either the normal everyday notation, as discussed above, or in e notation. Your function should decide whether or not the input is in e notation by reading the input, *not* by asking the user whether she or he will use e notation.

4   Write a program that reads a person's name in the format: first name, then middle name or initial, and then last name. The program then outputs the name in the format:

```
Last_Name, First_Name, Middle_Initial.
```

For example, the input

Mary Average User

should produce the output:

```
User, Mary A.
```

The input

Mary A. User

should also produce the output:

```
User, Mary A.
```

Your program should work the same and place a period after the middle initial, even if the input did not contain a period. Your program should allow for users who give no middle name or middle initial. In that case, the output, of course, contains no middle name or initial. For example, the input

Mary User

should produce the output:

User, Mary

Assume that each name is at most 20 characters long. Hint: You may want to use three string variables rather than one large string variable for the input. You may find it easier to *not* use `cin.getline`.

5 Write a program that reads in a line of text and replaces all four-letter words with the word `"love"`. For example, the input string

I hate you, you dodo!

should produce the output:

I love you, you love!

Of course, the output will not always make sense. For example, the input string

John will run home.

should produce the output:

Love love run love.

If the four-letter word starts with a capital letter, it should be replaced by `"Love"`, not by `"love"`. You need not check capitalization, except for the first letter of a word. A word is any string consisting of the letters of the alphabet and delimited at each end by a blank, the end of the line, or any other character that is not a letter. Your program should repeat this action until the user says to quit.

6 (This project is meant to be done with the material in Section 10.1. Programming Project 7 is a version of this project that uses the class `string` defined in Section 10.3.)

Give the function definition for the function with the following prototype:

```
int match(const char target[], const char pattern[]);
//Precondition: Both target and pattern contain string
//   values
```

```
// properly terminated with the null character, '\0'.
//Postcondition: If the string in pattern occurs as a
//substring of the string in target, then this function
//returns the index of the  array element where the first
//occurrence of pattern starts in target.
//If the string in pattern does not occur in target, then
//-1 is returned.
```

For example, consider the following code (and assume it is embedded in a complete and correct program that includes your definition):

```
char target[20] = "DoBeDoBe";
cout << match(target, "Be");
```

The output should be 2, because the first occurrence of "Be" begins with the 'B' in target[2]. (Remember, array indexes start with 0.) Embed your definition in a suitable test program.

7   (This project is meant to be done with the material in Section 10.3. Programming Project 6 is a version of this project that uses the kind of strings discussed in Section 10.1.)

Give the function definition for the function with the following prototype:

```
int match(const string& target, const string& pattern);
//Precondition: Both target and pattern contain string
//values
//Postcondition: If the string in pattern occurs as a
//substring of the string in target, then this function
//returns the position of the character where the first
//occurrence of pattern starts in target.
//If the string in pattern does not occur in target, then
//-1 is returned.
```

For example, consider the following code (and assume it is embedded in a complete and correct program that includes your definition):

```
String target("DoBeDoBe");
cout << match(target, "Be");
```

The output should be 2, because the first occurrence of "Be" begins with the 'B' in position 2 of target. (Remember, character positions start with 0.) Embed your definition in a suitable test program.

8 Write a program that can be used to train the user to use less sexist language by suggesting alternative versions of sentences given by the user. The program will ask for a sentence, read the sentence into a string variable, and replace all occurrences of masculine pronouns with gender neutral pronouns. For example, it will replace "he" by "she or he". Thus the input sentence:

See an adviser, talk to him, and listen to him.

should produce the following suggested changed version of the sentence:

See an adviser, talk to her or him, and listen to her or him.

Be sure to preserve uppercase letters for the first word of the sentence. The pronoun "his" can be replaced by "her(s)"; your program need not decide between "her" and "hers". Allow the user to repeat this for more sentences until the user says she or he is done. This will be a long program that requires a good deal of patience. Your program should not replace the string "he" when it occurs inside another word such as "here". A word is any string consisting of the letters of the alphabet and delimited at each end by a blank, the end of the line, or any other character that is not a letter. Allow your sentences to be up to 100 characters long. It will help to do Programming Project 6 or 7 before doing this project.

9 Enhance the program given in Display 10.5 so that it contains the following two additional features:

   a. Add an input function (omitted in Display 10.5) so that the program is complete.

   b. Enhance the program so that it reads in each student's name and displays the student names as well as student numbers. Store the names in an array of strings.

10   Write a program that will allow two users to play tic-tac-toe. The program should ask for moves alternately from player X and player O. The program displays the game positions as follows:

```
1   2   3
4   5   6
7   8   9
```

The players enter their moves by entering the position number they wish to mark. After each move, the program displays the changed board. A sample board configuration is:

```
X   X   0
4   5   6
0   8   9
```

11   Write a program to assign passengers seats in an airplane. Assume a small airplane with seat numbering as follows:

```
1    A B   C D
2    A B   C D
3    A B   C D
4    A B   C D
5    A B   C D
6    A B   C D
7    A B   C D
```

The program should display the seat pattern, with an 'X' marking the seats already assigned. For example, after seats 1A, 2B, and 4C are taken, the display should look like:

```
1    X B   C D
2    A X   C D
3    A B   C D
4    A B   X D
5    A B   C D
6    A B   C D
7    A B   C D
```

After displaying the seats available, the program prompts for the seat desired, the user types in a seat, and then the display of available seats is updated. This continues until all seats are filled or until the user signals that the program should end. If the user types in a seat that is already assigned, the program should say that that seat is occupied and ask for another choice.

12 Write a program that accepts input like the program in Display 9.9 and that outputs a bar graph like the one in that figure except that your program will output the bars vertically rather than horizontally. A two-dimensional array may be useful.

13 (This project is meant to be done with the material from Section 10.2 on two-dimensional arrays.) The mathematician, John Horton Conway, invented the "Game of Life." Though not a "game" in any traditional sense, it provides interesting behavior that is specified with only a few rules. The project asks you to write a program that allows you to specify an initial configuration. The program follows the rules of Life (listed shortly) to show the continuing behavior of the configuration.

LIFE is an organism that lives in a discrete, two-dimensional world. While this world is actually unlimited, we don't have that luxury, so we restrict the array to 80 characters wide by 22 character positions high. If you have access to a larger screen, by all means use it.

This world is an array with each cell capable of holding one LIFE cell. Generations mark the passing of time. Each generation brings births and deaths to the LIFE community.

The births and deaths follow this set of rules:

1. We define each cell to have eight **neighbor** cells. The neighbors of a cell are the cell directly above, below, to the right, to the left, diagonally above to the right and left, and diagonally below, to the right and left.

2. If an occupied cell has 0 or 1 neighbors, it dies of **loneliness.** If an occupied cell has more than 3 neighbors, it dies of **overcrowding.**

3. If an empty cell has exactly three occupied neighbor cells, there is a **birth** of a new cell to replace the empty cell.

4. Births and deaths are instantaneous, and occur at the changes of generation. A cell dying for whatever reason may help cause birth, but a newborn cell cannot resurrect a cell that is dying, nor will a cell's death prevent the death of another, say, by reducing the local population.

```
                              *
Examples:    *** becomes  *  then becomes  ***  again, and so on.
                              *
```

Notes: Some configurations grow from relatively small starting configurations. Others move across the region. It is recommended that for text output you use a rectangular array of char with 80 columns and 22 rows to store the LIFE world's successive generations. Use a * to indicate a living cell and use a blank to indicate an empty (or dead) cell. If you have a screen with more rows than that, by all means make use of the whole screen.

Suggestions: Look for stable configurations. That is, look for communities that repeat patterns continually. The number of configurations in the repetition is called the period. There are configurations that are fixed, that continue without change. A possible project is to find such configurations.

Hints: Define a void function named generation that takes the array we call world, an 80 column by 22 row array of char, which contains the initial configuration. The function scans the array and modifies the cells, marking the cells with births and deaths in accord with the rules listed above. This involves examining each cell in turn, either killing the cell, letting it live, or if the cell is empty, deciding whether a cell should be born. There should be a function display that accepts the array world and displays the array on the screen. Some sort of time delay is appropriate between calls to generation and display. To do this, your program should generate and display the next generation when you press return. You are at liberty to automate this, but automation is not necessary for the program. See the example configurations.

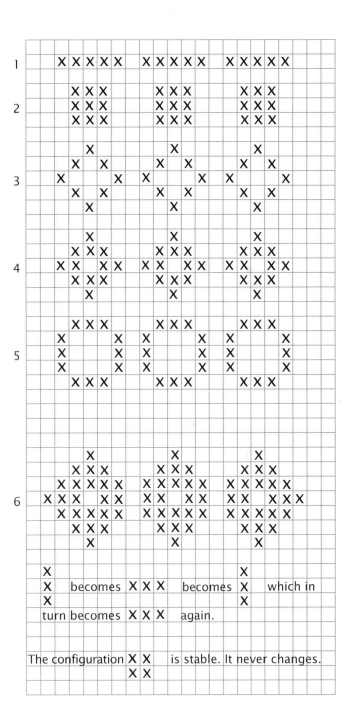

Curiosity: the three columns do not interfere with one another until Generation 6.

GLIDER

	1	2	3
1		X	
2			X
3	X	X	X

Count neighbors, both occupied and unoccupied cells:

0	0	1	1	1	0
1		1	x_1	2	1
2	1	3	3	x_3	2
3	1	x_1	x_3	x_2	2
4	1	2	3	2	1

Replace empty cells with count of 3 by new-born cells, living cells with count of 0 or 1 die. Others live. Observe that the whole organism has moved down one cell position.

Second Generation:

1				
2	X		X	
3		X	X	
4		X		

Neighbors counted:

1	1	1	0	1	1
2	1	x_1	4	x_2	2
3	1	3	x_4	x_3	2
4	0	2	x_3	3	1
5	0	1	1	1	0

Replace empty cells with count of 3 by new-born cells, living cells with neighbor count of 0, 1, or 4 die. Others live.

Third Generation:

1				
2			X	
3	X		X	
4		X	X	

Neighbors counted. You figure out the next two generations. The Fifth Generation is identical to the first.

1	0	0	1	1	1
2	1	1	3	x_1	1
3	1	x_1	5	x_2	3
4	1	2	x_3	x_2	2
5	0	1	2	2	1

14 English to Pig Latin Translator, "Igpay Atinlay." That is "pig latin" written in pig latin. To create the pig latin form of a word, take the first letter, move it to the end, and if the letter is a consonant (not a, e, i, o, or u) then add an "ay" suffix to the remainder of the word. If the first letter is a vowel: a, e, i, o, u, then add an "yay" to the end of the otherwise unchanged word. The second and third sentences in this paragraph should be rendered.

Examples:

Atthay isyay igpay atinlay orfay "pig latin." Otay ormfay hetay ormfay ofyay ayay ordway, aketay hetay irstfay etterlay, ovemay ityay otyay hetay endyay andyay addyay anyay ayyay uffixsay.

Commentary:

A first pass at this problem might be to blindly remove the first letter, regardless of whether it is a vowel, and add the suffix "ay" to the rest of the word. This won't fit the full rules, but will get you started. Once this program is running, then you can decide how to use the vowel-consonant rule.

CHAPTER
11

Pointers and Dynamic Arrays

11 Pointers and Dynamic Arrays

Memory is necessary for all the operations of reason.

BLAISE PASCAL, PENSÉES

Introduction

A *pointer* is a construct that gives you more control of the computer's memory. In this chapter we will show you how pointers are used with arrays and will introduce a new form of array called a *dynamic array.* **Dynamic arrays** are arrays whose size is determined while the program is running, rather than being fixed when the program is written.

11.1 Pointers

Do not mistake the pointing finger for the moon.

ZEN SAYING

A **pointer** is the memory address of a variable. Recall that the computer's memory is divided into numbered memory locations (called bytes), and that variables are implemented as a sequence of adjacent memory locations. Recall also that sometimes the C++ system uses these memory addresses as names for the variables. If a variable is implemented as, say, three memory locations, then the address of the first of these memory locations is sometimes used as a name for that variable. For example, when the variable is used as a call-by-reference argument, it is this address, not the identifier name of the variable, that is passed to the calling function. An address that is used to name a variable in this way (by giving the address in memory where the variable starts) is called a *pointer* because the address can be thought of as "pointing" to the variable. The address "points" to the variable because it identifies the variable by telling *where* the variable is, rather than telling what the variable's name is. A variable that is, say, at location number 1007 can be pointed out by saying "it's the variable over there at location 1007."

You have already been using pointers in a number of situations. As we noted in the previous paragraph, when a variable is a call-by-reference argument in a function call, the function is given this argument variable in the form of a pointer to the variable. As we noted in Chapter 9, an array is given to a function (or to anything else for that matter) by giving a pointer to the first array element. These are two powerful uses for pointers, but they are all done automatically for you by the C++ system. In this chapter we will show you how to write programs that manipulate pointers in any way you want, rather than relying on the system to manipulate the pointers for you.

Pointer Variables

A pointer can be stored in a variable. However, even though a pointer is a memory address and a memory address is a number, you cannot store a pointer in a variable of type *int* or *double*. A variable to hold a pointer must be declared to have a pointer type. For example, the following declares p to be a pointer variable that can hold one pointer that points to a variable of type *double*:

declaring pointer variables

    double *p;

The variable p can hold pointers to variables of type *double*, but it cannot normally contain a pointer to a variable of some other type, such as *int* or *char*. Each variable type requires a different pointer type.

In general, to declare a variable that can hold pointers to other variables of a specific type, you declare the pointer variable just as you would declare an ordinary variable of that type, but you place an asterisk in front of the variable name. For example, the following declares the variables p1 and p2 so they can hold pointers to variables of type *int*; it also declares two ordinary variables v1 and v2 of type *int*:

    int *p1, *p2, v1, v2;

There must be an asterisk before *each* of the pointer variables. If you omit the second asterisk in the above declaration, then p2 will not be a pointer variable; it will instead be an ordinary variable of type *int*. The asterisk is the same symbol you have been using for multiplication, but in this context it has a totally different meaning.

When discussing pointers and pointer variables, we usually speak of *pointing* rather than speaking of *addresses*. When a pointer variable, such as p1, contains the address of a variable, such as v1, the pointer variable is said to *point to the variable* v1 or to be *a pointer to the variable* v1.

Pointer variables, like p1 and p2 declared above, can contain pointers to variables like v1 and v2. You can use the operator & to determine the address of a

the & operator

Pointer Variable Declarations

A variable that can hold pointers to other variables of type *Type_Name* is declared the same way you declare a variable of type *Type_Name*, except that you place an asterisk at the beginning of the variable name.

Syntax:

Type_Name *Variable_Name1 , *Variable_Name2 , . . . ;

Example:

```
double *pointer1, *pointer2;
```

Addresses and Numbers

A pointer is an address, an address is an integer, but a pointer is not an integer— That is not crazy. That is abstraction! C++ insists that you use a pointer as an address and that you not use it as a number. A pointer is not a value of type *int* or of any other numeric type. You normally cannot store a pointer in a variable of type *int*. If you try, most C++ compilers will give you an error message or a warning message. Also, you cannot perform the normal arithmetic operations on pointers. (You can perform a kind of addition and a kind of subtraction on pointers, but they are not the usual integer addition and subtraction.)

---

variable, and you can then assign that address to a pointer variable. For example, the following will set the variable p1 equal to a pointer that points to the variable v1:

```
p1 = &v1;
```

*the * operator*

You now have two ways to refer to v1: you can call it v1 or you can call it "the variable pointed to by p1." In C++, the way that you say "the variable pointed to by p1" is *p1. This is the same asterisk that we used when we declared p1, but now it has yet another meaning. When the asterisk is used in this way it is often called the **dereferencing operator** and the pointer variable is said to be **dereferenced.**

dereferencing

Putting these pieces together can produce some surprising results. Consider the following code:

```
v1 = 0;
p1 = &v1;
*p1 = 42;
cout << v1 << endl;
cout << *p1 << endl;
```

This code will output the following to the screen

```
42
42
```

As long as p1 contains a pointer that points to v1, then v1 and *p1 refer to the same variable. So when you set *p1 equal to 42, you are also setting v1 equal to 42.

The symbol & that is used to obtain the address of a variable is the same symbol that you use in function prototypes to specify a call-by-reference parameter. This is not a coincidence. Recall that a call-by-reference argument is implemented by giving the address of the argument to the calling function. So, these two uses of the symbol & are very much the same. However, the usages are slightly different and we will consider them to be two different (although very closely related) usages of the symbol &.

The * and & Operators

The * operator in front of a pointer variable produces the variable it points to. When used this way, the * operator is called the **dereferencing operator.**

The operator & in front of an ordinary variable produces the address of that variable; that is, produces a pointer that points to the variable. The & operator is simply called the **address of operator.**

For example, consider the declarations

```
double *p, v;
```

The following sets the value of p so that p points to the variable v:

```
p = &v;
```

*p produce the variable pointed to by p, so after the above assignment, *p and v refer to the same variable. For example, the following sets the value of v to 9.99, even though the name v is never explicitly used:

```
*p = 9.99;
```

Display 11.1 Uses of the Assignment Operator

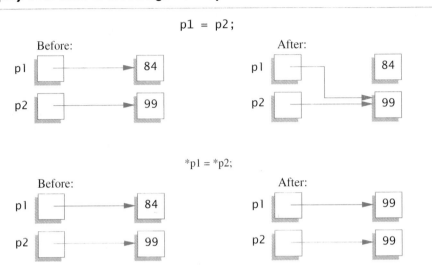

You can assign the value of one pointer variable to another pointer variable. This copies an address from one pointer variable to another pointer variable. For example, if p1 is still pointing to v1, then the following will set p2 so that it also points to v1:

```
p2 = p1;
```

Provided we have not changed v1's value, the following will also output a 42 to the screen:

```
cout << *p2;
```

Be sure you do not confuse

```
p1 = p2;
```

and

```
*p1 = *p2;
```

When you add the asterisk, you are not dealing with the pointers p1 and p2, but with the variables that the pointers are pointing to. This is illustrated in Display 11.1.

new   Since a pointer can be used to refer to a variable, your program can manipulate variables even if the variables have no identifiers to name them. The operator *new* can be used to create variables that have no identifiers to serve as their names. These nameless variables are referred to via pointers. For example, the following creates a new variable of type *int* and sets the pointer variable p1 equal to the address of this new variable (that is, p1 points to this new, nameless variable):

```
p1 = new int;
```

This new, nameless variable can be referred to as *p1 (that is, as the variable pointed to by p1). You can do anything with this nameless variable that you can do with any other variable of type *int*. For example, the following reads a value of type *int* from the keyboard into this nameless variable, adds 7 to the value, then outputs this new value:

```
cin >> *p1;
*p1 = *p1 + 7;
cout << *p1;
```

The *new* operator produces a new nameless variable and returns a pointer that points to this new variable. You specify the type for this new variable by writing the type name after the *new* operator. Variables that are created using the *new* operator are called **dynamic variables,** because they are created and destroyed while the program is running. The program in Display 11.2 demonstrates some simple operations on pointers and dynamic variables. Display 11.3 illustrates the working of the program in Display 11.2. In Display 11.3 variables are represented as boxes and the value of the variable is written inside the box. We have not shown the actual numeric addresses in the pointer variables. The actual numbers are not important. What is important is that the number is the address of some particular variable. So, rather than use the actual number of the address, we have merely indicated the address with an arrow that points to the variable with that address. For example, in illustration (b) in Display 11.3, p1 contains the address of a variable that has a question mark written in it.

SELF-TEST EXERCISES

1 Explain the concept of pointer in C++. Account for the fact that objects of different types occupy different amounts of memory.

2 What unfortunate misinterpretation can occur with the following declaration?

```
int* int_ptr1, int_ptr2;
```

Display 11.2 Basic Pointer Manipulations

```cpp
//Program to demonstrate pointers and dynamic variables.
#include <iostream>
using namespace std;

int main()
{
    int *p1, *p2;

    p1 = new int;
    *p1 = 42;
    p2 = p1;
    cout << "*p1 == " << *p1 << endl;
    cout << "*p2 == " << *p2 << endl;

    *p2 = 53;
    cout << "*p1 == " << *p1 << endl;
    cout << "*p2 == " << *p2 << endl;

    p1 = new int;
    *p1 = 88;
    cout << "*p1 == " << *p1 << endl;
    cout << "*p2 == " << *p2 << endl;

    cout << "Hope you got the point of this example!\n";
    return 0;
}
```

Sample Dialogue

```
*p1 == 42
*p2 == 42
*p1 == 53
*p2 == 53
*p1 == 88
*p2 == 53
Hope you got the point of this example!
```

Display 11.3 Explanation of Display 11.2

(a)
int *p1, *p2;

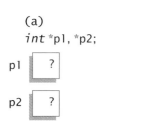

(b)
p1 = *new int*;

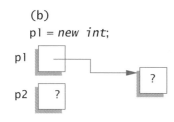

(c)
*p1 = 42;

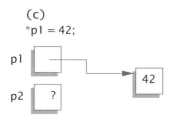

(d)
p2 = p1;

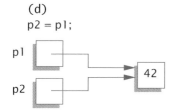

(e)
*p2 = 53;

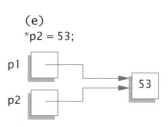

(f)
p1 = *new int*;

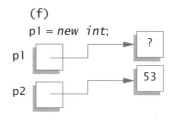

(g)
*p1 = 88;

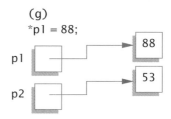

Pointer Variables Used with =

If p1 and p2 are pointer variables, then the statement

```
p1 = p2;
```

will change p1 so that it points to the same thing that p2 is currently pointing to.

The *new* Operator

The *new* operator creates a new dynamic variable of a specified type and returns a pointer that points to this new variable. For example, the following creates a new dynamic variable of type MyType and leaves the pointer variable p pointing to this new variable:

```
MyType *p;
p = new MyType;
```

If the type is a class with a constructor, the default constructor is called for the newly created dynamic variable. Initializers can be specified that cause other constructors to be called:

```
int *n;
n = new int(17); // initializes n to 17
MyType *mtPtr;
mtPtr = new MyType(32.0, 17); // calls MyType(double, int);
```

With earlier C++ compilers, if there is not sufficient available memory to create the new variable, then *new* returns a special pointer named NULL. The C++ Standard provides that if there is not sufficient available memory to create the new variable, then the *new* operator, by default, terminates the program.[1]

---

3   Give at least three uses of the * operator. State what the * is doing, and name the use of the * that you present.

4   What is the output produced by the following code?

```
int *p1, *p2;
p1 = new int;
```

---

[1]Technically, the *new* operator throws an exception, which, if not caught, terminates the program. It is possible to "catch" the exception or install a new handler, but these topics are beyond the scope of this book.

```
p2 = new int;
*p1 = 10;
*p2 = 20;
cout << *p1 << " " << *p2 << endl;
p1 = p2;
cout << *p1 << " " << *p2 << endl;
*p1 = 30;
cout << *p1 << " " << *p2 << endl;
```

How would the output change if you were to replace

```
*p1 = 30;
```

with the following?

```
*p2 = 30;
```

5 What is the output produced by the following code?

```
int *p1, *p2;
p1 = new int;
p2 = new int;
*p1 = 10;
*p2 = 20;
cout << *p1 << " " << *p2 << endl;
*p1 = *p2; //This is different from Exercise 4
cout << *p1 << " " << *p2 << endl;
*p1 = 30;
cout << *p1 << " " << *p2 << endl;
```

Basic Memory Management

A special area of memory, called the **heap,**[2] is reserved for dynamic variables. Any new dynamic variable created by a program consumes some of the memory in the heap. If your program creates too many dynamic variables, it will consume all of the memory in the heap. If this happens, any additional calls to *new* will fail.

the heap

---

[2]Note that **heap** is a word we use that comes from C++'s C heritage. The Standard and several other textbooks call this the **freestore**. Presumably, this is because there is an important data structure also named heap, which could cause confusion. When you read C++ literature be aware of this alternate usage. The use of the term heap is a tradition that we will continue.

NULL

NULL is a special constant pointer value that is used to give a value to a pointer variable that would not otherwise have a value. NULL can be assigned to a pointer variable of any type. The identifier NULL is defined in a number of libraries including the library with header file cstddef. With earlier compilers, the operator *new* returned a NULL pointer value whenever *new* failed in its attempt to create a dynamic variable. Current compilers "throw the exception *std::bad alloc*." The effect is to abort the program with an error message.

---

delete

The size of the heap will vary from one implementation of C++ to another. It is typically large and a modest program is not likely to use all the memory in the heap. However, even on modest programs it is a good practice to recycle any heap memory that is no longer needed. If your program no longer needs a dynamic variable, the memory used by that dynamic variable can be returned to the heap to be reused to create other dynamic variables. The *delete* operator eliminates a dynamic variable and returns the memory that the dynamic variable occupied to the heap, so the memory can be reused. Suppose that p is a pointer variable that is pointing to a dynamic variable. The following will destroy the dynamic variable pointed to by p and return the memory used by the dynamic variable to the heap:

```
delete p;
```

The *delete* Operator

The *delete* operator eliminates a dynamic variable and returns the memory that the dynamic variable occupied to the heap. The memory can then be reused to create new dynamic variables. For example, the following eliminates the dynamic variable pointed to by the pointer variable p:

```
delete p;
```

After a call to *delete*, the value of the pointer variable, like p above, is undefined. (A slightly different version of *delete*, discussed later in this chapter, is used when the dynamic variable is an array.)

● *PITFALL*   Dangling Pointers

When you apply *delete* to a pointer variable, the dynamic variable it is pointing to is destroyed. At that point, the value of the pointer variable is undefined, which means that you do not know where it is pointing, nor what the value is where it is pointing. Moreover, if some other pointer variable was pointing to this dynamic variable that was destroyed, then this other pointer variable is also undefined. These undefined pointer variables are called **dangling pointers.** If p is a dangling pointer and your program applies the dereferencing operator * to p (to produce the expression *p), the result is unpredictable, and usually disastrous. Before you apply the dereferencing operator * to a pointer variable, you should be certain that the pointer variable points to some variable.

Static Variables and Automatic Variables

Variables created with the *new* operator are called *dynamic variables* because they are created and destroyed while the program is running. When compared to these dynamic variables, ordinary variables seem *static,* but the terminology used by C++ programmers is a bit more involved than that and ordinary variables are not called *static variables.*

dynamic variables

The ordinary variables we have been using in previous chapters are not really static. If a variable is local to a function, then the variable is created by the C++ system when the function is called and is destroyed when the function call is completed. Since the main part of a program is really just a function called main, this is even true of the variables declared in the main part of your program. (Since the call to main does not end until the program ends, the variables declared in main are not destroyed until the program ends, but the mechanism for handling local variables is the same for main as it is for any other function.) The ordinary variables that we have been using (that is, the variables declared within main or within some other function definition) are called **automatic variables,** because their dynamic properties are controlled automatically for you; they are automatically created when the function in which they are declared is called and automatically destroyed when the function call ends. We will usually call these variables **ordinary variables,** but other books call them *automatic variables.*

automatic variables

There is one other category of variables, namely global variables. Global variables are variables that are declared outside of any function definition (including being outside of main). We discussed global variables briefly in Chapter 3. As it turns out, we have no need for global variables and have not used them.

global variables

typedef

PROGRAMMING TIP
Define Pointer Types

You can define a pointer type name so that pointer variables can be declared like other variables without the need to place an asterisk in front of each pointer variable. For example, the following defines a type called `IntPtr`, which is the type for pointer variables that contain pointers to *int* variables:

```
typedef int* IntPtr;
```

Thus, the following two pointer variable declarations are equivalent:

```
IntPtr p;
```

which is equivalent to

```
int *p;
```

You can use *typedef* to define an alias for any type name or definition. For example, the following defines the type name `Kilometers` to mean the same thing as the type name *double*:

```
typedef double Kilometers;
```

Once you have given this type definition, you can define a variable of type *double* as follows:

```
Kilometers distance;
```

Renaming existing types this way can occasionally be useful. However, our main use of *typedef* will be to define types for pointer variables.

There are two advantages to using defined pointer type names, such as `IntPtr` defined above. First, it avoids the mistake of omitting an asterisk. Remember, if you intend p1 and p2 to be pointers, then the following is a mistake:

```
int *p1, p2;
```

Since the * was omitted from the p2, the variable p2 is just an ordinary *int* variable, not a pointer variable. If you get confused and place the * on the *int*, the problem is the same but is more difficult to notice. C++ allows you to place the * on the type name, such as *int*, so that the following is legal:

```
int* p1, p2;
```

Although the above is legal, it is misleading. It looks like both p1 and p2 are pointer variables, but in fact only p1 is a pointer variable; p2 is an ordinary *int* variable. As far as the C++ compiler is concerned, the * that is attached to the identifier *int* may as well be attached to the identifier p1. One correct way to declare both p1 and p2 to be pointer variables is

```
int *p1, *p2;
```

An easier and less error-prone way to declare both p1 and p2 to be pointer variables is to use the defined type name IntPtr as follows:

```
IntPtr p1, p2;
```

The second advantage of using a defined pointer type, such as IntPtr, is seen when you define a function with a call-by-reference parameter for a pointer variable. Without the defined pointer type name, you would need to include both an * and an & in the prototype for the function, and the details can get confusing. If you use a type name for the pointer type, then a call-by-reference parameter for a pointer type involves no complications. You define a call-by-reference parameter for a defined pointer type just like you define any other call-by-reference parameter. Here's a sample:

```
void sample_function(IntPtr& pointer_variable);
```

Type Definitions

You can assign a name to a type definition and then use the type name to declare variables. This is done with the keyword *typedef*. These type definitions are normally placed outside of the body of the main part of your program (and outside the body of other functions) in the same place as *struct* and class definitions. We will use type definitions to define names for pointer types, as shown in the example below.

Syntax:

```
typedef Known_Type_Definition New_Type_Name;
```

Example:

```
typedef int* IntPtr;
```

The type name IntPtr can then be used to declare pointers to dynamic variables of type *int*, as in:

```
IntPtr pointer1, pointer2;
```

SELF-TEST EXERCISES

6 Suppose a dynamic variable were created as follows:

```
char *p;
p = new char;
```

Assuming that the value of the pointer variable p has not changed (so it still points to the same dynamic variable), how can you destroy this new dynamic variable and return the memory it uses to the heap so that the memory can be reused to create other new dynamic variables?

7 Write a definition for a type called NumberPtr that will be the type for pointer variables that hold pointers to dynamic variables of type *int*. Also, write a declaration for a pointer variable called my_point, which is of type NumberPtr.

8 Describe the action of the *new* operator. What does the operator *new* return?

11.2 Dynamic Arrays

In this section you will see that array variables are actually pointer variables. You will also find out how to write programs with dynamic arrays. A **dynamic array** is an array whose size is not specified when you write the program, but is determined while the program is running.

Array Variables and Pointer Variables

In Chapter 9 we described how arrays are kept in memory. At that point we had not learned about pointers, so we discussed arrays in terms of memory addresses. But, a memory address is a pointer. So, in C++ an array variable is actually a pointer variable that points to the first indexed variable of the array. Given the following two variable declarations, p and a are the same kinds of variables:

```
int a[10];
typedef int* IntPtr;
IntPtr p, p2;
```

The fact that a and p are the same kinds of variable is illustrated in Display 11.4. Since a is a pointer that points to a variable of type *int* (namely the variable a[0]), the value of a can be assigned to the pointer variable p as follows:

```
p = a;
```

Display 11.4 Arrays and Pointer Variables

```cpp
//Program to demonstrate that an array variable is a kind of pointer variable.
#include <iostream>
using namespace std;

typedef int* IntPtr;

int main( )
{
    IntPtr p;
    int a[10];
    int index;

    for (index = 0; index < 10; index++)
        a[index] = index;

    p = a;

    for (index = 0; index < 10; index++)
        cout << p[index] << " ";
    cout << endl;

    for (index = 0; index < 10; index++)
        p[index] = p[index] + 1;

    for (index = 0; index < 10; index++)
        cout << a[index] << " ";
    cout << endl;

    return 0;
}
```

Note that changes to the array p *are also changes to the array* a

Output

```
0 1 2 3 4 5 6 7 8 9
1 2 3 4 5 6 7 8 9 10
```

After this assignment, p points to the same memory location that a points to. So, p[0], p[1], ... p[9] refer to the indexed variables a[0], a[1], ... a[9]. The square bracket notation you have been using for arrays applies to pointer variables as long as the pointer variable points to an array in memory. After the above assignment, you can treat the identifier p as if it were an array identifier. You can also treat the identifier a as if it were a pointer variable, but there is one important reservation. *You cannot change the pointer value in an array variable, such as* a. If the pointer variable p2 has a value, you might be tempted to think the following is legal, but it is not:

```
a = p2;//ILLEGAL. You cannot assign a different address to a.
```

Creating and Using Dynamic Arrays

One problem with the kinds of arrays you have used thus far is that you must specify the size of the array when you write the program—but, you may not know what size array you need until the program is run. For example, an array might hold a list of student identification numbers, but the size of the class may be different each time the program is run. With the kinds of arrays you have used thus far, you must estimate the largest possible size you may need for the array, and hope that size is large enough. There are two problems with this. First, you may estimate too low, and then your program will not work in all situations. Second, since the array might have many unused positions, this can waste computer memory. Dynamic arrays avoid these problems. If your program uses a dynamic array for student identification numbers, then the size of the class can be entered as input to the program and the dynamic array can be created to be exactly that size.

creating a dynamic array

Dynamic arrays are created using the *new* operator. The creation and use of dynamic arrays is surprisingly simple. Since array variables are pointer variables, you can use the *new* operator to create dynamic variables that are arrays and treat these dynamic array variables as if they were ordinary arrays. For example, the following creates a dynamic array variable with 10 array elements of type *double*:

```
typedef double* DoublePtr;
DoublePtr d;
d = new double[10];
```

To obtain a dynamic array of elements of any other type, simply replace *double* with the desired type. In particular, you can replace the type *double* with a *struct* or class type. To obtain a dynamic array variable of any other size, simply replace 10 with the desired size.

There are also a number of less obvious things to notice about this example. First the pointer type that you use for a pointer to a dynamic array is the same as the

---

How to Use a Dynamic Array

- **Define a pointer type:** Define a type for pointers to variables of the same type as the elements of the array. For example, if the dynamic array is an array of *double*, you might use the following:

  ```
  typedef double* DoubleArrayPtr;
  ```

- **Declare a pointer variable:** Declare a pointer variable of this defined type. The pointer variable will point to the dynamic array in memory and will serve as the name of the dynamic array.

  ```
  DoubleArrayPtr a;
  ```

- **Call *new*:** Create a dynamic array using the *new* operator:

  ```
  a = new double[array_size];
  ```

  The size of the dynamic array is given in square brackets as in the above example. The size can be given using an *int* variable or other *int* expression. In the above example, `array_size` can be a variable of type *int* whose value is determined while the program is running.

- **Use like an ordinary array:** The pointer variable, such as a, is used just like an ordinary array. For example, the indexed variables are written in the usual way, a[0], a[1], and so forth. The pointer variable should not have any other pointer value assigned to it, but should be used like an array variable.

- **Call *delete* [ ]:** When your program is finished with the dynamic variable, use *delete* and empty square brackets along with the pointer variable to eliminate the dynamic array and return the storage that it occupies to the heap for reuse. For example:

  ```
  delete [] a;
  ```

---

pointer type you would use for a single element of the array. For instance, the pointer type for an array of elements of type *double* is the same as the pointer type you would use for a simple variable of type *double*. The pointer to the array is actually a pointer to the first indexed variable of the array. In the above example, an entire array with 10 indexed variables is created and the pointer p is left pointing to the first of these 10 indexed variables.

Also notice that, when you call *new*, the size of the dynamic array is given in square brackets after the type, which in this example is the type *double*. This tells the computer how much storage to reserve for the dynamic array. If you omit the square brackets and the 10, the computer will allocate enough storage for only one variable of type *double*, rather than for an array of 10 indexed variables of type *double*.

Display 11.5 contains a program that sorts a list of numbers. This program works for lists of any size because it uses a dynamic array to hold the numbers. The size of the array is determined when the program is run. The user is asked how many numbers there will be and then the *new* operator creates a dynamic array of that size. The size of the dynamic array is given by the variable array_size. The size of the dynamic array need not be given by a constant. It can, as in Display 11.5, be given by a variable whose value is determined when the program is run.

delete []

Notice the *delete* statement which destroys the dynamic array variable a in Display 11.5. Since the program is about to end anyway, we did not really need this *delete* statement; but if the program went on to do other things with dynamic variables, you would want such a *delete* statement so that the memory used by this dynamic array is returned to the heap. The *delete* statement for a dynamic array is similar to the *delete* statement you saw earlier, except that with a dynamic array you must include an empty pair of square brackets like so:

    delete [] a;

The square brackets tell C++ that a dynamic array variable is being eliminated, so the system checks the size of the array and removes that many indexed variables. If you omit the square brackets you would be telling the computer to eliminate only one variable of type *int*. For example:

    delete a;

is not legal, but the error is not detected by any compiler this author knows about. The ANSI C++ Standard says that what happens when you do this is "undefined." That means the author of the compiler can have this do anything that is convenient—for the compiler writer, not for us. Even if it does something useful, you have no guarantee that either the next version of that compiler or any other compiler you compile this code with will do the same thing. Moral: Always use the

    delete [] arrayPtr;

syntax when you are deleting memory that was allocated with something like

    arrayPtr = *new* MyType[37];

Display 11.5 A Dynamic Array (part 1 of 2)

```
//Sorts a list of numbers entered at the keyboard.
#include <iostream>
#include <cstdlib>
#include <cstddef>
using namespace std;

typedef int* IntArrayPtr;

void fill_array(int a[], int size);
//Precondition: size is the size of the array a.
//Postcondition: a[0] through a[size-1] have been
//filled with values read from the keyboard.

void sort(int a[], int size);
//Precondition: size is the size of the array a.
//The array elements a[0] through a[size-1] have values.
//Postcondition: The values of a[0] through a[size-1] have been rearranged
//so that a[0] <= a[1] <= ... <= a[size-1].

int main()
{
    cout << "This program sorts numbers from lowest to highest.\n";

    int array_size;
    cout << "How many numbers will be sorted? ";
    cin >> array_size;

    IntArrayPtr a;
    a = new int[array_size];

    fill_array(a, array_size);
    sort(a, array_size);
```

ordinary array parameters

Display 11.5 A Dynamic Array (part 2 of 2)

```
    cout << "In sorted order the numbers are:\n";
    for (int index = 0; index < array_size; index++)
        cout << a[index] << " ";
    cout << endl;

    delete [] a;

    return 0;
}


//Uses the library iostream:
void fill_array(int a[], int size)
{
    cout << "Enter " << size << " integers.\n";
    for (int index = 0; index < size; index++)
        cin >> a[index];
}


void sort(int a[], int size)
    <Any implementation of sort may be used. This may or may not require some
     additional function definitions. The implementation need not even know that
     sort will be called with a dynamic array. For example, you can use the
     implementation in Display 9.13 (with suitable adjustments to parameter
     names).>
```

The dynamic array a *is used like an ordinary array.*

You create a dynamic array with a call to *new* using a pointer, such as the pointer a in Display 11.5. After the call to *new*, you should not assign any other pointer value to this pointer variable, because that can confuse the system when the memory for the dynamic array is returned to the heap with a call to *delete*.

Dynamic arrays are created using *new* and a pointer variable. When your program is finished using a dynamic array, you should return the array memory to the heap with call to *delete*. Other than that, a dynamic array can be used just like any other array.

SELF-TEST EXERCISES

9 Write a type definition for pointer variables that will be used to point to
   dynamic arrays. The array elements are to be of type *char*. Call the type
   CharArray.

10 Suppose your program contains code to create a dynamic array as follows:

```
int *entry;
entry = new int[10];
```

   so that the pointer variable entry is pointing to this dynamic array. Write code
   to fill this array with 10 numbers typed in at the keyboard.

11 Suppose your program contains code to create a dynamic array as in Self-
   Test Exercise 10, and suppose the pointer variable entry has not had its
   (pointer) value changed. Write code to destroy this new dynamic array and
   return the memory it uses to the heap.

12 Given the following code, which is assumed to be embedded in a correct and
   complete program:

```
int array_size = 10;
int a[array_size];
int *p = a;
int i;
for (int i = 0; i < array_size; i++)
   a[i] = i;
```

   What is the output of the following code fragment?

```
for (int i = 0; i < array_size; i++)
   cout << p[i] << " ";
cout << endl;
```

Pointer Arithmetic *(Optional)*

There is a kind of arithmetic you can perform on pointers, but it is an arithmetic of
addresses, not an arithmetic of numbers. For example, suppose your program contains the following code:

```
typedef double* DoublePtr;
DoublePtr d;
d = new double[10];
```

After these statements, d contains the address of the indexed variable d[0]. The expression d + 1 evaluates to the address of d[1], d + 2 is the address of d[2], and so forth. Notice that although the value of d is an address and an address is a number, d + 1 does not simply add one to the number in d. If a variable of type *double* requires eight bytes (eight memory locations) and d contains the address 2001, then d + 1 evaluates to the memory address 2009. Of course, the type *double* can be replaced by any other type, and then pointer addition moves in units of variables for that type.

This pointer arithmetic gives you an alternative way to manipulate arrays. For example, if array_size is the size of the dynamic array pointed to by d, then the following will output the contents of the dynamic array:

```
for (int i = 0; i < array_size; i++)
    cout << *(d + i)<< " ";
```

The above is equivalent to the following:

```
for (int i = 0; i < array_size; i++)
    cout << d[i] << " ";
```

You may not perform multiplication or division of pointers. All you can do is add an integer to a pointer, subtract an integer from a pointer, or subtract two pointers of the same type. When you subtract two pointers the result is the number of indexed variables between the two addresses. Remember, for subtraction of two pointer values, *these values must point into the same array!* It makes little sense to subtract a pointer that points into one array from another pointer that points into a different array. You can use the increment and decrement operators ++ and --. For example, d++ will advance the value of d so that it contains the address of the next indexed variable, and d-- will change d so it contains the address of the previous indexed variable.

11.3 Classes and Dynamic Arrays

With all appliances and means to boot.

WILLIAM SHAKESPEARE, KING HENRY IV, PART III

A dynamic array can have a base type which is a class. A class can have a member variable which is a dynamic array. You can combine the techniques you learned about classes and the techniques you learned about dynamic arrays in just about any combination. There are a few more things to worry about when using classes and dynamic arrays, but the basic techniques are the ones that you have already used. Let's start with an example.

■)) *PROGRAMMING EXAMPLE*
A String Variable Class

In Chapter 10 we showed you how to define array variables to hold Standard strings. In the previous section you learned how to define dynamic arrays so that the size of the array can be determined when your program is run. In this example, we will define a class called `StringVar`, whose objects are string variables. An object of the class `StringVar` will be implemented using a dynamic array whose size is determined when your program is run. So objects of type `StringVar` will have all the advantages of dynamic arrays, but they will also have some additional features. We will define `StringVar`'s member functions so that if you try to assign a string that is too long to an object of type `StringVar`, you will get an error message. The version we define here provides only a small collection of operations for manipulating string objects. In Programming Project 1 you are asked to enhance the class definition by adding more member functions and over-loaded operators.

Since you could use the standard *class* string, as discussed in Chapter 10, you do not really need the *class* StringVar, but it will be a good exercise to design and code it.

The interface for the type `StringVar` is given in Display 11.6. One constructor *constructors* for the class `StringVar` takes a single argument of type *int*. This argument determines the maximum allowable length for a string value stored in the object. A default constructor creates an object with a maximum allowable length of 100. Another constructor takes an array argument that contains one of the standard C++ strings of the kind discussed in Chapter 10. Note that this means the argument to this constructor can be a quoted string. This constructor initializes the object so that it can hold any string whose length is less than or equal to the length of its argument, and it initializes the object's string value to the value of its argument. For the moment, ignore the constructor which is labeled *Copy constructor.* Also ignore the member function named ~`StringVar`. Although it may look like a constructor, ~`StringVar` is not a constructor. We will discuss these two new kinds of member functions in later subsections. The meaning of the remaining member functions for the class `StringVar` are straightforward.

A simple demonstration program is given in Display 11.7. Two objects, *size of string value* your_name and our_name, are declared within the definition of the function conversation. The object your_name can contain any string that is max_name_size or fewer characters long. The object our_name is initialized to the string value "Borg" and can have its value changed to any other string of length 4 or less.

Display 11.6 Interface File for the StringVar Class (part 1 of 2)

```
//This is the HEADER FILE strvar.h. This is the INTERFACE for the class StringVar whose values
//are strings. An object is declared as follows. Note that you use (max_size), not [max_size]
//       StringVar the_object(max_size);
//where max_size is the longest string length allowed. The argument max_size can be a variable.
#ifndef STRVAR_H
#define STRVAR_H
#include <iostream>
using namespace std;
namespace savitchstrvar
{

    class StringVar
    {
    public:
        StringVar(int size);
        //Initializes the object so it can accept string values up to size in length.
        //Sets the value of the object equal to the empty string.

        StringVar();
        //Initializes the object so it can accept string values of length 100 or less.
        //Sets the value of the object equal to the empty string.

        StringVar(const char a[]);
        //Precondition: The array a contains characters terminated with '\0'.
        //Initializes the object so its value is the string stored in a and
        //so that it can later be set to string values up to strlen(a) in length

        StringVar(const StringVar& string_object);
        //Copy constructor.

        ~StringVar();
        //Returns all the dynamic memory used by the object to the heap.

        int length() const;
        //Returns the length of the current string value.

        void input_line(istream& ins);
        //Precondition: If ins is a file input stream, then ins has been connected to a file.
        //Action: The next text in the input stream ins, up to '\n', is copied to the calling
        //object. If there is not sufficient room, then only as much as will fit is copied.
```

Display 11.6 Interface File for the StringVar Class *(part 2 of 2)*

```
        friend ostream& operator <<(ostream& outs, const StringVar& the_string);
        //Overloads the << operator so it can be used to output values of type StringVar
        //Precondition: If outs is a file output stream, then outs
        //has already been connected to a file.
    private:
        char *value; //pointer to the dynamic array that holds the string value.
        int max_length; //declared max length of any string value.
    };
}//savitchstrvar


#endif //STRVAR_H
```

As we indicated at the beginning of this subsection, the class StringVar is implemented using a dynamic array. The implementation is shown in Display 11.8. When an object of type StringVar is declared, a constructor is called to initialize the object. The constructor uses the *new* operator to create a new dynamic array of characters for the member variable value. The string value is stored in the array value as an ordinary string value, with '\0' used to mark the end of the string. Notice that the size of this array is not determined until the array is declared, at which point the constructor is called and the argument to the constructor determines the size of the dynamic array. As indicated in Display 11.7, this argument can be a variable of type *int*. Look at the declaration of the object your_name in the definition of the function conversation. The argument to the constructor is the call-by-value parameter max_name_size. Recall that a call-by-value parameter is a local variable so max_name_size is a variable. Any *int* variable may be used as the argument to the constructor in this way.

implementation

In this example, we have chosen to indicate the end of a string differently from what we did in the class String defined in Chapter 10 (Display 10.9 and Display 10.11). In Chapter 10 we used a separate member variable of type *int* to record the array index where the string of characters ends. In this example, we are using the symbol '\0' in the array to indicate the end of the string of characters. Each approach has its advantages and disadvantages.

The implementation of the member functions length, input_line, and the overloaded output operator << are all straightforward. In the next few subsections we discuss the function ~StringVar and the constructor labeled *Copy constructor.*

Display 11.7 Program Using the StringVar Class

```cpp
//Program to demonstrate use of the class StringVar.
#include <iostream>
#include "strvar.h"
using namespace std;
using namespace savitchstrvar;

void conversation(int max_name_size);
//Carries on a conversation with the user.

int main( )
{
    conversation(30);
    cout << "End of demonstration.\n";
    return 0;
}

// This is only a demonstration function:
void conversation(int max_name_size)
{
    StringVar your_name(max_name_size), our_name("Borg");

    cout << "What is your name?\n";
    your_name.input_line(cin);
    cout << "We are " << our_name << endl;
    cout << "We will meet again " << your_name << endl;
}
```

Memory is returned to the heap when the function call ends.

Determines the size of the dynamic array.

Sample Dialogue

```
What is your name?
Kathryn Janeway
We are Borg
We will meet again Kathryn Janeway
End of demonstration
```

Display 11.8 Implementation of StringVar *(part 1 of 2)*

```
//This is the IMPLEMENTATION FILE: strvar.cxx
//(Your system may require some suffix other than .cxx.)
//This is the IMPLEMENTATION of the class StringVar.
//The interface for the class StringVar is in the header file strvar.h.
#include <iostream>
#include <cstdlib>
#include <cstddef>
#include <cstring>
#include "strvar.h"

namespace savitchstrvar
{
    //Uses cstddef and cstdlib:
    StringVar::StringVar(int size)
    {
        max_length = size;
        value = new char[max_length + 1];//+1 is for '\0'.

        value[0] = '\0';
    }

    //Uses cstddef and cstdlib:
    StringVar::StringVar( )
    {
        max_length = 100;
        value = new char[max_length + 1];//+1 is for '\0'.

        value[0] = '\0';
    }

    //Uses cstring, cstddef, and cstdlib:
    StringVar::StringVar(const char a[])
    {
        max_length = strlen(a);
        value = new char[max_length + 1];//+1 is for '\0'.

        strcpy(value, a);
    }
```

Display 11.8 Implementation of StringVar *(part 2 of 2)*

```
//Uses cstring, cstddef, and cstdlib:
StringVar::StringVar(const StringVar& string_object)
{
    max_length = string_object.length( );
    value = new char[max_length + 1];//+1 is for '\0'.

    strcpy(value, string_object.value);
}

StringVar::~StringVar( )
{
    delete [] value;
}

//Uses cstring:
int StringVar::length( ) const
{
    return strlen(value);
}

//Uses iostream:
void StringVar::input_line(istream& ins)
{
    ins.getline(value, max_length + 1);
}

//Uses iostream:
ostream& operator <<(ostream& outs, const StringVar& the_string)
{
    outs << the_string.value;
    return outs;
}

}//savitchstrvar
```

Destructors

There is one problem with dynamic variables. They do not go away unless your program makes a suitable call to *delete*. Even if the dynamic variable was created using a local pointer variable and the local pointer variable goes away at the end of a function call, the dynamic variable will remain unless there is a call to *delete*. If you do not eliminate dynamic variables with calls to *delete*, the dynamic variables will continue to occupy memory space which may cause your program to abort by using up all the memory in the heap. Moreover, if the dynamic variable is embedded in the implementation of a class, the programmer who uses the class does not know about the dynamic variable and cannot be expected to perform the call to *delete*. In fact, since the data members are normally private members, the programmer normally *cannot* access the needed pointer variables and so *cannot* call *delete* with these pointer variables. To handle this problem, C++ has a special kind of member function called a *destructor*.

A **destructor** is a member function that is called automatically when an object of the class passes out of scope. This means that if your program contains a local variable that is an object with a destructor, then when the function call ends, the destructor will be called automatically. If the destructor is defined correctly, the destructor will call *delete* to eliminate all the dynamic variables created by the object. This may be done with a single call to *delete* or it may require several calls to *delete*. You may also want your destructor to perform some other clean-up details as well, but returning memory to the heap is the main job of the destructor. *destructor calls*

The member function ~StringVar is the destructor for the class StringVar shown in Display 11.6. Like a constructor, a destructor always has the same name as the class it is a member of, but the destructor has the tilde symbol ~ at the beginning of its name (so you can tell that it is a destructor and not a constructor). Like a constructor, a destructor has no type for the value returned, not even the type *void*. A *destructor name*

Destructor

A **destructor** is a member function of a class that is called automatically when an object of the class goes out of scope. Among other things, this means that if an object of the class type is a local variable for a function, then the destructor is automatically called as the last action before the function call ends. Destructors are used to eliminate any dynamic variables that have been created by the object so that the memory occupied by these dynamic variables is returned to the heap. Destructors may perform other clean-up tasks as well. The name of a destructor must consist of the tilde symbol ~ followed by the name of the class.

destructor has no parameters. Thus, a class can have only one destructor; you cannot overload the destructor for a class. Otherwise, a destructor is defined just like any other member function.

~StringVar

Notice the definition of the destructor ~StringVar given in Display 11.8. ~StringVar calls *delete* to eliminate the dynamic array pointed to by the member pointer variable value. Look again at the function conversation in the sample program shown in Display 11.7. The local variables your_name and our_name both create dynamic arrays. If this class did not have a destructor, then after the call to conversation has ended, these dynamic arrays would still be occupying memory, even though they are useless to the program. This would not be a problem here because the sample programs ends soon after the call to conversation is completed; but if you wrote a program that made repeated calls to functions like conversation, and if the class StringVar did not have a suitable destructor, then the function calls could consume all the memory in the heap and your program would then end abnormally.

● PITFALL   Pointers as Call-by-Value Parameters

When a call-by-value parameter is of a pointer type, its behavior can be subtle and troublesome. Consider the function call shown in Display 11.9. The parameter temp in the function sneaky is a call-by-value parameter, and hence it is a local variable. When the function is called, the value of temp is set to the value of the argument p and the function body is executed. Since temp is a local variable, no changes to temp should go outside of the function sneaky. In particular, the value of the pointer variable p should not be changed. Yet the sample dialogue makes it look like the value of the pointer variable p has changed. Before the call to the function sneaky, the value of *p was 77 and after the call to sneaky the value of *p is 99. What has happened?

The situation is diagrammed in Display 11.10. Although the sample dialogue may make it look like p was changed, the value of p was not changed by the function call to sneaky. Pointer p has two things associated with it: p's pointer value and the value stored where p points. Now the value of p is a pointer (that is, a memory address). After the call to sneaky, the variable p contains the same pointer value (that is, the same memory address). The call to sneaky has changed the value of the variable pointed to by p, but it has not changed the value of p itself.

If the parameter type is a class or structure type that has member variables of a pointer type, the same kind of surprising changes can occur with call-by-value arguments of the class type. However, for class types, you can avoid (and control) these surprise changes by defining a *copy constructor,* as described in the next subsection.

Display 11.9 A Call-by-Value Pointer Parameter

```
//Program to demonstrate the way call-by-value parameters
//behave with pointer arguments.
#include <iostream>
using namespace std;

typedef int* IntPointer;

void sneaky(IntPointer temp);

int main( )
{
    IntPointer p;

    p = new int;
    *p = 77;
    cout << "Before call to function *p == "
         << *p << endl;

    sneaky(p);

    cout << "After call to function *p == "
         << *p << endl;

    return 0;
}

void sneaky(IntPointer temp)
{
    *temp = 99;
    cout << "Inside function call *temp == "
         << *temp << endl;
}
```

Sample Dialogue

```
Before call to function *p == 77
Inside function call *temp == 99
After call to function *p == 99
```

Display 11.10 The Function Call sneaky(p);

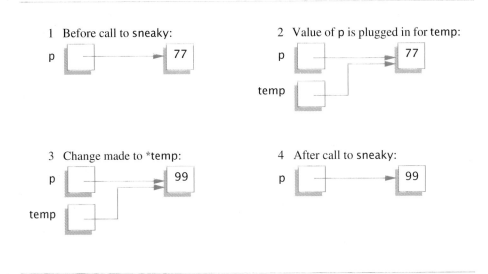

1   Before call to sneaky:

p [   ]———▶ [77]

2   Value of p is plugged in for temp:

p [   ]———▶ [77]

temp [   ]

3   Change made to *temp:

p [   ]———▶ [99]

temp [   ]

4   After call to sneaky:

p [   ]———▶ [99]

Copy Constructors

A **copy constructor** is a constructor that has one parameter that is of the same type as the class. The one parameter must be a call-by-reference parameter, and normally the parameter is preceded by the *const* parameter modifier, so it is a constant parameter. In all other respects a copy constructor is defined in the same way as any other constructor and it can be used just like other constructors. For example, a program that uses the class StringVar defined in Display 11.6 might contain the following:

called when an object is declared

```
StringVar line(20), motto("Constructors can help.");
cout << "Enter a string of length 20 or less:\n";
line.input_line(cin);
StringVar temp(line);//Initialized by the copy constructor.
```

The constructor used to initialize each of the three objects of type StringVar is determined by the type of the argument given in parentheses after the object's name. The object line is initialized with the constructor that has a parameter of type *int*; the object motto is initialized by the constructor that has a parameter of type *const char* a[]. Similarly, the object temp is initialized by the constructor that has one argument of type *const* StringVar&. When used in this way a copy constructor is being used just like any other constructor.

A copy constructor should be defined so that the object being initialized becomes a complete, independent copy of its argument. So, in the declaration

```
StringVar temp(line);
```

The member variable temp.value is not simply set to the same value as line.value; that would produce two pointers pointing to the same dynamic array. The definition of the copy constructor is shown in Display 11.8. Note that in the definition of the copy constructor, a new dynamic array is created and the contents of one dynamic array are copied to the other dynamic array. Thus, in the above declaration, temp is initialized so that its string value is equal to the string value of line, but temp has a separate dynamic array. Thus, any change that is made to temp will have no effect on line.

As you have seen, a copy constructor can be used just like any other constructor. A copy constructor is also called automatically in certain other situations. Roughly speaking, whenever C++ needs to make a copy of an object, it automatically calls the copy constructor. In particular, the copy constructor is called automatically in three circumstances: 1) when a class object is being defined and is initialized by another object of the same type, 2) when a function returns a value of the class type, and 3) whenever an argument of the class type is "plugged in" for a call-by-value parameter. In this case, the copy constructor defines what is meant by "plugging in."

call-by-value parameters

To see why you need a copy constructor, let's see what would happen if we did not define a copy constructor for the class StringVar. *Suppose we did not include the copy constructor in the definition of the class* StringVar and suppose we used a call-by-value parameter in a function definition, for example:

why a copy constructor is needed

```
void show_string(StringVar the_string)
{
    cout << "The string is: "
         << the_string << endl;
}
```

Consider the following code, which includes a function call:

```
StringVar greeting("Hello");
show_string(greeting);
cout << "After call: " << greeting << endl;
```

Assuming there is no copy constructor, things proceed as follows: When the function call is executed, the value of greeting is copied to the local variable the_string, so `the_string.value` is set equal to `greeting.value`. But these are pointer variables, so during the function call `the_string.value` and `greeting.value` point to the same dynamic array, as follows:

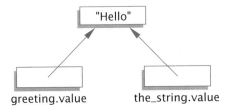

When the function call ends, the destructor for `StringVar` is called to return the memory used by `the_string` to the heap. The definition of the destructor contains the following statement:

delete [] value;

Since the destructor is called with the object `the_string`, this statement is equivalent to:

delete [] the_string.value;

which changes the picture to:

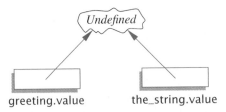

Since `greeting.value` and `the_string.value` point to the same dynamic array, deleting `the_string.value` is the same as deleting `greeting.value`. Thus, `greeting.value` is undefined when the program reaches the statement:

cout << "After call: " << greeting << endl;

so this `cout`-statement is undefined. The `cout`-statement may by chance give you the output you want, but sooner or later the fact that `greeting.value` is undefined will produce problems. One major problem occurs when the object `greeting` is a local variable in some function. In this case the destructor will be called with `greeting` when the function call ends. That destructor call will be equivalent to:

```
delete [] greeting.value;
```

But, as we just saw, the dynamic array pointed to by `greeting.value` has already been deleted once, and now the system is trying to delete it a second time. Calling *delete* twice to delete the same dynamic array (or other variable created with *new*) can produce a serious system error that can cause your program to crash.

That was what would happen if there were no copy constructor. Fortunately, we included a copy constructor in our definition of the class `StringVar`, so the copy constructor is called automatically when the following function call is executed:

```
StringVar greeting("Hello");
show_string(greeting);
```

The copy constructor defines what it means to "plug in" the argument `greeting` for the call-by-value parameter `the_string` so that now the picture is as follows:

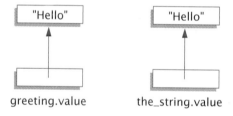

greeting.value   the_string.value

Thus, any change that is made to `the_string.value` has no effect on the argument `greeting`, and there are no problems with the destructor. If the destructor is called for `the_string` and then called for `greeting`, each call to the destructor deletes a different dynamic array.

When a function returns a value of a class type, the copy constructor is called automatically to copy the value specified by the return statement. If there is no copy constructor, then problems similar to what we described for value parameters will occur.

returned value

If a class definition involves pointers and dynamically allocated memory using the *new* operator, then you need to include a copy constructor. Classes that do not involve pointers or dynamically allocated memory do not need a copy constructor.

when you need a copy constructor

assignment statements
Contrary to what you might expect, the copy constructor is *not* called when you set one object equal to another using the assignment operator.[3] However, if you do not like what the default assignment operator does, you can redefine the assignment operator in the way described in the subsection that follows the self-test exercises.

Copy Constructor

A **copy constructor** is a constructor that has one call-by-reference parameter that is of the same type as the class. The one parameter must be a call-by-reference parameter; and normally the parameter is also a constant parameter, i.e., preceded by the *const* parameter modifier. The copy constructor for a class is called automatically whenever a function returns a value of the class type. The copy constructor is also called automatically whenever an argument is "plugged in" for a call-by-value parameter of the class type. A copy constructor can also be used in the same ways as other constructors.

Any class that uses pointers and the *new* operator should have a copy constructor.

The BIG Three

The **copy constructor,** the **= operator,** and the **destructor** are called the **big three** because experts say if you need any of them you need all three. If any of these is missing, the compiler will create it, but it may not behave as you want. So it pays to define them yourself. The copy constructor and overloaded = operator that the compiler generates for you will work fine if all member variables are of predefined types such as *int* and *double*, but it may misbehave on classes that have class member variables. For any class that uses pointers and the new operator, it is safest to define your own copy constructor, overloaded =, and a destructor.

Caveat: Good design says you need all three or none. Clearly, you can omit any one of these that you can guarantee you are not going to use.

---

[3]C++ makes a careful distinction between initialization (the three cases where the copy constructor is called) and assignment. Initialization uses the copy constructor to create a new object; the assignment operator takes an existing object and modifies it so that it is an identical copy (in all but location) with the right-hand side of the assignment.

SELF-TEST EXERCISES

13 If a class is named MyClass and it has a constructor, what is the constructor named? If MyClass has a destructor what is the destructor named?

14 Suppose you change the definition of the destructor in Display 11.8 to the following. How would the sample dialogue in Display 11.7 change?

```
StringVar::~StringVar( )
{
    cout << endl
        << "Good-bye cruel world! The short life of\n"
        << "this dynamic array is about to end.\n";
    delete [] value;
}
```

15 The following is the first line of the copy constructor definition for the class StringVar. The identifier StringVar occurs three times and it means something slightly different each time. What does it mean in each of the three cases?

```
StringVar::StringVar(const StringVar& string_object)
```

16 Answer these questions about destructors.

a. What is a destructor and what must the name of a destructor be?

b. When is a destructor called?

c. What does a destructor actually do?

d. What *should* a destructor do?

Overloading the Assignment Operator

Suppose string1 and string2 are declared as follows:

```
StringVar string1(10), string2(20);
```

The class StringVar was defined in Display 11.6 and Display 11.8. If string2 has somehow been given a value, then the following assignment statement is defined, but its meaning may not be what you would like it to be:

```
string1 = string2;
```

As usual, this predefined version of the assignment statement copies the value of each of the member variables of `string2` to the corresponding member variables of `string1` so the value of `string1.max_length` is changed to be the same as `string2.max_length` and the value of `string1.value` is changed to be the same as `string2.value`. But this can cause problems with `string1` and probably even cause problems for `string2`.

The member variable `string1.value` contains a pointer, and the assignment statement sets this pointer equal to the same value as `string2.value`. Thus, both `string1.value` and `string2.value` point to the same place in memory. Thus, if you change the string value in `string1`, you will also change the string value in `string2`. If you change the string value in `string2`, that will change the string value in `string1`.

In short, the predefined assignment statement does not do what we would like an assignment statement to do with objects of type `StringVar`. Using the predefined version of the assignment operator with the class `StringVar` can only cause problems. The way to fix this is to overload the assignment operator = so that it does what we want it to do with objects of the class `StringVar`.

= must be a member

The assignment operator cannot be overloaded in the way we have overloaded other operators, such as << and +. When you overload the assignment operator it must be a member of the class; it cannot be a friend of the class. To add an overloaded version of the assignment operator to the class `StringVar`, the definition of `StringVar` should be changed to the following:

```
class StringVar
{
public:
    void operator =(const StringVar& right_side);
    //Overloads the assignment operator = to copy a string
    //from one object to another.
    <The rest of the definition of the class can be the same as in
    Display 11.6.>
```

The assignment operator is then used just as you always use the assignment operator. For example, consider the following:

```
string1 = string2;
```

calling object for =

In the above call, `string1` is the calling object and `string2` is the argument to the member operator =.

The definition of the assignment operator can be as follows:

```
//The following is acceptable, but we will give a better
//definition:
void StringVar::operator =(const StringVar& right_side)
{
    int new_length = strlen(right_side.value);
    if ((new_length) > max_length)
        new_length = max_length;

    for (int i = 0; i < new_length; i++)
        value[i] = right_side.value[i];
    value[new_length] = '\0';
}
```

Notice that the length of the string in the object on the right side of the assignment operator is checked. If it is too long to fit in the object on the left side of the assignment operator (which is the calling object), then only as many characters as will fit are copied to the object receiving the string. But, suppose you do not want to lose any characters in the copying process. To fit in all the characters, you can create a new larger dynamic array for the object on the left-hand side of the assignment operator. You might try to redefine the assignment operator as follows:

```
//This version has a bug:
void StringVar::operator =(const StringVar& right_side)
{
    delete [] value;
    int new_length = strlen(right_side.value);
    max_length = new_length;

    value = new char[max_length + 1];

    for (int i = 0; i < new_length; i++)
        value[i] = right_side.value[i];
    value[new_length] = '\0';
}
```

This version has a problem when used in an assignment with the same object on both sides of the assignment operator, like the following:

```
my_string = my_string;
```

When this assignment is executed, the first statement executed is

```
delete [] value;
```

But, the calling object is my_string, so this means

> *delete* [] my_string.value;

So, the string value in my_string is deleted and the pointer my_string.value is undefined. The assignment operator has corrupted the object my_string and this run of the program is probably ruined.

One way to fix this bug is to first check to see if there is sufficient room in the dynamic array member of the object on the left-hand side of the assignment operator and to only delete the array if extra space is needed. Our final definition of the overloaded assignment operator does just such a check:

```
//This is our final version:
void StringVar::operator =(const StringVar& right_side)
{
    int new_length = strlen(right_side.value);
    if (new_length > max_length)
    {
        delete [] value;
        max_length = new_length;
        value = new char[max_length + 1];
    }

    for (int i = 0; i < new_length; i++)
        value[i] = right_side.value[i];
    value[new_length] = '\0';
}
```

For many classes, the obvious definition for overloading the assignment operator does not work correctly when the same object is on both sides of the assignment operator. You should always check this case, and be careful to write your definition of the overloaded assignment operator so that it also works in this case.

SELF-TEST EXERCISE

17 a. Explain carefully why no overloaded assignment operator is needed when the only data consist of built-in types.

  b. Same as part a for copy constructor.

  c. Same as part a for destructor.

CHAPTER SUMMARY

- A **pointer** is a memory address, so a pointer provides a way to indirectly name a variable by naming the address of the variable in the computer's memory.

- **Dynamic variables** are variables that are created (and destroyed) while a program is running.

- Memory for dynamic variables is in a special portion of the computer's memory called the **heap.** When a program is finished with a dynamic variable, the memory used by the dynamic variable can be returned to the heap for reuse; this is done with a *delete* statement.

- A **dynamic array** is an array whose size is determined when the program is running. A dynamic array is implemented as a dynamic variable of an array type.

- A **destructor** is a special kind of member function for a class. A destructor is called automatically when an object of the class passes out of scope. The main reason for destructors is to return memory to the heap so the memory can be reused.

- A **copy constructor** is a constructor that has a single argument that is of the same type as the class. If you define a copy constructor it will be called automatically whenever a function returns a value of the class type and whenever an argument is "plugged in" for a call-by-value parameter of the class type. Any class that uses pointers and the operator *new* should have a copy constructor.

Answers to Self-Test Exercises

1   A pointer is the memory address of a variable. A variable may occupy more than one address because pointers have a type, which specifies the type of object to which they can point. This controls what type object(s) a pointer may address.

2   To the unwary, or to the neophyte, this looks like two objects of type pointer to *int*, i.e., *int**. Unfortunately, the * binds to the *identifier*, not to the type (i.e., not to the *int*). The result is that this declaration declares int_ptr1 to be an *int* pointer, while int_ptr2 is an *int*.

3

```
int *p;    // The answer expected is "This declares a pointer
           //to int." The language lawyers call * as used
           //here a "pointer declarator."
*p = 17;   //Here, * is the dereference operator. This assigns
           //17 to the memory location WHERE p POINTS. (We
           //have not specified a memory location for p to point
           //to, but this should be specified in practice.)
void func(int *p) // Declares p to be a pointer value
                  // parameter. Language lawyers call this
                  // use of * a "pointer declarator."
```

4
```
10 20
20 20
30 30
```

If you replace *p1 = 30;

with *p2 = 30;, the output would be the same.

5
```
10 20
20 20
30 20
```

6

```
delete p;
```

7

```
typedef int* NumberPtr;
NumberPtr my_point;
```

8 The *new* operator takes a type for its argument. *new* allocates space on the heap (or free store) of an appropriate size for a variable of the type of the argument. It returns a pointer to that memory, if there was enough space.

9

```
typedef char* CharArray;
```

10

```
cout << "Enter 10 integers:\n";
for (int i = 0; i < 10; i++)
    cin >> entry[i];
```

11

```
delete [] entry;
```

12   0 1 2 3 4 5 6 7 8 9

13   The *constructor* is named MyClass, the same name as the name of the class.
The *destructor* is named ~MyClass.

14   The dialogue would change to the following:

```
What is your name?
Cathryn Janeway
We are Borg
We will meet again Cathryn Janeway
Good-bye cruel world! The short life of
this dynamic array is about to end.

Good-bye cruel world! The short life of
this dynamic array is about to end.
End of demonstration
```

15   The StringVar before the :: is the name of the class. The StringVar right
after the :: is the name of the member function. (Remember, a constructor is
a member function that has the same name as the class.) The StringVar
inside the parentheses is the type for the parameter string_object.

16 a. A destructor is a member function of a class. A destructor's name always begins with a tilde, ~, followed by the class name. It isn't a destructor unless it is named in this manner.

b. A destructor is called when a class object goes out of scope.

c. A destructor actually does whatever the class author programs it to do!

d. A destructor is *supposed* to delete dynamic variables that have been allocated by constructors for the class. Destructors may do other cleanup tasks.

17 In the case of the assignment operator = and the copy constructor, if there are only built-in types for data, the copy mechanism is exactly what you want, so the default works fine. In the case of the destructor, no dynamic memory allocation is done (no pointers) so the default do-nothing action is again what you want.

Programming Projects

1 Enhance the definition of the class StringVar given in Display 11.6 and Display 11.8 by adding all of the following: member functions copy_piece, one_char, and set_char, which return a specified substring, return a single character, and change a single character, respectively; an overloaded version of the == operator (note that only the string values have to be equal, the values of max_length need not be the same.); an overloaded version of + that performs concatenation of strings of type StringVar; an overloaded version of the extraction operator >> that reads one word (as opposed to input_line, which reads a whole line). If you did the section on overloading the assignment operator, then add it as well. Also write a suitable test program and thoroughly test your class definition.

2 Do Programming Project 9 in Chapter 9 using a dynamic array. In this version of the class the constructor should have a single argument of type *int* that specifies the maximum number of entries in the list.

3 Do Programming Project 8 in Chapter 9 using dynamic arrays. The program will ask the user the number of checks in each category and use this information to determine the sizes of the dynamic arrays.

4 In Chapter 8, Programming Project 8, you were asked to write an *int* class that has a single *int* data member. Rewrite that program using a private *int** data member. This class is to behave exactly like the built-in *int* type. Hints: You need all of the BIG THREE (copy constructor, operator =, and destructor). The rest of the hints in that problem should be followed.

CHAPTER 12

Recursion

12 Recursion

After a lecture on cosmology and the structure of the solar system, William James
was accosted by a little old lady.

"Your theory that the sun is the center of the solar system, and the earth is a ball
which rotates around it has a very convincing ring to it, Mr. James, but it's
wrong. I've got a better theory," said the little old lady.

"And what is that, madam?" inquired James politely.

"That we live on a crust of earth which is on the back of a giant turtle."

Not wishing to demolish this absurd little theory by bringing to bear the masses of
scientific evidence he had at his command, James decided to gently dissuade his
opponent by making her see some of the inadequacies of her position.

"If your theory is correct, madam," he asked, "what does this turtle stand on?"

"You're a very clever man, Mr. James, and that's a very good question" replied the
little old lady, "but I have an answer to it. And it is this: the first turtle stands on
the back of a second, far larger, turtle, who stands directly under him."

"But what does this second turtle stand on?" persisted James patiently.

To this the little old lady crowed triumphantly. "It's no use, Mr. James — it's turtles
all the way down."

J. R. ROSS, CONSTRAINTS ON VARIABLES IN SYNTAX

Introduction

You have encountered a few cases of circular definitions that worked out satisfactorily. The most prominent examples are the definitions of certain C++ statements. For example, the definition of a *while*-statement says that it can contain other (smaller) statements. Since one of the possibilities for these smaller statements is another *while*-statement, there is a kind of circularity in that definition. The definition of the *while*-statement, if written out in complete detail, will contain a reference to *while*-statements. In mathematics this kind of circular definition is called a **recursive definition.** In C++ a function may be defined in terms of itself in the same way. To put it more precisely, a function definition may contain a call to itself. In such cases the function is said to be **recursive.** In this chapter we will discuss recursion in C++, and more generally we will discuss recursion as a programming and problem-solving technique.

12.1   Recursive Functions for Tasks

> *I remembered too that night which is at the middle of the Thousand and One Nights when Scheherazade (through a magical oversight of the copyist) begins to relate word for word the story of the Thousand and One Nights, establishing the risk of coming once again to the night when she must repeat it, and thus to infinity.*

JORGE LUIS BORGES, THE GARDEN OF FORKING PATHS

When you are writing a function to solve a task, one basic design technique is to break the task into subtasks. Sometimes it turns out that at least one of the subtasks is a smaller example of the same task. For example, if the task is to search an array for a particular value, you might divide this into the subtask of searching the first half of the array and the subtask of searching the second half of the array. The subtasks of searching the halves of the array are "smaller" versions of the original task. Whenever one subtask is a smaller version of the original task to be accomplished you can solve the original task using a recursive function. It takes a little training to easily decompose problems this way, but once you learn the technique, it can be one of the quickest ways to design an algorithm, and ultimately a C++ function. We begin with a simple case study to illustrate this technique.

Recursion

In C++ a function definition may contain a call to the function being defined. In such cases the function is said to be **recursive.**

Case Study   Vertical Numbers

In this case study we design a recursive *void*-function that writes numbers to the screen with the digits written vertically, so that, for example, 1984 would be written as:

```
1
9
8
4
```

PROBLEM DEFINITION

The prototype and header comment for our function is

```
void write_vertical(int n);
//Precondition: n >= 0.
//Postcondition: The number n is written to the screen
//vertically with each digit on a separate line.
```

ALGORITHM DESIGN

One case is very simple. If n, the number to be written out, is only one digit long, then simply write out the number. As simple as it is, this case is still important, so let's keep track of this case.

Simple Case: If n < 10, then write the number n to the screen.

Now let's consider the more typical case in which the number to be written out consists of more than one digit. Suppose you want to write the number 1234 vertically so the result is:

```
1
2
3
4
```

One way to decompose this task into two subtasks is the following:

1 Output all the digits except the last digit like so:

```
1
2
3
```

2 Output the last digit, which in this example is 4.

Subtask 1 is a smaller version of the original task, so we can implement this subtask with a recursive call. Subtask 2 is just the simple case we listed above. Thus, an outline of our algorithm for the function write_vertical with parameter n is given by the following pseudocode:

```
if (n < 10)
{
    cout << n << endl;
}
else //n is two or more digits long:
{                         ⟋ recursive subtask
    write_vertical(the number n with the last digit removed);
    cout << the last digit of n << endl;
}
```

In order to convert this pseudocode into the code for a C++ function, all we need to do is translate the following two pieces of pseudocode into C++ expressions:

the number n with the last digit removed
         and
the last digit of n

But these expressions can easily be translated into C++ expressions using the integer division operators / and % as follows:

```
n/10 //the number n with the last digit removed
n%10 //the last digit of n
```

For example, 1234/10 evaluates to 123 and 1234%10 evaluates to 4.

Several factors influenced our selection of the two subtasks we used in this algorithm. One was that we could easily compute the argument for the recursive call to write_vertical (shown in color) that we used in the above pseudocode. The number n with the last digit removed is easily computed as n/10. As an alternative, you might have been tempted to divide the subtasks as follows:

1 Output the first digit of n.
2 Output the number n with first digit removed.

This is a perfectly valid decomposition of the task into subtasks, and it can be implemented recursively. However, it is difficult to calculate the result of removing the first digit from a number, while it is easy to calculate the result of removing the last digit from a number.

Another reason for choosing this decomposition is that one of the two subcases does not involve a recursive call. A successful definition of a recursive function always includes at least one case that does not involve a recursive call (as well as one or more cases that do involve at least one recursive call). This aspect of the recursive algorithm is discussed in the subsections that follow this case study.

Display 12.1 A Recursive Output Function *(part 1 of 2)*

```
//Program to demonstrate the recursive function write_vertical.
#include <iostream>
using namespace std;

void write_vertical(int n);
//Precondition: n >= 0.
//Postcondition: The number n is written to the screen vertically
//with each digit on a separate line.

int main( )
{
    cout << "write_vertical(3):" << endl;
    write_vertical(3);

    cout << "write_vertical(12):" << endl;
    write_vertical(12);

    cout << "write_vertical(123):" << endl;
    write_vertical(123);

    return 0;
}

//uses iostream:
void write_vertical(int n)
{
    if (n < 10)
    {
        cout << n << endl;
    }
    else //n is two or more digits long:
    {
        write_vertical(n/10);
        cout << (n%10) << endl;
    }
}
```

Display 12.1 A Recursive Output Function *(part 2 of 2)*

Sample Dialogue

```
write_vertical(3):
3
write_vertical(12):
1
2
write_vertical(123):
1
2
3
```

CODING

We can now put all the pieces together to produce the recursive function `write_vertical` shown in Display 12.1. In the next subsection we will explain more details of how recursion works in this example.

TRACING A RECURSIVE CALL

Let's see exactly what happens when the following function call is made:

```
write_vertical(123);
```

When this function call is executed the computer proceeds just as it would with any function call. The argument 123 is substituted for the parameter n and the body of the function is executed. After the substitution of 123 for n, the code to be executed is:

```
if (123 < 10)
{
    cout << 123 << endl;
}
else //n is two or more digits long:
{
    write_vertical(123/10);
    cout << (123%10) << endl;
}
```

Computation will stop here until the recursive call returns

Since 123 is not less than 10, the logical expression in the *if-else*-statement is *false,* so the *else* part is executed. However, the *else* part begins with the following function call:

```
write_vertical(n/10);
```

which (since n is equal to 123) is the call

```
write_vertical(123/10);
```

which is equivalent to:

```
write_vertical(12);
```

When execution reaches this recursive call, the current function computation is placed in suspended animation and this recursive call is executed. When this recursive call is finished, the execution of the suspended computation will return to this point and the suspended computation will continue from this point.

The recursive call

```
write_vertical(12);
```

is handled just like any other function call. The argument 12 is substituted for the parameter n and the body of the function is executed. After substituting 12 for n, there are two computations, one suspended and one active as follows:

```
if (123 < 10)
{
        cout
}
else //n
{
        writ
        cout
}
```

```
if (12 < 10)
{
        cout << 12 << endl;
}
else //n is two or more digits long:
{                                        Computation will
        write_vertical(12/10);  ←─── stop here until
        cout << (12%10) << endl;        the recursive call
}                                        returns.
```

Since 12 is not less than 10, the Boolean expression in the *if-else*-statement is *false* and so the *else* part is executed. However, as you already saw, the *else* part begins with a recursive call. The argument for the recursive call is n/10 which in this case is equivalent to 12/10. So this second computation of the function `write_vertical` is suspended and the following recursive call is executed

```
write_vertical(12/10);
```

which is equivalent to:

```
write_vertical(1);
```

At this point there are two suspended computations waiting to resume and the computer begins to execute this new recursive call, which is handled just like all the previous recursive calls. The argument 1 is substituted for the parameter n and the body of the function is executed. At this point, the computation looks like the following:

```
if (123 < 10)
{

}
els
{


}
```

```
if (12 < 10)
{

}
els
{


}
```

```
if (1 < 10)
{
    cout << 1 << endl;                     No recursive
}                                           call this time
else //n is two or more digits long:
{
    write_vertical(1/10);
    cout << (1%10) << endl;
}
```

When the body of the function is executed this time something different happens. Since 1 is less than 10, the Boolean expression in the *if-else*-statement is *true,* so the statement before the *else* is executed. That statement is simply a `cout`-statement that writes the argument 1 to the screen and so the call `write_vertical(1)` writes 1 to the screen and ends without any recursive call.

output the digit 1

When the call `write_vertical(1)` ends, the suspended computation that is waiting for it to end resumes where that suspended computation left off, as shown by the following:

```
if (123 < 10)
{
                if (12 < 10)
                {
}                   cout << 12 << endl;
els
{               }
                else //n is two or more digits long:
                {
}                   write_vertical(12/10);        ← Computation resumes
                    cout << (12%10) << endl;          here.
                }
```

output the digit 2   When this suspended computation resumes, it executes a cout-statement that
outputs the value 12%10, which is 2. That ends that computation, but there is yet
another suspended computation waiting to resume. When this last suspended
computation resumes, the situation is:

```
if (123 < 10)
{
    cout << 123 << endl;
}
else //n is two or more digits long:
{
    write_vertical(123/10);        ← Computation
    cout << (123%10) << endl;        resumes here.
}
```

output the digit 3   When this last suspended computation resumes it outputs the value 123%10, which is
3, and the execution of the original function call ends. And, sure enough, the digits 1,
2, and 3 have been written to the screen one per line, in that order.

A Closer Look at Recursion

The definition of the function `write_vertical` uses recursion. Yet we did nothing new or different in evaluating the function call `write_vertical(123)`. We treated it just like any of the function calls we saw in previous chapters. We simply substituted the argument 123 for the parameter n and then executed the code in the body of the function definition. When we reached the recursive call

```
write_vertical(123/10);
```

we simply repeated this process one more time.

The computer keeps track of recursive calls in the following way. When a function is called, the computer plugs in the arguments for the parameter(s) and begins to execute the code. If it should encounter a recursive call, then it temporarily stops its computation. This is because it must know the result of the recursive call before it can proceed. It saves all the information it needs to continue the computation later on, and proceeds to evaluate the recursive call. When the recursive call is completed, the computer returns to finish the outer computation.

how recursion works

The C++ language places no restrictions on how recursive calls are used in function definitions. However, in order for a recursive function definition to be useful, it must be designed so that any call of the function must ultimately terminate with some piece of code that does not depend on recursion. The function may call itself, and that recursive call may call the function again. The process may be repeated any number of times. However, the process will not terminate unless eventually one of the recursive calls does not depend on recursion in order to return a value. The general outline of a successful recursive function definition is as follows:

how recursion ends

- One or more cases in which the function accomplishes its task by using recursive call(s) to accomplish one or more smaller versions of the task.

- One or more cases in which the function accomplishes its task without the use of any recursive calls. These cases without any recursive calls are called **base cases** or **stopping cases.**

base case
stopping case

Often an *if-else*-statement determines which of the cases will be executed. A typical scenario is for the original function call to execute a case that includes a recursive call. That recursive call may in turn execute a case that requires another recursive call. For some number of times each recursive call produces another recursive call, but eventually one of the stopping cases should apply. *Every call of the function must eventually lead to a stopping case, or else the function call will never end because of an infinite chain of recursive calls.* (In practice, a call that includes an infinite chain of recursive calls will usually terminate abnormally rather than actually running forever.)

The most common way to ensure that a stopping case is eventually reached is to write the function so that some (positive) numeric quantity is decreased on each recursive call and to provide a stopping case for some "small" value. This is how we designed the function `write_vertical` in Display 12.1 When the function `write_vertical` is called, that call produces a recursive call with a smaller argument. This continues with each recursive call producing another recursive call until the argument is less than `10`. When the argument is less than `10`, the function call ends without producing any more recursive calls and the process works its way back to the original call and the process ends.

General Form of a Recursive Function Definition

The general outline of a successful recursive function definition is as follows:

- One or more cases that include one or more recursive calls to the function being defined. These recursive calls should solve "smaller" versions of the task performed by the function being defined.

- One or more cases that include no recursive calls. These cases without any recursive calls are called **base cases** or **stopping cases.**

⬢ PITFALL   Infinite Recursion

In the example of the function `write_vertical` discussed in the previous subsections, the series of recursive calls eventually reached a call of the function that did not involve recursion (that is, a stopping case was reached). If, on the other hand, every recursive call produces another recursive call, then a call to the function will, in theory, run forever. This is called **infinite recursion.** In practice, such a function will typically run until the computer runs out of resources and the program terminates abnormally. Phrased another way, a recursive definition should not be "recursive all the way down." Otherwise, like the lady's explanation of the universe given at the start of this chapter, a call to the function will never end, except perhaps in frustration.

Examples of infinite recursion are not hard to come by. The following is a syntactically correct C++ function definition, which might result from an attempt to define an alternative version of the function `write_vertical`:

```
void new_write_vertical(int n)
{
    new_write_vertical(n/10);
    cout << (n%10) << endl;
}
```

If you embed this definition in a program that calls this function, the compiler will translate the function definition to machine code and you can execute the machine code. Moreover, the definition even has a certain reasonableness to it. It says that to output the argument to new_write_vertical, first output all but the last digit and then output the last digit. However, when called, this function will produce an infinite sequence of recursive calls. If you call new_write_vertical(12), that execution will stop to execute the recursive call new_write_vertical (12/10), which is equivalent to new_write_vertical(1). The execution of that recursive call will, in turn, stop to execute the recursive call

```
new_write_vertical(1/10);
```

which is equivalent to

```
new_write_vertical(0);
```

That, in turn, will stop to execute the recursive call new_write_vertical(0/10); which is also equivalent to

```
new_write_vertical(0);
```

and that will produce another recursive call to again execute the same recursive function call new_write_vertical(0); and so on, forever. Since the definition of new_write_vertical has no stopping case, the process will proceed forever (or until the computer runs out of resources).

SELF-TEST EXERCISES

1 What is the output of the following program?

```
#include <iostream>
using namespace std;
void cheers(int n);

int main()
{
    cheers(3);
    return 0;
}
```

```
void cheers(int n)
{
    if (n == 1)
    {
        cout << "Hurray\n";
    }
    else
    {
        cout << "Hip ";
        cheers(n - 1);
    }
}
```

2   Write a recursive *void*-function that has one parameter which is a positive integer and that writes out that number of asterisks '*' to the screen all on one line.

3   Write a recursive *void*-function that has one parameter which is a positive integer. When called, the function writes its argument to the screen backward. That is, if the argument is 1234, it outputs the following to the screen:

    4321

4   Write a recursive *void* function that takes a single *int* argument n and writes the integers 1, 2, . . . , n.

5   Write a recursive *void* function that takes a single *int* argument n and writes integers n, n-1, . . . , 3, 2, 1. Hint: Notice that you can get from the code for Exercise 4 to that for Exercise 5 (or vice versa) by an exchange of as little as two lines.

Stacks for Recursion

stack

In order to keep track of recursion, and a number of other things, most computer systems make use of a structure called a *stack*. A **stack** is a very specialized kind of memory structure that is analogous to a stack of paper. In this analogy there is an inexhaustible supply of extra blank sheets of paper. In order to place some information in the stack, it is written on one of these sheets of paper and placed on top of the stack of papers. To place more information in the stack, a clean sheet of paper is taken, the information is written on it, and this new sheet of paper is placed on top of the stack. In this straightforward way more and more information may be placed on the stack.

Getting information out of the stack is also accomplished by a very simple procedure. The top sheet of paper can be read, and when it is no longer needed, it is thrown away. There is one complication: Only the top sheet of paper is accessible. In order to read, say, the third sheet from the top, the top two sheets must be thrown away. Since the last sheet that is put on the stack is the first sheet taken off the stack, a stack is often called a **last-in/first-out** memory structure.

last-in/first-out

Using a stack, the computer can easily keep track of recursion. Whenever a function is called, a new sheet of paper is taken. The function definition is copied onto this sheet of paper, and the arguments are plugged for the function parameters. Then the computer starts to execute the body of the function definition. When it encounters a recursive call, it stops the computation it is doing on that sheet in order to compute the value returned by the recursive call. But before computing the recursive call, it saves enough information so that, when it does finally determine the value returned by the recursive call, it can continue the stopped computation. This saved information is written on a sheet of paper and placed on the stack. A new sheet of paper is used for the recursive call. The computer writes a second copy of the function definition on this new sheet of paper, plugs in the arguments for the function parameters, and starts to execute the recursive call. When it gets to a recursive call within the recursively called copy, it repeats the process of saving information on the stack and using a new sheet of paper for the new recursive call. This process is illustrated in the subsection entitled "Tracing a Recursive Call." Even though we did not call it a stack at the time, the illustrations of computations placed one on top of the other illustrate the actions of the stack.

recursion

This process continues until some recursive call to the function completes its computation without producing any more recursive calls. When that happens, the computer turns its attention to the top sheet of paper on the stack. This sheet contains the partially completed computation that is waiting for the recursive computation that just ended. So, it is possible to proceed with that suspended computation. When that suspended computation ends, the computer discards that sheet of paper and the suspended computation that is below it on the stack becomes the computation on top of the stack. The computer turns its attention to the suspended computation that is now on the top of the stack, and so forth. The process continues until the computation on the bottom sheet is completed. Depending on how many recursive calls are made and how the function definition is written, the stack may grow and shrink in any fashion. Notice that the sheets in the stack can only be accessed in a last-in/first-out fashion, but that is exactly what is needed to keep track of recursive calls. Each suspended version is waiting for the completion of the version directly above it on the stack.

Needless to say, computers do not have stacks of paper of this kind. This is just an analogy. The computer uses portions of memory rather than pieces of paper. The contents of one of these portions of memory ("sheets of paper") is called an **activation frame.** These activation frames are handled in the last-in/first-out manner we just

activation frame

discussed. (These activation frames do not contain a complete copy of the function definition, but merely reference a single copy of the function definition. However, an activation frame contains enough information to allow the computer to act as if the activation frame contained a complete copy of the function definition.)

Stack

A **stack** is a *last-in/first-out* memory structure. The first item referenced or removed from a stack is always the last item entered into the stack. Stacks are used by computers to keep track of recursion (and for other purposes).

⬥ PITFALL   Stack Overflow

There is always some limit to the size of the stack. If there is a long chain in which a function makes a recursive call to itself, and that call results in another recursive call, and that call produces yet another recursive call, and so forth, then each recursive call in this chain will cause another activation frame to be placed on the stack. If this chain is too long, then the stack will attempt to grow beyond its limit. This is an error condition known as a **stack overflow.** If you receive an error message that says *stack overflow,* it is likely that some function call has produced an excessively long chain of recursive calls. One common cause of stack overflow is infinite recursion. If a function is recursing infinitely, then it will eventually try to make the stack exceed any stack size limit.

Recursion versus Iteration

iterative version

Recursion is not absolutely necessary. In fact, some programming languages do not allow it. Any task that can be accomplished using recursion can also be done in some other way without using recursion. For example, Display 12.2 contains a nonrecursive version of the function given in Display 12.1. The nonrecursive version of a function typically uses a loop (or loops) of some sort in place of recursion. For that reason, the nonrecursive version is usually referred to as an **iterative version.** If the definition of the function write_vertical given in Display 12.1 is replaced by the version given in Display 12.2, then the output will be the same. As is true in this case, a recursive version of a function can sometimes be much simpler than an iterative version.

efficiency

A recursively written function will usually run slower and use more storage than an equivalent iterative version. Although the iterative version of write_vertical given in Display 12.2 looks like it uses more storage and does more computing than the recursive version in Display 12.1, the two versions of write_vertical actually use comparable storage and do comparable amounts of computing. In fact, the recursive version may use more storage and run somewhat slower, because the computer must do a good deal of work manipulating the stack in order to keep track of the recursion. However, since the system does all this for you automatically, using recursion can sometimes make your job as a programmer easier, and can sometimes produce code that is easier to understand. As you will see in the examples in this chapter and in the Self-Test Exercises and Programming Projects, sometimes a recursive definition is simpler and clearer; other times an iterative definition is simpler and clearer.

Display 12.2 Iterative Version of the Function in Display 12.1

```
//Uses iostream:
void write_vertical(int n)
{
    int tens_in_n = 1;
    int left_end_piece = n;
    while (left_end_piece > 9)
    {
        left_end_piece = left_end_piece/10;
        tens_in_n = tens_in_n*10;
    }
    //tens_in_n is a power of ten that has the same number
    //of digits as n. For example, if n is 2345, then
    //tens_in_n is 1000.

    for (int power_of_10 = tens_in_n;
            power_of_10 > 0; power_of_10 = power_of_10/10)
    {
        cout << (n/power_of_10) << endl;
        n = n%power_of_10;
    }
}
```

SELF-TEST EXERCISES

6 If your program produces an error message that says *stack overflow,* what is a likely source of the error?

7   Write an iterative version of the function cheers defined in Self-Test Exercise 1.

8   Write an iterative version of the function defined in Self-Test Exercise 2.

9   Write an iterative version of the function defined in Self-Test Exercise 3.

10   Trace the recursive solution you made to Self-Test Exercise 4.

11   Trace the recursive solution you made to Self-Test Exercise 5.

12.2   Recursive Functions for Values

To iterate is human, to recurse divine.

ANONYMOUS

General Form for a Recursive Function That Returns a Value

The recursive functions you have seen thus far are all *void*-functions, but recursion is not limited to *void*-functions. A recursive function can return a value of any type. The technique for designing recursive functions that return a value is basically the same as what you learned for *void*-functions. An outline for a successful recursive function definition that returns a value is as follows:

- One or more cases in which the value returned is computed in terms of calls to the same function (i.e., using recursive calls). As was the case with *void*-functions, the arguments for the recursive calls should intuitively be "smaller."

- One or more cases in which the value returned is computed without the use of any recursive calls. These cases without any recursive calls are called **base cases** or **stopping cases** (just as they were with *void*-functions).

This technique is illustrated in the next programming example.

■)) PROGRAMMING EXAMPLE
Another Powers Function

In Chapter 3 we introduced the predefined function pow that computes powers. For example, pow(2.0, 3.0) returns $2.0^{3.0}$ so the following sets the variable x equal to 8.0:

double x = pow(2.0, 3.0);

Display 12.3 The Recursive Function power

```cpp
//Program to demonstrate the recursive function power.
#include <iostream>
#include <cstdlib>
using namespace std;

int power(int x, int n);
//Precondition: n >= 0.
//Returns x to the power n.

int main( )
{
    for (int n = 0; n < 4; n++)
        cout << "3 to the power " << n
                << " is " << power(3, n) << endl;

    return 0;
}

//uses iostream and cstdlib:
int power(int x, int n)
{
    if (n < 0)
    {
        cout << "Illegal argument to power.\n";
        exit(1);
    }

    if (n > 0)
        return ( power(x, n - 1)*x );
    else // n == 0
        return (1);
}
```

Sample Dialogue

```
3 to the power 0 is 1
3 to the power 1 is 3
3 to the power 2 is 9
3 to the power 3 is 27
```

The function pow takes two arguments of type *double* and returns a value of type *double*. Display 12.3 contains a recursive definition for a function that is similar but that works with the type *int*, rather than *double*. This new function is called power. For example, the following will set the value of y equal to 8, since 2^3 is 8:

    int y = power(2, 3);

Our main reason for defining the function power is to have a simple example of a recursive function, but there are situations in which the function power would be preferable to the function pow. The function pow returns values of type *double*, which are only approximate quantities. The function power returns values of type *int*, which are exact quantities. In some situations, you might need the additional accuracy provided by the function power.

The definition of the function power is based on the following formula:

x^n is equal to x^{n-1} * x

Translating this formula into C++ says that the value returned by power(x, n) should be the same as the value of the expression

    power(x, n - 1)*x

The definition of the function power given in Display 12.3 does return this value for power(x, n), provided n > 0.

The case where n is equal to 0 is the stopping case. If n is 0, then power(x, n) simply returns 1 (since x^0 is 1).

Let's see what happens when the function power is called with some sample values. First consider the simple expression:

    power(2, 0)

When the function is called, the value of x is set equal to 2, the value of n is set equal to 0 and the code in the body of the function definition is executed. Since the value of n is a legal value, the *if-else*-statement is executed. Since this value of n is not greater than 0, the *return*-statement after the *else* is used, so the function call returns 1. Thus, the following would set the value of y equal to 1.

    int y = power(2, 0);

Now let's look at an example that involves a recursive call. Consider the expression

    power(2, 1)

When the function is called, the value of x is set equal to 2, the value of n is set equal to 1, and the code in the body of the function definition is executed. Since this value of n is greater than 0, the following *return*-statement is used to determine the value returned:

```
return ( power(x, n - 1)*x );
```

which in this case is equivalent to

```
return ( power(2, 0)*2 );
```

At this point the computation of power(2, 1) is suspended, a copy of this suspended computation is placed on the stack, and the computer then starts a new function call to compute the value of power(2, 0). As you have already seen, the value of power(2, 0) is 1. After determining the value of power(2, 0), the computer replaces the expression power(2, 0) with its value of 1 and resumes the suspended computation. The resumed computation determines the final value for power(2, 1) from the above *return*-statement as follows:

```
power(2, 0)*2 is 1*2 which is 2
```

and so the final value returned for power(2, 1) is 2. So, the following would set the value of z equal to 2.

```
int z = power(2, 1);
```

Larger numbers for the second argument will produce longer chains of recursive calls. For example, consider the statement:

```
cout << power(2, 3);
```

The value of power(2, 3) is calculated as follows:

```
power(2, 3) is power(2, 2)*2
  power(2, 2) is power(2, 1)*2
    power(2, 1) is power(2, 0)*2
      power(2, 0) is 1 (stopping case)
```

When the computer reaches the stopping case power(2, 0), there are three suspended computations. After calculating the value returned for the stopping case, it resumes the most recently suspended computations to determine the value of power(2, 1). After that, the computer completes each of the other suspended computations, using each value computed as a value to plug into another suspended computation, until it reaches and completes the computation for the original call power(2, 3). The details of the entire computation are illustrated in Display 12.4.

Display 12.4 Evaluating the Recursive Function Call power(2,3)

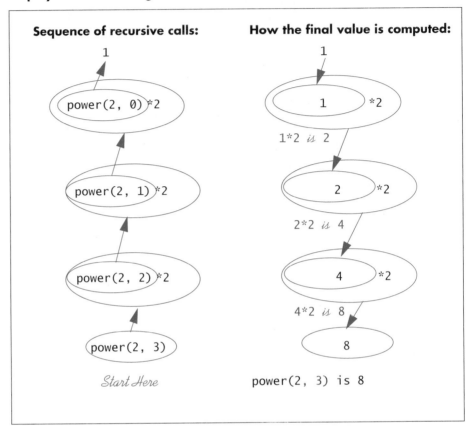

SELF-TEST EXERCISES

12   What is the output of the following program?

```cpp
#include <iostream>
using namespace std;
int mystery(int n);
//Precondition n >= 1.

int main( )
{
    cout << mystery(3);
    return 0;
}
```

```
int mystery(int n)
{
    if (n <= 1)
        return 1;
    else
        return ( mystery(n - 1) + n );
}
```

13 What is the output of the following program? What well-known mathematical function is rose?

```
#include <iostream>
using namespace std;
int rose(int n);
//Precondition: n >= 0.

int main( )
{
    cout << rose(4);
    return 0;
}
int rose(int n)
{
    if (n <= 0)
        return 1;
    else
        return ( rose(n - 1) * n );
}
```

14 Redefine the function power so that it also works for negative exponents. In order to do this you will also have to change the type of the value returned to *double*. The prototype and header comment for the redefined version of power is as follows:

```
double power(int x, int n);
//Precondition: If n < 0, then x is not 0.
//Returns x to the power n.
```

Hint: x^{-n} is equal to $1/(x^n)$.

12.3 Thinking Recursively

There are two kinds of people in the world, those who divide the world into two kinds of people and those who do not.

ANONYMOUS

Recursive Design Techniques

When defining and using recursive functions you do not want to be continually aware of the stack and the suspended computations. The power of recursion comes from the fact that you can ignore that detail and let the computer do the bookkeeping for you. Consider the example of the function power in Display 12.3. The way to think of the definition of power is as follows:

```
power(x, n) returns power(x, n - 1)*x
```

Since x^n is equal to x^{n-1}*x, this is the correct value to return, provided that the computation will always reach a stopping case and will correctly compute the stopping case. So, after checking that the recursive part of the definition is correct, all you need check is that the chain of recursive calls will always reach a stopping case and that the stopping case always returns the correct value.

When you design a recursive function you need not trace out the entire sequence of recursive calls for the instances of that function in your program. If the function returns a value, all that you need do is check that the following three properties are satisfied:

criteria for functions that return a value

1 There is no infinite recursion. (A recursive call may lead to another recursive call and that may lead to another and so forth, but every such chain of recursive calls eventually reaches a stopping case.)

2 Each stopping case returns the correct value for that case.

3 For the cases that involve recursion: *if* all recursive calls return the correct value, *then* the final value returned by the function is the correct value.

For example, consider the function power in Display 12.3:

1 **There is no infinite recursion:** The second argument to power(x, n) is decreased by one in each recursive call, so any chain of recursive calls must eventually reach the case power(x, 0), which is the stopping case. Thus, there is no infinite recursion.

2 **Each stopping case returns the correct value for that case:** The only stopping case is power(x, 0). A call of the form power(x, 0) always returns 1, and the correct value for x^0 is 1. So the stopping case returns the correct value.

3 For the cases that involve recursion: *if* all recursive calls return the correct value, *then* the final value returned by the function is the correct value: The only case that involves recursion is when n > 1. When n > 1, power(x, n) returns

$$power(x, n - 1)*x.$$

To see that this is the correct value to return, note that: *if* power(x, n – 1) returns the correct value, *then* power(x, n – 1) returns x^{n-1} and so power(x, n) returns

$$x^{n-1} * x, \text{ which is } x^n$$

and that is the correct value for power(x, n).

That's all you need to check in order to be sure that the definition of power is correct. (The above technique is known as *mathematical induction,* a concept that you may have heard about in a mathematics class. However, you do not need to be familiar with the term *mathematical induction* in order to use this technique.)

We gave you three criteria to use in checking the correctness of a recursive function that returns a value. Basically the same rules can be applied to a recursive *void*-function. If you show that your recursive *void*-function definition satisfies the following three criteria, then you will know that your *void*-function performs correctly:

1 There is no infinite recursion.

2 Each stopping case performs the correct action for that case.

3 For each of the cases that involve recursion: *if* all recursive calls perform their actions correctly, *then* the entire case performs correctly.

*criteria for
void-functions*

| *Case Study* | **Binary Search—
An Example of Recursive Thinking** |

In this case study we will develop a recursive function that searches an array to find out whether it contains a specified value. For example, the array may contain a list of the numbers for credit cards that are no longer valid. A store clerk needs to search the list to see if a customer's card is valid or invalid. In Chapter 9 (Display 9.11) we discussed a simple method for searching an array by simply checking every array element. In this section we will develop a method for searching a sorted array that is much faster.

The indexes of the array a are the integers 0 through `final_index`. In order to make the task of searching the array easier, we will assume that the array is sorted. Hence, we know the following:

```
a[0] <= a[1] <= a[2] <= ... <= a[final_index]
```

When searching an array, you are likely to want to know both whether the value is in the list and, if it is, where it is in the list. For example, if we are searching for a credit card number, then the array index may serve as a record number. Another array indexed by these same indexes may hold a phone number or other information to use for reporting the suspicious card. Hence, if the sought-after value is in the array, we will want our function to tell where that value is in the array.

PROBLEM DEFINITION

We will design our function to use two call-by-reference parameters to return the outcome of the search. One parameter, called `found`, will be of type *bool*. If the value is found, then `found` will be set to *true*. If the value is found, then another parameter, called `location`, will be set to the index of the value found. If we use key to denote the value being searched for, the task to be accomplished can be formulated precisely as follows:

Precondition: `a[0]` through `a[final_index]`
    are sorted in increasing order.
Postcondition: if `key` is not one of the values `a[0]` through
    `a[final_index]`, then `found` == *false*; otherwise
    `a[location]` == `key` and `found` == *true*.

ALGORITHM DESIGN

Now let us proceed to produce an algorithm to solve this task. It will help to visualize the problem in very concrete terms. Suppose the list of numbers is so long that it takes a book to list them all. This is in fact how invalid credit card numbers are distributed to stores that do not have access to computers. If you are a clerk and are handed a credit card, you must check to see if it is on the list and hence invalid. How would you proceed? Open the book to the middle and see if the number is there. If it is not and it is smaller than the middle number, then work backward toward the beginning of the book. If the number is larger than the middle number, you work your way toward the end of the book. This idea produces our first draft of an algorithm:

```
found = false;//so far.
mid = approximate midpoint between 0 and final_index;
if (key == a[mid])
{
    found = true;
    location = mid;
}
else if (key < a[mid])
    search a[0] through a[mid - 1];
else if (key > a[mid])
    search a[mid + 1] through a[final_index];
```

Since the searchings of the shorter lists are smaller versions of the very task we are designing the algorithm to perform, this algorithm naturally lends itself to the use of recursion. The smaller lists can be searched with recursive calls to the algorithm itself.

Our pseudocode is a bit too imprecise to be easily translated into C++ code. The problem has to do with the recursive calls. There are two recursive calls shown:

```
search a[0] through a[mid - 1];
        and
search a[mid + 1] through a[final_index];
```

To implement these recursive calls we need two more parameters. A recursive call specifies that a subrange of the array is to be searched. In one case it is the elements indexed by 0 through mid - 1. In the other case it is the elements indexed by mid + 1 through final_index. The two extra parameters will specify the first and last indices of the search, so we will call them first and last. Using these parameters for the lowest and highest indices, instead of 0 and final_index, we can express the pseudocode more precisely as follows:

To search a[first] through a[last] do the following:
found = *false*;//*so far.*
mid = approximate midpoint between first and last;
if (key == a[mid])
{
    found = *true*;
    location = mid;
}
else if (key < a[mid])
    search a[first] through a[mid − 1];
else if (key > a[mid])
    search a[mid + 1] through a[last];

Display 12.5 Pseudocode for Binary Search

int a[*Some_Size_Value*];

Algorithm to search a[first] **through** a[last]

    //*Precondition:*
    //*a[first]<= a[first + 1] <= a[first + 2] <= ... <= a[last]*

To locate the value key:
    if (first > last) //*A stopping case*
        found = *false*;
    else
    {
        mid = approximate midpoint between first and last;
        if (key == a[mid]) //*A stopping case*
        {
            found = *true*;
            location = mid;
        }
        else if key < a[mid] //*A case with recursion*
            search a[first] through a[mid − 1];
        else if key > a[mid] //*A case with recursion*
            search a[mid + 1] through a[last];
    }

To search the entire array, the algorithm would be executed with `first` set equal to 0 and `last` set equal to `final_index`. The recursive calls will use other values for `first` and `last`. For example, the first recursive call would set `first` equal to 0 and `last` equal to the calculated value `mid – 1`.

As with any recursive algorithm we must ensure that our algorithm ends rather than producing infinite recursion. If the sought-after number is found on the list, then there is no recursive call and the process terminates, but we need some way to detect when the number is not on the list. On each recursive call the value of `first` is increased or the value of `last` is decreased. If they ever pass each other and `first` actually becomes larger than `last`, then we will know that there are no more indexes left to check and that the number `key` is not in the array. If we add this test to our pseudocode, we obtain a complete solution as shown in Display 12.5.

stopping case

algorithm—final version

CODING

Now we can routinely translate the pseudocode into C++ code. The result is shown in Display 12.6. The function `search` is an implementation of the recursive algorithm given in Display 12.5. A diagram of how the function performs on a sample array is given in Display 12.7.

Notice that the function `search` solves a more general problem than the original task. Our goal was to design a function to search an entire array. Yet the function will let us search any interval of the array by specifying the index bounds `first` and `last`. This is common when designing recursive functions. Frequently, it is necessary to solve a more general problem in order to be able to express the recursive algorithm. In this case, we only wanted the answer in the case where `first` and `last` are set equal to 0 and `final_index`. However, the recursive calls will set them to values other than 0 and `final_index`.

solve a more general problem

CHECKING THE RECURSION

In the subsection entitled "Recursive Design Techniques" we gave three criteria that you should check to ensure that a recursive *void*-function definition is correct. Let's check these three things for the function `search` given in Display 12.6.

1 **There is no infinite recursion:** On each recursive call the value of `first` is increased or the value of `last` is decreased. If the chain of recursive calls does not end in some other way, then eventually the function will be called with `first` larger than `last`, and that is a stopping case.

2 **Each stopping case performs the correct action for that case:** There are two stopping cases, when `first > last` and when `key == a[mid]`. Let's consider each case.

If `first > last`, there are no array elements between `a[first]` and `a[last]` and so `key` is not in this segment of the array. (Nothing is in this

Display 12.6 Recursive Function for Binary Search (part 1 of 2)

```
//Program to demonstrate the recursive function for binary search.
#include <iostream>
using namespace std;
const int ARRAY_SIZE = 10;


void search(const int a[], int first, int last,
                    int key, bool& found, int& location);
//Precondition: a[first] through a[last] are sorted in increasing order.
//Postcondition: if key is not one of the values a[first] through a[last],
//then found == false; otherwise a[location] == key and found == true.


int main( )
{
    int a[ARRAY_SIZE];
    const int final_index = ARRAY_SIZE - 1;

            <This portion of the program contains some code to fill and sort
             the array a. The exact details are irrelevant to this example.>

    int key, location;
    bool found;
    cout << "Enter number to be located: ";
    cin >> key;
    search(a, 0, final_index, key, found, location);

    if (found)
        cout << key << " is in index location "
            << location << endl;
    else
        cout << key << " is not in the array." << endl;

    return 0;
}
```

Display 12.6 Recursive Function for Binary Search *(part 2 of 2)*

```cpp
void search(const int a[], int first, int last,
                          int key, bool& found, int& location)
{
    int mid;
    if (first > last)
    {
        found = false;
    }
    else
    {
        mid = (first + last)/2;

        if (key == a[mid])
        {
            found = true;
            location = mid;
        }
        else if (key < a[mid])
        {
            search(a, first, mid - 1, key, found, location);
        }
        else if (key > a[mid])
        {
            search(a, mid + 1, last, key, found, location);
        }
    }
}
```

Display 12.7 Execution of the Function search

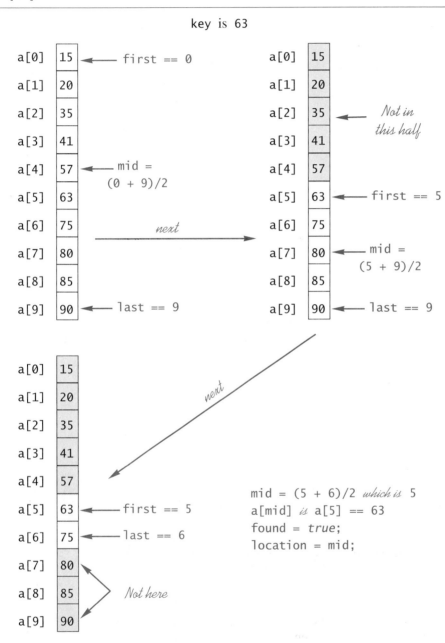

key is 63

a[0] 15 ← first == 0
a[1] 20
a[2] 35
a[3] 41
a[4] 57 ← mid = (0 + 9)/2
a[5] 63
a[6] 75
a[7] 80
a[8] 85
a[9] 90 ← last == 9

next

a[0] 15
a[1] 20
a[2] 35 ← *Not in this half*
a[3] 41
a[4] 57
a[5] 63 ← first == 5
a[6] 75
a[7] 80 ← mid = (5 + 9)/2
a[8] 85
a[9] 90 ← last == 9

a[0] 15
a[1] 20
a[2] 35
a[3] 41
a[4] 57
a[5] 63 ← first == 5
a[6] 75 ← last == 6
a[7] 80
a[8] 85 ⟩ *Not here*
a[9] 90

next

mid = (5 + 6)/2 *which is* 5
a[mid] *is* a[5] == 63
found = *true*;
location = mid;

segment of the array!) So, if first > last, the function search correctly sets found equal to *false*.

If key == a[mid], the algorithm correctly sets found equal to *true* and location equal to mid. Thus, both stopping cases are correct.

3 For each of the cases that involve recursion, *if* all recursive calls perform their actions correctly, *then* the entire case performs correctly: There are two cases in which there are recursive calls, when key < a[mid] and when key > a[mid]. We need to check each of these two cases.

First suppose key < a[mid]. In this case, since the array is sorted, we know that if key is anywhere in the array, then key is one of the elements a[first] through a[mid − 1]. Thus, the function need only search these elements, which is exactly what the recursive call
search(a, first, mid − 1, key, found, location);
does. So if the recursive call is correct, then the entire action is correct.

Next, suppose key > a[mid]. In this case, since the array is sorted, we know that if key is anywhere in the array, then key is one of the elements a[mid + 1] through a[last]. Thus, the function need only search these elements, which is exactly what the recursive call
search(a, mid + 1, last, key, found, location);
does. So if the recursive call is correct, then the entire action is correct. Thus, in both cases the function performs the correct action (assuming that the recursive calls perform the correct action).

The function search passes all three of our tests, so it is a good recursive function definition.

EFFICIENCY

The binary search algorithm is extremely fast compared to an algorithm that simply tries all array elements in order. In the binary search, you eliminate about half the array from consideration right at the start. You then eliminate a quarter, then an eighth of the array, and so forth. These savings add up to a dramatically fast algorithm. For an array of 100 elements, the binary search will never need to compare more than seven array elements to the key. A simple serial search could compare as many as 100 array elements to the key and on the average will compare about 50 array elements to the key. Moreover, the larger the array is, the more dramatic the savings will be. On an array with 1,000 elements, the binary search will only need to compare about ten array elements to the key value, as compared to an average of 500 for the simple serial search algorithm.

An iterative version of the function search is given in Display 12.8. On some systems the iterative version will run more efficiently than the recursive version. The algorithm for the iterative version was derived by mirroring the recursive version. In

iterative version

Display 12.8 Iterative Version of Binary Search

Function Prototype

```
void search(const int a[], int low_end, int high_end,
                           int key, bool& found, int& location);
//Precondition: a[low_end] through a[high_end] are sorted in increasing
//order.
//Postcondition: If key is not one of the values a[low_end] through
//a[high_end], then found == false; otherwise a[location] == key and
//found == true.
```

Function Definition

```
void search(const int a[], int low_end, int high_end,
                           int key, bool& found, int& location)
{
    int first = low_end;
    int last = high_end;
    int mid;

    found = false;//so far
    while ( (first <= last) && !(found) )
    {
        mid = (first + last)/2;
        if (key == a[mid])
        {
            found = true;
            location = mid;
        }
        else if (key < a[mid])
        {
            last = mid - 1;
        }
        else if (key > a[mid])
        {
            first = mid + 1;
        }
    }
}
```

the iterative version, the local variables `first` and `last` mirror the roles of the parameters in the recursive version, which are also named `first` and `last`. As this example illustrates, it often makes sense to derive a recursive algorithm even if you expect to later convert it to an iterative algorithm.

■)) PROGRAMMING EXAMPLE
A Recursive Member Function

A member function of a class can be recursive. Member functions can use recursion in the exact same way that ordinary functions do. Display 12.9 contains an example of a recursive member function. The class `BankAccount` used in that display is the same as the class named `BankAccount` that was defined in Display 6.6 except that we have overloaded the member function name `update`. The first version of `update` has no arguments and posts one year of simple interest to the bank account balance. The other (new) version of `update` takes an *int* argument that is some number of years. This member function updates the account by posting the interest for that many years. The new version of `update` is recursive. This new function `update` has one parameter, called `years`, and uses the following algorithm:

> If the number of `years` is 1, then //*Stopping case:*
> > call the other function named `update` (the one with no arguments).
>
> If the number of `years` is greater than 1, then //*Recursive case:*
> > make a recursive call to post `years` – 1 worth of interest, and then
> > call the other function called `update` (the one with no arguments)
> > to post one more year's worth of interest.

It is easy to see that this algorithm produces the desired result by checking the three points given in the subsection entitled "Recursive Design Techniques."

1 There is no infinite recursion: Each recursive call reduces the number of `years` by one until the number of `years` eventually becomes 1, which is the stopping case. So there is no infinite recursion.

2 Each stopping case performs the correct action for that case: The one stopping case is when `years == 1`. This case produces the correct action, since it simply calls the other overloaded member function called `update`, and we checked the correctness of that function in Chapter 6.

3 For the cases that involve recursion, *if* all recursive calls perform correctly, *then* the entire case performs correctly: The recursive case, i.e., `years > 1`, clearly works correctly, because if the recursive call correctly posts `years` – 1 worth of interest, then all that is needed is to post one additional year's worth of interest, and the call to the

Display 12.9 A Recursive Member Function *(part 1 of 2)*

```
//Program to demonstrate the recursive member function update(years). The class BankAccount
// in this program is an improved version of the class BankAccount given in Display 6.6.
#include <iostream>
using namespace std;

//Class for a bank account:
class BankAccount
{
public:
    BankAccount(int dollars, int cents, double rate);
    //Initializes the account balance to $dollars.cents and
    //initializes the interest rate to rate percent.

    BankAccount(int dollars, double rate);
    //Initializes the account balance to $dollars.00 and
    //initializes the interest rate to rate percent.

    BankAccount( );
    //Initializes the account balance to $0.00 and
    //initializes the interest rate to 0.0%.

    void update( );
    //Postcondition: One year of simple interest
    //has been added to the account balance.

    void update(int years);
    //Postcondition: Interest for the number of years given has been added to the
    //account balance. Interest is compounded annually.

    double get_balance( );
    //Returns the current account balance.

    double get_rate( );
    //Returns the current account interest rate as a percent.

    void output(ostream& outs);
    //Precondition: If outs is a file output stream, then outs has already been connected
    //to a file.
    //Postcondition: Account balance and interest rate have been written to the stream outs.
private:
    double balance;
    double interest_rate;

    double fraction(double percent);
    //Converts a percent to a fraction. For example, fraction(50.3) returns 0.503.
};
```

*two different functions
with the
same name*

Display 12.9 A Recursive Member Function *(part 2 of 2)*

```
int main( )
{
    BankAccount your_account(100, 5);
    your_account.update(10);
    cout.setf(ios::fixed);
    cout.setf(ios::showpoint);
    cout.precision(2);
    cout << "If you deposit $100.00 at 5% interest, then\n"
         << "in ten years your account will be worth $"
         << your_account.get_balance( ) << endl;
    return 0;
}

void BankAccount::update( )
{
    balance = balance + fraction(interest_rate)*balance;
}

void BankAccount::update(int years)
{
    if (years == 1)
    {
        update( );
    }
    else if (years > 1)
    {
        update(years – 1);
        update( );
    }
}
```

overloading (i.e., calls to ANOTHER function with the same name)

recursive function call

<Definitions of the other member functions are given in Display 6.5 and Display 6.6, but you need not read those definitions in order to understand this example.>

Sample Dialogue

```
If you deposit $100.00 at 5% interest, then
in ten years your account will be worth $162.89
```

overloading

overloaded zero-argument version of update will correctly post one year's worth of interest. Thus, *if* the recursive call performs the correct action, *then* the entire action for the case of years > 1 will be correct.

In this example, we have overloaded update so that there are two different functions named update: one that takes no arguments and one that takes a single argument. Do not confuse the calls to the two functions named update. These are two different functions that, as far as the compiler is concerned, just coincidentally happen to have the same name. When the definition of the function update with one argument includes a call to the version of update that takes no arguments, that is not a recursive call. Only the call to the version of update with the *exact* same prototype is a recursive call. To see what is involved here, note that we could have named the version of update that takes no argument post_one_year( ), instead of naming it update( ), and then the definition of the recursive version of update would read as follows:

```
void BankAccount::update(int years)
{
    if (years == 1)
    {
        post_one_year( );
    }
    else if (years > 1)
    {
        update(years – 1);
        post_one_year( );
    }
}
```

Recursion and Overloading

Do not confuse recursion and overloading. When you overload a function name you are giving two different functions the same name. If the definition of one of these two functions includes a call to the other, that is not recursion. In a recursive function definition the definition of the function includes a call to the *exact* same function with the *exact same definition,* not simply to some other function that coincidentally uses the same name. It is not too serious an error if you confuse overloading and recursion, since they are both legal. It is simply a question of getting the terminology straight so that you can communicate clearly with other programmers, and so that you understand the underlying processes.

SELF-TEST EXERCISES

15   Write a recursive function definition for the following function:

```
int squares(int n);
//Precondition: n >= 1
//Returns the sum of the squares of the numbers 1 through n.
```

For example, squares(3) returns 14 because $1^2 + 2^2 + 3^2$ is 14.

16   Write an iterative version of the one argument member function
BankAccount::update(*int* years) that is described in Display 12.9.

CHAPTER SUMMARY

- If a problem can be reduced to smaller instances of the same problem, then a recursive solution is likely to be easy to find and implement.

- A recursive algorithm for a function definition normally contains two kinds of cases: one or more cases that include at least one recursive call and one or more stopping cases in which the problem is solved without any recursive calls.

- When writing a recursive function definition, always check to see that the function will not produce infinite recursion.

- When you define a recursive function, use the three criteria given in the subsection "Recursive Design Techniques" to check that the function is correct.

- When you design a recursive function to solve a task it is often necessary to solve a more general problem than the given task. This may be required to allow for the proper recursive calls, since the smaller problems may not be exactly the same problem as the given task. For example, in the binary search problem, the task was to search an entire array, but the recursive solution is an algorithm to search any portion of the array (either all of it or a part of it).

Answers to Self-Test Exercises

```
1  Hip Hip Hurray
```

2

```
void stars(int n)
{
    cout << '*';
    if (n > 1)
        stars(n - 1);
}
```

The following is also correct, but is more complicated:

```
void stars(int n)
{
    if (n <= 1)
    {
        cout << '*';
    }
    else
    {
        stars(n - 1);
        cout << '*';
    }
}
```

3

```
void backward(int n)
{
    if (n < 10)
    {
        cout << n;
    }
    else
    {
        cout << (n%10);//write last digit
        backward(n/10);//write the other digits backward
    }
}
```

4–5 The answer to 4 is write_up(*int*);. The answer to 5 is write_down(*int*);

```
#include <iostream>
using namespace std;
void write_down( int n )
{
    if (n >= 1)
    {
        cout << n << " "; //write while the
                          //recursion winds
        write_down(n - 1);
    }
}

// 5
void write_up(int n)
{
    if (n >= 1)
    {
        write_up(n - 1);
        cout << n << " "; //write while the
                          //recursion unwinds
    }
}
//testing code for both #4 and #5
int main()
  {
    cout << "calling write_up(" << 10 << ")\n";
    write_up(10);
    cout << endl;
    cout << "calling write_down(" << 10 << ")\n";
    write_down(10);
    cout << endl;
  }
/* Test results
calling write_up( 10)
1 2 3 4 5 6 7 8 9 10
calling write_down( 10)
10 9 8 7 6 5 4 3 2 1
*/
```

6 An error message that says *stack overflow* is telling you that the computer has attempted to place more activation frames on the stack than are allowed on your system. A likely cause of this error message is infinite recursion.

7

```
void cheers(int n)
{
    while (n > 1)
    {
        cout << "Hip ";
        n--;
    }
    cout << "Hurray\n";
}
```

8

```
void stars(int n)
{
    for (int count = 1; count <= n; count++)
        cout << '*';
}
```

9

```
void backward(int n)
{
    while (n >= 10)
    {
        cout << (n%10);//write last digit
        n = n/10;//discard the last digit
    }
    cout << n;
}
```

10

Trace for Exercise 4: If n = 3, the code to be executed is:

```
if ( 3 >= 1 )
{
    write_down( 3 - 1);
}
```

Next recursion, n = 2, the code to be executed is:

```
if ( 2 >= 1 )
{
    write_down( 2 - 1)
}
```

Next recursion, n = 1, the code to be executed is:

```
if ( 1 >= 1 )
    {
        write_down( 1 - 1)
    }
```

Final recursion, n = 0, and the "true" clause is not executed:

```
if (1 >= 1 ) // condition false
{
            // this clause is skipped
}
```

The recursion unwinds, the cout << n << " "; line of code is executed for each recursion that was wound up, with n = 3 then n = 2, then 1 is written. The output is 3 2 1.

11

Trace for Exercise 5: If n = 3, the code to be executed is:

```
if ( 3 >= 1 )
{
    cout << 3 << " ";
    write up( 3 - 1  );
}
```

On the next recursion, n = 2; the code to be executed is

```
if ( 2 >= 1 )
{
    cout << 2 << " ";
    write up( 2 - 1 );
}
```

On the next recursion, n = 1 and the code to be executed is:

```
if ( 1 >= 1 )
{
    cout << 1 << " ";
    write up( 1 - 1 );
}
```

On the final recursion, n = 0 and the code to be executed is:

```
if ( 0 >= 1 ) // condition false, body skipped
{
    // skipped
}
```

The recursions unwind; the output (obtained while recursion was winding up) is 1 2 3.

12 6

13 The output is 24. The function is the factorial function, usually written *n!* and defined as follows:

n! is equal to $n*(n-1)*(n-2)*...*1$

14

```
//Uses iostream and cstdlib:
double power(int x, int n)
{
    if (n < 0 && x == 0)
    {
        cout << "Illegal argument to power.\n";
        exit(1);
    }
```

```
        if (n < 0)
            return ( 1/power(x, -n));
        else if (n > 0)
            return ( power(x, n - 1)*x );
        else // n == 0
            return (1.0);
    }
```

15

```
    int squares(int n)
    {
        if (n <= 1)
            return 1;
        else
            return ( squares(n - 1) + n*n );
    }
```

16

```
    void BankAccount::update(int years)
    {
        for (int count = 1; count <= years; count++)
            update( );
    }
```

Programming Projects

1 Write a recursive function definition for a function that has one parameter n of type *int* and that returns the nth Fibonacci number. See Programming Project 8 in Chapter 7 for the definition of Fibonacci numbers. Embed the function in a program and test it.

2 Write a recursive version of the function index_of_smallest that was used in the sorting program in Display 9.13 of Chapter 9. Embed the function in a program and test it.

3 The formula for computing the number of ways of choosing r different things from a set of n things is the following:

$$C(n, r) = n!/(r!*(n - r)!)$$

The factorial function $n!$ is defined by

$$n! = n*(n-1)*(n-2)*...*1.$$

Discover a recursive version of the above formula and write a recursive function that computes the value of the formula. Embed the function in a program and test it.

4   Write a recursive function that has an argument that is an array of characters and two arguments that are bounds on array indices. The function should reverse the order of those entries in the array whose indices are between the two bounds. For example, if the array is:

a[1] == 'A' a[2] == 'B' a[3] == 'C' a[4] == 'D' a[5] == 'E'

and the bounds are 2 and 5, then after the function is run the array elements should be:

a[1] == 'A' a[2] == 'E' a[3] == 'D' a[4] == 'C' a[5] == 'B'

Embed the function in a program and test it. After you have fully debugged this function, define another function that takes a single argument which is an array that contains a string value and that reverses the spelling of the string value in the array argument. This function will include a call to the recursive definition you did for the first part of this project. Embed this second function in a program and test it.

5   Write an iterative version of the recursive function in the previous exercise. Embed it in a program and test it.

6   Write a recursive function to sort an array of integers into ascending order using the following idea: Place the smallest element in the first position, then sort the rest of the array by a recursive call. This is a recursive version of the selection sort algorithm discussed in Chapter 9. (Note: Simply taking the program from Chapter 9 and plugging in a recursive version of index_of_smallest will not suffice. The function to do the sorting must itself be recursive and not merely use a recursive function.)

7

Towers of Hanoi. There is a story about Buddhist monks who are playing this puzzle with 64 stone disks. The story claims that when the monks finish moving the disks from one post to a second via the third post, time will end. Eschatology (concerns about the end of time) and Theology will be left to those better qualified; our interest is limited to the recursive solution to the problem.

A stack of n disks of decreasing size is placed on one of three posts. The task is to move the disks one at a time from the first post to the second. To do this, any disk can be moved from any post to any other post, subject to the rule that you can never place a larger disk over a smaller disk. The (spare) third post is provided to make the solution possible. Your task is to write a recursive function that describes instructions for a solution to this problem. We don't have graphics available, so you should output a sequence of instructions that will solve the problem.

Hint: If you could move up n-1 of the disks from the first post to the third post using the second post as a spare, the last disk could be moved from the first post to the second post. Then by using the same technique (whatever that may be) you can move the n-1 disks from the third post to the second post, using the first disk as a spare. There! You have the puzzle solved. You only have to decide what the nonrecursive case is, what the recursive case is, and when to output instructions to move the disks.

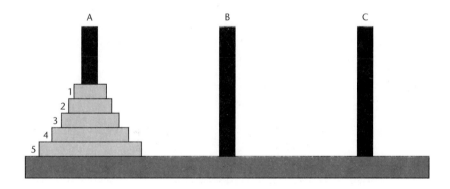

CHAPTER

13

Templates for More Abstraction

13 Templates for More Abstraction

All men are mortal.
Aristotle is a man.
Therefore, Aristotle is mortal.

All X's are Y.
Z is an X.
Therefore, Z is Y.

All cats are mischievous.
Garfield is a cat.
Therefore, Garfield is mischievous.

A SHORT LESSON ON SYLLOGISMS

Introduction

In this chapter we discuss C++ templates. Templates allow you to define functions and classes that have parameters for type names. This will allow you to design functions that can be used with arguments of different types and to define classes that are much more general than those you have seen before this chapter.

13.1 Templates for Algorithm Abstraction

Many of our previous C++ function definitions have an underlying algorithm that is much more general than the algorithm we gave in the function definition. For example, consider the function `swap_values` which we first discussed in Chapter 4. For reference, we now repeat the function definition:

```
void swap_values(int& variable1, int& variable2)
{
    int temp;

    temp = variable1;
    variable1 = variable2;
    variable2 = temp;
}
```

However, most function templates require only one type parameter. You cannot have unused template parameters, that is, each template parameter must be used in your template function.

● *PITFALL*   **Compiler Complications**

Many compilers do not allow separate compilation of templates, so you may need to include your template definition with your code that uses it. As usual, at least the prototype must precede any use of the template function.

Your safest strategy is not to use function template prototypes, and to be sure the function template definition appears in the same file in which it is used and appears before the function template is called. However, the function template definition can appear via a #include directive. You can give the function template definition in one file and then #include that file in a file that uses the template function.

Some C++ compilers have additional special requirements for using templates. If you have trouble compiling your templates, check your manuals or check with a local expert. You may need to set special options or rearrange the way you order the template definitions and the other items in your files.

Function Template

The function definition and the function prototype for a function template are each prefaced with the following:

```
template<class Type_Parameter>
```

The prototype (if used) and definition are then the same as any ordinary function prototype and definition, except that the *Type_Parameter* can be used in place of a type.

For example, the following is a prototype for a function template:

```
template<class T>
void show_stuff(int stuff1, T stuff2, T stuff3);
```

The definition for this function template might be:

```
template<class T>
void show_stuff(int stuff1, T stuff2, T stuff3)
{
    cout << stuff1 << endl
         << stuff2 << endl
         << stuff3 << endl;
}
```

The function template given in this example is equivalent to having one function prototype and one function definition for each possible type name. The type name is substituted for the type parameter (which is T in the example above). For instance, consider the following function call:

```
show_stuff(2, 3.3, 4.4);
```

When this function call is executed, the compiler uses the function definition obtained by replacing T with the type name *double*. A separate definition will be produced for each different type for which you use the template, but not for any types you do not use. Only one definition is generated for a specific type regardless of the number of times you use the template.

Algorithm Abstraction

As we saw in our discussion of the swap_values function, there is a very general algorithm for interchanging the value of two variables and this more general algorithm applies to variables of any type. Using a function template we were able to express this more general algorithm in C++. This is a very simple example of *algorithm abstraction*. When we say we are using **algorithm abstraction** we mean that we are expressing our algorithms in a very general way so that we can ignore incidental detail and concentrate on the substantive part of the algorithm. Function templates are one feature of C++ that supports algorithm abstraction.

SELF-TEST EXERCISES

1 Write a function template named maximum. The function takes two values of the same type as its arguments and returns the larger of the two arguments (or either value if they are equal). Give both the function prototype and the function definition for the template. You will use the operator < in your definition. Therefore, this function template will apply only to types for which < is defined. Write a comment for the prototype that explains this restriction.

2 We have used three kinds of absolute value function: abs, labs, and fabs. These functions differ only in the type of their argument. It might be better to have a function template for the absolute value function. Give a function template for an absolute value function called absolute. The template will apply only to types for which < is defined, for which the unary negation operator is defined, and for which the constant 0 can be used in a comparison with a value of that type. Thus, the function absolute can be called with any of the number types, such as *int*, *long*, and *double*. Give both the function prototype and the function definition for the template.

3 Define or characterize the template facility for C++.

4 In the template prefix,

```
template <class T>
```

what kind of variable is the parameter T?

a. T must be a class.

b. T must *not* be a class.

c. T can be only types built into the C++ language.

d. T can be any type, whether built into C++ or defined by the programmer.

■)) *PROGRAMMING EXAMPLE*
A Generic Sorting Function

In Chapter 9 we gave a simple sorting algorithm to sort an array of values of type *int*. The algorithm was realized in C++ code as the function sort which we gave in Display 9.13. Below we repeat the definitions of this function sort:

```
void sort(int a[], int number_used)
{
    int index_of_next_smallest;
    for (int index = 0; index < number_used – 1; index++)
    {//Place the correct value in a[index]:
        index_of_next_smallest =
                index_of_smallest(a, index, number_used);
        swap_values(a[index], a[index_of_next_smallest]);
        //a[0] <= a[1] <=...<= a[index] are the smallest of the original array
        //elements. The rest of the elements are in the remaining positions.
    }
}
```

If you study the above definition of the function sort you will see that the base type of the array is never used in any significant way. If we replace the base type of the array in the function header with the type *double*, then we would obtain a sorting function that applies to arrays of values of type *double*. Of course, we also must adjust the helping functions so they apply to arrays of elements of type *double*. So let's consider the helping functions that are called inside the body of the function sort. The two helping functions are swap_values and index_of_smallest.

helping functions

We already saw that swap_values can apply to variables of any type, provided we define it as a function template (as in Display 13.1). Let's see if

index_of_smallest depends in any significant way on the base type of the array
being sorted. The definition of index_of_smallest is repeated below so you can
study its details.

```
int index_of_smallest(const int a[], int start_index,
                       int number_used)
{
    int min = a[start_index];
    int index_of_min = start_index;
    for (int index = start_index + 1; index < number_used; index++)
        if (a[index] < min)
        {
            min = a[index];
            index_of_min = index;
            //min is the smallest of a[start_index] through
            //a[index]
        }

    return index_of_min;
}
```

The function index_of_smallest also does not depend in any significant way
on the base type of the array. If we replaced the two highlighted instances of the type
int with the type *double*, then we will have changed the function
index_of_smallest so that it applies to arrays whose base type is *double*.

To change the function sort so that it can be used to sort arrays with the base type
double, we only needed to replace a few instances of the type name *int* with the type
name *double*. Moreover, there is nothing special about the type *double*. We can do a
similar replacement for many other types. The only thing we need to know about the
type is that the operator < is defined for that type. This is the perfect situation for function templates. If we replace a few instances of the type name *int* (in the functions
sort and index_of_smallest) with a type parameter, then the function sort can sort
an array of values of any type provided that the values of that type can be compared
using the < operator. In Display 13.2 we have written just such a function template.

Notice that the function template sort shown in Display 13.2 can be used with
arrays of values that are not numbers. In the demonstration program, the function
template sort is called to sort an array of characters. Characters can be compared
using the < operator. Although the exact meaning of the < operator applied to character values may vary somewhat from one implementation to another, some things are
always true about how < orders the letters of the alphabet. When applied to two
uppercase letters, the operator < tests to see if the first comes before the second in
alphabetic order. Also, when applied to two lowercase letters, the operator < tests to

Display 13.2 A Generic Sorting Function

```
// This is file sortfunc.cxx

template<class T>
void swap_values(T& variable1, T& variable2)
            <The rest of the definition of swap_values is given in Display 13.1.>

template<class T>
int index_of_smallest(const T a[], int start_index, int number_used)
{
    T min = a[start_index];
    int index_of_min = start_index;

    for (int index = start_index + 1; index < number_used; index++)
        if (a[index] < min)
        {
            min = a[index];
            index_of_min = index;
            //min is the smallest of a[start_index] through a[index]
        }

    return index_of_min;
}


template<class T>
void sort(T a[], int number_used)
{
int index_of_next_smallest;
for(int index = 0; index < number_used - 1; index++)
    {//Place the correct value in a[index]:
        index_of_next_smallest =
            index_of_smallest(a, index, number_used);
        swap_values(a[index], a[index_of_next_smallest]);
    //a[0] <= a[1] <=...<= a[index] are the smallest of the original array
    //elements. The rest of the elements are in the remaining positions.
    }
}
```

Display 13.3 Using a Generic Sorting Function (*part 1 of 2*)

```
//Demonstrates a generic sorting function.
#include <iostream>
using namespace std;

//The file sortfunc.cxx defines the following function:
//template<class T>
//void sort(T a[], int number_used);
//Precondition: number_used <= declared size of the array a.
//The array elements a[0] through a[number_used - 1] have values.
//Postcondition: The values of a[0] through a[number_used - 1] have
//been rearranged so that a[0] <= a[1] <= ... <= a[number_used - 1].

#include "sortfunc.cxx"

int main( )
{
    int i;
    int a[10] = {9, 8, 7, 6, 5, 1, 2, 3, 0, 4};
    cout << "Unsorted integers:\n";
    for (i = 0; i < 10; i++)
        cout << a[i] << " ";
    cout << endl;
    sort(a, 10);
    cout << "In sorted order the integers are:\n";
    for (i = 0; i < 10; i++)
        cout << a[i] << " ";
    cout << endl;

    double b[5] = {5.5, 4.4, 1.1, 3.3, 2.2};
    cout << "Unsorted doubles:\n";
    for (i = 0; i < 5; i++)
        cout << b[i] << " ";
    cout << endl;
    sort(b, 5);
    cout << "In sorted order the doubles are:\n";
    for (i = 0; i < 5; i++)
        cout << b[i] << " ";
    cout << endl;
```

Many compilers will allow this prototype to appear as a prototype and not merely as a comment. However, including the prototype is not needed, since the definition of the function is in the file sortfunc.cxx, *and so the definition effectively appears before* main.

Display 13.3 Using a Generic Sorting Function *(part 2 of 2)*

```
char c[7] = {'G', 'E', 'N', 'E', 'R', 'I', 'C'};
cout << "Unsorted characters:\n";
for (i = 0; i < 7; i++)
    cout << c[i] << " ";
cout << endl;
sort(c, 7);
cout << "In sorted order the characters are:\n";
for (i = 0; i < 7; i++)
    cout << c[i] << " ";
cout << endl;

    return 0;
}
```

Output

```
Unsorted integers:
9 8 7 6 5 1 2 3 0 4
In sorted order the integers are
0 1 2 3 4 5 6 7 8 9
Unsorted doubles:
5.5 4.4 1.1 3.3 2.2
In sorted order the doubles are:
1.1 2.2 3.3 4.4 5.5
Unsorted characters:
G E N E R I C
In sorted order the characters are:
C E E G I N R
```

see if the first comes before the second in alphabetic order. When you mix uppercase and lowercase letters, the situation is not so well behaved, but the program shown in Display 13.2 deals only with uppercase letters. In that program an array of uppercase letters is sorted into alphabetical order with a call to the function template sort. (The function template sort will even sort an array of objects of a class that you define, provided you overload the < operator to apply to objects of the class.)

↪ *PROGRAMMING* TIP
How to Define Templates

When we defined the function templates in Display 13.2, we started with a function that sorts an array of elements of type *int*. We then created a template by replacing the base type of the array with the type parameter T. This is a good general strategy for writing templates. If you want to write a function template, first write a version that is not a template at all but is just an ordinary function. Then completely debug the ordinary function, and then convert the ordinary function to a template by replacing some type names with a type parameter. There are two advantages to this method. First, when you are defining the ordinary function you are dealing with a much more concrete case, which makes the problem easier to visualize. Second, you have fewer details to check at each stage; when worrying about the algorithm itself, you need not concern yourself with template syntax rules.

SELF-TEST EXERCISE

5 Display 9.11 shows a function called search, which searches an array for a specified integer. Give a function template version of search that can be used to search an array of elements of any type. Give both the function prototype and the function definition for the template. Hint: It is almost identical to the function given in Display 9.11.

6 In Programming Project 9 of Chapter 3 you were asked to overload the abs function so that the name abs would work with several of the built-in types that had been studied at the time. Compare and contrast function overloading of the abs function with the use of templates for this purpose in Self-Test Exercise 2.

13.2 **Templates for Data Abstraction**

As you saw in the previous section, function definitions can be made more general by using templates. In this section you will see that templates can also make class definitions more general.

Syntax for Class Templates

The syntax for class templates is basically the same as that for function templates. The following is placed before the template definition

```
template<class T>
```

The type parameter T is used in the class definition just like any other type. As with function templates, the type parameter T represents a type that can be any type at all; the type parameter does not have to be replaced with a class type. As with function templates, you may use any (nonkeyword) identifier instead of T, although it is traditional to use T.

type parameter

For example, the following is a class template. An object of this class contains a pair of values of type T; if T is *int*, the object values are pairs of integers, if T is *char*, the object values are pairs of characters, and so on.

```
//Class for a pair of values of type T:
template<class T>
class Pair
{
public:
    Pair( );

    Pair(T first_value, T second_value);

    void set_element(int position, T value);
    //Precondition: position is 1 or 2.
    //Postcondition: The position indicated has been set to value.

    T get_element(int position) const;
    //Precondition: position is 1 or 2.
    //Returns the value in the position indicated.
private:
    T first;
    T second;
};
```

Once the class template is defined, you can declare objects of this class. The declaration must specify what type is to be filled in for T. For example, the following declares the object score so it can record a pair of integers and declares the object seats so it can record a pair of characters:

declaring objects

```
Pair<int> score;
Pair<char> seats;
```

13 TEMPLATES FOR MORE ABSTRACTION

The objects are then used just like any other objects. For example, the following sets the `score` to be 3 for the first team and 0 for the second team:

```
score.set_element(1, 3);
score.set_element(2, 0);
```

defining member functions

The member functions for a class template are defined the same way as member functions for ordinary classes. The only difference is that the member function definitions are themselves templates. For example, the following are appropriate definitions for the member function `set_element` and for the constructor with two arguments:

```
//Uses iostream and cstdlib:
template<class T>
void Pair<T>::set_element(int position, T value)
{
    if (position == 1)
        first = value;
    else if (position == 2)
        second = value;
    else
    {
        cout << "Error: Illegal pair position.\n";
        exit(1);
    }
}
template<class T>
Pair<T>::Pair(T first_value, T second_value)
{
    first = first_value;
    second = second_value;
}
```

Notice that the class name before the scope resolution operator is `Pair<T>`, not simply `Pair`.

The name of a class template may be used as the type for a function parameter. For example, the following is a possible prototype for a function with a parameter for a pair of integers:

```
int add_up(const Pair<int>& the_pair);
//Returns the sum of the two integers in the_pair.
```

Class Template Syntax

The class definition and the definitions of the member functions are prefaced with the following:

template<class Type_Parameter>

The class and member function definitions are then the same as for any ordinary class, except that the *Type_Parameter* can be used in place of a type.

For example, the following is the beginning of a class template definition:

```
template<class T>
class Pair
{
public:
    Pair( );
    Pair(T first_value, T second_value);
        . . .
```

Member functions and overloaded operators are then defined as function templates. For example, the definition of the two argument constructor for the above sample class template would begin as follows:

```
template<class T>
Pair<T>::Pair(T first_value, T second_value)
{
    . . .
```

Note that we specified the type, in this case *int*, that is to be filled in for the type parameter T.

You can even use a class template within a function template. For example, rather than defining the specialized function add_up given above, you could instead define a function template as follows so that the function applies to all kinds of numbers:

```
template<class T>
T add_up(const Pair<T>& the_pair);
//Precondition: The operator + is defined for values of type T.
//Returns the sum of the two values in the_pair.
```

Type Definitions

You can specialize a class template by giving a type argument to the class name, as in the following example:

    Pair<*int*>

The specialized class name, like Pair<*int*>, can then be used just like any class name. It can be used to declare objects or to specify the type of a formal parameter.

You can define a new class type name that has the same meaning as a specialized class template name, such as Pair<*int*>. The syntax for such a defined class type name is as follows:

    typedef Class_Name<Type_Argument> New_Type_Name;

For example:

    typedef Pair<*int*> PairOfInt;

The type name PairOfInt can then be used to declare objects of type Pair<*int*>, as in the following example:

    PairOfInt pair1, pair2;

The type name PairOfInt can also be used to specify the type of a formal parameter.

■)) *PROGRAMMING* EXAMPLE
   An Array Class

Display 13.4 contains the interface for a class template whose objects are lists. Since this class definition is a class template, the lists can be lists of items of any type whatsoever. You can have objects that are lists of values of type *int*, or lists of values of type *double*, or lists of objects of type string, or lists of items of any other type.

Display 13.5 contains a demonstration program that uses this class template. Although this program does not really do anything much, it does illustrate how the class template is used. Once you understand the syntax details, you can use the class template in any program that needs a list of values. The implementation of the class template is given in Display 13.6.

Display 13.4 Interface for the Class Template List *(part 1 of 2)*

```
//This is the HEADER FILE list.h. This is the INTERFACE for the class List.
//Objects of type List can be a list of items of any type for which the operators
//<< and = are defined. All the items on any one list must be of the same type. A
//list that can hold up to max items all of type Type_Name is declared as follows:
//      List<Type_Name> the_object(max);
#ifndef LIST_H
#define LIST_H
#include <iostream>
using namespace std;

namespace savitchlist
{
    template<class T>
    class List
    {
    public:
        List(int max);
        //Initializes the object to an empty list that can hold up to max items
        //of type T.

        ~List();
        //Returns all the dynamic memory used by the object to the heap.

        int length() const;
        //Returns the number of items on the list.

        void add(T new_item);
        //Precondition: The list is not full.
        //Postcondition: The new_item has been added to the list.

        int full() const;
        //Returns true if the list is full.

        void erase();
        //Removes all items from the list so that the list is empty.
```

Display 13.4 Interface for the Class Template List *(part 2 of 2)*

```
        friend ostream& operator <<(ostream& outs, const List<T>& the_list);
        //Overloads the << operator so it can be used to output the
        //contents of the list. The items are output one per line.
        //Precondition: If outs is a file output stream, then outs has already
        //been connected to a file.
    private:
        T *item; //pointer to the dynamic array that holds the list.
        int max_length; //max number of items allowed on the list.
        int current_length; //number of items currently on the list.
    };
}//savitchlist
#endif //LIST_H
```

Display 13.5 Program Using the List **Class Template**

```
//Program to demonstrate use of the class template List.
#include <iostream>
#include "list.h"
#include "list.cxx"
using namespace std;
using namespace savitchlist;

int main( )
{
    List<int> first_list(2);
    first_list.add(1);
    first_list.add(2);
    cout << "first_list = \n"
        << first_list;

    List<char> second_list(10);
    second_list.add('A');
    second_list.add('B');
    second_list.add('C');
    cout << "second_list = \n"
        << second_list;

    return 0;
}
```

Since list.cxx *is included, you need only compile this one file (the one with the* main.*)*

Output

```
first_list =
1
2
second_list =
A
B
C
```

Display 13.6 Implementation of List *(part 1 of 3)*

```
//This is the IMPLEMENTATION FILE: list.cxx
//This is the IMPLEMENTATION of the class template named List.
//The interface for the class template List is in the header file list.h.
#ifndef LIST_CXX
#define LIST_CXX
#include <iostream>
#include <cstdlib>
#include "list.h"//This is not needed when used as we are using this file,
                 //but the #ifndef in list.h makes it safe.
using namespace std;

namespace savitchlist
{
    //Uses cstdlib:
    template<class T>
    List<T>::List(int max)
    {
        max_length = max;
        current_length = 0;
        item = new T[max];
    }

    template<class T>
    List<T>::~List( )
    {
        delete [] item;
    }
```

Display 13.6 Implementation of List *(part 2 of 3)*

```cpp
template<class T>
int List<T>::length( ) const
{
    return (current_length);
}

//Uses iostream and cstdlib:
template<class T>
void List<T>::add(T new_item)
{
    if ( full( ) )
    {
        cout << "Error: adding to a full list.\n";
        exit(1);
    }
    else
    {
        item[current_length] = new_item;
        current_length = current_length + 1;
    }
}

template<class T>
int List<T>::full( ) const
{
    return (current_length == max_length);
}

template<class T>
void List<T>::erase( )
{
    current_length = 0;
}
```

Display 13.6 Implementation of List *(part 3 of 3)*

```
//Uses iostream:
template<class T>
ostream& operator <<(ostream& outs, const List<T>& the_list)
{
    for (int i = 0; i < the_list.current_length; i++)
        outs << the_list.item[i] << endl;

    return outs;
}
}//savitchlist
#endif // LIST_CXX Notice that we have enclosed all the template
       // definitions in #ifndef... #endif.
```

A note is in order about compiling the code from Display 13.4, 13.5, and 13.6. A safe solution to the compilation of this code is to #include the template class definition and the template function definitions before use, as we did. In that case only the file in Display 13.5 needs to be compiled. Be sure that you use the #ifndef #define #endif mechanism to prevent multiple file inclusion of all the files you are going to #include.

a friend

Notice that we have overloaded the insertion operator << so it can be used to output an object of the class template List. To do this we made the operator << a friend of the class. In order to have a parameter that is of the same type as the class, we used the expression List<T> for the parameter type. When the type parameter is replaced by, for example, the type *int*, this list parameter will be of type List<*int*>.

SELF-TEST EXERCISES

7 Give the definition for the member function get_element for the class template Pair discussed in the section "Syntax for Class Templates."

8 Give the definition for the constructor with zero arguments for the class template Pair discussed in the subsection "Syntax for Class Templates."

9 Discuss briefly, indicating whether *true* or *false* and justify:

   Friends are used exactly the same for template and nontemplate classes.

CHAPTER SUMMARY

■ Using function templates you can define functions that have a parameter for a type.

■ Using class templates you can define a class with a type parameter for sub-parts of the class.

Answers to Self-Test Exercises

1

Prototype:

```
template<class T>
T maximum(T first, T second);
//Precondition: The operator < is defined for the type T.
//Returns the maximum of first and second.
```

Definition:

```
template<class T>
T maximum(T first, T second)
{
    if (first < second)
        return second;
    else
        return first;
}
```

2

Prototype:

```
template<class T>
T absolute(T value);
//Precondition: The expressions x < 0 and –x are defined
//whenever x is of type T.
//Returns the absolute value of its argument.
```

Definition:
```
template<class T>
T absolute(T value)
{
    if (value < 0)
        return -value;
    else
        return value;
}
```

3 Templates provide a facility to allow the definition of functions and classes that have parameters for type names.

4 d. Any type whether a primitive type (provided by C++) or a type defined by the user (a *class* or *struct* type, an *enum* type, or a typedefined array, or *int*, *float*, *double*, etc.).

5 The prototype and function definition are given below. They are basically identical to those for the versions given in Display 9.11 except that two instances of *int* are changed to T in the parameter list.

Prototype:
```
template<class T>
int search(const T a[], int number_used, T target);
//Precondition: number_used is <= the declared size of a.
//Also, a[0] through a[number_used -1] have values.
//Returns the first index such that a[index] == target,
//provided there is such an index, otherwise returns -1.
```

Definition:
```
template<class T>
int search(const T a[], int number_used, T target)
{

    int index = 0, found = false;
    while ((!found) && (index < number_used))
    if (target == a[index])
        found = true;
    else
        index++;
```

```
        if (found)
            return index;
        else
            return -1;
    }
```

6   Function overloading only works for types for which an overloading is pro-
    vided. Overloading may work for types that automatically convert to some
    type for which an overloading is provided, but may not do what you expect.
    The template solution will work for any type that is defined at the time of
    invocation, provided that the requirements for a definition of < are satisfied.

7

```
    //Uses iostream and cstdlib:
    template<class T>
    T Pair<T>::get_element(int position) const
    {
        if (position == 1)
            return first;
        else if (position == 2)
            return second;
        else
        {
            cout << "Error: Illegal pair position.\n";
            exit(1);
        }
    }
```

8   There are no natural candidates for the default initialization values, so this
    constructor does nothing, but it does allow you to declare (uninitialized)
    objects without giving any constructor arguments.

```
    template<class T>
    Pair<T>::Pair( )
    {
    //Do nothing.
    }
```

9   True. The only difference is the use of

```
    class name<type_argument>
```

    for the name of the class rather than just the class name.

Programming Projects

1 Write a function template for a function that has parameters for a partially filled array and for a value of the base type of the array. If the value is in the partially filled array, then the function returns the index of the first indexed variable that contains the value. If the value is not in the array, the function returns –1. The base type of the array is a type parameter. Notice that you need two parameters to give the partially filled array: one for the array and one for the number of indexed variables used. Also, write a suitable test program to test this function template.

2 Rewrite the definition of the class template List given in Display 13.4 and Display 13.6 so that it is more general. This more general version has the added feature that you can step through the items on the list in order. One item is always the current item. You can ask for the current item, you can change the current item to the next item, you can change the current item to the previous item, you can start at the beginning of the list by making the first item on the list the current item, and you can ask for the nth item on the list. To do this you will add the following members: An additional member variable that records the position on the list of the current item, a member function that returns the current item as a value, a member function that makes the next item the current item, a member function that makes the previous item the current item, a member function that makes the first item on the list the current item, and a member function that returns the nth item on the list given n as an argument. (Number items as in arrays so that the first item is the 0th item, the next is item number 1, and so forth.) Note that there are situations in which some of these function actions are not possible. For example, an empty list has no first item, and there is no item after the last item in any list. Be sure to test for the empty list and handle it appropriately. Be sure to test for the beginning and end of the list and handle these cases appropriately. Write a suitable test program to test this class template.

3 Write a template for a function that has parameters for a list of items and for a possible item on the list. If the item is on the list, then the function returns the position of the first occurrence of that item. If the item is not on the list, the function returns –1. The first position on the list is position 0, the next is position 1, and so forth. The type of the items on the list is a type parameter. Use the class template List that you defined in Project 2. Write a suitable program to test this function template.

4 Write a template version of the iterative binary search from Display 12.8. Specify requirements on the template parameter type. Discuss the requirements on the template parameter type.

5 Write a template version of the recursive binary search from Display 12.6. Specify requirements on the template parameter type. Discuss the requirements on the template parameter type.

CHAPTER

14

Pointers and Linked Lists

14 Pointers and Linked Lists

If somebody there chanced to be
Who loved me in a manner true
My heart would point him out to me
And I would point him out to you.

GILBERT AND SULLIVAN, RUDDIGORE

Introduction

A *linked list* is a list constructed using pointers. A linked list is not fixed in size but can grow and shrink while your program is running. In this chapter we show you how to define and manipulate linked lists, which will serve to introduce you to a new way of using pointers.

14.1 Nodes and Linked Lists

Useful dynamic variables are seldom of a simple type such as *int* or *double*, but are normally of some complex type such as an array, *struct*, or class type. You saw that dynamic variables of an array type can be useful. Dynamic variables of a *struct* or class type can also be useful, but in a different way. Dynamic variables that are either *struct*s or classes normally have one or more member variables that are pointer variables that connect them to other dynamic variables. For example, one such structure, which happens to contain a shopping list, is diagrammed in Display 14.1.

Nodes

node structures

A structure like the one shown in Display 14.1 consists of items which we have drawn as boxes connected by arrows. The boxes are called **nodes** and the arrows represent pointers. Each of the nodes in Display 14.1 contains a cstring, an integer, and a pointer that can point to other nodes of the same type. Note that pointers point

Display 14.1 Nodes and Pointers

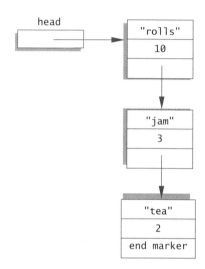

to the entire node, not to the individual items (such as 10 or "rolls") that are inside the node.

    Nodes are implemented in C++ as *struct*s or classes. For example, the *struct* type definitions for a node of the type shown in Display 14.1, along with the type definition for a pointer to such nodes, can be as follows:

node type definition

```
const int STRING_SIZE = 10;

struct ListNode
{
    char item[STRING_SIZE];
    int count;
    ListNode *link;
};

typedef ListNode* ListNodePtr;
```

The order of the type definitions is important. The definition of ListNode must come first, since it is used in the definition of ListNodePtr.

The box labeled head in Display 14.1 is not a node but is a pointer variable that can point to a node. The pointer variable head is declared as follows:

```
ListNodePtr head;
```

Even though we have ordered the type definitions to avoid some illegal forms of circularity, the above definition of the *struct* type ListNode is still blatantly circular. The definition of the type ListNode uses the type name ListNode to define the member variable link. There is nothing wrong with this particular circularity and it is allowed in C++. One indication that this definition is not logically inconsistent is the fact that you can draw pictures, like Display 14.1, that represent such structures.

We now have pointers inside of *struct*s and have these pointers pointing to *struct*s that contain pointers, and so forth. In such situations the syntax can sometimes get involved, but in all cases the syntax follows those few rules we have described for pointers and *struct*s. As an illustration, suppose the declarations are as above, the situation is as diagrammed in Display 14.1 and you want to change the number in the first node from 10 to 12. One way to accomplish this is with the following statement:

changing node data

```
(*head).count = 12;
```

The expression on the left side of the assignment operator may require a bit of explanation. The variable head is a pointer variable. So, the expression *head is the thing it points to, namely the node (dynamic variable) containing "rolls" and the integer 10. This node, referred to by *head, is a *struct*, and the member variable of this *struct*, which contains a value of type *int*, is called count, and so (*head).count is the name of the *int* variable in the first node. The parentheses around *head are not optional. You want the dereferencing operator * to be performed before the dot operator. However, the dot operator has higher precedence than the dereferencing operator *, and so without the parentheses, the dot operator would be performed first (and that would produce an error). In the next paragraph, we will describe a shortcut notation that can avoid this worry about parentheses.

the -> operator

C++ has an operator that can be used with a pointer to simplify the notation for specifying the members of a *struct* or a class. The **arrow operator** -> combines the actions of a dereferencing operator * and a dot operator to specify a member of a dynamic *struct* or object that is pointed to by a given pointer. For example, the above assignment statement for changing the number in the first node can be written more simply as

```
head->count = 12;
```

This assignment statement and the previous one mean the exact same thing, but this one is the form normally used.

Display 14.2 Accessing Node Data

```
head->count = 12;
strcpy(head->item, "bagels");
```

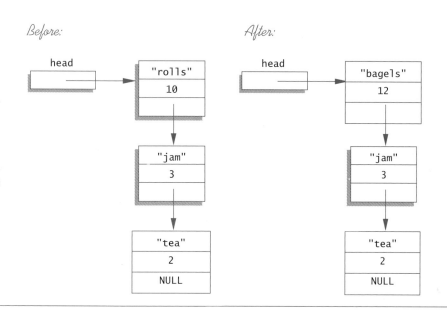

Before: *After:*

The `cstring` in the first node can be changed from `"rolls"` to `"bagels"` with the following statement:

```
strcpy(head->item, "bagels");
```

Remember, you have to use `strcpy` instead of the assignment operator for `cstrings`. The result of these changes to the first node in the list is diagrammed in Display 14.2.

Look at the pointer member in the last node in the lists shown in Display 14.2. This last node has the word NULL written where there should be a pointer. In Display 14.1 we filled this position with the phrase "end marker," but "end marker" is not a C++ expression. In C++ programs we use the constant NULL as an end marker to signal the end of a linked list. This is the same constant NULL that we introduced when we discussed the *new* operator in Chapter 11. As we noted there, the constant NULL is actually the number 0, but it is best to think of it and spell it as NULL, so that it is clear that you mean this special-purpose pointer value.

NULL

The Arrow Operator ->

The arrow operator -> specifies a member of a *struct* (or a member of a class object) that is pointed to by a pointer variable. The syntax is:

Pointer_Variable->Member_Name

The above refers to a member of the *struct* or object pointed to by the *Pointer_Variable*. Which member it refers to is given by the *Member_Name*. For example, suppose you have the following definition:

```
struct Record
{
    int number;
    char grade;
};
```

The following creates a dynamic variable of type Record and sets the member variables of the dynamic *struct* variable to 2001 and 'A':

```
Record *p;
p = new Record;
p->number = 2001;
p->grade = 'A';
```

The pointer NULL is used for a number of different purposes, but most usage falls into one of two overlapping categories. NULL is used to give a value to a pointer variable that otherwise would not have any value. This prevents an inadvertent reference to memory, since NULL is not the address of any memory location. The second category of use is that of an end marker. A program can step through the list of nodes shown in Display 14.2, and when the program reaches the node that contains NULL it knows that it has come to the end of the list.

A pointer can be set to NULL using the assignment operator, as in the following, which declares a pointer variable called there and initializes it to NULL:

```
double *there = NULL;
```

The constant NULL can be assigned to a pointer variable of any pointer type.

SELF-TEST EXERCISES

1   Suppose your program contains the following type definitions:

NULL

NULL is a special constant pointer value that is used to give a value to a pointer variable that would not otherwise have a value. NULL can be assigned to a pointer variable of any type. The identifier NULL is defined in a number of libraries including the library with header file cstddef. With earlier compilers, the operator *new* returned a NULL pointer value whenever *new* failed in its attempt to create a dynamic variable. Current compilers "throw the exception *std::bad alloc*." The effect is to abort the program with an error message.

```
struct Box
{
    char name[20];
    int number;
    Box *next;
};

typedef Box* BoxPtr;
```

What is the output produced by the following code?

```
BoxPtr head;
head = new Box;
strcpy(head->name, "Sally");
head->number = 18;
cout << (*head).name << endl;
cout << head->name << endl;
cout << (*head).number << endl;
cout << head->number << endl;
```

2 Suppose that your program contains the type definitions and code given in Exercise 1. That code creates a node that contains the cstring "Sally" and the number 18. What code would you add in order to set the value of the member variable next of this node equal to NULL?

3 Suppose that your program contains the type definitions and code given in Exercise 1. Assuming that the value of the pointer variable head has not been changed, how can you destroy the dynamic variable pointed to by head and return the memory it uses to the heap so that it can be reused to create other new dynamic variables?

4 Given the structure definition:

```
const int STRING_SIZE = 30;
struct ListNode
{
    char item[STRING_SIZE];
    int count;
    ListNode *link;
};
ListNode *head = new ListNode;
```

Give code to assign the string `"Wilbur's brother Orville"` to the member item of the variable to which `head` points.

Linked Lists

Lists such as those shown in Display 14.2 are called *linked lists*. A **linked list** is a list of nodes in which each node has a member variable that is a pointer that points to the next node in the list. The first node in a linked list is called the **head,** which is why the pointer variable that points to the first node is named `head`. Note that the pointer named `head` is not itself the head of the list but only points to the head of the list. The last node has no special name, but it does have a special property. The last node has NULL as the value of its member pointer variable. To test to see whether a node is the last node you need only test to see if the pointer variable in the node is equal to NULL.

node type definition

Our goal in this section is to write some basic functions for manipulating linked lists. For variety, and to simplify the notation, we will use a simpler type of node than that used in Display 14.2. These nodes will contain only an integer and a pointer. The node and pointer type definitions that we will use are:

```
struct Node
{
    int data;
    Node *link;
};

typedef Node* NodePtr;
```

a one node linked list

As a warm-up exercise, let's see how we might construct the start of a linked list with nodes of this type. We first declare a pointer variable, called `head`, that will point to the head of our linked list:

```
NodePtr head;
```

To create our first node, we use the operator *new* to create a new dynamic variable that will become the first node in our linked list.

```
head = new Node;
```

We then give values to the member variables of this new node:

```
head->data = 3;
head->link = NULL;
```

Notice that the pointer member of this node is set equal to NULL. That is because this node is the last node in the list (as well as the first node in the list). At this stage our linked list looks like this:

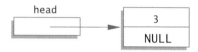

Our one-node list was built in a purely ad hoc way. To have a larger linked list, your program must be able to add nodes in a systematic way. We next describe one simple way to insert nodes in a linked list.

Inserting a Node at the Head of a List

In this subsection we assume that our linked list already contains one or more nodes, and we develop a function to add another node. The first parameter for the insertion function will be a call-by-reference parameter for a pointer variable that points to the head of the linked list, that is, a pointer variable that points to the first node in the linked list. The other parameter will give the number to be stored in the new node. The prototype for our insertion function is as follows:

```
void head_insert(NodePtr& head, int the_number);
```

Linked Lists as Arguments

You should always keep one pointer variable pointing to the head of a linked list. This pointer variable is a way to name the linked list. When you write a function that takes a linked list as an argument, this pointer (that points to the head of the linked list) can be used as the linked list argument.

To insert a new node into the linked list, our function will use the *new* operator to create a new node. The data is then copied into the new node and the new node is inserted at the head of the list. When we insert nodes this way, the new node will be the first node in the list (i.e., the head node), rather than the last node. Since dynamic variables have no names, we must use a local pointer variable to point to this node. If we call the local pointer variable `temp_ptr`, the new node can be referred to as `*temp_ptr`. The complete process can be summarized as follows:

algorithm

Pseudocode for `head_insert` function:

1 Create a new dynamic variable pointed to by `temp_ptr`. (This new dynamic variable is the new node. This new node can be referred to as `*temp_ptr`.)

2 Place the data in this new node.

3 Make the `link` member of this new node point to the head node (first node) of the original linked list.

4 Make the pointer variable named `head` point to the new node.

Display 14.3 contains a diagram of this algorithm. Steps 2 and 3 can be expressed by the C++ assignment statements given below:

```
temp_ptr->link = head;
head = temp_ptr;
```

The complete function definition is given in Display 14.4.

You will want to allow for the possibility that a list contains nothing. For example, a shopping list might have nothing in it because there is nothing to buy this week. A list with nothing in it is called an **empty list.** A linked list is named by naming a pointer that points to the head of the list, but an empty list has no head node. To specify an empty list you use the pointer NULL. If the pointer variable `head` is supposed to point to the head node of a linked list and you want to indicate that the list is empty, then you set the value of `head` as follows:

empty list

```
head = NULL;
```

Whenever you design a function for manipulating a linked list, you should always check to see if it works on the empty list. If it does not, you may be able to add a special case for the empty list. If you cannot design the function to apply to the empty list, then your program must be designed to handle empty lists some other way or to avoid them completely. Fortunately, the empty list can often be treated just like any other list. For example, the function `head_insert` in Display 14.4 was designed with nonempty lists as the model, but a check will show that it works for the empty list as well.

Display 14.3 Adding a Node to a Linked List

Set up new node:

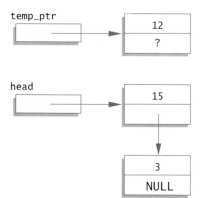

`temp_ptr->link = head;`

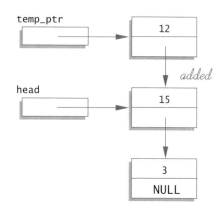

`head = temp_ptr;`

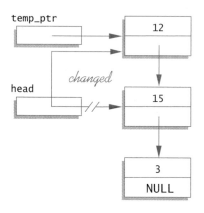

After function call:

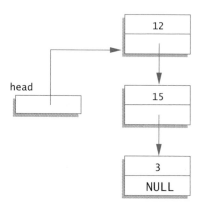

Display 14.4   Function to Add a Node at the Head of a Linked List

Prototype

```
struct Node
{
    int data;
    Node *link;
};

typedef Node* NodePtr;

void head_insert(NodePtr& head, int the_number);
//Precondition: The pointer variable head points to
//the head of a linked list.
//Postcondition: A new node containing the_number
//has been added at the head of the linked list.
```

Function Definition

```
//Uses cstddef:
void head_insert(NodePtr& head, int the_number)
{
    NodePtr temp_ptr;
    temp_ptr = new Node;

    temp_ptr->data = the_number;

    temp_ptr->link = head;
    head = temp_ptr;
}
```

⬢ PITFALL   Losing Nodes

You might be tempted to write the function definition for head_insert (Display 14.4) using the pointer variable head to construct the new node, instead of using the local pointer variable temp_ptr. If you were to try, you might start the function as follows:

```
head = new Node;
head->data = the_number;
```

At this point the new node is constructed, contains the correct data and is pointed to by the pointer head, all as it is supposed to be. All that is left to do is to attach the rest of the list to this node by setting the pointer member given below so that it points to what was formerly the first node of the list:

```
head->link
```

Display 14.5 shows the situation when the new data value is 12. That illustration reveals the problem. If you were to proceed in this way, there would be nothing pointing to the node containing 15. Since there is no named pointer pointing to it (or to a chain of pointers ending with that node), there is no way the program can reference this node. The node below this node is also lost. A program cannot make a pointer point to either of these nodes, nor can it access the data in these nodes, nor can it do anything else to the nodes. It simply has no way to refer to the nodes. Such an effect ties up memory for the duration of the program. A program that loses nodes is sometimes said to have a "memory leak." A significant memory leak can result in the program running out of memory, causing abnormal termination. Worse, a memory leak (lost nodes) in an ordinary users' program can cause the operating system to crash. To avoid such lost nodes, the program must always keep some pointer pointing to the head of the list, usually the pointer in a pointer variable like head.

Searching a Linked List

Next we will design a function to search a linked list in order to locate a particular node. We will use the same node type, called Node, that we used in the previous sub-sections. (The definition of the node and pointer types are given in Display 14.4.) The function we design will have two arguments: the linked lists and the integer we

Display 14.5 Lost Nodes

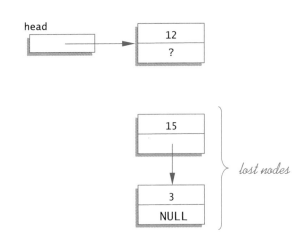

want to locate. The function will return a pointer that points to the first node that contains that integer. If no node contains the integer, the function will return the pointer NULL. This way our program can test to see whether the integer is on the list by checking to see if the function returns a pointer value that is not equal to NULL. The prototype and header comment for our function is as follows:

```
NodePtr search(NodePtr head, int target);
//Precondition: The pointer head points to the head of a linked
//list.
//The pointer variable in the last node is NULL.
//If the list is empty, then head is NULL.
//Returns a pointer that points to the first node that contains the
//target. If no node contains the target, the function returns NULL.
```

We will use a local pointer variable, called here, to move through the list looking for the target. The only way to move around a linked list, or any other data structure made up of nodes and pointers, is to follow the pointers. So we will start with here pointing to the first node and move the pointer from node to node following the pointer out of each node. This technique is diagrammed in Display 14.6. Since empty lists present some minor problems that would clutter our discussion, we

Display 14.6 Searching a Linked List

target *is* 6

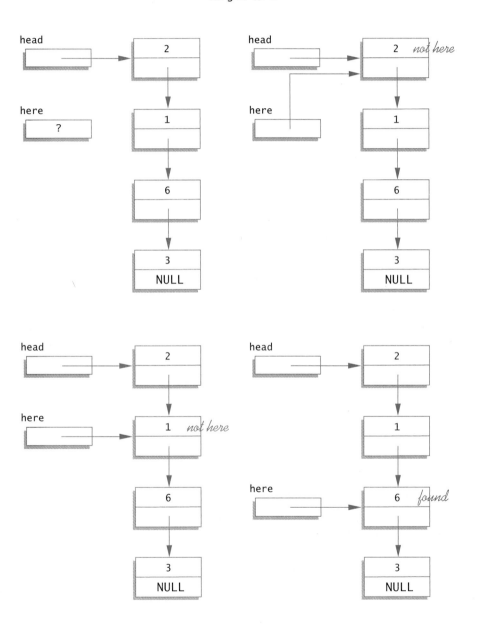

will at first assume that the linked list contains at least one node. Later we will come back and make sure the algorithm works for the empty list as well. This search technique yields the following algorithm:

algorithm

Pseudocode for search function:

Make the pointer variable here point to the head node (i.e., first node) of the linked list.

```
while (here is not pointing to a node containing target
                    and here is not pointing to the last node)
{
    Make here point to the next node in the list.
}
if (the node pointed to by here contains target)
    return here;
else
    return NULL;
```

In order to move the pointer here to the next node, we must think in terms of the named pointers we have available. The next node is the one pointed to by the pointer member of the node currently pointed to by here. The pointer member of the node currently pointed to by here is given by the expression:

```
here->link
```

To move here to the next node, we want to change here so that it points to the node that is pointed to by the above-named pointer (member) variable. Hence, the following will move the pointer here to the next node in the list:

```
here = here->link;
```

Putting these pieces together yields the following refinement of the algorithm pseudocode:

algorithm refinement

Preliminary version of the code for the search function:

```
here = head;
while (here->data != target &&
                        here->link != NULL)
    here = here->link;
if (here->data == target)
    return here;
else
    return NULL;
```

Notice the Boolean expression in the *while*-statement. We test to see if here is pointing to the last node by testing to see if the member variable here->link is equal to NULL.

We still must go back and take care of the empty list. If we check the above code we find that there is a problem with the empty list. If the list is empty, then here is equal to NULL and hence the following expressions are undefined:

empty list

```
here->data
here->link
```

When here is NULL, it is not pointing to any node, so there is no member named data nor any member named link. Hence, we make a special case of the empty list. The complete function definition is given in Display 14.7.

Inserting and Removing Nodes Inside a List

We next design a function to insert a node at a specified place in a linked list. If you want the nodes in some particular order, such as numeric order or alphabetical order, you cannot simply insert the node at the beginning or end of the list. We will therefore design a function to insert a node after a specified node in the linked list. We assume that some other function or program part has correctly placed a pointer called after_me pointing to some node in the linked list. We want the new node to be placed after the node pointed to by after_me, as illustrated in Display 14.8. The same technique works for nodes with any kind of data, but to be concrete, we are using the same type of nodes as in previous subsections. The type definitions are given in Display 14.7. The prototype for the function we want to define is given below:

inserting in the middle of a list

```
void insert(NodePtr after_me, int the_number);
//Precondition: after_me points to a node in a linked list.
//Postcondition: A new node containing the_number
//has been added after the node pointed to by after_me.
```

A new node is set up the same way it was in the function head_insert in Display 14.4. The difference between this function and that one is that we now wish to insert the node not at the head of the list but after the node pointed to by after_me. The way to do this is shown in Display 14.8 and is expressed as follows in C++ code:

```
//add a link from the new node to the list:
temp_ptr->link = after_me->link;
//add a link from the list to the new node:
after_me->link = temp_ptr;
```

Display 14.7 Function to Locate a Node in a Linked List

Prototype

```
struct Node
{
    int data;
    Node *link;
};


typedef Node* NodePtr;


NodePtr search(NodePtr head, int target);
//Precondition: The pointer head points to the head of a
//linked list.
//The pointer variable in the last node is NULL.
//If the list is empty, then head is NULL.
//Returns a pointer that points to the first node that
//contains the target. If no node contains the target,
//the function returns NULL.
```

Function Definition

```
//Uses cstddef:
NodePtr search(NodePtr head, int target)
{
    NodePtr here = head;

    if (here == NULL)
    {
        return NULL;                          empty list case
    }
    else
    {
        while (here->data != target &&
                              here->link != NULL)
            here = here->link;

        if (here->data == target)
            return here;
        else
            return NULL;
    }
}
```

Display 14.8 Inserting in the Middle of a Linked List

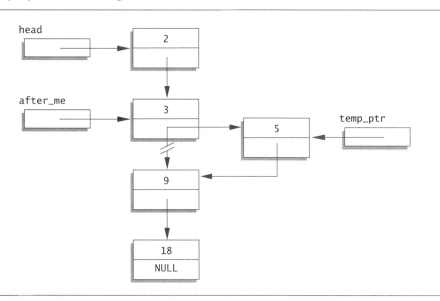

The order of these two assignment statements is critical. In the first assignment we want the pointer value `after_me->link` *before it is changed.* The complete function is given in Display 14.9.

insertion at the ends

If you go through the code for the function `insert` you will see that it works correctly even if the node pointed to by `after_me` is the last node in the list. However, `insert` will not work for inserting a node at the beginning of a linked list. The function `head_insert` given in Display 14.4 can be used to insert a node at the beginning of a list.

comparison to arrays

By using the function `insert` you can maintain a linked list in numerical order or alphabetical order or other ordering. You can "squeeze" a new node into the correct position by simply adjusting two pointers. This is true no matter how long the linked list is or where in the list you want the new data to go. If you instead used an array, much, and in extreme cases all, of the array would have to be copied in order to make room for a new value in the correct spot. Despite the overhead involved in positioning the pointer `after_me`, inserting into a linked list is frequently more efficient than inserting into an array.

removing a node

Removing a node from a linked list is also quite easy. Display 14.10 illustrates the method. Once the pointers `before` and `discard` have been positioned, all that is required to remove the node is the following statement:

```
before->link = discard->link;
```

Display 14.9 Function to Add a Node in the Middle of a Linked List

Prototype

```
struct Node
{
    int data;
    Node *link;
};

typedef Node* NodePtr;

void insert(NodePtr after_me, int the_number);
//Precondition: after_me points to a node in a linked
//list.
//Postcondition: A new node containing the_number
//has been added after the node pointed to by after_me.
```

Function Definition

```
//Uses cstddef:
void insert(NodePtr after_me, int the_number)
{
    NodePtr temp_ptr;
    temp_ptr = new Node;

    temp_ptr->data = the_number;

    temp_ptr->link = after_me->link;
    after_me->link = temp_ptr;
}
```

Display 14.10 Removing a Node

1   *position the pointer* discard *so that it points to the node to be deleted and position the pointer* before *so that it points to the node before the one to be deleted.*

2   `before->link = discard->link;`

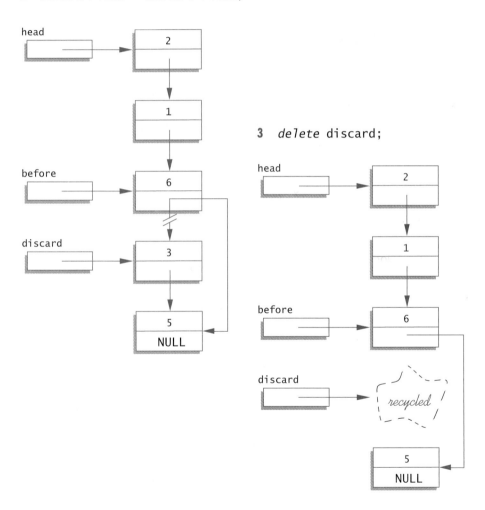

3   *delete* discard;

This is sufficient to remove the node from the linked list. However, if you are not using this node for something else, you should destroy the node and return the memory it uses to the heap; you can do this with a call to *delete* as follows:

    delete discard;

◆ *PITFALL*   **Using the Assignment Operator with Dynamic Data Structures**

If `head1` and `head2` are pointer variables and `head1` points to the head node of a linked list, the following will make `head2` point to the same head node and hence the same linked list:

    head2 = head1;

However, you must remember that there is only one linked list, not two. If you change the linked list pointed to by `head1`, then you will also change the linked list pointed to by `head2`, because they are the same linked lists.

If `head1` points to a linked list and you want `head2` to point to a second, identical *copy* of this linked list, the above assignment statement will not work. Instead, you must copy the entire linked list node by node. Alternatively, you can overload the assignment operator = so that it means whatever you want it to mean. Overloading = is discussed in the optional subsection of Chapter 11 entitled "Overloading the Assignment Operator."

SELF-TEST EXERCISES

5 Write type definitions for the nodes and pointers in a linked list. Call the node type `NodeType` and call the pointer type `PointerType`. The linked lists will be lists of letters.

6 A linked list is normally given by giving a pointer that points to the first node in the list, but an empty list has no first node. What pointer value is normally used to represent an empty list?

7 Suppose your program contains the following type definitions and pointer variable declarations:

    struct Node
    {
        double data;

```
    Node *next;
};

typedef Node* Pointer;
Pointer p1, p2;
```

Suppose p1 points to a node of the above type which is on a linked list. Write code that will make p1 point to the next node on this linked list. (The pointer p2 is for the next exercise and has nothing to do with this exercise.)

8 Suppose your program contains type definitions and pointer variable declarations as in Self-Test Exercise 7. Suppose further that p2 points to a node of the above type which is on a linked list and which is not the last node on the list. Write code that will delete the node *after* the node pointed to by p2. After this code is executed, the linked list should be the same, except that there will be one less node on the linked list. Hint: You may want to declare another pointer variable to use.

9 Choose an answer, and explain:

For a large array and large list holding the same type objects, inserting a new object at a known location into the middle of a linked list compared to insertion in an array is

a. more efficient.

b. less efficient.

c. about the same.

d. depends on the size of the two lists.

14.2 A Linked List Application

But many who are first now will be last,
and many who are last now will be first.

THE NEW TESTAMENT GOSPELS, MATTHEW 19:30

There are many applications of linked lists. In this section we will give you only a small sample of what they can be used for. We will present one *class* definition that uses a linked list as the heart of its implementation.

Stacks

A stack is a data structure that retrieves data in the reverse of the order in which the data is stored. Suppose you place the letters 'A', 'B', and then 'C' in a stack. When you take these letters out of the stack, they will be removed in the order 'C', then 'B', and then 'A'. This use of a stack is diagrammed in Display 14.11. As shown there, you can think of a stack as a hole in the ground. In order to get something out of the stack, you must first remove the items on top of the one you want. For this reason a stack is often called a *last-in/first-out* data structure.

Stacks are used for many language processing tasks. In Chapter 12 we discussed how the computer system uses a stack to keep track of C++ function calls. However, here we will do only one very simple application. Our goal in this example is to show you how you can use the linked list techniques to implement specific data structures and a stack is one simple example of the use of linked lists.

■)) *PROGRAMMING* EXACT *EXAMPLE*
A Stack ADT

The interface for our stack ADT is given in Display 14.12. This particular stack is used to store data of type *char*. You can define a similar stack to store data of any other type. There are two basic operations you can perform on a stack: adding an item to the stack and removing an item from the stack. Adding an item is called *pushing* the item onto the stack, and so we called the member function that does this push. Removing an item from a stack is called *popping* the item off the stack, and so we called the member function that does this pop.

The names push and pop derive from another way of visualizing a stack. A stack is analogous to a mechanism that is sometimes used to hold plates in a cafeteria. The mechanism stores plates in a hole in the countertop. There is a spring underneath the plates with its tension adjusted so that only the top plate protrudes above the countertop. If this sort of mechanism were used as a stack data structure, the data would be written on plates (which might violate some health laws, but still makes a good analogy). To add a plate to the stack, you put it on top of the other plates, and the weight of this new plate *pushes* down the spring. When you remove a plate, the plate below it *pops* into view.

Display 14.13 shows a simple program that illustrates how the stack ADT is used. This program reads a word one letter at a time and places the letters in a stack. The program then removes the letters one by one and writes them to the screen. Because data is removed from a stack in the reverse of the order in which it enters the stack, the output shows the word written backward.

Display 14.11 A Stack

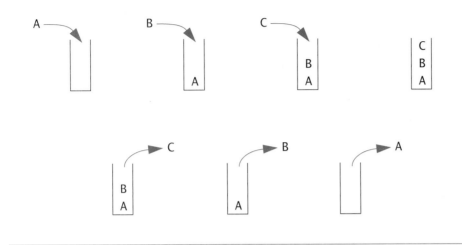

As shown in Display 14.14, our stack ADT is implemented as a linked list in which the head of the list serves as the top of the stack. The member variable `top` is a pointer that points to the head of the linked list.

implementation

Writing the definition of the member function `push` is Self-Test Exercise 10. However, we have already given the algorithm for this task. The code for the `push` member function is essentially the same as the function `head_insert` shown in Display 14.4, except that in the member function `push` we use a pointer named `top` in place of a pointer named `head`.

An empty stack is just an empty linked list, so an empty stack is implemented by setting the pointer `top` equal to NULL. Once you realize that NULL represents the empty stack, the implementations of the default constructor and of the member function `empty` are obvious.

default constructor

The definition of the copy constructor is a bit complicated but does not use any techniques we have not already discussed. The details are left to Self-Test Exercise 11.

copy constructor

The `pop` member function first checks to see if the stack is empty. If the stack is not empty, it proceeds to remove the top character in the stack. It sets the local variable `result` equal to the top symbol on the stack. That is done as follows:

pop

```
char result = top->data;
```

Display 14.12   Interface File for a Stack Class

```
//This is the HEADER FILE stack.h. This is the INTERFACE for the class Stack,
//which is an ADT for a stack of symbols.
#ifndef STACK_H
#define STACK_H
namespace savitchstack
{
    struct StackFrame
    {
        char data;
        StackFrame *link;
    };

    typedef StackFrame* StackFramePtr;

    class Stack
    {
    public:
        Stack();
        //Initializes the object to an empty stack.

        Stack(const Stack& a_stack);
        //Copy constructor.

        ~Stack();
        //Destroys the stack and returns all the memory to the heap.

        void push(char the_symbol);
        //Postcondition: the_symbol has been added to the stack.

        char pop();
        //Precondition: The stack is not empty.
        //Returns the top symbol on the stack and removes that
        //top symbol from the stack.

        bool empty() const;
        //Returns true if the stack is empty. Returns false otherwise.
    private:
        StackFramePtr top;
    };
}//savitchstack

#endif //STACK_H
```

Display 14.13 Program Using the Stack ADT (part 1 of 2)

```
//Program to demonstrate use of the Stack ADT.
#include <iostream>
#include "stack.h"
using namespace std;
using namespace savitchstack;

int main( )
{
    Stack s;
    char next, ans;

    do
    {
        cout << "Enter a word: ";
        cin.get(next);
        while (next != '\n')
        {
            s.push(next);
            cin.get(next);
        }

        cout << "Written backward that is: ";
        while ( ! s.empty( ) )
            cout << s.pop( );
        cout << endl;

        cout << "Again?(y/n): ";
        cin >> ans;
        cin.ignore(10000, '\n');
    }while (ans != 'n' && ans != 'N');

    return 0;
}

//The ignore member of cin is discussed in Chapter 10. It discards input remaining
//on the current input line up to 10,000 characters or until a return is entered.
//It also discards the return ('\n') at the end of the line.
```

Display 14.13 Program Using the Stack ADT *(part 2 of 2)*

Sample Dialogue

```
Enter a word: straw
Written backward that is: warts
Again?(y/n): y
Enter a word: C++
Written backward that is: ++C
Again?(y/n): n
```

Display 14.14 Implementation of the Stack ADT *(part 1 of 2)*

```cpp
//This is the IMPLEMENTATION FILE stack.cxx.
//This is the IMPLEMENTATION of the class Stack.
//The interface for the class Stack is in the header file stack.h.
#include <iostream>
#include <cstddef>
#include "stack.h"
using namespace std;

namespace savitchstack
{
    //Uses cstddef:
    Stack::Stack()
    {
        top = NULL;
    }

    Stack::Stack(const Stack& a_stack)
        <The definition of the copy constructor is Self-Test Exercise 11.>
```

Display 14.14 Implementation of the Stack ADT *(part 2 of 2)*

```
Stack::~Stack( )
{
    char next;
    while (! empty( ))
        next = pop( );//pop calls delete.
}


//Uses cstddef:
bool Stack::empty( ) const
{
    return (top == NULL);
}


void Stack::push(char the_symbol)
  <The rest of the definition is Self-Test Exercise 10.>

//Uses iostream:
char Stack::pop( )
{
    if (empty( ))
    {
        cout << "Error: popping an empty stack.\n";
        exit(1);
    }

    char result = top->data;

    StackFramePtr temp_ptr;
    temp_ptr = top;
    top = top->link;

    delete temp_ptr;

    return result;
}
}//savitchstack
```

After the symbol in the top node is saved in the variable `result`, the pointer `top` is moved to the next node on the linked list, effectively removing the top node from the list. The pointer `top` is moved with the statement:

```
top = top->link;
```

However, before the pointer `top` is moved, a temporary pointer, called `temp_ptr`, is positioned so that it points to the node that is about to be removed from the list. The node can then be removed with the following call to *delete*:

```
delete temp_ptr;
```

destructor

Each node that is removed from the linked list by the member function `pop` is destroyed with a call to *delete*. So all that the destructor needs to do is remove each item from the stack with a call to `pop`. Each node will then have its memory returned to the heap.

SELF-TEST EXERCISES

10 Give the definition of the member function `push` of the class `Stack` described in Display 14.12.

11 Give the definition of the copy constructor for the class `Stack` described in Display 14.12.

CHAPTER SUMMARY

- A **node** is a *struct* or class object that has one or more member variables that are pointer variables. These nodes can be connected by their member pointer variables to produce data structures that can grow and shrink in size while your program is running.

- A linked list is a list of nodes in which each node contains a pointer to the next node in the list.

- The end of a linked list is indicated by setting the pointer member variable equal to NULL.

Answers to Self-Test Exercises

1
```
Sally
Sally
18
18
```

Note that `(*head).name` and `head->name` mean the same thing. Similarly, `(*head).number` and `head->number` mean the same thing.

2 The best answer is

```
head->next = NULL;
```

However, the following is also correct:

```
(*head).next = NULL;
```

3 `delete head;`

4 `strcpy(head->item, "Wilbur's brother Orville");`

5

```
struct NodeType
{
    char data;
    NodeType *link;
};

typedef NodeType* PointerType;
```

6 The pointer value `NULL` is used to indicate an empty list.

7 `p1 = p1-> next;`

8

```
Pointer discard;
discard = p2->next;//discard points to the node to be deleted.
p2->next = discard->next;
```

This is sufficient to delete the node from the linked list. However, if you are not using this node for something else, you should destroy the node with call to *delete* as follows:

```
delete discard;
```

9 a. Inserting a new item at a known location into a large linked list is more efficient than inserting into a large array. If you are inserting into a list, you have about five operations, most of which are pointer assignments, regardless of the list size. If you insert into an array, on the average you have to move about half the array entries to insert a data item.

For small lists, the answer is c, about the same.

10

```
//Uses cstddef:
void Stack::push(char the_symbol)
{
    StackFramePtr temp_ptr;
    temp_ptr = new StackFrame;

    temp_ptr->data = the_symbol;

    temp_ptr->link = top;
    top = temp_ptr;
}
```

11

```
//Uses cstddef:
Stack::Stack(const Stack& a_stack)
{
    if (a_stack.top == NULL)
        top = NULL;
    else
    {
        StackFramePtr temp = a_stack.top;//temp moves
            //through the nodes from top to bottom of
            //a_stack.
        StackFramePtr end;//Points to end of the new stack.

        end = new StackFrame;
        end->data = temp->data;
        top = end;
        //First node created and filled with data.
        //New nodes are now added AFTER this first node.
```

```
        temp = temp->link;
        while (temp != NULL)
        {
            end->link = new StackFrame;
            end = end->link;
            end->data = temp->data;
            temp = temp->link;
        }
        end->link = NULL;
    }
}
```

Programming Projects

1 Write a *void*-function that takes a linked list of integers and reverses the order of its nodes. The function will have one call-by-reference parameter that is a pointer to the head of the list. After the function is called this pointer will point to the head of a linked list that has the same nodes as the original list, but in the reverse of the order they had in the original list. Note that your function will neither create nor destroy any nodes. It will simply rearrange nodes. Place your function in a suitable test program.

2 Write a function called merge_lists that takes two call-by-reference arguments that are pointer variables that point to the heads of linked lists of values of type *int*. The two linked lists are assumed to be sorted so the number at the head is the smallest number, the number in the next node is the next smallest, and so forth. The function returns a pointer to the head of a new linked list that contains all of the nodes in the original two lists. The nodes in this longer list are also sorted from smallest to largest values. Note that your function will neither create nor destroy any nodes. When the function call ends, the two pointer variable arguments should have the value NULL.

3 Design and implement a class that is an ADT for polynomials. The polynomial

$$a_n x^n + a_{n-1} x^{n-1} + \ldots + a_0$$

will be implemented as a linked list. Each node will contain an *int* value for the power of x and an *int* value for the corresponding coefficient. The ADT operations should include addition, subtraction, multiplication, and evaluation of a polynomial. Overload the operators +, −, and * for addition, subtraction, and multiplication. Evaluation of a polynomial is implemented as a member function with one argument of type *int*. The evaluation member function returns the value obtained by plugging in its argument for x and performing the indicated operations. Include four constructors: a default constructor, a copy constructor, a constructor with a single argument of type *int* that produces the polynomial that has only one constant term that is equal to the constructor argument, and a constructor with two arguments of type *int* that produces the one-term polynomial whose coefficient and exponent are given by the two arguments. (In the above notation the polynomial produced by the one argument constructor is of the simple form consisting of only a_0. The polynomial produced by the two-argument constructor is of the slightly more complicated form $a_n x^n$.) Include a suitable destructor. Include member functions to input and output polynomials. When the user inputs a polynomial, the user types in the following:

```
aₙx^n + aₙ₋₁x^n–1 +...+ a₀
```

However, if a coefficient a_i is zero, the user may omit the term $a_i x^ i$. For example, the polynomial

$$3x^4 + 7x^2 + 5$$

can be input as

```
3x^4 + 7x^2 + 5
```

It could also be input as

```
3x^4 + 0x^3 + 7x^2 + 0x^1 + 5
```

If a coefficient is negative, a minus sign is used in place of a plus sign, as in the following examples:

```
3x^5 – 7x^3 + 2x^1 – 8
–7x^4 + 5x^2 + 9
```

A minus sign at the front of the polynomial, as in the second of the above two examples, applies only to the first coefficient; it does not negate the entire polynomial. Polynomials are output in the same format. In the case of output, the terms with zero coefficients are not output. To simplify input you can assume that polynomials are always entered one per line and that there will always be a constant term a_0. If there is no constant term, the user enters zero for the constant term as in the following:

```
12x^8 + 3x^2 + 0
```

4   Refer to Programming Project 9 from Chapter 9. Redo this project, using a linked list instead of a dynamic array. As noted there, this is a linked list of

double items. This fact may imply changes in some of the member functions. The members are: a default constructor; an insertion member: add_item; a test for a full list: *bool* full(); and a *friend* function overloading the insertion operator.

5   A harder version of Programming Project 4 would be to write a *class* List, similar to Project 4, with the following members:

> default constructor, List();
>
> *double* List::front(); that returns the first item in the list.
>
> *double* List::back(); that returns the last item in the list.
>
> *double* List::current(); that returns the "current" item.
>
> *void* List::advance(); that advances the item that current() returns.
>
> *void* List::reset(); to make current() return the first item in the list.
>
> *void* List::insert(*double* after_me, *double* insert_me); that inserts insert_me into the list after after_me, and, incidentally, increments the *private:* variable count.
>
> *int* size(); that returns the number items in the list, and, finally:
>
> *friend* istream& *operator*<< (istream& ins, *double* write_me);.

The private data members should include the following:

```
node* head;
node* current;
int count;
```

You will need a struct (outside the list class) for the linked list nodes:

```
struct node
{
    double item;
    node *next;
}
```

Incremental development is essential to all projects of any size, and this is no exception. Write the definition for *class* List, but *do not implement any members yet.* Place this *class* definition in a file list.h. Then #include "list.h" in a file that contains *int* main(){}. Compile your file. This will find syntax errors and many typographical errors that will cause untold difficulty if you attempt to implement members without this check. Then you should implement and compile *one member at a time,* until you have enough to write test code in your main function.

6 A harder version of this Programming Project 5 is to use templates (Chapter 13) to allow lists of any type object. Note the requirements that your implementation demands of the template parameter type. Test your list with a `struct` such as this:

```
struct person
{
    string name;
    string phoneNumber;
};
```

CHAPTER

15

Inheritance

15 Inheritance

With all appliances and means to boot.

William Shakespeare, King Henry IV, Part III

Introduction

Object-oriented programming is a popular and powerful programming technique. Among other things, it provides for a new dimension of abstraction known as **inheritance**. This means that a very general form of a class can be defined and compiled. Later more specialized versions of that class may be defined and can inherit all the properties of the previous class. Provisions for **object-oriented programming** were a part of the initial design of C++, and facilities for inheritance are available in all versions of C++.

The first section of this chapter, 15.1 which covers the basics of inheritance, does not depend in any way on the material in Chapters 11–14. This section can be covered whether or not you have read those chapters.

Section 15.2 provides an introduction to polymorphic functions through virtual functions. Further, Section 15.2 deals with accessing member functions through pointers and dynamic binding. Hence, Chapters 11 and 14 should be covered before covering Section 15.2.

15.1 Inheritance Basics

If there is anything that we wish to change in the child, we should first examine it and see whether it is not something that could better be changed in ourselves.

CARL GUSTAV JUNG, THE INTEGRATION OF THE PERSONALITY

One of the most powerful features of C++ is the use of inheritance to derive one class from another. Inheritance is the process by which a new class—known as a **derived class**—is created from another class, called the **base class.** A derived class automatically has all the member variables and functions that the base class has, and can have additional member functions and/or additional member variables.

In Chapter 5, we noted that to say that class D is derived from another class B means that class D has all the features of class B and some extra, added features as well. When a class D is derived from a class B, we say that B is the base class and D is the derived class. We also say that D is the **child class** and B is the **parent class**.[1]

For example, we discussed the fact that the predefined class ifstream is derived from the (predefined) class istream by adding member functions such as open and close. The stream cin belongs to the class of all input streams (i.e., the class istream), but it does not belong to the class of input-file streams (i.e., does not belong to ifstream), partly because it lacks the member functions open and close of the derived class ifstream.

Derived Classes

Suppose we are designing a record-keeping program that has records for salaried employees and hourly employees. There is a natural hierarchy for grouping these classes. These are all classes of people who share the property of being employees.

Employees who are paid an hourly wage are one subset of employees. Another subset consists of employees who are paid a fixed wage each week. Although the program may not need any type corresponding to the set of all employees, thinking in terms of the more general concept of employees can be useful. For example, all employees have names, and the member functions for initializing and changing names will be the same for salaried and hourly employees.

Within C++ you can define a class type called Employee that includes all employees, whether salaried or hourly, and then use this class to define classes for hourly employees and salaried employees. (We could add temporary, permanent, professional, and administrator employees as well as others, but will leave some of that for the exercises.)

The class Employee also contains member functions that manipulate the data fields of the class Employee. Displays 15.1 and 15.2 show one possible definition for the class Employee.

You can have an (undifferentiated) Employee object, but our reason for defining the class Employee is so that we can define derived classes for different kinds of employees. In particular, the functions print_check will always have its definition changed in derived classes so that different kinds of employees can have different kinds of checks. This is reflected in the definition of the function print_check for the class Employee (Display 15.2). It makes little sense to print a check for such an (undifferentiated) Employee. We know nothing about this employee. Consequently we implemented the function print_check of the class Employee so that the program stops with an error message if print_check is called for a base class

---

[1] Some authors speak of a subclass D and superclass B instead of derived class D and base class B. However we have found the terms derived class and base class to be less confusing. We only mention this in an effort to help you to read other texts.

Display 15.1 Interface for the Base Class Employee

```
//This is the HEADER FILE employee.h.
//This is the INTERFACE for the class Employee.
//This is primarily intended to be used as a base class to derive
//classes for different kinds of employees.
#ifndef EMPLOYEE_H
#define EMPLOYEE_H

#include <string>
using namespace std;

namespace savitchemployees
{

    class Employee
    {
    public:
        Employee();
        Employee(string new_name, string new_ssn);
        string get_name();
        string get_ssn();
        void change_name(string new_name);
        void change_ssn(string new_ssn);
        void print_check();
        void give_raise(double amount);
    protected:
        string name;
        string ssn;
        double net_pay;
    };

}//savitchemployees

#endif //EMPLOYEE_H
```

Display 15.2 Implementation for the Base Classes Employee *(part 1 of 2)*

```
//This is the IMPLEMENTATION FILE: employee.cxx
//This is the IMPLEMENTATION for the class Employee.
//The interface for the class Employee is in the header file employee.h.
#include <iostream>
#include <string>
#include <cstdlib>
#include "employee.h"
using namespace std;

namespace savitchemployees
{

    Employee::Employee() // default is to fetch data from keyboard
    {
        cout << "Enter employee name, followed by return.:\n";
        getline(cin, name);
        cout<< endl << "Enter employee social security number,"
            << " followed by return.:\n";
        getline(cin, ssn);
        cin.ignore(10000, '\n');
        cout << endl;
    }

    Employee::Employee(string new_name, string new_number) :
        name(new_name), ssn(new_number) //initializer list
    {
        //deliberately empty
    }

    string Employee::get_name()
    {
        return name;
    }
```

If the member function ignore *is not familiar to you, see the section on the* ignore *member function in Chapter 10.*

Display 15.2 Implementation for Classes Employee *(part 2 of 2)*

```
string Employee::get_ssn()
{
    return ssn;
}

void Employee::change_name(string new_name)
{
    name = new_name;
}

void Employee::change_ssn (string new_ssn)
{
    ssn = new_ssn;
}

void Employee::print_check()
{
    cout<< "\nERROR: print_check FUNCTION CALLED FOR AN \n"
        << "UNDIFFERENTIATED EMPLOYEE. Aborting the program.\n"
        << "Check with the author of the program about this bug.\n";
    exit(1);
}

void Employee::give_raise(double amount)
{
    cout << "\nERROR: give_raise FUNCTION CALLED FOR AN \n"
        << "UNDIFFERENTIATED EMPLOYEE. Aborting the program.\n"
        << "Check with the author of the program about this bug.\n";
    exit(1);
}

}//savitchemployees
```

Employee object. As you will see, derived classes will have enough information to redefine the function print_check to produce meaningful employee checks.

A class that is derived from the class Employee will automatically have the all the member variables of the class Employee (name, ssn, and net_pay). A class that is derived from the class Employee will also have all the member functions of the class Employee, such as print_check, get_name, change_name, give_raise, and the other member functions listed in Display 15.1. This is usually expressed by saying that the derived class **inherits** the member variables and member functions.

Notice that we have used the keyword *protected* where you might expect *private*. A *protected* member is the same as a *private* member to any other class except a class derived from the base class (or derived from a class derived from the base class, etc). For example, a derived class of the class employee inherits the member variables name, ssn, and net_pay and can access them directly. More precisely, any class that is derived from the class Employee, derived from a class derived from the class Employee, or derived from Employee by some longer chain of "derived from" can directly access these protected variables in the derived classes' function definitions. However, to any other classes these member variables are treated as if they were marked *private*.

protected

The member function give_raise and print_check that belongs to the class Employee need to be implemented differently in the derived classes. We compute wages and print checks differently for salaried employees than we do for hourly employees. So we must redefine these two functions when we defined derived classes of the class Employee for different kinds of employees.

The interface files with the class definitions of two derived classes of the class Employee are given in Displays 15.3 (HourlyEmployee) and 15.4 (SalariedEmployee). We have placed the class Employee and the two derived classes in the same namespace. C++ does not require that they be in the same namespace, but since they are related classes, it makes sense to put them in the same namespace. We will first discuss the derived class HourlyEmployee given in Display 15.3.

Note that the definition of a derived class begins like any other class definition but adds a colon, the reserved word *public*, and the name of base class to the first line of the class definition, as in the following (from Display 15.3):

```
class HourlyEmployee : public Employee
{
```

The derived class (such as HourlyEmployee) automatically receives all the member variables and member functions of the base class (such as Employee) and it can add additional member variables and member functions.

Display 15.3 Interface for the Derived Class HourlyEmployee

```
//This is the HEADER FILE hourlyemployee.h.
//This is the INTERFACE for the class HourlyEmployee.
#ifndef HOURLYEMPLOYEE_H
#define HOURLYEMPLOYEE_H

#include <string>
#include "employee.h"

using namespace std;

namespace savitchemployees
{

    class HourlyEmployee : public Employee
    {
    public:
        HourlyEmployee();
        HourlyEmployee(string new_name, string new_ssn,
                       double new_wage_rate, double new_hours);
        void set_rate(double new_wage_rate);
        double get_rate();
        void set_hours(double hours_worked);
        double get_hours();
        void give_raise(double amount);
        void print_check();
    private:
        double wage_rate;
        double hours;
    };

}//savitchemployees

#endif //HOURLYEMPLOYEE_H
```

Display 15.4 Interface for the Derived Class SalariedEmployee

```
//This is the HEADER FILE salariedemployee.h.
//This is the INTERFACE for the class SalariedEmployee.
#ifndef SALARIEDEMPLOYEE_H
#define SALARIEDEMPLOYEE_H

#include <string>
#include "employee.h"

using namespace std;

namespace savitchemployees
{

    class SalariedEmployee : public Employee
    {
    public:
        SalariedEmployee();
        SalariedEmployee (string new_name, string new_ssn,
                          double new_weekly_salary);
        double get_salary();
        void change_salary(double new_salary);
        void print_check();
        void give_raise(double amount);
    private:
        double salary;//weekly
    };

}//savitchemployees

#endif //SALARIEDEMPLOYEE_H
```

The definition of the class HourlyEmployee does not mention the member variables name, ssn, and net_pay, but every object of the class HourlyEmployee has member variables named name, ssn, and net_pay. The member variables name, ssn, and net_pay are inherited from the class Employee. The class HourlyEmployee declares two additional member variables named wage_rate and hours. Thus, every object of the class HourlyEmployee has five member variables named name, ssn, net_pay, wage_rate, and hours. Note that the definition of a derived class (such as HourlyEmployee) lists only the added member variables. The member variables defined in the base class are not mentioned; they are provided automatically to the derived class.

Just as it inherits the member variables of the class Employee, the class HourlyEmployee inherits all the member functions from the class Employee. So, the class HourlyEmployee inherits the member functions get_name, get_ssn, change_name, change_ssn, print_check, and give_raise from the class Employee. The class HourlyEmployee also adds the new member functions named set_rate, get_rate, set_hours, and get_hours.

When you define a derived class, such as HourlyEmployee, you need to give the prototypes for all the new member functions. (In the case of HourlyEmployee these are the member functions named set_rate, get_rate, set_hours, and get_hours.) When defining a derived class, you do not give the names of member functions inherited from the base class unless you want to change the definitions of the inherited member functions. This is discussed in a following subsection.

Inherited Members

A derived class automatically has all the member functions and member variables of the base class. These members from the base class are said to be **inherited**. These inherited member functions and inherited member variables are not mentioned in the definition of the derived class, but they are automatically members of the derived class. (As we will see, you do mention an inherited member function in the definition of the derived class if you want to change the definition of the inherited member function.)

SalariedEmployee is another example of a derived class of the class Employee. The interface for the class SalariedEmployee is given in Display 15.4. An object declared to be of type SalariedEmployee has all the member functions and member variables of Employee and the new members given in the definition of the class SalariedEmployee. This is true even though the class Salaried-

Employee lists only two constructors, a few accessor functions, and the one member variable `salary`. The class `SalariedEmployees`, nonetheless, has the three member variables `name`, `ssn`, and `net_pay`, as well as the member variable `salary`. Notice that you do not have to declare the member variables and member functions of the class `Employee`, such as `name` and `change_name`, in order for a `SalariedEmployee` to have these members. The class `SalariedEmployee` gets these inherited members automatically without the programmer doing anything.

Note that the class `Employee` has all the code that is common to the two classes `HourlyEmployee` and `SalariedEmployee`. This saves you the trouble of writing identical code twice, once for the classes `HourlyEmployee` and once for the class `SalariedEmployee`. Inheritance allows you to reuse the code in the class `Employee`.

We still need to discuss the implementations of the derived classes `HourlyEmployee` and `SalariedEmployee`. This will require covering some preliminary information on constructor definitions, which we do in the next subsection.

An Object of a Derived Class Is also an Object of the Base Class

In everyday experience an hourly employee is an employee. In C++ the same sort of thing holds. Since `HourlyEmployee` is a derived class of the class `Employee`, every object of the class `HourlyEmployee` can be used anyplace an object of the class `Employee` can be used. In particular, you can use an argument of type `HourlyEmployee` when a function requires an argument of type `Employee`. You can assign an object of the class `HourlyEmployee` to a variable of type `Employee`. (But be warned: You cannot assign a plain old `Employee` object to a variable of type `HourlyEmployee`. After all, an `Employee` is not necessarily and `HourlyEmployee`.) Of course, the same remarks apply to any base class and its derived class. You can use an object of a derived class any place that an object of its base class is allowed.

This relationship between a derived class and its base class is often referred to as the "Is-A" relationship. An `HourlyEmployee` *is an* `Employee`.

Constructor Base Initialization List

When we use inheritance, we will need to initialize the inherited members of derived class as well as the members defined directly in the derived class. We will discuss a slightly different way of initializing variables in constructors in preparation for the way that the inherited members of a derived class must be initialized.

When defining a constructor you can initialize member variables in a **base initialization list**. This initialization section is part of the heading for the function definition for a constructor. For example, suppose you have the following class definition:

```
class Rational
{
public:
    Rational( );
    Rational(int whole_number);
    Rational(int numerator, int denominator);
// other details omitted
private:
    int top;
    int bottom;
};
```

The three constructors can be defined as follows:

```
Rational::Rational( ) : top(0), bottom(1)
//Initializes top to 0 and bottom to 1:
{
    //Empty body
}


Rational::Rational(int whole_number)
                : top(whole_number), bottom(1)
//Initializes top to whole_number and bottom to 1:
{
    //Empty body
}


Rational::Rational(int numerator, int denominator)
                : top(numerator), bottom(denominator)
//Initializes top to numerator and bottom to denominator:
{
    //Empty body
}
```

As these examples show, the initialization section goes after the parenthesis that ends the parameter list and before the opening brace of the function body. The initialization section consists of a colon followed by a list of some or all the member variables separated by commas; each member variable is followed by its initializing value in parentheses. Notice that the initializing values can be given in terms of the constructor parameters.

These examples recall an alternate initialization discussed briefly in Chapter 2 for ordinary variables:

```
int x(2);
```

as a variant for

```
int x = 2;
```

The function body need not be empty as in the above examples. For example, the second of the above constructor definitions is equivalent to the following:

```
Rational::Rational(int whole_number) : top(whole_number)
{
    bottom = 1;
}
```

There need not be any initialization section, but as we shall shortly see, when we define a derived class constructor, most of the time we must invoke a base class constructor to accomplish the required initialization. This invocation of the base class constructor can only be done in a base initializer list with syntax that is almost exactly as in these examples. We recommend that you get into the habit of using the base initializer list to initialize data members in a constructor.[2]

When it becomes difficult to squeeze the necessary logic to test constructor arguments into an initializer, you move to the constructor body. For example, the above constructor definition is, in turn, equivalent to the following:

```
Rational::Rational(int whole_number)
{
    top = whole_number;
    bottom = 1;
}
```

Normally we use the version with the initialization section, although either is acceptable. However, if we want to add an extra check, as in the following redefined constructor, then it is best to make the initialization inside the body of the function definition:

```
Rational::Rational(int numerator, int denominator)
//Initializes top to numerator and bottom to denominator:
{
```

---

[2] There are two circumstances in which you must use base initializer lists to initialize members: one when the member is a const, and the second when the member is a reference to another variable. These situations are sufficiently obscure that it may not be easy to find how to initialize them. If you use base initializer lists consistently, you won't run into this problem.

```
    if (denominator != 0)
    {
        top = numerator;
        bottom = denominator;
    }
    else
    {
        cout << "Error: denominator of zero.\n" << endl;
        exit(1);
    }
}
```

As we shall shortly see, when we inherit, most of the time we must invoke a base class constructor to accomplish the required initialization. Consistency in coding suggests the use of the base initializer list whether or not it is required.

Constructors in Derived Classes

A constructor for a derived class uses a constructor from the base class in a special way. A constructor for the base class initializes all the data inherited from the base class. Thus, a constructor for a derived class begins with an invocation of a constructor for the base class. There is a special syntax for invoking the base class constructor that is illustrated by the constructor definitions for the class HourlyEmployee given in Display 15.5. In what follows we have reproduced one of the constructor definitions for the class HourlyEmployee taken from that display:

```
HourlyEmployee::HourlyEmployee() : Employee()
{
    cout << "Enter HourlyEmployee wage rate, followed by return.:\n";
    cin >> wage_rate;
    cout << "Enter number of hours worked, followed by return:\n";
    cin >> hours;
}
```

The portion : Employee() is the initialization section of the constructor definition for the constructor HourlyEmployee::HourlyEmployee(). The part Employee() is an invocation of the zero argument constructor for the base class Employee. You should always include an invocation of the base class constructor in the initialization section of a derived class constructor.

On page 853 we reproduce the other constructor for the class HourlyEmployee (from Display 15.5).

Display 15.5 Implementations for the Derived Class HourlyEmployee (part 1 of 2)

```
//This is the IMPLEMENTATION FILE: hourlyemployee.cxx
//This is the IMPLEMENTATION for the class HourlyEmployee.
//The interface for the class HourlyEmployee is in
//the header file hourlyemployee.h.
#include <iostream>
#include <string>
#include "hourlyemployee.h"
using namespace std;

namespace savitchemployees
{

    HourlyEmployee::HourlyEmployee() : Employee()
    {
        cout << "Enter HourlyEmployee wage rate, followed by return.:\n";
        cin >> wage_rate;
        cout << "Enter number of hours worked, followed by return:\n";
        cin >> hours;
    }

    HourlyEmployee::HourlyEmployee(string new_name, string new_number,
                                   double new_wage_rate, double new_hours)
        : Employee(new_name, new_number),
          wage_rate(new_wage_rate), hours(new_hours)
    {
        //deliberately empty
    }

    void HourlyEmployee::set_rate(double new_wage_rate)
    {
        wage_rate = new_wage_rate;
    }

    double HourlyEmployee::get_rate()
    {
        return wage_rate;
    }
```

Display 15.5 Implementations for the Derived Class HourlyEmployee *(part 2 of 2)*

```
void HourlyEmployee::set_hours(double hours_worked)
{
    hours = hours_worked;
}

double HourlyEmployee::get_hours()
{
    return hours;
}


void HourlyEmployee::give_raise( double amount)
{
    wage_rate = wage_rate + amount;
}


void HourlyEmployee::print_check()
{
    net_pay = hours * wage_rate;

    cout << "\n_____\n";
    cout << "Pay to the order of " << name << endl;
    cout << "The sum of        " << net_pay << " Dollars\n";
    cout << "_____\n";
    cout << "Check Stub: NOT NEGOTIABLE\n";
    cout << "Employee Number: " << ssn << endl;
    cout << "Hourly Employee. \nHours worked: " << hours
         << " Rate: " << wage_rate << " Pay: " << net_pay << endl;
    cout << "_____\n";
}


}//savitchemployees
```

```
HourlyEmployee::HourlyEmployee(string new_name, string
              new_number, double new_wage_rate, double new_hours)
    : Employee(new_name, new_number),
      wage_rate(new_wage_rate), hours(new_hours)
{

    //deliberately empty

}
```

In this case all the work is done in the initialization section and so the body of the function definition is empty.

The *protected* Qualifier

In the definition of the base class Employee (Display 15.1) we used the keyword *protected* where you might expect *private*. A *protected* member is the same as a *private* member to any other class except a class derived from the base class (or derived from a derived class of the base class etc.). For example, a derived class of the class Employee inherits the member variables name, ssn, and net_pay and can access them directly in definitions of member functions of the derived class. More generally, any class that is derived from the class Employee, derived from a class derived from the class Employee, or derived from Employee by some longer chain of "derived from" can directly access these protected variables in the derived classes' function definitions. However, to any other classes these member variables are treated as if they were marked *private*.

protected

The meaning of the protected qualifier is illustrated in the definition of the function print_check of the derived class HourlyEmployee (Display 15.5), which we reproduce in what follows:

```
void HourlyEmployee::print_check()
{
    net_pay = hours * wage_rate;

    cout << "\n_____\n";
    cout << "Pay to the order of " << name << endl;
    cout << "The sum of " << net_pay << " Dollars\n";
    cout << "_____\n";
    cout << "Check Stub: NOT NEGOTIABLE\n";
    cout << "Employee Number: " << ssn << endl;
    cout << "Hourly Employee. \nHours worked: " << hours
         << " Rate: " << wage_rate << " Pay: " << net_pay <<
    endl;
    cout << "_____\n";
}
```

Since the inherited member variables net_pay, name, and ssn are marked *protected* in the base class Employee, you can use them by name in the definition of functions for the derived class HourlyEmployee, as illustrated in the definition of the function print_check. If they had been marked *private* in the definition of the base class Employee, this direct use of the inherited member variables net_pay, name, and ssn in the derived class HourlyEmployee would be illegal. If they had been marked *private* in the definition of the base class Employee, the class HourlyEmployee would still have the inherited member variables net_pay, name, and ssn, but they could not be mentioned by name in the definition of functions in the derived class HourlyEmployee; you would have to access and manipulate these inherited member variables by means of inherited functions such as get_name and change_name.

Suppose you define a derived class PartTimeHourlyEmployee of the class HourlyEmployee. The class PartTimeHourlyEmployee inherits all the member variables of the class HourlyEmployee including the member variables that HourlyEmployee inherits from the class Employee. So, the class PartTimeHourlyEmployee will have the member variables net_pay, name, and ssn. Since these member variables were marked *protected* in the class Employee they can be used by name in the definitions of functions of the class PartTimeHourlyEmployee.

Except for derived classes (and derived classes of derived classes etc.) a protected member variable that is marked *protected* is treated the same as if it were marked *private*. For example, the following would not be allowed in a program:

```
Employee joe;
joe.net_pay = 1000;  //ILLEGAL!
```

We include a discussion of *protected* member variables primarily because you will see them used and should be familiar with them. However, many programming authorities say it is bad style to use *protected* member variables. They say that all member variables should be marked *private*. If all member variables are marked *private*, the inherited member variables cannot be accessed by name in derived class function definitions. However, this is not as bad as its sounds. The inherited *private* member variables can be accessed indirectly by invoking inherited functions that either read or change the *private* inherited variables. You may or may not choose to use *protected* member variables. If you are in a course, then follow your instructor's guidelines on this point.

Redefinition of Member Functions

In the definition of the derived class HourlyEmployee (Display 15.3) we gave the prototypes for the new member functions set_rate, get_rate, set_hours, and get_hours. We also gave the prototypes for some, but not all, the member functions

Display 15.6 Implementations for the Derived Class SalariedEmployee *(part 1 of 2)*

```
//This is the IMPLEMENTATION FILE: salariedemployee.cxx
//This is the IMPLEMENTATION for the class SalariedEmployee.
//The interface for the class SalariedEmployee is in
//the header file salariedemployee.h.
#include <iostream>
#include <string>
#include "salariedemployee.h"
using namespace std;

namespace savitchemployees
{
    SalariedEmployee::SalariedEmployee():Employee()
    {
        cout << " Enter Salaried Employee's weekly salary\n";
        cin >> salary;
    }

    SalariedEmployee::SalariedEmployee(string new_name, string new_number,
                                double new_weekly_pay)
                    : Employee(new_name, new_number), salary(new_weekly_pay)
    {
        //deliberately empty
    }

    void SalariedEmployee::give_raise(double amount)
    {
        salary = salary + amount;
    }

    double SalariedEmployee::get_salary()
    {
        return salary;
    }

    void SalariedEmployee::change_salary(double new_salary)
    {
        salary = new_salary;
    }
```

Display 15.6 Implementations for the Derived Class SalariedEmployee *(part 2 of 2)*

```
void SalariedEmployee::print_check()
{
    net_pay = salary;
    cout << "\n_____\n";
    cout << "Pay to the order of " << name << endl;
    cout << "The sum of " << net_pay << " Dollars\n";
    cout << "_____\n";
    cout << "Check Stub NOT NEGOTIABLE \n" ;
    cout << "Employee Number: " << ssn << endl;
    cout << " Salaried Employee. Regular Pay: "
         << salary << endl;
    cout<< "_____\n";
}
}//savitchemployees
```

redefined
function

inherited from the class Employee. The inherited member functions whose prototypes were not given (such as change_name and change_ssn) are inherited
unchanged. They have the exact same definition in the class HourlyEmployee as
they do in the base class Employee. When you define a derived class like Hourly-
Employee, you list only the prototypes for the inherited member functions whose
definition you want to change to have a different definition in the derived class. If
you look at the implementation of the class HourlyEmployee, given in Display
15.5, you will see that we have redefined the inherited member functions
print_check, and give_raise. The class SalariedEmployee also gives new definitions to the member functions print_check and give_raise, as shown in Display 15.6. Moreover, the two classes give different definitions from each other. The
functions print_check and give_raise are **redefined** in the derived classes.

You can go on and derive another derived class from a derived class. Suppose
you want to add a class for company officers. You can have a class derived from
SalariedEmployee that adds the title (and perhaps nothing else). You will need to
write constructors that set the new information and add a member function to change
the title. You will need to redefine the change_name member function to insert a title
into the employee's name. You will be asked to do this in a programming problem.

Display 15.7 Using Derived Classes *(part1 of 2)*

```
#include <iostream>
#include "hourlyemployee.h"
#include "salariedemployee.h"
using namespace std;
using namespace savitchemployees;

int main()
{
    cout << "Data for hourly employee \n";
    HourlyEmployee h;
    cout << "Check for " << h.get_name()
        << " for " << h.get_hours() << " hours.\n";
    h.print_check();
    SalariedEmployee doc("Doc Adams", "345-12-3456", 1234.45);
    cout << "Check for " << doc.get_name() << endl;
    doc.print_check();

    return 0;
}
```

The function get_name *is inherited unchanged from the class* Employee.
The function print_check *is redefined.*
The function get_hours *was added to the derived class* HourlyEmployee.

If you define the class for company officers as we suggested, then only the member function change_name would be changed, and all other member functions would be inherited unchanged from the class SalariedEmployee.

Display 15.7 gives a demonstration programs that illustrates the use of the derived classes HourlyEmployee and SalariedEmployee.

Redefining an Inherited Function

A derived class inherits all the member functions (and data members as well) that belong to the base class. However, if a derived class requires a different implementation for an inherited member function, the function may be redefined in the derived class. When a member function is redefined, you must list its prototype in the definition of the derived class, even though the prototype is the same as in the base class. If you do not wish to redefine a member function that is inherited from the base class, then it is not listed in the definition of the derived class.

Display 15.7 Using Derived Classes *(part 2 of 2)*

Sample Dialogue

```
Data for hourly employee
Enter employee name, followed by return:
   Frank Black
Enter employee social security number, followed by return:
   123-45-6789
Enter hourly employee wage rate, followed by return:
   12.50
Enter number of hours worked, followed by return:
   20
Check for Frank Black for 20 hours
_____
Pay to the order of Frank Black
The sum of         250 Dollars
_____
Check Stub: NOT NEGOTIABLE
Employee Number: 123-45-6789
Hourly Employee.
Hours worked: 20 Rate: 12.5 Pay: 250
_____
Check for Doc Adams
_____
Pay to the order of Doc Adams
The sum of         1234.45 Dollars
_____
Check Stub NOT NEGOTIABLE
Employee Number: 345-12-3456
Salaried Employee. Regular Pay: 1234.45
_____
```

Redefining versus Overloading

Do not confuse *redefining* a function definition in a derived class with *overloading* a function name. When you redefine a function definition, the new function definition given in the derived class has the exact same number and types of parameters. On the other hand, if the function in the derived class were to have a different number of parameters or a parameter of a different type from the function in the base class, then the derived class would have both functions. That would be overloading. For example, suppose we added a function with the following prototype to the definition of the class HourlyEmployee:

```
void change_name(string first_name, string last_name);
```

The class HourlyEmployee would have this two-argument function change_name, and it would also inherit the following one-argument function change_name:

```
void change_name(string new_name);
```

The class HourlyEmployee would have two functions named change_name. This would be *overloading* the function name change_name.

On the other hand, both the class Employee and the class HourlyEmployee define a function with the following prototype:

```
void print_check();
```

In this case, the class HourlyEmployee has only one function named print_check, but the definition of the function print_check for the class HourlyEmployee is different from its definition for the class Employee. In this case, the function print_check has been *redefined*.

If you get redefining and overloading confused, you do have one consolation. They are both legal. So, it is more important to learn how to use them than it is to learn to distinguish between them. Nonetheless, you should learn the difference between them.

Signature

A function's **signature** is the function's name with the sequence of types in the parameter list, including things like the *const* keyword. When you redefine a function, the function in the base class and the redefined function in the derived class have the same signature. If a function has the same name in a derived class as in the base class, but has a different signature, that is overloading not redefinition.

SELF-TEST EXERCISES

1   The class `SalariedEmployee` inherits both of the functions `get_name` and `print_check` (among other things) from the base class `Employee`, yet only the function prototype for the function `print_check` is given in the definition of the class `SalariedEmployee`. Why isn't the prototype for the function `get_name` given in the definition of `SalariedEmployee`?

2   Give a definition for a class `TitledEmployee` that is a derived class of the base class `SalariedEmployee` given in Display 15.4. The class `TitledEmployee` has one additional member variable of type `string` called `title`. It also has two additional member functions: `get_title` that takes no arguments and returns a `string`, and `set_title` that is a *void* function that takes one argument of type `string`. It also redefines the member function `change_name`. You do not need to give any implementations, just the class definition. However, do give all needed #include directives and all *using namespace* directives. Place the class `TitledEmployee` in the namespace `savitchemployees`.

3   Give the definitions of the constructors for the class `TitledEmployee` that you gave as the answer to Exercise 2. Also, give the redefinition of the member function `change_name`. The function `change_name` should insert the title into the name. Do not bother with #include directives or namespace details.

4   Give a definition for a *class* `SmartBut` that is a derived class of the base class `Smart`, which we reproduce for you here. Do not bother with #include directives or namespace details.

```
class Smart
{
public:
    Smart();
    void print_answer();
protected:
    int a;
    int b;
};
```

This class should have an additional data field, `crazy`, of type *bool* and one additional member function that takes no arguments and returns a value of type *bool*. The new function is named `is_crazy`. You do not need to give any implementations, just the class definition.

15.2   Polymorphism

I did it my way.

FRANK SINATRA

In its most general meaning, *polymorphism* refers to the ability to associate multiple meanings to one function name. When used in this general sense, overloading, for example, is considered a form of polymorphism. The term is also used in a more narrow sense. When used in the more restricted sense, the term *polymorphism* refers to the ability to associate multiple meanings to one function name *by means of* a special mechanism known as *late binding*. We have not yet seen any examples of polymorphism in this narrow sense. It is polymorphism in this more restricted sense that we will discuss in this section.

Late Binding

A virtual function is one that, in some sense, may be used before it is defined. For example, a graphics program may have several kinds of figures, such as rectangles, circles, ovals, and so forth. Each figure might be an object of a different class. For example, the `Rectangle` class might have member variables for a height, width, and center point, while the `Circle` class might have member variables for a center point and a radius. In a well-designed programming project, all of them would probably be descendants of a single parent class called, for example, `Figure`. Now, suppose you want a function to draw a figure on the screen. To draw a circle, you need different instructions from those you need to draw a rectangle. So, each class needs to have a different function to draw its kind of figure. However, because the functions belong to the classes, they can all be called `draw`. If `r` is a `Rectangle` object and `c` is a `Circle` object, then `r.draw()` and `c.draw()` can be functions implemented with different code. All this is not news, but now we move on to something new: *virtual functions* defined in the parent class `Figure`.

Now, the parent class `Figure` may have functions that apply to all figures. For example, it might have a function called `center` that moves a figure to the center of the screen by erasing it and then redrawing it in the center of the screen. `Figure::center` might use the function `draw` to redraw the figure in the center of the screen. When you think of using the inherited function `center` with figures of the classes `Rectangle` and `Circle`, you begin to see that there are complications here.

To make the point clear and more dramatic, let's suppose the class `Figure` is already written and in use and at some later time we add a class for a brand new kind of figure, say, the class `Triangle`. Now `Triangle` can be a derived class of the class `Figure`, and so the function `center` will be inherited from the class `Figure` and so the function `center` should apply to (and perform correctly for!) all `Triangle`s. But there is a complication. The function center uses draw, and the function draw is different for each type of figure. The inherited function center (if nothing special is done) will use the definition of the function draw given in the class Figure, and that function draw does not work correctly for Triangles. We want the inherited function center to use the function Triangle::draw rather than the function Figure::draw. But the class Triangle and so the function Triangle::draw was not even written when the function center (defined in the class Figure) was written and even compiled! How can the function center possibly work correctly for Triangles? The compiler did not know anything about Triangle::draw at the time that center was compiled! The answer is that it can apply provided draw is a *virtual function*.

virtual function

late binding

When you make a function **virtual**, you are telling the compiler "I do not know how this function is implemented. Wait until it is used in a program, and then get the implementation from the object instance." The technique of waiting until run time to determine the implementation of a procedure is called **late binding** or **dynamic binding**. Virtual functions are the way C++ provides late binding. But, enough introduction. We need an example to make this come alive (and to teach you how to use virtual functions in your programs). In order to explain the details of virtual functions in C++, we will use a simplified example from an application area other than drawing figures.

Virtual Functions in C++

Suppose you are designing a record-keeping program for an automobile parts store. You want to make the program versatile, but you are not sure you can account for all possible situations. For example, you want to keep track of sales, but you cannot anticipate all types of sales. At first, there will only be regular sales to retail customers who go to the store to buy one particular part. However, later you may want to add sales with discounts or mail-order sales with a shipping charge. All these sales will be for an item with a basic price and ultimately will produce some bill. For a simple sale, the bill is just the basic price, but if you later add discounts, then some kinds of bills will also depend on the size of the discount. Now your program will need to compute daily gross sales, which intuitively should just be the sum of all the individual sales bills. You may also want to calculate the largest and smallest sales of the day or the average sale for the day. All these can be calculated from the individual bills, but the functions for computing the bills will not be added until later, when you decide what types of sales you will be dealing with. To accommodate this, we make the function for computing the bill a virtual function. (For simplicity in this first example, we assume that each sale is for just one item, although with derived classes and virtual functions we could, but will not here, account for sales of multiple items.)

Displays 15.8 and 15.9 contain the interface and implement for the class Sale. All types of sales will be derived classes of the class Sale. The class Sale correspond to simple sales of a single item with no added discounts or charges. Notice the

Display 15.8 Interface for the Base Class Sale

```
//This is the HEADER FILE sale.h.
//This is the INTERFACE for the class Sale.
//Sale is a class for simple sales.
#ifndef SALE_H
#define SALE_H

#include <iostream>
using namespace std;

namespace savitchsale
{

    class Sale
    {
    public:
        Sale();
        Sale(double the_price);
        virtual double bill() const;
        double savings(const Sale& other) const;
        //Returns the savings if you buy other instead of the calling object.
    protected:
        double price;
    };

    bool operator < (const Sale& first, const Sale& second);
    //Compares two sales to see which is larger.

}//savitchsale

#endif // SALE_H
```

Display 15.9 Implementation of the Base Class Sale

```
//This is the IMPLEMENTATION FILE: sale.cxx
//This is the IMPLEMENTATION for the class Sale.
//The interface for the class Sale is in
//the header file sale.h.
#include "sale.h"

namespace savitchsale
{

    Sale::Sale() : price(0)
    {}

    Sale::Sale(double the_price) : price(the_price)
    {}

    double Sale::bill() const
    {
        return price;
    }

    double Sale::savings(const Sale& other) const
    {
        return ( bill() - other.bill() );
    }

    bool operator < (const Sale& first, const Sale& second)
    {
        return (first.bill() < second.bill());
    }

}//savitchsale
```

reserved word *virtual* in the prototype for the function bill (Display 15.8). Notice (Display 15.9) that the member function savings and the overloaded operator < each use the function bill. Since bill is declared to be a virtual function, we can later define derived classes of the class Sale and define their versions of the function bill, and the definitions of the member function savings and the overloaded operator <, which we gave with the class Sale, will use the version of the function bill that corresponds to the object of the derived class.

For example, Display 15.10 shows the derived class DiscountSale. Notice that the class DiscountSale requires a different definition for its version of the function bill. Nonetheless, when the member function savings and the overloaded operator < are used with an object of the class DiscountSale, they will use the version of the function definition for bill that was given with the class DiscountSale. This is indeed a pretty fancy trick for C++ to pull off. Consider the function call d1.savings(d2) for objects d1 and d2 of the class DiscountSale. The definition of the function savings (even for an object of the class DiscountSale) is given in the implementation file for the base class Sale, which was compiled before we ever even thought of the class DiscountSale. Yet, in the function call d1.savings(d2), the line that calls the function bill knows enough to use the definition of the function bill given for the class DiscountSale.

How does this work. In order to write C++ programs you can just assume it happens by magic, but the real explanation was given in the introduction to this section. When you label a function *virtual*, you are telling the C++ environment "Wait until this function is used in a program, and then get the implementation corresponding to the calling object."

Display 15.11 gives a sample program that illustrates how the virtual function bill and the functions that use bill work in a complete program.

There are a number of technical details you need to know in order to use virtual functions in C++. We list them in what follows:

> If a function will have a different definition in a derived class than in the base class and you want it to be a virtual function, you add the keyword *virtual* to the function prototype in the base class. You do not need to add the reserved word *virtual* to the prototype in the derived class. If a function is virtual in the base class, then it is automatically virtual in the derived class. (It is a good idea to label the function prototype in the derived class *virtual*, even though it is not required.)

> The reserved word *virtual* is added to the function prototype and not to the function definition.

> You do not get a virtual function and the benefits of virtual functions unless you use the keyword *virtual*.

Display 15.10 the Derived Class DiscountSale

```
//This is the INTERFACE for the class DiscountSale.
#ifndef DISCOUNTSALE_H
#define DISCOUNTSALE_H
#include "sale.h"

namespace savitchsale                          This is the file discountsale.h.
{
    class DiscountSale : public Sale
    {
    public:
        DiscountSale();
        DiscountSale(double the_price, double the_discount);
        //Discount is expressed as a percent of the price.
        double bill() const;
    protected:
        double discount;
    };
}//savitchsale
#endif //DISCOUNTSALE_H
```

```
//This is the IMPLEMENTATION for the class DiscountSale.
#include "discountsale.h"                      This is the file discountsale.cxx.

namespace savitchsale
{
    DiscountSale::DiscountSale() : Sale(), discount(0)
    {}

    DiscountSale::DiscountSale(double the_price, double the_discount)
             : Sale(the_price), discount(the_discount)
    {}

    double DiscountSale::bill() const
    {
        double fraction = discount/100;
        return (1 - fraction)*price;
    }
}//savitchsale
```

Display 15.11 Use of a Virtual Function

```
//Demonstrates the performance of the virtual function bill.
#include <iostream>
#include "sale.h" //Not really needed, but safe due to ifndef.
#include "discountsale.h"
using namespace std;
using namespace savitchsale;

int main()
{
    Sale simple(10.00);//One item at $10.00.
    DiscountSale discount(11.00, 10);//One item at $11.00 with a 10% discount.

    cout.setf(ios::fixed);
    cout.setf(ios::showpoint);
    cout.precision(2);

    if (discount < simple)
    {
        cout << "Discounted item is cheaper.\n";
        cout << "Savings is $" << simple.savings(discount) << endl;
    }
    else
        cout << "Discounted item is not cheaper.\n";

    return 0;
}
```

Sample Dialogue

```
Discounted item is cheaper.
Savings is $0.10
```

Since virtual functions are so great, why not make all member functions virtual? Almost the only reason for not always using virtual functions is efficiency. The compiler and the run-time environment need to do much more work for virtual functions, and so if you label more member function *virtual* than you need to, then your programs will be less efficient.

Overriding

When a virtual function definition is changed in a derived class, programmers often say the function definition is **overridden**. In the C++ literature a distinction is sometimes made between the terms *redefined* and *overridden*. Both terms refer to changing the definition of the function in a derived class. If the function is a virtual function it's called *overriding*. If the function is not a virtual function, it's called *redefining*. This may seem like a silly distinction to you the programmer, since you do the same thing in both cases, but the two cases are treated differently by the compiler.

Polymorphism

In its most general meaning, **polymorphism** refers to the ability to associate multiple meanings to one function name. The term is also used in a more narrow sense. When used in the more restricted sense, the term **polymorphism** refers to the ability to associate multiple meanings to one function name *by means of* late binding. Thus, when we use *polymorphism* in this restricted sense, polymorphism, late binding, and virtual functions are really all the same topic.

SELF-TEST EXERCISES

5   Suppose you modify the definitions of the class Sale (Display 15.8) by deleting the reserved word *virtual*. How would that change the output of the program in Display 15.11?

Virtual Functions and Extended Type Compatibility

We will discuss some of the further consequences of declaring a class member function to be *virtual* and do one example that uses some of these features.

C++ is a fairly strongly typed language. This means that the types of items are always checked and an error message is issued if there is a type mismatch, such as a type mismatch of an argument and a formal parameter when there is no conversion that can be automatically invoked. This also means that normally the value assigned to a variable must match the type of the variable, although in a few well-defined cases C++ will perform an automatic type cast (called a **coercion**) so that it appears that you can assign a value of one type to a variable of another type.

For example, C++ allows you to assign a value of type *char* or *int* to a variable of type *double*. However, C++ does not allow you to assign a value of type *double* or *float* to a variable of any integer type (*char*, *short*, *int*, *long*).

However, as important as the strong typing is, this strong type checking interferes with the very idea of inheritance in object-oriented programming. Suppose you have defined *class* A and *class* B and have defined objects of type *class* A and *class* B. You cannot always assign between objects of these types. For example suppose a program or unit contains the following type declarations:

```
class Pet
{
public:
    virtual void print();
    string name;
};

class Dog : public Pet
{
public:
    virtual void print(); //keyword virtual not needed, but is
            //put here for clarity. (It is also good style!)

    string breed;
};

Dog vdog;
Pet vpet;
```

Now concentrate on the data members, name and breed. (To keep this example simple, we have made the member variables *public*. In a real application, they should be *private* and have functions to manipulate them.)

Anything that is a Dog is also a Pet. It would seem to make sense to allow programs to consider values of type Dog to also be values of type Pet and hence the following should be allowed:

```
vdog.name = "Tiny";
vdog.breed = "Great Dane";
vpet = vdog;
```

C++ does allow this sort of assignment. You may assign a value, such as the value of vdog to a variable of a parent type, such as vpet, but you are not allowed to perform the reverse assignment. Although the above assignment is allowed, the value that is assigned to the variable vpet loses its breed field. This is called the "**slicing problem**." The following attempted access will produce an error message:

```
cout << vpet.breed;
          // Illegal: class Pet has no member named breed
```

You can argue that this makes sense, since once a Dog is moved to a variable of type Pet it should be treated like any other Pet and not have properties peculiar to Dogs. This makes for a lively philosophical debate, but it usually just makes for a nuisance when programming. The dog named Tiny is still a Great Dane and we would like to refer to its breed, even if we treated it as a Pet someplace along the line.

Fortunately, C++ does offer us a way to treat a Dog as a Pet without throwing away the name of the breed. To do this, we use pointers to dynamic object instances. Suppose we add the following declarations:

```
Pet *ppet;
Dog *pdog;
```

If we use pointers and dynamic variables we can treat Tiny as a Pet without losing his breed. The following is allowed.

```
pdog = new Dog;
pdog->name = "Tiny";
pdog->breed = "Great Dane";
ppet = pdog;
```

Moreover, we can still access the breed field of the node pointed to by ppet. Suppose that

```
Dog::print();
```

has been defined as follows:

```
//uses iostream.h members
void Dog::print()
{
    cout << "name: " << name << endl;
    cout << "breed: " << breed << endl;
}
```

The statement

```
ppet->print();
```

will cause the following to be printed on the screen:

```
name: Tiny
breed: Great Dane
```

This by virtue of the fact that print() is a *virtual* member function. (No pun intended.) We have included test code in Display 15.12.

◆ **PITFALL**   **The Slicing Problem**

Although it is legal to assign a derived class object into a base class variable, assigning a derived class object to a base class object slices off data. Any data members in the derived class object that are not also in the base class will be lost in the assignment, and any member functions that are not defined in the base class are similarly unavailable to the resulting base class object.

If we make the declarations and assignment,

```
Dog vdog;
Pet vpet;
vdog.name = "Tiny";
vdog.breed = "Great Dane";
vpet = vdog;
```

then vpet cannot be a calling object for a member function introduced in Dog, and the data member, Dog::breed, is lost.

◆ **PITFALL**   **Not Using Virtual Member Functions**

In order to get the benefit of the extended type compatibility we discussed earlier you must use *virtual* member functions. For example, suppose we had not used member functions in the example in Display 15.7. Suppose that in place of

```
ppet->print();
```

we had used the following:

```
cout << "name: " << ppet->name
     << " breed: " << ppet->breed << endl;
```

This would have precipitated an error message. The reason for this is that the expression

```
*ppet
```

Display 15.12 More Inheritance with Virtual Functions (*part 1 of 2*)

```
//Program to illustrate use of a virtual function
//to defeat the slicing problem.

#include <string>
#include <iostream>
using namespace std;

class Pet
{
public:
    virtual void print();
    string name;
};

class Dog : public Pet
{
public:
    virtual void print();//keyword virtual not needed, but put
                          //here for clarity. (It is also good style!)
    string breed;
};

int main()
{
    Dog vdog;
    Pet vpet;

    vdog.name = "Tiny";
    vdog.breed = "Great Dane";
    vpet = vdog;

    //vpet.breed; is illegal since class Pet has no member named breed

    Pet *ppet;
    ppet = new Pet;
```

Display 15.12 More Inheritance with Virtual Functions (*part 2 of 2*)

```
        Dog *pdog;
        pdog = new Dog;

        pdog->name = "Tiny";
        pdog->breed = "Great Dane";

        ppet = pdog;
        ppet->print(); // These two print the same output:
        pdog->print(); // name: Tiny breed: Great Dane

        //The following, which accesses member variables directly
        //rather than via virtual functions would produce an error:
        //cout << "name: " << ppet->name << "  breed: "
        //<< ppet->breed << endl;
        //generates an error message: 'class Pet' has no member
        //named 'breed' .
        //See Pitfall section "Not Using virtual member functions"
        //for more discussion on this.

        return 0;
    }

void Dog::print()
{
    cout << "name: " << name << endl;
    cout << "breed: " << breed << endl;
}

void Pet::print()
{
    cout << "name: " << endl;//Note no breed mentioned
}
```

Sample Dialogue

```
name: Tiny
breed: Great Dane
name: Tiny
breed: Great Dane
```

has its type determined by the pointer type of ppet. It is a pointer type for the type Pet and the type Pet has no field named breed.

But, print() was declared *virtual* by the base class, Pet. So, when the compiler sees the call

```
ppet->print();
```

it checks the *virtual* table for classes Pet and Dog, and sees that ppet points to an object of type Dog and so uses the code generated for

```
Dog::print(),
```

rather than the code for

```
Pet::print();
```

Object-oriented programming with dynamic variables is a very different way of viewing programming. This can all be bewildering at first. It will help if you keep two simple rules in mind:

1. If the domain type of the pointer p_ancestor is a base class for the domain type of the pointer p_descendant, then the following assignment of pointers is allowed:

   ```
   p_ancestor = p_descendant;
   ```

   Moreover, none of the data members or member functions of the dynamic variable being pointed to by p_descendant will be lost.

2. Although all the extra fields of the dynamic variable are there, you will need *virtual* member functions to access them.

◆ PITFALL   Attempting to Compile Class Definitions without Definitions for Every Virtual Member Function

It is wise to develop incrementally. This means code a little then test a little, then code a little more and test a little more, and so forth. However, if you try to compile classes with *virtual* member functions, but do not implement each member, you may run into some very-hard-to-understand error messages, even if you do not call the undefined member functions!

If any virtual member functions are not implemented before compiling, then the compilation fails with error messages similar to this:

"undefined reference to *Class_Name* virtual table".

Even if there is *no derived class* and there is *only one* `virtual` member, but that function does not have a definition, then this kind of message still occurs.

What makes the error messages very hard to decipher is that without definitions for the functions declared `virtual`, there will be further error messages complaining about an undefined reference to default constructors, even if these constructors really are already defined.

SELF-TEST EXERCISES

6   Why can't we assign a base class object to a derived class variable?

7   What is the problem with the (legal) assignment of a derived class object to a base class variable?

8   Suppose the base class and the derived class each have a member function with the same signature. When you have a pointer to a base class object and call a function member through the pointer, discuss what determines which function is actually called, the base class member function or the derived-class function.

CHAPTER SUMMARY

- Inheritance provides a tool for code reuse by deriving one class from another, adding features to the derived class.

- Derived class objects inherit all the members of the base class, and may add members.

- Late binding means that the decision of which version of a member function is appropriate is decided at runtime. Virtual functions are what C++ uses to achieve late binding.

- A `protected` member in the base class is directly available to a publicly derived class's member functions.

Answers to Self-Test Exercises

1   The prototype for the function `get_name` is not given in the definition of `SalariedEmployee` because it is not redefined in the class `Salaried-Employee`. It is inherited unchanged from the base class `Employee`.

2

```cpp
#include <iostream>
#include "salariedemployee.h"
using namespace std;
namespace savitchemployees
{
    class TitledEmployee : public SalariedEmployee
    {
    public:
        TitledEmployee();
        TitledEmployee(string new_name, string new_title,
                       string new_ssn, double new_salary);
        string get_title();
        void set_title(string new_title);
        void change_name(string new_name);
    private:
        string title;
    };
}//savitchemployees
```

3

```cpp
TitledEmployee::TitledEmployee():SalariedEmployee()
{
    cout << " Enter employee's title:\n";
    cin >> title;
}

TitledEmployee::TitledEmployee(string new_name,
                   string new_title,
                   string new_ssn, double new_salary)
: SalariedEmployee(new_name, new_ssn, new_salary),
title(new_title)
{
        //deliberately empty

}
void TitledEmployee::change_name(string new_name)
{
    name = title + new_name;
}
```

4

```
class SmartBut : public Smart
{
public:
    SmartBut();
    SmartBut( int new_a, int new_b, bool new_crazy);
    bool is_crazy();
private:
    bool crazy;
};
```

5 The output would change to:

   ```
   Discounted item is not cheaper.
   ```

6 There would be no member to assign to the derived class's added members.

7 While it is legal to assign a derived class object to a base class variable, this discards the parts of the derived class object that are not members of the base class. This situation is known as the "slicing problem."

8 If the base class function carries the *virtual* modifier, then the type of the object to which the pointer was initialized determines whose member function is called. If the base class member function does not have the *virtual* modifier, then the type of the pointer determines whose member function is called.

Programming Projects

1 Write a program that uses the class in Display 15.4. Your program is to define a derived class called Administrator, which is to be derived from the class SalariedEmployee. You will likely need to change *private* in the base class to *protected*. Part of your job is to explain why you make this change. You are to supply the following additional data and function members:

   A data member of type string that contains the administrator's title, (such as Director or Vice President).

   A data member of type string that contains the company area of responsibility, (such as Production, Accounting, or Personnel).

   A data member of type string that contains the name of this administrator's immediate supervisor.

A *protected:* data member of type *double* that holds the administrator's annual salary. It is possible for you to use the existing salary member if you did the change recommended above.

A member function called `change_supervisor`, which changes the supervisor name.

A member function for reading in an administrator's data from the keyboard.

A member function called `print`, which outputs the programmer's data to the screen.

Finally, an overloading of the member function `print_check()` with appropriate notations on the check.

2 (Stroustrup) Consider the class

```
class base
{
public:
    virtual void iam()
    { cout << "base\n";}
};
```

a. Derive two classes from *class* base, and for each define `iam()` to write out the name of the class.

b. Declare objects of each class, and call `iam()` from them.

c. Assign the address of objects of the derived classes to base pointers and call `iam()` through the pointers.

d. Remove the *virtual* keyword from the base class member function, run your code again, and compare the results.

3 Add temporary, administrative, permanent and other classifications of employee to the hierarchy from Displays 15.1, 15.3, and 15.4. Implement and test this hierarchy. Test all member functions. A menu user interface with a menu would be a nice touch for your test program. (See Chapter 7 for a brief discussion of menus.)

CHAPTER

16

Exception Handling

16 Exception Handling

It's the exception that proves the rule.

COMMON MAXIM (POSSIBLY A CORRUPTION OF
SOMETHING LIKE: *IT'S THE EXCEPTION THAT TESTS THE RULE.*)

Introduction

One way to write a program is to first assume that nothing unusual or incorrect will happen. For example, if the program takes an entry off of a list, you might assume that the list is not empty. Once you have the program working for the core situation where things always go as planned, you can then add code to take care of the exceptional cases. In C++, there is a way to reflect this approach in your code. Basically, you write your code as if nothing very unusual happens. After that, you use the C++ exception-handling facilities to add code for those unusual cases.

Exception handling is commonly used to handle error situations, but perhaps a better way to view exceptions is as a way to handle "exceptional situations." After all, if your code correctly handles an "error," then it no longer is an error.

Perhaps the most important use of exceptions is to deal with functions that have some special case that is handled differently depending on how the function is used. Perhaps the function will be used in many programs and some will handle the special case in one way, while others will handle it in some other way. For example, if there is a division by zero in the function, then it may turn out that for some invocations of the function, the program should end, but for other invocations of the function something else should happen. You will see that such a function can be defined to throw an exception if the special case occurs, and that exception will allow the special case to be handled outside of the function. That way, the special case can be handled differently for different invocations of the function.

In C++, exception handling proceeds as follows: Either some library software, or your code, provides a mechanism that signals when something unusual happens. This is called **throwing an exception**. At another place in your program you place the code that deals with the exceptional case. This is called **handling the exception**. This method of programming makes for cleaner code. Of course, we still need to explain the details of how you do this in C++.

16.1 Exception-Handling Basics

Well, the program works for most cases. I didn't know it had to work for that *case.*

COMPUTER SCIENCE STUDENT, APPEALING A GRADE

Exception handling is meant to be used sparingly and in situations that are more involved than what is reasonable to include in a simple introductory example. So, we will teach you the exception handling details of C++ by means of simple examples that would not normally use exception handling. This makes a lot of sense for learning about exception handling, but do not forget that these first examples are toy examples, and in practice, you would not use exception handling for anything that simple.

A Toy Example of Exception Handling

For this example, suppose that milk is such an important food in our culture that people almost never run out of it, but still we would like our programs to accommodate the very unlikely situation of running out of milk. The basic code, which assumes we do not run out of milk, might be as follows:

```
cout << "Enter number of donuts:\n";
cin >> donuts;
cout << "Enter number of glasses of milk:\n";
cin >> milk;
dpg = donuts/double(milk);
cout << donuts << " donuts.\n"
     << milk << " glasses of milk.\n"
     << "You have " << dpg
     << " donuts for each glass of milk.\n";
```

If there is no milk, then this code will include a division by zero, which is an error. To take care of the special situation in which we run out of milk, we can add a test for this unusual situation. The complete program with this added test for the special situation is shown in Display 16.1. The program in Display 16.1 does not use exception handling. Now, let's see how this program can be rewritten using the C++ exception-handling facilities.

In Display 16.2, we have rewritten the program from Display 16.1 using an exception. This is only a toy example, and you would probably not use an exception in this case. However, it does give us a simple example. Although the program as a whole is not simpler, at least the part between the words *try* and *catch* is cleaner, and this hints at the advantage of using exceptions. Look at the code between the

Display 16.1 Handling a Special Case without Exception Handling

```cpp
#include <iostream>
using namespace std;

int main()
{
    int donuts, milk;
    double dpg;
    cout << "Enter number of donuts:\n";
    cin >> donuts;
    cout << "Enter number of glasses of milk:\n";
    cin >> milk;

    if (milk <= 0)
    {
        cout << donuts << " donuts, and No Milk!\n"
             << "Go buy some milk.\n";
    }
    else
    {
        dpg = donuts/double(milk);
        cout << donuts << " donuts.\n"
             << milk << " glasses of milk.\n"
             << "You have " << dpg
             << " donuts for each glass of milk.\n";
    }

    cout << "End of program.\n";
    return 0;
}
```

Sample Dialogue

```
Enter number of donuts:
12
Enter number of glasses of milk:
0
12 donuts, and No Milk!
Go buy some milk.
End of program.
```

Display 16.2 Same Thing Using Exception Handling *(part 1 of 2)*

```cpp
#include <iostream>
using namespace std;

int main()
{
    int donuts, milk;
    double dpg;

    try
    {
        cout << "Enter number of donuts:\n";
        cin >> donuts;
        cout << "Enter number of glasses of milk:\n";
        cin >> milk;

        if (milk <= 0)
                throw donuts;

        dpg = donuts/double(milk);
        cout << donuts << " donuts.\n"
             << milk << " glasses of milk.\n"
             << "You have " << dpg
             << " donuts for each glass of milk.\n";
    }
    catch(int e)
    {
        cout << e << " donuts, and No Milk!\n"
             << "Go buy some milk.\n";
    }

    cout << "End of program.\n";
    return 0;
}
```

Display 16.2 Same Thing Using Exception Handling *(part 2 of 2)*

Sample Dialogue 1

```
Enter number of donuts:
12
Enter number of glasses of milk:
6
12 donuts.
6 glasses of milk.
You have 2 donuts for each glass of milk.
```

Sample Dialogue 2

```
Enter number of donuts:
12
Enter number of glasses of milk:
0
12 donuts, and No Milk!
Go buy some milk.
End of program.
```

words *try* and *catch*. That code is basically the same as the code in Display 16.1, but rather than the big *if-else*-statement (shown in color in Display 16.1) this new program has the following smaller *if*-statement (plus some simple nonbranching statements):

```
if (milk <=0)
    throw donuts;
```

This *if*-statement says that if there is no milk, then do something exceptional. That something exceptional is given after the word *catch*. The idea is that the normal situation is handled by the code following the word *try*, and that the code following the word *catch* is used only in exceptional circumstances. So we have separated the normal case from the exceptional case. In this toy example, that does

Display 16.2 Same Thing Using Exception Handling *(part 1 of 2)*

```cpp
#include <iostream>
using namespace std;

int main()
{
    int donuts, milk;
    double dpg;

    try
    {
        cout << "Enter number of donuts:\n";
        cin >> donuts;
        cout << "Enter number of glasses of milk:\n";
        cin >> milk;

        if (milk <= 0)
                throw donuts;

        dpg = donuts/double(milk);
        cout << donuts << " donuts.\n"
            << milk << " glasses of milk.\n"
            << "You have " << dpg
            << " donuts for each glass of milk.\n";
    }
    catch(int e)
    {
        cout << e << " donuts, and No Milk!\n"
            << "Go buy some milk.\n";
    }

    cout << "End of program.\n";
    return 0;
}
```

Display 16.2 Same Thing Using Exception Handling (part 2 of 2)

Sample Dialogue 1

```
Enter number of donuts:
12
Enter number of glasses of milk:
6
12 donuts.
6 glasses of milk.
You have 2 donuts for each glass of milk.
```

Sample Dialogue 2

```
Enter number of donuts:
12
Enter number of glasses of milk:
0
12 donuts, and No Milk!
Go buy some milk.
End of program.
```

words *try* and *catch*. That code is basically the same as the code in Display 16.1, but rather than the big *if-else*-statement (shown in color in Display 16.1) this new program has the following smaller *if*-statement (plus some simple nonbranching statements):

```
if (milk <=0)
    throw donuts;
```

This *if*-statement says that if there is no milk, then do something exceptional. That something exceptional is given after the word *catch*. The idea is that the normal situation is handled by the code following the word *try*, and that the code following the word *catch* is used only in exceptional circumstances. So we have separated the normal case from the exceptional case. In this toy example, that does not really buy us too much, but in other situations, it will prove to be very helpful. Let's look at the details.

The basic way of handling exceptions in C++ consists of the *try-throw-catch* threesome. A *try*-**block** has the syntax

try-block

```
try
{
    Some_Code
}
```

This *try*-block contains the code for the basic algorithm that tells the computer what to do when everything goes smoothly. It is called a *try*-block because you are not 100% sure that all will go smoothly, but you want to "give it a try."

Now if something does go wrong, you want to throw an exception, which is a way of indicating that something went wrong. So the basic outline, when we add a *throw*, is as follows:

```
try
{
    Code_To_Try
    Possibly_Throw_An_Exception
    More_Code
}
```

The following is an example of a *try*-block with a *throw*-statement included (copied from Display 16.2):

```
try
{
    cout << "Enter number of donuts:\n";
    cin >> donuts;
    cout << "Enter number of glasses of milk:\n";
    cin >> milk;

    if (milk <= 0)
            throw donuts;

    dpg = donuts/double(milk);
    cout << donuts << " donuts.\n"
         << milk << " glasses of milk.\n"
         << "You have " << dpg
         << " donuts for each glass of milk.\n";
}
```

throw-statement

The following statement **throws** the *int* value donuts:

```
throw donuts;
```

exception

The value thrown, in this case donuts, is sometimes called an **exception**, and the execution of a *throw*-statement is called **throwing an exception**. You can throw a value of any type. In this case an *int* value is thrown.

---

throw-Statement

Syntax:

```
throw Expression_for_Value_to_Be_Thrown;
```

When the *throw*-statement is executed, the execution of the enclosing *try*-block is stopped. If the *try*-block is followed by a suitable *catch*-block, then flow of control is transferred to the *catch*-block. A *throw*-statement is almost always embedded in a branching statement, such as an *if*–statement. The value thrown can be of any type.

Example:

```
if (milk <= 0)
    throw donuts;
```

As the name suggests, when something is "thrown," something goes from one place to another place. In C++ what goes from one place to another is the flow of control (as well as the value thrown). When an exception is thrown, the code in the surrounding *try*-block stops executing and another portion of code, known as a *catch*-**block**, begins execution. This executing of the *catch*-block is called **catching the exception** or **handling the exception**. When an exception is thrown, it should ultimately be handled by (caught by) some *catch*-block. In Display 16.2, the appropriate *catch*-block immediately follows the *try*-block. We repeat the *catch*-block in what follows:

catch-block

```
catch(int e)
{
    cout << e << " donuts, and No Milk!\n"
         << "Go buy some milk.\n";
}
```

This *catch*-block looks very much like a function definition that has a parameter of a type *int*. It is not a function definition, but in some ways, a *catch*-block is like a function. It is a separate piece of code that is executed when your program encounters (and executes) the following (within the preceding *try*-block):

```
throw Some_int;
```

So, this *throw*-statement is similar to a function call, but instead of calling a function, it calls the *catch*-block and says to execute the code in the *catch*-block. A *catch*-block is often referred to as an **exception handler**, which is a term that suggests that a *catch*-block has a function-like nature.

What is that identifier e in the following line from a *catch*-block?

```
catch(int e)
```

That identifier e looks like a parameter, and acts very much like a parameter. So, we will call this e the *catch*-**block parameter**. (But remember, this does not mean that the *catch*-block is a function.) The *catch*-block parameter does two things:

catch-block parameter

1. The *catch*-block parameter is preceded by a type name that specifies what kind of thrown value the *catch*-block can catch.

2. The *catch*-block parameter gives you a name for the thrown value that is caught, so you can write code in the *catch*-block that does things with the thrown value that is caught.

We will discuss these two functions of the *catch*-block parameter in reverse order. In this subsection, we will discuss using the *catch*-block parameter as a name for the value that was thrown and is caught. In the subsection entitled "Multiple Throws and Catches," later in this chapter, we will discuss which *catch*-block (which exception handler) will process a value that is thrown. Our current example has only one *catch*-block. A common name for a *catch*-block parameter is e, but you can use any legal identifier in place of e.

Let's see how the *catch*-block in Display 16.2 works. When a value is thrown, execution of the code in the *try*-block ends and control passes to the *catch*-block (or blocks) that are placed right after the *try*-block. The *catch*-block from Display 16.2 is reproduced here:

```
catch(int e)
{
    cout << e << " donuts, and No Milk!\n"
         << "Go buy some milk.\n";
}
```

When a value is thrown, the thrown value must be of type *int* in order for this particular *catch*-block to apply. In Display 16.2, the value thrown is given by the variable donuts, and since donuts is of type *int*, this *catch*-block can catch the value thrown.

Suppose the value of donuts is 12 and the value of milk is 0, as in the second sample dialogue in Display 16.2. Since the value of milk is not positive, the *throw*-statement within the *if*-statement is executed. In that case the value of the variable donuts is thrown. When the *catch*-block in Display 16.2 catches the value of donuts, the value of donuts is plugged in for the *catch*-block parameter e and the code in the *catch*-block is executed, producing the following output:

```
12 donuts, and No Milk!
Go buy some milk.
```

If the value of donuts is positive, the *throw*-statement is not executed. In this case the entire *try*-block is executed. After the last statement in the *try*-block is executed, the statement after the *catch*-block is executed. Note that if no exception is thrown, then the *catch*-block is ignored.

---

catch-Block Parameter

The *catch*-block parameter is an identifier in the heading of a *catch*-block that serves as a placeholder for an exception (a value) that might be thrown. When a (suitable) value is thrown in the preceding *try*-block, that value is plugged in for the *catch*-block parameter. You can use any legal (nonreserved-word) identifier for a *catch*-block parameter.

Example:

```
catch(int e)
{
    cout << e << " donuts, and No Milk!\n"
        << "Go buy some milk.\n";
}
```

e is the *catch*-block parameter.

This makes it sound like a *try-throw-catch*-setup is equivalent to an *if-else*-statement. It almost is equivalent, except for the value thrown. A *try-throw-catch*-setup is similar to an *if-else*-statement *with the added ability to send a message to one of the branches*. This does not sound much different from an *if-else*-statement, but it turns out to be a big difference in practice.

To summarize in a more formal tone, a *try*-block contains some code that we are assuming includes a *throw*-statement. The *throw*-statement is normally executed only in exceptional circumstances, but when it is executed, it throws a value of some type. When an exception (a value like donuts in Display 16.2) is thrown, that is the end of the *try*-block. All the rest of the code in the *try*-block is ignored and control passes to a suitable *catch*-block. A *catch*-block applies only to an immediately preceding *try*-block. If the exception is thrown, then that exception object is plugged in for the *catch*-block parameter, and the statements in the *catch*-block are executed. For example, if you look at the dialogues in Display 16.2, you will see that as soon as the user enters a nonpositive number, the *try*-block stops and the *catch*-block is executed. For now, we will assume that every *try*-block is followed by an appropriate *catch*-block. We will later discuss what happens when there is no appropriate *catch*-block.

Next, we summarize what happens when no exception is thrown in a *try*-block. If no exception (no value) is thrown in the *try*-block, then after the *try*-block is completed, program execution continues with the code after the *catch*-block. In other words, if no exception is thrown, then the *catch*-block is ignored. Most of the time when the program is executed, the *throw*-statement will not be executed, and so in most cases, the code in the *try*-block will run to completion and the code in the *catch*-block will be ignored completely.

SELF-TEST EXERCISES

1   What output is produced by the following code?

```
int wait_time = 46;

try
{
    cout << "Try-block entered.\n";
    if (wait_time > 30)
        throw wait_time;
    cout << "Leaving try-block.\n";
}

catch(int thrown_value)
{
    cout << "Exception thrown with\n"
         << "wait_time equal to " << thrown_value << endl;
}
cout << "After catch-block" << endl;
```

2   What would be the output produced by the code in Self-Test Exercise 1 if we make the following change? Change the line

```
int wait_time = 46;
```

try-throw-catch

This is the basic mechanism for throwing and catching exceptions. The ***throw-statement*** throws the exception (a value). The ***catch-block*** catches the exception (the value). When an exception is thrown, the *try*-block ends and then the code in the *catch*-block is executed. After the *catch*-block is completed, the code after the *catch*-block(s) is executed (provided the *catch*-block has not ended the program or performed some other special action).

If no exception is thrown in the *try*-block, then after the *try*-block is completed, program execution continues with the code after the *catch*-block(s). (In other words, if no exception is thrown, then the *catch*-block(s) are ignored.)

Syntax:

```
try
{
    Some_Statements
  < Either some code with a throw-statement or
        a function invocation that might throw an exception>
    Some_More_Statements
}
catch(Type e)
{
  < Code to be performed if a value of the
        catch-block parameter type is thrown in the try-block>
}
```

Example:

See Display 16.2.

to

```
int wait_time = 12;
```

3 In the code given in Self-Test Exercise 1, what is the *throw*-statement?

4 What happens when a *throw*-statement is executed? This is a general question. Tell what happens in general, not simply what happens in the code in Self-Test Question 1 or some other sample code.

5 In the code given in Self-Test Exercise 1, what is the *try*-block?

6 In the code given in Self-Test Exercise 1, what is the *catch*-block?

7 In the code given in Self-Test Exercise 1, what is the *catch*-block parameter?

Defining Your Own Exception Classes

A *throw*-statement can throw a value of any type. A common thing to do is to define a class whose objects can carry the precise kind of information you want thrown to the *catch*-block. An even more important reason for defining a specialized exception class is so that you can have a different type to identify each possible kind of exceptional situation.

An exception class is just a class. What makes it an exception class is how it's used. Still, it pays to take some care in choosing an exception class's name and other details.

Display 16.3 contains an example of a program with a programmer-defined exception class. This is just a toy program to illustrate some C++ details about exception handling. It uses much too much machinery for such a simple task, but it is an otherwise uncluttered example of some C++ details.

Notice the *throw*-statement, reproduced in what follows:

```
throw NoMilk(donuts);
```

The part `NoMilk(donuts)` is an invocation of a constructor for the class `NoMilk`. The constructor takes one *int* argument (in this case `donuts`) and creates an object of the class `NoMilk`. That object is then "thrown."

Multiple Throws and Catches

A *try*-block can potentially throw any number of exception values, and they can be of differing types. In any one execution of the *try*-block only one exception will be thrown (since a thrown exception ends the execution of the *try*-block), but different types of exception values can be thrown on different occasions when the *try*-block is executed. Each *catch*-block can only catch values of one type, but you can catch exception values of differing types by placing more than one *catch*-block after a *try*-block. For example, the program in Display 16.4 has two *catch*-blocks after its *try*-block.

Note that there is no parameter in the *catch*-block for `DivideByZero`. If you do not need a parameter, you can simply list the type with no parameter. This case is discussed a bit more in the programming tip section entitled "Exception Classes Can Be Trivial."

Display 16.3 Defining Your Own Exception Class (part 1 of 2)

```
#include <iostream>
using namespace std;

class NoMilk
{
public:
    NoMilk();
    NoMilk(int how_many);
    int get_donuts();
private:
    int count;
};

int main()
{
    int donuts, milk;
    double dpg;

    try
    {
        cout << "Enter number of donuts:\n";
        cin >> donuts;
        cout << "Enter number of glasses of milk:\n";
        cin >> milk;

        if (milk <= 0)
                throw NoMilk(donuts);

        dpg = donuts/double(milk);
        cout << donuts << " donuts.\n"
            << milk << " glasses of milk.\n"
            << "You have " << dpg
            << " donuts for each glass of milk.\n";
    }
    catch(NoMilk e)
    {
        cout << e.get_donuts() << " donuts, and No Milk!\n"
            << "Go buy some milk.\n";
    }
    cout << "End of program.";
    return 0;
}
```

This is just a toy example to learn C++ syntax. Do not take it as an example of good typical use of exception handling.

Display 16.3 Defining Your Own Exception Class *(part 2 of 2)*

```
NoMilk::NoMilk()
{}
NoMilk::NoMilk(int how_many) : count(how_many)
{}

int NoMilk::get_donuts()
{
    return count;
}
```

The sample dialogues are the same as in Display 16.2.

◆ *PITFALL*   Catch the More Specific Exception First

When catching multiple exceptions, the order of the *catch*-blocks can be important. When an exception value is thrown in a *try*-block, the following *catch*-blocks are tried in order, and the first one that matches the type of the exception thrown is the one that is executed.

For example, the following is a special kind of *catch*-block that will catch a thrown value of any type:

```
catch (...)
{
   <Place whatever you want in here>
}
```

The three dots do not stand for something omitted. You actually type in those three dots in your program. This makes a good default *catch*-block to place after all other *catch*-blocks. For example, we could add it to the *catch*-blocks in Display 16.4 as follows:

(Text continues on page 897.)

Display 16.4 Catching Multiple Exceptions *(part 1 of 3)*

```
#include <iostream>
#include <string>
using namespace std;

class NegativeNumber
{
public:
    NegativeNumber();
    NegativeNumber(string take_me_to_your_catch_block);
    string get_message();
private:
    string message;
};

class DivideByZero
{};

int main()
{
    int jem_hadar, klingons;
    double portion;

    try
    {
        cout << "Enter number of Jem Hadar warriors:\n";
        cin >> jem_hadar;
        if (jem_hadar < 0)
            throw NegativeNumber("Jem Hadar");

        cout << "How many Klingon warriors do you have?\n";
        cin >> klingons;
        if (klingons < 0)
            throw NegativeNumber("Klingons");
```

The exception classes can have their own interface and implementation files and can be put in a namespace.

This is another toy example.

Display 16.4 Catching Multiple Exceptions *(part 2 of 3)*

```
            if (klingons != 0)
                portion = jem_hadar/double(klingons);
            else
                throw DivideByZero();
            cout << "Each Klingon must fight "
                 << portion << " Jem Hadar.\n";
        }
        catch(NegativeNumber e)
        {
            cout << "Cannot have a negative number of "
                 << e.get_message() << endl;
        }
        catch(DivideByZero)
        {
            cout << "Today is a good day to die.\n";
        }

        cout << "End of program.\n";
        return 0;
    }


    NegativeNumber::NegativeNumber()
    {}

    NegativeNumber::NegativeNumber(string take_me_to_your_catch_block)
        : message(take_me_to_your_catch_block)
     {}

    string NegativeNumber::get_message()
    {
        return message;
    }
```

Display 16.4 Catching Multiple Exceptions *(part 3 of 3)*

Sample Dialogue 1

```
Enter number of Jem Hadar warriors:
1000
How many Klingon warriors do you have?
500
Each Klingon must fight 2.0 Jem Hadar.
End of program
```

Sample Dialogue 2

```
Enter number of Jem Hadar warriors:
-10
Cannot have a negative number of Jem Hadar
End of program.
```

Sample Dialogue 3

```
Enter number of Jem Hadar warriors:
1000
How many Klingon warriors  do you have?
0
Today is a good day to die.
End of program.
```

```
catch(NegativeNumber e)
{
    cout << "Cannot have a negative number of "
        << e.get_message() << endl;
}
catch(DivideByZero)
{
    cout << "Today is a good day to die.\n";
}
catch (...)
{
    cout << "Unexplained exception.\n";
}
```

However, it only makes sense to place this default *catch*-block at the end of a list of *catch*-blocks. For example, suppose we instead used:

```
catch(NegativeNumber e)
{
    cout << "Cannot have a negative number of "
        << e.get_message() << endl;
}
catch (...)
{
    cout << "Unexplained exception.\n";
}
catch(DivideByZero)
{
    cout << "Today is a good day to die.\n";
}
```

With this second ordering, an exception (a thrown value) of type NegativeNumber will be caught by the NegativeNumber *catch*-block as it should be. However, if a value of type DivideByZero were thrown, it would be caught by the block that starts *catch*(...). So, the DivideByZero *catch*-block could never be reached. Fortunately, most compilers tell you if you make this sort of mistake.

↝ PROGRAMMING TIP
Exception Classes Can Be Trivial

Here we reproduce the definition of the exception class DivideByZero from Display 16.4:

```
class DivideByZero
{};
```

This exception class has no member variables and no member functions (other than the default constructor). It has nothing but its name, but that is useful enough. Throwing an object of the class `DivideByZero` can activate the appropriate *catch*-block as it does in Display 16.4.

When using a trivial exception class you normally do not have anything you can do with the exception (the thrown value) once it gets to the *catch*-block. The exception is just being used to get you to the *catch*-block. Thus, you can omit the *catch*-block parameter. (You can omit the *catch*-block parameter anytime you do not need it, whether the exception type is trivial or not.)

Throwing an Exception in a Function

Sometimes it makes sense to delay handling an exception. For example, you might have a function with code that throws an exception if there is an attempt to divide by zero, but you may not want to catch the exception in that function. Perhaps some programs that use that function should simply end if the exception is thrown, and other programs that use the function should do something else. So you would not know what to do with the exception if you caught it inside the function. In these cases, it makes sense to not catch the exception in the function definition, but instead to have any program (or other code) that uses the function place the function invocation in a *try*-block and catch the exception in a *catch*-block that follows that *try*-block.

Look at the program in Display 16.5. It has a *try*-block, but there is no *throw*-statement visible in the *try*-block. The statement that does the throwing in that program is

```
if (bottom == 0)
    throw DivideByZero();
```

This statement is not visible in the *try*-block. However, it is in the *try*-block in terms of program execution, because it is in the definition of the function `safe_divide` and there is an invocation of `safe_divide` in the *try*-block.

If a function does not catch an exception, it should at least warn programmers that any invocation of the function might possibly throw an exception. If there are exceptions that might be thrown, but not caught, in a function definition, then those exception types should be listed in a *throw*-list, which is illustrated by the following prototype from Display 16.5.

throw-list

```
double safe_divide(int top, int bottom) throw (DivideByZero);
```

As illustrated in Display 16.5, the *throw*-list should appear in both the function prototype and the function definition.

Display 16.5 Throwing an Exception inside a Function (part 1 of 2)

```cpp
#include <iostream>
#include <cstdlib>
using namespace std;

class DivideByZero
{};

double safe_divide(int top, int bottom) throw (DivideByZero);

int main()
{
    int numerator;
    int denominator;
    double quotient;
    cout << "Enter numerator:\n";
    cin >> numerator;
    cout << "Enter denominator:\n";
    cin >> denominator;

    try
    {
        quotient = safe_divide(numerator, denominator);
    }
    catch(DivideByZero)
    {
        cout << "Error: Division by zero!\n"
             << "Program aborting.\n";
        exit(0);
    }

    cout << numerator << "/" << denominator
         << " = " << quotient << endl;

    cout << "End of program.\n";
    return 0;
}
```

Display 16.5 Throwing an Exception inside a Function *(part 2 of 2)*

```
double safe_divide(int top, int bottom) throw (DivideByZero)
{
    if (bottom == 0)
        throw DivideByZero();

    return top/double(bottom);
}
```

Sample Dialogue 1

```
Enter numerator:
5
Enter denominator:
10
5/10 = 0.5
End of Program.
```

Sample Dialogue 2

```
Enter numerator:
5
Enter denominator:
0
Error: Division by zero!
Program aborting.
```

If there is more than one possible exception that can be thrown in the function definition, then the exception types are separated by commas as illustrated in what follows:

```
void some_function() throw (int, DivideByZero);
```

A function can throw an exception that is not listed in a throw list, but in that case the program will terminate. (Technically speaking, if an exception is thrown but not caught, then the function std::terminate() is called, but unless you do something to change defaults, that will end the program.) Also, a function that has no throw list at all (not even an empty one) can throw any exception and it will be treated normally. Thus, the effect of listing a type in a throw list is to change what happens when exceptions are thrown. If there is a throw list, then all exceptions of the listed types that are thrown are treated normally and all exceptions of unlisted types end the program. By way of summary:

```
void some_function() throw (int, DivideByZero);
//Exceptions of type int or DivideByZero treated normally
//All other exceptions end the program

void some_function() throw ();
//Empty exception list so all exceptions end the program.

void some_function();
//All exceptions of all types treated normally.
```

Keep in mind that an object of a derived class is also an object of its base class. So, if D is a derived class of class B and B is on a *throw*-list, then a thrown object of class D will be treated normally, since it is an object of class B, and B is on the *throw*-list

Also keep in mind that a *throw*-list is for exceptions that "get outside" the function. If they do not get outside the function, they do not belong on the *throw*-list. If they get outside the function, they belong on the *throw*-list no matter where they originate. If an exception is thrown in a *try*-block that is inside a function definition and is caught in a *catch*-block inside the function definition, then its type need not be listed on the *throw*-list. If a function definition includes an invocation of another function and that other function can throw an exception that is not caught, then the type of the exception should be placed on the *throw*-list.

One final warning: Not all compilers treat the *throw*-list as they are supposed to. Some compilers essentially treat the *throw*-list as a comment, and so with those compilers, the *throw*-list has no effect on your code.

● PITFALL   Throw List in Derived Classes

When you redefine or override a function definition in a derived class, it should have the same *throw*-list as it had in the base class, or it should have a *throw*-list whose exceptions are a subset of those in the base class *throw*-list. Put another way, when you redefine or override a function definition, you cannot add any exceptions to the *throw*-list (but you can delete some exceptions if you want). This makes sense, since an object of the derived class can be used any place an object of the base class can be used, and so a redefined or overwritten function must fit any code written for an object of the base class.

SELF-TEST EXERCISES

8 What is the output produced by the following program?

```
#include <iostream>
using namespace std;

void sample_function(double test) throw (int);

int main()
{
    try
    {
        cout << "Trying.\n";
        sample_function(98.6);
        cout << "Trying after call.\n";
    }
    catch(int)
    {
        cout << "Catching.\n";
    }

    cout << "End program.\n";
    return 0;
}
void sample_function(double test) throw (int)
{
    cout << "Starting sample_function.\n";
    if (test < 100)
        throw 42;
}
```

9 What is the output produced by the program in Self-Test Exercise 8 if the following change were made to the program?

change

```
sample_function(98.6);
```

in the *try*-block to

```
sample_function(212);
```

16.2 Programming Techniques for Exception Handling

Only use this in exceptional circumstances.

WARREN PEACE, THE LIEUTENANT'S TOOLS

So far we have shown you lots of code that explains how exception handling works in C++, but we have not yet shown even one example of a program that makes good and realistic use of exception handling. However, now that you know the mechanics of exception handling, this section can go on to explain exception-handling techniques.

When to Throw an Exception

We have given some very simple code in order to illustrate the basic concepts of exception handling. However, our examples were unrealistically simple. A more complicated but better guideline is to separate throwing an exception and catching the exception into separate functions. In most cases, you should include any *throw*-statement within a function definition, list the exception in a *throw*-list in that function, and place the *catch*-clause in *a different function*. Thus, the preferred use of the *try-throw-catch*-triple is as illustrated here:

```
void functionA() throw (MyException)
{
        .
        .
        .
    throw MyException(<Maybe an argument>);
        .
        .
        .
}
```

Then, in *some other function* (perhaps even some other function in some other file), you have

```
void functionB()
{
        .
        .
        .

    try
    {
            .
            .
            .

        functionA();
            .

            .

            .

    }
    catch(MyException e)
    {
            <Handle exception.>
    }
            .
            .
            .

}
```

Moreover, even this kind of use of a *throw*-statement should be reserved for cases in which it is unavoidable. If you can easily handle a problem in some other way, do not throw an exception. Reserve *throw*-statements for situations in which the way the exceptional condition is handled depends on how and where the function is used. If the way that the exceptional condition is handled depends on how and where the function is invoked, then the best thing to do is to let the programmer who invokes the function handle the exception. In all other situations, it is almost always preferable to avoid throwing exceptions.

When to Throw an Exception

For the most part, *throw*-statements should be used within functions and listed in a *throw*-list for the function. Moreover, they should be reserved for situations in which the way the exceptional condition is handled depends on how and where the function is used. If the way that the exceptional condition is handled depends on how and where the function is invoked, then the best thing to do is to let the programmer who invokes the function handle the exception. In all other situations, it is almost always preferable to avoid throwing an exception.

◆ PITFALL   Uncaught Exceptions

Every exception that is thrown by your code should be caught someplace in your code. If an exception is thrown but not caught anywhere, then your program ends. Technically speaking, if an exception is thrown but not caught, then the function `std::terminate()` is called. The default meaning for `std::terminate()` is to end your program. You can change the meaning from the default, but that is beyond the scope of this book.

◆ PITFALL   Nested *try-catch*-Blocks

You can place a *try*-block and following *catch*-blocks inside a larger *try*-block or inside a larger *catch*-block. In rare cases this may be useful, but if you are tempted to do this, you should suspect that there is a nicer way to organize your program. It is almost always better to place the inner *try-catch*-blocks inside a function definition and place an invocation of the function in the outer *try*- or *catch*-block (or maybe just eliminate one or more *try*-blocks completely).

If you place a *try*-block and following *catch*-blocks inside a larger *try*-block, and an exception is thrown in the inner *try*-block but not caught in the inner *try-catch*-blocks, then the exception is thrown to the outer *try*-block for processing and might be caught there.

◆ PITFALL   Overuse of Exceptions

Exceptions allow you to write programs whose flow of control is so involved that it is almost impossible to understand the program. Moreover, this is not hard to do. Throwing an exception allows you to transfer flow of control from any place in your program to almost any place else in your program. In the early days of programming, this sort of unrestricted flow of control was allowed via a construct known as a goto. Programming experts now agree that such unrestricted flow of control is very poor programming style. Exceptions allow you to revert to these bad old days of unrestricted flow of control. Exceptions should be used sparingly and only in certain ways. A good rule is the following: If you are tempted to include a *throw*-statement, then think about how you might write your program or class definition without this *throw*-statement. If you think of an alternative that produces reasonable code, then you probably do not want to include the *throw*-statement.

Exception Class Hierarchies

It can be very useful to define a hierarchy of exception classes. For example, you might have an ArithmeticError exception class and then define an exception class DivideByZeroError that is a derived class of ArithmeticError. Since a Divide-ByZeroError is an ArithmeticError, every *catch*-block for an ArithmeticError will catch a DivideByZeroError. If you list ArithmeticError in a *throw*-list, then you have, in effect, also added DivideByZeroError to the *throw*-list, whether or not you list DivideByZeroError by name on the *throw*-list.

Testing for Available Memory

In Chapter 14 we created new dynamic variables with code such as the following:

```
struct Node
{
    int data;
    Node *link;
};
typedef Node* NodePtr;
    ...
NodePtr pointer = new Node;
```

This works fine as long as there is sufficient memory available to create the new node. But, what happens if there is not sufficient memory? If there is not sufficient memory to create the node, then a bad_alloc exception is thrown. The type bad_alloc is part of the C++ language. You do not need to define it.

Since *new* will throw a bad_alloc exception when there is not enough memory to create the node, you can check for running out of memory as follows:

```
try
{
    NodePtr pointer = new Node;
}
catch (bad_alloc)
{
    cout << "Ran out of memory!";
}
```

Of course, you can do other things besides simply giving a warning message, but the details of what you do will depend on your particular programming task.

Rethrowing an Exception

It is legal to throw an exception within a *catch*-block. In rare cases you may want to catch an exception, and then, depending on the details, decide to throw the same or a different exception for handling farther up the chain of exception handling blocks.

SELF-TEST EXERCISES

10 What happens when an exception is never caught?

11 Can you nest a *try*-block inside another *try*-block?

CHAPTER SUMMARY

- Exception handling allows you to design and code the normal case for your program separately from the code that handles exceptional situations.

- An exception can be thrown in a *try*-block. Alternatively, an exception can be thrown in a function definition that does not include a *try*-block (or does not include a *catch*-block to catch that type of exception). In this case, an invocation of the function can be placed in a *try*-block.

- An exception is caught in a *catch*-block.

- A *try*-block may be followed by more than one *catch*-block. In this case, always list the *catch*-block for a more specific exception class before the *catch*-block for a more general exception class.

- Do not overuse exceptions.

Answers to Self-Test Exercises

1
```
Try block entered.
Exception thrown with
wait_time equal to 46
After catch-block.
```

2

```
Try-block entered.
Leaving try-block.
After catch-block.
```

3

```
throw wait_time;
```

Note that the following is an *if*-statement, not a *throw*-statement, even though it contains a *throw*-statement:

```
if (wait_time > 30)
    throw wait_time;
```

4   When a *throw*-statement is executed, that is the end of the enclosing *try*-block. No other statements in the *try*-block are executed, and control passes to the following *catch*-block(s). When we say control passes to the following *catch*-block, we mean that the value thrown is plugged in for the *catch*-block parameter (if any), and the code in the *catch*-block is executed.

5

```
try
{
    cout << "Try-block entered.";
    if (wait_time > 30)
        throw wait_time);
    cout << "Leaving try-block.";
}
```

6

```
catch(int thrown_value)
{
    cout << "Exception thrown with\n"
         << "wait_time equal to" << thrown_value << endl;
}
```

7   thrown_value is the *catch*-block parameter.

8

```
Trying.
Starting sample_function.
Catching.
End of program.
```

9

```
Trying.
Starting sample_function.
Trying after call.
End of program.
```

10 If an exception is not caught anywhere, then your program ends. Technically speaking, if an exception is thrown but not caught, then the function `std::terminate()` is called. The default meaning for `std::terminate()` is to end your program.

11 Yes, you can have a *try*-block and corresponding *catch*-blocks inside another larger *try*-block. However, it would probably be better to place the inner *try*- and *catch*-blocks in a function definition and place an invocation of the function in the larger *try*-block.

Programming Projects

1 Write a program that converts from 24-hour time to 12-hour time. The following is a sample dialogue:

```
Enter time in 24-hour notation:
13:07
That is the same as
1:07 PM
Again?(y/n)
y
Enter time in 24-hour notation:
10:15
That is the same as
10:15 AM
Again?(y/n)
y
Enter time in 24-hour notation:
10:65
```

```
There is no such time as 10:65
Try Again:
Enter time in 24-hour notation:
16:05
That is the same as
4:05 PM
Again?(y/n)
n
End of program
```

You will define an exception class called `TimeFormatMistake`. If the user enters an illegal time, like `10:65` or even gibberish like `8&*68`, then your program will throw and catch a `TimeFormatMistake`.

2 Write a program that converts dates from numerical month/day format to alphabetic month/day (e.g. 1/31 or 01/31 corresponds to January 31). The dialogue should be similar to that in Programming Exercise 1. You will define two exception classes, one called `MonthError` and another called `DayError`. If the user enters anything other than a legal month number (integers from 1 to 12) then your program will throw and catch a `MonthError`. Similarly, if the user enters anything other than a valid day number (integers from 1 to either 29, 30, or 31, depending on the month), then your program will throw and catch a `DayError`. To keep things simple, always allow 29 days for February.

The following keywords should not be used for anything other than their predefined purposes in the C++ language. In particular, do not use them for variable names or names for programmer-defined functions. In addition to the keywords listed below, identifiers containing a double underscore (__) are reserved for use by C++ implementations and standard libraries and should not be used in your programs.

asm	do	inline	return	typedef
auto	double	int	short	typeid
bool	dynamic_cast	log	signed	typename
break	else	long	sizeof	union
case	enum	mutable	static	unsigned
catch	explicit	namespace	static_cast	using
char	extern	new	struct	virtual
class	false	operator	switch	void
const	float	private	template	volatile
const_cast	for	protected	this	wchar_t
continue	friend	public	throw	while
default	goto	register	true	
delete	if	reinterpret_cast	try	

These alternative representations for operators and punctuation are reserved and also should not be used otherwise.

and &&	and_eq &=	bitand &	bitor |	compl ^	not ~
not_eq !=	or ||	or_eq |=	xor ^	xor_eq ^=	

APPENDIX 2
PRECEDENCE OF OPERATORS

All the operators in a given box have the same precedence. Operators in higher boxes have higher precedence than operators in lower boxes. Unary operators and the assignment operator are done right to left when operators have the same precedence. For example, x = y = z means x = (y = z). Other operators that have the same precedences are done left to right. For example, x+y+z means (x+y)+z.

```
:: scope resolution operator
```

```
. dot operator
-> member selection
[] array indexing
( ) function call
++ postfix increment operator (placed after the variable)
-- postfix decrement operator (placed after the variable)
```

```
++ prefix increment operator (placed before the variable)
-- prefix decrement operator (placed before the variable)
! not
- unary minus
+ unary plus
* dereference
& address of
new
delete
delete[]
sizeof
```

* multiply
/ divide
% remainder (modulo)

+ addition
- subtraction

<< insertion operator (output)
>> extraction operator (input)

< less than   <= less than or equal
> greater than   >= greater than or equal

== equal
!= not equal

&& and

|| or

= assignment
+= add and assign   -= subtract and assign
*= multiply and assign
/= divide and assign   %= modulo and assign

highest precedence (done first)

lowest precedence (done last)

APPENDIX 3

THE ASCII CHARACTER SET

Only the printable characters are shown. Character number 32 is the blank.

32		56	8	80	P	104	h
33	!	57	9	81	Q	105	i
34	"	58	:	82	R	106	j
35	#	59	;	83	S	107	k
36	$	60	<	84	T	108	l
37	%	61	=	85	U	109	m
38	&	62	>	86	V	110	n
39	'	63	?	87	W	111	o
40	(	64	@	88	X	112	p
41	)	65	A	89	Y	113	q
42	*	66	B	90	Z	114	r
43	+	67	C	91	[	115	s
44	,	68	D	92	\	116	t
45	–	69	E	93	]	117	u
46	.	70	F	94	^	118	v
47	/	71	G	95	_	119	w
48	0	72	H	96	'	120	x
49	1	73	I	97	a	121	y
50	2	74	J	98	b	122	z
51	3	75	K	99	c	123	{
52	4	76	L	100	d	124		
53	5	77	M	101	e	125	}
54	6	78	N	102	f	126	~
55	7	79	O	103	g		

APPENDIX 4
SOME LIBRARY FUNCTIONS

The following lists are organized according to what the function is used for, rather than what library it is in. The function prototype gives the number and types of arguments as well as the type of the value returned. In most cases, the prototypes give only the type of the parameter and do not give a parameter name. (See the section "Alternate Form for Function Prototypes" in Chapter 3 for an explanation of this kind of prototype.) Depending on your implementation of C++, you may or may not need to use the .h in the header file name.

Arithmetic Functions

Prototype	Description	Header File
int abs(*int*);	Absolute value.	cstdlib
long labs(*long*);	Absolute value.	cstdlib
double fabs(*double*);	Absolute value.	cmath
double sqrt(*double*);	Square root.	cmath
double pow(*double, double*);	Returns the first argument raised to the power of the second argument.	cmath
double exp(*double*);	Returns e (base of the natural logarithm) to the power of its argument.	cmath
double log(*double*);	Natural logarithm (ln).	cmath
double log10(*double*);	Base 10 logarithm.	cmath

Arithmetic Functions (continued)

Prototype	Description	Header File
double ceil(*double*);	Returns the smallest integer that is greater than or equal to its argument.	cmath
double floor(*double*);	Returns the largest integer that is less than or equal to its argument.	cmath

Input and Output Member Functions

Form of a Function Call	Description	Header File
Stream_Var.open(*External_File_Name*);	Connects the file with the *External_File_Name* to the stream named by the *Stream_Var*. The *External_File_Name* is a string value.	fstream
Stream_Var.fail( );	Returns *true* if the previous operation (such as open) on the stream *Stream_Var* has failed.	fstream or iostream
Stream_Var.close( );	Disconnects the stream *Stream_Var* from file it is connected to.	fstream
Stream_Var.bad( );	Returns *true* if the stream *Stream_Var* is corrupted.	fstream or iostream
Stream_Var.eof( );	Returns *true* if the program has attempted to read beyond the last character in the file connected to the input stream *Stream_Var*. Otherwise, it returns *false*.	fstream or iostream
Stream_Var.get(*Char_Variable*);	Reads one character from the input stream *Stream_Var* and sets the *Char_Variable* equal to this character. Does *not* skip over whitespace.	fstream or iostream

Input and Output Member Functions *(continued)*

Form of a Function Call	Description	Header File
Stream_Var.getline(*String_Var*, *Max_Characters* +1);	One line of input from the stream *Stream_Var* is read and the resulting string is placed in *String_Var*. If the line is more than *Max_Characters* long, only the first *Max_Characters* are read. The declared size of the *String_Var* should be *Max_Characters* +1 or larger.	fstream or iostream
Stream_Var.peek();	Reads one character from the input stream *Stream_Var* and returns that character. But, the character read is *not* removed from the input stream; the next read will read the same character.	fstream or iostream
Stream_Var.put(*Char_Exp*);	Writes the value of the *Char_Exp* to the output stream *Stream_Var*.	fstream or iostream
Stream_Var.putback(*Char_Exp*);	Places the value of *Char_Exp* in the input stream *Stream_Var* so that that value is the next input value read from the stream. The file connected to the stream is not changed.	fstream or iostream
Stream_Var.precision(*Int_Exp*);	Specifies the number of digits output after the decimal point for floating point values sent to the output stream *Stream_Var*.	fstream or iostream
Stream_Var.width(*Int_Exp*);	Sets the field width for the next value output to the stream *Stream_Var*.	fstream or iostream
Stream_Var.setf(*Flag*);	Sets flags for formatting output to the stream *Stream_Var*. See Display 5.4 for the list of possible flags.	fstream or iostream
Stream_Var.unsetf(*Flag*);	Unsets flags for formatting output to the stream *Stream_Var*. See Display 5.4 for the list of possible flags.	fstream or iostream

Character Functions

For all of these the actual type of the argument is *int*, but for most purposes you can think of the argument type as *char*. If the value returned is a value of type *int*, you must perform an explicit or implicit typecast to obtain a *char*.

Prototype	Description	Header File
bool isalnum(*char*);	Returns *true* if its argument satisfies either `isalpha` or `isdigit`. Otherwise returns *false*.	cctype
bool isalpha(*char*);	Returns *true* if its argument is an upper- or lowercase letter. It may also return true for other arguments. The details are implementation dependent. Otherwise returns *false*.	cctype
bool isdigit(*char*);	Returns *true* if its argument is a digit. Otherwise returns *false*.	cctype
bool ispunct(*char*);	Returns *true* if its argument is a printable character that does not satisfy `isalnum` and that is not white space. (These characters are considered punctuation characters.) Otherwise returns *false*.	cctype
bool isspace(*char*);	Returns *true* if its argument is a white space character (e.g., blank, tab, newline). Otherwise returns *false*.	cctype
bool iscntrl(*char*);	Returns *true* if its argument is a control character. Otherwise returns *false*.	cctype
bool islower(*char*);	Returns *true* if its argument is a lowercase letter. Otherwise returns *false*.	cctype
bool isupper(*char*);	Returns *true* if its argument is an uppercase letter. Otherwise returns *false*.	cctype

Character Functions *(continued)*

Prototype	Description	Header File
int tolower(*char*);	Returns the lowercase version of its argument. If there is no lowercase versions, returns its argument unchanged.	cctype
int toupper(*char*);	Returns the uppercase version of its argument. If there is no uppercase versions, returns its argument unchanged.	cctype

String Functions

Prototype	Description	Header File
int atoi(*const char* a[]);	Converts a string of characters to an integer.	cstdlib
long atol(*const char* a[]);	Converts a string of characters to a *long* integer.	cstdlib
double atof(*const char* a[]);	Converts a string of characters to a *double*.	cstdlib[a]
Form of a Function Call	**Description**	**Header File**
strcat(*String_Variable*, *String_Expression*);	Appends the value of the *String_Expression* to the end of the string in the *String_Variable*.	cstring

a. Some implementations place it in cmath.

String Functions (continued)

Form of a Function Call	Description	Header File
strcmp(*String_Exp1*, *String_Exp2*)	Returns *true* if the values of the two string expressions are different; otherwise, returns *false.*[a]	cstring
strcpy(*String_Variable*, *String_Expression*);	Changes the value of the *String_Variable* to the value of the *String_Expression*.	cstring
strlen(*String_Expression*)	Returns the length of the *String_Expression*.	cstring
strncat(*String_Variable*, *String_Expression*, *Limit*);	Same as strcat except that at most *Limit* characters are appended.	cstring
strncmp(*String_Exp1*, *String_Exp2*, *Limit*)	Same as strcmp except that at most *Limit* characters are compared.	cstring
strncpy(*String_Variable*, *String_Expression*, *Limit*);	Same as strcat except that at most *Limit* characters are copied.	cstring
strstr(*String_Expression*, *Pattern*)	Returns a pointer to the first occurrence of the string *Pattern* in *String_Expression*. Returns the NULL pointer if the *Pattern* is not found.	cstring
strchr(*String_Expression*, *Character*)	Returns a pointer to the first occurrence of the *Character* in *String_Expression*. Returns the NULL pointer if *Character* is not found.	cstring
strrchr(*String_Expression*, *Character*)	Returns a pointer to the last occurrence of the *Character* in *String_Expression*. Returns the NULL pointer if *Character* is not found.	cstring

a. Returns an integer that is less than zero, zero, or greater than zero accordingly as *String_Exp1* is less than, equal to, or greater than *String_Exp2*, respectively. The ordering is lexicographic ordering.

Random Number Generator

Prototype	Description	Header File
int random(*int*);	The call random(n) returns a pseudorandom integer greater than or equal to 0 and less than or equal to n-1. (Not available in all implementations. If not available, then you must use rand.)	cstdlib
int rand( );	The call rand( ) returns a pseudorandom integer greater than or equal to 0 and less than or equal to RAND_MAX. RAND_MAX is a predefined integer constant that is defined in cstdlib. The value of RAND_MAX is implementation dependent but will be at least 32767.	cstdlib
void srand(*unsigned int*); (The type *unsigned int* is an integer type that only allows nonnegative values. You can think of the argument type as *int* with the restriction that it must be nonnegative.)	Reinitializes the random number generator. The argument is the seed. Calling srand multiple times with the same argument will cause rand or random (whichever you use) to produce the same sequence of pseudorandom numbers. If rand or random is called without any previous call to srand, the sequence of numbers produced is the same as if there had been a call to srand with an argument of 1.	cstdlib

Trigonometric Functions

These functions use radians, not degrees.

Prototype	Description	Header File
double acos(*double*);	Arc cosine	cmath
double asin(*double*);	Arc sine	cmath
double atan(*double*);	Arc tangent	cmath
double cos(*double*);	Cosine	cmath
double cosh(*double*);	Hyperbolic cosine	cmath
double sin(*double*);	Sine	cmath
double sinh(*double*);	Hyperbolic sine	cmath
double tan(*double*);	Tangent	cmath
double tanh(*double*);	Hyperbolic tangent	cmath

APPENDIX 5

THE assert-STATEMENT

In Chapter 5 we used the following to test to see if a file named `in_stream` was opened successfully:

```
if (in_stream.fail())
{
    cout << "Input file opening failed.\n";
    exit(1);
}
```

The `assert`-statement can be used to write the same test as follows:

```
assert(!in_stream.fail());
```

Note that in this case we needed to insert a *not* in order to get the equivalent meaning, because we are asserting that the file opening did *not fail*.

The `assert`-statement consists of the identifier `assert` followed by a logical expression in parentheses and ends with a semicolon. Any logical expression may be used. If the logical expression is *false*, then the program ends and an error message is issued. If the logical expression is *true*, nothing happens and the program proceeds to the next statement after the `assert`-statement. Thus `assert`-statements are a compact way to include error checks within your program.

The `assert`-statement is defined in the library `cassert`, so any program that uses an `assert`-statement must contain the following `include` directive:

```
#include <cassert>
```

`assert` is a macro, which is a construct similar to a function, and so it makes sense to define it in a library.

One advantage of using `assert`-statements is that you can turn them off. You can use the `assert`-statements in your program to debug your program, and then turn them off so that users do not get error messages that they might not understand, and so that you reduce the overhead performed by your program. To turn off all the `assert`-statements in your program, you add `#define NDEBUG` before the `include` directive, as follows:

```
#define NDEBUG
#include <cassert>
```

Thus, if you insert `#define NDEBUG` in your program after it is fully debugged, then all assert-statements in your program are turned off. If you later change your program and need to debug it again, you can turn the assert-statements back on by deleting the `#define NDEBUG` (or commenting it out).

APPENDIX 6
INLINE FUNCTIONS

When a member function definition is short, you can give the function definition within the definition of the class. You simply replace the member prototype by the member function definition; however, since the definition is within the class definition, you do not include the class name and scope resolution operator. For example, the class `Pair` defined below has inline function definitions for its two constructors:

```
class Pair
{
public:
    Pair( )
    {}
    Pair(char first_value, char second_value)
    {first = first_value; second = second_value;}
        ...
private:
    char first;
    char second;
};
```

Note that there is no semicolon after the closing brace in an inline function definition, though it is not incorrect to have a semicolon there.

Inline function definitions are treated differently by the compiler and so they usually run more efficiently, although they consume more storage. With an inline function, each function call in your program is replaced by a compiled version of the function definition, so calls to inline functions do not have the overhead of a normal function call.

APPENDIX 7
CONSTRUCTOR INITIALIZATION SECTION

When defining a constructor you can initialize member variables in an **initialization section.** This initialization section is part of the heading for the function definition for the constructor. For example, suppose you have the following class definition:

```
class Rational
{
public:
    Rational( );
    Rational(int whole_number);
    Rational(int numerator, int denominator);
        . . .
private:
    int top;
    int bottom;
};
```

The three constructors can be defined as follows:

```
//Initializes top to 0 and bottom to 1:
Rational::Rational( ) : top(0), bottom(1)
{
    //Empty body
}
//Initializes top to whole_number and bottom to 1:
Rational::Rational(int whole_number)
                : top(whole_number), bottom(1)
{
    //Empty body
}
```

```
//Initializes top to numerator and bottom to denominator:
Rational::Rational(int numerator, int denominator)
                : top(numerator), bottom(denominator)
{
    //Empty body
}
```

As these examples show, the initialization section goes after the parentheses that ends the parameter list and before the opening brace of the function body. The initialization section consists of a colon followed by a list of some or all the member variables separated by commas; each member variable is followed by its initializing value in parentheses. Notice that the initializing values can be given in terms of the constructor parameters.

The function body need not be empty as in the above examples. For example, the second of the above constructor definitions is equivalent to the following:

```
Rational::Rational(int whole_number) : top(whole_number)
{
    bottom = 1;
}
```

There need not be any initialization section. For example, the above constructor definition is, in turn, equivalent to the following:

```
Rational::Rational(int whole_number)
{
    top = whole_number;
    bottom = 1;
}
```

APPENDIX 8

OVERLOADING THE ARRAY INDEX SQUARE BRACKETS

You can overload the square brackets [] for a class so that the square brackets can be used with objects of the class. If you want to use [] in an expression on the left-hand side of an assignment operator, then the operator must be defined to return a reference, which is indicated by adding & to the returned type. (This has some similarity to what we discussed for overloading the I/O operators << and >>.) When overloading [], the operator [] *must* be a member function; the overloaded [] *cannot* be a friend operator. (In this regard [] is overloaded in a way that is similar to the way that the assignment operator = is overloaded; overloading = is discussed in the optional section of Chapter 11 entitled "Overloading the Assignment Operator.")

For example, the following defines a class called Pair whose objects behave like arrays of characters with the two indexes 1 and 2 (*not* 0 and 1):

```
class Pair
{
public:
    Pair();
    Pair(char first_value, char second_value);
    char& operator[](int index);
private:
    char first;
    char second;
};
```

The type of the parameter must be an integer type, i.e., *enum, char, short, int, long*, or an *unsigned* version of one of these types.

The definition of the member function [] can be as follows:

```
char& Pair::operator[](int index)
{
    if (index == 1)
        return first;
    else if (index == 2)
        return second;
    else
    {
        cout << "Illegal index value.\n";
        exit(1);
    }
}
```

Objects are declared and used as follows:

```
Pair a;
a[1] = 'A';
a[2] = 'B';
cout << a[1] << a[2] << endl;
```

Note that in a[1], a is the calling object and 1 is the argument to the member function [].

APPENDIX 9

THE *this* POINTER

When defining member functions for a class you sometimes want to refer to the calling object. The *this* pointer is a predefined pointer that points to the calling object. For example, consider a class like the following:

```
class Sample
{
public:
        ...
    void show_stuff( );
        ...
private:
    int stuff;
        ...
};
```

The following two ways of defining the member function show_stuff are equivalent:

```
void Sample::show_stuff( )
{
    cout << stuff;
}
//Not good style, but this illustrates the this pointer:
void Sample::show_stuff( )
{
    cout << (this->stuff);
}
```

Notice that *this* is not the name of the calling object, but is the name of a pointer that points to the calling object. The *this* pointer cannot have its value changed; it always points to the calling object.

As the comment before the previous sample use of *this* indicates, you normally have no need for the pointer *this*. However, in a few situations it is handy.

One place where the *this* pointer is commonly used is in overloading the assignment operator =. For example, consider the following class:

*overloading the
assignment operator*

```
class StringClass
{
public:
    ...
    StringClass& operator=(const StringClass& right_side);
    ...
private:
    char *a;//Dynamic array for a string value ended with '\0.'
};
```

The following definition of the overloaded assignment operator can be used in chains of assignments like

```
s1 = s2 = s3;
```

This chain of assignments means

```
s1 = (s2 = s3);
```

The definition of the overloaded assignment operator uses the *this* pointer to return the object on the left side of the = sign (which is the calling object):

```
//This version does not work in all cases. Also see the next version.
StringClass& StringClass::operator=(const StringClass& right_side)
{
    delete [] a;
    a = new char[strlen(right_side.a) + 1];
    strcpy(a, right_side.a);
    return *this;
}
```

The above definition does have a problem in one case: if the same object occurs on both sides of the assignment operator (like s = s;), then the array member will be deleted. To avoid this problem, you can use the *this* pointer to test this special case as follows:

```
//Final version with bug fixed:
StringClass& StringClass::operator=(const StringClass&
right_side)
{
    if (this == &right_side)
    {
        return *this;
    }
    else
    {
        delete [] a;
        a = new char[strlen(right_side.a) + 1];
        strcpy(a, right_side.a);
        return *this;
    }
}
```

In the optional section of Chapter 11 entitled "Overloading the Assignment Operator," we overloaded the assignment operator for a string class called StringVar. In that section, we did not need the *this* pointer because we had a member variable called max_length which we could use to test whether or not the same object was used on both sides of the assignment operator =. With the class StringClass, discussed above, we have no such alternative because there is only one member variable. In this case we have essentially no alternative but to use the *this* pointer.

APPENDIX 10

SIMULATING
THE *bool* TYPE

Early compilers did not have the Boolean type, *bool*. Instead of the *bool* type these earlier compilers used *int* values to represent *true* and *false*. Any nonzero *int* value represented *true* and 0 represented *false*. To simulate the *bool* type, we *typedef int* to Boolean; then, define named constants:

```
//file: boolean.h
#ifndef BOOLEAN_H
#define BOOLEAN_H
typedef int Boolean;
const int TRUE = 1;
const int FALSE = 0;
#endif //BOOLEAN_H
```

You then #include "boolean.h", and use Boolean as if it were a built-in type with TRUE and FALSE as Boolean literals.

Note that the "real" *bool* type uses the lowercase version of *true* and *false*, and the keyword *bool*. If you define the lowercase versions of *bool*, *true*, and *false*, you will have a conflict if you compile your program with a compiler in which the *bool* type is defined. For this reason, we have not typedefed *int* to *bool*.

If in fact you *do* wish to use the standard lowercase *bool*, *true*, and *false* with these older compilers, then you can use this version of the boolean.h header file:

```
//file: boolean.h
#ifndef BOOLEAN_H
#define BOOLEAN_H
typedef int bool;
const int true = 1;
const int false = 0;
#endif  //BOOLEAN_H
```

OLD AND NEW HEADER FILES

In this book we have used the header files for standard libraries that are part of the new ANSI/ISO C++ standard. If you have an older compiler you may need to use the older header files. Below we list the new header file names that we have used in this book along with their corresponding older header file names. If the new header files do not work for you, then try the older header file names instead.

If your compiler requires the older header file names, then it also may not accommodate namespaces. In that case, you may have to eliminate all references to namespaces. If you have a compiler that requires the older header file names and/or does not support namespaces, you should consider obtaining a new compiler that comes closer to meeting the new standard.

New Header File	Corresponding Older Header File
cassert	assert.h
cctype	ctype.h
cstddef	stddef.h
cstdlib	stdlib.h
cmath	math.h
cstring	string.h
fstream	fstream.h
iomanip	iomanip.h
iostream	iostream.h

APPENDIX 12

OVERLOADING OPERATORS
AS MEMBER OPERATORS

In this book we have normally overloaded operators by treating them as friends of the class. For example, in Display 8.5 of Chapter 8 we overloaded the + operator as a friend. We did this by labeling the operator a friend inside the class definition, as follows:

```
//Class for amounts of money in U.S. currency.
class Money
{
public:
    friend Money operator +(const Money& amount1,
                                    const Money& amount2);
```

. . .

We then defined the overloaded operator + outside the class definition (as shown in Display 8.5).

It is also possible to overload the operator + (and other operators) as **member operators**. To overload the + operator as a member operator, the class definition would instead begin

```
//Class for amounts of money in U.S. currency.
class Money
{
public:
    Money operator +(const Money& amount2);
```

Note that when a binary operator is overloaded as a member operator, there is only one (not two) parameters. The calling object serves as the first parameter. For example, consider the following code:

```
Money cost(1, 50), tax(0, 15), total;
total = cost + tax;
```

When + is overloaded as a member operator, then in the expression cost + tax, the variable cost is the calling object and tax is the one argument to +.

The definition of the member operator + would be as follows:

```
Money Money::operator +(const Money& amount2)
{
    Money temp;
    temp.all_cents = all_cents + amount2.all_cents;
    return temp;
}
```

Notice the following line from this member operator definition:

```
temp.all_cents = all_cents + amount2.all_cents;
```

The first argument to + is an unqualified `all_cents` and so it is the member variable `all_cents` *of the calling object.*

Overloading an operator as a member variable can seem strange at first, but it is easy to get used to the new details. Many experts advocate always overloading operators as member operators rather than as friends. That is more in the spirit of object-oriented programming. However, there is a big disadvantage to overloading a binary operator as a member operator. When you overload a binary operator as member operator, the two arguments are no longer symmetric. One is a calling object and only the second "argument" is a true argument. This is unaesthetic, but it also has a very practical shortcoming. Any automatic type conversion will only apply to the second argument. So, for example, the following would be legal:

```
Money base_amount(100, 60), full_amount;
full_amount = base_amount + 25;
```

This is because `Money` has a constructor with one argument of type *long*, and so the value 25 will be considered a *long* value that is automatically converted to a value of type `Money`.

However, if you overload + as a member operator, then you cannot reverse the two arguments to +. The following is illegal:

```
full_amount = 25 + base_amount;
```

This is because 25 cannot be a calling object. Conversion of *long* values to type `Money` works for arguments but not for calling objects.

On the other hand, if you overload + as a friend, then the following is perfectly legal:

```
full_amount = 25 + base_amount;
```

AN ANNOTATED BIBLIOGRAPHY FOR C++ LANGUAGE AND LIBRARY ISSUES

For some of the details about who and what influenced the development of the C++ language, and some of the reasons behind the decisions, we recommend Bjarne Stroustrup, *The Design and Evolution of C++,* Addison Wesley Longman, © 1994 ISBN 0-201-54330-3.

For difficult points of the language presented in an understandable way, see Marshall Cline and Greg Lomow, *C++ FAQs Frequently Asked Questions,* Addison Wesley Longman, © 1994, ISBN 0-201-58958-3.

The base document for the ANSI C++ Standard is Margaret Ellis and Bjarne Stroustrup, *The Annotated C++ Reference Manual,* Addison Wesley Longman, © 1990. Each reprinting of this book includes the ANSI C++ Committee's resolutions to date. This document, though dated, is a surprisingly accurate description of the present language. It omits any reference to libraries. At the time of printing, no libraries were part of the language.

The final authority on what the language *should be* is the ISO/IEC FDIS 14882 *Information Technology—Programming Languages, Their Environments and System Software Interfaces—Programming Language C++,* available from ANSI, Attention: Customer Service, 11W 42nd Street, New York, NY 10036. This is an International Standards Organization document, so it is quite expensive. There are essentially correct machine-readable copies of the December 1996 Draft Standard on the World Wide Web. Search with Altavista, for C++, ANSI, Standard. There is, at this printing, some indication that ANSI may provide a machine-readable copy of this document for a lower price than the printed copy. An announcement should be made to the comp.std.c++ news group, should this occur.

Of course, the final authority on what language you are dealing with is your compiler. (Even your compiler documentation may not be right!) Learn to ask your compiler questions of syntax and semantics.

Bjarne Stroustrup, *The C++ Programming Language,* 3rd edition, Addison Wesley Longman, © 1997, ISBN: 0-201-88954-4 is the most recent in a series of definitive books on the C++ language, its history, and some of the reasons why the design proceeded as it did. It has a wealth of easy to difficult exercises. The exercises are marked with a measure of the difficulty of the exercise.

The book by Andrew Koenig and Barbara Moo, *Ruminations on C++,* Addison Wesley Longman, © 1997, ISBN 0-201-42339-1 is not curriculum-based. It is a compendium of updated and corrected articles written over several years for the journal *Object-Oriented Programming,* the *C++ Report,* and the *C++ Journal.* Koenig and Moo started using C++ when the entire user community would fit into one room (circa 1986). This book is both enlightening and enjoyable.

For the libraries, see P. J. Plauger, *The Draft Standard C++ Library,* Prentice Hall, © 1995, ISBN 0-13-117003-1. This was the base document for the ANSI Standard C++ library. In spite of the fact that this book is dated, this is a useful book when referenced with care. Dr. Plauger is the foremost authority on C and C++ libraries in the world. He is president of Dinkumware, a library company in Australia. He worked for Bell Labs when C was being developed and wrote one of the first commercial C compilers. See the Dinkumware Web page, at www.dinkumware.com.

A dated but still very useful addition to any library is the "Trout Book": Steve Teale, *C++ IO Streams,* Addison Wesley Longman, © 1993, ISBN 0-201-59641-5. The book is based on a version of the C++ iostreams library that came with a fairly early version of the AT&T C-Front C++ translator. Nevertheless, this is a book we still consult, along with the December 1996 ANSI C++ Draft Standard.

Standard Template Library was written by Ming Lee and Alex Stepanov of Hewlett Packard Corp. It was presented to the ANSI Standards committee in 1994. HP has made the STL available as freely redistributable code. Silicon Graphics also has a version of the STL they have made freely available and freely redistributable. Both are available on the World Wide Web.

P. J. Plauger *Standard Template Library: A Definitive Approach to C++ Programming,* Prentice Hall, © 1996, ISBN 0-13-417633-1. I have not read this book, but I know the author. The book is likely a good read.

Other useful references are:

Tim Budd, *Data Structures in C++ Using the Standard Template Library,* Addison Wesley Longman, © 1998, ISBN 0-201-30879-7. This book is very nearly unique in that it treats many of the Standard Template Library's container classes and generic algorithms. It is written at a level that should be accessible to students who have completed through Chapter 10 or 11 of this book.

Graham Glass and Brett Schuschert, *The STL PRIMER,* Prentice Hall, © 1996. ISBN 0-13-454976-7. This is a book designed to supplement a professional STL course taught by the authors. It is very good once you have mastered the overview and a few of the details in, say, Budd's book.

David R. Musser and Atul Saini, *STL Tutorial and Reference Guide,* Addison Wesley Longman, © 1996, ISBN 0-201-63398-1. This book uses the full gamut of C++. It will allow you to learn the full Standard Template library from scratch to a professional level if you know enough C++ to read it.

Mark Nelson, *A C++ Programmer's Guide to the Standard Template Library,* IDG Books, © 1995, ISBN 1-56884-314-3.

Mark Allen Weiss, *Algorithms, Data Structures, and Problem Solving with C++,* Addison Wesley Longman, © 1996, ISBN 0-8053-1666-3. Like Budd's book, Weiss's book should be accessible to anyone who has completed this book. It has a very different flavor than Budd's book, however. It expends more effort in teaching C++ along with implementations of the major classic data structures, programming techniques, and object-oriented programming.

Frank M. Carrano, Paul Veroff, and Robert Helman, *Data Abstractions and Problem Solving with C++—Walls and Mirrors,* 2nd edition, Addison Wesley, © 1998, ISBN 0-201-87402-4.

Style, pitfalls, and idiomatic C++ are discussed in the following:

Scott Meyers, *Effective C++,* Addison Wesley Longman, © 1992, ISBN 0-201-56364-9.

Scott Meyers, *More Effective C++,* Addison Wesley Longman, © 1996, ISBN 0-201-63371-X.

Tom Cargill, *C++ Programming Style,* Addison Wesley Longman, © 1992, ISBN 0-201-56365-7.

James Coplein, *Advanced C++ Programming Styles and Idioms,* Addison Wesley Longman, © 1992, ISBN 0-201-54855-0.

Grady Booch, *Object-Oriented Design and Analysis with Applications,* 2nd edition, Benjamin-Cummings, © 1994, ISBN 0-8053-5340-2. This is one of the classic object-oriented programming books. Booch has been doing object-oriented analysis, design, and programming since the early days of the Ada programming language. He switched his company library efforts to C++ soon after good C++ compilers became available.

Other excellent books at approximately the level of this text that bear examination follow. These books represent diverse approaches to beginning C++ and beginning computer science. Each is worth reading.

Rick Mercer, *Computing Fundamentals with C++,* Franklin-Beedle, © 1995, ISBN 0-938661-72-8.

Cay Horstmann, *Computing Concepts with C++ Essentials,* Wiley, © 1997, ISBN 0-471-13779-7.

Joel Adams, Sanford Leestma, and Larry Nyhoff, *C++ An Introduction to Computing,* Prentice Hall, © 1998, ISBN 0-13-744392-7.

Owen Astrachan, *A Computer Science Tapestry,* McGraw Hill, © 1997, ISBN 0-07-0022036-1.

INDEX

SYMBOLS

!, 77, 79, 367, 372

--, 87, 369, 402, 473, 474, 700
    See Decrement operator

/, 67, 68, 69, 70, 369, 470, 471

/=, 74, 92, 367, 369

\n, 54, 55, 59

"\n", 29, 52, 54, 257

#, 26

#ifndef, 498-501

#include directives, 20, 26, 112, 269

%, 68, 69, 369, 470, 471

%=, 72

&, 183, 185, 479, 681

& operator, 679

&&, 76, 77, 78, 367, 368, 369, 370

'\0', 607, 608, 610, 703

n!, 154

*, 46, 67, 68, 69, 369, 680, 681, 804

-=, 72

*=, 72

+, 46, 67, 69, 87, 158, 369, 467, 470, 471, 512, 716

++, 87, 400, 402, 473, 474, 700
    See Increment operator

+=, 72

-, 67, 68, 87, 369, 470, 471

/*, 94

*/, 94

//, 94

/=, 72

\t, 54

\a, 54

::, 316
    See Scope resolution operator

<, 51, 77, 112, 366, 367, 369

<<, 22, 51, 226, 234, 244, 256, 269, 477, 478
    overloading, 474, 476, 480, 512, 716, 794

<=, 74, 367, 369, 404

<assert.h>, 923

-=, 72

=, 47, 67, 72, 77, 79-80, 367, 611, 651, 714
    pointer variables with, 686

==, 74, 79, 80, 92, 512, 611, 651

== operator, 366, 368, 369

->, 471, 804, 806

>, 77, 112, 368, 369

>=, 74, 369

>>, 22, 225, 234, 256, 258, 269, 476, 477
    overloading, 474, 480, 512

[], 471, 530, 531, 532, 695, 928-929

\", 54

\n, 54

\n and endl, 54, 59

\", 54

{}, 25, 81, 94, 129, 374, 376-377

or operator ||, 76, 77, 78, 367, 369, 370, 911

~, 707, 911

Z